A SOCIAL HISTORY OF TRUTH

Science and Its Conceptual Foundations
David L. Hull, Editor

STEVEN SHAPIN

A
Social History
of Truth

Civility and Science
in Seventeenth-Century England

THE UNIVERSITY OF

CHICAGO PRESS

CHICAGO AND LONDON

Steven Shapin is professor in the Department of Sociology and the Science Studies Program at the University of California, San Diego. He is the coauthor, with Simon Schaffer, of *Leviathan and the Air-Pump* (1985).

This book has been brought to publication with the support of a grant from the National Endowment for the Humanities, an independent federal agency, and both author and publisher acknowledge this support with thanks.

The University of Chicago Press, Chicago 60637
The University of Chicago Press, Ltd., London
© 1994 by The University of Chicago
All rights reserved. Published 1994
Printed in the United States of America

03 02 01 00 99 98 97 96 95 94   1 2 3 4 5

ISBN: 0-226-75018-3   (cloth)

Library of Congress Cataloging-in-Publication Data

Shapin, Steven.
    A social history of truth : civility and science in seventeenth-century
England / Steven Shapin.
        p.   cm. — (Science and its conceptual foundations)
    Includes bibliographical references and index.
    1. Science—Social aspects—England—History—17th century.
    2. Science—Moral and ethical aspects—England—History—17th
century.   I. Title.   II. Series.
    Q175.52.G7S48   1994
    306.4′5′094109032—dc20   93-41950
                                                                    CIP

For T. L. Martin, Gent.

Sayest thou this of thyself,
or did others tell it thee . . . ?

—John 18:34

It is a fundamental belief of all aristocrats that the common
people are untruthful. "We truthful ones"—the nobility in
ancient Greece called themselves.
It is obvious that everywhere the designations of
moral value were at first applied to *men*, and were only
derivatively and at a later period applied to *actions*.

—Nietzsche, *Beyond Good and Evil*

Contents

Illustrations

Figures

Table

Acknowledgments

A book so long in the making acquires many intellectual debts. Most of these obligations are acknowledged in formal citations, but I fear that some are not, or are, at best, inadequately recognized. Versions of some of the material presented here were inflicted on a great many tolerant audiences over the past eight years or so. These include seminars at the universities of Cambridge, California at Berkeley, California at Los Angeles, Chicago, Cornell, Griffith, Harvard, the Hebrew University of Jerusalem, Johns Hopkins, London (University College), Manchester, Melbourne, New South Wales, Notre Dame, Oxford, Pittsburgh, Princeton, Tel-Aviv, and Wollongong. Members of all these audiences must have assisted this project in more ways than I can readily recall.

Individuals who have offered valuable information, criticisms, or comments are, again, too numerous for properly inclusive enumeration, but they include J. A. Bennett, Mario Biagioli, Jeffrey Brown, H. M. Collins, Lorraine J. Daston, Michael Aaron Dennis, Yaron Ezrahi, Mordechai Feingold, Daniel Garber, J. V. Golinski, Rob Hagendijk, Willem Halffman, Hans Harbers, John Henry, Michael Hunter, Robert Iliffe, Adrian Johns, Robert Kohler, Bruno Latour, John Law, Julian Martin, David Philip Miller, Iwan Rhys Morus, Andrew Pickering, Trevor Pinch, Theodore Porter, Jacques Revel, John Schuster, Susan Leigh Star, Sharon Traweek, Jay Tribby, and Andrew Wayne. I have discussed some of the ideas in this book with Peter Dear and Simon Schaffer over so many years, and in so many places, that I cannot confidently estimate the extent of my debt to them. A series of friendly arguments with my colleague Philip Kitcher over the past several years has considerably sharpened an exercise which he will still, no doubt, regard as lamentably fuzzy and philosophically naive. I hope he will not object to being thanked in this connection. At an early stage of writing, portions of the manuscript were read by David Bloor and Michael Lynch, each of whom offered detailed and enormously constructive criticisms at a time when I was most able to benefit from them. Charles Rosenberg, Andrew Scull, and Philip Kitcher kindly read over much of the completed manuscript and made a number of penetrating criticisms, some of which only pressure of time made me decline to take up. My friend Christopher Martyn is a scientist who has (at times unwittingly) taught me some common sense about the moral economy of modern science which I was happy to dress up in fancy language and present as my own.

I owe far more than the usual debt to three very diligent and very competent readers for the University of Chicago Press. My editor Susan Abrams has been a continuing and much-valued source of support, encouragement, and sound advice. It has been a pleasure and a moral education working with her. My copy editor Michael Koplow has my gratitude for caring as much about getting it right as I do.

Interlibrary loan staff at my own university were extremely helpful: without their assistance this book would have taken very much longer to complete. I also thank staff at the University Library of Cambridge University, the Whipple Museum of the History of Science at Cambridge University, the National Library of Scotland, and the Royal Society of London. I thank the Fellows and Council of the Royal Society for permission to use and quote from the Boyle Papers and other manuscripts in their possession.

A slightly different version of Chapter 4—"Who Was Robert Boyle?"—was presented to the William Andrews Clark Memorial Library, UCLA, conference on "Civility, Court Society, and Scientific Discourse" on 23 November 1991, and to the Stalbridge Boyle Symposium on 14 December 1991. I am grateful to the organizers—Mario Biagioli and Michael Hunter respectively—for allowing me to publish this material for the first time here. Chapter 7 is a greatly revised version of "Robert Boyle and Mathematics: Reality, Representation, and Experimental Practice," *Science in Context* 2 (1988), 23–58. I thank Cambridge University Press for permission to use some of that material here.

This book was largely written during academic leave from the University of California, San Diego, in 1991–1992, supported by fellowships from the National Science Foundation and the University of California President's Initiative in the Humanities. Small summer research grants from the University of California, San Diego Academic Senate, supported an early stage of this work. I am honored to acknowledge a very special debt to Mr. Gerry Martin and the Renaissance Trust.

September 1992
Lochinver, Sutherland

Notes on Genres,
Disciplines, and Conventions

What Kind of Book?

A Social History of Truth is concerned with questions about the grounds of scientific knowledge which have traditionally been the preserve of philosophers; it uses evidence and techniques customarily owned by historians; and the conclusions it arrives at are broadly sociological in form and substance. For all that, it was not initiated with any special intent to celebrate interdisciplinarity or deliberately to mix, merge, or mangle disciplinary procedures. Rather, it is the upshot of years of engagement with questions whose exploration has taken me at some angle from the trajectories of colleagues more comfortable in their disciplinary identities. I have followed the questions, and the resources for addressing them, wherever they happened to be in the academic culture. My purpose is not to blur the genres of history, sociology, and philosophy of science, but to assist in the reconstitution of what might count as historical practice, and to make a theoretically driven detailed historical narrative the sort of thing which engages the attention of philosophers and sociologists because they recognize it as a significant way of dealing with their problems. There seems no good reason why practitioners, including myself, writing about the past should not be called 'historians,' but I cannot insist on that honor.

I wanted to explore the bases upon which factual scientific knowledge is held. It was natural that I should do so in relation to a setting I knew relatively well, and that lends the book its historical character. It is 'about' a particular past setting. Unlike some postmodernist and reflexivist friends, I write in the confident conviction that I am less interesting than the subjects I write 'about,' and, accordingly, much of this book can be read in the mode of old-fashioned historical realism. Yet the resources to conduct an inquiry about the grounds of credibility do not presently belong to any one academic discipline, and my efforts to explore and assess these resources lend the book its appar-

ently sociological and, to a lesser extent, philosophical character. I do
not doubt that many historians reading this book will be irritated by
the generalities of the first chapter. I hope, nevertheless, that they will
give it a go, and I argue below why they ought to try. However, failure
to tolerate this chapter is not terminal, and the book may, if absolutely
necessary, be read from chapter 2, with only intermittent intrusions of
sociological theory. Chapter 1 may then, if desired, be taken on after
'properly historical' sensibilities have been addressed. Conversely,
many philosophers and sociologists, their interest perhaps whetted by
the first chapter, will no doubt be exasperated by the detailed historical
treatments that constitute the bulk of the book. I will also give arguments why they ought to persist, but, alas, there is no way of reading
this book as an abstract exercise, nor are chapters 2 to 8 to be regarded
simply as the testing of some theory about knowledge and order which
can subsist independently of the detailed narratives which make it
visible.

Members of audiences exposed to early versions of the material in
this book posed questions which at first I had difficulty in understanding but which I now realize merit concise and clear responses. I was
asked why, if my enterprise was, as I said, historical in form, I continually referred to modern microsociological studies of the forms of interaction in the Los Angeles, Philadelphia, or Shetland Islands of the
twentieth century. Was I claiming that the aspects of the modern condition addressed by present-day microsociologists were 'brought into
being' in seventeenth-century England? And, if so, how could I switch
back and forth between widely separated temporal settings without
any significant attention to the successive transformations of the *longue
durée?* Furthermore, how could I justify such close attention to the
English setting unless I was claiming that the English were unique or
that English practices were totally insulated from Continental counterparts?

These are good questions, the first very penetrating indeed, and the
last perhaps not quite so telling. I respond in reverse order. My concern here is to open a historicist window upon the practices by which
types of scientific knowledge were made and their credibility secured
in early modern England, to show how this was done in as much detail
as I felt the subject merited and the general reader could be expected
to bear.[1] A historical ethnography is, strictly speaking, an impossibility,
but this is *inter alia* an attempt at one. Obviously, the gentle and learned
worlds with which I am concerned interacted significantly across na-

1. Here and elsewhere I use *historicism* in its loose 'new' sense: the practice devoted
to interpreting historical action in historical actors' terms.

tional boundaries, and many of their attributed characteristics were common to several national settings. I use evidence deriving from non-English cultures when such sources importantly circulated in England, whether in translation or not. Where there is evidence that English patterns significantly diverged from those obtaining elsewhere, or that the English accounted themselves different in relevant respects, I draw attention to such evidence. I make no claim of the sort that the English were 'wholly unique' or that every national culture was 'essentially the same,' although I am happy that, so far as its historical dimension is concerned, this book should be taken substantially to support accumulating evidence of the relative 'peculiarities of the English.'[2] I offer no special justification for focusing upon the English context and upon the probabilistic empirical and experimental practices which were characteristic of that setting. Historians of early modern England will need no such justification. Searchers after the 'origins of modernity' have in recent years found much of interest in seventeenth-century English science and allied cultural practices, and, for that reason, their attention may be engaged by my story about the relationship between science and gentlemanly conduct. What happened in England was, by any standards, 'important' for scientific change. I am well aware that, in significant ways, matters were arranged differently in other European settings, and that these too were 'important' for the development of science.

Indeed, this book does not contain a great deal about knowledge-making practices obtaining in early modern France or Italy or Norway. Nor does it address the career of these practices in England into the eighteenth and nineteenth centuries. My relative ignorance of these cultural settings and periods is culpable, but not, I hope, fatal to the inquiry I have framed here. My apology for this restriction requires some comment about how the arguments and narratives in this book stand with respect to the interests and conventions of various academic disciplines.

One argument contained here has some chance of being visible as straightforwardly historical. It is a claim about the *origins* of the practice known as English experimental philosophy. I say that this new culture emerged partly through the purposeful relocation of the conventions, codes, and values of gentlemanly conversation into the domain of natural philosophy. I show how this relocation was formulated and assisted by the gentlemanly identities of such key advocates as Francis Bacon and Robert Boyle. Scholarship of a certain sort might

2. E.g., Macfarlane, *Origins of English Individualism;* idem, "Socio-economic Revolution in England."

be made suitable for early modern gentlemen through a reformulation of the very idea of philosophy such that it became recognizable as a form of gentlemanly conversation. I display the local advantages accruing from this move for practical solutions to endemic problems of credibility. Accordingly, insofar as history is taken to be defined by 'origins stories,' I offer this one. It is about the gentlemanly origins of seventeenth-century English experimental and observational natural philosophy. If one wants to read this book as a story about the 'gentlemanly origins of modern science,' I cannot prevent that reading, although I need to insist that we still know relatively little about the complex processes through which seventeenth-century practices were successively transformed into those of the present day. Any such version of this 'origins story' ought, therefore, to be argued with due modesty.

Other arguments (and, in my view, by far the most interesting ones) are not at all about specific historical origins or transformations. Rather, they draw attention to (what, fearful of pretentiousness, I suppose I must call) 'the human condition.' I mean to open a window on the historical past in order to show what modern scientists and everyday actors share with it. No doubt, we share practices with the early modern English because we are its particular cultural legatees. Yet part of my concern is to argue—and, if necessary, freely to speculate—that all people living and working in a collective state are obliged to address and practically to solve a range of problems about the relations between self and others, subjects and objects, knowledge and the moral order. What are the cognitive and moral conditions for intersubjectivity? What social conditions have to be satisfied for the collective good called knowledge to exist? That is the framework within which I offer a synthetic account of relevant bits of philosophy and sociological theory as chapter 1, and require the historical reader to suffer intermittent eruptions of such concerns throughout the narrative. I do so not because I wish specially to intrude the theorizing of these disciplines into historical narrative, but because I conceive of history as one of the human sciences. History can provide materials to discern the possibly universal as well as to illuminate the possibly particular.

The speculative dimension of this book is meant to stimulate reaction, critical or otherwise, from scholars knowledgeable about other cultural and temporal settings. It is a depressing view of historical inquiry that would define its goal as the ceaseless identification of particularities. Yet the very possibility that history can contribute to the general understanding of human behavior arises from the depth of detail it can dredge up from the past. If there are cultural universals arising from the human condition, then only a series of detailed accounts can display the temporal and cultural diversity with which such universal predicaments have been addressed and resolved, and, accordingly, identify pattern among particulars. Universals can be discerned only by pressing the historical study of particularities as far as it can practically go. If I claim that this exercise remains a work of history, it is in the hope that a space can be created for the conception of history as a human science represented here. And, after all, such a conception need not be created *de novo;* it can be creatively reconstituted from the most constructive features of historical traditions dominant in past centuries.

As I have indicated, loose usage often distinguishes historical from philosophical or sociological inquiry in respect of the greater concern with particularities and detail represented in historical writing and the greater abstractness of the schemes proffered by philosophy and sociology. There is a further reason why such a distinction is increasingly unfortunate. Many strands of modern philosophy and social theory, including those I find most appealing, argue that epistemic judgment depends upon local contexts of use, and that it is 'embedded in streams of practical activity.' In one way or another, such sensibilities characterize American pragmatist philosophy of science and its symbolic interactionist sociological heirs, much Continental phenomenology, some variants of English idealism, the late writings of Wittgenstein, many strands of cultural anthropology, and ethnomethodology.

Knowledge, it is rightly said, does not stand outside of practical activity: it is made and sustained through situated practical activity. Yet, despite the chorus of modern voices commending detailed study of the particularities by which knowledge is made, protected, and transmitted, advocacy largely remains at a programmatic and abstract level. A view about knowledge and practical activity which seems to demand the historian's finest microscope is largely fobbed off with traditional philosophers' toy-examples and social theorists' impenetrably airy generalities. This is both odd and deeply unsatisfactory. Michael Oakeshott's account of the conditions for learning a "tradition of behaviour" is apt in this connection: "[K]nowledge of it is unavoidably knowledge of its detail: to know only the gist is to know nothing. What has to be learned is not an abstract idea, or a set of tricks, not even a ritual, but a concrete, coherent manner of living in all its intricateness."[3] I offer this book as my appreciation of one way those committed to the view that 'knowledge is embedded in streams of practical activity' might consider making that case.

---

3. Oakeshott, "Political Education," 129.

Notes on Sources and Their Interpretation

In my efforts to retrieve some understanding of early modern modes of gentlemanly interaction I have made much use of the so-called 'courtesy literature.' This was a corpus of practical ethical texts—in its most mundane form 'books of manners'—describing how gentlemen ought to behave and intended in the main to represent how authentic gentlemen did behave. The general nature of this literature is detailed in chapter 3, and there is no need here to preview that account.[4] Nevertheless, reaction to early versions of that chapter has convinced me that I ought to say a few words about how I use such material and how I conceive of the relationship between actual past behavior and historical texts describing and enjoining behavior.

Certainly, I do not make the mistake of simply assuming that early modern English gentlemen behaved as they were ideally supposed to do. Courtesy texts did indeed represent an ideal, and we are all thoroughly familiar with gaps between normatively stipulated and actually occurring behavior in the present day. Accordingly, a literature specifying ideal behaviors cannot be expected to serve in itself, and untheorized, as an adequate account of real behavior. However, just because such literature represents a reiterated stock of norms, it *may* (together with other evidence) be taken as a more or less reliable indication of the cultural forms actually used by early modern gentlemen to call each other to account, to extend praise or blame.[5] These uses are entirely consistent with evidence of transgressions, and it is likely that reiterated insistence upon the rightness of certain forms of behavior is a sign that there is a problem with the observance of that behavior. For these reasons, I triangulate the ideals contained in courtesy texts with as many other sources of information as possible—letters, diaries, dramatic and poetic works, ethical glosses in philosophical and historical tracts, and so on. What I mean to retrieve from the courtesy literature, and related texts, is the general shape of a culture, a set of repertoires of what was accounted good and bad, decorous and indecorous, in gentlemanly conversation.[6] To that end, at times I quote densely from such texts, not, as is often the case in historical writing, to display unusual, or unusually revealing, formulations, but to help build up in the reader's mind a sense of what was *conventional*.

I draw particular attention to the role of truthfulness and mendacity

---

4. For a survey of the English courtesy genres, see, e.g., Mason, *Gentlefolk in the Making*, and, for a well-known treatment of the relationship between courtesy literature and European macrosocial change, see Elias, *The Civilizing Process*, esp. I, ch. 2.

5. Whigham (*Ambition and Privilege*, 27), e.g., writes about the relative homogeneity of the courtesy literature as "a corpus of strategic gestures."

6. For broadly parallel usage, see, notably, Revel, "Uses of Civility," esp. 168.

in this culture. The relevant literature indicates a special relationship between the idea of a gentleman and the idea of truth-telling. To acquire the reputation of a liar was to endanger membership in gentlemanly society. Note, however, that I do not make any claim of the sort that early modern English gentlemen were more truthful—told fewer lies—than any other sector of their society, or people in other times and in other places. I would have no way of knowing whether this was so or not, and I very much doubt that any other historian or sociologist would be better placed to acquire such knowledge. As I characterize the lie, and, indeed, as many early modern actors regarded it, a culpably uttered untruth must proceed from an awareness that the matter was untrue and from an intention to deceive. My historical practice avoids claiming reliable access to individual states of mind. Therefore, while I cannot say whether English gentlemen were statistically more honest than Italian courtiers or English merchants, I can seek to display the shape of a culture which valued truthfulness very highly and whose members were apparently prepared and able to identify veracity and mendacity in the context of practical action.[7] Moreover, similar empirical methods serve to display the differential social *cost* in that culture of impugning the veracity of various speakers. The culture was characterized not only by members' knowledge of what counted as truth and untruth in specific contexts of action but also by members' knowledge of the likely consequences of offering or withholding assent to the relations of different sorts of people. Those kinds of knowledge are, I argue, endemically employed in practical social relations. Normative repertoires are, therefore, not simply to be set against 'real behavior'; properly established and theorized, they can be viewed as a constitutive feature of 'real behavior.' They were the resources used to evaluate action and to make action visible as action-of-a-certain-sort.[8]

This is a story about the gentlemanly constitution of scientific truth. I concentrate upon the role of gentle cultural practices in the making of factual knowledge. I argue that preexisting gentlemanly practices provided working solutions to problems of credibility and trust which presented themselves at the core of the new empirical science of seventeenth-century England. To the extent that I focus on the society of gentlemen, this is a story told 'from their point of view.' I am not so confident (nor, perhaps, so foolish) a historian as to suppose that mine is a story that early modern gentlemen 'could be brought to accept as

7. For pertinent methodological discussion, see Collins, "The Meaning of Lies," esp. 71–73.

8. For amplification of these comments, see, e.g., Shapin and Barnes, "Darwin and Social Darwinism: Purity and History"; and Mills, "Situated Action and Vocabularies of Motive."

correct,' not least because subjecting the art of gentility to analysis is the sort of thing done by the vulgar and the pedantic.[9]

I am both well aware of, and deeply sympathetic towards, the new cultural history of the disenfranchised and the voiceless. That much ought to be apparent from my treatment of support personnel in chapter 8 and of women intermittently. Nevertheless, if my basic claim about the significance of the gentle in the formal culture of science is correct, then there need be no apologies for the fact that this is a book about a small group of powerful and vocal actors; that is, as the current sneer has it, about Dead White European Males. Given the nature of the cultural practice in question, if there are past voices—of women, of servants, of savages—in the practice to be attended to and made audible, then there is every reason why historians should, if they choose, concern themselves with them. However, if there are no such voices, or if they are almost inaudible, then the same sensibility should induce historians to attend to the local *practices of inclusion and exclusion* through which some speak and others are spoken for, some act and others are acted upon. These practices will, by definition, be those implemented and enforced by those who have put their mark upon the cultural form one proposes to interpret. Nor is there any reason to dismiss as 'politically incorrect' the possibility that the legitimacy of gentlemanly practices was locally conceded beyond the bounds of gentlemanly society. If that was so—and it is a matter for inquiry to determine—then historians can also, if they want, ask what that legitimacy consisted in and how far it extended. I draw attention to some evidence that gentlemanly conclusions, if not codes, were rejected by others, while I am provisionally satisfied that gentlemanly forms were quite widely regarded as legitimate outwith the bounds of gentlemanly recognitions.

Deciding that question is, fortunately, not a task I need to take up here. I am, however, very much concerned in this connection to establish a basic point about historical genres: there is no necessary opposition between writing the history of elites and of the masses. Furthermore, since I argue that formal scientific knowledge is made through mundane processes of social interaction, there is no necessary opposition between the study of 'high' (even the 'highest') forms of elite culture and the study of the everyday modes in which people deal with each other. Extraordinarily highly valued forms of knowledge are made by and through ordinary courses of social interaction. I hope *inter alia* that this book will be taken as an exercise in establishing these generic possibilities. Indeed, the desire to signal this view about genres is one reason for my perhaps overly ambitious title. Just as we have

9. Skinner, "Meaning and Understanding in the History of Ideas," esp. 6, 28, 49.

social histories of eating, dying, breeding, and getting and spending, so too we can have a social history of truth-making.

A Note on 'Belief'

This book deals with questions of assent to factual knowledge-claims. Common or garden English usage—in the seventeenth as in the late twentieth century—refers to such assent as 'belief,' and so, occasionally, shall I. To 'believe,' from this book's point of view, is to 'profess belief' or to 'act as if one believed.' I see no great harm in using such locutions as 'belief' and 'assent' more or less interchangeably. Nevertheless, as I have already indicated, I make no claims as to the psychological states of historical actors, and nothing here depends upon such diagnoses.

A Note on Referencing

This book uses an economical footnoting and referencing convention identical to that employed in Shapin and Schaffer's *Leviathan and the Air-Pump* and similar to that of Elizabeth Eisenstein's *The Printing Press as an Agent of Change*. Bibliographic information is kept to a minimum in notes, apart from the occasional addition of publication dates where that information is germane and is not indicated in the accompanying text. Full titles and publication details are provided in the bibliography. Complete details of unpublished manuscript sources and early modern periodical articles are, however, given in the notes and not repeated in the bibliography.

A Note on Dating

During the period with which this book is concerned, the British Isles employed a calendar different from that used in most Continental countries, especially Catholic ones. The former used the Julian (old style) calendar, which was ten days behind the Gregorian (new style) calendar used on the Continent. In addition, the British new year was reckoned to begin on 25 March, so that dates between 1 January and 24 March were commonly given as, for example, 2 February 1666/67. I have not bothered with reconciling such usages, save in one long section of chapter 6 where the timing of astronomical communications between England, France, Italy, and Danzig was significant for the actors. In that context alone, I give relevant dates in both new- and old-style form, adjusting years to correspond with a new year commencing 1 January. Thus, the English 2 February 1666/67 is here rendered 2/12 February 1667, and the French 15 August 1670 is given as 5/15 August 1670.

The Argument Summarized

Chapter One

The book is loosely structured as a series of explorations of central arguments about the grounds of factual knowledge which are systematically presented in the first chapter. There is a massive mismatch between dominant characterizations of the sources of our factual knowledge and the ways in which we actually secure that knowledge. Both seventeenth-century and present-day 'moderns' widely advertise direct experience as the surest grounds for factual knowledge, just as they identify reliance upon the testimony of others as an insecure warrant for such knowledge. Similarly, both sets of 'moderns' celebrate proper science as a culture which has indeed rectified knowledge by rejecting what others tell us and seeking direct individual experience. In contrast, I argue that no practice has accomplished the rejection of testimony and authority and that no cultural practice recognizable as such could do so. I set myself the dual task of showing the ineradicable role of what others tell us and of saying how reliance upon testimony achieves invisibility in certain intellectual practices.

Knowledge is a collective good. In securing our knowledge we rely upon others, and we cannot dispense with that reliance. That means that the relations in which we have and hold our knowledge have a moral character, and the word I use to indicate that moral relation is *trust*. I offer a critical synthesis of well-established appreciations of trust in the building and maintaining of social order, and I introduce less well-known traditions in philosophy and social science which identify the role of trust in building and maintaining cognitive order. These traditions suggest that the fabric of our social relations is made of knowledge—not just knowledge of other people, but also knowledge of what the world is like—and, similarly, that our knowledge of what the world is like draws on knowledge about other people—what they are like as sources of testimony, whether and in what circumstances they may be trusted. Accordingly, the making of knowledge in general takes place on a moral field and mobilizes particular appreciations of the virtues and characteristics of types of people. I review some phenomenological and ethnomethodological appreciations of the ways in which knowledge of the world and knowledge of other people are drawn together in social interaction, paying special attention to the processes of *mundane reason,* in which presuppositions about the nature of an objective external world are embedded within ordinary social interaction and within practices inquiring about that world.

Whom to trust? I argue that the identification of trustworthy agents is necessary to the constitution of any body of knowledge. I do not thereby claim that this is all there is to knowledge-making. Here and elsewhere in the book, I argue that absolutely everything which individuals know about the world—natural and social—is potentially relevant to their assessments of new knowledge-claims. I draw attention to the ineradicable role of people-knowledge in the making of thing-knowledge just because the stabilization of the latter pervasively involves rendering the former invisible. What we recognize as people-knowledge is a necessary, not a sufficient, condition for the making of thing-knowledge. It follows therefore that what we call 'social knowledge' and 'natural knowledge' are hybrid entities: what we know of comets, icebergs, and neutrinos irreducibly contains what we know of those people who speak for and about these things, just as what we know about the virtues of people is informed by their speech about things that exist in the world.

Chapter Two

The end of chapter 1 introduces the importance of conceptions of *free action* and *virtue* as quite general indicators of reliable truth-tellers and knowledge-sources. While the role of trust and social knowledge in the building up of natural knowledge is treated as a general matter, this book seeks to show how that global problem was particularly solved in the scientific culture of early modern England. To this end, chapter 2 introduces the *gentleman,* that culture's paradigm of the type of individual one could trust to speak truth. This chapter is recognizably written in the idiom of economic and social history—describing the relevant concrete 'facts of the matter' about early modern English gentlemen—but is best read as a survey of the sorts of things that gentlemen wanted to *know* in order to 'place' each other. Contemporary culture was importantly shaped by the exercise of identifying the gentleman in social and economic frames. How much money did one have to have to be a gentleman? How much discretionary action? How much breeding and how might that breeding be made visible and audible in cultural practice? What was the presumed and proper relationship between one's ascribed standing and one's deportment?

Here I critically summarize social-historical literature establishing the role of birth and material circumstances in making the English gentleman, and I sketch features of the culture in which birth, wealth, and behavior were described, defined, and made manifest. I draw particular attention to the transformation of free action from a presumption about persons specially placed in the social and economic system to a symbolic cultural display of such placement. I show how those circumstances were available to be read as guarantees of the truth of what the gentleman avowed. He was accounted to be such a man as had no inducement to misrepresent the case, no forces working on him that would shift his utterances out of correspondence with reality.

Chapter Three

While the circumstances of the early modern English gentleman may be spoken about as economic and social facts, it was a matter of interpretative cultural practice to read those facts as warrants for truth. This chapter, accordingly, offers a detailed account of the cultural practices by which the gentleman was recognized as, and enjoined to be, a truth-teller, as well as the practices which massively *costed* imputations that he might not be. I situate the recognition of truthfulness within a traditional culture of *honor,* and I indicate how the practices of an honor culture stood in relation to alternative ways of specifying gentle identity, with special reference to Christian and humanist patterns. This chapter begins the move from social history to practical epistemology. What was it about the placement of English gentlemen that was adduced to explain and enjoin truthfulness? What guarantees were there for the veracity of the gentleman's word, and what sanctions were available if his relations were gainsaid? I describe how an honor culture stressed the significance of gentlemanly truthfulness and identified the imputation of lying as incompatible with membership in civil society. Lying was understood to proceed from constrained circumstances; hence he who lied revealed himself to be base, ignoble, and unfree. The same culture which explained why one might rely upon a gentleman's word and build one's sense of the world upon that word also provided a picture of the social order and its distinctions of rank. Practical epistemology was embedded within practical social theory.

This chapter paints a picture of the discursive culture which was elaborated by the general desire to prevent dissent from provoking disaster. I show how broadly *probabilistic* discursive practices were institutionalized in English gentle society before they appeared in empirical scientific culture, and I argue that the perceived standing and worth of these practices made them available for importation into new cultural practices—such as experimental natural philosophy—whose members required solutions to the problems of managing credibility. I describe how the cultural practices attending the English gentleman fit him for the role of being a reliable spokesman for reality. A relatively well-working solution to problems of order in one uniquely authoritative domain was purposefully transferred to the new domain of experimental philosophy, where it was constituted as a solution to problems of order in special scholarly practice.

Chapter Four

This chapter traces a connection between biography and practical epistemology. It explores the personal identity of a major English scientific practitioner and the ways in which that identity figured in solutions to endemic problems of credibility. Chapters 1 to 3 argue that assent to factual testimony mobilizes local knowledge of trustworthy sources: what sorts of people count as reliable truth-tellers? Here I draw attention to perhaps the greatest seventeenth-century master of scientific credibility, and, by offering a detailed picture of his local identity and the cultural materials out of which it was put together, I show personal identity at epistemological work.

Who was Robert Boyle? In general terms, what was the ideal identity of the new experimental practitioner and how did that identity figure in the production and warranting of scientific truth? I indicate how Boyle, with others' assistance, constructed a usable new identity out of existing cultural materials, employing the understood facts of his birth and standing, and the understood characters of gentlemen, Christians, and scholars, to fashion a new and valued character for the experimental philosopher. I lay particular stress upon the use of gentle identity to protect against the damage that attribution of professional *special interest* might do to the credibility of testimony. The physician, the chemist, the schoolman, the priest, and the professional author might all be presumed to speak out of trade or mercenary interest, while Boyle and his associates repeatedly pointed to his gentlemanly status as an argument against imputing any such interest to him. I construe the identity of the "Christian Virtuoso" as a purposeful assemblage of cultural elements warranting truth-telling, and I show how Boyle's acknowledged identity as Christian gentleman and Christian scholar meant that he was one whose experimental relations might be relied upon with security, who could speak for empirical realities inaccessible to other practitioners, and whose representations might be accepted as corresponding to things themselves.

Chapter Five

English 'moderns' repeatedly insisted upon the epistemic inadequacy of testimony and authority. Truth could be guaranteed by going on individual direct experience and individual reason; reliance upon others' testimony was a sure way to error. That much is well known, and that much is what allows present-day 'moderns' to speak about seventeenth-century individualistic empiricists as the 'founders of modernity.' This chapter seeks to specify in just what ways English seventeenth-century scientific practitioners and their allies proposed to jettison authority and in what ways their concrete knowledge-making practices utterly depended upon testimony. I introduce the problems posed for those practices by the ontological opening represented in the 'modern' critique of ancient authority. I describe practitioners' recognition that prudence sat poised between skepticism and credulity, and I show how they came to terms with a central and legitimate role for testimony in the constitution of that culture's most valued forms of knowledge, including empirical natural science and religion. Some forms of trust and authority were rendered invisible as such, and I argue that these were the forms which were effectively transported from gentlemanly culture into the domains of scientific knowledge-making.

I give an account of John Locke's philosophical reflections upon the management of testimony as the articulation of widely distributed *maxims of prudence*. I show how the recommended assessment of testimony according to its multiplicity, plausibility, directness, knowledge-ability, and the like was the systematization of prudential wisdom circulating in gentlemanly culture. I display the skill-like character of gentlemen's undoubted ability to sort out reliable and unreliable testimonial sources, and I indicate how the interpretative circle created by Locke's rules for assessing testimony was effectively closed by members' ability to recognize disinterested, trustworthy sources. The notion of *epistemological decorum* is here introduced to indicate the expectation that knowledge will be evaluated according to its appropriate place in practical cultural and social action, and I show how the skill of doing the proper thing in the proper setting informed the assessment of knowledge-claims as well as the evaluation of social conduct.

Chapter Six

Here I offer a moral history of scientific credibility by following a series of factual knowledge-claims through their short- to medium-term careers. I show how the constitution of knowledge of things and their properties mobilized knowledge of people and their virtues. I work through cases having to do with the practice of natural history, hydro-statics, and cometary astronomy. In the last case, I revert to discussions of 'mundane reason' introduced in chapter 1, arguing that the establishment of the identity, number, and trajectories of comets proceeded on a moral field. The nature of discrepantly testified physical objects was decided through consideration of the skill and veracity of testifying sources and the likely consequences of impugning skill and veracity. I relate various actors' credibility troubles to nongentle identity, and I return to the career of Robert Boyle to show how mastery of credibility functioned in day-to-day scientific practice. I draw attention to the epistemic significance of face-to-face interaction, and I discuss the civil significance of various means of *avoiding* the deliberative assessment of the truth or falsity of testimony.

Chapter Seven

At several points in the book I invite consideration of the modes of gentlemanly interaction as *conversation*. Chapter 3, for example, argues that forms of probabilistic discourse were institutionalized in gentlemanly civil conversation before the emergence of the new experimental science. Gentlemanly society greatly valued the means to dissent without disaster and just those institutionalized means were, I argue, purposefully transferred to a reformed philosophical practice where they constituted solutions to problems of epistemic and moral order. I lay special stress upon gentlemanly rejections of notions of truth, certainty, rigor, and precision which were judged to be suitable for scholarly inquiry but out of place in civil conversation. In chapter 7, I proceed to show how such conversational sensibilities and practices were put to work even in those areas of experimental natural philosophy that appeared to pose the greatest obstacles to civil conversation and decorum. Here I explore some objections to the place of *mathematics* in strands of experimental natural philosophy, and especially to the confidence of mathematicians' claims and the certainty with which those claims were made. I document and interpret Robert Boyle's unease about mathematical confidence and certainty. I argue that Boyle's proffered alternative to forms of mathematical practice linked epistemology, ontology, and civility. If the world was constituted in a specific way, then specific ways of interrogating it were indicated, specific types of confidence were to be expected, and specific modes in which members of a community might converse and collaborate were to be morally preferred. Manners, mores, and mundane ontology were implicated together in a moral economy of truth. I examine the practices by which hypothetical expectations about the behavior of nature were juxtaposed to experimental findings, and I show how *adequate and reasonable agreement* between theory and findings was constituted as experimental *conversation*.

Chapter Eight

Chapter 4 introduces the power of gentlemanly personal identity as a solution to endemic problems of credibility within experimental practice. Here I return to issues concerning authorial identity and the making of natural knowledge. Chapter 8 describes the *human agents* for whom experimentalists like Boyle spoke. I display the seventeenth-century laboratory as a collective workplace, but one in which one human agent spoke for others. This chapter studies technicians and other support personnel, documenting what they did in the making of experimental knowledge, the grounds on which their work and relations might be trusted or distrusted, the circumstances which licensed others speaking on their behalf, and the continuing culture which renders their work invisible, subsumed in that of their masters. I show how the moral economy of the laboratory embedded practical social theory as well as practical epistemology. Mastery and servitude are categories in the understanding of society and its power relations; I show that the same categories also figured in resolutions of practical problems in the constitution and validation of knowledge.

Epilogue

A Social History of Truth concludes with some speculations about *longue durée* change and stability in the means used to assess the truth of what we are told about the world. Is modernity distinguished from the seventeenth century by a qualitatively different way we now accord trust? Do we now trust faceless institutions rather than familiar persons whom we look in the face? Insofar as individuals' capacities are pointed to as justifications of trust, have the gentleman's integrity and virtue been replaced by the specialist's expertise? What vouches for the truthfulness of modern knowledge-sources? I suggest that trust in familiar persons continues to be important in the making of modern scientific knowledge while vigilance has supplanted virtue in lay understanding of what guarantees scientific truthfulness.

A SOCIAL HISTORY OF TRUTH

CHAPTER ONE

The Great Civility:
Trust, Truth, and Moral Order

Suppose men imagined there was no obligation to veracity,
and acted accordingly; speaking as often against
their own opinion as according to it; would not
all pleasure of conversation be destroyed,
and all confidence in narration?

—Francis Hutcheson, *System of Moral Philosophy*

A social history of truth is not supposed to be possible. When people refer to some statement or belief as 'true,' they customarily mean that it 'corresponds' to 'the facts of the matter,' to how 'things really are.' In that sense, within our own scheme of things, 'truth,' 'knowledge,' and 'the facts' indicate similar judgments, enabling us to sort out, and differentially to evaluate, a range of beliefs and statements. In all probability, every community needs some such sorting mechanism, and usages of this kind may even be universal, despite the fact that what is locally meant by 'correspondence' may be vague and varying.

That same sorting function can embed a distinction between what is 'true' and what is merely taken to be so, by some people at some time. Indeed, there is a special community of language-users called 'academic philosophers' who insist very vigorously on such a distinction. The body of locally credible knowledge—what is taken to be true—cannot be the same as 'truth,' since truth is one and what people have taken to be true is known to be many. Whatever changes over time, whatever varies from one community to another, cannot be truth and honored as such: "If truth has many faces, then not one of them deserves trust and respect."[1]

---

1. Gellner, "Relativism and Universals," 83. For a review of dominant philosophical views of truth, see, e.g., Davidson, "Structure and Content of Truth"; and R. Campbell, *Truth and Historicity;* and, for sociological criticism, see McHugh, "Failure of Positivism." Pragmatist philosophers count as a major exception to this disciplinary generalization, though they routinely fail to appreciate the locally obligatory character of

3

This is a restrictive notion of truth and nothing in this book counts as an argument against its legitimacy. The restrictive sensibility, after all, performs an enormously important sorting function. However, restrictive sensibilities carry with them considerable costs, and those costs become more visible as one's purpose moves from sorting and evaluating on the one hand to understanding and interpreting an array of beliefs on the other. I want to preserve from the restrictive sensibility the loose equation between truth, knowledge, and the facts of the matter, while defending the practical interest and legitimacy of a more liberal notion of truth, a notion in which there is indeed a social-historical story to be told about truth.

, Communities making truth-judgments mean to distinguish statements or beliefs which correspond to reality from those which do not, and as they do so they create an automatic bias in favor of their own stock of current knowledge. We assume that all people live in a common external world and that this world has a determinate structure. So the notion of truth can point to 'what the world is like' and therefore to the culture that corresponds to it. Accordingly, this 'materialist' sense of truth grants correspondence to the beliefs we have attached to the world and may withhold correspondence from those that others have attached. This illiberality is no fault of such judgments, since sorting and differential evaluation are often just what is intended. Yet the same illiberality blocks curiosity about *how it is* that, if truth is one and the same, it has so many, and so various, claimants, how it is that truth comes always to be on 'our side,' whoever 'we' are.[2]

Consequently, the distinction between 'truth' and 'what locally counts as truth' can be adequate for some purposes while being fatal to others. There are groups of people dedicated to the disinterested understanding of cultural variation in belief, and for them the restrictive sensibility lacks both value and legitimacy. For historians, cultural anthropologists, and sociologists of knowledge, the treatment of truth as accepted belief counts as a maxim of method, and rightly so. If one means to interpret variation in belief, then it seems prudent to ask how it is that truth speaks in different voices, how it is that what 'they' account to be true comes to be so accounted, and to approach those inquiries with a methodological disposition towards charity. The same maxim of method cautions us momentarily to set aside what 'we' know to be true in the interest of understanding what 'they' know to be true, even to entertain the possibility that, for methodological purposes, 'we' are

truth-judgments: see, e.g., W. James, "Pragmatism's Conception of Truth," in idem, *Pragmatism*, 87–104.

2. Bloor, *Knowledge and Social Imagery*, 37–45.

another form of 'them.' The liberal sensibility towards truth, therefore, while optimistic about the potential scope of understanding, is modest when compared to the restrictive view. As ordinary social actors, truth-liberals know no less than their restrictive colleagues about the world to which knowledge-claims do or do not correspond, but they aim to set evaluation to one side in the special activity of interpreting cultural variation. The special-purpose nature of truth-liberalism is no argument against it: many of our society's most highly valued beliefs and practices, including those of the natural sciences, are adapted to quite specialized purposes. This book proceeds from the view that a social-historical approach to truth is possible, adequate, and methodologically valuable. With respect to other conceptions of truth, it is tolerant.

Set against the overall modesty of a social-historical engagement with truth is the particular nature of the knowledge to be interpreted here. I am concerned with a body of knowledge which members of our own culture routinely recognize as having special claims to truth. I will be focusing on science, on science in a setting where many aspects of what now count as reliable truth-generating practices were put in place and institutionalized, and, in general, with epistemic items widely taken to be the hardest and most fundamental elements of scientific knowledge—statements of fact, observation-reports, and the like. Olive oil freezes in a Russian winter. A comet is near the first star of Aries on the night of 18 February 1665. Minuscule 'eels' multiply in a bottle of vinegar in Delft. If such claims were judged to correspond to actual states of affairs, then seventeenth-century actors deemed them to be true and took them into their stock of natural knowledge. What we know about seventeenth-century comets draws massively on what seventeenth-century practitioners knew and therefore on how they came to know it.

If truth is not supposed to change over time—to have a history—neither is it supposed to have a sociology. Whatever bears the marks of collective production cannot be truth and honored as such, and few cultural-historical topics are more pervasive than the equation between truth, solitude, passivity, and impersonality.[3] In contrast, I want to argue the adequacy and legitimacy of a thoroughgoing social conception of truth. What counts for any community as true knowledge is a collective good and a collective accomplishment. That good is always in others' hands, and the fate of any particular claim that something 'is the case' is never determined by the individual making the claim.

3. E.g., Durkheim, *Elementary Forms of the Religious Life*, 436–47; Arendt, *The Human Condition*, 15–16, 301–04; Mannheim, *Ideology and Utopia*, 150–151, 254–56, 265–68; Shapin, "'The Mind Is Its Own Place.'"

This is a sense in which one may say that truth is a matter of collective judgment and that it is stabilized by the collective actions which use it as a standard for judging other claims.[4] In short, truth is a social institution and is, therefore, a fit and proper topic for the sociologist's investigation.

The history of truth can be a social history because what we know about the world is arrived at, sustained, and recognized through collective action. Against dominant romantic and heroic views, it is argued that no single individual can constitute knowledge: all the individual can do is offer claims, with evidence, arguments, and inducements, to the community for its assessment. Knowledge is the result of the community's evaluations and actions, and it is entrenched through the integration of claims about the world into the community's institutionalized behavior. Since the acts of knowledge-making and knowledge-protecting capture so much of communal life, communities may be effectively described through their economies of truth. Indeed, there is a variety of sociological and philosophical idioms for drawing attention to such codependencies. Wittgenstein's later philosophical writings insisted that all justifications for our judgments of the proper and the improper, the true and the false, must come to an end. All such judgments are ultimately terminated not in a way of seeing but in a collective way of acting.[5] What is accepted as a justification for the truth of a proposition is shown by how communities go on together: "The danger here, I believe, is one of giving a justification of our procedure when there is no such thing as a justification and we ought simply to have said: *that's how we do it.*"[6]

Pragmatist philosophers reject a static conception of truth as epistemological equilibrium and, in so doing, set truth in motion: "True ideas are those we can assimilate, validate, corroborate and verify. . . . truth *happens* to an idea." Truth consists of the actions taken by practical communities to *make* the idea true, to *make* it agree with reality: "the possession of true thoughts means everywhere the possession of invaluable instruments of action." William James brilliantly noted that truth lives "on a credit system": "Our thoughts and beliefs 'pass,' so long as nothing challenges them, just as bank-notes pass so long as nobody refuses them."[7] Richard Rorty argues that there is "nothing to be said about either truth or rationality apart from descriptions of

---

4. For a philosophical framework broadly compatible with the position developed here, see Welbourne, *Community of Knowledge.*

5. Wittgenstein, *On Certainty*, sects. 110, 192, 204; see also Bloor, *Wittgenstein*, esp. 116, 119, 162.

6. Wittgenstein, *Remarks on the Foundations of Mathematics*, Pt. II, 74; see also idem, *Philosophical Investigations*, Pt. I, sects. 325, 485.

7. W. James, "Pragmatism's Conception of Truth," in idem, *Pragmatism*, 88–91.

familiar procedures of justification which a given society—*ours*—uses in one or another area of enquiry."[8] The ethnomethodologist Peter McHugh stresses the "behavior of seeking truth . . . the institutional and public character of truth, in contrast to the usual psychological and semantic descriptions that depict private disembodiments of that behavior." For the sociologist there is no other way of *conceiving* truth save through the study of what people do collectively. "Truth resides in the rule-guided institutional procedures for conceding it"; we have to accept "that there are no adequate grounds for establishing criteria of truth except the grounds that are employed to grant or concede it," and truth's grip on us resides in the forms of collective life which produce and uphold it.[9] For either the analyst or the member to be radically skeptical would be "equivalent to challenging the rules to which members of a collectivity subscribe."[10]

This book aims to draw special attention to some moral aspects of the collective nature of knowledge. Different members of a community hold knowledge that individuals may need to draw upon in order to perform practical actions: to maneuver in the material world, to confirm the status of their knowledge, to make new knowledge, even to be skeptical about existing items of knowledge. Accordingly, in order for that knowledge to be effectively accessible to an individual—for an individual to *have* it—there needs to be some kind of moral bond between the individual and other members of the community.

The word I propose to use to express this moral bond is *trust*. I want to leave the notion of trust diffuse at this point, allowing its sense to emerge as the inquiry proceeds. Nevertheless, a caveat about recent technical treatments of trust needs to be entered. It has become customary to make distinctions among our usable notions of trust. There is said to be trust in the fulfillment of inductively generated expectations about events in the world, as when we might say that we trust (or are confident) that many people catch colds in Edinburgh winters or that it will be a nice day tomorrow in San Diego. This is identified as an amoral sense of trust: no one will be *blamed* if expectations are not realized or if the case turns out to be otherwise.

By contrast, there is said to be a distinct sense of trust which is recognized as morally consequential. If I trust that you will meet me as promised in my office at two o'clock, then I can blame you if you

---

8. Rorty, "Science as Solidarity," 11.

9. McHugh, "Failure of Positivism," 320–21, 333–35. McHugh's formulation was prominently cited by H. M. Collins early in the development of the sociology of scientific knowledge: Collins, "Seven Sexes," 205; cf. Collins and Yearley, "Epistemological Chicken," 303.

10. Blum, "The Corpus of Knowledge as a Normative Order," 125.

do not show up.[11] Both kinds of trust are systems of expectation about the world, yet only the latter is said to be morally textured. This book will mainly be concerned with the latter form, that is, trust in persons and their relations. Nevertheless, I want to suggest that this routine distinction between types of trust may be inadequately grounded. Here I will simply assert, but later will argue, that much of our sense of the world's contents and inductive regularities is built up and protected by the constitutively moral processes by which we credit others' relations and take their accounts into our stock of knowledge about the world. Indeed, the constitutive relation between the two forms of trust can be made more visible if one transforms the inductive confidence that 'many people are ill in Edinburgh in the winter' into the form '*you (and others) have told me* that this is the case.' Insofar as our factual knowledge is built up through assent to what we have been told, the two, allegedly distinct, notions of trust both belong within the same moral frame, the second routinely visible as such, the first routinely not. Moreover, I recognize, but wish to blur, a distinction between trust in affirmed *actions* (e.g., that you will meet me tomorrow) and trust in *relations* (e.g., that what you tell me about Edinburgh winters is true). Both forms of trust engender states of *belief,* and both may be implicated in schemes of coordinated *action.* My stock of knowledge provides the framework for my practical orientation to the world. Accordingly, while much writing about trust has focused directly upon promised *actions,* I will treat relevant views as equally applicable to *communications* about the world.

Trust and the Order of Society

The trust-dependency of social order has always been recognized.[12] The order of society depends upon (some sociologists would say that it *is*) a complex of normatively ordered expectancies. How could coordinated activity of any kind be possible if people could not rely upon others' undertakings? No goods would be handed over without prior payment, and no payment without goods in hand. There would be no point in keeping engagements, nor any reason to make engagements with people who could not be expected to honor their commitments.[13] The relationship between teacher and pupil, parent and child, would be impossible if the reliability of the former as sources of knowledge were not to be granted. In all cases, the order of knowledge is recognized to be part of the normative fabric of society, and our knowledge

---

11. B. Barber, *Logic and Limits of Trust,* esp. 9; Luhmann, "Familiarity, Confidence, Trust," esp. 97–98; Giddens, *Consequences of Modernity,* 29–34.

12. Holzner, "Sociological Reflections on Trust."

13. A derivation for the modern English *trust* is, indeed, *tryst*—an appointed meeting.

of what people will do is considered to be reliable insofar as we believe they operate in accordance with certain moral standards, enjoining truthfulness and condemning falsehood. And our knowledge of the world is also deemed reliable insofar as we consider that certain people are reputable and veracious sources, and act appropriately with respect to their testimony.

Social theorists from antiquity to the present, writing in the most abstract or the most practical idiom, have all recognized and approved the trust-dependency of social order. Cicero stressed the virtue of "justice" in upholding society. Social order would be impossible unless one were morally enjoined "to stand to one's word in all promises and bargains." The foundation of justice was faithfulness, "which consists in being constantly firm to your word, and a conscientious performance of all compacts and bargains." To be sure, the obligation to keep a promise was not absolute; for example, if keeping it was likely to injure an individual or society, one might have no legitimate commitment. And persons "overawed by fear" or otherwise unfree when they made a promise were not deemed to have entered into a moral commitment. Yet, like other Greek and Roman social theorists, Cicero understood that social order utterly depended upon trust being rightly reposed in morally bound truth-tellers and promise-keepers. Liars and dissimulators threatened the moral fabric of society: they were "knaves" and their actions were "attended with baseness and dishonour."[14]

Early modern ethical writers endorsed and developed the appreciation of the role of trust in social order. The sixteenth-century English humanist Sir Thomas Elyot categorized the types of faithfulness upon which moral order depended: "faith" was belief in the promises of God; "loyalty" was the keeping of promises made by a subject to his prince; and promise-keeping between "men of equal estate or condition" was "trust." All were equally essential to the maintenance of social order. There could be no such thing as civil society if there were no trust: "O what public weal should we hope to have there, where lacketh fidelity, which as [Cicero] saith is the foundation of justice?" Without trust "a public weal may not continue."[15] In France, Montaigne brilliantly analyzed untruthfulness and the breakdown of trust this caused and expressed as the most serious subversions of social order. Order was founded upon our knowledge of others' minds and intentions. Hence it was utterly dependent upon the reliability of our communications about ourselves and about the state of our knowledge:

14. Cicero, *Offices*, 8–14, 111, 136–39, 152–62. On "the power of promise" in antiquity, see Arendt, *The Human Condition*, 243–45.
15. Elyot, *The Governor* (1531), 181–82.

Lying is an accursed vice. We are men, and hold together, only by our word. . . . Since mutual understanding is brought about solely by way of words, he who breaks his word betrays human society. It is the only instrument by means of which our wills and thoughts communicate, it is the interpreter of our soul. If it fails us, we have no more hold on each other, no more knowledge of each other. If it deceives us, it breaks up all our relations and dissolves all the bonds of our society.[16]

The more practical ethical literature of early modern Europe pervasively rehearsed the relationship between trust, truthfulness, and social order. Lodowick Bryskett noted that untruthfulness destroyed "the societie and civill conversation of men, since no man can trust . . . a lyer." Those whose actions eroded trust did not properly belong to civil society, and, since man was (as Aristotle said) a political animal, the liar lost "the title of a man."[17] This judgment had proverbial status in seventeenth-century England: "He that hath lost his credit is dead to the world."[18] In the 1620s the Anglican divine Henry Mason observed that the lie "disturbeth humane society, and hindereth mutuall commerce": "societie and commerce must needs be disturbed, when men in wisedom may not belleue one another, vpon their words or oathes."[19] In mid-seventeenth-century Scotland the jurist Sir George Mackenzie said that untruthfulness "striks at the root of all humane society." Any society in which people could not routinely trust one another's relations would fall apart. It would be incapable of the complex coordination necessary for "great undertakings."[20] In Restoration England an archbishop of Canterbury preached that "truth and fidelity in all our dealings do create mutual love, and good-will, and confidence among men, which are the great bands of peace," and Sir Charles Wolseley argued for the necessity and propriety of trusting others' narratives: "The World it self is so framed, that Men cannot live and converse together, without putting *some trust* in each other. All the matters of the World cannot be made sure. *Trust,* is the first and chief ground of all humane Converse."[21] Just as trust in truth-telling was understood to be the cement of society, so untruthfulness was seen as a potent social solvent.

Explicit seventeenth-century theorizing about the proper basis of

16. Montaigne, "Of Liars" and "Of Giving the Lie," in idem, *Essays* (1580–1588), 23, 505.

17. Bryskett, *Discourse of Civill Life* (1606), 49; cf. MacIntyre, *After Virtue,* 151.

18. Ray, *Collection of English Proverbs* (1670), 6.

19. Mason, *New Art of Lying,* 88, 96.

20. Mackenzie, *Moral Paradox,* 18; idem, *Moral Essay Preferring Solitude,* 58–59.

21. Tillotson, "Sermon III. The Advantages of Religion to Societies," in idem, *Works,* I, 37; Wolseley, *Unreasonableness of Atheism* (1675), 153.

civil society occasionally formalized the role of trust. John Locke argued that the legitimate foundation of the obligation citizens owed to the sovereign power resided in a notion of trust—the sovereign's undertaking, commitment, or promise to the people to perform certain offices and to perform these within a specified domain of lawful action. Locke's political philosophy drew upon formal legal notions of "trust" and "trusteeship," but he also built upon a commonsensical understanding of what was involved in making a promise to another and in reposing trust in another's relations about the world. Civil society emerged out of the state of nature from people's desire to protect their property. That led them to erect an "indifferent Judge" with the authority to decide disputes "according to the established Law." The judge, or governing power, therefore accepted a trust to execute its task according to certain conditions, and in turn offered a promise that it would do so. The existing form of obligation, and of civil society, was thus coterminous with the honoring of that trust. If and when the people decided that the promise was not being honored, and the purportedly indifferent judge had lied to them, both the obligation and the social order that flowed from it were at a legitimate end. Society was made through an act of trust; it continued so long as the trust was being acquitted; and it was voided when trust was violated.[22]

For Locke, as John Dunn has observed, "the fundamental bond of human society—what makes it possible for human beings to associate with each other as human beings at all—is *fides,* the duty to observe mutual undertakings and the virtue of consistently discharging this duty. Truth and the keeping of faith . . . belong to 'Men, as Men, and not as Members of Society'."[23] Samuel Johnson reckoned that even the social order of hell was founded upon the general reliability of the utterances of the condemned: there were entirely pragmatic reasons why a society of the damned required trust no less than that of the virtuous.[24] The problem for social order created by untruthfulness was not lying in itself but the *unpredictable* reliability of the liar's relations. As Montaigne recognized, "If falsehood, like truth, had only one face, we would be in better shape. For we would take as certain the opposite of what the liar said. But the reverse of truth has a hundred thousand shapes and a limitless field."[25] The liar disoriented those who were obliged to cooperate with him or to act upon his relations.

No theorists attended more centrally to the role of trust in social

22. Locke, *Two Treatises of Government,* e.g., Bk. II, sects. 110, 155–56, 226–27; see also Dunn, "Concept of 'Trust'"; Silver, "'Trust' in Social and Political Theory," 52–54.
23. Dunn, "Trust and Political Agency," 80–81. Dunn here quotes Locke's *Two Treatises of Government,* Bk. II, sect. 14.
24. Johnson, *Adventurer* 50 (20 April 1753), quoted in Bok, *Lying,* 19–20.
25. Montaigne, *Essays,* 24.

order than the eighteenth-century Scots. All the Common Sense philosophers agreed that social order was predicated upon trust in others'
truthfulness. Francis Hutcheson reckoned that this most basic principle
of sociality was innate, one of the "immediate principles in our nature."
Our fellows have a natural desire to know the truth from us, and we
have a natural disposition to tell it: "Truth is the natural production
of the mind when it gets the capacity of communicating it, dissimulation and disguise are plainly artificial effects of design and reflection."
So great are "the general advantages of sincerity and of the mutual
confidence then arising in society," and so pernicious are the "effects
of insincerity and falsehood," that the necessity must be very great for
any breach of truthfulness to be justified. Breaches of faith, "were they
frequent in society, must destroy all social commerce."[26] Adam Smith
likewise identified a natural disposition to believe which was likely always to prevail over tendencies to doubt and distrust others' relations.
The attribution of truthfulness was fundamental to membership in the
moral community:

> To tell a man that he lies, is of all affronts the most mortal. But
> whoever seriously and wilfully deceives is necessarily conscious to him-
> self that he merits this affront, that he does not deserve to be believed,
> and that he forfeits all title to that sort of credit from which alone he
> can derive any sort of ease, comfort, or satisfaction in the society of
> his equals. The man who had the misfortune to imagine that nobody
> believed a single word he said, would feel himself the outcast of hu-
> man society, would dread the very thought of going into it, or of
> presenting himself before it, and could scarce fail, I think, to die of
> despair.

To wish to be believed by one's fellows was "a natural desire." To
believe another was to give him respect and to endow him with authority: "The man whom we believe is necessarily, in the things concerning
which we believe him, our leader and director. . . ."[27] David Hume
dissented from this position only in the denial that fidelity, promise-
keeping, and truthfulness followed from anything innate in human
nature. Fidelity was a convention, not a "natural human virtue," but
being a convention made it no less fundamental to the maintenance
of social order. There will be no society if there is no well-reposed
trust in members' commitments and relations, no moral obligation to
keep promises and speak truth.[28] For Hume it was a defensible conclusion of *experience* that men were "commonly" inclined towards truthful-

---

26. Hutcheson, *System of Moral Philosophy* (1755), II, 2–3, 28–29, 35.
27. Smith, *Theory of Moral Sentiments* (1759), 336–37.
28. Hume, *Treatise of Human Nature* (1739–40), 519–22.

ness and felt "shame when detected in a falsehood": "A man delirious, or noted for falsehood and villany, has no manner of authority with us."[29]

Modern social theorists have elaborated the old theme. For Durkheim the organic solidarity of modern societies was possible only because cooperative behavior was saturated with moral sentiments,[30] while a modern Scottish philosopher of sociability has revived an innatist version of the Common Sense tradition. Barry Barnes rejects the idea that the social-order problem is solved by insinuating society's norms into calculative asocial individuals. Infants' translation into competent adults proceeds via learning, and learning presupposes trust in the reliability of knowledge-sources: "Trust and co-operation are manifest, [as is] the quest for standing as a competent member in the relevant context. In the acquisition of language and in the acquisition of knowledge, the child reveals an inherent sociability. That sociability is essential; verbally mediated learning would be impossible in its absence."[31] Alasdair MacIntyre argues that members of any given social "practice," sharing the standards and values of that practice, define their relationships with each other "by reference to standards of truthfulness and trust." Without those virtues no practice has integrity.[32] In late twentieth-century America imputations of insincerity and dishonesty threaten to become the institutionalized language of politics, resulting not only in the further debasement of public discourse but also in renewed academic attention to the role of trust in social order. Some have noted that the force of such imputations indicates that the norms survive, while other commentators suggest that the accusation of lying is beginning to lose some of its potency. The moral philosopher Sissela Bok understands that "trust is a social good. . . . When it is damaged the community as a whole suffers; and when it is destroyed, societies falter and collapse."[33] Approaching the problem of wider social order from the other end, the political scientist Yaron Ezrahi has drawn attention to the ways in which scientific and technical norms in modern democratic societies have made it possible "to substitute technical discipline for moral, organizational and political controls as socially trusted guarantors of the integrity of public actions." The public order which

29. Hume, *Enquiry Concerning Human Understanding* (1748), 112.

30. Durkheim, *Division of Labor in Society,* esp. 280.

31. Barnes, *Nature of Power,* 33–34, 88–89 (drawing upon social-psychological work by Colwyn Trevarthen, e.g., "Foundations of Intersubjectivity"); cf. Polanyi, *Science, Faith and Society,* 45. Wittgenstein speculated (*Zettel,* sect. 566) that "the attitude, the behaviour, of trusting" might be a human universal.

32. MacIntyre, *After Virtue,* 192–93.

33. Bok, *Lying,* 28–29, 185–91, quoting 28; see also B. Barber, *Logic and Limits of Trust,* esp. chs 1–2, 7–8.

now characterizes modern Western society is, in this view, largely grounded in trust in institutionalized bodies of instrumental expertise.[34]

The central role of truthfulness and trust in the constitution of society continues to preoccupy present-day micro- and macrosociological theorists. Erving Goffman's work on small-scale social interaction noticed that the dealings of individuals in the immediate presence of others have "a promissory character." Individuals present themselves to others as persons of a certain kind, likely to behave in certain ways, and, in so doing, request others actively to accept them as that kind of person. Trust in self-presentation is essential to interaction, yet only the future will tell whether that trust has been well reposed. The working consensus of social life depends upon morally textured inference: you do not know, but only infer, that if you invite me into your home, I will not steal the spoons.[35] The practical stability of social interaction is partly sustained by my knowledge of the expectations my presentation has generated in you. If I claim to be a certain sort of person, I acknowledge the appropriate moral expectations you have of me. Thus, as Howard Becker observes, "If one claims implicitly, in presenting himself to others, to be truthful, he cannot allow himself to be caught in a lie and is in this way committed to truth-telling."[36] Even writing in a game-theoretic mood, Goffman noted that "the willingness of an individual to credit another's unconditional and conditional avowals is an entirely necessary thing for the maintenance of collaborative social activity and, as such, a central and constant feature of social life."[37]

Trust has also been central to sociological theorizing about the nature of modernity and postmodernity. Georg Simmel recognized that truth-telling was "of the most far-reaching significance for relations among men," and that social systems varied enormously in their tolerance for lying and distrust. Very simple societies were said to be relatively tolerant of untruthfulness, whereas deceit and distrust worked lethal effects on highly differentiated and interdependent modern societies. Modern life, Simmel said, "is a 'credit economy' in a much

---

34. Ezrahi, *Descent of Icarus*, ch. 2, quoting 44; see also T. Porter, "Quantification and the Accounting Ideal in Science"; idem, "Objectivity as Standardization." I return to this theme in the epilogue.

35. E.g., Goffman, *Presentation of Self*, 1–14; idem, *Interaction Ritual*, esp. 5–45; idem, "Interaction Order," 3.

36. Becker, "Notes on the Concept of Commitment," in idem, *Sociological Work*, 269.

37. Goffman, *Strategic Interaction*, 104. It might also be added that social *occasions* vary enormously in their tolerances: contrast dealing with salespeople, teasing, and flirting with formal oath-giving. Truth-telling is policed according to what is understood and expected in the circumstances.

broader than a strictly economic sense." Here social existence "rests on a thousand premises which the single individual cannot trace and verify to their roots at all, but must take on faith." Indeed, for Simmel, trust was simply a form of faith, a normative expectation about probable outcomes.[38] Niklas Luhmann treats trust within a broadly functional perspective. It is a necessary mechanism for dealing with and reducing complexity. It is "a basic fact of social life" without which one could not get out of bed in the morning, still less function as a competent member of any conceivable social order. We take a necessary risk in reposing trust; we anticipate a future containing others' actions, treating it as though it were certain, with the result that it *can be* about as certain as anything else. Trust offers us a basis for action, considering only certain possibilities in the future instead of an infinite range.[39]

Trust is integral to social order, yet the manner in which trust is reposed is said to distinguish modern from premodern order. Modernity produces a highly complex array of social information while reducing the familiarity with people that was the basis of traditional trust. In the past, we made judgments of other people; now we are obliged to trust in impersonal systems, for the cost of doing otherwise is unbearable. Anthony Giddens diagnoses the modern condition as a set of "disembedding mechanisms" by which relations more and more take place between individuals separated in space and in which social relations in a given space and time are more and more infiltrated by physically absent others. Social relations are lifted out of local scenes of interaction and restructured in abstract time-space. All disembedding mechanisms—think of money—depend upon trust. Like Simmel and Luhmann, Giddens sees modernity as the shift from reposing trust in individuals in contexts of face-to-face interaction to trust in systems and abstract capacities. We board a plane trusting it to get us safely to our destination not because we have familiarity with the design engineer or the pilot but because we trust that reliable *systems of expertise* were brought to bear in constructing the plane and will be devoted to flying it.[40]

38. Simmel, "The Lie," in idem, *The Sociology of Georg Simmel*, 312–13; idem, *Philosophy of Money*, esp. 179; see also Holzner, "Sociological Reflections on Trust," 337–38.

39. Luhmann, *Trust and Power*, esp. 4, 7–8, 10, 21–22; see also idem, "Familiarity, Confidence, Trust"; Holzner, "Sociological Reflections on Trust," 333–34, 340–41; B. Barber, *Logic and Limits of Trust*, 10–11; Silver, "'Trust' in Social and Political Theory," 59–63; Dunn, "Trust and Political Agency," 85; and, for extended treatment of the relationship between trust, credibility, and social order, see Elster, *The Cement of Society*, 272–87.

40. Giddens, *Consequences of Modernity*, esp. 21–27, 79–85. To be sure, if planes routinely crashed we would not place much trust in these systems of expertise, and I will deal later with the source of the factual knowledge we might use to make a judgment

Trust and the Order of Knowledge

There is no missing the role of trust in thinking about the problem of social order. Social theorists have always noted it, commented upon it, and practically addressed themselves to threats to social order posed by abusing trust or unwarrantably withholding trust. What could social order be without the interdependence signaled and enabled by the allocation of trust? By contrast, the role of trust and authority in the constitution and maintenance of systems of valued *knowledge* has been practically invisible. The problem, indeed, has not been one of neglect. Rather, much modern epistemology has systematically argued that legitimate knowledge is defined precisely by its rejection of trust. If we are heard to say that we know something on the basis of trust, we are understood to say that we do not possess genuine knowledge at all. It is unwise to take the world on trust. Fools, cowards, and quacks do that sort of thing, and that is one way we recognize them as such. Trust and authority stand against the very idea of *science*. While Montaigne claimed that there was "no harm" in the fact that "almost all the opinions we have are taken on authority and on credit,"[41] the seventeenth-century 'moderns' distinguished themselves from the Scholastic 'ancients' precisely through the opposite view. From Gilbert and Bacon to Descartes and Boyle, the new philosophers of nature and their cultural allies avowed the supremacy of direct individual experience or intuition over trusting the authority of previous writers. Natural knowledge, properly so called, was founded in the evidence of nature or of individual reason, not in the say-so of traditionally trusted sources, and chapter 5 will briefly review the terms in which seventeenth-century scientific practitioners sought to reject or discipline the role of trust.

This was the optimistic and individualistic epistemology parodied by Sir Karl Popper: "there was no need for any man to appeal to authority in matters of truth because each man carried the sources of knowledge in himself."[42] The Restoration natural theology of Edward Stillingfleet lamented the distorting effects of collective practices upon truth: "There are *few* in the world that *look* after *truth* with their own *eyes,* most make use of *spectacles* of others making, which makes them so seldom *behold* the proper *lineaments* in the *face* of truth; which the several *tinctures* from *education, authority, custom,* and *predisposition* do

---

of that sort. The epilogue picks up an important claim Giddens briefly makes in this connection about personal "access points" in one's relationship with the institutions that house expertise.

41. Montaigne, "Of Physiognomy," in idem, *Essays,* 792.
42. Popper, *Conjectures and Refutations,* 5, also 15–18.

exceedingly *hinder* men from *discerning* of."[43] John Locke laid it down that "in the sciences, every one has so much as he really knows and comprehends. What he believes only, and takes upon trust, are but shreds." There was no more common, or more defective, way men used to "regulate their assent" than to pin their faith on "the opinion of others." That way lay both epistemic error and moral danger: "If the opinions and persuasions of others, whom we know and think well of, be a ground of assent, men have reason to be Heathens in Japan, Mahometans in Turkey, Papists in Spain, Protestants in England, and Lutherans in Sweden."[44] Knowledge is supposed to be the product of a sovereign individual confronting the world; reliance upon the views of others produces error. The very distrust which social theorists have identified as the most potent way of dissolving social order is said to be the most potent means of constructing our knowledge.

A Skeptical Experiment

Let us, therefore, conduct an experiment with distrust. Take an item of present-day factual knowledge which we know with as much confidence as any other. This item will then stand for the epistemic result of whatever processes constitute and maintain the knowledge we consider most true and most reliable. I propose that we take the factual proposition that 'DNA contains cytosine.' I assume that many readers—having encountered elements of molecular biology in common or specialized cultures—give their assent to this claim and regard it as true. I further assume that a sizable proportion of the same group do not hold this knowledge on the basis of their own direct experience and have never had occasion to attempt individual verification. Given modern individualistic epistemological preferences, that group ought to be satisfied that they do not possess genuine knowledge at all, although they may be disposed to say that there are *other* individuals who are properly entitled to that knowledge on grounds of direct experience. This expert group would presumably include all those people who apparently do not hold their knowledge of DNA on the basis of trusted sources but are satisfied that they have checked out the relevant bit of reality firsthand.

As it happens, I belong to the latter group. When I worked in a genetics laboratory many years ago, I extracted DNA from mammalian cells and then subjected it to chemical analysis. It may therefore be

43. Stillingfleet, *Origines Sacræ* (1662), 7.
44. Locke, *Essay Concerning Human Understanding*, Bk. I. ch. 3, sect. 24; Bk. IV, ch. 15, sect. 6; see also ibid., ch. 17, sect. 19; ch. 20, sect. 17. Locke's formulation closely paralleled that of Boyle ("Christian Virtuoso, Appendix to First Part," 712).

said that I enjoy firsthand, and properly founded, knowledge of the identity of DNA. Here was what I did:[45] I was given some pieces of rat liver which I then minced and froze in liquid nitrogen; I ground the frozen tissue and suspended it in digestion buffer; I incubated the sample at 50° C for 16 hours in a tightly capped tube; I then extracted the sample with a solution of 25 : 24 : 1 phenol/chloroform/isoamyl alcohol and centrifuged it for 10 minutes at 1700 × *g* in a swinging bucket rotor. Transferring the top (aqueous) layer to a new tube, I added ½ volume of 7.5 M ammonium acetate and 2 volumes of 100% ethanol. A stringy precipitate then formed in the tube, which was recovered by centrifugation at 1700 × *g* for 2 minutes. I rinsed the pellet with 70% ethanol, decanted the ethanol, and air-dried the pellet. I went on to hydrolyze the sample and to perform a chemical test confirming the presence of the nucleotide cytosine. This was DNA; I had it in my hand; and I had verified the facts of its composition.

A moment's reflection about this experience gives grounds for skepticism about the 'firsthand' character of my knowledge. I knew that a certain outcome of a chemical test stood for the presence of cytosine, just as I knew that the dried precipitate which I held in my hand was DNA. I do not recall that I, or any other worker in that laboratory, expressed any skepticism about the nature of the precipitate or the adequacy of the test for cytosine, but, of course, I could have. I could, for example, have sought further to verify the identity of the precipitate by subjecting it to additional chemical, as well as biological and physical, assays. It would have been very time-consuming and I would have made myself a nuisance by requiring the appropriate verification, but there was no reason in principle why I could not have done so. I might then have considered that I was *finally* entitled to say that I had my factual knowledge of DNA directly, without reliance upon trustworthy sources.[46]

Skepticism is always a possible move, but its possibility derives from a system in which we take other relevant knowledge on trust. My extraction of DNA took on trust the identity of the animal tissue sup-

---

45. Or, to be absolutely truthful, this is an updated protocol of the general procedure I *must* have used, since I cannot now remember the technical details and my laboratory notebooks have been lost: "Preparation and Analysis of DNA," in *Current Protocols in Molecular Biology*, Supplement 9, eds F. M. Ausubel et al., New York: Wiley, 1990. (I thank Joshua Jorgensen for pointing out how out-of-date my scientific training had become.) As a general matter, when people say that they warrant knowledge on the basis of firsthand experience, they should almost always be heard to say that they do so on the basis of their *memory* of that experience—an argument well made by John Locke, *Essay Concerning Human Understanding*, Bk. IV, ch. 16, sects. 1–2.

46. Here I set aside treatment of the trust-dependency of the *generalization* involved in the move from my factual findings about *this sample of DNA* to the fact about cytosine in *the genus DNA*.

plied, the speed of the centrifuge, the reliability of thermometric readings, the qualitative and quantitative makeup of various solvents, the
rules of arithmetic. Of course, I could have, in principle and at considerable cost of time and money, adopted a skeptical posture about the
truthfulness of the label on the 'ethanol' bottle, and consequently about
the competence and honesty of whoever prepared the liquid. I could
have tested the putative ethanol for its chemical and physical properties. In so doing, I would probably have relied upon the competence
and honesty of whoever prepared the instruments and chemicals I
would then be using in distrusting the identity of the alleged ethanol.
It should, therefore, be obvious that each act of distrust would be
predicated upon an overall framework of trust, and, indeed, all distrust
presupposes a system of takings-for-granted which make *this instance*
of distrust possible. Distrust is something which takes place on the
margins of trusting systems.[47] While actors' schemes may set trust and
skepticism in opposition, the invitation to the analyst is to envisage a
relationship between trust and skepticism in which the character of
skepticism depends upon the extent and quality of trust.

   This experiment in distrust was, of course, wholly imaginary. It is
safe to assume that no practicing scientist has ever carried skepticism
so far. Both pragmatic and moral considerations weigh against even
considering such thoroughgoing skepticism. Commitment to distrust
on that scale would oblige skeptics to work backwards through their
community's accumulated knowledge. Cultural change, and what
counted as progress in the field, would be forced, against considerable
resistance, to run in reverse. Counterlaboratories would have to be
constructed and grant proposals would have to be written for the announced purpose not of securing new knowledge but of subjecting
some of the community's hard-won and stable knowledge to systematic
scrutiny. Indeed, the very identity and solidarity of the scientific community stem from members' need to trust each other if each individual
is to add to the stock of credible knowledge.[48] If skeptics were able,
and enabled, to persist, they could, however, envisage an outcome to
their indefinite perseverance: they would ultimately succeed in knowing nothing at all. A piece of suggestive, if disputable, etymology links

47. See Barnes's concise account of the knowledge-dependency of skepticism with
respect to anomalous scientific findings: *About Science*, 59–63; and, for practical trust in
the black boxes of modern science, see Jordan and Lynch, "The Sociology of a Genetic
Engineering Technique," esp. 93, 102.
   48. The exposition of Bruno Latour's network-theory of scientific knowledge (*Science
in Action*, ch. 1) utilizes such an imaginary exercise in distrust while preferring an apparently coercive to a moral-pragmatic conception of the limits to skepticism. For an ethno-
graphic engagement with trust and credibility in modern science, see Latour and
Woolgar, *Laboratory Life*, ch. 5.

the English words *trust* and *truth* through a Germanic word for
"tree"[49]—as firm and straight as a tree. Trust/truth is therefore, like
a tree, something to be relied upon, something which is durable, which
resists and will support you. Without that durable thing to lean on,
you could not do anything.

There are moral as well as pragmatic reasons which make distrust
difficult. It is at least uncivil, and perhaps terminally so, to decline to
take knowledge from authoritative sources. And if it is considered
discourteous to distrust professors of biochemical genetics, it is not
much less ill-mannered to express skepticism about the reliability and
sincerity of the suppliers of the instruments and reagents on which
the smooth running of the laboratory (and the discipline) depend.
Skeptics run the real risk of being ejected from the practical communities of which they are members. Their skepticism expresses an uncooperativeness which invites uncooperativeness from others. Persistent
distrust, therefore, has a moral terminus: expulsion from the community. If you will not know, and accept the adequate grounds for, what
the community knows, you will not belong to it, and even your distrust
will not be recognized as such. Radical skepticism cannot survive the
short trip from the solitude of the study to the street, as, indeed, David
Hume recognized: "The great subverter of *Pyrrhonism* or the excessive
principles of scepticism is action, and employment, and the occupations
of common life." What may flourish "in the schools" vanishes "like
smoke" in everyday conversation.[50] However far the skeptic pushes his
principles, "he must act . . . and live, and converse like other men; and
for this conduct he is not obliged to give any other reason than the
absolute necessity he lies under of so doing."[51] Mary Douglas's observation that radical skepticism is incompatible with "the commitment to
ordering and organizing" people is, therefore, a moral expansion of
Wittgenstein's dictum that "doubting has an end."[52]

Skepticism and the search for independent verification are, without
doubt, real and substantial features of both lay and scientific systems
of empirical knowledge. We can, and many people do, distrust what
some authoritative source says about the world, though such distrust is
certainly a far less pervasive and systematic feature of natural scientific
practice than some of the more fanciful textbook sociologies and phi-

49. Partridge, *Origins*, 740.
50. Hume, *Enquiry Concerning Human Nature*, 158–59; see also idem, *Treatise of Human Nature*, 183; and Toulmin, *The Uses of Argument*, 163–66, 230–32.
51. Hume, *Dialogues Concerning Natural Religion* (comp. *ca.* 1751–55), 134.
52. M. Douglas, "Social Preconditions of Radical Scepticism," 78; Wittgenstein, *Philosophical Investigations*, Pt. II, v.

losophies would have us believe.[53] Replication *happens,* and the claims of even the most prestigious scientist are occasionally subjected to independent trial. I do not argue for the role of trust *against* that of experience and its modes (including replication), though, indeed I want to draw attention to how much of our empirical knowledge is held solely on the basis of what trustworthy sources tell us. Rather, I want to establish the ineradicable role of trust, even in skeptical search for an individual and independent grounding of knowledge. Insofar as experience is obliged to transit a nexus of trust in order to become a part of our knowledge, then there is no aspect of our knowledge we can speak about which can be set apart from our moral order.

Neither scientists nor laypeople have experience, as it were, by itself: whenever experiments are performed and the results of empirical engagement with the world are reported and assessed, this is done within some system in which trust has been reposed and background knowledge taken for granted. When we have experience, we recognize it as experience-of-a-certain-sort only by virtue of a system of trust through which our existing state of knowledge has been built up. In everyday speech it is, indeed, sensible to say that there is trust and there is experience, and in this book I am content, for the most part, to use the categories of common speech in order to understand how those categories are constituted. But it is incorrect to say that we can ever have experience outside a nexus of trust *of some kind.* Such skepticism as we choose to exercise is not a stepping outside of trust; it is, instead, the attempted calibration of one dubiously trustworthy source by others assumed to be trustworthy. This is, no doubt, not how the search for independent verification appears to skeptics. They may seek to discipline trust by *plausibility,* by comparing the claim in question with an overall ordered sense of what the world is like.[54]

In *actors' schemes* the plausibility of a claim and the trustworthiness of a claimant can appear as independent variables, which, when summed, factored, or compared together, yield a reliable judgment of credibility. Hume's argument that it was more likely that tellers of miracle-tales

53. A number of sociologists of science have, for example, drawn attention to the relative rarity of experimental replication. Polanyi (*Personal Knowledge,* 217) noted that if we attempted to replicate any appreciable part of the observations of science and failed to do so, "we would quite rightly ascribe our failure to our lack of skill"; see also Collins, *Changing Order,* esp. chs 2, 4. Mertonian sociologists have established what a large proportion of scientific papers are never even cited: Cole and Cole, *Social Stratification in Science,* 228; Hagstrom, "Production of Culture in Science," 762; see also Ziman, *Reliable Knowledge,* 130; Hull, *Science as a Process,* 348, 394.

54. An early attempt to assess the role of plausibility schemes in scientific judgment is B. Harvey, "Plausibility and the Evaluation of Knowledge," and in chapters 5 and 6 I offer a detailed account of the role of plausibility judgments.

were deceived or deceitful than that their alleged matters of fact had really happened is perhaps the most celebrated instantiation of this binary credibility-testing scheme.[55] Yet that apparently independent sense of plausibility was not, as Wittgenstein noted, acquired by "satisfying myself of its correctness; nor do I have it because I am satisfied of its correctness. No: it is the inherited background against which I distinguish between true and false."[56] Our schemes of plausibility, which become so naturalized that they appear wholly independent of trust, were themselves built up by crediting the relations of trusted sources. The *appearance* of plausibility as an independent criterion is the result of a massively consequential *evaluation*, splitting judgments of what is the case from the everyday relations by which knowledge is made, sustained, and transmitted. Plausibility incorporates judgments of trustworthiness *at a remove*. It is trust institutionalized.

Trust and the Order of Scientific Knowledge

Some theorists opposed to individualistic and empiricist accounts of knowledge have pointed to the constitutive role of trust in systems of knowledge generally. The phenomenologist Alfred Schutz's account of everyday knowledge stressed that "only a small part of my knowledge of the world originates within my personal experience. The greater part is socially derived, handed down to me by my friends, my parents, my teachers and the teachers of my teachers." In all cases, that knowledge only becomes 'mine' through a prior allocation of trust in others.[57] In everyday life, we take our knowledge from a friend who "knows what he's talking about," and from sources treated as "the eyewitness," "the insider," "the analyst," and "the commentator."[58] Wittgenstein reckoned that all knowledge grew from foundations in trust: "The child learns by believing the adult. Doubt comes *after* belief." As children "we learn facts; e.g., that every human being has a brain, and we take them on trust." And as adults we continue to take authoritative knowledge on trust, believing "what people transmit to me in a certain manner." Skepticism can only be carried so far before

55. Hume, *Enquiry Concerning Human Understanding*, sect. 10 ("Of Miracles"). Welbourne (*Community of Knowledge*, 5–6) usefully notes that deliberative weighing of testimony is probably relatively rare: "*All* that is required of a listener who understands a knowledgeable teller if the knowledge is to be successfully transmitted to him is that he *believe* the teller." Later chapters dwell upon episodes of deliberative assessment while also analyzing the cultural schemes which *justify* belief in particular sorts of narrators.

56. Wittgenstein, *On Certainty*, sect. 94.

57. Schutz, *Collected Papers*, I, 13–14; see also idem, *On Phenomenology and Social Relations*, 236–42; Fleck, *Genesis and Development of a Scientific Fact*, 38, 41–43.

58. Schutz, *Collected Papers*, II, 131–34; Embree, "Schutz on Science," 255–57.

it collapses in the face of our commitments to a shared way of acting: "The difficulty is to realize the groundlessness of our believing."[59]

The exercise of retrieving the role of trust in the construction and maintenance of our most valued systems of knowledge is beset with particular difficulties. I have already noted seventeenth-century 'modern' rhetoric identifying trust-dependency as a massive epistemic fault. In the nineteenth century, commentators noted, and usually lamented, the growing differentiation and specialization of scientific culture, which made it impossible for any one individual to hold the whole of science in his head. Some writers even doubted whether it was right to refer to a 'corpus of knowledge' if no one person knew it, while others drew attention to the forms of social solidarity which made collectively held knowledge possible.[60] While modern orthodox philosophy of science tends to presume a solitary knower confronting reality, several naturalistically inclined philosophers have acknowledged the facts of cognitive differentiation and division of labor in systems of knowledge.[61] Hilary Putnam, for instance, points to the universal fact "that there is a *division of linguistic labor*." Members of the English-speaking community can reliably use the word *gold* without being able on their own to distinguish the genuine from the fake metal. In everyday usage, it is sufficient that we are aware that there are people who possess the relevant knowledge and who may be considered to vouch for the genuineness of the piece of jewelry we propose to buy. The various parts of the meaning of the word *gold* are distributed across a collectivity. Knowledge may be held by a community even if it is possessed by very few individuals in it. Language-use in lay and scientific contexts alike "require[s] the cooperative activity of a number of persons," and cooperation presupposes a moral bond.[62] Richard Rorty has proposed that such epistemological differentiating notions as "objective truth" be replaced by "unforced agreement" among practically acting communities. "Rationality" is a mode of "civility," and "truth" is given an intersubjective reading as knowledge-freely-held-in-common, which is but another way of identifying the role of trust in the production and maintenance of knowledge: "The only sense in which science is exemplary is that it is a model of human solidarity."[63]

59. Wittgenstein, *On Certainty*, sects. 159–62, 166, 170; see also 23, 34, 196, 204, 220, 263, 600: "What kind of grounds have I for trusting text-books of experimental physics? I have no grounds for not trusting them."

60. E.g., Durkheim, *Division of Labor in Society*, 356–64 (esp. the treatment of Comte and recommendation that philosophy act as "the collective conscience of science").

61. After this book was completed two fine philosophical treatments of trust and testimony appeared which bear significantly upon these arguments: Coady's important *Testimony* and Hardwig's concise account of "The Role of Trust in Knowledge."

62. Putnam, "The Meaning of 'Meaning,'" 227–29.

63. Rorty, "Science as Solidarity," 12, 14–15.

A number of modern philosophers have drawn back from the full-blooded individualist skeptical model which informed so much traditional philosophy of science. Popper's assault on empiricist epistemologies pointed out that most of our assertions about the world "are not based upon observations, but upon all kinds of other sources," including being told the thing by an alleged eyewitness. Yet if you went on to question these eyewitnesses about the sources of their knowledge, "you would in fact never arrive at all those observations by eyewitnesses in the existence of which the empiricist believes. You would find, rather, that with every single step you take, the need for further steps increases in snowball-like fashion."[64] Popper's knockabout criticisms of "Vulgar Marxist" and Mannheimian sociologies of knowledge vigorously attacked what he took to be their *individualism:* "objectivity is closely bound up with the *social aspect of scientific method,* with the fact that science and scientific objectivity do not result from the attempts of individual scientists to be 'objective,' but from the cooperation of many scientists. Scientific objectivity can be described as the intersubjectivity of scientific method."[65] Popper's later location of "epistemology without a knowing subject" in a Platonic "Third World" was a retreat: a naturalistic epistemology requires cooperating collectivity, not *a* knowing subject or a Third World.[66]

Philip Kitcher's recent work represents a sustained, articulate, and powerful philosophical assault on the doctrine of the solitary scientific knower. In an apparently sociological mood, Kitcher argues against those who would deny, or deny the epistemological relevance of, the social character of scientific and mathematical knowledge. He draws attention to the fact that individuals' knowledge is rooted in the authoritative knowledge of their community, which knowledge is, in turn, historically grounded in the authoritative knowledge of preceding communities: "There is very little that we know without reliance on the testimony and support of others. Even in the case of empirical science, most of the knowledge of each individual is based, not on direct experience, but on the communications of others." Even those

64. Popper, *Conjectures and Refutations,* 22–23. Popper here conceived an exercise in distrusting a factual report in *The Times* roughly parallel to my DNA example. Phone *The Times* and you are informed that a reporter was told the matter of fact by the prime minister's office. The dedicated empiricist-skeptic would wind up requiring suitable responses to demands for the reporter's name and for assurance that the voice that informed him did indeed come from Downing Street, *ad infinitum.*

65. Popper, *The Open Society and Its Enemies,* ch. 23 ("The Sociology of Knowledge"), quoting 403 (italics in original).

66. Popper, *Objective Knowledge,* chs. 3–4; cf. Bloor, "Popper's Mystification of Objective Knowledge."

"happy few" enjoying direct experience "are dependent on their colleagues. . . . Their knowledge is sustained, in part, by community
approval of their techniques and background assumptions."[67]

Kitcher approaches the sociological cliff, but draws back just in time:
those "very littles," "mosts," and "in parts" emerge as crucial. There is
a division of cognitive labor in science, but, in Kitcher's view, the
grounds on which individuals are trusted and deemed to be authoritative are empirically adjudicable and rationally explicable. There is, to
be sure, plenty of room for authority and trust in science, and a philosophical project can supposedly instruct scientists whether or not it is
proper to rely on authority and go on trust. But rational scientists in
Kitcher's account can sometimes—even if it is judged impractical—'do
better' than that. Kitcher's scientists are cognitive maximizers who, in
the interests of enhancing output, *may* rationally decide to jettison authority and trust.[68] Using a game-theoretic idiom, Kitcher envisages a
process called "direct calibration," which permits scientists' "earned
authority" to be computed by individual inspection of their historic
"truth-ratio."[69]

The work of Michael Polanyi has been notably invisible even to those
philosophers of science who have alluded to the social character of
scientific knowledge. Polanyi stressed the cognitive differentiation of
scientific culture and the trusting relationships that differentiation enjoined and expressed. If scientists only knew what was available to
them via direct experience, they would, Polanyi observed, know very
little indeed. No scientist, however expert, encompasses the knowledge
of his or her science *as an individual:* "The overwhelming proportion
of our factual beliefs continue therefore to be held at second hand
through trusting others." Scientists, like the laity, hold the bulk of their
knowledge, so to speak, by courtesy. The learner "must believe before
he can know." Trusting is a form of faith indispensable to the holding
and growth of scientific knowledge: it is "a passionate pouring of oneself into untried forms of existence." Trust is a creative as well as a
conservative force in science. Since each acceptance of authoritative
knowledge at the same time modifies existing usage, trusting is an
unending means for the extension and modification of knowledge.
And even the most radical forms of scientific skepticism operate "by
partial submission to an existing consensus: for the revolutionary must

67. Kitcher, *Nature of Mathematical Knowledge*, 5, 91.

68. Kitcher, *Advancement of Science*, ch. 8 ("The Organization of Cognitive Labor");
idem, "Authority, Deference, and the Role of Individual Reason."

69. Kitcher, *Advancement of Science*, 306–18. My chapters 5 and 6 will argue that our
knowledge of others' 'track-records' is itself trust mediated.

speak in terms that people can understand."[70] For all Polanyi's emphasis upon the pervasiveness of trust in science, he did not accept its foundational role. Even though scientist A was obliged to take the knowledge of scientist C on trust, he or she was able directly to check over the knowledge of B who was, in turn, competent to assess C. In this way, Polanyi claimed, direct experience connected the elements of a scientific system, and guaranteed its reliability, even though an individual's experience did not extend very far through the system.[71]

By contrast, Barry Barnes has no such reservations about the role of trust and authority at all points in a scientific system of belief and practice. If, as is usually the case, one conceives of a solitary individual as the unit of action, then knowledge and action can be directly related to each other. Barnes offers a vividly instructive example from our knowledge of elementary geometry:

> If an individual knows Euclid's geometry up to the twentieth theorem we can straightforwardly say that he is in a position to prove the twenty-first theorem: he knows all it is necessary to know. But imagine that this knowledge is spread over the members of a society, some known by some individuals, some by others. We cannot say of this society that it knows enough to prove the twenty-first theorem. To think of the society as an individual writ large in this way would be quite misconceived. Suppose that the different individuals, with the different necessary bits of knowledge, did not know each other, or how to find each other. Or suppose they did not trust each other, or know how to check on each other's trustworthiness. In both cases, the twenty-first theorem would remain unproven. The technical knowledge would have been present in the society, but not the necessary internal ordering—the necessary social relationships—for the proof

---

70. Polanyi, *Personal Knowledge*, 207–08; see also 216, 240–41, 375; idem, *Knowing and Being*, 55; and the less-known work of Yves Simon (e.g., *General Theory of Authority*, ch. 3). The creativity involved in recognizing a new situation as one of a certain kind has been stressed in Howard Becker's sociological view of culture: *Doing Things Together*, ch. 1, esp. 16–19. Bernard Barber ("Trust in Science"; *Logic and Limits of Trust*, 156–62) argues that the modern scientific community has witnessed a resurgence of awareness of members' fiduciary responsibilities to their closest colleagues and to the scientific community as a whole, and, indeed, recent American preoccupation with scientific sloppiness and dishonesty has publicly underscored the trust-dependency of scientific knowledge: e.g., Broad and Wade, *Betrayers of the Truth;* Stewart and Feder, "The Integrity of the Scientific Literature"; Turner, "Forms of Patronage"; Chubin, "Scientific Malpractice"; cf. Bodewitz, Buurma, and de Vries, "Regulatory Science and the Social Management of Trust."

71. Polanyi, *Personal Knowledge*, 217; idem, *Science, Faith and Society*, 48–49 (a claim endorsed in Kitcher, *Advancement of Science*, ch. 8, sect. 7); cf. Ziman, *Public Knowledge*, 65–66, 137–38. This argument, of course, sets aside the foundational role of trust identified in the imaginary skeptical experiment regarding DNA.

to be executed. Individuals would have known enough mathematics,
but not known enough about themselves.[72]

The example is, of course, fully generalizable to empirical systems
of knowledge.[73] To have knowledge that DNA contains cytosine, it is
necessary to have at hand not only solutions of chemicals but solutions
to the problem of trust. And the same is the case if one means to be
skeptical about the composition of DNA. Take any practical action or
cultural move in science; then imagine that all trusting social relationships were canceled. Consider the void that would be left. Our prevalent understanding of science—though not, of course, science itself—is
thus deeply paradoxical. We traditionally and formally warrant scientific truth by pointing to individual empirical foundations, yet nothing
recognizable as scientific knowledge would be possible were that knowledge actually to be individually sought and held. Nor would the paradox be resolved if we conceived of scientific knowledge as the aggregate of what individuals hold in their heads. To the aggregate of
individuals we need to add the morally textured relations between
them, notions like authority and trust and the socially situated norms
which identify who is to be trusted, and at what price trust is to be
withheld. The epistemological paradox can be repaired only by removing solitary knowers from the center of knowledge-making scenes and
replacing them with a moral economy.

Trust and the Problem of Order

I have now drawn attention to the relatively well-understood role of
trust in underwriting social order; I have sketched some obstacles
which stand in the way of acknowledging the role of trust in the production and protection of valued systems of knowledge; and I have
pointed to some resources available for extending that appreciation.
Solutions to the problem of trust are necessary for building both social
and cognitive order; indeed, there must be such practical solutions as
a condition for actors' or analysts' being able to recognize social or
cognitive order. But it would be incorrect to assume that these solutions are distinct: the problems of social order and cognitive order are
addressed together. There is a variety of academic idioms in which
the social order–cognitive order dualism has been criticized. I want
briefly to offer a rather abstract account of these critiques, not as a
self-contained exercise in theoretical synthesis, but so that some fully

72. Barnes, *About Science*, ch. 3, quoting 82. A relatively attenuated, but still interesting, engagement with the collectivism of science is Ziman, *Public Knowledge*.
73. Bloor (*Knowledge and Social Imagery*, 168–69) works through a parallel argument
for the case of Boyle's law.

general problems and themes *will resonate in the reader's mind through the historical narratives which follow.*

In social theory and the sociology of knowledge, the neo-Durkheimian tradition has provided one of the most powerful solvents of the opposition that makes the relationship of culture and society problematic. Mary Douglas has consistently pressed the case for treating culture as a set of instruments for making and unmaking social order. The order of society can be conceived of as an order of shared knowledge. The construction and maintenance of a system of knowledge can be treated in the same way as any other collective good.[74] Similarly, Barnes invites us to consider society "as a persisting distribution of knowledge": "How people act depends upon what they know. Anything that is known may affect how people act. Therefore, everything that people know is constitutive of their existence as a society."[75] Even the cognitive processes that generate beliefs and representations are unintelligible in individualistic terms, since, in Douglas's striking phrase, "our colonization of each other's minds is the price we pay for thought."[76] Social institutions require sources and grounds of legitimacy: every institution needs a bit of culture that testifies to "its rightness in reason and in nature."[77]

If society is to be conceived as a distribution of knowledge, how is that network of distribution possible? And if knowledge is generated and upheld by a communal moral order, how is that community possible? Questions of this sort informed the phenomenological tradition in philosophy and social theory, and I want, by way of sketching some characteristic procedures and presuppositions in phenomenology, to prepare the ground for a well-founded historical inquiry into the role of trust in the production of credible factual knowledge. Phenomenological inquiry has been centrally concerned with the texture of everyday relationships between moral and cognitive order. What is it that we have to suppose—about ourselves and about the world—for both social order and held-in-common knowledge to be possible? What, indeed, is it that we have to presume to allow arguments over variation

74. M. Douglas, *How Institutions Think*, esp. 8, 19, 32, 45.
75. Barnes, *Nature of Power*, 45–46; see also idem, "Ostensive Learning and Self-referring Knowledge," esp. 197–99.
76. M. Douglas, *Implicit Meanings*, xx, or, less elegantly: "In his very negotiating activity, each [individual] is forcing culture down the throats of his fellow men" (idem, "Cultural Bias," 189). Cf. Fleck, *Genesis and Development of a Scientific Fact*, 42: "Cognition is the most socially-conditioned activity of man, and knowledge is the paramount social creation."
77. M. Douglas, *How Institutions Think*, 45–47, 55; see also Barnes, *Nature of Power*, 46; Wuthnow, *Meaning and Moral Order*, esp. chs 3–5. Douglas uses "institution" to refer to any legitimized social group, irrespective of size or level of organization—the Conservative party or the 'core-set' of expert nucleic acid biochemists.

in knowledge to proceed and communal membership to be contested or rejected?

From Edmund Husserl to Maurice Merleau-Ponty and Alfred Schutz, the phenomenological tradition has pointed to two related primordial suppositions embedded in the practices of everyday life. First, commonsense action supposes that there is a world external to us, that this world has a certain objective determinate order, and that this order is independent of the acts of observation or representation by which it is known and reported. Everyday thought and action, therefore, are predicated upon robust and confident commonsense realism. Skepticism is, of course, possible within this everyday realism, but it is that robust realism which permits skepticism to happen: "The attitude of everyday life sustains particular doubts, but never global doubts. Indeed, that the existence of the world is never brought into question is an essential requirement for any particular doubt."[78] Doubting, as Bloor puts it, is parasitic on trust.[79] Second, everyday action supposes that we and other human beings are so constituted that this objective and determinate external world is, *ceteris paribus*, available to the perceptions of all of us, and that when we are satisfied that each of us is attending to the same spatiotemporal region, we are seeing an instance of 'the same thing' together.

Taken together, these presuppositions amount to what phenomenologists have called "the natural attitude" of everyday life.[80] And in everyday life this is an *attitude* and not an object of reflective thought. The

78. Zimmerman and Pollner, "The Everyday World as a Phenomenon," 84 (following Schutz); see also Zimmerman, "Facts as a Practical Accomplishment," 133; Bloor, *Knowledge and Social Imagery*, 41–42. Cf. Wittgenstein, *On Certainty*, sect. 105: "All testing, all confirmation and disconfirmation of a hypothesis takes place already within a system. . . . The system is not so much the point of departure, as the element within which arguments have their life"; also sect. 232.

79. Bloor, *Wittgenstein*, 162.

80. This discussion draws upon Husserl, *Ideas*, 101–11; Schutz, *Collected Papers*, I, 7–19, 208–09, 218–22; Berger and Luckmann, *Social Construction of Reality*, ch. 1; Pollner, *Mundane Reason*, ix–xv, 2–16; Heritage, *Garfinkel and Ethnomethodology*, 41–43, 75–102, 212–21. Aspects of this basic phenomenological orientation have also been integrated into symbolic interactionist sociology; e.g., Becker, *Sociological Work*, 312: "One of the ways we know that we are normal human beings is that our perceptual world, on the evidence available to us, seems to be pretty much the same as other people's. We see and hear the same things, make the same kind of sense of them, and where perceptions differ, can explain the difference by a difference in situation or perspective." Early phenomenologists assumed a distinction between the natural attitude of everyday life and the posture of scientific action (see, e.g., Schutz, *Collected Papers*, I, 3–47), while a number of modern sociologists working within that broadly construed tradition have persuasively shown the natural sciences to embody forms of everyday reasoning (e.g., Lynch, "Schutz and the Sociology of Science"; Garfinkel, Lynch, and Livingston, "The Work of a Discovering Science"; Lynch, Livingston, and Garfinkel, "Temporal Order in Laboratory Work").

natural attitude is a practical condition for both action and reflection, including such phenomenological reflection as may take the natural attitude as an intellectual object. For some phenomenologists the commonsense realism of the natural attitude is to be treated as "inherent in thought."[81] The very notion of truth as correspondence between the real and a perception or description presupposes the natural attitude.[82] Social interaction is thus predicated upon the adoption of an informal ontological view, while our sense of what things exist in the world is built upon a moral foundation—a moral expectation about intersubjectivity.

The presumption of an independent, external, and communally knowable world is a precondition for communication. The natural attitude is what makes communication possible and what allows communication reliably to be taken as *referring* to the world. Community is, as it were, built into the natural attitude we employ to accomplish collective action. Through what Schutz calls "the idealization of the interchangeability of the standpoints," one takes for granted, and assumes the other does the same, that, were we to change biographical and physical places, we would enjoy the same perceptual access to the world.[83] Through the conversations of everyday life we *show* each other that this is our presumption. Communication is the mutual display of our assumption of the attitude of everyday life; hence our sense of the value of everyday life proceeds from its being held in common.[84] For the phenomenologist the natural attitude that presupposes the existence of an intersubjectively knowable external world is not treated as a decisive proof that such a world exists: through what Husserl called "the phenomenological reduction," or "putting the world in brackets," the natural attitude is made into a central topic of inquiry.[85] How does it act as the foundation of cognitive and moral order? How is it sustained in the face of challenges, and how, in fact, does the natural attitude provide a powerful resource for the artful repair of cognitive and social order?[86]

81. See, e.g., W. Earle, *Objectivity*, 16. For a suggestion that it is, at any rate, inherent in *language*, see, in a different idiom, Quine, "The Scope and Language of Science," in idem, *Ways of Paradox*, 216–17.

82. Schutz, *Collected Papers*, I, 227; Pollner, *Mundane Reason*, 16–18, 22, 126–27.

83. Schutz, *Collected Papers*, I, 12; see also Garfinkel, "Conception of, and Experiments with, 'Trust,'" 212; Heritage, *Garfinkel and Ethnomethodology*, 54–61; Pollner, *Mundane Reason*, 50–51.

84. Mullin, "Phenomenology and Friendship," 31–32.

85. Schutz, *Collected Papers*, I, 104.

86. For linguistic philosophers' orientation to the fundamental presuppositions of conversational acts, see, e.g., Austin, *How to Do Things with Words*, 14–15 (for "felicity conditions"); Searle, *Speech Acts*, esp. ch. 3 (for "sincerity conditions"); Grice, "Logic

The ethnomethodologist Melvin Pollner uses the term "mundane reason" to designate the repertoire of practices by which presumptions about the nature of an objective external world are embedded within practice and inquiry about that world. It is reasoning about the world, self, and others which presupposes the world and its relationship to the observer. It is a set of presuppositions about the subject, the object, and the nature of their relations. Its legitimacy cannot be demonstrated from within mundane inquiry, since it is incorrigibly presupposed "by virtually any form of praxis." Nor, strictly speaking, is mundanity an object, since "it is the work which provides for the possibility of objects in the first place."[87] Even the sociologists who have placed mundane reason at the center of their account of social and cognitive order have been drawn to talk about it in a functional idiom. The commonsense realism of mundane reason is "profoundly functional": "The social world would undoubtedly collapse if the actors simply shrugged their shoulders every time someone came up with a different version of the events going on before their eyes."[88]

The natural attitude embeds the norm that accounts of the world will *not* be significantly discrepant: the world exists, and exists in a certain way; people have competent access to such a world, and their accounts are presumed reliably to report upon it. Nevertheless, everyday actors are wholly familiar with the fact that variation in reports is endemic.[89] The natural attitude is not therein compromised in any way. First, actors within the natural attitude may help themselves to informal theories about perspective and circumstance to account for discrepant reports about a determinate and in-principle-accessible external world. Reports may vary because individuals are differently situated in space and time (e.g., you were not present when the phenomena were on display), because observational conditions vary (e.g., cloud cover obscured your sight of the comet), or because others may be observing from different angles (e.g., a geometrical figure may present different forms depending upon the face at which one looks). One observer or the other may lack a requisite aid to perception (a telescope or one of sufficient quality), may be perceptually compromised

and Conversation," 43–45 (cf. Schiffrin, "Management of Self," 243); see also Lakoff, "Language in Context," 916; Bolinger, "Truth Is a Linguistic Question," 543. And for sociological assimilation, see esp. Goffman, "Felicity's Conditions," 25–26; and idem, *Forms of Talk*, 14–15.

87. Pollner, *Mundane Reason*, 14, 16, 29.

88. Heritage, *Garfinkel and Ethnomethodology*, 213. Chapter 6 below is an extended exploration of mundane reason at work in passages of seventeenth-century science.

89. Compare, for example, Barnes's concise treatment of discrepant late-nineteenth-century accounts of the existence of an intermediate layer of marine fauna: "Problems of Intelligibility and Paradigm Instances," esp. 119–20.

(myopia, cataracts), or may, in extreme cases, be suffering from a delusionary or hallucinatory condition. Second, there may be a discrimination between 'the same' perception and varying 'interpretations' of that perception. One may grant that 'something' of a determinate structure was observed but not the thing proposed in another's intepretation. Moreover, the natural attitude acknowledges the possibility that observing may be an expert act. Biology pupils learn from teachers to see through a microscope; we accept that only expert geologists can see the parallel roads of Glen Roy. Everyday actors understand that cognition may be distributed across fields of expertise, and that there is such a thing as "the properly accredited witness."[90] Third, a distinction is available between perception and cognition, on the one hand, and representation and reporting, on the other. As John Heritage says, "discrepancies between accounts may be held to result from the fact that one or the other was 'poorly phrased,' metaphorical, ironic, a joke or a lie. In some cases, specific interests may be invoked as a basis for the proposedly discrepant account."[91]

Far from being threatened by the existence of discrepant accounts of the world, mundane reason contains within itself the resources which can repair or resolve variation and further entrench itself as the necessary set of tools for accomplishing social and cognitive order. In the course of this repair, decisions may be taken about what the world is like such that *these* discrepant reports have been made by *these* people. Michael Lynch's study of observational reports in a modern neurobiological laboratory documents the pervasive use of the three repair mechanisms just noted: individuals may cite perspectival circumstances; they may mobilize the gaps between perceptions, cognitions, and representations; and they may proffer uncertainty stipulations ('it may be,' 'I think') so as to defuse conflict between discrepant accounts. Interestingly, they may also negotiate the properties of the object discrepantly reported upon so as to reach agreement upon a stable object whose properties allow varying accounts that are morally and technically competent: "Speakers often show great cleverness in providing for the object in consistent ways which nonetheless reconcile initially contrary assertions. . . . In such explanations the object is not haphazardly reformulated but is provided with qualities, aspects, or implications which show a sensitivity to what a recipient . . . might agree with."[92] Given varying accounts of the object, individuals interact so as

90. Schutz, *Collected Papers*, I, 11–12, 15. The quoted phrase is from Heritage, *Garfinkel and Ethnomethodology*, 215.

91. Heritage, *Garfinkel and Ethnomethodology*, 214–15. This summary draws extensively on Heritage's chapter on "'World Maintenance' as an Institutionalized Activity."

92. Lynch, *Art and Artifact in Laboratory Science*, 214; cf. Garfinkel, Lynch, and Livingston, "The Work of a Discovering Science," esp. 137–38.

to reach agreement about what the object was all along. If A says that a cell is elongated, and B describes it as circular, their subsequent conversation may, for instance, stabilize upon reference to a cell that is, and always was, oval. The conversation need not, though it may, invoke perspectival differences or distinctions of instrumental access or skill. Knowledge of the world is given its shape as conversation proceeds.[93]

Conversation does not necessarily have to reach consensus, nor does it have to 'split the difference' in accounts, as the price of peace. Lynch describes an interactive setting in which there are strong institutional inducements towards peaceable and innocuous resolutions of discrepant accounts, and in which imputations of technical incompetence or insincerity are strongly interdicted. The 'shop-workers' of a scientific laboratory have, after all, to live with each other. Consider, however, the 'reality disjunctures' depicted in Jeff Coulter's study of interaction between a mental welfare officer (MWO) and a former mental patient, currently living in the community.[94] Coulter's transcript of an exchange between patient and MWO has the former reporting that he is being "knocked up" every night. The patient's claim, as it emerges, is that other tenants at his residence have been making noise with the intention of causing the patient to lose sleep, consequently to lose weight, and, ultimately, to be subject to an unwanted and unpleasant medical regime. The "knocking up" reported by the patient *is* that set of intentional acts and no other.

The MWO takes upon himself the role of suggesting some other interpretation of an objectively existing state of affairs which gave rise to the patient's obviously unsatisfactory and unsustainable account: perhaps "variations in your sleep pattern," perhaps the sound of pipes changing temperature, but *not* a purposefully malevolent "knocking up" conspiracy. One has here an "interpretive asymmetry," the proposal of divergent, and differently evaluated, accounts of some acknowledged, actor-independent feature of the world. The patient, as it happened, declined the range of permissible interpretations offered to him, all the while expressing his awareness that another type of accounting was potentially available to the MWO: a decision that the patient was suffering from a delusional condition. Indeed, this was

93. For important work along these lines in the social psychology of perception and belief, see, e.g., Gruber, "From Epistemic Subject to Unique Creative Person at Work," 178–81; Tryphon et al., "De l'ombre à l'objet"; Gruber, "The Cooperative Synthesis of Disparate Points of View"; D. Campbell, "Asch's Moral Epistemology for Socially Shared Knowledge."

94. Coulter, "Perceptual Accounts and Interpretive Asymmetries," esp. 385–91; see also Lynch, *Art and Artifact in Laboratory Science*, 211; Heritage, *Garfinkel and Ethnomethodology*, 215–19.

how the exchange ended—with a morally unpalatable version of interpretative agreement about an existent-in-the-world. The MWO continued to credit the patient's perceptual account while disallowing his
explanation of that perception. However, another outcome, with even
graver consequences for interaction, was possible. Had the MWO concluded that the patient was hallucinatory, he might have denied that
a relevant state of affairs in the world (as reported by the patient)
did exist and was available for perception. Interpretative asymmetries
constitute a rich resource for avoiding ruptures, and, in most social
interactions, they are deployed by participants highly motivated to prevent them. Had the MWO enforced a rupture, he would *at the same
time* have denied that he and the patient reliably reported upon a
world-held-in-common,[95] have concluded that conversation between
himself and the patient could not be sustained, and have assisted in
labeling the patient a paranoid schizophrenic, that is, someone so damaged as not to be a competent member of the community. Ontology—
taken as a sense of what kinds of things exist in the world—is therefore
inscribed within even the smallest-scale of moral economies.

Trust, Manners, and Mundanity

Much commentary on the role of trust in social order has rightly
pointed to its routine, even automatic, quality. How could trust, for
instance, be regarded as a device for reducing social complexity if
certain outcomes or courses of action could not simply be taken for
granted and moved out of the domain of deliberation and inspection?
Yet it is also right to point to highly reflective processes by which
decisions may be taken about whom to trust, in what respects, and in
what circumstances. Here the relationship between trust and explicit
moral discourse becomes more apparent. Some analysts might want to
distinguish, even use a different word for, trust-as-a-routine and *decisions* to grant or withhold trust. I prefer not to, partly because, as I
shall note, skepticism can appear as the purposive movement from
taking an item for granted to subjecting the same item to inspection
and reflection.

Consider some celebrated investigations about the relationship between moral and cognitive order conducted by the ethnomethodologist
Harold Garfinkel. These were not designed as rigorous scientific experiments but as "aids to a sluggish imagination," devices to loosen
up reflection about the problem of order considered quite generally.
Garfinkel asked some of his graduate students to go away and perform
some skepticism with respect to their everyday lives. Put another way,

95. For the MWO this presumed world still existed, though the assumption that it
was equally accessible to, and reportable by, the other was withdrawn.

they were requested to act on the assumption that another person was attempting to lie to them about a reported state of affairs. Almost all students elected to try their experiment in distrust with friends or relatives as there was considerable intuitive worry that the situation might become uncontrollable with strangers. Likewise, students reported that convincing displays of distrust were extremely difficult to perform and maintain. One student distrusted a bus driver's assurance about the route that would be taken, while a "housewife" student distrusted her husband's account of why he was home late the night before. Both situations immediately "turned serious"—reaction to even the most straightforward and apparently inconsequential distrust was often hostility of a quite explosive kind—and in the latter case even acknowledgment that the distrust was in the nature of a "sociology experiment" failed to restore preexisting order in the marriage.[96]

For present purposes these so-called "breaching experiments" help to develop three points about the maintenance of everyday order. First, since, as is evident, order is disrupted with such spectacular ease, it arguably follows that everyday order is actively maintained by a complex set of practices that motivated actors use to constitute "interpretative trust." These practices notably include trusting as a routine, *not* inquiring too far or too much, *not* seeking to go too deeply beyond the 'face value' of things, letting the quality of knowledge be 'sufficient unto the day.' The experiments artificially rend the fabric of everyday ordered life to show how utterly trust-dependent it is. Second, what is breached in these exercises in distrust is not cognitive order *or* moral order (as we are accustomed to make the distinction), but *both at once.* It is not the case that the moral order fails and then the cognitive order fails, or the reverse. They fail together, just as they stabilize together. The same distrust that is understood as an act of hostility is an effective denial of the right of another to colonize one's mind, one's sense of what the world is like. Distrusting the bus driver means that buses reliably running from Westwood to Santa Monica may not be part of one's world; distrusting the husband's account of why he arrived home at 2 A.M. means that a 'husband-working-late-at-the-office' is not an unequivocal fact about the wife's world while a 'husband-having-an-affair' might be; and, similarly, distrusting the biochemist's claims about nucleic acids means that 'DNA contains cytosine' may not be a proposition that describes the world-as-it-is. Third, trust appears

96. Garfinkel, *Studies in Ethnomethodology,* 38, 49–53; see also idem, "Conception of, and Experiments with, 'Trust,'" 217–35. For a critical appreciation of these and related experiments, see Heritage, *Garfinkel and Ethnomethodology,* ch. 4, esp. 97–101. Note that requests for information or justification breed hostility when one is expected to know or accept the matter in question. Presumably, a foreigner's request for reassurance about bus routes would be dealt with differently.

as the cement of social and cognitive order whether it is reposed rou-tinely—taking matters just as they seem to be—or whether it is allo-cated through more or less formal and reflective exercises of delibera-tion. Order may be maintained by routine trusting and it may be ruptured by *deciding* that one does not wish to continue in the same moral community as another, or that another has *decided* to terminate conversation with oneself. The distribution of trust is therefore coex-tensive with the community, and its boundaries are the community's boundaries.

Trust is, quite literally, the great civility. Mundane reason is the space across which trust plays. It provides a set of presuppositions about self, others, and the world which embed trust and which permit both consensus and civil dissensus to occur. A world-known-in-common is built up through acts of trust, and its properties are decided through the civil conversations of trusting individuals. The root of all civility and good manners is therefore the presumption of that basic perceptual competence and sincerity which provide warrants for our conversation as being reliably oriented towards and about the realities upon which we report. The ultimate incivility is the public withdrawal of trust in another's access to the world and in another's moral commit-ment to speaking truth about it: those who cannot be trusted to report reliably and sincerely about the world may not belong to our commu-nity of discourse. It is not just that we do not agree with them; it is that we have withdrawn the possibility of disagreeing with them. The external determinate world is preserved across this great incivility; what is lost is the presumption of a world-known-in-common between the participants to such a rupture. The great civility, therefore, is granting the conditions in which others can colonize our minds and expecting the conditions which allow us to colonize theirs. It is in this sense that a world-known-in-common is part of the moral fabric of ordinary social interaction.

Truth and Consequences

Phenomenological insistence upon the social character of truth con-nects with a currently better-known Foucauldian idiom. Naturally, truth is not "outside of power"; it is not "the reward of free spir-its," or "the child of protracted solitude." Truth is produced and maintained in what Foucault called "régimes," each with its "'general politics' of truth." Foucault too wanted to conceive of truth as a collec-tive way of acting: truth is power in the same way that it is a social institution: "'Truth' is . . . a system of ordered procedures for the production, regulation, distribution, circulation and operation of state-ments. 'Truth' is linked in a circular relation with systems of power which produce and sustain it, and to effects of power which it induces and which extend it. A 'régime' of truth." The "political question," says Foucault, "is not error, illusion, alienated consciousness or ideology; it is truth itself."[97] "Every point in the exercise of power is at the same time a site where knowledge is formed. And conversely every established piece of knowledge permits and assures the exercise of power."[98] The practices by which we accomplish truth amount to our moral order.

Trust builds social and cognitive order; trust is unimaginable in the absence of such order; yet it also proceeds by way of working knowledge of the state of that order at any time. Whom to trust, what to trust, and in what circumstances? And as we perform the next instance of trust, so do we check, make manifest, instantiate, protect, or modify the understood order on the basis of which we trust. The knowledge involved in trust has, of course, a provisional character and an empirical component. Circumstances can induce us to reflect upon our previous routines, to inspect our stock of knowledge for ways of handling problematic instances. We can find that *this* act of trusting was misplaced and, revising our working knowledge accordingly, the scheme of things upon which we reposed that routine trust can change, with the result that the next similar situation may yield a different result. Nevertheless, such empirical feedback as we receive and act upon can have only a partial character. It is information to be assessed against the large background of knowledge we have on trust and continue to take for granted. We might very loosely say that actors have a working picture of the world, and instances can be judged as confirming or disconfirming only in light of *everything else they know* which bears upon the validity of that picture.

One feature of such a picture is knowledge of the likely *consequences* of trusting or distrusting. What will be the probable outcomes of expressions of assent or of skepticism? Consideration of such questions is arguably a prominent feature of a reflective mood, but they may also be thought to feature as part of routine behavior. Certainly, pragmatic considerations are important here. For example, another's skepticism about claims which fit into, support, and extend some scientific theory I hold dear will diminish me. And these are presumably the interested grounds upon which scientists rarely check claims that favor their preferred views or techniques, while they sometimes rigorously check or reject claims conflicting with them. Yet pragmatic considerations of this sort scarcely define the map of likely outcomes upon which trust

97. Foucault, "Truth and Power," in idem, *Power/Knowledge*, 131–33; see also idem, "The Order of Discourse," esp. 54–56; and Latour and Woolgar, *Laboratory Life*, 229.
98. Foucault, "Power and Norm," 62.

is reposed or withheld. The working schemes involved in such judgments also include what can be called knowledge of the distribution of
power in the social world.

True Knowledge and Free Action

To accept the relations of another is, as I have noted, to give that other
the right to furnish our minds and to provide guides for our actions,
while to withhold that right is to deny the other's ability to contribute
to a world-known-in-common. Such judgments are enormously consequential. To trust is to join with others and to show estimation of their
worth; to distrust is to disrupt cooperative relations and to dishonor.
To trust people is to perform a moral act, proceeding on the basis of
what we know about people, their makeup and probable actions with
respect to our decisions. Insofar as knowledge comes to us via other
people's relations, taking in that knowledge, rejecting it, or holding
judgment in abeyance involves knowledge of *who these people are.* What
are their circumstances and characteristics? What, in general and in
this case, do those circumstances and characteristics testify about the
likely reliability of what they say? What of relevance to credibility assessment do we know about them as individuals and as members of
some collectivity? What will probably happen if I assent to this person's
narration and dispute that person's? What do I know about the likely
behavior of these people, as individuals, as representatives of types of
individual, and as members of certain collectivities? Of course, knowledge of people and their natures, individually and collectively, makes
up an enormous portion of our culture. The application of that knowledge to specific instances of claim assessment may likewise involve complex and subtle judgments of what characteristics are relevant to the
case at hand. There is, in principle, no limit to the knowledge deemed
relevant to the giving or withholding of assent to knowledge-claims.
Nevertheless, I want to point to one type of knowledge we may have
of others which has had a distinctive place in credibility assessments in
a wide variety of contexts and which, as I shall argue, was specially
attended to and picked out in the culture of early modern England.

That circumstance is *free action* and the characteristics that might
reliably be attributed to people enjoying free action. By free action I
mean to draw attention to the imputation of unconstrained volition
vis-à-vis others in a social system. Free actors do, and are regarded as
doing, what they judge best, natural, most right, or most pleasing, as
they freely judge these actions to be. By contrast, the judgments and
behavior of the unfree are seen as being constrained—by circumstances or by the consequences of what free actors do. Barnes has
argued that to speak of the powerful agents in society is to speak of

discretionary actors: "Social power *is* the capacity for action in a society, and hence is predominantly but not wholly identifiable as that which is routinely possible therein. Social power is *possessed* by those with discretion in the direction of social action."[99] Recognition and attribution of free action are at the heart of practical social theory. Indeed, Barnes's theory of power is revisionist only with respect to modern social theory. Much early modern culture put free action at the center of its practice of power and its theorizing about power. Society's free actors were considered to be society's powers. There were circumstances which were understood to make it possible to act freely, and the culture was importantly shaped by efforts to define, discern, and display those circumstances. Thus, free action was one of the materials out of which practical and theoretical political culture was constructed.

Even more fundamentally, understandings of free action figure in much reflection about whether or not a person may safely be trusted as a truth-teller. Persons giving a promise bind themselves to others: their word, as the commonplace has it, becomes their bond. To that extent, trusted persons make some set of their future actions predictable by agreeing to forgo a certain amount of free action. And, because those who trust them may forgo relevant precaution or skepticism, they facilitate the free actions of others. Thus, free action appears as a problem to which trust is a solution. If people did and said just as they liked, without regard for others' interests or how things stood in reality, there could be no secure or, indeed, recognizable social order. As Luhmann says, "You cannot trust chaos": "Freedom is the source of the need for trust."[100] Or, in a nonfunctionalist idiom, the concepts of freedom and trust are codependent: neither makes sense without the other.

Since antiquity, ethical writers were generally agreed that promises offered under duress were void and that lies might legitimately be told in order to secure one's life or the good of society. One's word was one's bond only if one was not bound in giving it. The forgoing of free action was considered effective and reliable only if that course was freely decided upon.[101] In that sense, free action was part of the solution to the unpredictability of behavior and word that free action itself engendered. Free action had to be freely disciplined: "Trust, then, is the generalized expectation that the other will handle his freedom."[102] The identification of that appropriate other is an element of practical social theory: only certain types of people, specially placed in the social

99. Barnes, *Nature of Power*, ch. 3, quoting 58.
100. Luhmann, *Trust and Power*, 41.
101. Among many examples, see Cicero, *Offices*, 15–19; A. Smith, *Theory of Moral Sentiments*, 330–33.
102. Luhmann, *Trust and Power*, 39.

system, can be relied upon practically to resolve the paradox involved in the free forgoing of free action.

The recognition of free action, therefore, is inscribed at the center of the culture which justifies trust, which allows trust to be accomplished and social order to be built and sustained. The free actor is a responsible power. And just as free action is fundamental to social order, so free action figures largely in the construction of systems of knowledge: practical social theory and practical epistemology make use of the same materials. Georg Simmel identified what he took to be the peculiar social circumstances of those capable of taking an "objective" view of the world. The stranger was not an isolated individual or one innocent of the customs and conventions of a particular social order: such a person would be not objective but ignorant. Rather, objectivity was said to be the characteristic attitude of those who could freely come and go, belong to and disengage from a society and its system of knowledge: "it is a particular structure composed of distance and nearness, indifference and involvement." That kind of mobility was visible as free action with respect to some particular set of situated ties and constraints. The "objective individual is bound by no commandments which could prejudice his perception, understanding, and evaluation of the given." For Simmel the social circumstance which permitted this kind of truth to be apprehended and spoken belonged to the "stranger," and, locally, to the European Jew. The stranger was "freer"; he was "not tied down in his action by habit, piety, and precedent." It was the stranger's free action which allowed him to see and say truth. In this way, Simmel participated in the great cultural-historical tradition which assigned truth to disengagement and error or distortion to membership in the polity. Particular social ties pulled seeing and saying out of correspondence with the true state of affairs, while freedom from those ties allowed truth to be looked directly in the face and told to others.[103] The solitary intellectual and the stranger are major actors in both practical social theory and practical epistemology.

This book starts by identifying another sort of supposed free actor in the making of knowledge. Unlike Simmel's stranger or Jew, this free actor was not to be found on the periphery of a social system. Instead, his characteristic setting was right at its center. He was the English gentleman, and this book is largely concerned with the cultural practices which recruited patterns of gentlemanly recognition and con-

103. Simmel, "The Stranger," in idem, *Sociology of Simmel*, 402–08, quoting 405, 407. Karl Mannheim's views on the "*freischwebende Intelligenz*" (the term originated with Alfred Weber) recognizably belong to same cast of mind; see, e.g., Mannheim, *Ideology and Utopia*, 136–46; Ringer, "Origins of Mannheim's Sociology of Knowledge," 63–64; Popper, *The Open Society and Its Enemies*, 400–01, 706 n. 3. For Alexandre Koyré's reflections upon lying and unfreedom, see Forrester, "Lying on the Couch," 153–55.

versation for the enterprise of making and maintaining scientific knowledge. How was the English gentleman placed in social and economic culture, and what was the shape of the culture which identified his circumstances, his powers, and his virtues? How did that culture talk about, explain, and enjoin a relationship between gentility and veracity?

CHAPTER TWO

"Who Was Then a Gentleman?"
Integrity and Gentle Identity
in Early Modern England

Every man is not a proper Champion for Truth,
nor fit to take up the Gauntlet in the cause of Verity.

—Sir Thomas Browne, *Religio Medici.*

Gentility was a massively powerful instrument in the recognition, constitution, and protection of truth. In early modern culture the definition of gentility implied a conception of truth, just as the location of
truth in that culture might invoke a notion of gentility. Subsequent
chapters will argue that the cultural practices linking truth to honor
in gentle society were adapted and transferred to provide substantial
practical solutions to problems of credibility in seventeenth-century
English science. A working solution in one area of the culture (gentlemanly society) was transported into another (the new practice of empirical science) to act as a local resolution of a pervasive problem about
the grounds and adequacy of knowledge. How, and with what warrants, might one reliably move from what is said to be the case to what
is the case, from testimony to truth? Whom to trust? Whose relations
about the world to take into one's stock of knowledge? Or, to put it
another way, who had the right to speak for those that did not speak
for themselves? Who might be a reliable spokesman for reality? These
are questions about the identity of cultural actors and about the bases
of reliable knowledge. Accordingly, they belong to practical social theory as well as to practical epistemology.

   This stick can be picked up from either end. There are, nevertheless,
special reasons to begin the inquiry with discussions of the concrete
and the material: social and economic circumstances. Much contemporary social theorizing differentially ascribed characteristics to the gentle
and nongentle on the basis of how they were situated in the social and
economic orders. Contemporary actors understood the gentleman's

qualities, including the guarantees of his truthfulness, to be grounded largely in his placement in social, economic, and biological circumstances. These were considered to be structural realities, which, to be sure, individuals might struggle with, negotiate, respecify, and, even, on occasion, be thought to transcend. They were realities about which culture spoke and which, indeed, were made manifest through institutionalized cultural practices. Nevertheless, early modern actors regarded such structural realities as external to individuals and as relatively resistant to individuals' negotiations. These were the realities which were talked about, and justified, as the causes of gentlemanly traits. As that talk was institutionalized in early modern culture, so the structural realities it referred to were constituted as constraints upon what an individual could do or be. Members of early modern gentle society were highly skilled at discovering the relevant realities and using that knowledge to enforce the boundaries and conditions of social membership. This chapter will concentrate upon materials usually considered the preserve of social and economic historians, while chapter 3 will move to more recognizable cultural-historical terrain. The question, however, remains the same: what were the bases upon which the gentleman was recognized as a reliable truth-teller?

Chapter 1 introduced the ascription relating free action and integrity to truthfulness. Here I want to show how that quite widely distributed identification was grounded and worked out in the specific historical setting of early modern England. I briefly sketch the contours of a culture which recognized the gentleman through that placement in the social and economic orders which was considered most effectively to enable an individual to act free of necessity and constraint. I treat the significance of the demarcation between gentle and nongentle for the overall shape of contemporary culture and for contemporary actors' general understanding of their social order. I introduce the significance for practical social theorizing and action of the distinction between free and unfree, between those who might do as they liked and those who labored under constraint. I sketch the roles of wealth, birth, and virtue in making a gentleman and how early modern culture was shaped by continuing discussions of their respective significance. Finally, I confront the deep uncertainty frequently expressed in early modern English society about who indeed was a gentleman and whether any system of entitlements and recognitions was functioning effectively.

The Grounds of Gentlemanly Free Action

Few boundaries in sixteenth- and seventeenth-century England were at once as substantial, as consequential, and as contested as that dividing society into its gentle and nongentle portions. Contemporary commentators on Tudor and Stuart English society were agreed in seeing the social order as a matter of "degrees," "orders," and "conditions." While views on the bases and origins of these categories varied, at the upper levels of society there was a simple assumption that the social order was, and ought to be, hierarchically structured.[1] *Vade mecums* of the English social order traced the scale of "preeminence" and honor, and were widely available to those who might require periodic reminders of the more subtle gradations. In 1577 William Harrison's *Description of England* followed broadly Aristotelian patterns in sketching the orders of English society; in 1583 portions of his account were closely followed by Sir Thomas Smith's *De Republica Anglorum,* which in turn provided a model for such later writers as John Ferne, Sir William Segar, Thomas Wilson, and John Selden. The map of English society had the character of an institution.

The king headed all; the "nobilitas maior" encompassed dukes, marquesses, viscounts, and barons; the "nobilitas minor" were those knighted by the king; "esquires" were a variously defined group including untitled sons of knights, gentlemen "of the better Rank," and the otherwise "armigerous";[2] and the yeomanry included nongentle freeholders of land. Thus, for Smith, the "policie of England" was made up of four "estates": king, major and minor nobility, gentlemen, and yeoman.[3] All of the above (except the yeomanry) counted as "gentlemen" and, until the late sixteenth century, no distinction was commonly made between the notions of nobility and gentility.[4] In 1581 Richard Mulcaster attempted to distinguish nobility from gentility,

1. M. James, *English Politics and the Concept of Honour,* 63; Fletcher and Stevenson, "Introduction," esp. 1–15.

2. F. Markham, *Booke of Honour* (1625), 61–64; Selden, *Titles of Honor* (1614), 339–51 (for esquires). A visible sign of gentle standing was the coat of arms, as displayed about an individual's real and movable property or on his clothing (traditionally his armor). Arms were, of course, handed down through the lineage, but in the late sixteenth and early seventeenth centuries were increasingly awarded upon petition after an inquiry by the heralds; see, e.g., M. James, *English Politics and the Concept of Honour,* esp. 22–27, 64–65, 87. The title of "baronet" was not created until 1611. Grantees technically had to be from families entitled to bear arms for three generations and who possessed lands with the rental value of £1,000 per annum, but Stuart kings sold the title in a much looser fashion: Wrightson, *English Society,* 21–23; Stone, *Crisis of the Aristocracy,* ch. 3.

3. Harrison, *Description of England* (1577; comp. 1560s), ch. 5; T. Smith, *De Republica Anglorum* (1583; comp. 1565–77), 29–33; Wilson, *State of England* (1601), 38–39. For varying conceptions of the "esquire," see T. Smith, *De Republica Anglorum,* 25–26; Selden, *Titles of Honor;* Wilson, *State of England,* 23.

4. E.g., Ferne, *Blazon of Gentrie* (1586), 4; see also Smythe-Palmer, *Ideal of a Gentleman,* 17–18. By *ca.* 1600 the word *nobility* was increasingly taken to refer to the upper ranks of the aristocracy, though aspects of its more general usage continued through the seventeenth century: Kelso, *Doctrine of the English Gentleman,* 18–20.

partly in terms of preeminence ("*nobilitie* being the flower and *gentilitie* the roote"), but mainly through a discrimination between common inner qualities and their varying expression, "nobilitie emplying the outward note of inward value, and gentilitie signifying the inward value of the outward note."[5] According to Thomas Smith, those referred to simply as "gentlemen" were "those whom their blood and race both make noble and knowne." Whatever the basis of gentility was, it was ascribed to all the grades of nobility in equal measure: "simple gentlemen" possessed it in the same degree as did the greatest of the aristocracy. Gentlemen were divided into their "conditions," but what distinguished the duke from the simple gentleman was a degree of honor accorded by the sovereign to mark out and reward some deed or individual characteristic and then passed on through the lineage.[6] Thus, although inequality in standing and in "authority" was a fact of gentle society—a duke took ritual precedence over an earl and an earl over a simple gentleman—it was not accepted that there was any inequality in the authentic bases of gentility: "Whosoeuer was borne noble (vnder which word is comprised all sorts of Gentlemen) then were they euer reputed equall."[7] In *Henry V*, the King asks Pistol what he is and gets the reply: "As good a gentleman as the Emperor" (IV, i). The normative presumption of gentlemanly equality endured well into the nineteenth century. Thus, the wealthy archdeacon Grantley of Trollope's Barsetshire assured the impecunious Mr. Crawley that "we stand on the only perfect level on which such men can meet each other. We are both gentlemen."[8]

By contrast, the division between the gentle and the nongentle was widely considered to be both evident and (literally) essential. In Peter Laslett's view "the term gentleman marked the exact point at which the traditional social system divided up the population into two extremely unequal sections," and Lawrence Stone agrees that "the division between the gentleman and the rest was basic to Elizabethan society." In that system, and well into the seventeenth century, the distinction between gentle and nongentle was second in cultural significance only

5. Mulcaster, *Positions*, 200. By the 1620s English commentators noted ambiguity and varying uses of nobility and gentility, both domestically and between England and other European countries: see, e.g., F. Markham, *Booke of Honour*, 43–44.

6. T. Smith, *De Republica Anglorum*, 18–28, quoting 26. Harrison, *Description of England*, ch. 5, at 113, follows Smith's formulation, adding "or at least their virtues" to "blood and race."

7. Segar, *Honor Military and Civill* (1602), 121; idem, *Booke of Honor and Armes* (1590), 35–36; cf. Smythe-Palmer, *Ideal of a Gentleman*, 18; Macfarlane, *Origins of English Individualism*, 177–78. On the continuing culture presuming and enjoining gentlemanly equality into the eighteenth century, see, e.g., Clark, *English Society*, 103.

8. Trollope, *Last Chronicle of Barset* (1867), 885.

to that between Christian and heathen.[9] The inequality of the cut de-
marcating gentle and nongentle degrees needs to be stressed. According to Thomas Smith and Thomas Wilson the relevant division
did (and ought to) sharply separate simple gentlemen and above from
yeomen, citizens and burgesses, merchants, artificers, laborers, and
servants. In 1600 Wilson guessed that there were about 500 knights
and about 16,000 gentlemen in the whole of the country. In 1688
Gregory King counted 12,000 simple gentlemen plus 4,500 of higher
condition. If the population of England and Wales at 1600 is taken at
4 million, and at 1700 at 5.5 million, then the proportion of gentry
(provided the estimate is not taken too seriously) is probably no more
than 1 to 5 percent.[10]

That tiny fraction of the people of England regarded themselves as
the political nation, and, so far as having a voice in the sanctioned
public forums was concerned, they *were* the political nation. It was
their voices that were heard in national political deliberations; they
effectively exercised their individual wills in economic, legal, and political deliberations; and they legally spoke for all the rest. In practice,
however, the location of consequential free action and spokesmanship
in the society of gentlemen was not absolutely clear-cut. Yeomen were
also "freemen borne English," who could freely dispose of their own
land and who "have a certaine preheminence" in the shires. In urban
settings "citizens and burgesses" were "free and received as officers
within the cities," though "generally in the shyres they be of none
accompt, save onely in the common assembly of the realme to make
lawes."[11] That is to say, it was recognized that gentlemen were (for all
practical purposes) being made by informal processes which were either not adequately justified by principles of legitimacy or which might
even be in conflict with those principles. As I shall later note, social
mobility made the distinction between gentlemen, on the one hand,
and yeomen and mercantile citizens, on the other, both much contested
and much insisted upon.

In principle, however, the differential possession of the capacity for
economic and political free action grounded the richly varying culture

9. Laslett, *World We Have Lost*, 27; Stone, *Crisis of the Aristocracy*, 34, 49–53; see also
Smythe-Palmer, *Ideal of a Gentleman*, 40.

10. Wilson, *State of England*, 23–24; King, *Natural and Political Observations*, 48–49;
Laslett, *World We Have Lost*, 30–33.

11. T. Smith, *De Republica Anglorum*, 29–33, and, closely following Smith, Harrison,
Description of England, 115–18, and Wilson, *State of England*, 38–39 (though more vehement than the others on the gap between gentlemen and yeomen). John Ferne (*Blazon
of Gentrie*, 7) ambiguously qualified perceptions of craftsmen's free action by stressing
the servility of the extended apprenticeship process; see also M. James, *English Politics
and the Concept of Honour*, 64–65.

that debated the bases of gentility in durable realities of social life. Below the level of gentlemen, yeomen, and citizens there were the masses of laborers, poor husbandmen, merchants who did not possess free land, copyholders, artificers, and craftsmen. These made up the "Sort of Men which doe not rule": "These have no voice nor authoritie in our common wealth, and no account is made of them but onelie to be ruled, not to rule other."[12] This is the circumstance that inclined Laslett to conceive of preindustrial England as a "one-class society." The traditional gentry was "this tiny minority" that "owned most of the wealth, wielded the power and made all the decisions, political, economic and social for the national whole." These alone were the people who acted upon a national stage. If you were not of this degree, "then you counted for little in the world outside your own household, and for almost nothing outside your small village community and its neighbourhood." Your opinion was of no consequence, and you exerted no power over anyone outside your own family. Thus, to exercise power—"to be free of the society of England"—and to count as a relevant political actor in Tudor and Stuart society was (with some necessary qualifications) to be a gentleman.[13] So basic was this identification of the society of gentlemen with the political nation that (as Hill, Macpherson, Laslett, and others have argued) references to "the people" in seventeenth-century political writings (even by the radical writers of the Civil War period) have to be understood in light of taken-for-granted equations between the politically relevant sector of the population and those who enjoyed the freeman's political agency, independence, and integrity. In traditional usage, therefore, "England" meant "a small minority of the English [people]" and "the point of transformation was the change which came with the transition from the commonalty to the gentry."[14]

12. T. Smith, *De Republica Anglorum,* 33–34, though even in their case Smith recognized that in cities, "for default of yeomen" jury panels might include "such manner of people," and "in villages they be commonly made Churchwardens, alecunners, and manie times Constables." This qualification was culturally important, since it was persistently claimed that, unlike the polities of other nations, that of England did not include slaves or bondsmen; see also Harrison, *Description of England,* 118.

13. Laslett, *World We Have Lost,* 27–28. Laslett's view has been disputed by, among others, Hill (see, e.g., "A One-Class Society?"); Neale (*Class in English History,* ch. 3); and Stone (*Crisis of the Aristocracy,* ch. 2). The basic point at issue regarding the application of class terminology is not the facts of inequality or of the distribution of power, but the existence of relevant forms of collective consciousness, especially among the nongentle.

14. Laslett, *World We Have Lost,* 19–20, 27–29; see also Hill, *Society and Puritanism,* 459–63; idem, "Pottage for Free-born Englishmen," 223–27, 342 n. 24; Macpherson, *Political Theory of Possessive Individualism,* ch. 3; Underdown, *Revel, Riot, and Rebellion,* 3 (usefully documenting referential variation in uses of "the people").

Wealth, Work, and Will

Free action and spokesmanship were in turn considered to be grounded in economic structures and social relations. Indeed, the culture that specified who was and who was not a gentleman laid great emphasis on how individuals were placed *vis-à-vis* wealth, work, and the production of goods and services. Recognition, authority, and the political rights of spokesmanship flowed locally from the control of land and the disposition of labor on that land. Wilson reckoned that his five hundred knights enjoyed between £1,000 and £2,000 annual income, and at this level controlled wealth equal to many of the higher nobility. He estimated the rental income of his "esquires" at £500 to £1,000 per year, and guessed that, at least in the north, "a gentleman of good reputation may be content with £300 and £400 yearly." These were the elder brothers, and Wilson bewailed the "most miserable" state of the younger brothers, shifting for even less.[15] Gregory King's late seventeenth-century survey estimated the average annual income of hereditary knights (baronets) at £880; simple knights at £650; esquires at £450; and simple gentlemen at £280. But living in London or maintaining a politically and socially leading position in the shires came more expensively.[16] (When a poll tax was introduced in 1660, it was, unlike Thatcher's modern incarnation, graduated according to rank [and thus, in general, ability to pay]: a common person paid sixpence, a gentleman £5, and a duke £100 per annum.)[17]

Here are some scattered but locally relevant contrasts: Robert Hooke's remuneration as curator of experiments for the Royal Society in the 1660s was around £30 per annum; one of Hooke's talented young apprentice mechanics in the 1670s was offered a plum position worth approximately £150 to £200; the vicar of a rural Essex parish from 1641 to 1683 averaged £165 per annum, of which £60 to £80 came from his living; a year at Oxford or Cambridge might wind up costing £60 (if you had to pay for it); the earl of Cork (Robert Boyle's father) allowed £1,000 per annum to support two sons on their Continental grand tour; annual rent for a typical merchant's London house was £20 to £30; a London shopkeeper might spend 4 to 5 shillings a week on food and drink, while a laborer got by on half that sum; domestic servants could be engaged for £2 to £8 per annum, all found, depending upon sex and grade; an income of about £50 constituted a

15. Wilson, *State of England*, 23–24; see also Ap-Robert, *The Younger Brother* (1618), 33; cf. Wrightson, *English Society*, 25–27.

16. King, *Natural and Political Observations*, 48–49; J. R. Jones, *Country and Court*, 86–87; Mingay, *The Gentry*, 4–5.

17. Laslett, *World We Have Lost*, 35–36.

lower boundary for the middle station of London society; and £50 was from three to five times the annual income of a laborer.[18]

The English gentleman's income was overwhelmingly in the form of land rents, and his capital wealth was in agricultural land tilled and husbanded by unfree others.[19] Thus, his economic position meant that the gentleman was (and was supposed to be) free of want and that he was under no mundane necessity to labor. The culture that testified to the gentleman's identity and that explained and justified his characteristics laid particular stress upon the facts of his independence and integrity relative to individuals in other social categories.[20] A Restoration courtesy text typically observed that a gentleman *"fears* nothing, he *despiseth* nothing, he *admires* nothing."[21] In English Christian conceptions of gentility *"a Gentleman* is a Man of himself," one "that is God's *Servant, the Worlds Master,* and his *own man."*[22] While, as I shall indicate, *discipline* was central to the identity of the early modern English gentleman, it was valued and legitimate only insofar as it was visible as self-imposed, not exacted by any other save God and the sovereign.

The recognized facts of economic circumstance were taken substantially to distinguish the gentle from the nongentle. Most early modern commentators endorsed or adapted Aristotle's definition of gentility as ancient riches and virtue.[23] Romei's *Courtiers Academie* (translated into English in 1598) elaborated an extended argument for the essentiality of riches in making and recognizing nobility. Since, as the Greeks agreed, the mechanical arts (and remunerated labor in general) were base and ignoble, and since virtue was the ultimate cause of nobility, wealth was necessary to purchase the quiet and leisure for the pursuit of the liberal arts and their virtuous fruit. "Though Nobility hath vertue for foundation, yet can it not be nourished without riches; the which, the greater antiquitie they be of in a familie, the more speciall token giue they of Nobility and vertue: that Nobility is by riches preserued, and through want thereof lost, experience and reason mani-

18. The economic position of early modern scientific technicians is addressed in chapter 8 below. The best source for the circumstances of London's middling sorts is P. Earle, *Making of the English Middle Class,* esp. chs 1, 10; see also Hole, *English Housewife,* 130–33; Macfarlane, *Family Life of Ralph Josselin,* 36–39.

-19. Mingay, *The Gentry,* chs 1, 4. Wrightson (*English Society,* 27) notes that "in the final analysis the establishment and maintenance of gentility depended upon the acquisition and retention of landed wealth."

20. Watson, *Shakespeare and the Renaissance Concept of Honor,* 97–101.

21. Walker, *Of Education* (1673), 55; see also Britaine, *Humane Prudence* (1686), 66.

22. Brathwait, *English Gentleman,* sig. Nnnr; Ellis, *Gentile Sinner,* 178.

23. Aristotle, *Politics,* IV. 1294ª 21–22; see also Smythe-Palmer, *Ideal of a Gentleman,* 209–34.

festeth it."[24] Guazzo agreed that riches enabled a gentleman effectively to exercise the virtues of liberality and hospitality, while poverty weakens and "disfurnishes" him.[25]

Lord Burghley's famous definition of gentility as "nothing but ancient riches" also combined the criteria of lineage and lucre (and R. H. Tawney noted that in practice the riches need not be all that ancient).[26] William Petty wrote that a gentleman was "understood many wayes," one criterion stipulating that he "have and enjoy annuel riches, especially in Terra Firma," and another that he possess "such estate, reall and personall, as whereby hee is able to subsist without the practise of any mercenary employments."[27] Henry Peacham's influential *The Complete Gentleman* codified the ancient philosophical consensus, saying that "whosoever labor for their livelihood and gain have no share at all in nobility or gentry."[28] And Segar noted that "commonly no man is accompted worthy much honour, or of great trust and credit, vnlesse he be rich."[29] The more cynical ethical texts of Tudor and Stuart England commented upon the gap between the professed importance of virtue and the practical significance of wealth in making a gentleman: "I must needs allow that a vertuous man (though hee bee poore) deserueth to bee respected, and honored: yet experience teacheth the contrary, that men of Title and wealth, are euer honored, and the poorer sorte (though full fraught with vertue) doo passe without reputation: As for example, when we . . . accompt him more or lesse honorable or worshipfull, as hee is more or lesse landed or wealthy."[30] The point was emphatically not that it was necessary to possess very great wealth or power. Most commentators broadly endorsed an Aristotelian notion that it was best for a gentleman to have a "mediocrity" of means and standing. Montaigne's view was that princes gave up much personal freedom in exchange for very little worth having.[31] It was an opinion widely echoed in England, where many ethical writers reck-

24. Romei, *Courtiers Academie*, 199–200.

25. Guazzo, *Civile Conversation* (trans. 1581), I, 188–89. For treatment of the significance of hospitality in the constitution and recognition of gentlemen, see Heal, *Hospitality in Early Modern England*, esp. ch. 1.

26. Quoted in Mingay, *The Gentry*, 4–5 (for Burghley and Tawney); cf. F. Markham, *Booke of Honour*, 22–23; and Smythe-Palmer, *Ideal of a Gentleman*, 186.

27. Petty, "Of Civility and a Gentleman," in idem, *The Petty Papers*, II, 186–89, quoting 187; see also [Allestree], *Gentleman's Calling* (1668), 11. In Lawrence Stone's version the gentleman's independence was "the capacity to live idly without the necessity of undertaking manual, mechanic, or even professional tasks": Stone, *Crisis of the Aristocracy*, 5; also 39–40.

28. Peacham, *Complete Gentleman* (1622), 23.

29. Segar, *Honor Military and Civill*, 228.

30. Anon., *Cyuile and Uncyuile Life* (1586), 44–45.

31. Montaigne, "Of the Inequality That Is between Us" and "Of Experience," in idem, *Essays*, 194–96, 826.

oned that the condition of the simple English gentleman *was* at the social golden mean: "It is then more safe to be in a middle condition, better to be in low Valleys than upon the top of high Mountains."[32]

Some contemporary commentators even formally dissociated wealth and legitimate gentility. Thus, Mulcaster said that "of all the meanes to make a gentleman, it is the most vile, to be made for money," and Peacham insisted that "riches are an ornament, not the cause of gentility."[33] In late Tudor and early Stuart England, those "whose Honors haue no other assent or Scale to rise by, but onely their wealth," were known as "Dunghill" knights. No English writer to my knowledge argued that wealth in itself rightly made a gentleman (and many lamented the effects of new money on traditional patterns), yet the effective control of sufficient wealth was very widely recognized as a practical necessity. Riches allowed the gentleman to "supply his King, and to doe benefit to the Commonwealth."[34] In early modern usage *generosity* and *gentle behavior* were practically synonymous terms.[35] Thomas Smith said that a gentleman, to be known as such, must show "bountifuller liberalitie than others, and keepe aboute him idle servaunts, who shall doe nothing but waite upon him."[36] A commonly expressed English opinion was that "a niggard is not worthy to be called a gentleman," and an early seventeenth-century courtesy text warned that "a Gentleman without meanes, is a painted bardge without oares; faire to looke on, but there is no vse of him, neither in calm, nor storme." Lack of means made a man a fawner and a panderer; it compromised both the liberality and the independence stipulated for the gentlemanly role.[37]

The gentleman was a master for whom others labored. He could be recognized by his idleness, and the practical equation between leisure and gentility was acknowledged even by commentators who argued in favor of vocation and virtue. The Jacobean physician Richard Burton diagnosed idleness as "the badge of gentry" and the cause of gentle melancholy: "idleness is an appendix to nobility, they count it a disgrace to work, and spend all their days in sports, recreations, and

32. Gailhard, *Two Discourses* (1682), 62–65; see also Anon., *Cyuile and Uncyuile Life*, 16–17; Bacon, "Of Great Place," in idem, *Moral and Historical Works*, 28–29.

33. Mulcaster, *Positions*, 194; Peacham, *Complete Gentleman*, 20.

34. F. Markham, *Booke of Honour*, 39, 69.

35. E.g., [Gainsford], *Rich Cabinet* (1616), 57v–58r.

36. T. Smith, *De Republica Anglorum*, 29. For humanist criticisms of these patterns, see Heal, *Hospitality in Early Modern England*, 95–97.

37. Sir William Vaughan of Carmarthenshire (1626), quoted in Mingay, *The Gentry*, 2; [Gainsford], *Rich Cabinet*, 51v, 52r, 55v; see also Ray, *Collection of English Proverbs* (1670), 96 ("A *Gentleman* without living, is like a pudding without sewet"); Kelso, *Doctrine of the English Gentleman*, 28.

pastimes, and will therefore take no pains, be of no vocation."[38] Indeed, the gentleman's leisured control of others' labor was continuously audible in sixteenth- and seventeenth-century speech. His form of address was "Master" (abbreviated to "Mr.," as "Mistress" was to "Mrs."), and, while the appellation became increasingly debased during the course of the seventeenth century, usurpers were occasionally sharply reminded of their trespass.[39] A Restoration viscount famously observed that "we eat and drink and rise up to play and this is to live like a gentleman, for what is a gentleman but his pleasure?"[40] Although many seventeenth-century English voices argued that "pleasure" was an illegitimate criterion for proper gentility,[41] few commentators disagreed that the gentleman was so placed that he might do as he pleased, or denied that this freedom of action was a defining circumstance of the gentle condition. Thomas Hobbes construed a free man as "he, that in those things, which by his strength and wit he is able to do, is not hindred to doe what he has a will to."[42] It was a definition which, to the seventeenth-century 'period eye,' summoned up the image of a gentleman. Financial independence was not only a substantial fact about gentlemen, it also was a sign (with others) that allowed a gentleman to be recognized and that explained and justified certain attributes he was presumed and enjoined to possess.

Inheriting Gentility

The role of blood was treated along lines similar to that of wealth. No one doubted that descent was an extremely important qualification for gentility, even if few English social commentators defended its

---

38. Burton, *Anatomy of Melancholy* (1628), 210–12. Note that *leisure* (or even *idleness*) in contemporary usage did not mean the absence of activity, only the absence of *valued* activity; cf. Veblen, *Theory of the Leisure Class*, ch. 3.

39. Harrison, *Description of England*, 114; T. Smith, *De Republica Anglorum*, 27; Peacham, *Complete Gentleman*, 25–26; Laslett, *World We Have Lost*, 26–27, 38–39; Stone, *Crisis of the Aristocracy*, 50.

40. This was the rakish husband of Anne Conway, philosopher and friend of Cambridge Platonist Henry More, as quoted in Ashley, *England in the Seventeenth Century*, 18, and Walzer, *Revolution of the Saints*, 252. "What is a gentleman but his pleasure?" was a contemporary commonplace: see, e.g., Barrow, "Sermon LIII," in idem, *Works*, III, 335; [Allestree], *Gentleman's Calling* (1668), sig. A3r.

41. For example, the author of *The Whole Duty of Man* lectured against the view that "a *Gentleman* is now supposed to be only a thing of pleasure": [Allestree], *Gentleman's Calling*, sig. A3r.

42. Hobbes, *Leviathan* (1651), 262. Ferne (*Blazon of Gentrie*, 8) expressed the widespread English anti-Aristotelian view that such liberty was universally distributed to all men by "the law of nature," and that it was "the law of nations" which brought in servitude.

sufficiency. Peacham expressed a highly traditional view in reckoning "the genuine sense" of nobility to be "the honor of blood in a race or lineage"; Thomas Gainsford's *Rich Cabinet* noted that "the auncestrie of bloud must needes haue preheminence ouer a familie newly erected"; and William Petty's list of criteria also included "consanguinity or affinity by marriage to and with many other gentlemen, and for many yeares past."[43] Into the eighteenth century even Daniel Defoe's critical assessment of English gentlemen as they then were did not scruple to define a gentleman as "a person *Born* (for there lies the Essence of Quality) of some known, or Ancient Family; whose Ancestors have at least from some time been rais'd above the Class of Mechanicks."[44]

Tudor and Stuart heralds customarily insisted upon descent from "three degrees of gentry, both on the mothers and fathers side," and a seventeenth-century proverb had it that "it takes three generations to make a gentleman," even if ways were frequently found to finesse that requirement in the award of arms.[45] Although the practical ethical literature of the sixteenth and seventeenth centuries developed systematic arguments against the adequacy of blood, it was fully accepted that "vulgar" opinion—within and without gentle society—laid greatest stress on descent. Guazzo's *Civile Conversation* (1574, trans. 1581) acknowledged that "the world commonly reputeth gentry by byrth as legitimate, and gentry by vertue as bastardily, and farre inferiour to the other."[46] As Mervyn James writes, "There could be no wholehearted rejection of blood and lineage in a society for which this was still a central concept. . . . The hierarchical grouping of the social order, and its basis in heredity . . . was taken for granted."[47] Despite the contrast traced by contemporary writers between the criteria of "blood" and "virtue," lineage might also be mobilized in the cause of virtue—to account for and enjoin proper standards of gentlemanly

43. Peacham, *Complete Gentleman*, 12; [Gainsford], *Rich Cabinet*, 64v; Petty, "Of Civility and a Gentleman," in idem, *The Petty Papers*, II, 186–89, quoting 187; see also M. James, *English Politics and the Concept of Honour*, 85–86. Early modern commentators here echoed Aristotle's view (*Rhetoric* II. 1387ᵃ 16–17) that anciently established gentility was better than recent ennoblement because it aroused less indignation: "what is long established seems akin to what exists by nature."

44. Defoe, *Compleat English Gentleman* (comp. *ca.* 1728), 13.

45. Segar, *Booke of Honor and Armes*, 35–36; idem, *Honor Military and Civill*, 121; Romei, *Courtiers Academie*, 187; see also Kelso, *Doctrine of the English Gentleman*, 25–27; M. James, *English Politics and the Concept of Honour*, 23; and Palliser, *Age of Elizabeth*, 69–70: "The heralds could register anyone of free birth and £10 a year in land or £300 in movable goods, and they made nearly 4,000 such grants of arms between 1560 and 1640."

46. Guazzo, *Civile Conversation*, I, 179.

47. M. James, *English Politics and the Concept of Honour*, 59; see also Stone, *Crisis of the Aristocracy*, 23–27; Kelso, *Doctrine of the English Gentleman*, 22–24.

conduct. Pride in one's ancestors might act as an inducement to virtuous and valorous behavior. Indeed, such pride and jealousy of reputation were central to the self-assertiveness and competitiveness of the
traditional honor culture.

Many stories were told in the sixteenth and seventeenth centuries
about the historical origins of the idea of gentility and the gentle degree. One common variant traced gentility to Adamic roots and thus
sought scriptural warrant for gross features of social hierarchy. Thus,
Ferne eclectically drew upon more recent Tudor commentators as well
as the late fifteenth-century *Boke of St. Albans* in arguing that nobility
originated in a divine gift of virtue to Adam, and others saw in Seth
and Cain the beginning of "gentle" and "ungentle." Ancestors' nobility
or ignobility were then effectively propagated through the line of descent by natural processes of emulation in an honor culture.[48] (This
argument was, plausibly, a response to the uncomfortable question
posed by the rebellious English peasants of the fourteenth century
and kept alive in seventeenth-century radical sectarian thought: "When
Adam delved and Eve span, Who was then a gentleman?")[49]

Another version (elaborated in 1531 by Sir Thomas Elyot) posited
a primitive equality of degree and common ownership of goods. When
private possessions were then granted, they were given to those of
recognized virtue and those who had benefited the community. "And
that promptitude or readiness in employing that benefit was then
named in English gentleness . . . and the persons were called gentlemen, more for the remembrance of their virtue and benefit, than for
discrepance of estates." God's providence worked to ensure that these
good men brought up good children, "who being brought up in virtue,
and perceiving the cause of the advancement of their progenitors,
endeavoured themselves by imitation of virtue to be equal to them in
honour and authority. . . . Thus I conclude that nobility is not after
the vulgar opinion of men, but is only the praise and surname of

---

48. Ferne, *Blazon of Gentrie*, 2–4; [Gainsford], *Rich Cabinet*, 50v; F. Markham, *Booke
of Honour*, 21–22; see also M. James, *English Politics and the Concept of Honour*, 64; Stone,
Crisis of the Aristocracy, 49; Whigham, *Ambition and Privilege*, 82–84; Kelso, *Doctrine of the
English Gentleman*, 22–25, 32–35. Of course, there were problems with tracing nobility
back to Adam (or Seth), since if that principle alone operated then all (or half) the
population would have to be considered noble.

49. See, e.g., Anon., *The Institucion of a Gentleman* (1555), sig. A.i–ii, confuting "this
old objection of the commune people. When Adam delued and Eve span, who was then
a gentleman? To whom it may be sayd, that so much grace and vertue as Adam our
first father received of God at his creation, so much nobility and gentry he receyued";
see also Cleland, *Instruction of a Young Noble-man* (1612), 2; Smythe-Palmer, *Ideal of a
Gentleman*, 165–66, 173, 176; Vogt, "Gleanings for the History of a Sentiment"; and
Hill, *World Turned Upside Down*, 35.

virtue; which the longer it continueth in a name or lineage, the more is nobility extolled and marvelled at."[50]

An old lineage had, so to speak, repeatedly distilled the inclination to virtue over the course of many generations. As with traditional hereditary theories, what was thought to be inherited was not the trait (virtue) but a disposition towards it. Yet that distilled, and continually reinforced, disposition might be regarded as so strong that a practical equation could be made between the fact of old blood and the attribution of virtue. In its strongest formulation it might be claimed that "the noble seemeth borne with a better inclination, and disposition unto vertue, then a plebeian, or one extracted from the common sorte."[51] In the 1570s the new earl of Essex was told by his father's secretary that the aristocratic virtues could be considered innate in his blood: they were "peculiar to your house, and grafted as it were in your principles."[52] John Selden eclectically drew on Galenic sources in arguing that mental and moral qualities might be inherited in connection with physical traits: "in the Seed are alwaies potentially seuerall indiuiduating Qualities deriued from diuers of the neere Ancestors. . . . The Minds inclination follows the Bodies Temperature."[53]

Lineage was, therefore, important in identifying gentlemen, though not necessarily for reasons "vulgarly" posited. There were, of course, other theories of the origin of nobility current in the early modern period. Machiavellian "triumphant force" theory traced nobility to superior power and cunning, since forgotten and dressed up with the lineaments of virtue, though this was not, for obvious reasons, a popular strategy for the public justification of social hierarchy. Still another theory—especially fashionable among the clergy—offered the hope that it might overcome the legitimacy-troubles experienced by rivals. This was the view that hierarchical order and submission of rank was the first law of heaven. Adapted from Thomist origins, divine hierarchy was pressed into service in even the most practical ethical literature. Gouge's *Domesticall Duties* of 1622 was one of a host of popular

50. Elyot, *The Governor* (1531), 103–06; see also Guazzo, *Civile Conversation*, I, 182; Kelso, *Doctrine of the English Gentleman*, 33–34.

51. Romei, *Courtiers Academie* (1598), 185; see also Kelso, *Doctrine of the English Gentleman*, 22–24, 29; Watson, *Shakespeare and the Renaissance Concept of Honor*, 79–81.

52. Edward Waterhouse to second earl of Essex, quoted in M. James, *Society, Politics and Culture*, 432.

53. Selden, *Titles of Honor*, "Preface," sig. b3. 2r. Selden rejected the view that nobility derives only from the father's seed: both sexes are "equally to be regarded"; see also F. Markham, *Booke of Honour*, 10, for a similar argument about the heritability of "the vertues of [parents'] minds, being a thing so neere conioyned to the body." The association between physical constitution and intellectual capacity is treated in more detail in chapter 3.

texts noting that "God in generall ordained degrees of superiorities and inferioritie, of authority and subjection: and in particular gaue to masters the authorities which they haue, and put seruants in that subjection wherein they are."[54]

Contesting Gentility

At this point one practically exhausts the signs and criteria of gentility about which early modern English commentators were substantially agreed. At any given time from the middle of the sixteenth to the middle of the eighteenth century, a variety of conflicting opinions was expressed and maintained about who a gentleman was, who he ought to be, and what the legitimate bases of gentle standing were. Indeed, it is not too much to claim that English culture as a whole from the Elizabethan age to the Augustan was more profoundly shaped by inquiries into the nature of gentility than by any other concern. The fundamental ground of dissensus concerned whether lineage or some notion of "virtue" was most important, and most legitimate, as the basis of gentle standing. English writing on this subject tended overwhelmingly to support the case for virtue, or at least some admixture of blood and virtue, though it is a plausible conjecture that the formal literature argued against deeply entrenched informal criteria and social practices that supported the case for blood.[55] The secondary literature on the contested constitution of the early modern English gentleman is far too large even to be summarized here.[56] I must, however, at least touch on several of the major issues important in connection with the culture of virtue, honor, truthfulness, and credibility to be discussed in the next chapter.

English commentators repeatedly expressed uncertainty about how gentlemen were made in practice and about what legitimate and dura-

---

54. Gouge, *Of Domesticall Duties,* 591; see also Kelso, *Doctrine of the English Gentleman,* 34–37. For the classic seventeenth-century defense of patriarchy, see Filmer, *Patriarcha* (1680).

55. Stone (*Crisis of the Aristocracy,* 23–27, quoting p. 27), discusses lay Tudor obsession with antiquity of lineage, noting that "one of the paradoxes of the age was that . . . excessive adulation of ancient lineage took place at precisely the time when political theorists were laying increasing emphasis upon virtue, education, and the capacity to serve the State as the supreme test of and justification for a leisured class living off the labours of others."

56. Among very many useful sources, see especially C. Barber, *The Theme of Honour's Tongue;* Brauer, *The Education of a Gentleman;* Caspari, *Humanism and the Social Order;* Einstein, *The Italian Renaissance in England;* Greenblatt, *Renaissance Self-fashioning;* M. James, *English Politics and the Concept of Honour;* Kelso, *Doctrine of the English Gentleman;* Mason, *Gentlefolk in the Making;* Stone, *Crisis of the Aristocracy;* Ustick, "Changing Ideals of Aristocratic Character"; and Watson, *Shakespeare and the Renaissance Concept of Honor.*

ble principles might be rescued and rehabilitated from complex and shifting social realities. In the Elizabethan period, Harrison, Smith, Ferne, and others acknowledged, with varying degrees of disapprobation, that traditional criteria identifying gentlemen were being put under severe pressure by thrusting yeomen, merchants, and profesionals. While the monarch customarily, and increasingly, created knights, barons, and the higher degrees of nobility as a mark of favor or recognition or as a mercenary *quid pro quo,* simple gentlemen were, it was said, being manufactured uncontrollably by diffuse processes of social mobility. Segar worried about the role of vulgar opinion in the matter: "by common opinion some ignoble persons are called Gentlemen. Of these the number is infinite, yet they are not indeed Noble, but vulgarly so esteemed."[57] A formulation much quoted and paraphrased during Elizabeth's reign noted that

> as for gentlemen, they be made good cheape in England. For whosoever studieth the lawes of the realm, who studieth in the universities, who professeth liberall sciences, and to be shorte, who can live idly and without manuall labour, and will beare the port, charge and countenaunce of a gentleman, he shall be called master, for that is the title which men give to esquires and other gentlemen, and shall be taken for a gentleman.[58]

It was a view that described (and rather exaggerated) substantial facts about the mobility of late Tudor society. In practice it was possible to become gentle (or at least for one's progeny to become so) through a variety of vehicles: marriage, money, education, professional standing (especially legal and clerical), court and military service, and, very rarely indeed, displays of virtue unconnected with any of the above. In 1602 Segar carefully qualified the alleged rights of the educated to gentility: "knowledge or learning doth not make a Gentleman, vnlesse hee be dignified with the title of Doctor, or graced by some office of reputation, and if that be taken away, he shal be reputed a common person." Insofar as they counted at all, the learned were to be regarded only as *ex officio* gentlemen.[59] The educationalist Richard Mulcaster judged that "the vilest diuises be the readiest meanes to become most wealthy, and ought not to looke honour in the face."[60] Into the Resto-

57. Segar, *Honor Military and Civill,* 227.

58. T. Smith, *De Republica Anglorum,* 27; see also versions in Harrison, *Description of England,* 114; Segar, *Honor Military and Civill,* 228.

59. Segar, *Honor Military and Civill,* 226 (Segar here approvingly quoted Bartolus); cf. Wrightson, *English Society,* 26–31; Smythe-Palmer, *Ideal of a Gentleman,* 146–48 (quoting a Royal Commission judgment of 1699 "to the effect that the gentlemen of the long robe and of physic were not to be interfered with or hindered in their claims to be entitled noble, but such title was not to carry with it real privileges").

60. Mulcaster, *Positions,* 195.

ration period, social commentators continued to repeat the conventional judgment that learning was a practical route to gentility while mildly deploring the scheme of things that made it so.[61]

Some Tudor and Stuart ethical texts endorsed without reservation the Aristotelian view that the life of "artisans or tradesmen" was "ignoble and inimical to virtue," while others were more persuaded that at least certain forms of such employment might be compatible with gentility.[62] In 1600 Wilson deplored the blurring of the gap between authentic gentlemen and rich yeomen, and an early seventeenth-century courtesy text bemoaned the loss of traditional distinctions between gentlemen and citizens, while acknowledging the fact of new criteria: "Citizens in time past did not marry beyond their degrees, nor would a Gentleman make affinitie with a Burgesse: but wealth hath taught vs now another lessin; and the Gentleman is glad to make his younger sonne a tradsman, and match his best daughter with a rich Citizen for estate and liuing."[63] To Henry Peacham the worst abuse of contemporary society was "the purchase of arms and honor for money, . . . every undeserving and base peasant aiming at nobility." We must not "honor or esteem those ennobled or made gentle in blood who by mechanic and base means have raked up a mass of wealth."[64] In 1634 another text judged that "there is no Country under the Sunne, that hath such an Apochryphall Gentry as the *English,* where the sonnes of Brokers blend with, and outbrave, and precede the most Ancient of it, as if clothes had the guift to ennoble blood."[65] Several Restoration writers carried on John Ferne's balanced defense of the potential gentility of trade, while others considered tradesmen "a baser sort of people" and accounted the blurring of boundaries between the gentleman and the merchant to be "the shame of our Nation."[66]

61. E.g., Waterhouse, *Discourse and Defence of Arms* (1660), 138, 148; Chamberlayne, *Angliæ Notitia* (1673), I, 318–19; see also M. James, *English Politics and the Concept of Honour,* 60–62.

62. Aristotle, *Politics,* VII. 1328[b] 38–39; see also idem, *Rhetoric,* I. 1367[a] 31–32: "It is noble not to practise any sordid craft, since it is the mark of a free man not to live at another's beck and call"; see also Watson, *Shakespeare and the Renaissance Concept of Honor,* 89. For assessments of the actual interrelations of the gentry and the mercantile classes, see, e.g., Stone, *Crisis of the Aristocracy,* ch. 7; Mingay, *The Gentry,* 104–07; P. Earle, *Making of the English Middle Class,* 6–10.

63. Wilson, *State of England,* 38–39; [Gainsford], *Rich Cabinet,* 27v (cf. 89–90 for condemnation of trade); see also Powell, *Tom of All Trades* (1631), 163–64: "To my knowledge, a great *Earle* lately of this land, did thinke it no scorne to indeavour the attaining of the Craft and trade of a Farrier, wherein he grew excellent."

64. Peacham, *Complete Gentleman,* 13, 25–26; see also F. Markham, *Booke of Honour,* 11–12.

65. Stafford, *Guide of Honour,* 59–60.

66. For positive comments on trade, see, e.g, Waterhouse, *Discourse and Defence of Arms,* 179–84 (following Ferne, *Blazon of Gentrie,* 72–73); and for criticisms, see,

By the 1640s, forms of address distinguishing the gentle and non-gentle had audibly eroded. Many took to describing themselves as "gent." or "master," without, as Stone says,

> reference to the Heralds, and without any pretension to a coat of arms. Small merchants, shopkeepers in provincial towns, and minor officials in government office were so styled, although they were still below the line in public repute, and would hardly have considered themselves in a position to converse on equal terms with, marry their children to, or challenge to a duel, a true landed gentleman or esquire.[67]

In the early eighteenth century *The Tatler* blamed the heralds' office for permitting the use of titles of honor by "small quillmen, and transcribing clerks": England had allegedly become *"populus armigerorum, a people of esquires."*[68]

Deep dissension, even incoherence, in treating the identity of the English gentleman was one reaction to this state of affairs.[69] The practical constitution of gentility was as important as its legitimate principles were contested. Palliser notes that "it was precisely because the title of gentleman mattered so much that some prospering commoners were desperately keen to assume it."[70] Thus, one response to a society in flux was a range of discrepant cultural enterprises aimed at stating clearly the legitimate principles of gentility.[71] Another response was the free acknowledgment that there was a large element of uncontrolled attribution in the constitution of the English gentleman and that nothing could (or should) be done about this. An Interregnum gentleman observed that "in these days he is a gentleman who is commonly taken and reputed," and John Selden wrote that "what a Gentleman is; tis hard wth us [the English] to define. In other Countrys he is known by his priviledges: In Westminster Hall he is one yt is

---

e.g., Anon., *Cyuile and Uncyuile Life*, 19–20; Peacham, *Complete Gentleman*, 22; Chamberlayne, *Angliæ Notitia*, I, 320–22; see also M. James, *English Politics and the Concept of Honour*, 64–65; Walzer, *Revolution of the Saints*, 247–50; G. Holmes, *Augustan England*, 5–15; Stone, *Crisis of the Aristocracy*, 39–40.

67. Stone, *Crisis of the Aristocracy*, 49–50. Visual distinctions between gentle and non-gentle were also said to be disappearing. The decline of sumptuary laws and habits was widely noted by contemporary commentators: "All are permitted to weare what they can get, and their owne vallue depends on that of their raiment" (Stafford, *Guide of Honour*, 60).

68. Addison and Steele, *The Tatler*, I, 175 (26–28 May 1709).

69. As Walzer says (*Revolution of the Saints*, 247), "general uncertainty as to the nature of gentility" went hand in hand "with a considerable confusion as to the actual membership of the English gentry."

70. Palliser, *Age of Elizabeth*, 70–71.

71. See the fine account of the relationship of Elizabethan courtesy literature to social change in Whigham, *Ambition and Privilege*, 6–31.

reputed one: In ye Court of Honour he yt has Arms; ye King can not make A Gentleman of blood . . . but he can make A Gentleman by creacon."[72]

Flux and uncertainty about the nature of gentility were countered by attempts to locate and display anciently established criteria that could be made to answer to new realities while defending elements of the traditional hierarchy and traditional distinctions between the gentle and nongentle. The facts of mobility and the erosion of many customary demarcation criteria meant that actors—whatever attitude they took—were confronted with major problems: how (if they wished) to justify the situation? how to argue against it? what generally warrantable principles of legitimacy might, in this context, serve best to justify, criticize, or explain? should new criteria of gentility be created or could more traditional ones—in whole or part—serve as a common language to justify and preserve basic features of a hierarchy that served old and new gentry alike?

Indeed, this is precisely the role played by various notions of *virtue*.[73] I have already noted attempts to seek biblical warrants for the noble/ignoble distinction. While by no means all writers concerned to explain and justify nobility helped themselves to sacred history, all were agreed that gentle and nongentle conditions were both anciently established and justifiable using ancient cultural resources. Aristotle's attempt to derive the gross orders of society—master and slave—from individuals' natures was not widely endorsed by early modern English thinkers, even if few went so far as Hobbes in insisting upon natural equality.[74] But the Ciceronian tradition of unambiguously equating gentility with virtue was a robust, if eclectically deployed, ancient resource. Ancient stresses on virtue powerfully assisted in both the interpretation and legitimization of increasingly acknowledged contemporary tensions in the constitution and identification of gentry. The enumeration and

72. Doderidge, *Honors Pedigree* (1652), 147–48 (quoted in Stone, *Crisis of the Aristocracy*, 49); Selden, *Table Talk*, 50–51.

73. For the heroic and classical origins of the concept of virtue, see MacIntyre, *After Virtue*, chs 10–12. Pocock notes (*The Machiavellian Moment*, 37) that the original Latin notion *virtus* "consisted both in the quality of personality that commanded good fortune and in the quality that dealt effectively and nobly with whatever fortune might send." By the early modern period, however, *virtue* had substantially shed the former sense. Because of the routine opposition between virtue (as a masculine active intelligence) and fortune (a feminine passive capriciousness), *virtus* "could therefore carry many of the connotations of virility, with which it is etymologically linked; *vir* means man"; see also F. R. Bryson, *Point of Honor*, 104–10.

74. E.g., Aristotle, *Politics*, I. 1254^a 18–1255^b 15; cf. Gouge, *Of Domesticall Duties*, 591–92; for Hobbesian egalitarianism see *Leviathan*, Part I, ch. 13, and Osborne, *Advice to a Son* (1656), 31; and, for Lockean endorsement of natural freedom and equality, see, e.g., Locke, *Two Treatises of Government*, Bk. II, sects. 4, 54.

annotation of the virtues found in almost all early modern ethical literature derived overwhelmingly from Aristotle's *Nicomachean Ethics,* Cicero's *Offices,* and Seneca.[75] While virtue was a concept mobilized to justify the existing social order, it was also widely recruited to make sense of and legitimate the acknowledged facts of social change. The newly risen man could argue that, as founder of an honorable line, the association between individual virtue and social standing was stronger in him than in the offspring of anciently gentle families.[76] As Peacham observed, "Neither are the truly valorous or any way virtuous ashamed of their so mean parentage, but rather glory in themselves that their merit hath advanced them above so many thousands far better descended."[77] A Restoration courtesy text advised the newly risen man of virtue what to say to the debased gentleman of ancient lineage: "In me my Gentility begins, in thee thine ends."[78]

On the one hand, the recognized facts of social mobility, the accelerating and at times uncontrolled recruitment of new men to the gentry, required justification and reconciliation with traditional understandings of the bases of gentility. On the other, it was pervasively acknowledged that there were at least occasional mismatches between inherited standing and individual merit. Not all gentlemen behaved as they ought to; some men of base and common parentage behaved nobly. Many commentators, accordingly, developed typologies which carved up the social and cultural order into categories of people whose virtues matched their standing ("gentle gentle," "ungentle ungentle") and those whose did not ("ungentle gentle," and "gentle ungentle").[79]

Virtually all writers on the subject were perfectly able to dissociate and juxtapose distinct discursive repertoires explaining and justifying gentle standing on the basis of blood or merit.[80] For instance, the anonymous 1555 *Institucion of a Gentleman* accounted the contemporary gentry to be debased, and, consequently, in danger of losing their legitimacy: "suche corruption of maners hathe taken place, that almost the name of gentry is quenched, and handycrafte men haue obtayned the tytle of honour." A hereditary gentry could be defended only by the outer display of inner virtue: "noble and gentle men must dili-

<hr>

75. Among many endorsements of Ciceronian virtue, see Brathwait, *English Gentleman,* "To the Knowing Reader"; see also Ustick, "Changing Ideals of Aristocratic Character," 147–52; Watson, *Shakespeare and the Renaissance Concept of Honor,* 21–29, 60–71, 95–96.

76. E.g., Guazzo, *Civile Conversation,* I, 177–79.

77. Peacham, *Complete Gentleman,* 14–15; see also Osborne, *Advice to a Son,* 84–85.

78. Dare, *Counsellor Manners* (1672), 13; see also [Ramesey], *Gentlemans Companion* (1676), 3–4.

79. Smythe-Palmer, *Ideal of a Gentleman,* 32.

80. See, among many examples, Peacham, *Complete Gentleman,* 13–16.

gently labour to excell others in vertues, or els there wil rise compari-
son of worthynes. . . . No man becometh gentle without vertue, (as
cause efficient of his gentlenes)."[81] In the 1630s Sir Thomas Browne
reckoned that contingent secular arrangements had almost quenched
a natural (but divinely endowed) hierarchy of individual virtue:

> There is a Nobility without Heraldry, a natural dignity, whereby one
> man is ranked with another, another filed before him, according to
> the quality of his Deesert, and the preheminence of his good parts. . . .
> Thus it was in the first and primitive Commonwealths, and is yet in
> the integrity and Cradle of well-order'd Polities, till corruption getteth
> ground.[82]

Throughout the early seventeenth century much of the courtesy
literature was still overwhelmingly lamenting the alleged corruption—
even the "depraved effeminancie"—of gentlemanly conduct.[83] The ancient trope *Generositas virtus, non sanguis* had long been familiar in
scholarly circles, and now it was vigorously popularized by the humanists.[84] By the early seventeenth century the prescription of virtue had
become a commonplace in the practical ethical literature: "Vertue the
greatest Signall and Symbol of *Gentry:* is rather expressed by *goodnesse*
of *Person,* than *greatnesse* of Place." Honor without virtue was accounted
no honor at all.[85] And even texts which elsewhere recognized the case
for wealth and birth commended virtue as the most legitimate sign
and entitlement of gentility:

> [One ought] not account him a gentleman, which is onely descended
> of noble bloud, in power great, in iewels rich, in furniture fine, in
> attendants brave: for all these are found in Merchants and Iewes. But
> to be a perfect Gentleman, is to bee measured in his words, liberall
> in giuing, sober in diet, honest in liuing, tender in pardoning, and
> valiant in fighting.[86]

81. Anon., *The Institucion of a Gentleman,* "Epistle Dedicatory," sig. *.iiir–*.iiiir, A. iiii
3v; see also Stone, *Crisis of the Aristocracy,* 672–77, and Todd, *Christian Humanism,* chs 2,
6 (for humanist contributions to the culture of virtue).

82. Browne, *Religio Medici* (publ. 1643; comp. 1635), 66.

83. E.g., Brathwait, *English Gentleman,* "To the Knowing Reader," [1]; see also
Peacham, *Complete Gentleman,* 8, 19; Stafford, *Staffords Niobe* (1611), 8: "Our men are
growen so effeminate, and our women so man-like, that (if it might be) I think they
woulde exchange genders."

84. Vogt, "Gleanings for the History of a Sentiment"; M. James, *English Politics and
the Concept of Honour,* 60–62.

85. Brathwait, *English Gentleman,* "Epistle Dedicatory," [1], 69 and sig. Nnnr; see also
F. Markham, *Booke of Honour,* 1, 9–10.

86. [Gainsford], *Rich Cabinet,* 51v. For general treatments of virtue in the fashioning
of a gentleman, see, e.g., Brauer, *Education of a Gentleman,* ch. 2; Mason, *Gentlefolk in the
Making,* ch. 2; Childs, "Prescriptions for Manners"; Kelso, *Doctrine of the English Gentleman,* esp. ch. 5.

Humanist educators tried, with some success, to link virtue with the case for learning: study was intended to make gentlemen as magnanimous, humble, and self-controlled as would render them technically able to serve the Crown and protect the interests of the state.[87] Thus, by the Stuart period English culture was strongly marked by a concern to define gentility, to display legitimate signs by which it might be recognized, and to offer resources to justify and maintain it.

By the late sixteenth and early seventeenth centuries, a further element was introduced into the English culture concerned with the description and justification of gentility. In the traditional honor culture, chivalric sentiments sat in uneasy tension with Christian ethics. The knightly code, which enjoined the gentleman jealously to guard his honor, to resent slights to his reputation, and to fight to repair the effects of injury, was formally contradicted by religious injunctions to meekness and stress on the transitoriness of earthly concerns. In practice, traditional gentlemanly culture found ways of keeping both codes in play, typically by reserving pious commitments to old age, by formally supporting religious institutions and rites, and by making a distinction between "the world" and "the world to come," while ensuring that no secular insult derogating from earthly honor was permitted to go unchallenged. As James says, "the horizontally demarcated lines marking off one Christian profession from another, with the vertical gradations of the hierarchy leading up from nature to supernature, all helped to clear a space for honour. As a result the warrior values of ancient Germanic society continued to flourish as a corporate way of life in a setting whose dominant tone was Christian."[88]

The Reformation, however, brought about a new conjuncture of state and religion which made the untrammeled individualism of an honor society increasingly untenable. Demands were made, and powerfully supported, for the Christianization of the code regulating gentlemanly society. And, while practical ethical writers from Elyot onward had formally equated virtue with elements of Christian religiosity, by the 1620s and 1630s a Puritan courtesy genre brought piety and religious self-assessment to center-stage and developed a detailed picture of "the Christian gentleman" which remained influential in England into the Restoration.[89] Richard Brathwait's *The English Gentleman* (1630) was explicitly written against the perceived secularism of ex-

87. E.g., Caspari, *Humanism and the Social Order,* esp. chs 1, 4, 6; Stone, *Crisis of the Aristocracy,* ch. 12; Shapin, "'A Scholar and a Gentleman.'"

88. M. James, *English Politics and the Concept of Honour,* 8–15, quoting 11; but cf. Watson, *Shakespeare and the Renaissance Concept of Honor,* 4–5, 38–50, 102–35 (for stress on the "basic duality" of Renaissance values).

89. Ustick, "Changing Ideals of Aristocratic Character," 154–63; Kelso, *Doctrine of the English Gentleman,* 74, 106–08.

isting conceptions of gentility. Where Peacham's earlier *The Complete Gentleman* practically equated virtue with decorum, self-discipline, and perfection in the humanistic arts, Brathwait saw virtue in primarily religious terms. The same self-control that made a man agreeable (in the humanistic idiom) made him holy (in the religious canon). A gentleman displayed his legitimacy by emulating, not his fellows or his noble ancestors, but Christ. Brathwait argued that meekness was "the first marke I tooke to distinguish true *Gentilitie*" and that "*Modestie* surely becommeth men of all *Degrees,* but especially men of eminent and noble ranke, to the end they may understand and acknowledge in every action, that there is a God, from whom all things proceed and are derived." Accordingly, there was no truer gentleman than one who was sovereign over his own passions and who displayed his calm indifference to attempted injury and insult.[90] By the Restoration, an increasingly confident Puritan courtesy literature announced that traditionally dominant principles of gentlemanly conduct were radically at odds with Christianity and with truly legitimate codes of gentility: "the readiest meanes of *making* the *Christian,* is to *vex* the *Gentleman.*"[91] In chapter 4, I offer an extended treatment of Robert Boyle's presentation of self as Christian gentleman, showing how this identity was potently deployed in the making of scientific truth.

Thus, by the mid-seventeenth century the culture which treated the nature of gentility, and which circulated in practical form as guides to gentlemanly conduct, contained three overlapping repertoires: a secular knightly code which laid great stress upon blood, individual honor, and reputation; a partly secular humanist culture of virtue which sought to define and defend gentry by displaying anciently sanctioned codes of social behavior; and a highly Christianized culture of virtue which encouraged many of the same social virtues as the humanist code while stimulating systematic self-interrogation of the state of the soul. The next chapter shows how these cultures, together with understood facts about the social, economic, and political situation of gentlemen, were mobilized to explain and enjoy the telling of truth.

90. Brathwait, *English Gentleman,* 61–65.
91. Ellis, *Gentile Sinner,* 7; see also [Allestree], *Gentleman's Calling,* 8.

A Social History of Truth-Telling: Knowledge, Social Practice, and the Credibility of Gentlemen

To believe, to trust, to rely on another,
is to Honour him; signe of opinion of his vertue and power.
To distrust, or not believe, is to Dishonour.

—Hobbes, *Leviathan*

Thomas Hobbes was one of many early modern commentators who identified the possession of honor and power with others' belief in one's word. In the contemporary commonplace, a gentleman's word was his bond. No other bond but that which the gentleman freely imposed upon himself was held to be necessary to guarantee that what he said was the case or to secure his obligation to do what he promised. To require any further surety was to express doubt that he was indeed a gentleman. Hence, insofar as others acted as if a man's word was sufficient to secure their commitment, belief, or assent, they gave publicly visible signs that the individual was gentle. Trusting a man's word was to do a man honor, and, as Hobbes suggested, to establish him as a man of honor. The same trust recognized and constituted the trusted individual as a man of power, for those who bound others without being bound by others were indeed powerful agents. Honor was translated into power by way of knowledge. If the relations of a man of honor were to be believed, then such a man might unconditionally colonize others' minds, constituting their sense of what was the case. An honor culture molded truth to the contours of power.

This chapter explores the cultural bases of gentlemanly truthfulness, the social practices mobilized around the description of gentlemen as truth-tellers, and the prescription that they ought to be so. I trace the outlines of the early modern culture which explained why the gentleman's word was presumed to be reliable, drawing out the understood relationship between birth, wealth, and virtue (as treated in chapter 2) and the depiction of truthfulness as a circumstance of integrity and free action. These repertoires for the interpretation of gentlemanly truthfulness constituted valuable resources in practical interaction. I show how departures from truthfulness were condemned by the presumption that the liar gave publicly understood indications of constraint and weakness, stressing the disastrous significance of those attributions within civil society and traditional honor culture. The chapter then describes how the culture of truth-telling discriminated men of honor from other categories in the social order, examining those types of people whose truthfulness might routinely be impugned or who labored under the necessity of establishing the veracity of their relations. Imputations of mendacity were explosive within gentlemanly culture: I describe the elaborate social practices by which a gentleman's word might be gainsaid, and I pay special attention to the means by which modification or negation might be done without impugning truthfulness. Finally, I offer a brief synopsis of the broadly *probabilistic* discourse institutionalized within early modern gentle society which permitted dissension without disaster, and I show how those institutionalized practices were made available for the practical resolution of problems of credibility within the new culture of English empirical science.[1] Credible knowledge was established through the practices of civility.

Honor, Word, Truth

So far I have glossed over a feature of the concepts of gentility and honor fundamental to recognizing the use to which they were put in context, and, therefore, to their historical meaning. Each of these concepts possessed, as it were, an 'internal' and an 'external' sense. For example, honor might be treated as one's public reputation and gentility as one's acknowledged standing in the social order or occupation of certain *ex officio* positions.[2] Conceived this way, the notions of honor and gentility gestured at criteria external to the individuals concerned and certainly external to their mental lives. Yet criteria were also available which mapped the concepts onto states regarded as internal to the actors. Honor might be taken as awareness of one's own integrity and uprightness, and gentility as the virtuous behavior which testified to that internal state. From antiquity through the early modern period, the relative importance and legitimacy of external and internal senses

1. Detailed treatments of credibility management in experimental and observational science are in chapters 5–8 below.
2. Fletcher, "Honour, Reputation and Local Officeholding," 93–94.

were continuously debated.[3] Although it might be argued that Renaissance culture stressed reputation and that late Tudor and Stuart England witnessed a resurgence of internal criteria, the concepts of honor and gentility always possessed these dual aspects. In some accounts internal and external senses were causally connected, and the competent ascription of honor might conveniently be taken as a reliable sign of its internal existence. A typical early seventeenth-century definition had it that "*Honor* ys a certeine testemonie of vertue shining of yt self, geven of some man by the iudgement of good men: For when any one ys of such and so apparant vertue that he turneth others into admiracion and love of him . . . then he ys called honorable."[4] Indeed, it was that very duality which allowed the concepts to function effectively both as organizing descriptive and prescriptive terms.

In this connection the anthropologist Ernest Gellner offers a useful fictional aid to reflection. He imaginatively encounters a tribe routinely using the term "bobility." He observes that tribal members use the appellation "boble" both to designate persons displaying appropriate virtues (uprightness, generosity) *and* to indicate individuals holding certain positions in society even if their behavior is manifestly mean and nasty. There are not *two* concepts of "bobility" in this society, only the one, used in these different ways. The incoherence is genuinely there for the analyst to identify, yet it is a socially functional incoherence, since members of that society may do a variety of things with it: they may enjoy the prestige of "bobility" without having to behave "bobly"; they may reinforce "bobility" by associating it with power and authority"; they may remind individuals in a certain social condition of how they *ought* to behave; and they may be able to "find" authentically "boble" persons outside officially "boble" society.[5] The extension of this argument to the materials presently under study should need no further comment.[6]

The concept and practice of truth were inscribed at the heart of traditional honor culture. The social practices mobilized around the recognition of truthfulness, the injunction to truth-telling, and the interpretation of why gentlemen were, and ought to be, truthful were central to the very notions of both honor and gentility. According to Mulcaster, "*truth* [is] the priuate protest of a gentleman, *honour*, of a noble man, *fayth* of a Prince, yet generally they do all ioyne in this:

3. See, especially, Watson, *Shakespeare and the Renaissance Concept of Honor,* 81 and ch. 4 passim; MacIntyre, *After Virtue,* 115–16; Kelso, *Doctrine of the English Gentleman,* 18–19.

4. Ashley, *Of Honour* (1607–10), 34; see also ibid., 52.

5. Gellner, "Concepts and Society," 38–39.

6. The example is treated in the mode of historical realism in Skinner, "Meaning and Understanding in the History of Ideas," 36–37.

As they be true gentlemen."[7] The practices recognizing and prescribing truthfulness formed a solid basis for the production and maintenance of social order in gentlemanly society, just as social order might be violently breached by refusals to recognize veracity in members' relations according to the prescribed forms.

A series of classical and pagan virtues—fortitude, fidelity, valor—were expressed in the notion of a gentleman's *word*. A man whose word might be consistently credited was a man to whom the virtues were imputed and a man upon whom others might rely. Montaigne said that "truth is the first and fundamental part of virtue." The genuine and steadfast truth-teller was one who was understood to do so because his soul "hates even to think a lie."[8] Behavior which built and protected social order was reckoned to flow from an individual's inner nature, even as that behavior offered a visible warrant for attributing the virtues as inner qualities. This is the scheme in which two senses of *honor* coexisted: one external, public, and reputational (having to do with one's standing *vis-à-vis* others), the other internal, personal, and private (referring to indwelling virtues and one's awareness of having those virtues).[9]

Chapter 1 described the general scheme in terms of which ascribed consistency between word and deed, word and reality, generates trust and makes collective social order possible. In the early modern context, such consistency was considered to offer a public token of one's innate nobility. The honor code thus laid very great stress upon consistency, and especially consistency in standing by a professed position or committed course of action. Insofar as the code was a public resource, there was, as Mervyn James writes, "the need to define the position to which honour was committed by a public gesture. This took the form of promise and oath, the giving of one's word, the 'word of honour'." The 'giving of one's word' freely bound individual honor to a future course of action, or, more generally, to a future interrogation of an averred state of affairs. Failure to perform, or revelation that one had knowingly misled, was pervasively read as an admission of *weakness:* "the will had been overruled, and the autonomy of honour cancelled." A gentleman was thus substantially defined by his reliability, his promise, his word.[10] "His words are bonds, his oaths are oracles."[11]

---

7. Mulcaster, *Positions*, 200.

8. Montaigne, "Of Presumption," in idem, *Essays*, 491.

9. Watson, *Shakespeare and the Renaissance Concept of Honor*, 11–12; Pitt-Rivers, "Honour and Social Status," esp. 21–23.

10. M. James, *English Politics and the Concept of Honour*, 8, 15, 28–31; see also C. Barber, *The Theme of Honour's Tongue;* Watson, *Shakespeare and the Renaissance Concept of Honor*.

11. Shakespeare, *Two Gentlemen of Verona*, II, vii, 75.

The imputed constancy, steadfastness, and reliability of an authentic gentleman was a master-figure of the traditional honor culture of medieval Europe, a trope by which the official interpreters of feudal society identified and justified its hierarchical order.[12] Yet while conceptions of gentility changed, and while the honor culture underwent substantial alterations in early modern Europe, the description and injunction of gentlemanly constancy, reliability, and truthfulness continued, recruiting and assimilating new resources all the while. The justifications changed, but the outcome was recognizably the same: the distribution of imputed credit and reliability followed the contours of authority and power.

The credibility and presumed reliability of gentlemen's utterances could survive without the chivalric ritual forms of oath and promise. The rhetorical query "What is a gentleman but his pleasure?" was itself a variant of the commonplace "What is a man but his promise?"[13] James Cleland, describing "How a Nobleman should keep his promise," argued a relationship between the distribution of power and the moral push towards faithfulness:

> The authoritie, puissance, and safety of al Princes dependeth vpon faith, & promise keeping. Keep therfore your faith preciselie, as the onelie badge, and marke of your honour: for the greater men you are, the more are you bound to performe it, in respect your libertie is the greater in making of it: Wherefore wee saie that the simple word of a Prince is as good as a subjects oath.[14]

Segar's treatment of the "Priuileges anciently appertaining to Gentlemen" simply noted that "in giuing witnesse, the testimony of a Gentleman ought to be receiued and more credited than the word of a common person. *Quia promissa Nobilium, pro factis habentur.*"[15] Peacham reported it as routinely accepted that "we ought to give credit to a noble or gentleman before any of the inferior sort."[16] Modern historians note that "one of the traditional privileges of the aristocrat had been his right to testify in court without bond and without witnesses."[17] His word might be taken as sufficient in itself, requiring no voucher and no external support. The notion of truthfulness was thus central to the description of gentle qualities. Through the Renaissance and into the eighteenth century an *honorable man* and an *honest man* were

12. Canfield, *Word as Bond*, xi–xii.
13. M. James, *English Politics and the Concept of Honour*, 29.
14. Cleland, *Instruction of a Young Noble-man*, 199.
15. Segar, *Honor Military and Civill*, 229 ("Because the promises of nobles are taken for deeds").
16. Peacham, *Complete Gentleman*, 24.
17. Watson, *Shakespeare and the Renaissance Concept of Honor*, 97. I return to this topic in chapter 5.

interchangeable designations: "honesty" *included* the notion of truth-telling but was understood far more broadly to include concepts of probity, uprightness, fair-dealing, and respectability.[18] Thus, a late six-teenth-century ethical text argued that "touching honesty & iustice, I accompt them as one: for indeed, an honest man is a iust man: & a iust man is honest."[19] As late as the 1720s, Defoe wrote matter-of-factly that "honesty and honour are the same."[20] Indeed, while the differenti-ation of *honesty*, narrowly considered as truthfulness, from its more general senses was apparently under way by the late seventeenth cen-tury, throughout the period of this book's concern the attribution of truth-telling was firmly embedded within a culture associating it with the characteristics of gentlemen.

The courtesy literature of early modern England sought to lay out for gentlemanly society the grounds and practices of a happy and virtuous life. While few such texts treated truthfulness in systematic detail, fewer still failed to treat it in some way. While explanations and justifications of gentlemanly truthfulness varied between courtesy genres (especially between English secular and Christian forms), there was virtual unanimity in condemning mendacity and applauding truth-telling: the character of a liar was said to be radically incompatible with legitimate gentility. The practical task taken up by the courtesy literature was, on the one hand, to enjoin the gentleman not to lie or dissimulate, to remind him of the consequences of doing so, to inform him of the costs of impugning the veracity of other gentlemen's rela-tions, and, on the other, to situate the injunction not to lie in a system of generally understood and approved ethical principles regulating the happy and virtuous life and justifying the gentle condition.

What understandings and justifications were available to sustain the prescription that gentlemen ought to be truthful? The Bible and the valued secular writings of antiquity, of course, provided major re-sources for specifying and enjoining truthfulness. In both the Judeo-Christian and the Greek philosophical traditions, the deity was identi-fied with the notion of pure truth. The idea of God was incompatible with mendacity.[21] Pythagoras was supposed to have said that men did anything which resembled the divine nature only when they told the truth.[22] For Plato, "from every point of view the divine and the divinity are free from falsehood." There is no *motive* for God to deceive. Since the gods have perfect and complete knowledge, and since they have

18. Cicero, *Offices*, 8.
19. Anon., *Cyuile and Uncyuile Life*, 16.
20. Defoe, *Compleat English Gentleman*, 33.
21. This despite Jehovah's intermittent dirty-tricks and the biblical register of mendac-ity among some of His chosen.
22. Stanley, *History of Philosophy*, I, 83–84.

no necessities which might induce them to depart from truthfulness, they must be considered as absolutely reliable truth-tellers. Divine freedom and integrity were the circumstances of divine truthfulness. Mortal imitation of the divine nature implicated not only the search for truth, but an intention in secular life to be a truth-teller and not to play one's fellows false.[23] A man who thus imitated the gods gave visible signs of his integrity. As a Restoration courtesy text put it, "nothing makes a man more like God than these two things, Holiness and Truth."[24]

Aristotle's *Nicomachean Ethics* distinguished between the virtue of fidelity to one's promise (which was binding in a judicial sense) and the more general matter of truthfulness in everyday life. Truth-telling instantiated the general ethical rule of "mediocrity" or the golden mean. The truthful man was said to be positioned between the two extremes of undue humility and undue boastfulness. Both extremes were vicious. We may rely upon the sort of man who tells truth when nothing is at stake, for he gives a visible moral token that he will be truthful when passions and interests are engaged. Falsehood is base in itself, but it is more base when falsehood is uttered for advantage. (In fact, the liar's sought-for advantage was said to be at most short-lived.) The boaster's lie was the most despicable sort. Either he tells untruths for their own sake—"because he enjoys the lie itself"—or he does so "for money, or the things that lead to money." The attributed meanness of lying was in this way joined to ugliness of character. Intentional and designed departures from truthfulness were ignoble acts; noble men were distinguished from mean and base men *inter alia* by the reliability of their truth-telling. That reliability gave a public sign of their integrity, the fact that—like the gods—they labored under no constraint that would induce them to seek advantage.[25]

Cicero's gloss on these themes was among the most influential sources for early modern ethical literature. Truth-telling and bond-keeping counted as one of Cicero's "four parts of honesty." Insofar as one acquired the character of an unreliable narrator, so one lost reputation and standing among one's fellows. Ultimately, a reputation for integrity could not survive the imputation of culpable untruthfulness. Like Aristotle, Cicero considered lying mean and vile in itself, but he also depicted liars as ignobly seeking that which honesty en-

---

23. Plato, *Republic*, III. 382; I. 331; see also Forrester, "Lying on the Couch," 150–51; cf. Descartes's formulation ("Principles of Philosophy," 231): "Although the capacity for deceit would seem to be a mark of subtlety of mind amongst men, yet the will to deceive proceeds only from malice, or fear, or weakness, and it cannot consequently be ascribed to God."

24. Dare, *Counsellor Manners*, 52.

25. Aristotle, *Nicomachean Ethics*, V. 1127ᵃ 13-1127ᵇ 32.

joined them openly to disdain. The liar showed himself to be *in fear,* to be a man of compromised integrity.[26] Accordingly, Greek and Roman philosophers developed a practically usable map of the social distribution of truth-telling. One could, and one ought to, attribute truthfulness to individuals placed in positions of influence, just as one could, and one ought to, recognize nobility and integrity in those who reliably told the truth.

The early Christian tradition addressed the matter of lying in a discourse almost wholly disengaged from secular considerations of meanness, dishonor, ignominy, and ignobility. Theologians devoted much attention to discriminating among categories of untruthfulness, reaching no consensus on the question of whether lying was ever blameless or, indeed, what untruthfulness needed to be regarded as a lie. Augustine combated early heretics who condoned lying under special circumstances, for example when untruths were told to non-Christians in the service of the true faith. He appreciated the force of arguments exculpating the lie which harmed none and which benefited some meritorious cause, but Augustine nevertheless condemned all forms of lying, while acknowledging some as less blamable than others. Aquinas offered a categorization of lies ("officious" or useful, "jocose," and "mischievous" or malevolent) which mapped onto the Christian taxonomy of sin. Lies were more or less grievous and sinful according to the moral intentions animating them: "the greater the good intended, the more is the sin of lying diminished in gravity." Aquinas reckoned that, while lying was to be avoided, not every lie needed to be accounted a mortal sin.[27] While Thomist thinking on truthfulness and morality fed into the casuistical literature of the early modern Roman Catholic church, it appears to have had little impact on the practical ethical canon. Indeed, one sign of a gap between dominant Christian and secular ethical postures in early modern Europe was the contrast between the relatively judicious and temperate attitude towards truthfulness adopted by many theologians and the obsession with the purity of truth-telling manifested in the secular canon. So far as civil society was concerned, the connection of truth-telling with external conceptions of honor was evidently more powerful than its link with piety and the imitation of God.

26. Cicero, *Offices,* esp. 6–9, 15, 18–19, 30–31, 111, 136–38. The four "parts of honesty" were prudence; justice or promise-keeping; magnanimity or fortitude; and decorum.

27. For summaries of the historical development of early and medieval Christian thinking about mendacity, see Lipmann and Plaut, *Die Lüge;* Bok, *Lying,* 34–39, 265–85; Sommerville, "'New Art of Lying,'" 160–61; Zagorin, *Ways of Lying,* chs 1–2; Kerr, *Book of Lies,* 33–39, 61–63.

In its engagement with matters of truth-telling and mendacity the courtesy literature of early modern Europe recruited, rearranged, and creatively reworked tropes familiar from Aristotle and Cicero. Courtesy writers reminded the gentleman that he must not acquire the character of a liar; they offered him reasons why that character was disadvantageous and dishonorable; and they elaborated a culture which explained why it was that gentlemen were truthful and were so to be accounted. Castiglione's *Courtier* (in English translation from 1561) simply laid it down as a maxim that a man of noble condition shall be "no lyar."[28] Della Casa's *Galateo* (English translation 1576) deprecated lying as "vain" and misguided in those who wished to be accounted honorable.[29] Other practical ethical writing more expansively worked out the association between truthfulness and gentlemanly standing. In 1531 Elyot's *Governor* prohibited the nobleman from speaking "all thing which in visage or appearance pretendeth to be any other than verily it is": such an act is "a great reproach to . . . honour."[30] In the 1570s Guazzo's *Civile Conversation* (Englished 1581–1586) condemned lying and commended truth-telling as respective marks of a base or noble nature: "He, which plainly telleth the trueth, sheweth himself to be an honest man, and of noble condition; so he, which lieth, doth the act of a slave, and of a disloyal, unjust, and undiscrete person."[31] Lodowick Bryskett's early seventeenth-century English compilation of Italian ethical material judged verity to be "that excellent vertue that is of all others the best fitting a Gentleman, and maketh him respected and welcom in all companies."[32]

The equation between gentility and truth-telling persisted in content and force throughout the seventeenth century. *The Rich Cabinet* succinctly contrasted "generosity"—construed as the moral expression of a gentle nature—with lying, linking mendacity with "cowardliness," "maliciousness," and "niggardliness" as equally "worthy of reproach and infamy."[33] Francis Bacon adapted Plato's metallurgical metaphor for the composition of human natures: "Round dealing is the honour of man's nature; and a mixture of falsehood is like alloy in gold and silver, which make the metal work better, but it debaseth it."[34] Clement Ellis's *Gentile Sinner* stipulated that "the truly *Honourable Gentleman*"

28. Castiglione, *The Courtier*, 124, 368.
29. Della Casa, *Galateo*, 44.
30. Elyot, *The Governor*, 168.
31. Guazzo, *Civile Conversation*, I, 96.
32. Bryskett, *Discourse of Civill Life*, 180.
33. [Gainsford], *Rich Cabinet*, 57v.
34. Bacon, "Elegant Sentences," in idem, *Moral and Historical Works*, 193; see also F. Markham, *Booke of Honour*, 10. The source is Plato, *Republic*, III. 415.

shows "himself to be as *good* as his *word,* esteeming no *disgrace* like that of *deserving* the *Lie.*" He "looks upon no *disrespect* as comparable with that, of not being thought a person fit to be *trusted.*"[35]

Brathwait's Puritanical ethical writing picked out the manner in which suspicion of untruthfulness stained honor: "[Nor] can any thing disparage or lay a deeper aspersion upon the face of *Gentrie,* than to be taxed for fabulous relations." For that reason, those who valued their honor should study to speak in such a way as to avoid any sustainable imputation that what they were saying was not indubitably the case. Here one needed not just truthfulness but its warrantable appearance. "*Gentlemen,* of all others, ought to be most respective of their conversation: for a little soile is a great blemish in them. . . . Such men . . . gaine best authoritie or approbation in *Discourse,* who have beene ever observed to speak probably, and not of *Subjects* above the reach or pitch of humane conceit."[36] John Locke's tract on the practical education of gentlemen was unforgiving on the subject. Lying was

> a quality so wholly inconsistent with the name and character of a gentleman, that nobody of any credit can bear the imputation of a lye; a mark that is judged the utmost disgrace, which debases a man to the lowest degree of a shameful meanness, and ranks him with the most contemptible part of mankind, and the abhorred rascality; and is not to be endured in any one, who would converse with people of condition, or have any esteem or reputation in the world.[37]

The child must be made to understand, if necessary through corporal punishment, "that twenty faults are sooner to be forgiven, than the straining of truth, to cover any one by an excuse."[38] In the early eighteenth century still another courtesy writer fluently linked the Christian and the secular idioms: "It is sinful and ill Breeding to lie."[39]

The Bases of Believability

The practical ethical literature of the period from *ca.* 1550 to *ca.* 1700 therefore persistently argued that the gentleman ought to be a truth-teller and that the consequences of his acquiring a reputation for mendacity were disastrous. Why was the gentleman said to be a truth-teller?

35. Ellis, *Gentile Sinner,* 235–36.
36. Brathwait, *English Gentleman,* 83–84.
37. Locke, *Some Thoughts Concerning Education* (1690), 126–27.
38. Ibid., 131; see also Montaigne, "Of Liars," in idem, *Essays,* 23–24; Burnet, *Thoughts on Education* (comp. *ca.* 1668), 16, 34.
39. Petrie, *Rules of Good Deportment* (1720), 54; see also Brauer, *Education of a Gentleman,* 145–46.

What features of his nature, his situation, and his aspirations were said to underwrite the reliability of his truth-telling? I have indicated that the inquiries elaborated around these questions occupied a central position in early modern English culture. I want also to show that discourse concerned with these questions spread across a great swath of cultural terrain, stretching from thinking about human natures to social theory to formal and informal epistemology and ontology.

The first consideration implicated in the culture of gentlemanly veracity was rarely given explicit treatment in the practical ethical literature of early modern Europe. Nevertheless, it was an absolutely fundamental feature of the practical assessment of testimony, and one which might assist in discriminating the worth of testimony from gentle and nongentle sources. This was the ascription to gentlemen of *perceptual competence.* That is, it was assumed (without evident obligation to give justification) that all gentlemen not categorized as pertinently handicapped or defective were competent sensory agents. That which was available to be experienced, and thus reported upon, in the natural and social worlds was in fact registered by their senses and experienced in a manner deemed normal within the relevant community.

The assumption of perceptual competence seems banal, yet it was *not* one which gentlemanly culture extended without qualification to all sorts of human beings whatsoever. Formal and informal theorizing about the differential constitution of human natures can be traced back to antiquity. I have alluded to Aristotle's view that some people might be slaves or masters "by nature." Those natures might even be read off bodily appearances: "Nature indeed wishes to make the bodies of free persons and slaves different as well [as their souls]—those of the latter strong with a view to necessary needs, those of the former straight and useless for such tasks, but useful with a view to a political way of life."[40] While I have noted that there was considerable disagreement about whether social kinds were natural, the Greek view continued to be strongly represented in the Tudor and Stuart courtesy literature. Romei's *Courtiers Academie* vigorously asserted the importance of blood in making noble and ignoble kinds. Human beings were by nature "of diuers temperatures . . . and in their mindes different effects and affects are discouered: from whence it proceedeth in reason, that some are esteemed of noble race, and others of ignoble: some ingenious, others stupide: some preuaile with force of mind, and are truely worthy to command, and others be as it were lumpish sturdy, with

---

40. Aristotle, *Politics*, I. 1254[b] 26-31. Aristotle subsequently (I. 1255[a] 4–1255[b] 15) qualified the strong equation between the condition of slaves and their natural constitutions.

whome seruitude better befitteth."[41] And Jean Bodin explained "savagery" as "a lack of proportion in the mixing of humours."[42]

Moreover, ways of life had powerful effects in enhancing or diminishing what nature provided. Plato's prohibition against citizens entering into the arts and crafts derived from a view of the potency of labor and habit in forming skill and character. Those whose ways of life involved much manual labor were coarsened; those who gave themselves over to the political life were rendered more sensitive.[43] Aristotle asserted the necessity of leisure for the cultivation of virtue, and the ethical literature of early modern England intermittently argued that the body was "contaminated" by labor and base ways of life and that this contamination might be handed down to offspring.[44] In Hippocratic and Galenic thinking, the mind's functions were shaped by the body's temperament—including its humoral constitution and the physical state of bodily tissue—and these in turn might be determined by climate and way of life. Differences in "witt and vnderstanding" might arise from individual variation, but they could equally proceed from forms of collective life.[45] Late sixteenth-century Italian writers found occasion to observe that the bodies of men of honor were better "tempered" than those of the meaner sort: "they have a better mixture of heat, cold, dryness, and moisture. As a result, their flesh is more delicate, their 'humors' more refined, and their 'spirits' more subtle."[46] In 1669 Walter Charleton continued the Hippocratic tradition by associating intellectual ingenuity and acuity with hot and sanguine constitutions and dullness with cold and phlegmatic types.[47]

In *Twelfth Night* (I, v) Olivia used Viola's body as well as manner to recognize 'his' gentility: "Thy tongue, thy face, thy limbs, actions and spirit,/Do give thee five-fold blazon." The Rev. Isaac Barrow referred to the gentleman's "innate vigor of spirit" compared to that of the "rustic laborer, or a mechanic artisan."[48] And Daniel Defoe, ridiculing the notion "that there are some Globules in the Blood [of gentlemen],

41. Romei, *Courtiers Academie*, 193–94. For Guazzo's characterization of "base people" as "by nature uncivil, rude [and] rough," see *Civile Conversation*, II, 81–82, and, for recent general treatment of these themes, see A. Bryson, "The Rhetoric of Status," 150–51.

42. Bodin, *Methods for the Easy Comprehension of History* (1566), as quoted in J. R. Hale, "Sixteenth-Century Explanations of War and Violence," 12.

43. Plato, *Laws*, VIII. 847; idem, *Republic*, II. 374–76.

44. Aristotle, *Politics*, VII. 1328^b 40–1329^a 5; Romei, *Courtiers Academie*, 199–203.

45. Zilboorg, *History of Medical Psychology*, 89–91; Ashley, *Of Honour*, 48; Boyle, "Aretology" (1645), 33, 45.

46. F. R. Bryson, *Point of Honor*, 5, quoting tract by Francesco de Vieri (1580).

47. Charleton, *Discourse Concerning the Different Wits of Men*, 48–52; cf. Hobbes, *Human Nature* (1650), ch. 13.

48. Barrow, "Sermon LIII," in idem, *Works*, III, 337.

some sublime Particles in the Animal Secretion, which will not mix with the hated Stream of a mechanick Race," nevertheless recognized that "this is the Language of the Times."[49] Into the mid-eighteenth and nineteenth centuries environmental theories of human nature occasionally touched upon the coarsening or refining effects of ways of life on the nervous system, and, hence, upon perceptual sensitivity.[50] In addition, there was an even more diffuse sensibility that delusionary tendencies might be differentially distributed among types of human being. Sensations might need to be processed by higher intellectual faculties before they were rendered into properly reportable perceptions. Categories of people—women and the vulgar in particular—in whom those faculties were poorly developed might therefore be constitutionally prone to undisciplined and inaccurate perceptions.[51]

Peter Burke's account of the "withdrawal" of the polite world from popular culture in early modern Europe describes how university-trained physicians identified the tendencies of common people towards common cognitive errors.[52] Popular belief was conceived, as Jacques Revel has noted, to be a form of "popular illness."[53] Thus, the physician Sir Thomas Browne's *Pseudodoxia Epidemica* (1646) observed the "erroneous disposition of the people" which made them credulous and readily deceived by "fortune-tellers, jugglers, [and] geomancers." Sense needed to be tutored by knowledge, and, lacking knowledge, the common people were "but bad discerners of verity": "Their understanding is so feeble in the discernment of falsities, and averting the errors of reason, that it submitteth unto the fallacies of sence, and is unable to rectifie the error of its sensations." Worse, postlapsarian common people were so constituted that their animal natures dominated what reason and knowledge they possessed, further disposing them to error and delusion: "Their understanding thus weake in it selfe, and perverted by sensible delusions, is yet farther impaired by the dominion of their appetite; that is, the irrationall and brutall part of the soule, which lording it over the soveraigne facultie, interrupts the actions of that noble part, and choakes those tender sparkes, which

49. Defoe, *Compleat English Gentleman,* 17.

50. Lawrence, "Nervous System and Society." For nineteenth-century persistence of these general medical and biological views of heredity and nervous constitution, see, e.g., Rosenberg, *No Other Gods,* chs 1–2, 5.

51. See, e.g., Defoe's remarks on the tendency of the vulgar to "possession" and unreliable witnessing, as treated in Schaffer, "Defoe's Natural Philosophy," 20–22. Lack of learning, as well as innate dispositions, was also widely identified with delusion and credulity; see Hume's discussion of belief in miracles among "the ignorant" and "the barbarous," in *Enquiry Concerning Human Understanding,* 118–20.

52. P. Burke, *Popular Culture,* 273.

53. Revel, "Forms of Expertise," esp. 262.

Adam hath left them of reason."[54] In routine medieval and early modern English usage, an "idiot" was simply a lay, uneducated, or common person, and that was the major basis upon which "tales told by idiots" might signify nothing.[55] Later chapters will note that in fact some common people in seventeenth-century English society were, in specific circumstances and for specific reasons, treated as perceptually unreliable when compared with gentlemen. The possibility was thus opened up that their reports might not be trustworthy because, other considerations notwithstanding, they did not reliably sense that which was available-in-the-world-to-be-sensed or they did sense what did not exist in the world.

All 'normal' gentlemen were deemed to be perceptually competent—indeed, the reports of such people largely defined what perceptual competence was—but not all 'normal' members of other social categories were assumed to be so. Assessments of the reliability of empirical narratives in early modern society were therefore founded upon largely informal, but nonetheless hugely consequential, theories about the "natures," "temperaments," and "dispositions" of different types of people. While it was both possible and permissible to impugn the perceptual competence of categories of people outwith the boundaries of gentle conversation, it was obligatory within those boundaries to presume equality of basic competences. Thus, Obadiah Walker's Restoration tract on education urged the gentleman not to dispute another's empirical relations. (The language was, typically, universal, while the context makes it evident that *men* meant gentlemen.)

> All mens apprehensions naturally are alike; what one sees red, another sees not green; and Aloes is not bitter to one, and sweet to another; and their first thoughts upon them are the same. And that one man is more learned, is not because he knows otherwise then another; but it is because he knows more consequences, and more propositions by his greater industry and experience.[56]

The second consideration implicated in the culture of veracity was that gentlemen, in common with all other sorts of social actors, faced a *pragmatic* consideration that enjoined them to be, and to secure the reputation of, reliable truth-tellers, though gentlemanly society experi-

---

54. Browne, *Pseudodoxia Epidemica*, 8–12; see also E. R. Harvey, *The Inward Wits*, 39.

55. See *Oxford English Dictionary* and, for example, Webster, "Paracelsus and Demons," 4.

56. Walker, *Of Education* (1673), 237. The rough parallel with Hobbes's view of "naturall witte" and his ninth law of nature ("That every man acknowlege other for his Equall by Nature") (*Leviathan*, 134–35, 211) is a more likely indication of the commonplace character of such early modern sentiments than of philosophical 'influence,' while the 'egalitarianism' of Descartes's *Discourse on Method*, Part I, was probably meant as dry wit.

enced and interpreted this consideration in a special way. Aristotle noted that little genuine advantage could in fact be secured by frequent lying. Asked "what those who tell lies gain by it," he was said to have replied: "They gain this, that when they speak truth, they are not believed."[57] What would the reputed liar's practical dealings be like if all suspected that what he said—about his intentions, his future courses of action, his empirical experience—was of dubious veracity? The habitual liar put himself in the position of the boy who repeatedly cried "wolf": no one would believe him when there really was a wolf. Although this pragmatic interpretation and injunction towards truth-telling was not a dominant theme in early modern thinking, a number of well-known texts worked it through in repetitive detail. Guazzo echoed the Aristotelian form, and Della Casa observed that "in the long run liars are not only discredited, but no one listens to them any more than they listen to people whose words are meaningless."[58] Bryskett's *Discourse of Civill Life* noted that truth-tellers "purchase to themselues not onely honour and praise, but also trust and credit with all men, so as their words are obserued as oracles: whereas of the others, no man maketh more account then of the sound of bels, or old wives tales."[59] Josiah Dare enjoined the gentleman to "take heed of lying, for if thou usest this Vice often, thou wilt lose thy credit amongst all men."[60]

The Quaker gentleman William Penn was one of many seventeenth-century English writers mixing and recombining chivalric, pragmatic, and Christian idioms. He said that he could not "see the policy any more than the necessity of a man's mind always giving the lie to his mouth; or his mouth ever giving false alarms of his mind. For no man can be long believed that teaches all men to distrust him; and since the ablest have sometimes need of credit, where lies the advantage?"[61] Montaigne thought that lying was a difficult policy as well as a detestable vice. Truth is one; lies are many. Over a period of time it simply becomes too hard to keep one's lies in mind and in order. It followed that "anyone who does not feel sufficiently strong in memory should not meddle with lying." Ultimately, liars revealed themselves by the diversity of their accounts; truth-tellers by the simplicity of theirs.[62] Correspondingly, one might also take consistency and simplicity over an array of an individual's narrations as evidence not just of coherence

57. Diogenes Laërtius, *Lives of Philosophers*, 187.
58. Guazzo, *Civile Conversation*, I, 97; Della Casa, *Galateo*, 44–45.
59. Bryskett, *Discourse of Civill Life*, 179–80.
60. Dare, *Counsellor Manners* (1672), 41.
61. Penn, *Fruits of Solitude*, 73; see also [De Courtin], *Rules of Civility*, 287.
62. Montaigne, "Of Liars," in idem, *Essays*, 23; see also "Of Presumption," ibid., 491.

but also of truth.[63] The jurist Sir Matthew Hale endorsed Montaigne's pragmatic prohibition of mendacity: "an hypocrite, or dissembler, or double-hearted man, though he may shuffle it out for a while, yet at the long run, he is discovered, and disappointed, and betrays very much folly at the latter end; when a plain, sincere honest man holds it out to the last; so that the Proverb is most true, that *Honesty is the best Policy*."[64]

In 1660 *The Gentlemans Companion* picked out the practical advantages of scrupulous truth-telling: "Keep thy word and promise punctually, though but in slight, and small matters; so shall thou be believed in greater."[65] A Restoration jurist noted that "dissimulation thrives never but once"; the habitual liar is cut off from "that trust and confidence which is necessary" in interdependent social undertakings: "Who will depend on those whom they cannot trust?"[66] And an early eighteenth-century Scottish courtesy writer cautioned against acquiring the habit of lying: "Such are never credited, even when they speak Truth. To speak the Truth is one of the best and strongest Bonds of humane Society and Commerce."[67]

The practical consequences of credibility-loss, of course, bore upon all social actors and not just upon the gentle. Yet the social practices of early modern public gentlemen arguably involved the manipulation of more extended and more complex social networks than those of other sorts of individuals, and, in consequence, careful attention to their place on the civic map of credibility and trustworthiness was at a premium. He who needed to enlist many others had to ensure that many others trusted him, or, far more expensively, feared him. For this reason, the secular condemnation of lying was intermittently directed towards avoiding the *appearance* of untruthfulness if that appearance was avoided at the expense of strict veracity itself. Thus, Guazzo enjoined gentlemen in company to "be spare in speaking of thinges whiche are not easily beleeved," even if the narrator knew these things to be the case.[68] Castiglione warned the courtier "not to acquire the name of a liar or boaster": "Therefore, in all he says, let him be always careful not to exceed the limits of verisimilitude, and not to tell too often those truths that have the appearance of falsehoods."[69] Obadiah Walker advised against that surfeit of polite wit which led to fantastic relations: "Be not hyperbolic and extravagant . . . for the wit

---

63. See, e.g., Stillingfleet, *Origines Sacræ* (1662), 297.
64. M. Hale, *Contemplations Moral and Divine* (1676), 34–35.
65. [Ramesey], *Gentlemans Companion*, 71; cf. [De Courtin], *Rules of Civility*, 287.
66. Mackenzie, *Moral Essay Preferring Solitude*, 58–59.
67. Petrie, *Rules of Good Deportment*, 54; see also Gailhard, *Two Discourses*, 255.
68. Guazzo, *Civile Conversation*, I, 153–54.
69. Castiglione, *The Courtier*, 139–40.

takes away the credit; whereas the end of speech was first to make us understood, then believed."[70]

In the middle of the eighteenth century Lord Chesterfield admonished his son against acquiring the reputation of a teller of marvelous tales. Fashionable people regarded fable-telling as "a sort of lying, which they reckon innocent." But it was a far from trivial matter for a public gentleman, "for one must naturally conclude, that he who will tell any lie from idle vanity, will not scruple telling a greater for interest." Chesterfield said that if he himself had actually witnessed anything "so very extraordinary as to be almost incredible, I would keep it to myself, rather than, by telling it, give any one body to doubt for one minute of my veracity."[71] The normative texture of polite conversation was not argument but agreement. Accordingly, that which strained free and easy assent likewise stressed the bonds of gentle social order.[72]

A third explanation of gentle truthfulness crucially depended upon the cultural recognition of the identity of the *Christian* gentleman. From the early seventeenth century, it was increasingly argued in England that the gentleman, enjoying divine donatives, stood in a special relationship with God, and that the constitution of legitimate gentility proceeded through religious belief and observance. Although the fashioning and legitimation of the Christian gentleman was a major preoccupation of much English courtesy literature from *ca.* 1580 to *ca.* 1680, I have already noted that religious conceptions of gentlemen's nature and behavior always coexisted with rival codes. The Christian ethical tradition of seventeenth-century England indeed recommended truthfulness as the imitation of God, but vigorously condemned that sensitivity to reputation which in the honor culture so spectacularly linked veracity to violence. Truth-telling and the word of honor were systematically shifted away from the center of the Christian picture of authentic gentility. Nevertheless, throughout the seventeenth century the chivalric idiom continued to erupt in fundamentally Christian accounts of gentle truthfulness.

In the 1580s Montaigne, referring to ancient pagan authority, assimilated Christian sanctions against lying to the secular code of honor which made cowardice an unbearable shame for a gentleman. To lie was to be "a coward towards men and bold towards God," and nothing could be uglier than that imputation.[73] Montaigne was here endeav-

---

70. Walker, *Of Education*, 248.

71. Chesterfield, *Letters to His Son*, 149.

72. The *conversational* character of gentlemanly discourse, and the problematic place of truth within that conversation, is further treated in chapters 5–7 below.

73. Montaigne, "Of Giving the Lie," in idem, *Essays*, 505. Montaigne's *Essays* were translated into English in 1603 and enjoyed wide popularity in England.

oring to understand why gentle society regarded the accusation of lying as such a mortal affront, so his stress was upon the significance of the accusation of cowardice in civil society. When Francis Bacon, in his essay "Of Truth," endorsed Montaigne's sentiment, he picked out the accusation of impiety.[74] Indeed, there had always been a Christian element in English accounts of authentic gentlemanly truthfulness. In the 1530s Thomas Elyot had said that to God "nothing may be acceptable wherein lacketh verity, called commonly truth, He Himself being all verity, and all thing containing untruth is to Him contrarious and adverse. And the devil is called a liar, and the father of leasings [lies]."[75] Samuel Johnson had it that "while the world was yet in its infancy, Truth came among mortals from above, and Falsehood from below."[76] William Penn instructed his children to speak nothing but the truth: "For equivocation is half way to lying; as lying, the whole way to hell."[77] English courtesy writers had little difficulty locating scriptural warrant for the prohibition against lying: "Lying lips are an abomination to the Lord; but they that deal truely are his delight" (Proverbs 12:22); "Wherefore putting away lying, speak every man truth with his neighbour; for we are members of one another" (Ephesians 4:25).[78]

In general, Christian writing on this subject tended to extend secular endorsement of word-keeping into divine terrain. One idiom suggested that breaking faith with God would incur substantial secular penalties. The authentic Christian gentleman was reminded of the verbal commitments he had made to God, who was in this context made to assume the character of an omniscient prince. Legitimate reputation in gentlemanly society could not be secured if one was seen to break one's holy vows: "If the Gentleman be thus carelesse in maintaining his *Credit,* thus false in his *promises* to *God* and his *Soul,* I hope he will not think it strange, if others be so scrupulous and weak-faith'd, as not to believe him to be a *Gentleman* upon his own bare *word.*"[79] In another

74. Bacon, "Of Truth," in idem, *Moral and Historical Works,* 1–4. Cf. Stafford, *Staffords Niobe,* 34: "A Coward I call him, who slauishlie feareth any thing but God."

75. Elyot, *The Governor,* 168–69. The scriptural reference is to John 8:44; see also Bryskett, *Discourse of Civill Life,* 50; Stanley, *History of Philosophy,* I, 84, citing Porphyry. For an early eighteenth-century exploration of the devil's credibility problems, see Schaffer, "Defoe's Natural Philosophy," esp. 24–28.

76. Johnson, *The Rambler,* IV, 149 (16 February 1751).

77. Penn, *Fruits of Solitude,* 41.

78. Note that the Ninth Commandment (Exodus 20:16), which prohibits "bearing false witness," was sometimes, but not invariably, interpreted as a blanket prohibition against all forms of untruthfulness; see, especially, practical uses of a notion of a deity who could not lie and "would not suffer us to be deceived" in authentically divine testimony, in Stillingfleet, *Origines Sacræ,* 232, 240. For scriptural passages used by early Christian writers to *support* certain types of untruthfulness, see, e.g., Sommerville, "'New Art of Lying,'" 163–64; Zagorin, *Ways of Lying,* 21–23.

79. Ellis, *Gentile Sinner,* 236–37.

idiom the gentleman was told not to take the opinion of civil society at all seriously compared to that of God. William Darrell's *The Gentleman Instructed* reminded the Christian gentleman to think of the shame and dishonor of "receiving the lie" as residing in *meriting* the accusation. If he deserved the lie, then his own conduct was the cause of his shame; if he did not, then God was sufficient witness to his innocence.[80] As a practical Restoration ethical text put it, "he that Sins against Conscience, sins with a witness."[81] Genuine shame was considered not to be reputational but wholly internal to the self. Montaigne reckoned that the occasions of authentic truth-telling were not those when there is "some external obligation to do so" or when one's interests are served, but when "it is not important to anybody." The truthful man feels "inward shame and stinging remorse" when a lie escapes him.[82] Matthew Hale lectured Christian gentlemen on the meaning of divine omniscience. Whoever fears God "is under the sense of the introspection and animadversion of that God that searches the Heart, and therefore he knows the pure, all-seeing, righteous God, that loves truth and integrity, and hates lying and dissimulation, beholds and sees and observes him, and knows his thoughts, words and actions."[83] Insofar as gentlemen were, and were considered to be, Christian believers, thus far such considerations might count as explanations of their truthfulness.

The fourth major element brought to bear to explain the reliability of gentle testimony was arguably the most fundamental and consequential, since it drew upon the very integrity and independence figuring so largely in the mundane system by which early modern English gentlemen were recognized as such. Dr. Johnson reflected common wisdom in noting that "Truth is scarcely to be heard but by those from whom it can serve no interest to conceal it," and it was the *disinterestedness* of the English gentleman's situation that was most importantly identified as the basis of his truth-telling.[84] The specific circumstances of his economic, political, and social free action outlined in chapter 2 were mobilized as explanations of the integrity of a gentleman's narrations. The explanations could also function as normative resources: one *ought* to behave thus or it would be reliably concluded that one was not the type of person one claimed to be. Lying was vile, base, mean, and ignoble because it arose from circumstances attending the lives of ignoble people. An ignoble life was a *constrained* life, in which

80. [Darrell], *Gentleman Instructed* (1704–08), 22.
81. Britaine, *Humane Prudence* (1686), 9.
82. Montaigne, "Of Presumption," in idem, *Essays,* 491.
83. M. Hale, *Contemplations Moral and Divine* (1676), 35; cf. R. Baxter, *Autobiography* (1696), 88–89.
84. Johnson, *The Rambler,* V, 37 (24 August 1751).

one was at the will of another, in which passion or interest compromised the self's spontaneous free action. Gentlemen were truth-tellers because nothing could work upon them that would induce them to be otherwise. This was said to be the case, and this was what the canon of practical ethical writing enjoined one to act upon as if it were the case.

I have already noted the general association between mendacity and servility traced in the early modern courtesy literature. That same tradition intermittently spelled out just why it was that lying was an adequate sign of baseness. Guazzo, for example, noted that "though lying be unseemely for every man, yet is it more tollerable in one of base calling, and who is driven thereto by necessitie: And therefore in holy Scripture, a riche man being a lyar is greatly reproved." Lying was thus "a thynge of all others moste servile."[85] A Restoration Scots moralist inquired whether there is "anything more mean than dependence." All viciousness, and especially the vice of lying, betrays "a meanesse, because in all these we confesse want and infirmities." When we depart from the truth, we show that "we feare to speak openly."[86] La Rochefoucauld judged that "weak people cannot be sincere," and Gilbert Burnet diagnosed the causes of a lying disposition in children as "fear," "envy," and "malice."[87] This basic equation between truth-telling and integrity of life was even used by Christian apologists as a powerful motive for men to believe biblical testimony. Restoration courtesy texts argued, for instance, that we ought to credit the word of scriptural writers just because of who they were: "The Pen-men (throughout the *Bible*) were either Kings, Rulers, Men of Honour, and high Esteem among the People; and therefore, would not attest Lyes, to expose themselves to the contradiction, and scorn of the World, or Vulgar. [They were] Men of Integrity, Piety, and Fidelity, that could purchase nothing by that they delivered, if untrue."[88]

The association traced by Montaigne and Bacon between the liar and the coward was a potent resource for sixteenth- and seventeen-century moralists. As I shall show, the secular code of honor impelled the gentleman to resist any imputation of cowardice, if necessary by displaying his willingness to risk his body in order to protect his reputation. A number of seventeenth-century English and Scots writers labored to assimilate entrenched elements of that secular code to Christian principles. The Scots jurist Sir George Mackenzie elaborated the argument that true "gallantry" for the Christian gentleman con-

85. Guazzo, *Civile Conversation*, I, 96; II, 101.
86. Mackenzie, *Moral Gallantry*, 46–48; see also [Allestree], *Gentleman's Calling*, 117.
87. La Rochefoucauld, *Maxims* (1665), 93; Burnet, *Thoughts on Education*, 16.
88. [Ramesey], *Gentlemans Companion*, 53; see also Stillingfleet, *Origines Sacræ*, 419–20. This point is elaborated in chapter 5 below.

sisted in self-discipline and in the heroic avoidance of vice. In his view the fundamental vice spoiling gentle identity was mendacity. Indeed, so differently placed were the gentle and ungentle that Mackenzie conferred different names on their respective departures from truth. In the "meaner sort" he called it "falsehood," while "dissimulation" was "the peculiar sin of the Great." Whatever name it went by, it was a heinous vice, and those reputed gentlemen who committed it revealed that they were not gentlemen at all:

> What an ugly and ungentile Vice Dissimulation is, seing that he is no Gentleman who would not choise rather to die, or starve, then to be thought false. . . . Cowards dissemble best, gallant men laying that weight upon their Courage, which the others do upon Dissimulation. . . . Dissimulation is but a Courtly Cowardness, and a Stately Cheat. . . . [It is] this under-boord Game.[89]

Mackenzie vividly embroidered Christian ethics with a chivalric figure: "To deceive one who is not obliged to believe us is ill; but to cheat one whom our own fair pretences have induced to believe us, is much worse, for this is to murther one whom we have perswaded to lay aside his Arms." Dissimulation is but the "theory of Cut-pursing, and Assasination." Even if, as is regrettably the case, it has "great Patrons" at Court, "all who are Gallant there hate it." It subsists only in "a cowardly lurking, and shunning to be discovered."[90]

Trading upon the secular code in which such imputations fatally damaged honor, the Anglican divines Gilbert Burnet and John Tillotson and the Huguenot Pierre du Moulin identified fear and envy as among the chief motives to lying.[91] Moreover, in the Protestant culture which stressed the importance of continual self-interrogation, such imputations also spoke of a compromised *inner* integrity: the self was constrained and unfree. The liar, and the vicious man generally, displayed failure of *self-control.* One was understood to engage in vicious behavior because the rational, higher, and truly human part of one's nature had become a servant to the passions. Within one's own compound nature, what ought to be master had become servant. The person had become transformed from a well-ordered to a riotous household.[92]

Mackenzie claimed that the most powerful argument displaying "the

89. Mackenzie, *Moral Essay Preferring Solitude,* 56–57.

90. Ibid., 59–60; see also similar locutions in Britaine, *Humane Prudence,* 67.

91. Burnet, *Thoughts on Education,* 16; Tillotson, "Of the Education of Children," in idem, *Works,* I, 494; du Moulin, *Directions for the Education of a Young Prince,* quoted in Mason, *Gentlefolk in the Making,* 160.

92. For this theme, see, e.g., Mackenzie, *Moral Gallantry,* passim; idem, *Moral Essay Preferring Solitude,* 91–94, 104; Ellis, *Gentile Sinner,* 101, 115, 129–33, 234–42; Brathwait, *English Gentleman,* 13; Britaine, *Humane Prudence,* 31, 35.

meaness of Vice" arose from the fact "that Servants, without pains or
Art, equal us in them." To be virtuous was, however, to give a publicly
visible sign that we "deserve, and are by such as know us not, judged to
be Masters and well descended."[93] Brathwait's account of the authentic
English Christian gentleman was one of many which enlisted Stoical
conceptions of self-mastery in the argument against vice: "A true and
generous Moderation of his affections, hathe begot in him an absolute
command and conquest of himselfe."[94] The Anglican divine Edward
Stillingfleet recommended service to God over making oneself "a slave
to those *passions* and *lusts* which put men under continual hard service."[95] De Britaine urged self-control as the special and practical obligation of gentlemen: "He who commands himself, commands the
World too; and the more Authority you have over others, the more
command you must have over your self."[96] Sir Henry Wotton, diplomat and provost of Eton in the early seventeenth century, rhymed
"The Character of a Happy Life": "How happy is he born and taught,/
That serveth not anothers will?/Whose armour is his honest thought,/
And simple truth his utmost skill?"[97] And Defoe asked about the likely
public consequences of private viciousness: "If the gentleman . . . can
not govern himself, how should we expect any good œconomy in his
household?"[98]

Unreliable People

An account of the grounds on which certain categories of people were
deemed unreliable truth-tellers supports the general link between integrity of circumstance and integrity of word. Just as the ideal gentleman's integrity and independence were used to account for and enjoin
his truthfulness, so the unreliable truthfulness of others was pervasively referred to their constrained circumstances. Those whose placement in society rendered them dependent upon others, whose actions
were at others' bidding, or who were so placed as to need relative
advantage were *for these reasons* deemed liable to misrepresent real
states of affairs—what they were actually thinking, what their intentions were with respect to future action, how matters stood in the
world. Their word might not be relied upon; it might need to be

93. Mackenzie, *Moral Gallantry*, 46–47.
94. Brathwait, *English Gentleman*, sig. Nnn2v. For the significance of Stoicism in
sixteenth- and seventeenth-century conceptions of gentility, see Childs, "Prescriptions
for Manners," 61–67, 176–86.
95. Stillingfleet, *Origines Sacræ*, sig. a2v.
96. Britaine, *Humane Prudence*, 31 (also 35).
97. Wotton, "The Character of a Happy Life" (1651), in Grierson and Bullough,
Oxford Book of Seventeenth-Century Verse, 77–78.
98. Defoe, *Compleat English Gentleman*, 232.

vouched for or otherwise deliberately gauged against independently known standards of how things were. Accordingly, the culture which accounted for the unreliability of certain people's word figured in a massively consequential system of exclusion.

One such excluded category was, albeit ambiguously, part of gentle society itself, namely women. Undoubtedly, early modern people were able, with great reliability, to categorize members of their society as males and females, and, undoubtedly, these identities were regarded as interesting and as at least partly natural. Recent research by such historians as David Underdown and Susan Amussen establishes beyond question the significance in early modern English political theory of patriarchical models of the family.[99] But *just because* the characteristic view was that women took their social standing from men, that their identity was subsumed in that of their father or husband, and that they worked their will through men, the relevant category of analysis was not the natural one of *biological endowment* and its expression but the situated cultural one of *dependence*. And dependence was a circumstance that was understood to affect biological males in much the same way that it worked on biological females. That is to say, the historian who wants to accept and seriously act upon recommendations that we treat sex as a matter of biology and gender as a matter of culture[100] may well encounter settings wherein the attributions assigned to gender do not correspond wholly or significantly with our map of sex.

While some courtesy texts did indeed comment upon women's unreliable truthfulness, and while there was a sixteenth- and seventeenth-century ethical literature especially designed for a female readership,[101] it cannot be said that the cultural qualifications of women were as such a major preoccupation of early modern (male) ethical writing. In the main, women's conduct was addressed within a domestic context, as might be expected in settings where *institutional* obstacles to female participation in formally political or cultural affairs were so substantial that exclusion did not need to be elaborately justified.[102]

99. Underdown, "Taming of the Scold"; Amussen, *An Ordered Society*, 4; idem, "Gender, Family and Social Order." Both historians stress the role of gender while fully recognizing the cultural variability of what was understood by gender categories.

100. E.g., E. Keller, "Feminist Perspectives on Science Studies," esp. 236–37.

101. E.g., Brathwait, *English Gentlewoman* (1631).

102. In these connections see, esp., Amussen, *An Ordered Society;* Neale, *Class in English History*, ch. 7; and Stone, *Family, Sex and Marriage,* 195–206. There was, of course, much commentary on women's proper place within a patriarchal household and much attention to "scolds" and rebellious women. On the facts of the institutional exclusion of women from early modern scientific culture, I am here at one with Schiebinger, *The Mind Has No Sex?*, esp. chs 1–2, and Mendelson, *Mental World of Stuart Women,* esp. introduction and ch. 1, while I dissent from claims about the gender-specificity of that exclusion.

There were powerful institutions of exclusion that affected the cultural and political role of women, as well as of nongentle men. But precisely because those institutional systems were so effective, and because the justifications overwhelmingly picked out dependence as a disqualifying circumstance, the *literate culture* of early modern England was not nearly so significantly marked by identifications of gender disabilities as it was by commentary on "ignobility," "servility," and "baseness." In fact, much of the formal culture that addressed women's nature was ambivalent on this subject.[103] What need of systematic cultural legitimations when the institutions of exclusion worked well enough?[104]

Nevertheless, the relevant ethical literature sporadically did condemn women as endemic dissemblers and deceivers. Aristotle concluded that the female sex in all species was an imperfect or deformed version of the male. Regular sex differences evident throughout the animal realm were even more pronounced among humans: "[The female] is more prone to despondency and less hopeful than the man, more void of shame, more false of speech, more deceptive."[105] Women were commonly reckoned on humoral grounds to possess stronger powers of imagination and weaker reasoning faculties—they tended towards defective judgment and delusion—while minority voices in-

103. Castiglione's courtiers importantly *disagreed* in their assessments of women's mental capacities: *The Courtier*, esp. 189 (for Ottaviano's misogyny) and 214–15 (for Giuliano's view that women are "by nature better fitted for speculation than men are"); cf. Schiebinger, *The Mind Has No Sex?*, 17–19. Similarly, the Tudor educationalist Richard Mulcaster argued for the education of women as wholly right and natural. There was nothing in their makeup (apart from relative bodily weakness) that hindered their capacity to learn what men learned, and Mulcaster, like Giuliano, pointed to many instances of learned women (including the queen). Yet he only felt obliged to cite national "custom" as disqualifying women from participation in the activities that put learning to institutionalized cultural use: Mulcaster, *Positions*, 167–83, esp. 173; see also Stone, *Family, Sex and Marriage*, 196–97, 202–06. In the event, the tide of sentiment favoring learned gentlewomen was running out by the middle of the sixteenth century, and seventeenth-century Englishwomen were even more poorly educated than their mothers and grandmothers.

104. As Stone shows (*Family, Sex and Marriage*, 199), explicit feminist claims to equality did not surface until the Interregnum, in a context where radical groups were calling into question a range of hierarchies. I shall treat the role of specific women in Robert Boyle's scientific work in chapters 4 and 8.

105. Aristotle, *History of Animals*, IX. 608^b 10–13; cf. [Aristotle?], *Physiognomonics*, 809^a 27–809^b 14; see also Maclean, *Renaissance Notion of Woman*, ch. 3; Lloyd, *Science, Folklore and Ideology*, 94–105 (and see 76–78 for male Greek physicians' view that women were unreliable sources, even as to the stages of their own pregnancy); and Daston, "Naturalized Female Intellect," 214–18. Because the differences between men and women were generally considered to be matters of degree rather than essence, those adhering to this system need not have been surprised to find women with exceptional attributes, occasionally surpassing many men in personal integrity, courage, etc. For the alleged early modern dissolution of the traditional "one-sex" model, see Laqueur, *Making Sex*.

sisted upon a random distribution of mental characteristics among the sexes.[106] Women's physical size, weakness, and reproductive makeup were regarded as natural facts warranting cultural conclusions. Woman was, as scripture said (1 Peter 3:7), the "weaker vessel," her infirmities testifying to the natural plan or divine intention that the husband should be master in his own household, that the wife should do his bidding and act as his agent, and that social roles ought to be differentiated into a productive, publicly acting, and politically vocal male and a reproductive, privately acting, and politically silent female.[107] Although it was very occasionally debated whether or not women possessed independent wills and souls, it was much more widely accepted that women's wills were so circumstanced that they could only act through men's.[108]

Medieval, Renaissance, and early modern moralists argued about whether Adam or Eve was most responsible for the Fall. Some commentators excused her because women had weaker powers of reason while others stressed her capacity to be deceived and identified women accordingly as diabolic instruments.[109] Elizabethan male poets liked to conceive of love as an unequal contest between man's genuine devotion and woman's falseness. The earl of Essex wrote: "Now thou see'st, but all too late,/Love loves truth, which women hate." A contemporary typically complained that "A woman's face is full of wiles,/Her tears are like the crocadill . . ./Her tongue still chats of this and that,/Than aspen leaf it wags more fast;/And as she talks she knows not what,/There issues many a truthless blast."[110] Shakespeare's sonnet 138 is an

---

106. Maclean, *Renaissance Notion of Woman*, 41–46; see also E. R. Harvey's account of Costa ben Luca's early tenth-century views on the coarser bodily constitutions of women and "Ethiopians and Slavs," and their consequent inability to attain the soul's virtues: *The Inward Wits*, 37–39. It was in the context of a general argument in favor of learning-for-life that Montaigne said that the reason much learning was not required of women— and why in general they were ignorant—was simply that in practice they had little scope to *use* formal knowledge: "Of Pedantry," in idem, *Essays*, 103.

107. See the source in Aristotle, *Nicomachean Ethics*, VIII. 1160^b 23–1161^a 9; idem, *Politics*, I. 1252^b–1254^a; also Brathwait, *English Gentlewoman*, 40–55; see also Plato, *Republic*, V. 453–58; idem, *Laws*, VII. 805–06; Amussen, *An Ordered Society*, 43–44; Jordanova, "Natural Facts"; idem, *Sexual Visions*, ch. 2; and, above all, Maclean, *Renaissance Notion of Woman*, chs 2, 4. Of course, there is no reason uncritically to accept that injunctions towards female submissiveness accurately described social realities, and Stone suggests that there may have been considerable social variability in sex-role patterns (*Family, Sex and Marriage*, 199–202).

108. Stone, *Family, Sex and Marriage*, 196.

109. Maclean, *Renaissance Notion of Woman*, esp. 15; H. L. Smith, "Intellectual Bases for Feminist Analyses," esp. 24–29; Browne, *Pseudodoxia Epidemica*, 2–3, but Browne noted that both Adam and Eve were deceived by their shared desire for "Pleasure and profit."

110. Essex and Humfrey Gifford, in Ault, *Elizabethan Lyrics*, 281–84, 84–85.

extended play on the falsehood of women: "When my love swears that she is made of truth,/I do believe her, though I know she lies." Carroll Camden notes the contemporary opinion that "to get what she wants, a woman will do or say anything; thus she is deceiving, dissembling, and lying."[111]

For all that, there is considerable risk in identifying a too-coherent early modern English view of women's capacities and virtues. Strands of neo-Platonic thought celebrated female virtues, while much ethical writing manifested mixed, ambivalent, or ambiguous evaluations. Gainsford's *Rich Cabinet* developed a character of woman which, on the one hand, had no difficulty in acknowledging the moral and intellectual equality of *some* women, while, on the other, offering standard portrayals of female disabilities: "Woman is endued with the same vertues as man, for there hath beene as valiant, wise, godly, magnanimous, pollitick, iudicious, great spirited women as men." Yet "woman" was also "the weaknesse of vnderstanding," "the trouble of reason," and "the deceite of trust and confidency."[112] Delusionary tendencies were occasionally ascribed to women, as often as not owing to circumstances and traits they shared with some categories of men. Montaigne preceded Thomas Browne in reckoning that ignorance was the key to delusions and bad judgment: "The more a mind is empty and without counterpoise, the more easily it gives beneath the weight of the first persuasive argument. That is why children, common people, women, and the sick are most subject to being led by the ears."[113] Unreliable testimony was routinely labeled as "old wives' tales," and William Gilbert was one of very many early modern scientific practitioners who rhetorically rejected traditional natural historical testimony by assimilating it to "the maunderings of a babbling hag."[114]

Other commentators picked out the moral environment in which women were placed as the cause of their unreliability. A woman's "honor" was considered to reside wholly in the chastity of her body, or rather that body as the instrument and possession of her father or future or present husband.[115] Accordingly, women, just like male

111. Camden, *Elizabethan Woman*, 27; see also ibid., 123–24. There was also a (male) literature exculpating women from such charges, and still other commentators admitted that if women were in fact untruthful this was either because they imitated men or because "they have learned to lie in saving the reputations of their husbands" (ibid., 31).

112. [Gainsford], *Rich Cabinet*, 162–64.

113. Montaigne, "It is Folly to Measure the True and False by Our Own Capacity," in idem, *Essays*, 132.

114. Gilbert, *De Magnete* (1600), 6, 101, 103; see also Bacon, "Preparative towards a Natural and Experimental History," 255; idem, "Advancement of Learning," 288.

115. Romei, *Courtiers Academie*, 126–28; Brathwait, *English Gentlewoman*, 157–221; Watson, *Shakespeare and the Renaissance Concept of Honor*, 159–62, 437–47; Amussen, *An Ordered Society*, 104.

dependent persons, were recognized as lacking freedom of action and integrity in themselves. The wife was "at the will and disposition of the Husband" in the same way that servants (of whatever sex) were instruments of their master's will. She had no independence of view, and that was why she could not be a witness in courts of law either for or against her husband.[116] As Stone notes, by marriage "the husband and wife became one person in law—and that person was the husband."[117] In English common law a woman was deemed "covert," that is, subsumed in her husband's legal person. According to the author of *The Lawes Resolution of Womens Rights* (1632), "all of them are understood either married or to be married and their desires are subject to their husband."[118] Unfreedom was, therefore, identified as the key circumstance in women's cultural and political "muteness." Indeed, as far back as Aristotle, the dependent places of women and servants were treated in tandem.[119] Because women were so placed that they might not be reproached with accusations of cowardice or servility, the honor code could not act as a constraint on their behavior. The identification of deceit with fear and weakness was ineffective when directed at women, since their dependence and vulnerability could not be denied.[120]

Servants—by definition—were dependent and subject to the will of another.[121] Courtesy books, and practical guides to domestic management, routinely commented on the unreliability and mendacity of servants and advised how they should be selected, managed, and supervised. The gentleman's treatment of his servants was deemed

116. Chamberlayne, *Angliæ Notitia*, I, 330, 336. I briefly treat English political meanings of servitude and subsumption in chapter 8.

117. Stone, *Family, Sex and Marriage*, 195.

118. Quoted in Mendelson, *Mental World of Stuart Women*, 2.

119. Maclean, *Renaissance Notion of Woman*, 50, 54.

120. Mackenzie, *Moral Essay Preferring Solitude*, 60–65. A modern feminist writer recognizes, and condemns, the same predicament that confronted early modern women: "Women's honor, something altogether else: virginity, chastity, fidelity. . . . Honesty in women has not been considered important. We have typically been depicted as generically whimsical, deceitful, subtle, vacillating. And we have been rewarded for lying. . . . Women have been forced to lie, for survival, to men. . . . The liar is afraid" (Rich, "Women and Honor: Some Notes on Lying," in idem, *On Lies, Secrets, and Silence*, 185–94). I cannot here treat views on the untruthfulness of *children*, though some psychological work on particularly untruthful children has stressed their suggestibility, lack of self-control, and weakness relative to other children: Slaght, *Untruthfulness in Children*, esp. 22, 31.

121. *Servants* here designates persons from the lower ranks of society who were employed on a contractual basis and who had no effective expectation of becoming masters themselves. As I shall note in chapter 8, very many sons of the gentry and aristocracy went through a youthful period of transient servitude before setting up their own households.

important both as a practical and as a moral matter. His 'family' included his residential servants.[122] In the Puritan literature especially, the gentleman was urged to make himself responsible for their moral management, just as servants were responsible for his economic affairs and the safekeeping of his secrets.[123] The selection of servants was therefore a weighty business. What were servants in general like? How to read their characters? How far to trust them? What quality and quantity of supervision did they require? And to what extent did one's own conduct shape that of the dependent members of one's household?

Virtually all relevant sixteenth- and seventeenth-century English polite commentary agreed that servants were to be well treated, that they were to be given examples of responsible and truthful conduct, and that they were not to be used in improper and dishonest ventures. Some few even went so far as to assert the in-principle equality of masters and servants.[124] Nevertheless, there was wide agreement that the servant's word was *not* his bond, and that the reason for this distinction between masters and servants was the latter's dependence and compromised integrity of action. Servants had to come with recommendations and character references from previous masters. Their own testimony of their character, experience, and qualifications could not, obviously, be taken at face value, for they would say anything to secure advantageous employment. As one early seventeenth-century guide cautioned, "to take a man [servant] of his own word, is the worst of all."[125]

Since, as with women generally, there were no considerations of honor that worked on servants, the restraints that prevented them from lying and stealing had to be external, dependent upon the master's effective supervision and the servant's recognition that he would be detected and made accountable. There *were* indeed individual servants who were recognized as reliable and virtuous, but, owing to their circumstances, even these must not be trusted too far. Britaine, for

122. See, e.g., Gailhard, *Two Discourses*, 15–18; see also Hole, *English Housewife in the Seventeenth Century*, ch. 7; Kussmaul, *Servants in Husbandry*, ch. 1, esp. 7–9; Laslett, introduction to Filmer, *Patriarcha*, 24–26; Locke, *Two Treatises of Government*, Bk. II, sect. 86.

123. E.g., [Alestree], *Gentleman's Calling*, 89–98; Petrie, *Rules of Good Deportment*, 32–33; see also E. S. Morgan, *Puritan Family*; J. Morgan, *Godly Learning*, ch. 8; Todd, *Christian Humanism*, ch. 4; Hill, *Society and Puritanism*, ch. 13; Macfarlane, *Family Life of Ralph Josselin*, 145–49, 205–10 (especially for distant kin as domestic servants).

124. E.g., Penn, *Fruits of Solitude*, 44–45; Osborne, *Advice to a Son*, 31; Walker, *Of Education*, 265.

125. [Brydges?], *Horæ Subseciuæ* (1620), 85–102, quoting 86–87.

instance, warned that "your Servants . . . you may admit into your
Bed-Chamber, but never into your Closet."[126] A practical early eighteenth-century discussion of how gentlemen must deal with their servants argued that "Honesty is not always Proof against Temptation;
Men often cheat without Scruple, when they can do it without Fear."[127]
Literature produced for the instruction of servants pervasively recognized their temptation to lie for advantage and recruited divine resources to caution them against it: "*Lying* is in it selfe an hainous sinne:
yet so much the more hainous when it is told to one that hath authority
ouer vs, and by reason thereof standeth in Gods place."[128]

The testimony of the poor and the mean in general was widely
deemed by gentle society to be unreliable, even in legal settings where
testimony was taken on oath. Again, the accepted reason for this suspicion flowed from the compromised circumstances of dependent and
constrained people. Thus, early seventeenth-century legal proceedings
in Norfolk referred to "poor needy vile base people of no esteem
amongst their neighbours, . . . such as . . . for some small reward
may be procured to swear falsely."[129] Although this book is largely
concerned with the circulation of credibility in and from the point of
view of gentlemanly society, there is no reason simply to assume that
the relevant concepts were universally distributed and valued. Susan
Amussen notes that by the late sixteenth century, the notion of "credit"
described "both honesty and solvency; wealth and virtue were joined."
She argues that the poor of early modern England never used the
concept of credit, and certainly did not label each other as people
whose word and work were of no worth: "Credit was a concept of the
governors of early modern England, and it made their job easier; it
was not universally accepted."[130]

Still another group whose circumstances placed them in need of
gaining advantage, and indeed whose daily employment was the getting
of material advantage, was the mercantile and trading class. Accordingly, gentle commentators often observed that merchants systematically told untruths in their efforts to secure that advantage. Bacon, for
example, distinguished three motives for lying: the poet's lie (told for
pleasure), the general lie (for its own sake), and that told "for advan-

126. Britaine, *Humane Prudence*, 21.

127. [Darrell], *Gentleman Instructed*, 17; see also Defoe, *Complete English Tradesman*
(1726), 179–91 (for characteristics of servants and apprentices in trade).

128. Gouge, *Of Domesticall Duties*, 600; see also ibid., 622–35. For discussion of ethical
texts for servants, see Childs, "Prescriptions for Manners," ch. 6.

129. Quoted in Amussen, *An Ordered Society*, 152–53.

130. Ibid., 152–55; see also Schaffer, "Defoe's Natural Philosphy," 14 (for seven-
teenth- and early eighteenth-century changes in the notion of credit).

tage, as with the merchant."[131] From the early sixteenth to the eigh-teenth century, ethical tracts produced by and for the gentle classes noted and deplored the deceit and lying of merchants, even if mercan-tile activities were otherwise approved. Erasmus noted the "meanness" of merchants' methods: "their lies, perjury, thefts, frauds and decep-tions are everywhere to be found."[132] Ferne's *Blazon of Gentrie* de-scribed merchants' "condition of life" as consisting "of most vngentle parts, as doublenes of toong, violation of faith, with the rest of their tromperies and disceites."[133] *The Rich Cabinet* commended the mercan-tile classes for their value to the commonwealth while condemning their routine mendacity: "The Merchant is onely traduced in this, that the hope of wealth is his principall object whereby profite may arise, which is not vsually attained without corruption of heart, deceit-full protestations, vaine promises, idle oathes, paltry lyes, pedling de-ceit, simple denials, palpable leauing his friend, and in famous abuse of charitie."[134] And Thomas Hobbes criticized ministers who did not inveigh enthusiastically enough "against the lucrative vices of men of trade or handicraft; such as are feigning, lying, cozening, [or] hy-pocrisy."[135]

Even as the intermingling of gentle and mercantile families became increasingly common, fellows of the early Royal Society echoed the traditional sentiment. John Aubrey urged gentlemen to be vigilant in examining their merchants' bills: "a little honesty goes a great way with them: they make no conscience of telling a lie, and most of them are knaves."[136] Edward Chamberlayne observed that "Tradesmen in all Ages and Nations have been reputed ignoble in regard of the dou-bleness of their Tongue, without which they hardly grow rich." Mer-chants' mendacity and deceit might be taken as reliable signs that they were indeed "a baser sort of people." The son of a gentleman could be said to make himself base by going into trade just because he subjected himself to those circumstances which would make truth-telling impossi-ble.[137] Tradesmen's preference for lucre over the light of knowledge constituted a continuing practical problem for scientific practitioners devoted to public knowledge. Boyle said that he had "found by long and unwelcome experience, that very few tradesmen will, and can give

131. Bacon, "Of Truth," in idem, *Moral and Historical Works*, 1.

132. Erasmus, *Praise of Folly* (1511), 74.

133. Ferne, *Blazon of Gentrie* (1586), 7. This charge was specifically rebutted in Water-house, *Discourse and Defence of Arms* (1660), 178–79.

134. [Gainsford], *Rich Cabinet*, 89v.

135. Hobbes, *Behemoth* (1668), 25.

136. Aubrey, *Aubrey on Education* (comp. 1669–84), 133.

137. Chamberlayne, *Angliæ Notitia*, I, 320–21, 328.

a man a clear and full account of their own practices; partly out of envy, partly out of want of skill to deliver a relation intelligibly."[138]

In the 1720s Daniel Defoe dwelt at length on the practical problems of constituting and maintaining credit and credibility in trade and civil society generally.[139] He recognized that the exigencies of trade made departures from literal truth-telling practically necessary. While he vigorously argued the fundamental role of "credit" in making a cohesive and dynamic economic order, Defoe explicitly defended the permissibility of lying in the course of business. Every reasonable person understood, Defoe said, that the tradesman's word and promise had to be taken in the context of the "circumstances of trade," including his ability on the day to perform what he had undertaken. Similarly, everyone understood and accepted that when a tradesman swore that he would accept no less than a guinea for a piece of cloth, he knew that in fact he would accept less. Thus, Defoe argued that "the tradesman should indeed not be understood strictly and literally to his words." These "trading lies" were therefore literally untrue but contextually benign. Such mendacity in no way compromised the tradesman's "honesty." Indeed, Defoe was one of the first commentators systematically to identify the practical impossibility of telling 'the whole truth' to all men, on all occasions.[140] Defoe also commented upon the practices of Quaker businessmen, who publicly advertised their commitment to tell as much truth in their trading as they did in other aspects of life. Even so, the Quaker William Penn recognized how the nature of business compromised one's ability to tell truth. There are "few dealers but what are faulty, which makes trade difficult, and a great temptation to men of virtue." Merchants ask what they can get, not what the thing is worth; they point out perfections and conceal defects: "Big words are given where they are not deserved, and the ignorance or necessity of the buyer imposed upon for unjust profit."[141]

Unreliable Gentlemen

Imputations of unreliability were not, however, confined to the ungentle. There were people of undoubtedly gentle standing whose truthfulness was widely held in suspicion, at least for certain purposes and in certain circumstances. In each case, a view of their compromised integ-

138. Boyle, "Some Considerations Touching the Usefulness of Experimental Natural Philosophy. Second Tome," 396.

139. Schaffer, "Defoe's Natural Philosophy."

140. Defoe, *Complete English Tradesman*, 276, 279, 281, 285, 289–92; see also M. McKeon, *Origins of the English Novel*, 120–21.

141. Penn, *Fruits of Solitude*, 83, also 44.

rity and free action provided the basis for imputations of untruthfulness. In post-Reformation England there was widespread sentiment that the truth-telling of recusant Catholics might be questionable in any matter impinging upon their faith. In the 1620s the Anglican divine Henry Mason published *The New Art of Lying*, describing and denouncing the practices of "equivocation" and "mental reservation" recommended by Jesuit casuists.[142] This "new art" was propagated, for example, to enable English Catholics to mislead Protestant authorities without doing anything Rome was obliged to regard as sinful. Accordingly, a priest might properly tell an English magistrate that he was *not* a priest, by having the appropriate mental reservation—"so far as I am obliged to tell you," or "not a *Jewish* priest"—at the moment he said it. In Pascal's influential critique of Jesuit casuistry, it was supposed to be "the intention that determines the quality of the action." Casuists counseled that one might also, without sin, exploit the natural ambiguity of language or the indexical relationship between the context of utterances and their accepted meanings. For Catholic casuists "equivocation" might be a warranted misleading of the enemies of Rome. Protestant writers, of course, did not recognize these techniques of mental reservation and equivocation as legitimate. Mason wanted the "new art" called by its proper name of "lying," in contrast to "the practice of Protestants in using *plainesse and syncerity in speech*."[143] Nor did he think that the practitioners of the new art were confined to the ranks of the Jesuits, even though the English Jesuits "haue beene the chiefe Abettors, Defenders and Polishers of this *Arte*." In fact, "Secular Priests, and Laie Papists of all sorts, doe iumpe with the Iesuites in the practice of this Arte."[144] Insofar as Catholics were said to lie for Rome, it might be concluded that their integrity and freedom of action were compromised. In matters of the faith, and perhaps of civil policy that flowed from confessional considerations, they were said to be at the bidding of others, not free to do as they pleased.[145]

142. For recent studies of "mental reservation" and early modern attitudes to dissimulation, see Zagorin, *Ways of Lying*, chs 7–10, and Sommerville, "'New Art of Lying.'" For valuable recuperation of the casuistical tradition, see Jonsen and Toulmin, *Abuse of Casuistry*, esp. ch. 10.

143. Pascal, *Provincial Letters*, no. IX (1656), 443–44; Mason, *New Art of Lying*, 19; see also Jonsen and Toulmin, *Abuse of Casuistry*, ch. 12. For English *Protestant* use of equivocation, see Baxter, *Christian Dictionary* (1673), 430, quoted in Sommerville, "'New Art of Lying,'" 168. For a suggestive study of "theological lying" and the doctrine of "esotericism" among English deists, see Bagley, "On the Practice of Esotericism."

144. Mason, *New Art of Lying*, 19, 35, 39; see also Tillotson, "The Lawfulness and Obligation of Oaths," in idem, *Works*, I, 196–97; Gailhard, *Two Discourses*, 257; Baxter, *Autobiography*, 185 (for Restoration suspicion of Catholic truthfulness).

145. Almost needless to say, Catholicism was only one consideration among many that bore upon such imputations. Thus, I have seen no evidence that Catholic members

More generally, English commentators were suspicious of the integrity and truthfulness of Continental gentry. Roger Ascham's *Scholemaster* (1570) was one of a number of ethical tracts which vigorously criticized the growing fashionability of foreign travel in the education of the English gentleman, and, in particular, the effect of Italian manners and mores. Italian culture and society were said to be debased by papism and by court intrigue. Machiavellian morals were routinely associated with the hierarchical social relations of the Italian courts, and contrasted with the relative simplicity and equality of English gentlemanly society, especially in its "country" aspects. Italians were bred up to flatter, deceive, pander, backbite, and quarrel. And the Italian influence was seen as corrupting honest English manners, including plainness, sincerity, directness, simplicity, and openness. An "English man Italianated" was putting at risk the authentic moral basis of his gentility.[146] William Harrison protested that in Italy he is "accounted most wise and politic that can most of all dissemble."[147] Tudor and Stuart moralists worried that the English would put on Continental patterns of insincerity along with Continental fashions in dress and manner. In *Richard II* the upright duke of York ridiculed "Report of fashions in proud Italy,/Whose manners still our tardy apish nation/ Limps after in base imitation" (II, i).

While the influence of French and Italian models of gentility increased through the early seventeenth century and into the Restoration—for example, as elaborated in Peacham's *Complete Gentleman*—opposition persisted, much of which continued to juxtapose English ingenuousness to Continental deceit. Suspicion of the French and Italians was, unsurprisingly, particularly intense in the more religiously oriented literature, and Lewis Einstein has argued that much of the culture of English Puritanism was a specific reaction to the growing "Italianization" of the English gentry.[148] The earl of Cork sent his sons on the standard Continental grand tour in the 1630s and 1640s, while expressing an increasingly common Protestant wariness about the possibility of infection by "the Roman disease."[149] Thomas Browne identi-

---

of the higher aristocracy (e.g., the Howards of Arundel and Norfolk) were seriously burdened with charges of mendacity.

146. Ascham, *The Scholemaster*, 23–30; see also Stone, *Crisis of the Aristocracy*, 700–01; Whigham, *Ambition and Privilege*, 176–83.

147. Harrison, *Description of England* (1577), 447.

148. Einstein, *Italian Renaissance in England*, 173; see also Macfarlane, *Origins of English Individualism*, 172.

149. Stone, *Crisis of the Aristocracy*, 697–98; see also Mason, *Gentlefolk in the Making*, 151–52; Einstein, *Italian Renaissance in England*, ch. 4 ("The Italian Danger"). Cork had good reason to fear the effect of Italian mores: see Boyle, "Philaretus," 40–41, and chapter 4 below.

fied "generous Honesty, Valour, and plain Dealing" as the "Character-
istick" of "the true Heroick English Gentleman," warning of recent
"transforming degenerations"; Lingard praised "the *Sincerity* and *Generosity* of the *English Disposition*"; and Archbishop Tillotson criticized
the elaborateness of French manners which, he said, conflicted with
"The old *English* plainness and sincerity, that generous integrity of
nature and honesty of disposition, which always argues true greatness
of mind, and is usually accompanied by undaunted courage and resolution."[150]

Writing the history of the Royal Society, Thomas Sprat praised "the
general constitution of the minds of the *English*," uniquely fitting them
"to be the Head of a *Philosophical league*": "they have an unaffected
sincerity"; "they love to deliver their minds with a sound simplicity."
Subtle foreigners might mock them for their lack of polish and gloss,
but the English ought rather "to be commended for an honourable
integrity . . . for a scorn to deceive as well as to be deceiv'd."[151] Through
the early modern period, and, indeed, into modern times, the English
(and those of English stock) tended particularly to ascribe to themselves the virtues of integrity, straightforwardness, and honesty, and
to contrast those national characteristics with the slavish, deceitful, and
dissimulating ways of many Continentals.[152] In much English commentary Italian and French deceitfulness was associated with the Roman
Catholic church and with the excessively hierarchical and powerful
nature of Continental court societies. Compromised social and political
integrity was seen to yield compromised truthfulness.

Early modern ethical literature was deeply concerned with the position of the prince, the courtier, and other servants of the state. What
sort of power and integrity did they possess? What was the effect of
their position on sincerity and truthfulness? To whom did they owe
the truth? Commentary on court practices, especially in Continental
writing, displayed the most refined and discriminating early modern

150. Browne, *Religio Medici*, 249, 251; Lingard, *Advice to a Young Gentleman*, 22–23;
Tillotson, "Of Sincerity towards God and Man," in idem, *Works*, II, 6.

151. Sprat, *History of the Royal Society* (1667), 113–14. Sprat attributed this racial integrity partly to "the position of our climate, the air, the influence of the heaven, [and] the
composition of the English blood." In the 1680s the astronomer Edmond Halley refused
to believe French testimony about a transsexual, "tho it seems well attested . . . , but the
bantring ridiculing humour of that light nation makes me suspect all that comes from
thence": Halley to John Wallis, 9 April 1687, in Halley, *Correspondence and Papers*, 82.

152. See esp. Harrison, *Description of England*, 448 (ascribing the sincerity of the English—and other northern races—to their "phlegmatic" constitution); and Ralph Waldo
Emerson, "Truth," in idem, *English Traits*, ch. 7: "The Teutonic tribes have a national
singleness of heart, which contrasts with the Latin races" (quoting 116); see also Childs,
"Prescriptions for Manners," 93; Einstein, *Tudor Ideals*, 69.

sensibility towards truth-telling, its nature and warrant. I have already noted Castiglione's recommendation that the ideal courtier "take care not to acquire the name of a liar." Both Castiglione and Guazzo were well aware of the current "fashyon" of court flattery—to tell "Princes, Magistrates, and other our Superiours" what they wanted to hear. Yet they claimed that flattery proceeded from an unworthy and ignoble "distrustfull fearfulnesse." In the name of service it rendered disservice to the prince. It was therefore noble, necessary, and even advantageous for the ideal courtier to tell his prince the truth, if only because so few would take the risk of doing so. Truth would out and its source would ultimately be rewarded.[153]

For the most part, however, practical ethical writers simply acknowledged the real-world exigencies that led princes, courtiers, and other state servants to depart from truthfulness. Some attempted to distinguish the precise quality of truthfulness that the prince or courtier owed and to whom it was owed; some argued that the prince had no such overarching obligation; others recognized the court as just the sort of place where truth was compromised and sought to mark out a better place for the gentleman to inhabit. Indeed, much of the sixteenth- and seventeenth-century English debate over "court" and "country" crucially implicated truthfulness and its ideal site.[154] Machiavelli famously distinguished private morality and the necessities of public policy. *The Prince* (1532) justified deceit for an effective ruler. Men were by nature bad. In the world-as-it-was, it was imprudent and impolitic for the prince simply to rely upon their relations. If he wished to secure his position and to acquit his responsibilities to the good order of his state, he must not blindly keep faith. He might, if necessary, break treaties and promises; he might give his word in bad faith, and act contrary to the cardinal virtue of fidelity: "it is necessary . . . to be a great feigner and dissembler."[155]

While few English commentators endorsed this Machiavellian position, recognition that state servants might have a genuine obligation to tell untruths was widespread. Francis Bacon, for example, prohibited "false professions . . . except it be in great and rare matters," and the diplomat Sir Henry Wotton offered his celebrated definition of an

153. Castiglione, *The Courtier*, e.g., 71; Guazzo, *Civile Conversation*, II, 91; also Whigham, *Ambition and Privilege*, 130–36. For reasons sketched above I find it hard to agree with recent assessments that the dominant tone of even court manuals was the promotion and justification of dissimulation: see, e.g., Greenblatt, *Renaissance Self-fashioning*, 162–64, and, for a more qualified claim, Zagorin, *Ways of Lying*, 7–8.

154. Among many examples see Anon., *Cyuile and Uncyuile Life*, 14. The expositor of country virtues accounted "fraude and dissimulation" as things "little vsed among vs plaine men of the Country."

155. Machiavelli, *The Prince*, chs 15, 18–19, quoting 93; see also Whigham, *Ambition and Privilege*, 98–102.

ambassador as "an honest man, sent to lie abroad for the good of his country."[156] The poet Edmund Spenser said that the courtier "doth soonest rise that best can handle his deceitful arts"; a Jacobean gentleman wrote that court deceit was even worse than that which Machiavelli recommended ("Hee was for the Theorick; these men for the Practicke"); the moralist Jean Gailhard identified the "common Vices of the Court" as "Vanity, Mockery, [and] Dissembling"; and to John Evelyn the Restoration court was "a Stage of continual *Masquerade* . . . , where the art of dissimulation . . . is avow'd."[157]

For all that, many practical English moralists broadly agreed with Machiavelli that it was indeed politic to secure the *appearance* of one who told the truth and kept his promises. The result was that it was very widely understood in sixteenth- and seventeenth-century English society that the possession of great power and responsibility might compromise integrity, and that places of power were places where truth could thrive only with the greatest difficulty. The court was, therefore, the major target of claims that the early modern period was an 'age of dissimulation.' Despite much seventeenth-century English political theorizing insisting upon the scope of the sovereign's will and power, there was also recognition that those in positions of power were in fact *more* constrained in their actions than simple independent gentlemen. Bacon wrote that "men in great offices are servants, having no freedom compared to private men."[158] As men secure power so they lose liberty. Insofar as princes, courtiers, and state servants departed from truthfulness, they could be regarded as doing so *in service*, through the compromises their circumstances inflicted upon integrity and free action. By contrast, the middle position might be accounted the place where scope for free action was greatest. Here one might be content with one's portion and be free of the necessity to secure more; here one might have easy communication with those afraid of greater men; and here one might have no need of preferment and no fear of

156. Bacon, "Of Simulation and Dissimulation," in idem, *Moral and Historical Works*, 17; L. P. Smith, *Life and Letters of Wotton*, I, 109–10 (note, however, that Wotton elsewhere advised a prospective diplomat always to tell the truth, for "you shall never be believed; and by this means your truth will secure yourself, if you are ever called to any account; and 'twill also put your adversaries [who will still hunt counter] to a loss in all their disquisitions and undertakings"); see also Kelso, *Doctrine of the English Gentleman*, 75; Mason, *Gentlefolk in the Making*, 248–49.

157. Spenser quoted in Einstein, *Tudor Ideals*, 41; Stafford, *Staffords Niobe*, 21–24, 93–100, 106–09, quoting 107; Gailhard, *Two Discourses*, 133 (see also 183–85); Evelyn, *Publick Employments*, 39–40.

158. Bacon, "Of Great Place," in idem, *Moral and Historical Works*, 28; cf. Montaigne, "Of the Inequality That Is between Us" and "Of Experience," in idem, *Essays*, 194–96, 826.

superiors.[159] It was a good place for those wanting to speak truth and to hear truth.

Relative Truth

It was, however, widely agreed that the society of English gentlemen was not what it should be, that gentlemen were not as learned, virtuous, or truthful as the moralists urged and as they themselves reckoned they ought to be. This was a "dangerous age," which "seducest many to errour," but "reducest none to truth."[160] Hamlet told Polonius that "to be honest, as this world goes, is to be one man picked out of ten thousand" (II, ii), and John Aubrey quoted the scandalous earl of Rochester, saying "ingeniously somewhere, that for a man to be honest is as if one should play upon the square among rooks."[161] A popular Restoration courtesy text offered this account of the contemporary world: "shifting, lying, plotting, counter-plotting, temporizing, flattering, cozening, dissembling."[162] As I said in the introductory notes, the historian has no privileged knowledge of how much or how little the early modern period was marked by genuine truth-telling. What the courtesy literature and related writings do reliably tell us is that truthfulness continued to be an ideal. That ideal shaped a culture which enjoined gentlemanly veracity. It articulated aspirations and norms; it identified the consequences of impugning gentlemanly truthfulness; and it constituted the practical resources for self-fashioning.

The dominant tone in the popular ethical literature urged gentlemen to take acts of will to improve themselves, while more pragmatic sentiments pointed to circumstances and means-end calculations as the effective cause of departures from the norms. The exigencies confronting courtiers and those holding civic office were acknowledged to some extent to bear upon any gentleman who acted on a public stage and who wished to conduct his affairs efficiently in society-as-it-was as opposed to setting himself up as a pattern for society-as-it-ought-to-be. The most pervasive of these exigencies was inscribed within the great divisions of social hierarchy: gentlemen were enjoined to adapt their behavior to the setting in which they found themselves, and, specifically, to the form and quality of social relations in which behavior took place. 'Decorum' dictated this adaptability and the relations of hierarchy gave it shape. It was both prudent and civically virtuous to suit one's conduct to the company one was in. While the fundamental

159. See, among many examples, Montaigne, "Of Experience," in idem, *Essays*, 826.
160. Stafford, *Staffords Niobe* (1611), 18.
161. Aubrey, *Aubrey on Education*, 133.
162. [Ramesey], *Gentlemans Companion* (1669), 244.

principles of upright and civil behavior might be considered as universals, their manifestations in conventions of discourse were understood to be highly local.[163] Montaigne was one of many early modern ethical writers who reckoned that sincerity was handicapped by unequal social relationships: "There are few things on which we can give a sincere judgment, because there are few in which we have not in some way a private interest. Superiority and inferiority of position, mastery and subjection, are forced into a natural envy and contention; . . . I do not believe either one about the rights of the other."[164]

There were precise English terms indicating deportment appropriate to dealing with superiors (*deference*), inferiors (*condescension*), and equals (*complaisance*).[165] Inferiors were not entitled to know one's mind; superiors might be entitled to have their way regardless of what one believed to be true or prudent. Flattery, as I have noted, was as widely understood as it was deprecated.[166] Similarly, no courtesy text advocated lying to one's inferiors, even though the thrust of practical advice was that one did well to treat them with circumspection and cynicism. Yet behavior with one's equals was regarded as both more consequential and more difficult to prescribe. These were people like oneself; one's friends were drawn from their society; their capacities and rights were to be considered as one's own; their cooperation was essential to collective enterprises; and they held one's reputation in their hands. Just as gentle society was considered to be fundamentally a society of equals, so dissension and divisions within that society were most damaging and most difficult to repair. Guazzo endorsed Stoic social prescriptions: in company "wee must yeelde humbly to our Superiour, perswade gently with our inferiour, and agree quietly with our equall. And by that meanes there shall never bee any falling out."[167] *The Gentlemans Companion* was one of many courtesy texts amplifying this advice for a Restoration readership. One was to keep one's due distance from one's superiors, to show proper respect and submission, and to avoid, where possible, being entrusted with secrets that would compromise

163. See, e.g., Childs, "Prescriptions for Manners," 95–100; Heal, *Hospitality in Early Modern England*, 103–06; and, for a representative early modern English account of the requirements of decorum, see Ashley, *Of Honour*, 58ff. Chapter 5 below treats the role of decorum in epistemic judgments.

164. Montaigne, "Of the Disadvantage of Greatness," in idem, *Essays*, 701.

165. See, e.g., Whigham, *Ambition and Privilege*, 102–12. An interesting indicator of changing social realities as well as attitudes would be secured by dating the precise moment in English history when *condescension* became a pejorative. Certainly, as late as Jane Austen's time, it seems to have functioned mainly as a descriptive.

166. E.g., Montaigne, "Of the Inequality That Is between Us," in idem, *Essays*, 195: "What testimony of affection and good will can I extract from a man who, willy-nilly, owes me everything he can do?"

167. Guazzo, *Civile Conversation*, I, 164; see also I, 114.

one or expose one to vice or danger. One was to be civil to inferiors, without showing or encouraging familiarity, nor was one to expose to them the secrets of one's heart or purse. With equals one was enjoined to be constant and faithful, to avoid all contentious disputes, but, if unavoidable, to seek to keep them within manageable bounds, and to tell them the truth so far as prudence dictated.[168]

The obligation to truth-telling was therefore *relative to setting;* and truthfulness, and departures from it, was itself understood to have a relative character. Thus far, I have intentionally spoken loosely of *truthfulness* and *lying,* and I have not called special attention to a family of related locutions in early modern discourse. This is because I wanted to trace the general contours of a culture that associated integrity with veracity. Yet, as I have begun to indicate, that culture was a set of resources put to work in specific actions, in specific settings, and for specific purposes. Given the flux and complexity of practical social action in early modern society, the categories indicated by *truthfulness* and *lying* were widely qualified, graded, and supplemented. This was a culture that possessed a vocabulary for speaking about veracity and mendacity that was as rich as it was ambiguous and contested. Indeed, both the richness and the contested nature of this vocabulary indicate something important about how the culture worked in practice. I shall be arguing that this vocabulary was part of discursive repertoires which allowed actors to do the work of modification and negation without subjecting moral and cognitive orders to impossible tension, to dissent without disaster.

Many early modern moralists discriminated between types of falsehood: *secrecy* was a habit or policy of closeness that might or might not be benign depending upon circumstances; *dissimulation* was an intentional withholding of truth when truth-telling might be deemed appropriate, leading others to believe what was not true; *simulation* was a positive intentional act or utterance that led to the same effect. Writers varied in their notions of what each category was and how it was to be distinguished from wholly innocuous forms of behavior having the effect of blocking the free flow of truth. Bacon, for example, fully recognized the constraints acting upon the truth-telling of public men, but argued strongly against dissimulation. It was a public display of one's own compromised integrity: "it is the weaker sort of politicians that are the greatest dissemblers"; "the greatest politiques have in a natural and free manner professed their desires, rather than been reserved and disguised in them." Simulation—"false profession" or the act by which a man "industriously and expressly feigns and pretends to be that he is not"—was more culpable. It counted as an even more

168. [Ramesey], *Gentlemans Companion,* 67–91.

reliable mark of weakness, and its habitual use could be taken as a sign that the simulator was either naturally false or had a mind "that hath some main faults." Even so, Bacon judged that all the main forms of falsehood had their proper use and setting: "The best composition and temperature is, to have openness in fame and opinion; secrecy in habit; dissimulation in seasonable use; and a power to feign if there be no remedy."[169]

Bacon's predominantly pragmatic sensibility was, however, contested in the ethical literature, on one side by religiously oriented writers and, on the other, by rather more cynical Continental courtiers. The Puritan divine Richard Baxter refused to condone any form of untruthfulness so recognized. Condemning Cromwell's character, Baxter noted that the Great Protector "thought secrecy a virtue and dissimulation no vice, and simulation—that is, in plain English, a lie—or perfidiousness to be a tolerable fault in a case of necessity."[170] Some courtesy texts also wanted spades called spades: the *Wits Theater* listed all the categories of "Deceit, Dissimulation, Craft, Hipocrisie, Idolatry, and cousenage" under the heading "Of Lying."[171] Contrarily, Guazzo—who elsewhere censured lying—mobilized Thomist resources to distinguish between benign and malign forms. The difference was to hinge upon the quality of intention: "I denie not, but that it is commendable to coyne a lye at some time, and in some place, so that it tend to some honest [N.B.] ende."[172]

The issue of falsehood was most ambiguous in the case of the conventional contrast between an open and a reserved form of life. No one doubted that a reserved habit kept truth from circulating and that, as a style of life, it was hard to distinguish virtuous from vicious secrecy—in their effects and in their good or bad intentions. Where did innocuous closeness end and malevolent dissimulation begin? Indeed, the topic of how much openness was obligatory for a gentleman was intensely debated by ethical writers since antiquity. A few moralists did recommend a highly open disposition. Lingard unreservedly endorsed the norm, saying that the best behavior was one which expressed "the *Sincerity* of your heart":

> I think this Rule fails not, that that kind of Conversation that lets men into your Soul, to see the goodness of your Nature, and Integrity of your Mind is most acceptable; for be assured, every man loves

169. Bacon, "Of Simulation and Dissimulation," in idem, *Moral and Historical Works,* 15–17; idem, "Advancement of Learning," 467.

170. Baxter, *Autobiography,* 88–89.

171. [Allott], *Wits Theater* (1599), 120.

172. Guazzo, *Civile Conversation,* I, 97–98; see also Della Casa, *Galateo,* 45.

another for his *Honesty*; To this every *Knave* pretends, and with the *show* of this he *deceives*.[173]

I do not know of any early modern author who argued that gentlemen had an obligation to tell all their secrets to all, upon all occasions. Archbishop Tillotson, for example, condemned dissimulation while considering that one had no obligation "to tell every man all our mind."[174] I have already noted that the notion of 'the whole truth'—from which any true utterance is an interested and conventional selection—is arguably a more recent conception, but most early modern ethical writers apparently took for granted that truth-telling was some contextually informed excerpt of possibly relevant true statements. Much practical moralizing cautioned the gentleman to take care when and to whom to tell his secrets. Thus, the topic of openness and closeness was most extensively discussed in the context of friendship, what friends were, how they ought to be chosen and treated. Precisely because certain things that a person knew could decisively tip the balance of advantage in social transactions, one's statements in those transactions had carefully to be gauged according to complex calculations of interest, trust, and the principles of virtuous action.

Most writers, in fact, recommended that the gentleman be watchfully reserved and judged that careless openness was the mark of a fool. Bacon agreed with ancient moralists in counting judicious closeness a gentlemanly virtue: "nakedness is uncomely, as well in mind as in body"; more respect is usually paid to men "who are not altogether open."[175] Isaac Newton repeated conventional prudential wisdom in advising a Trinity colleague about to embark on a Continental tour: "When you come into any fresh company, 1, observe their humours; 2, suit your own carriage thereto, by wch insinuation you will make their converse more free & open: 3 let your discourse bee more in Quærys & doubtings yn peremptory assertions or disputings, it being ye designe of Travellers to learne not teach."[176] Brathwait was among many English courtesy writers who agreed that the public man should

173. Lingard, *Advice to a Young Gentleman,* 14–15. Yet some pages later (31–32) even this author commended a somewhat reserved temperament, allowing none to see all of one's thoughts.

174. Tillotson, "Of Sincerity towards God and Man," in idem, *Works,* II, 4.

175. Bacon, "Of Simulation and Dissimulation," in idem, *Moral and Historical Works,* 16; see also idem, "Advancement of Learning," 460, 466–68.

176. Newton to Francis Aston, 18 May 1669, in Newton, *Correspondence,* I, 9. The form in which this advice was offered was almost certainly cribbed from a 1658 manuscript on travel by Sir Robert Southwell found in Newton's papers (see editorial note in ibid., 12), but, in general terms, it shared sentiments with Polonius's advice to Laertes about to embark on his travels (*Hamlet,* I, iii): "Give thy thoughts no tongue,/Nor any unproportion'd thought his act./Be thou familiar, but by no means vulgar. . . ./Give every man thy ear, but few thy voice."

be neither "too credulous in *giving trust* to the relations of others, [nor] too credulous in *imparting his thoughts* to the secrecie of others"; "even a private man committing his secrecy to another, becomes his *slave* to whom he committed it."[177] Britaine's Restoration collection of prudential wisdom likewise reckoned that between credulity and skepticism, openness and secrecy, the gentleman ought to seek the golden mean: "Believe not all you hear, nor speak all you believe"; "It's an equal Mischief to distrust all, as to believe all"; "Make not your self a body of Christal, that all Men may look thorow you."[178] Early modern gentlemen evidently sought to become expert at reading the text of other men's discourse and gestures while making themselves at least a partly closed book.

Secrecy might be laudable, dissimulation circumstantially recommended, and simulation occasionally excused. But the falsehood that went under the name of *lie* found scarcely any defenders in ethical writing *per se* and very few in even the most practical English guides to conduct. Indeed, as I shall shortly show, the accusation of lying possessed a uniquely explosive capacity in the social relations of early modern gentlemanly society: it alone was considered effectively to break intellectual and moral order. What, then, was a lie? What was the accusation which, if directed at a gentleman, had to be resisted at the utmost cost? We understand that not just any departure from truthfulness was recognized as a lie in early modern culture, though a few commentators did, indeed, make such an abstract claim. I offer this version of the lie as one that might have been recognizable by the majority of early modern ethical writers and their gentlemanly audience. A lie was a communicative act identified by three features: an attributed state of awareness of the truth-status of a statement; an attributed purpose or end; and a recognized social setting or bit of social action in which it occurred. One had to have *knowledge* that the utterance (or other communicative act) was untrue;[179] one had to have the *intention* of misleading another and of doing so with the *purpose* of unfairly changing the distribution of advantage between oneself and the other; and, finally, one had to do these things with respect to another whom one should not in justice mislead and who had a sub-

177. Brathwait, *English Gentleman*, 137, 139; see also Gailhard, *Two Discourses*, 241–43.

178. Britaine, *Humane Prudence*, 15, 22, 27; see also Petrie, *Rules of Good Deportment*, 42–43. For the crystal metaphor in relation to Robert Boyle's sincerity of character, see chapter 4 below.

179. According to most sensibilities it did not matter whether the statement was in fact true so long as one believed it to be false. Nonverbal lying was sometimes referred to as simulation: see, e.g., Sommerville, "'New Art of Lying,'" 160–62.

stantial right to the truth.[180] Additionally, it was commonly reckoned that lying, and imputations that another had lied, were most insupportable when they were committed orally, in face-to-face interaction, and in a place which was the public resort of gentlemen or their superiors.

Giving the Lie

In late medieval and early modern gentlemanly society, the final defense of gentlemanly honor involved deadly violence. The duel was the ultimate means by which a gentleman adhering to the secular chivalric code acquitted himself—sometimes also his women, family, friends, and prince—from imputations of dishonor.[181] From the middle of the sixteenth century through the late seventeenth century, dueling was a pervasive and important institution in gentlemanly society, both on the Continent and in England. In late Tudor and Stuart England it was acknowledged as a serious threat to social order. Early Restoration commentators described the practice as running riotously out of control, this despite organized attempts by the English Crown to control the practice and massive cultural disapproval from religious circles.[182] In the early seventeenth century English lawyers sought arguments against the code accounting the duel a legitimate and even obligatory way of settling disputes. In 1614 Francis Bacon, as attorney general, reported that dueling then constituted a major threat to good order: it was "that euill which seemes vnbridled"; it proceeded from "a false and erronious imagination of honour and credit" carried along by a "streame of vulgar opinion." The king had to be acknowledged as the fountain of honor, and if he were to ban duelists from his presence, then those who engaged in the practice were truly dishonored.[183] Indeed, from James I to Charles II the Crown attempted to deal with the situation by making its disapproval known, by having agents stop impending duels of which the king had been made aware, and by occasionally banishing the dueling parties from court or country.

180. Pitt-Rivers, "Honour and Social Status," 33–34. For detailed discussion of conceptions of lying by a modern moral philosopher, see Bok, *Lying*, and idem, *Secrets*; cf. Bolinger, "Truth Is a Linguistic Question," 542: "When two parties are in communication, anything that may be used which clogs the channel, and is not the result of accident, is a lie," though this definition opens the possibility of unintentional lies. My usage is close to that arrived at by Rousseau's extended treatment of lying in the "Fourth Walk" of his *Reveries of the Solitary Walker*.

181. Pitt-Rivers, "Honour and Social Status," 29–34.

182. For recent accounts of the history, sociology, and culture of the duel, see, e.g., Kiernan, *The Duel*, esp. chs 4–6; Billacois, *The Duel;* Stone, *Crisis of the Aristocracy*, 242–50.

183. Bacon, *Charge Touching Duells* (1614), 5, 9, 12–13, 17; see also Bryskett, *Discourse of Civill Life*, 50–70.

Religiously oriented courtesy texts in seventeenth-century England almost without exception argued strenuously against the duel. It was considered to be the most typical expression of the secular code which Christian commentators saw as responsible for much of the immorality of the modern age. Bryskett said that the duel was odious and offensive to God; it was the work "of the divell himselfe."[184] Allestree condemned the code which equated "a *man of Honor*" with "one that can start and maintain a Quarrel." What was that reputation really worth that hangs "only at the point of a sword"? The duelist, he urged, was the genuine coward: he showed himself to be a man of compromised integrity, fearing mere men and their opinions.[185] Sir George Mackenzie's character of the "moral gallant" similarly identified a person secure in his own conscience and integrity, serenely unafraid of the world's opinion.[186] Josiah Dare instructed his son to shun violence, though "some will call thee a Coward, yet fear not shame so much as sin."[187] Clement Ellis's *Gentile Sinner* was a Christian hero whose authentic valor and courage made him fear not "the brand of a *Coward*," and William Ramesey's *Gentlemans Companion* described the practice of dueling as a "senseless" and dishonorable insult to God.[188] Britaine used Stoical and Christian resources to invert the traditional honor code: "If you have an injury done you, you do your Adversary too much Honour to take notice of it."[189] Even such a defender of the duel as the chief herald Sir William Segar acknowledged a tension between the single combat as ultimate protection of honor and the Christian's duties of forgiveness and meekness.[190]

The duel in early modern England was, on the one hand, the most typical and dramatic eruption of the fissiparous and aggressive traditional honor culture, and, on the other, an expression of social tensions and ambiguities brought on by massive social change. Just because there was practical uncertainty about how the gentle might be distinguished from the nongentle, the public culture of honor, resentment, and violence was a valuable resource for those wishing to make dramatic *display* of their entitlement. Indeed, the relevant practical

184. Bryskett, *Discourse of Civill Life*, 55–56; see also Einstein, *Italian Renaissance in England*, 74–75.
185. [Allestree], *Gentleman's Calling*, 105, 107–10.
186. Mackenzie, *Moral Gallantry* (1667).
187. Dare, *Counsellor Manners*, 100.
188. Ellis, *Gentile Sinner*, 144–46; [Ramesey], *Gentlemans Companion*, 80–85; see also [Darrell], *Gentleman Instructed*, sig. a2, 122; Stafford, *Staffords Niobe*, 34.
189. Britaine, *Humane Prudence*, 33.
190. Segar, *Booke of Honor and Armes*, "To the Reader," sig. A2; see also Stafford, *Guide of Honour*, 77. Writers disapproving the duel mobilized *historical* arguments against the institution; see, e.g., Bacon, *Charge Touching Duells;* Montaigne, "Of Giving the Lie," in idem, *Essays*, 503–06; Walker, *Of Education*, 244; cf. Selden, *The Duello* (1610), 14–15.

literature devoted much attention to discussing what sorts of people ought *not* to be allowed to participate in the institution and what sorts of people were *not* capable of injuring one's reputation.[191] Most guides encouraged gentlemen to ignore the insults of inferiors: "But if any man of your owne Ranke doe you an affront, shew that you are sensible of your Honour."[192] The display of resentment was, therefore, a way of claiming, as well as acknowledging, equality of standing.[193] As such, the duel and the nexus of social and cultural practices surrounding it occupied a position of unique importance in gentlemanly society. The institution of the duel contained a violent energy that worked its way through the social practices antecedent to it, and, indeed, through practices by which men argued against it and sought to avoid disruption and violent disorder.

There was a precise ritual form of words employed in early modern society to provoke a challenge to the single combat.[194] This was the 'giving of the lie' (in Italian *mentita*, in French *démenti*), that is, a direct accusation that another lied.[195] Accusing another gentleman of lying was understood to be the gravest insult and the utmost provocation. According to an early seventeenth-century English guide, "it is reputed so great a shame to be accounted a lyer, that any other injury is cancelled by giving the lie; and he that receiveth it, standeth so charged in his honor and reputation, that he cannot disburden himselfe of that imputation, but by striking of him that hath so giuen it, or by challenging him the combat."[196] While disparagements of "Honor, freedome, & Curtesie" were also injuries that might trigger a demand for revenge, the denial of "truth" had a special place in the entrained ritual behaviors leading to violence.[197] Ferne said that the legitimate purpose of a duel was "not for malice, or reuenge, thereby to dishonour or wrong an other: but onely, for the manifesting of truth." A man's truthfulness being impugned, he was considered to stand outside the

---

191. See, e.g., Ferne, *Blazon of Gentrie*, 84, 313–15; Segar, *Booke of Honor and Armes*, 30–34; idem, *Honor Military and Civill*, 118–19; see also J. R. Hale, "Sixteenth-Century Explanations of War and Violence," 11–12; Pitt-Rivers, "Honour and Social Status," 31. Bacon (*Charge Touching Duells*, 6) argued that men of quality ought to give up dueling on the grounds that it had been taken up by "Barber-surgeons and Butchers, and such base mechanicall persons."

192. Stafford, *Guide of Honour*, 76.

193. Kiernan, *The Duel*, 94, 102.

194. Pitt-Rivers, "Honour and Social Status," 32.

195. Lying is here understood to contain the elements of intentionality and injustice noted above.

196. Bryskett, *Discourse of Civill Life*, 50; see also Billacois, *The Duel*, 127–36; Baldick, *The Duel*, 33.

197. Selden, *The Duello*, 14. On the culture of insult, injury, and resentment, see esp. F. R. Bryson, *Point of Honor*, ch. 3.

moral order of gentlemanly society.[198] In that condition he forfeited
the trust which lay at the heart of cooperative enterprises; his promises
were worthless; and he was unable to contribute to the building up
and maintenance of the stock of knowledge which enabled men to
coordinate their activities.[199]

A challenge to combat might be instigated by a number of injuries—a physical attack on the integrity of one's body, an insult to a
woman to whom one was attached, an imputation of disloyalty or cowardice, and so on. The quarrel could reach serious proportions if, at
any point, one gentleman contested another's honor, for example, saying to the other, 'You have stolen from the prince'; 'You fled from
battle'; 'Your wife is a whore.' Any such insult had immediately to be
resented, or else its veracity might be publicly credited. The chivalric
code stipulated that a direct and significant resentment of such insults
was obligatory, agreeing with Aristotle that only people of a slavish
nature would allow themselves to be insulted without protest.[200] A rich
linguistic and gestural culture of resentment was available for gentlemen desiring to display the exact shade and degree of anger, pride,
or dissent deemed contextually appropriate. Whatever injury was the
initial cause of the quarrel, conflict might move into its physically violent phase only through the particular act of resentment constituted
by giving the lie. Thus, accusations of mendacity might in the great
majority of cases be only the 'occasion' for the duel. Yet the very fact
that truth occupied this formally central role is a further indication of
how deeply contemporary conceptions of epistemic and social order
implicated each other.

Sixteenth- and seventeenth-century gentlemanly culture made available a large number of highly detailed handbooks identifying and enjoining the appropriate means of displaying resentment, and describing how, in general, quarrels were to be conducted.[201] This literature
was as much part of the education of the typical gentleman and aristocrat as were the courtesy texts whose contents sometimes overlapped
with them. The Italians were the acknowledged masters of this form
of writing (and the associated practices), though French writers were

198. Ferne, *Blazon of Gentrie,* 316–18; see also Bryskett, *Discourse of Civill Life,* 49–50.
199. E.g., Segar, *Booke of Honor and Armes,* 2–3. Opinions varied on what form and
source of justice underwrote the outcome of a duel. Segar (ibid., sig. A2) supposed that
"God (who onelie knoweth the secret thoughts of all men) would giue victorie to him
that iustlie aduentured his life, for truth, Honor, and Iustice." Those arguing against
the duel claimed that the result went merely to the strong and skillful; e.g., Bryskett,
Discourse of Civill Life, 52–54.
200. Aristotle, *Rhetoric,* II. 1387[b] 13–14; ibid., III. 1416[a] 4–1416[b] 15; F. R. Bryson,
Point of Honor, 44.
201. The following paragraphs draw heavily on the work of F. R. Bryson (*Point of
Honor,* esp. ch. 4); see also Billacois, *The Duel,* and Kiernan, *The Duel.*

also important, and the English were avid translators, adapters, and readers of tracts on quarreling and dueling. These texts were almost wholly agreed in recommending the *mentita* as the ordinary means for resenting verbal injuries—*if* one wished to cancel the injury and press the quarrel on to a possibly violent end. The *mentita* was not just any negation of what was said, nor was it deemed appropriate for just any insult or injury. So one might, in certain carefully prescribed circumstances, respond to an insult by saying 'I do not agree,' or 'The truth is otherwise,' and this denial was sometimes considered not to constitute a *mentita*. An early seventeenth-century English source gave an indication of the fine, but deadly important, distinctions in negation: "If I say vnto another man, *Thou saiest not true*, thereby I reproue him, and consequentlie offer iniurie: but if I say, *That which thou saiest is not true*, that speach is not iniurious, and may be without burthen of him vnto whom it is spoken."

Such guides proffered a moral grammar of lies, each with its associated degree of injury and appropriate response. A few commentators contended that one might qualify the *mentita* with the phrase *saving your honor*, and thereby avoid a challenge, though most writers accounted this a contradiction. The so-called conditional *mentita* might, however, do some of the work of denial without necessarily provoking challenge: 'If you indeed said that I am a coward, then I would say that you lied.' However, some writers disapproved the conditional giving of the lie as ungentlemanly: matters ought to be brought straightforwardly to a head.[202] Furthermore, one might believe, or act as if one believed, that the insult was said in jest or that it was innocently believed to be true by the person uttering it. If this was the case, or if one wished to pretend it was so, then one would avoid giving the lie, but find a way of suggesting that an unintentional, humorous, or otherwise innocuous untruth had been uttered.

If, however, one believed that serious injury to one's honor had been done intentionally, then the *mentita* was deemed mandatory in order effectively to display resentment. Giving the lie could take various forms. One could simply say 'You lie,' or, more specifically, 'You lie in saying that I am a coward.' It was also widely considered that one could effectively give the lie without actually using the word by saying 'I am a man of honor,' or 'I am no coward.' Or one might embellish the basic *mentita* (without altering its quality or consequences) by such forms as

202. Segar, *Booke of Honor and Armes*, 5–11 (the quotation in the previous paragraph is from p. 5). This writer was concerned that quarrels might be needlessly complicated by such responses to the conditional lie as 'I never spake any such thing,' or, worse, 'Whosoever saith that I have spoken such words, he lieth,' and 'If thou or any man else will affirme I have so said, thou liest'; see also Herbert, *Autobiography*, 49–52; ibid., 179–82.

'You lie in your throat,' 'You lie to my face,' 'You lie a thousand times,' or 'You lie; I am no coward; it is you who are cowardly.' A late six-teenth-century Norfolk gentleman conducting an epistolary quarrel pulled out all the stops:

> I tell thee thou liest, thou liest and liest in thy throat . . . and I do by this my letter challenge thee as a lying knight . . . who doth first endamage the enemy, let the other be accounted recreant, a dastard, and a discredited person in all honourable and honest company. . . . But if thou shall refuse the performance of the one of these three, then I will secretly repute thee and openly blast thee as a dunghell spirited man, as one that did nothing participate in thy generation with the silver mould of thy honourable father.[203]

Such amplifications were, however, generally reckoned to be unneces-sary and even rather vulgar. Finally, the role of the *mentita* was embed-ded within the culture that imputed basic equality to all authentic gen-tlemen. Thus, it was thought that one could legitimately give the lie to the statement 'You are not as honorable as I.'

Within the relevant culture the only possible response to a *mentita* received by an appropriate person was considered to be a challenge to combat.[204] The challenge had to be delivered immediately but could either take the form of an explicit verbal invitation or some recognized gestural convention, such as striking a ritual blow with hand or glove. There was one noteworthy exception to the requirement of instant response to insult or *mentita:* if either was offered in the house or presence of a superior lord, it was deemed unseemly for the quarrel to be carried on in such a setting. Other gestures or forms of words might be used to signal that the injury was noted and resented and that an appropriate response would be forthcoming as soon as morally and practically feasible.[205]

He who delivered the challenge gave to the other the choice of arms, and that choice was recognized to be a very considerable advantage in the ensuing combat. For this reason, the exact form and sequencing of the discursive maneuverings in the performance of negation and modification of claims was understood to be highly significant and highly charged with dramatic energy.[206] Once a grave insult was given,

---

203. Thomas Lovell to Sir Nicholas Bacon (1586), quoted in Fletcher, "Honour, Repu-tation and Local Officeholding," 101.

204. Segar, *Booke of Honor and Armes,* 2–5.

205. Ibid., 12–14. For general injunctions against quarreling in one's superior's house, see Petrie, *Rules of Good Deportment,* 20.

206. See, e.g., Lord Herbert's accounts of his experiences *ca.* 1608–10: Herbert, *Auto-biography,* 49–52.

the risk of violence was greatly increased, and once the lie was given, the challenge and its violent realization were certain, unless prince or friends intervened, or, less likely, dishonor was accepted by one of the parties.[207] If one was aware that a quarrel might become violent, then several considerations had to be borne in mind. The first was whether one was ultimately willing to take part in violence, and therefore to continue participation in the entrained discursive forms which would lead to that outcome. If one was not willing to entertain that possibility, then one had to deploy linguistic repertoires which might prevent the quarrel from moving into its obligatory phase. Second, if one was willing in principle to fight for the issue at stake, then the question was how practically to conduct the quarrel so that one might offer the *mentita* oneself rather than receiving it from another, that is, to manage the dispute so as to avoid doing any injury that would elicit a direct denial. If one left to the other the performance of direct denial, then, if the matter was not pressed, violence might be avoided, and, if it was insisted upon, the choice of weapons would be one's own.[208]

Dueling was prevalent in seventeenth-century English gentlemanly society, and it was recognized as an institution central to certain conceptions of what authentic gentility consisted in. Yet it is no part of my argument to establish any particular incidence of quarrels in gentle (or in philosophical) society ending that way. No doubt, only a small proportion of gentlemanly disputes came to violence or were ever at serious risk of doing so. At the same time, there is also no doubt that the possibility of violence was always acknowledged whenever early modern gentlemen were in dispute, and no doubt that all gentlemen were thoroughly aware of the discursive practices by which quarrels might be managed, and dissent done, without incurring the risk of violence. My argument depends, first, upon the existence of a shared understanding that certain sorts of arguments *might* end in violence; second, upon a shared understanding of what forms of discursive behavior would increase or decrease the probability of a violent termination; and last, upon the shared availability of discursive resources that would permit utterances to be skeptically regarded, to be modified, or even negated, *without the risk of violence.*

The duel thus was a violent fact of gentle social relations, one effect of which was the elaboration and protection of means through which the duel might be avoided. This was one—very important—reason why early modern gentlemanly society possessed such an elaborated, subtle, and effective culture for performing skepticism, modification,

207. Segar, *Booke of Honor and Armes,* 10–11, 26–27.
208. Schematically, the practice is represented thus: A offers grave insult; B gives the lie; A challenges; and B receives choice of arms.

and negation. It was a culture that was available for appropriation by innovators wishing to translate and adapt aspects of gentlemanly social relations into new or reformed bodies of cultural practice. Indeed, that culture was well known to those who rejected its secular morality and to others who commented upon it from its margins.

In *As You Like It* (V, iv) Shakespeare gave to the clown Touchstone the role of dissecting and displaying the institutions of gentlemanly dispute. Touchstone tells the melancholic Jaques that he too has played the gentleman in his time: "I have been politic with my friend, smooth with mine enemy; I have undone three tailors; I have had four quarrels, and like to have fought one." Jaques asks him how that quarrel finally came to issue, and Touchstone tells him that it was enjoined "upon the seventh cause." The clown describes a quarrel he had with a certain courtier and how the *mentita* and violence were artfully avoided. "I durst go no further than the Lie Circumstantial, nor he durst not give me the lie; and so we measured swords and parted":

> O sir, we quarrel . . . by the book; as you have books for good manners: I will name you the degrees. The first, the Retort Courteous; the second, the Quip Modest; the third, the Reply Churlish; the fourth, the Reproof Valiant; the fifth, the Countercheck Quarrelsome; the sixth, the Lie with Circumstance; the seventh, the Lie Direct. All these you may avoid but the Lie Direct; and you may avoid that too, with an If. I knew when seven justices could not take up a quarrel, but when the parties were met themselves, one of them thought but of an If, as, 'If you said so, then I said so;' and they shook hands and swore brothers. Your If is the only peace-maker; much virtue in If.[209]

Conversation, Courtesy, and Contradiction

The courtesy literature of sixteenth- and seventeenth-century England offered gentlemen rules, recommendations, and repertoires for conducting decorous conversation—how to keep conversation going, how to adapt it to setting and purpose, how to avoid or manage dissent, how to turn conversation to one's own advantage. The point of princi-

209. Likely sources of this passage include Segar, *Booke of Honor and Armes*, 5–12, and Ferne, *Blazon of Honor*, 308–41. For contemporary legal practices of 'joining issue,' see Martin, *Francis Bacon, the State, and the Reform of Natural Philosophy*, 83–84. For further Shakespearean uses of the conventions of gentlemanly dispute and dueling, see, e.g., *Richard II* (I, i; IV, i). Several early modern English proverbs point to a widespread approval of probabilistic speech in everyday life: "Almost was never hang'd"; "Almost and very nigh, save many a lie" (Ray, *Collection of Proverbs*, 56).

ple was not itself principle but the continuance of civil conversation.[210] Indeed, there were few principles or interests that were deemed worth the risk of disrupting civil conversation or disturbing its even flow. Much of this advice was set within the relational frames constituted by one's dealings with inferiors, superiors, and equals, and the culture that presumed basic gentlemanly equality. Guides to manners elaborated the precise ceremonial forms in which condescension, deference, and complaisance ought to be expressed: rituals concerning the removal of hats, turn-taking in conversation, whether to scratch or knock at the door of someone one wished to see, the proper distance to escort one's visitors when leaving the house. And the same relational frame was brought to bear upon the speech acts of assenting, asserting, modifying, and negating.

To inferiors "nothing is lawful, but what is modest and agreeable to our prescriptions." By contrast, one should not contradict, or even seem to contradict, the claims of one's equals and *a fortiori* of one's superiors. To superiors "all things are lawful, because of their eminence and authority; and because we have no right of censuring them." Nor is it civil to correct a superior's factual errors, "it being little less than to upbraid his memory, if it be not a kind of giving him the lie." One should use care in qualifying superiors' narratives. One must not say "If what you speak be true," since "to suspect, what he says . . . is very disobliging." If one had to say "*no* in contradiction to some person of quality, you must not say bluntly or positively, *no*, but by way of Circumlocution."[211] Another courtesy text was only partly ironical in noting that "he is a Fool who gain sayes his Master, even when he saith, he hath seen the Sky full of Stars at noon, and the Sun at midnight."[212]

In the early eighteenth century Defoe deplored what he took to be the institutionalized expectation of assent to gentlemen's relations: "Nothing is more affronting to a gentleman than to contradict him when he takes the affirmatio upon him . . . ; good manners say I am oblig'd to believ it."[213] The understood consequences of giving the

210. In early modern usage, the sense of *conversation* was close to its Latin roots, meaning the whole repertoire of practices—including but not confined to discursive practices—involved in civically *living together:* cf. Warren, "Turning Reality Round Together," 67–69. I develop this theme in chapter 7.

211. [De Courtin], *Rules of Civility*, 17–18, 29, 40, 42. Montaigne ("Of the Art of Discussion," in idem, *Essays*, 705) played upon the strength of this sort of injunction against contradiction when he averred that we ought to embrace those who gainsay us, which is, of course, a position more comfortable for a Pyrrhonist skeptic than for that larger number of people who maintain that they do possess genuine knowledge.

212. Gailhard, *Two Discourses*, 184; see also Petrie, *Rules of Good Deportment*, 63; ibid., 67.

213. Defoe, *Compleat English Gentleman*, 42.

lie were extended to complaisant discourse in general. Josiah Dare cautioned his son to "give no man the Lye, lest thou be answered with a stab, or compelled to answer for it by a Duel; for few there are who can pass by such an affront." Even when one thought that an untruth had been uttered, one ought carefully to control one's body so as not even to suggest denial: "neither shall thou, if thou think anything that is reported by another, to be a Lye, in any wise upbraid him with it, wither in word or gesture, either by shaking thy head, or wresting aside thine eyes, or blaring out thy Tongue, for this is next of kin to the giving a man the Lye."[214]

In general, the practice of opposition was recognized as a serious threat to the good order of civil conversation. Means had to be found to account for and repair faulty utterances and acts without impugning credit, sincerity, or competence. If a man should not perform a promise, "you shall rather impute it to forgetfulnesse, then thrust out any stings of complaint, anger, or choller."[215] If a man should claim as original what was not novel, "say not, I knew this before, but accept what is said as new, and in good part."[216] The corrosive effects of opposition and obstinancy were not worth the cause of truth for which they were allegedly enlisted. In "disputing," do not "strive so much as if thou wert discussing and sifting out the truth; neither suffer the heat of disputation to cool and Extinguish that of Charity and love":

> Oppose no man whilst he is talking or disputing, which many use to do; there shall not a word drop from anothers Tongue, but they presently will take it up, and oppose him, and contend with him, and say it is not true, or it is not so as he reports it, the man was not so and so, nor the things thus; truly it is a sign of a man not well educated, nor well learned; for every one loves Victory and will hardly be overcome, as well in words as in deeds: besides it begets nothing but hatred and disdain: wherefore thou wert far better to yield to the opinion of others.[217]

"Obstinacy is contrary to the Laws of Civility."[218] If disputatious and wrangling scholars accounted truth well worth the price of social discord, gentlemanly civil society took a radically different view.[219] And

---

214. Dare, *Counsellor Manners*, 51, 54.
215. [Gainsford], *Rich Cabinet*, sig. A2.
216. Walker, *Of Education*, 226.
217. Dare, *Counsellor Manners*, 48–49.
218. Petrie, *Rules of Good Deportment*, 46.
219. "Be not thou like those who that they may shew themselves subtle, intelligent, and wise men, will always be giving of counsel unto others . . . , always disputing with others" (ibid., 49–50; see also Lingard, *Letter of Advice*, 21). For gentlemanly views of 'pedantry' and the attributed incivility of scholars from the late Renaissance through

if the philosopher's code was "A friend of Plato but more a friend of truth," early modern gentlemanly society accounted friendship and practical civil order a far stronger claim than philosophers' truth.[220]

Just as one was to avoid the spirit of contradiction, so one was to refrain from forms of speech that asserted too positively. Strong, precise, and certain claims demanded of one's fellows a forced and unnatural assent. It was an assent they might consider themselves obliged to yield, but it was not civil to demand it of them. Civil conversation might be recognized by the free consensus it generated. Obadiah Walker's eloquent defense of discursive moderation was typical of the resources used in late sixteenth- and seventeenth-century English gentlemanly society to reject overpositive and overenthusiastic ways of presenting knowledge:

> Be not magisterial in your dictates; nor contend pertinaceously in ordinary discourse for your opinion, nor for a truth of small consequence. Declare your reasons, if they be not accepted, let them alone; assure your self that you are not obliged to convert the whole world. It is also an uncivil thing . . . to confute every thing we think is false. . . . Also if what you report is not believed, do not swear it, . . . nor lay wagers, nor take yourself engaged to defend it, or that he who believes you not, affronts you. . . . The conceptions according to truth are alike and the same, but false are infinite; wherefore if you find a man single in his judgment, be wary of him; he either knows more then all others, or there is some ill principle in him.[221]

The "bold maintaining of any Argument doth conclude against your own civil Behaviour."[222] Similarly, discourse which was too precise and which demanded too much accuracy in following it, was a violation of the presumed equality of civil society: "to talk with such men, as are so, is rather a Bondage than an equal Society." Citations of authorities ought to be done circumspectly and with care for avoiding even the appearance of pedantry: "When you cite an Author, be not too precise in quoting the Chapter, or Page."[223]

---

the eighteenth century, see Shapin, "'A Scholar and a Gentleman'"; also A. Keller, "Renaissance Mathematical Duels."

220. The tag "Amicus Plato, amicus Aristoteles, magis amica veritas"—or versions thereof—appears in the work of many seventeenth-century authors, including Walter Charleton and Isaac Newton: see McGuire and Tamny, Certain Philosophical Questions, 336–37.

221. Walker, Of Education, 226, 237; see also ibid., 248–49.

222. Britaine, Humane Prudence, 22–23.

223. I read this somewhere. Interestingly, Boyle later acknowledged the force of just this code of decorum in excusing his occasionally exact citation practices: "I know it would be more acceptable to most readers, if I were less punctual and scrupulous in my

Civil conversation demanded that claims be made in the due forms of *imprecision,* presented with modesty, argued with circumspection, and proffered with due allowance for natural variation in men's wits and interests.[224] That way lay both cognitive and civil order. Temperately made claims had three positive recommendations: they would give a moral voucher of the honesty of the man who made them; they would prove agreeable to one's listeners; and they would allow gracious withdrawal if the claims needed to be retracted or if they prove untrue: "In matters of Dispute, apparel your Arguments in modesty; for so, finding your selfe in an errour, you may make an honorable retreate. Bold, and peremptory positions, being true, offend the opposer, and being false, shame the [proposer]."[225] Or, as Britaine put it, "Modesty in your discourses will give a Lustre to Truth, and an excuse to your Error." A judicious skepticism about the quality of knowledge and a temperate probabilism about its certainty were therefore resources for the constitution and protection of civil conversation. Britaine commended the view "that nothing in the World could be certainly known" as a lubricant for civil social relations.[226] In the early eighteenth century the earl of Shaftesbury developed a systematic philosophy of civil society which recommended a healthy, if mitigated, skepticism about the status and significance of any knowledge-claim or body of knowledge not directly involved with the stream of practical life.[227]

Moreover, it was widely recognized that civil conversation was highly vulnerable to forms of discourse which were demanding of technical competence or which bore upon men's passions and interests. "Academical Discourses," studded with "Terms of Art," were to be shunned, as was talking "of ones *Trade* or *Profession* to those that neither *mind* nor *understand it.*" Ways ought to be found to pitch discourse to the company's common ground. Let your discourse rather be "of *Things* than of *Persons,* of *Historical matters,* rather than the *present Age,* of things *distant & remote,* rather than at *Home,* and of your *Neighbours.*"[228] Obadiah Walker warned that one was not "in *ordinary* company [to] treat of matters too subtil and curious, nor too vile and

---

quotations; it being by many accounted a more genteel and masterly way of writing, to cite others but seldom, and then to name only the authors, or mention what they say in the words of him that cites, not theirs, that are cited": Boyle, "New Experiments Touching Cold" (1665), 476.

224. Walker, *Of Education,* 251. The moral significance of imprecision is treated in chapter 7 below.

225. Stafford, *Guide of Honour,* 117.

226. Britaine, *Humane Prudence,* 22–23.

227. Shaftesbury, *Characteristics* (1711), 88, 195–96, 214; see also Shapin, "'A Scholar and a Gentleman,'" 302–04.

228. Lingard, *Letter of Advice,* 11–14.

mean; nor of things unseasonable, as of Religion in mixed . . . company, or at table." Civil conversation demanded "subjects [that] concern no mans reputation."[229]

Science and Civil Conversation

Niklas Luhmann has offered a discerning account of the conversations of everyday life.[230] Conversation is not viewed as the means to an end, rather its pleasurable continuance *is* the end to which artful human endeavor strives. An unproblematically existing world—indeed "any world"—is "sufficient to provide the indispensable environment for friendship as long as it accords with the requirements of pleasant company." The conception of truth appropriate to conversational settings is a tolerant one. Matters that 'are the case' need only be so 'for all practical purposes.' The certainty of claims can be passed over or held in abeyance. As proposed in conversation, matters-that-are-the-case need not be formulated so as to survive testing, deliberation, or the rigors of reflective verification. Instead, their perspicuity for conversational purposes arises from their capacity to perpetuate and generate further conversation.

It is not simply that truth *can* be tolerantly construed; the truth of conversational matters *should* possess such a practically adequate character if it is not to have destructively divisive effects:

> [Conversation] selected what was essential for maintaining the readiness to continue contact and (to this end) for changing the topics of conversation continually. What mattered with respect to topics was not the attainment of conclusions; the imposition of either/or demands could therefore be avoided, and, because they were socially uncomfortable, also had to be avoided. Disagreement with beliefs expressed in a conversation was regarded as problematic, or even as an instance of unacceptable behavior. No articulated thought could be criticized, for it must never be forgotten that vulnerable persons were behind such thought: it must therefore only be commented upon, reviewed from another perspective, cautiously examined, and circumvented. What was permissible as a discourse was determined by the fact that the discourse itself was the sole reason why the most diverse persons took part in it.

229. Walker, *Of Education*, 250; cf. the concluding sentence of Hobbes's *Leviathan*, 729: "Such Truth, as opposeth no mans profit, nor pleasure, is to all men welcome."

230. Luhmann, "Differentiation of Advances in Knowledge." I discuss Michael Oakeshott's similar, and more systematic, account of conversation in chapter 7.

For Luhmann, conversation thus construed is "the purest form of so-ciability, a self-contained sociability which perpetuates and maintains itself."[231]

Luhmann's account of conversational conventions belongs to a spe-cifically historical inquiry. He wants to show how this code *conflicted with* the origins of science in early modern society. He asks "how knowl-edge is possible" in a society possessing such conversational expecta-tions, and his answer is that properly scientific knowledge required a differentiation of settings and the consequent creation of a space within which a radically different set of norms operated. Science neces-sitated *inter alia* a far less tolerant and far more deliberative approach to truth: empirical proof, certainty, and clarity. These were, Luhmann says, the conditions for the emergence of authentically scientific in-quiry, and they involved the splitting off of procedures for establishing scientific truth from the conventions for producing matters-that-are-the-case within civil conversation.[232]

Luhmann shares a widespread Continental tendency to associate 'sci-ence' simply with its Cartesian version, and, indeed, with formal meth-odological pronouncements concerning Cartesianism.[233] Science aimed to secure certainty; it possessed or pretended to possess a rigorously reliable method for arriving at indubitable knowledge and eliminating the merely probable; it sought truth through the precise framing of either/or questions, excluding alternatives and restricting the range of permissible responses; its ideals were sought in the demonstrative sciences of logic and geometry; assent to its propositions was bound by the iron rules of reason. Yet, as a generation of historical research has now taught us, early modern culture produced a range of scientific enterprises, some of which bore little resemblance to the Cartesian project, and some of which, indeed, were forcibly juxtaposed to its brand of the search for certainty.

Some of the best recent cultural studies of science display strands of early modern Italian science as a courtly version of civil conversation: scientific discourse was a species of *sprezzatura*. Tribby's studies of the seventeenth-century Florentine setting, for example, show Francesco Redi's experimental work on snakes as an exercise designed to delight, to amuse, and, overwhelmingly, to draw its gentle audience into affably decorous conversation with each other, with ancient authorities, and

231. Ibid., 108. Luhmann's account associates these conventions specifically with early modern lay conversation, but chapter 1 above strongly suggests their ubiquitous char-acter.

232. Ibid., 108–09. Luhmann was here indebted to Mertonian conceptions of the "norms of science" and Parsonian notions of "differentiation."

233. See, e.g., Schuster, "Methodologies as Mythic Structures"; idem, "Cartesian Method as Mythic Speech."

with the marvelous objects which were the occasion for courtly conversation.[234] Mario Biagioli's fine monograph on Galileo stresses has role
as Medici retainer, and hopeful courtier, striving to produce the cultural goods that would not only augment his prince's glory but also
contribute to the ongoing conversation of the court.[235] And Paula
Findlen's wide-ranging and detailed investigations of early modern
(and mainly) Italian natural history similarly establish the importance
of traditional codes of civil conversation in scientific communication:
"Politeness, affability, and the ability to put aside differences in order
to establish a 'neutral' ground for communication were central features
of the emerging scientific culture."[236]

In the present connection, however, Luhmann's assumptions about
science and civil conversation jar most markedly with our present appreciation of seventeenth-century *English* science, especially in its empirical and experimental forms. The practice which emerged with the
Interregnum work of Boyle and his Oxford associates, and which was
institutionalized at the Restoration in the Royal Society of London,
was strongly marked by its *rejection* of the quest for absolutely certain
knowledge, by its suspicion of logical methods and demonstrative models for natural science, and by its tolerant posture towards the character
of scientific truth. This chapter has described some cultural repertoires
which were available for English gentlemanly use in producing, sustaining, and modifying knowledge-claims in lay society. Much of the
remainder of the book will seek to show how these widely distributed
practices figured in the assessment of knowledge-claims within the relatively specialized culture of empirical and experimental English science. That is to say, conventions and codes of gentlemanly conversation were mobilized as practically effective solutions to problems of
scientific evidence, testimony, and assent.

I will argue that the appropriation and relocation of specific gentlemanly practices were relatively deliberate and purposeful moves:
(i) they were responses to problems in the control and validation of
testimony brought on partly by rejection of traditional authority and
the opening up of the realm of matters-that-might-be-the-case in the
natural world; (ii) they were the result of new modes of participation

234. Tribby, "Cooking (with) Clio and Cleo"; see also idem, "Body/Building"; idem,
"'It's All *Sprezzatura* to Me!'" For a concise account of *sprezzatura*—the art which conceals
art, effortless superiority—see, e.g., Whigham, *Ambition and Privilege*, 93–95.

235. Biagioli, *Galileo, Courtier.*

236. Findlen, "The Limits of Civility and the Ends of Science," 2; see also idem,
"Economy of Sciencific Exchange"; idem, "Museums, Collecting and Scientific Culture";
idem, "Jokes of Nature." For further recent studies of patronage and polite behavior
among Continental practitioners, see, e.g., P. H. Smith, "Curing the Body Politic"; idem,
Science and Culture in the Age of the Baroque; Eamon, "Court, Academy, and Printing
House."

by members of the gentle classes in natural philosophy and natural history, and of the possibilities that participation offered for legitimating and revaluing scholarly culture; and (iii) they were valuable resources increasingly looked to by scientific practitioners who viewed traditional scholarly behavior as scandalously divisive and unproductive.[237] Furthermore, I want to make the practical assessment of scientific knowledge-claims visible as a manifestation of the ubiquitously distributed "natural attitude" treated in chapter 1. What was purposefully taken from one cultural domain (gentlemanly conversation) and relocated to another (scientific culture) was the specific form in which the natural attitude was historically embedded. However, insofar as the natural attitude is a necessary presupposition of reliable communication and coordinated action, some version of it must be a concomitant of any institutionalized solutions to problems of knowledge and social order.

Later chapters will offer detailed accounts of truth-making and truth-warranting practices in seventeenth-century English science. Here is a sketch of some central features of that enterprise, summarized and stressed to prepare the ground for subsequent discussions of the relationship between gentlemanly codes and scientific practices. First, the English scientific enterprise centered upon the Royal Society of London was itself predominantly gentlemanly in its membership. There is nothing surprising in this. In the seventeenth-century English setting, almost all forms of literate organized culture matter-of-factly excluded the great majority of women and the great majority of nongentle men. It is probably pointless to search for particular grounds of exclusion, since the interlocked institutions of family, education, and religion ensured that few women or nongentle men would ever present themselves as possible participants. To be sure, the early Royal Society produced much rhetoric arguing the relative openness of this form of culture: Thomas Sprat, for example, described the Society as "an Assembly setled of many eminent men of all Qualities."[238]

However, while historians have been intermittently impressed with

237. Some fine recent scholarship has argued, with varying degrees of forcefulness, causal clarity, and specificity, that English scientific procedures for dealing with evidence and testimony were formally *legal* in origin; see, e.g., Shapiro, *Probability and Certainty*, esp. chs 2, 5; idem, "Law and Science"; idem, "'To a Moral Certainty,'" 155–68; Martin, *Francis Bacon, the State, and the Reform of Natural Philosophy*, esp. 72–73, 141–75; Sargent, "Scientific Experiment and Legal Expertise"; Daston, *Classical Probability*, esp. ch. 1; idem, "Baconian Facts." I have no reason to argue against the relevance of legal patterns, especially, as I indicate in chapter 5, with reference to jury trials. While it is undeniable that many English gentlemen were familiar with practical and academic jurisprudence, my case for the general significance of gentlemanly codes has their pervasiveness to recommend it.

238. Sprat, *History of the Royal Society* (1667), 431; see also ibid., 65–66, 407, 435.

that rhetoric of inclusion, we still lack any systematic comparisons between the social composition of the English natural scientific community and that of, for example, the membership of the universities, the inns of court, or the body of practicing poets and playwrights. It is by no means clear that such comparisons would show the Royal Society to be even relatively open to 'all classes.' Sprat elsewhere represented the Royal Society as an organization predominantly made up of "Gentlemen, free, and unconfin'd," and subsequent chapters will elaborate the significance of gentle constitution and gentlemanly codes for the making of empirical knowledge.[239]

Overwhelmingly, the fellows of the Royal Society possessed the circumstances, education, expectations, cultural heritage, and moral equipment of early modern English gentlemen. In insisting upon their individual freedom, integrity, and equality in the world of science, they mobilized the culture which stipulated the normative freedom, integrity, and equality of English gentlemen. What was understood of gentlemen generally, and what was routine and expected in their social relations, might effectively be appropriated to pattern and justify social relations within the new practice of empirical and experimental science. The Royal Society's 'modern' rejection of authority in scientific matters quite specifically mobilized codes of presumed equality operative in early modern gentle society. Just as each knowledge-claim was to make its way in the world without help or favoritism, so all participants played on a level field, no man lording it over another with respect to his ability to assist the transition from belief to knowledge. Authority—so recognized—was identified as both morally odious and epistemically dangerous. While the society of schools might put one man in fear of another, conjoining institutional standing and epistemic authority, the Royal Society insisted upon egalitarian codes operative in gentlemanly conversation. Conversation was, thus, not only a mark of epistemic efficiency, it was also a civil end in itself. No conception of truth could be legitimate if pursuing and maintaining it put civil conversation at risk.

Second, I will note the relative rarity of episodes in the Royal Society setting in which natural-historical or experimental reports were ne-

239. Ibid., 67; also 405–07; and for recent prosopographical research, see Hunter, *Royal Society and Its Fellows.* A reader of an early version of this chapter wondered why I should even refer to gentlemanly codes' being purposefully relocated to philosophy: to the extent that English natural philosophers *were* gentlemen, how else should they be expected to behave in philosophy but as gentlemen? Yet much later material in this book draws attention to the explicitness and pervasiveness of the local opposition between gentlemanly and scholarly codes of conduct, while there was no necessity that gentlemen should have come to see participation in what was traditionally scholars' practice as legitimate nor that their participation should have been on gentlemanly terms.

gated. It would be facile to say, as is traditional, that this was because of the 'credulity' of early modern practitioners, since they were quite able to express vigorous skepticism in specific circumstances, and since, in any case, it is the relationship between attitudes to reports and the texture of social relations I am concerned to document and interpret. Views of what the world is like are built up through the actions by which testimonies are accepted or rejected. Factual testimony from gentlemen-philosophers, I shall indicate, was almost never gainsaid in the public forums of seventeenth-century English science. Gentility powerfully assisted credibility.[240] The Royal Society was a place whose inhabitants had learnt to accomplish the assessment and modification of the great majority of knowledge-claims without doing anything visible as negation.

Third, the Royal Society's (and leading fellows') rejection of logical methods, pedantry, and esoteric language appropriated widespread gentle suspicion of, and contempt for, traditional scholarly modes of discourse. While the schools wrangled and disputed in the name of truth, the modern critique of Scholasticism construed such contention as a mean and ignoble quest for fame, unworthy of gentle ambition. Experimental truth, by contrast, was to be sought by selfless selves, seeking not celebrity or private advantage but the civic good. This was a conception of the gentlemanly civic actor thoroughly familiar from early modern ethical writing, and English scientific practitioners proposed to reconstitute the natural philosopher on just that civic model.

Most important, the practice of English empirical and experimental science institutionalized epistemic boundaries and evaluations which worked to solve problems of both knowledge and social order. Matters of fact were to be made into the foundations for properly scientific procedures. Practitioners assured themselves that they could be "morally certain" about the veridical status of fact-claims, even they were not themselves direct witnesses. By contrast, the correct posture *vis-à-vis* theoretical items which might count, for example, as causes of such facts was *probabilistic*. Facts might be made manifest or accessible through the morally adequate means gentlemanly actors used to assure themselves of matters-that-were-the-case, while theoretical items lacked equivalent vehicles for their consensual establishment.

Gentlemanly society well understood the risks of disputing members' fact-relations. To say that a man's relation of empirical experience was faulty was to say that he was a liar, perceptually damaged, or

240. Much that bears on these and related points was concisely noted by Peter Dear ("*Totius in Verba*," 156–57) some years ago, and I am indebted to him for many useful conversations on this subject; cf. Shapin, "Pump and Circumstance," 495–97; Shapin and Schaffer, *Leviathan and the Air-Pump*, esp. 55–76; Golinski, "Boyle: Scepticism and Authority," 71–72.

incompetent. Discrepant fact-reports had to be handled with extreme care. Precisely because practices historically adapted to protect the reliability of testimony and the integrity of the moral order existed as institutions in gentlemanly society, these practices were powerful resources for an enterprise which sought to build philosophical order on factual foundations. They simply had to be relocated from the gentlemanly to the philosophical setting. Moreover, the very gentlemanly practices which protected factual relations lightened the epistemic and moral load placed upon theoretical entities. Different theoretical schemes of nature might account for the same factual order. It was not to be expected that men could attain that certainty about theories that they could about facts. Accordingly, a characteristic mark of the English natural-philosophical enterprise was its vigilant protection of the factual domain combined with injunctions to speak modestly, diffidently, and doubtingly about the domain of the theoretical. It was philosophically and morally possible to do so, because the foundations of knowledge and of members' moral order were located elsewhere. For the English scientific community, as for Touchstone and the society of early modern gentlemen, there was "much virtue in If."

CHAPTER FOUR

Who Was Robert Boyle?
The Creation and Presentation
of an Experimental Identity

In all Actions, the Autority of the Person giues autority to the Example.

—Robert Boyle, "Aretology"

This chapter explores connections between the identity of individuals making claims and the credibility of what they claim. Previous chapters have introduced the idea that judgments of the truth or falsity of knowledge-claims incorporate assessments of the knowledge-source. Knowledge of who speaks is pervasively pertinent to decisions about whether what is spoken may be relied upon, and acted upon as true. I need now to offer a detailed examination of the constitution of personal identity and of its consequences for a philosophical project. I aim to trace the trajectory between the making of a personal identity and the making of items of public knowledge. Thus, the chapter will reach the general role of identity in the constitution of knowledge only through a detailed examination of the constitution of a particular identity. I want to arrive at practical epistemology through an exercise customarily called biography.

The individual in question is of special significance. Robert Boyle was, of course, one of the most influential practitioners of the new experimental philosophy. His particular natural-philosophical and natural-historical claims provided much of the factual stuff of the world upon which late seventeenth-century experimentalists operated: facts about the physical and vital properties of air, about specific gravity, color, cold, and chemical combination. Boyle arguably entered more matters of fact in the register of the seventeenth-century English experimental community than any other individual. Yet Boyle's role in the establishment of experimental practice was even more fundamental. For he, more than any other early experimentalist, spelled out and exemplified the matter, form, and power of the new practice. He offered it an embodied identity. Boyle did not *take on* the identity of experimental philosopher, he was a major force in *making* that identity. And as he made the role, so he proffered ostensive arguments for the validity and legitimacy of what that role produced. If one wished to believe what an experimental philosopher believed, then *this* was what the world was like and this was the certainty with which such beliefs might be held. If one wished to make experimental knowledge, then *here* were the technical, social, and discursive means with which it might be made. And if one wished to be an experimental philosopher, then the identity of Robert Boyle offered a paradigm of the new role. The legitimacy and validity of mid- to late seventeenth-century English experimental knowledge traded importantly upon the person of Robert Boyle and upon his personal presentation of gentlemanly identity.[1] Thanks to the fine research of other historians, that much is now well known. I do not here intend to go over old ground, though some of the facts here related about Boyle's life and work will probably be familiar to specialists.[2]

Collective Biography

No genre is better established in the history of science and ideas than that of individual biography. My purpose here is also biographical, yet it proceeds from orientations at odds with individualistic assumptions informing most biographical writing. I want, and for present purposes I need, to insist that individual biography is a sociological and social-historical topic. My subject is the achievement of identity and the cultural work done by and through that identity. Identity at once belongs to an individual *and* to the collectivities of which that individual is a part. The latter claim may seem as implausible as the former appears self-evident. The sociological case has four major components.[3]

First, a personal identity has to be continually made, and is continually revised and remade, throughout an individual career in contingent social and cultural settings. Such a claim runs counter to ways of ac-

1. Elsewhere, I have explored the role of *collective* identity, the recognized polity of knowledge-making places, in warranting the knowledge emerging from those places: Shapin, "House of Experiment," esp. 390–93; idem, "'The Mind Is Its Own Place,'" esp. 201–08.

2. Although I will refer to their work repeatedly, I want specially to acknowledge the extent of my indebtedness here to the writings of R. E. W. Maddison, James Jacob, Michael Hunter, and John T. Harwood. After this book was copyedited, an account of Boyle's early development which has many similarities to that developed in this chapter was published by Malcolm Oster, "Biography, Culture, and Science: The Formative Years of Robert Boyle."

3. Here I summarize arguments developed in Shapin, "Personal Development and Intellectual Biography: The Case of Robert Boyle."

counting for personal development deeply entrenched in present-day academic and lay cultures. In a popular psychological idiom, individual character is seen as *laid down* in infancy or childhood, perhaps massively shaped by the individual textures of universal sexual traumas and rites of passage. The most prevalent sociological perspectives similarly conceive individual personality to be predominantly shaped by early exposure to and internalization of *social values,* thereafter reinforced by the reiterations of those values in *social institutions.* Thus, for example, an enterprise aimed at establishing Robert Boyle's identity would traditionally look to the 'influence' of his early socialization, and especially of his family and schooling. These would be regarded as the forces that shaped Boyle's character, which, thus shaped, might be treated as a stable (and stabilizing) structure 'possessed' by Boyle throughout his life.

Yet, for all the commonsensical appeal of such theories in our culture, they have at best a patchy record of success. Psychoanalytic theories have such trouble in accounting for personal change in adult life that they sometimes seem to conceive the adult as a permanent child, to whom nothing interesting happens after puberty. And theories that point to the internalization of social values fail massively in accounting for deviance and cultural change. For these and other reasons, there seem to be no adequate reasons not to explore more dynamic sociological frameworks for understanding the development of personal identity which at once recognize the reality of personal change in adult life and acknowledge those patterns of consistent action which individuals undeniably manifest. I have particularly in mind the rich but underexplored resources for biography provided by the work of such symbolic interactionist sociologists as Howard Becker.[4] Becker argues, with evidence, that individuals adapt to the varying circumstances encountered through their adult lives, and that their sequential adaptation generates 'side bets' which contingently stabilize behavior in ways radically different from those supposed by psychoanalytic or sociological internalization theories.[5] In the case of the individual Robert Boyle, there would be no reason to identify a moment at which his identity was 'laid down.' Stories identifying the springs of his stable makeup which emerge from him and others in his setting would be treated as

4. See esp. Becker's "Notes on the Concept of Commitment" and "Personal Change in Adult Life," as well as Barnes's utilization of Becker's work in his critique of Mertonian socialization theories: "Making Out in Industrial Research."

5. One may, for example, take a job intending to leave after only a few years, but realizing the consequences of departure for one's pension may induce one to stay. Alternatively, one may develop routines of work and patterns of living which one comes to value and which would cost effort to reconstruct.

normative resources in *stipulations* of what sort of person he was and
how his actions ought to be understood and valued.

Second, while Boyle systematically made himself available as a pattern, his effective constitution into a template for others' emulation
was a collective enterprise. Practitioners and publicists associated with
the early Royal Society of London advertised Boyle as a founder of the
experimental philosophy. They accredited his programmatic writings
about how the new philosophy ought to be practiced; they approved
his views of its value and cultural relations; they helped him fashion a
self which helped fashion collective philosophical identity. And, of
course, that collective work did not cease with Boyle's death: through
the eighteenth and nineteenth centuries, his appropriated reputation
remained a resource for assessing philosophical conduct.

No personal identity can be made without the cooperation of others,
nor can it be stably possessed by an individual should its validity be
disputed by those to whom he presents it. In this connection Erving
Goffman's work offers the richest and most systematic understanding
of the presentation of self in face-to-face interaction. The "front" that
an individual presents to others is, on the one hand, the result of
internal deliberations about what others will make of it, and, on the
other, an experiment in a potential course of cooperative action. An
individual's definition of himself, as Goffman puts it, "exerts a moral
demand upon the others, obliging them to value and treat him in the
manner that persons of this kind have a right to expect." Yet that
definition is a hedged bet about what presentations can be successfully
brought off in specified circumstances.[6]

Third, personal identity is constructed out of materials at hand. The
stuff out of which identity can be made is presented by the local culture. Cultures vary in their repertoires for recognizing roles, in their
distribution of value to different sorts of activity, in their acknowledgment of different conceptions of selfhood, and in the legitimacy they
accord to conceptions of motive.[7] This means that the biographer of
a historical individual (or one belonging to another contemporaneous
culture) can treat the creation and presentation of personal identity
within a general historicist framework. What materials were available
in *this* culture for making identity? What vocabularies of motive and

6. E.g., Goffman, *Presentation of Self*, esp. 8–13. The primary source for conceptions
of "the social self" emerging in the capacity of the individual to conduct conversations
with internalized others is the work of George Herbert Mead; see, e.g., "The Social
Self," in Mead, *Selected Writings*.

7. See, esp., Mills, "Situated Actions and Vocabularies of Motive" (on motive); and
Elias, *The Society of Individuals*, and Taylor, *Sources of the Self* (on early modern conceptions
of the self).

purpose were present for warranting behavior and rendering it comprehensible as behavior *of a certain kind?* What roles preexisted against the background of which individual presentations might be understood and evaluated? Goffman's microsociological focus upon face-to-face interaction can and should be supplemented by inquiries into the codified knowledge historical actors possessed about what *sorts* of people there were in society, what forms of conduct might be expected of them, what entitlements they had by virtue of their understood occupancy of certain roles or positions in society. The knowledge that people have of others, and that which they can assume others have of them, accompanies them into face-to-face interaction. It may be revised in microinteraction, but it is relatively durable to such revisions. In the present connection, for example, I insist upon the importance of Boyle's recognized identity as a great gentleman, knowledge of which preceded him into any specific interaction.

Fourth, it follows from this basic historicist perspective that changes in roles and conceptions of identity can be viewed as a form of bricolage, respecifying and revaluing existing repertoires into new roles and new types of personal identity. This chapter is therefore mainly structured by a serial typology of existing roles that were available for occupancy by *someone like Boyle* in seventeenth-century England: philosopher, Christian, gentleman. Yet I do not make out Boyle to be a 'dope' of his culture and the passive recipient of values and plans inculcated by family, books, and schools. I present him as a major artful creator of a new identity assembled out of the materials his culture offered someone like him, helped by others to do so, and continually monitoring that developing identity throughout his adult life. The Boyle that emerges through this inquiry is no less an individual and no less creative. What it means to be an individual, and what it means to be creative, may, however, have shifted, arguably in a more historically defensible direction. My purpose is to reconstruct a personal identity as an element in the making and legitimizing of knowledge. And insofar as that knowledge has to be seen as collective property, so too must inquiries into Boyle's identity be treated as collective biography.

The Origins of Robert Boyle's Honor

The honor attached to Boyle was a valuable symbolic and practical resource for the experimental community of mid- to late seventeenth-century England. I want here to explore the origins and quality of that honor. Robert Boyle was a younger son of Richard Boyle, first earl of Cork, the next to last of his father's sixteen children, and the youngest surviving son.[8] For his contemporaries, including the vast majority of fellow English gentlemen who knew little and cared less about the philosophy of nature, that was how Boyle was known, recognized, and described. His father was sixty years old when Robert was born and would die during Robert's adolescence. Robert's mother, Katherine Fenton, died when he was three. In early seventeenth-century English society, to identify Boyle as the younger son of his father was to speak (contested) volumes. First, it was the basis of his title as "Honourable." By the time of his father's death, there were three surviving sons ahead of Robert in line of succession: Richard, Viscount Dungarvan, succeeded to his father's earldom in 1643 and was raised to the English peerage as Baron Clifford and, later, as earl of Burlington; Roger was created Baron Broghill as a boy in 1628 and earl of Orrery in 1660; Francis was created Viscount Shannon in 1660. All sons of earls were minimally styled "Honourable": no hereditary title was apparently intended for Robert nor did he ever take steps to secure one.[9] Second, although Robert had no hereditary title, he ultimately received a significant portion of his father's vast landholdings in Ireland and England. Although, as I shall note, the Irish rebellion of the 1640s momentarily placed the bulk of his inheritance in jeopardy, he controlled, and was known to control, independent means entirely adequate to support the leisured life of a gentleman, to sustain normal standards of hospitality and largesse, and to marry and to continue to live appropriately if he chose to do so.

If early modern gentlemanly identity hinged upon integrity and freedom of action, that integrity could, without question, be attributed to Robert Boyle. (By the mid-1630s, for example, we know that Robert was being assigned at least £2,000 per annum from his father's rents, and on Cork's death he inherited the estate of Stalbridge, one of the five largest manor houses in Dorset and his father's chosen point-of-entry into English aristocratic society.)[10] These facts about Boyle's

8. Cork had a stillborn son by his first wife (who died in childbirth in 1599). Eleven children survived to adulthood. Biographical details summarized are from: Budgell, *Memoirs of the Life of the Earl of Orrery*, 1–114; Fell-Smith, *Mary Rich;* Maddison, *Boyle,* esp. 289–97; Canny, *Upstart Earl,* esp. ch. 5; Jacob, *Boyle,* chs 1–2; Ranger, "Richard Boyle"; Mendelson, *Mental World of Stuart Women,* ch. 2.

9. Eighteenth-century biographers claim that, as an adult, Robert "was several times offered a peerage, which he constantly refused to accept": Birch, "Life of Boyle," cxliii; Budgell, *Memoirs of the Life of the Earl of Orrery,* 24, 145.

10. Maddison, *Boyle,* 54, 60; Canny, *Upstart Earl,* 98–99; Fell-Smith, *Mary Rich,* 17; I. Jones, *Boyle: Lord of Stalbridge,* [2]–[5]. As Gilbert Burnet acknowledged, Boyle "had a great and noble fortune": Burnet, "Character of a Christian Philosopher," 351. John Evelyn thought that Boyle also enjoyed "an honorary pay of a troop of horse" (Evelyn to William Wotton, 30 March 1696, in Evelyn, *Diary and Correspondence,* III, 349), and

standing in society provided, as it were, his basic social identity: every-one who knew Robert Boyle also knew his standing and degree and adjusted their behavior in light of that knowledge; they acknowledged certain rights, privileges, and circumstances as pertaining to that stand-ing, and these were relatively independent of his specific behavior or others' assessments of his personal virtue. While that basic identity said little about Boyle's individuality, it was a powerful resource which might be mobilized by him and others to make significant stipulations about the status and worth of what he did as an individual.

Boyle's father was not just any English earl. Indeed, his career, cir-cumstances, and behavior were very well known in English polite soci-ety. He was one of many rising new men of late Tudor and early Stuart England, and one of a large number who made their fortune in, and out of, Ireland. A self-made man, Cork was regarded as a pattern, even a caricature, of the type. He was the founder, not the inheritor, of his family's honor. His own origins remain somewhat obscure, but it is probable that his parents were of yeoman stock.[11] The second son of a younger brother, Richard Boyle was born in Canterbury and attended Bene't (now Corpus Christi) College in Cambridge. He left Cambridge without a degree and acquired some legal and administra-tive experience in London. Arriving in Dublin from England at age twenty-one with, so it was said, little more than the clothes on his back,[12] he launched a career whose ambition and acquisitiveness were matched only by its spectacular success. Appointed deputy to the es-cheator general for Crown lands in Ireland, Boyle rapidly accumulated a large fortune on the foundations of which he established his and his family's claims to nobility.

All this was not achieved without making many enemies. In their view, and in that of most Irish historians, Boyle was a robber baron of heroic stature, using his position to defraud Irish landowners, espe-cially in Munster, of their existing titles and to pass title to himself at absurdly deflated prices.[13] He then expelled the Irish tenants and replaced them with more pliable and profitable English settlers. By the late 1590s Boyle was not only a target of the righteous anger of indige-nous Irish Catholic landowners and farmers, he was also facing a series

Hooke told Aubrey that he had seen Cork's will, in which Robert was assigned £3,000 per annum in rentals (Aubrey, *Brief Lives*, 37).

11. An 'official' version of the Boyle family lineage is in Birch, "Life of Boyle," vi, and a sympathetic latter-day account is in Fell-Smith, *Mary Rich*, ch. 1.

12. It was typical of the man that he kept accounts—to the penny—of the money then in his pocket and the exact fabric and cut of the clothes he wore. The relative poverty from which Cork emerged passed into Boyle family tradition: in 1671 his daugh-ter, Mary, was able to record the exact sum—£27 3s—he possessed upon arrival in Ireland: Rich, *Autobiography*, 1.

13. Ranger, "Richard Boyle," is a detailed source for Cork's early land-dealings.

of legal actions brought by senior Anglo-Irish officials taken aback by the rapaciousness of his land-grabs. Boyle was twice imprisoned, and he was obliged to use his considerable connections to obtain a royal pardon for the actions which had attracted charges of fraud. His marriage to Robert's mother (the daughter of the surveyor general) was a shrewd move, allowing him to rebuild his fortune, and his subsequent aggressive manipulation of his children's marriages marked his continuing vigilance in expanding that fortune. The latter part of his life represents, as Canny has put it, the poacher turned gamekeeper, Boyle using his extensive knowledge of Irish land-titles to ensure the inviolability of his own tenure. By 1614 his rents amounted to £4,000 a year, but by the 1630s they had swollen to £20,000, giving him a rental income *larger than that of any other Crown subject.* Translating turf into title, Boyle had himself knighted in 1603, raised to the baronage in 1616, and finally created Viscount Dungarvan and first earl of Cork (for a fee of £4,500) in 1620.[14] In the early 1640s Cork had to endure a further investigation of his activities by the governor of Ireland, Sir Thomas Wentworth (later earl of Strafford), and another Irish rebellion. But he emerged triumphant from the former, and was under a garishly vulgar family funerary monument in Youghal by the time the Irish were effectively put back in their place.[15]

His Anglo-Irish enemies saw him as an appalling little arriviste, totally untrustworthy, immoral, and cynically calculative. Wentworth (who, to be sure, had his reasons to do so) blackened Cork's reputation throughout Ireland and England. He told all who would listen that Cork was mean and mean-spirited, minding his purse even more than his family's welfare. While boasting that "he was a better gentleman" than any in Ireland, Cork's behavior was said to be base and ignoble. He was coarse, abusive, and insulting. Wentworth reported that whenever Cork entertained guests they would "have half a dozen good loud storms from him in despite of who soever says nay." Most damagingly, Wentworth distributed a portrait of Cork as an untrustworthy, manipulative liar: "How can honest men ever admit of his company with honour and safety[?]"; "[I have] never known [Cork] to deliver one truth."[16]

Cork was not only a self-made man, he was a man who worked assiduously to make an appropriate self. First he sought to make himself a gentleman, then a Christian. Antiquaries were commissioned to establish the Boyles as "ancient and well-descended" and, when that

14. For the young Robert Boyle's unself-conscious condemnation of the purchase of titles, see his "Aretology," 116.

15. Canny, *Upstart Earl,* ch. 1; see also Stone, *Crisis of the Aristocracy,* 112–13, 116, 140, 580; Fell-Smith, *Mary Rich,* 8.

16. Canny, *Upstart Earl,* ch. 2.

did not succeed, his wife's family was made to serve as a credible source of his children's gentle ancestry. Distant relatives were sought out and rewarded with land and office in order to constitute Cork as chief of a potent kinship network. An elder brother was made bishop of Cork and cousins were strategically planted in other Irish clerical offices. While still infants, children were pressed into advantageous marriage alliances with noble court-connected families and care was taken with their education "not to have their youth infected with the leaven of Ireland." The sons were, of course, to have all the advantages he never had, Cork designing for them a systematically "religious, learned and noble breeding." While Ireland was the source of his fortune, Cork apparently despised "this barren and remote kingdom" and labored to translate Irish money into English land and repute. Despite his general vigilance in money matters, ostentatious residences were bought up and done up, both in Ireland and England, to serve Cork as fitting settings in which to play his new role of liberal and generous country gentleman. Robert and his sister Mary later remembered Cork in London "living extraordinarily high," surrounded by almost "constant crowds of company." While formally disapproving of such vices, Cork sought social acceptability by beginning to gamble on a grand scale.[17]

From the 1630s, Cork circulated his autobiographical "True Remembrances," which represented a mature view of the self through which he wished to be known. As well as a great gentleman, Cork was a Protestant moral hero. His remarkable rise was referred not to mastery of the Machiavellian arts but to extraordinary manifestations of divine providence. Upon his ennoblement, Cork adopted as family motto "God's providence is mine inheritance," a sentiment which he intended to be taken quite literally. "Divine providence" directed his steps towards Ireland, delivered him from prison, made his fortune and supervised its reestablishment. Providence was evident in his fecundity and was invoked to ensure that his many children lived in virtue: "The great God of heaven I do humbly and heartily beseech, to bless all these my children, whom he hath in his mercy so graciously bestowed upon me, with long and religious lives, and that they may be fruitful in virtuous children and good works."[18] There were indeed

17. Ibid., ch. 4 (quoting 42, 71–73, 177 n. 120). Rich, *Autobiography*, 4; see also Palgrave, *Mary Rich*, 43; Stone, *Crisis of the Aristocracy*, 568, 571. As a young man, Robert Boyle came to share his father's view of Ireland as a "barbarous country": Boyle to Frederick Clodius, *ca.* 1648, in Boyle, *Works*, VI, 54–55.

18. Richard Boyle, "True Remembrances," xi (comp. 1632). The general form of thanksgiving was not, of course, unique to Cork, but the detailed way in which providence was invoked to explain and justify economic success is noteworthy. Particulars of

friends and allies (usually linked with his political and financial adventures) who endorsed Cork's presentation of self. They referred his enemies' condemnation to envy and interest, cited his religious endowments as proof of piety, and praised the efficiency with which he sought to make Ireland safe for Protestantism. His providentialist motto, according to one memorialist, "shews, from whence he derived all his blessings; the greatest of which was the numerous and noble posterity he had to leave his estate unto."[19]

Robert said he loved his father. Writing an autobiographical essay at age twenty-two, Robert introduced himself as the much-loved son of a providence-favored father, "who, by God's blessing on his prosperous Industry, vpon very inconsiderable Beginnings built so plentifull & and so eminent a Fortune, that his prosperity has found many Admirers, but fewe Parallels. . . . To be such Parent's Son . . . was a Happinesse."[20] In fact, almost everything that Robert knew of his father was known through others' testimony, and whatever 'impression' his family exerted upon his personality in early development must have acted indirectly. The teat which suckled him was not his mother's; the paternal admonitions which corrected his early behavior were not his father's; and the language he learned to speak was inflected by others' tongues. Like Cork's other children, Robert was sent out to a country wet nurse shortly after being born, remaining there until perhaps three years of age.[21] He was probably summoned back to Lismore Castle in County Waterford for intermittent checkings-over until Christmas 1634, when he and brother Francis returned to the parental home for private tuition by a Frenchman. He remained there for less than a year, during which Cork was in residence no more than a few months, before being sent first to Eton and then on the grand tour of the Continent. Even when, in the brief interval between Eton and Europe, Robert and Cork were both at Stalbridge, his father took care not to have his son lodge in the manor house but with a parson several miles distant.[22] Thus, young Robert probably spent no more than a

---

Cork's personal providentialism are in Canny, *Upstart Earl*, ch. 3, esp. 28–29; see also Burnet, "Character of a Christian Philosopher," 351.

19. Richard Cox, *History of Ireland* (quoted in Birch, "Life of Boyle," xii); see also Canny, *Upstart Earl*, 24–25. For endorsement of Cork's "integrity" and "probity," see Aubrey, *Brief Lives*, 34, and Evelyn, *Diary and Correspondence*, III, 349; also ibid., 395–97. (Evelyn was related to the Boyles by marriage and much insisted on the importance of that connection.)

20. Boyle, "Philaretus," 2–3.

21. Wet-nursing may have been in part a strategy to increase the fertility of aristocratic marriages, and, if so, it was an unusually successful one in Cork's case: Stone, *Crisis of the Aristocracy*, 168–69.

22. Boyle, "Philaretus," 18–20; Fell-Smith, *Mary Rich*, 52.

few months in the same house as his father, and it is unlikely that he
ever had more than a few conversations with him.

For all that, Robert ("Robin" to his brothers and sisters) reported
himself to have been the family pet, beloved of father and elder siblings. Perhaps, he speculated, this paternal fondness might be ascribed
"to a likenesse obseru'd in [Robert] both to his Fathers body & his
mind."[23] The spartan nature of his country breeding was accounted
for by Cork's solicitous regard for his children's welfare. If modern
ears will inevitably hear sarcasm in young Robert's story, there is no
external evidence to suggest any intended tone of voice but earnest
sincerity:

> When once [I] was able without Danger to support the Incommoditys
> of a Remoue, [my] Father, who had a perfect auersion for their Fond-
> nesse, who vse to breed their Children so nice & tenderly, that a hot
> Sun, or a good Showre of Raine as much endangers them as if they
> were made of Butter or of Sugar; sends [me] away from home; &
> commits [me] to the Care of a Cuntry-nurse; who by early invring
> [me] by slow degrees to a Coarse (but cleanly) Dyet, & to the Vsuall
> Passions of the Aire, gaue [me] so vigorous a Complexion, that both
> Hardships were made easy to [me] by Custome, & the Delights of
> conveniencys & ease, were endear'd to [me] by their Rarity.[24]

Among the most ambiguous of the legacies Robert inherited from
his early socialization was his cultural identity. He was certainly not
Irish, but neither were the Anglo-Irish colonials accepted as genuinely
English. I have noted Cork's contempt for the land out of which he
made his fortune. Nevertheless, he evidently recognized that ability to
negotiate one's way through Irish culture, and facility with the Irish
language, might be useful acquirements. He arranged tuition for his
sons in Irish Gaelic, of which Roger and Robert are thought to have
acquired some command.[25] Whether Robert's country nurse and childhood governors were Irish is uncertain,[26] but there is some basis for
speculating that conflicted linguistic and cultural identity may have
been at the root of the speech impediment that proved both a disability
and a resource in Robert's later life. Robert said that his impediment
was a providential punishment for ridiculing his (Irish?) childhood
playfellows for their "stuttring Habitude," which "he so long Counter-
feited that he at last contracted it." I like to think (with little additional

23. Boyle, "Philaretus," 18–19; see also Jacob, *Boyle*, 8.
24. Boyle, "Philaretus," 4; see also Canny, *Upstart Earl*, 95–99, and Rich, *Autobiography*,
2 (for sister Mary's parallel sentiments about her separation at age three from Cork's
presence).
25. Canny, *Upstart Earl*, 126–27; Maddison, *Boyle*, 11n.; Fell-Smith, *Mary Rich*, 43–44.
26. Aubrey (*Brief Lives*, 36)—none too reliable a source in this connection—said that
Boyle "was nursed by an Irish Nurse, after the Irish manner."

evidence to support the notion) that Robert was making fun of them for their Irishness, and that the shock of finding the Lismore household making fun of *him* for *his* accent caused the stutter. Diligent efforts were apparently made to extinguish the stutter and, perhaps, the residual Irish accent. At Eton, the master of choristers was engaged "to correct the errors of voices and pronunciation," evidently with little effect, and throughout his life Boyle's impediment became an audible emblem of a man doubtfully fitted for normal civil conversation.[27]

In revering Cork's memory, Robert endorsed the identity his father disseminated through the "True Remembrances." Indeed, the two siblings with whom Robert remained the closest each made themselves into living memorials to Cork's identity as Christian hero. Mary, a vivacious and flirtatious young girl who doggedly refused her father's plans for her marriage, won a ferocious battle in 1641 to marry the man of her choice, Charles Rich, the second son of the earl of Warwick (who, improbably, succeeded to the earldom in 1659). But, some years after the marriage, he developed a debilitating chronic illness—ostensibly gout, possibly tertiary syphilis—which turned him into an irritably abusive invalid and Mary into one of great female Puritan meditators and diarists of her generation.[28] Katherine, eleven years older than Robert, accepted an orthodox Cork-arranged marriage to Arthur Jones, Viscount Ranelagh. And while Cork concerned himself little with his daughters' education—one was said to be scarcely literate at marriage—under Katherine's influence the Ranelagh London residences developed into major midcentury resorts for Anglo-Irish, parliamentary, and Puritan intellectuals. John Milton, Henry Oldenburg, and Francis Tallents served as family tutors, and members of the Samuel Hartlib circle were frequent visitors. Katherine supervised a devout household, committed to godly learning and its melioristic propagation.[29]

27. Boyle, "Philaretus," 4, 11n. (letters from Sir Henry Wotton and Robert Carew to Cork). For a friendly account of Boyle's mature impediment, see John Evelyn to William Wotton, 30 March 1696, in Evelyn, *Diary and Correspondence*, III, 351: "In his first addresses . . . he did sometimes a little hesitate, rather than stammer, or repeat the same word. . . . This . . . made him somewhat slow and deliberate." Evelyn imputed this infirmity "to the frequent attack of palsies, contracted . . . by his often attendance on chemical operations." Burnet's observations that Boyle never uttered the name of God "without a pause, and a visible stop in his discourse" may possibly be an attempt to give a divine gloss to this impediment: Burnet, "Character of a Christian Philosopher," 354.

28. Rich, *Autobiography;* Mendelson, *Mental World of Stuart Women*, ch. 2; Palgrave, *Mary Rich*, esp. 36–81, 111, 260; Fell-Smith, *Mary Rich*, esp. chs 3–4, 6, 10, 13. Mary Rich worked on, but never completed, a biography of her father.

29. The best source for Katherine's role in Interregnum London intellectual life is Webster, *Great Instauration*, 62–67; see also Turnbull, *Hartlib, Dury and Comenius*, 27–29, 245–49, 258; Maddison, *Boyle*, 61–63; Fraser, *The Weaker Vessel*, 131–34. The Ranelagh

Not all Cork's children were living testaments to their father's Christian piety. Roger, Lord Broghill and later earl of Orrery, made his reputation as soldier, as Irish politician, and especially as Restoration court wit, literatus, and gallant. Cork vigorously forbade the reading of romances to all his children, with the result that most of them, including the young Robert, became infatuated with romantic fiction and its effect on the imagination, and Broghill became a noted romantic author and playwright. If, as one historian suggests, Robert, Mary, and Katherine sought to reproduce Cork-as-he-wanted-himself-known, Broghill may have responded more to Cork-as-he-was.[30] An ardent Royalist adventurer, Broghill had little time for Puritan soul-searching and moralizing. Like his brother Lewis, the young Broghill was an active member of the Caroline smart set. Contemporary comment had it that both of them were "very debauched": Lewis was unable to consummate his marriage because of venereal disease, and London rumormongers, including his own fiancée, speculated that Broghill also had gonorrhea. In 1640, Broghill took his gallantry to its logical conclusion, fighting a duel over the honor of his mistress (even though, as it turned out, he eventually married another). As earl of Orrery, he wrote 'heroic' plays that enjoyed a mixed success on the London stage. The king liked them and Orrery was a regular royal playmate, together with such cronies as Shadwell and Rochester, in some of Whitehall's and St. James's louchest settings.[31] Young Robert periodically, and gently, reminded his brother of his Christian duties, but Broghill paid little attention. In fact, one of Orrery's later plays was allusively rude about the "modern natural philosophy" and the doings of chemists.[32] When Orrery died in 1679, Gilbert Burnet, who later preached Robert's funeral sermon, left a character of a typical Restoration debauchee: "Orrery pretended to knowledge, but was very

---

marriage made Robert a relation of John Dury, a leading member of the Hartlib circle. I briefly treat Katherine's significance for Boyle's intellectual work in chapter 8.

30. For relations between the Boyles and the theatrical Killigrew family, see M. Butler, *Theatre and Crisis*, 117; for remarks on family reactions to the Cork pattern, see Mendelson, *Mental World of Stuart Women*, 62.

31. For Orrery's life, see Clark, "Historical Preface," in Orrery, *Dramatic Works*, I, 3–60 (see comment on his morality on 9–10); see also Mendelson, *Mental World of Stuart Women*, 72.

32. E.g., *Mr. Anthony* (act I, 85, 155; act II, sc. i, 416–18; act II, sc. ii, 380–81), in Orrery, *Dramatic Works*, II, 521–22, 540, 558. For Boyle on Broghill, see, e.g., Boyle to [Broghill?], 18 April 1647, in Harwood, *Early Essays*, 66 n. 63; Boyle to Isaac Marcombes, 22 October 1646, in Boyle, *Works*, I, xxxii; Boyle to Broghill, 20–21 December 1649, in ibid., VI, 50–52; Boyle to Lady Orrery, October 1649, in ibid., 52–53; and "The Epistle Dedicatory" to Boyle's "Some Considerations Touching the Style of the Holy Scriptures" (1661), 247–50. For Boyle's youthful censure of the bodily ill-effects of debauchery, see Boyle to unknown nobleman, *ca.* 1647, in Boyle, *Works*, I, xliii.

ignorant, and to wit, but it was very luscious; . . . and to religion, but was thought a very fickle and false man."[33]

While Cork sought energetically to press his children (or at least the sons) into a mold of heroic virtue, it is not clear what in the Boyle children's environment most importantly shaped their personalities. If there was an 'impression' through their brief familiarity with the father and early family socialization, it was such as to have produced the widely varying characters of Robert and Roger. In any case, Cork's enduring significance for Robert would largely have been mediated by others' continuing testimony and evaluations of his character, a deeply ambiguous legacy. In all probability, throughout his life Robert would have encountered as many people who regarded Cork as a criminal "dunghill earl" as those who honored the basis of his nobility. Among elder male figures in Robert's life, his tutor Isaac Marcombes was arguably the most lasting source of moral influence. Robert traveled and lodged with Marcombes for almost five years, from September 1639 to ca. June 1644, and continued to correspond with him thereafter. In general, Robert carefully invigilated his various tutors' characters, and seems never to have forgotten their status as employees or family retainers: Robert Carew he found a debauched dissembler, the Eton tutor John Harrison kind and encouraging but lax in discipline, the Dorset parson William Douche careful and civil, while Marcombes, criticized for being a bit cynical and irritable, was applauded for his soundness in Protestant religion and knowing "what belong'd to a Gentleman."[34] If, therefore, Robert's personality was 'shaped' by an effective direct paternal model, one might look not to Cork but to Marcombes.[35] Yet Marcombes also tutored Broghill, without equivalent moral and intellectual consequences. For these, and related, reasons it is best to set aside an 'impression model' of Boyle's developing identity and to see family and early environment as a set of patterns and resources (among many others) which might be drawn upon to equip himself with a defensible identity as he followed his unique biographical trajectory.

The rest of Robert's childhood and adolescent formation was in no way remarkable for someone of his standing and condition. Cork in-

33. Burnet, *Supplement to History of My Own Time*, 63.
34. Boyle, "Philaretus," 8–15, 20–23 (quoting 22). For Harrison, see Birley, "Boyle's Headmaster at Eton." Marcombes was French but a resident of Geneva and a nephew by marriage of the Genevan theologian Jean Diodati. Having been recommended to Cork by Wotton, he took Broghill and Lewis on the grand tour before picking up Francis and Robert on his return (Maddison, *Boyle*, 21n.; Fell-Smith, *Mary Rich*, 39–41, 57–58).
35. Boyle's own youthful ponderings about the moral importance of paternal exemplars indicate little self-consciousness about his own experience: "Domestick Examples ar heer both most necessary and most to be regarded: not onely for their frequency (tho that be very considerable [!])" ("Aretology," 76–77).

tended to shape all his sons into paragons of learned Christian gentility: "all the rarest that this world can lay upon me, are farr inferior to
my Study and endeavors which I have, to give my Sons a religious,
learned and noble breeding."[36] At age eight, Robert was shipped with
his twelve-year-old brother Francis to Eton, where they enjoyed the
personal supervision of Cork's appointed tutor as well as the attention
of the provost Sir Henry Wotton, who generally functioned as trusted
advisor on the education of Cork's sons.[37] Eton was then, as Robert
said, "very much throng'd with young Nobility" and the tutor's breath-
less letters to Cork repeatedly noted his sons' growing intimacy with
the children of ancient English aristocratic houses.[38] Whether or not
Robert was specially marked out for his withdrawn and earnest personality before going to Eton, his studious seriousness, discipline, and
self-control began then to attract comment. His tutor reported to Cork
that Francis was "not soe much giuen to his booke as my most honored
and affectionate Mr Robert, who looseth noe houre without a line of
his idle time, but one Scooldays he doth compose his exercises as well
as them of double his yeares and experience." The nine-year-old Robert was deeply censorious of his brother's infatuation with hunting and
horses, and lectured him on the honor and virtue of youthful learning.
Although Robert was reported to be enjoying chubby good health, "his
delight is in his learning . . . for he takes noe pleasure in playing with
boyes nor running abroad."[39] Apart from the usual Latin studies, the
pedantic character of which did not impress Robert, he continued his
French lessons, and received some instruction in playing the viol and
singing.

   The grand tour which commenced in October 1639 continued Robert's cultural furnishing and introduced him to Continental polite and
learned society. Until autumn of 1641, Robert and his just-married
brother Francis lodged with Marcombes in his Genevan home, studying rhetoric, logic, languages, and the "practicke parts of mathematickes" (surveying and fortification). Robert had lessons in fencing
(which he loved) and dancing (which he loathed), but reported himself
to be still too young for the "rude & violent" traditional chivalric exer-

36. Cork to William Perkins (Cork's London agent), 2 June 1635, in Chatsworth
Devonshire Collections, quoted in Jacob, *Boyle*, 7. Boyle acknowledged that while his
father was not learned, he "supply'd what he wanted in Schollership himselfe by being
both a Passionate Affecter & eminent Patron of it" (Boyle, "Philaretus," 6).
37. Canny, *Upstart Earl*, 70–71, 98.
38. Boyle, "Philaretus," 19.
39. Robert Carew to Cork, December 1635 and 29 February 1636, quoted in Maddison, *Boyle*, 10n–12n. Isaac Marcombes later contrasted Francis's use of Eton—where he
was said to have learned little but "to drinke with other deboice [debauched]
scholers"—with Robert's, who "is ye finest gentleman of ye worlde" (Marcombes to
[Cork?], *ca.* 1640, quoted in ibid., 14n).

cise of riding the 'Great Horse.'[40] Although Cork was uneasy about
the theological and moral risks of Italy, the Marcombes entourage was
in Florence when Galileo died in January 1642. They saw the usual
antiquities, inspected the usual curiosities, and had all the usual unusual foreign experiences: in Padua Robert may have seen a human
dissection, in Rome he witnessed the operation of Athanasius Kircher's
wind-engine, and in Florence he disputed with rabbis and ("out of bare
Curiosity") agreed to be taken to the "famousest Bordellos," whence
he emerged disgusted but with "an vmblemish't Chastity." Cork's fears
about papist immorality were abundantly and instructively confirmed:

> For being at that Time not above 15, & the Cares of the World hauing
> not yet faded a Complexion naturally fresh enuf; as he was once
> vnaccompany'd diuerting himselfe abroad, he was somewhat rudely
> presst by the Preposterous Courtship of 2 of those Fryers, whose Lust
> makes no distinction of Sexes; but that which it's Preference of their
> owne creates; & not without Difficulty, & Danger, forc't a scape from
> these gown'd Sodomites.[41]

While Robert's standing as the son of an aristocrat provided much
of his basic identity, his position as *younger* brother constituted a major
generic identity-problem which required practical resolution. Within a
primogeniture system younger sons were either dependent upon the
father's or eldest son's largesse or given a helping hand into a military,
professional, or trade career. As I have indicated, Cork's intention was
to secure his youngest son's integrity and independence, if not through
his own generosity then certainly through an advantageous marriage.
While it was not uncommon for younger sons of the aristocracy to
remain unmarried and heirless for economic reasons, this was apparently not a consideration in Robert's case. More generally, for younger
sons the problem of vocation presented itself whether or not it was
given a Protestant moral charge. If the younger son was so fortunately
situated that he might live at pleasure, how was he to structure his
day, discipline his self, and forge a publicly warrantable identity in
gentlemanly society? It was widely recognized that the freedom and
formal irresponsibility of the younger son inclined him more to "idle
courses."[42] While within one conception of gentle identity a gentleman

40. Young Robert was still enough of a gallant to pester Marcombes (a former soldier)
for a new and fashionable sword (Marcombes to Cork, 20 December 1641 and 7 January
1640, in Maddison, *Boyle*, 27n., 31n.; Boyle, "Philaretus," 31).

41. Boyle, "Philaretus," 40–41. Robert reported that the hypocrisy and immorality of
papist Italy were such that direct experience was the Protestant's best fortification (ibid.,
42).

42. Ap-Robert, *The Younger Brother* (1618), 2, 32–33; Stone, *Crisis of the Aristocracy*,
169, 599–600; Harwood, *Early Essays*, xlv.

was "nothing but his pleasure," within another code pleasure and idleness were substantial social and cultural *problems.*

In fact, the matter of Robert's identity and vocation became acutely problematic in the years immediately spanning his father's death. James R. Jacob has vividly described the trauma brought on for all those dependent upon Cork's fortunes by the Irish rebellion of 1641–1642. The immediate loss of land-rent reduced Cork to penury, and, until those lands could be secured, only marriage to an heiress or earned income could save Robert from ruin.[43] His party had only just returned from Italy to France in the spring of 1642 when word of Cork's catastrophe was received. Normal prospects of a life of gentlemanly leisure were suddenly shaken by circumstances that might force Robert, as he now realized, "honorably [to] gaine my liuing."[44] Cork forbade either son to appear in England suffering from straitened circumstances: it was either Ireland or the Continent until they could cut the proper figure in the setting where their figures mattered to the paternal reputation: "For into England I will not consent they shall yet come, . . . for I haue neither present money nor meanes to defray their expences there: And for them that haue been soe well maintayned to appeare there with out money, would deiect their spirits, and grieue and disgrace me, and draw contempt vpon vs all."[45]

Cork suggested the possibility of shipping the brothers off to the Low Countries where they might find military careers. Robert delicately turned that idea aside, protesting that he was too young, too tired, and "too weake" for such an adventure, and elsewhere expressing revulsion and fear of the company of such "debaucht" persons as were normally found in army camps.[46] While Francis hastened back to his father's side to see what use he might be in Ireland, Robert elected to stay on with Marcombes in Geneva, gathering his strength, studying, suffering the presumed embarrassment of living on his tutor's credit, and waiting for money to arrive and the Irish situation to be resolved. It was during this period that Cork died and Robert came into his vexed inheritance. He remained in Geneva almost two more years, returning to England in mid-1644 in order to take possession

43. Jacob, *Boyle,* 10–12. Just before the rebellion broke out, Cork was laying plans to marry Robert to Anne Howard, daughter of Edward, Lord Howard of Esrick. It was intended that Robert reside at Mallow in County Cork, but a revised will was made necessary by brother Lewis's death: Maddison, *Boyle,* 54–55.

44. Boyle to Cork, 25 May 1642, quoted in Maddison, *Boyle,* 48–49.

45. Cork to Marcombes, 9 March 1642, quoted in Maddison, *Boyle,* 46–48.

46. Birch, "Life of Boyle," xxvii; Maddison, *Boyle,* 48, 53–54; Jacob, *Boyle,* 13. Later, Boyle recommended ("Aretology," 87) that the choice of vocation suit the individual's innate temperament: "We must not . . . send a soft contemplatiue Nature to the Warres; nor one that delihts but in Drums and Trumpets and Armes and Blood, to the Vniversity."

of his Dorset estate and to proceed there as quickly as possible. He would be a leisured country gentleman—and something else yet to be decided.

The basic features of Boyle's mature life are so well known that only a bare summary is necessary here. He spent about ten years in residence at his Stalbridge manor, visiting friends and relations in Ireland, London (most often staying with Katherine), and the Leese, Essex, home of his sister Mary Rich. Throughout this period he kept in close personal contact with the Hartlib circle, worked away on a series of moral and theological essays, developed networks of charitable and religious patronage, spent time in a chemical laboratory he had built in Stalbridge, and continued to lay in a disorganized stock of utilitarian knowledge with special attention to medical receipts. By the early to mid-1650s, Boyle had acquired a considerable English natural- and moral-philosophical identity without having as yet published anything. Books were dedicated to him, and the general form of his philosophically flavored piety was well known in the local culture.[47]

By late 1655 or early 1656, Boyle took up residence at Oxford, where he became an important member of the philosophical circle including John Wilkins, John Wallis, Seth Ward, Christopher Wren, and Thomas Willis. Robert Hooke became his scientific assistant in 1658, and Boyle's first series of air-pump experiments was published in 1660. That work, quickly followed by a collection of essays on the proper practice of an experimental natural philosophy, securely established Boyle's identity in the republic of letters. The founding of the Royal Society of London, and its effective international information-exchange system, distributed Boyle's example throughout the world. By his midthirties Boyle had become a highly visible pattern for the making of a proper experimental identity. The triple conjunction of birth and wealth, learning, and piety that had been so long recommended by Christian humanist writers was now taken to be exemplified in the remarkable person of the Honourable Robert Boyle. He was much talked about, written about, and visited. However privately he lived, his life had become public property, a public resource for warranting experimental philosophy and producing experimental philosophers.

In 1668, responding to the repeated entreaties of his sister Katherine, Boyle moved to London, where he shared her Pall Mall house and worked in a laboratory especially constructed for him there. After an initial period of relatively frequent attendance at the meetings of the Royal Society, Boyle withdrew to a more private form of life, protected by his sister, and removing from London to Leese or Oxford when

---

47. A 1655 essay (to be discussed below) was published anonymously.

the press of visitors became too great. After his recovery from a stroke in 1670, Boyle entered into one of the most experimentally productive periods of his life, fortunate in a series of exceptionally able technicians and the editorial assistance of his neighbor Henry Oldenburg until Oldenburg's death in 1677. Boyle's health declined in the mid-1680s, and he died on 30 December 1691, one week after the death of the person to whom he was closest throughout his life, his sister Katherine. He was much mourned, and, if no monument was ever erected to his memory (even his bones were lost by the mid-eighteenth century), the philosophical identity continued a usable template well into this century. He became the pattern of a moral, humble, selfless, disinterested, public-spirited, and inductive natural scientist.

Historians have laid great emphasis upon the period of perhaps four months that Boyle spent with his sister Lady Ranelagh after arriving back in London from the Continent.[48] Katherine's parliamentary connections helped him secure some of his Irish and English estates, though his financial affairs remained tangled for years thereafter. I have already noted that her house in Holborn was a center of Puritan intellectual debate, and it was almost certainly there that Boyle was introduced to the Hartlib circle, whose Christian-reformist program proved so immediately attractive to him.[49] The timing could not have been better, both for Boyle and for the Hartlibians. Boyle was a young man, already of earnestly Christian bent, newly come into much of his fortune, and looking for a vocation and an agenda of activity which suited his retired but civically concerned temperament. By the time Boyle made his way to Stalbridge late in 1644, he was already exploring a program of chemical and ethical work closely connected to that of Hartlib, Clodius, Worsley, and the Boate brothers. He was barely eighteen years old, and he had the funds to buy the furnaces and apparatus to do chemistry, the leisure to write ethical systems, and the largesse to support the activities of others in the circle. Simply by virtue of his basic identity, he was already recognized as a great prize. Together with his new Hartlibian associates he now embarked on a series of experiments in forging a personal identity which testified to his religiosity and to the legitimacy of his emerging cultural practice.[50]

48. Birch, "Life of Boyle," xxvii; Jacob, *Boyle*, 13–25; Maddison, *Boyle*, 61–63, 69–72; Webster, *Great Instauration*, 57–67.

49. Major figures of that circle were Samuel Hartlib himself, John Dury, Frederick Clodius, Gabriel Plattes, and Benjamin Worsley. As Jacob notes (*Boyle*, 16; also Trevor-Roper, "The Great Tew Circle," 171–79), Lady Ranelagh had also been a friend of the irenic aristocrat Lucius Cary, center of the Great Tew circle.

50. Thanks to the fine editorial work of John T. Harwood (*Early Essays*), we now possess diplomatic editions of a number of ethical and moral essays which Boyle produced at Stalbridge from *ca.* 1645 to *ca.* 1650, and I draw on this material extensively in the following sections. This includes the extended tract called "The Aretology" as

What Sort of Gentleman?

Chapters 2 and 3 identified different repertoires circulating in six-teenth- and seventeenth-century England which treated the bases of gentility, and which offered resources for those who wished to present themselves as gentlemen or who wished to recognize legitimate repre-sentatives of the type. The culture thus presented individuals a degree of choice over how gentility, and their claims to it, might be justified—if, indeed, justification was deemed right or necessary. The more traditional chivalric repertoire was seen to be in tension with newer humanist and Christian stresses upon virtue, piety, and learn-ing. Some writers even said that the codes were in irreconcilable con-flict with each other, while others worked to bring them into alignment. Cultural tension might be addressed, and decisions might be made about which repertoire to embrace. Or it might be lived with, glossed over, or ignored. Quite possibly, the majority of English gentlemen did not bother the literate record with justifications for their standing, paying their dues to chivalric and Christian institutions as occasions demanded. Yet the cultural legacy handed down to posterity was over-whelmingly shaped by those gentlemen, and other social commenta-tors, who reckoned that justification was required. Robert Boyle was one of those. Many of his early ethical writings were experiments in locating and collating cultural resources appropriate to his own partic-ular situation and defensible in general terms. In this section and the two following I want to treat some aspects of those experiments, noting how his preferred solutions bore upon the personal gentle, Christian, and philosophical identity that was emerging by the 1660s. I intend to keep the narrative moving, therefore, from an individual's experi-ments in gentle identity to the credibility of his experiments.

An early manuscript called "The Gentleman" (probably dating from around the same time as "The Aretology") rummaged among different criteria for identifying and defending gentle standing.[51] (Although this

---

well as a series of essays on sin, piety, the moral management of time, the control of thinking, and the practice of meditation. Harwood's editorial introduction is a valuable exercise in situating Boyle's ethical views within a general European humanist cultural context. For extended historiographic treatment of Boyle's early ethical essays, see Shapin, "Personal Development and Intellectual Biography: The Case of Robert Boyle."

51. Boyle Papers, Vol. 37, ff. 160–63 (all quotations in the following three para-graphs—except where otherwise indicated—are from this manuscript). J. R. Jacob (*Boyle*, 48–49) argues strongly that this document must have preceded "The Aretology" since it represents a more traditionally chivalric conception and is "clearly in conflict" with the other tract. I plead nescience about its precise date, nor does it much matter to my case whether the one preceded the other. I see all the early ethical writings as eclectic and synthetic experiments in making an identity rather than as the expressions of a *made* identity. The "conflict" Jacob refers to is, in any case, one which was not acknowledged by many late Tudor and Stuart gentlemen.

manuscript was not published, I take it—together with other materials—as evidence of how Boyle presented himself as a gentleman, and, indeed, sentiments expressed therein resonate through texts printed until the end of his life.) Despite his father's pedigree, Boyle saw no reason to dispute the role played by blood and birth in producing the circumstances in which gentility might be expressed. It was a matter of "Custome" that "the Title of Gentleman" was practically confined "to them that are so by Descent," just as custom was pleased to justify the role of birth on grounds of informal hereditary theory: "Great Persons are beleev'd, together with the Lives they give their Posterity, to transmit to them very effective Seeds or Sparkes of that Greatnesse of Courage & Desseins that was eminent in themselves."[52] Boyle did *not* disagree with the humanist case that the "true Seat of Nobility" was "much more properly establish't in the mind then in the Blood." Yet, since the institutions of gentlemanly recognition acknowledged, and traded upon, the signs of descent, Boyle's ideal gentleman might as well be born one. The more ancient the descent the better. Boyle noted the envy of anciently established gentlemen at the fast-rising "Mushroom-Nobility."

"Nobility of Extraction" was a serviceable condition. It endowed an individual with a prior presumption of moral character that was independent of his own actions. He did not have to *win* attributions of valor, magnanimity, faithfulness, or truthfulness; he merely had not to give occasion for such attributions to be withdrawn: "he has little else to do, but to conserve by his Actions, that Esteem that his Birth has given which makes Men presume to have merit, till his owne Indiscretion declare the Contrary." He who lacked gentle birth needed "Some Time to purchase that Esteeme that the Sole Knowledge of the other's Extraction shall have præacquir'd him." Literally and figuratively, birth opened doors. Noble descent gives the gentleman "a Free Admittance into many Companys, whence Inferior Persons (tho never so Deserving) are commonly excluded."[53] Birth enhanced the ascription of goodness, as it increased the power of doing good. Noble descent disposed princes to award places of power and influence. Boyle acknowledged that the gentleman's integrity and freedom of action contained a large element of cultural attribution. Actions performed by a nobleman may appear as "very high Civilitys" which, performed by a meaner man, will "looke like bare Dutys; if not Necessity." Yet

52. Unlike Jacob, I do not read these passages necessarily as endorsing the role of birth, merely stating the views and consequent constraints of custom.

53. Cf. Boyle, "Philaretus," 3: "A man of meane Extraction (Tho neuer so aduantag'd by Greate meritts) is seldome admitted to the Priuacy & the secrets of greate ones promiscuously; & scarce dares pretend to it, for feare of being censur'd sawcy, or an Intruder."

"an Illustrious Descent" was itself an objective circumstance working in favor of integrity and free action: he who possessed gentility by birth was free of the necessity of laboring to secure it. Effortless superiority came more easily to those whose superiority cost no effort.

For many of the same reasons, Boyle recommended his ideal gentleman to be rich. Following sentiments widely expressed in the contemporary courtesy literature, Boyle did not value magnificence so much as means well adapted to one's condition in life: "a Good Fortune is not any thing of Absolute but onely Relative: consisting in a Competency . . . proportion'd to a Man's Condition & his Birth. . . . his Estate ought to be suitable to his Condition." On the whole, it was better to be somewhat richer than one's condition, for then one could support "New Titles." And, Boyle pertinently added, this was especially important "in Familys whose Honors are of a fresh Creation," where wealth is needed to "purchase Alliances," and "where men are oblig'd to live with more Eclats . . .; to derive from that Splendor an Eminence it owes not to its Antiquity; & leave men no reason to suspect, that their Humors retaine any thing of the meanesse of the Quality of their Ancestors."

Nothing binds the sentiments in Boyle's early ethical manuscripts more firmly to consensual early modern ethical thinking than the commendation of Aristotelian "mediocrity." It is, however, remarkable that Boyle reckoned that his own birth was so precisely positioned at the golden mean of basic social identities. He congratulated himself upon not being the eldest son, and, hence, not having to assume the responsibilities attached to the heir to the Cork title. Analyzing his "Humor" as one which "indispose[d] him to the distracting Hurry of the World," he said that heirship would have been, for him, "but a Glittering kind of Slauery," committing him to a course of public life for which he was temperamentally unfitted. Interestingly, Boyle accounted himself of sufficiently modest social standing that epistemic sources were open to him that would be closed to someone of grander condition. Gesturing at the distinctive patterns of discourse obtaining in relations between a man and his inferiors, superiors, and equals, Boyle noted that

> titular Greatnesse is euer an impediment to the Knowledge of many
> retir'd Truths, that cannot be attain'd without Familiarity with meaner
> Persons, & such other Condiscentions, as fond opinion in greate men
> disapproues & makes Disgracefull. But now our Philaretus was borne
> in a Condition, that neither was high enuf to proue a Temptation to
> Lazinesse; nor low enuf to discourage him from aspiring.[54]

A sharper image of Boyle's self-presentation and its cultural location

---

54. Ibid. Chapter 8 below treats Boyle's mature relations with tradesmen and artisans.

emerges from private and public writings about contemporary gentle-manly practices which he *rejected* and against which he systematically argued. A related early manuscript drew an ugly portrait of "A Mere Fine Gentleman" as a bragging, boozing, swearing, and wenching oaf.[55] He was a man who boasted of the nobility of his family while doing everything within his compass to bring disgrace upon it. He was "a constant frequenter of Taverns" and it was there that his true demerits were most visible and audible: "When his Belly begins to swell, he opens his Doublet & his Brest together, Wine alone having the Power to wash away this point of Dissimulation, & make him more candid Drunke then Sober." He "uses God's most Sacred Name" merely as punctuation, and sex as a form of animal amusement. From a posture of professed chastity, Boyle lectured the gentle gallant on his immoral conduct of romantic love:

> Wenching hee esteems a most Gentile quality. . . . He is so generall a Sectary of the French, that he wil not Bate [?] them so much as the Pox it self, but wil needs be Frenchify'd to the very Bones. . . . He usually devotes himself to such a one, who, with the richness of the Booty, promises him (by her Behavior) the easyness of the Conquest. Ladys, that weare the Chastity of their Harts in their very Lookes, he seldom dares so much as attempt.

All of these themes identifying contemporary fashionable society as debauched and debased were prominent in the Christian courtesy literature of seventeenth-century England and all were further devel-oped in the "Aretology" and in such published Boyle tracts as *Seraphic Love* and *A Free Discourse against Customary Swearing*. True Christian "moral gallantry" was forcefully juxtaposed to traditional practices by which honor and reputation were established. The "mere fine" gentle-man was identified as the servant of his animal nature, as unfree in the ostensible taking of his "pleasure" as any servant acting at the behest of a human master: "Passions, as they ar Excellent Seruants, so they ar Very bad Masters"; "To ouercom ordinary Temptations is Comendable but to ouercom Gyant-like Temptations is Glorious."[56] By contrast, the Christian gentleman who sought and attained moral con-trol of himself displayed the authentic emblems of internal command and integrity. The foundations of genuine honor were wholly internal, yet piety, charity, and sincerity gave unmistakable external signs of one's internal state.[57]

If swearing by God's name was considered a fashionable means of

55. Boyle Papers, Vol. 37, f. 169. All quotations in this paragraph are from this manuscript.
56. Boyle, "Aretology," 24, 116–17.
57. Ibid., esp. 7–8, 24, 72–74, 105, 130–33, 136.

stressing commitment and stipulating sincerity, then Boyle judged that
the man who refrained from swearing secured the greatest credibility:

> How unlikely is it that (by believing you speak truth, because you use
> to swear you do not lye) [men] should take your readiness to trans-
> gress one of God's commandments, for a proof that you dare not
> break another. . . . For in oaths (as in most other things) too constant
> a frequency depreciates that authority, which their rareness, as well
> as nature, gives them. . . . No, no; he needs not many oaths, that uses
> few; for to be known to make a conscience of an oath, will gain your
> words more credit than the swearing of a thousand.[58]

Moral gallantry proceeded from a more defensible conception of gentlemanly valor: "true Infamy is the Offspring of our [own] Actions not
other men's bad Opinions," and "an excessive feare of Dishonor it
self is Dishonorable." Boyle dissented from the pervasive aristocratic
admiration of military courage, celebrated the valor of a philosophical
and moral character, and deemed the most manly virtue to be fortitude.[59]

Boyle's conception of gentility therefore rejected some major features of the contemporary system of recognitions and entitlements
while accepting and respecifying others. For example, the significance
of birth and wealth as matter-of-fact criteria was not disputed, and,
while Christian morality was stressed, its practice was identified as a
genuine expression of traditional chivalric virtues—courage, magnanimity, faithfulness, and so on. Nevertheless, Boyle's endorsement of
Christian virtue and learning precipitated a series of practical problems
in situating himself within gentle culture. The most fundamental of
these problems involved finding and displaying a warrantable solution
to the ancient debate over whether the happy and virtuous gentle
life was to be lived actively or contemplatively, in public or in private
disengagement from civic forums.[60]

If, as Boyle said, the world of contemporary polite society was debased and corrupt, was the Christian gentleman to separate himself
from it? Was he, like traditional Christian hermits and philosophers,
to express his engagement with the divine by his rejection of the civic?
Boyle grappled with this problem throughout his adolescence and

58. Boyle, "Free Discourse against Customary Swearing," 10; see also 8, 11, 14. Cf.
Browne, *Pseudodoxia Epidemica*, 25: "Certainly of all men a Philosopher, should be
no swearer: for an oath which is the end of controversies in Law cannot determine
any[thing] here." For fashionable swearing in Restoration culture there are few better
examples than some of the plays of Boyle's elder brother the earl of Orrery. Boyle's
brother-in-law, Charles Rich, was also said to be a notorious swearer.

59. Boyle Papers, Vol. 196, ff. 63–67 ("Of Valour"), quoted in Jacob, *Boyle*, 63.

60. For a fuller account of these traditions and the ways in which seventeenth-century
scientific culture engaged with them, see Shapin, "'The Mind Is Its Own Place.'"

adult life. Nor was the problem purely conceptual: day by day he
was presented with decisions about commitment versus retirement,
fulfilling the normal social obligations of a considerable aristocrat versus insisting upon the philosopher's culturally understood rights of
disengagement. Where he placed himself, and how he advertised the
reasons for that placement, constituted bases for establishing identity
and for justifying the cultural goods produced from that placement.

Boyle's early ethical writings acknowledged the helps to virtue that
were offered by a life of solitary disengagement. At the same time,
he recognized the requirements of civic duty and experimented with
placements that acquitted both virtue and gentlemanly obligation. If
the tavern and the gaming-house were inconducive to virtue, then they
must be shunned as temptations. The virtuous man must learn how
to be alone, enjoying divine and self-conversation. There was no need
to go out of oneself for pleasure: "The Gallant he makes it his Plesure
to frolicke it in good Company; but Vertu teaches him how to meet
with good Company when he is alone":

> In sensual Plesures a man is for the most part forc'd to go [out of
> himself; and to go] abroad . . . to fetch in external Objects to furnish
> out his Delihts. The miser must haue his Bags, the Glutton his Dishes,
> the Drunkard his good-Company, and the wencher his Courtisane to
> satisfy their Appetites: and all this must they go seek for out of them-
> selues: whereas the Vertuus man finds . . Daintys, his Company, his
> Treasure, and his Mistres, always about him in his Breast.[61]

In "The Dayly Reflection" Boyle told his sister Katherine that "in
[his] solitary retirements" he "neuer thought the World but a greate
Bedlam, peopled with fooles and Knaues" with which he neither
wanted nor needed any traffic.[62] The posture of the disengaged
searcher after truth was commended as an antidote to temptation:
"[Knowledge] withdraws and diuerts our thouhts oftentimes from
Erthly and sensuall Objects, and so deliuers vs from many occasions
of Sinning."[63] Boyle also acknowledged the attractions of solitude as a
creative situation: "Solitary Friars" lose themselves in private contemplation, and "poets and amorists . . . loue those Places that sequester
them from all other Company."[64]

Yet Boyle did not in fact simply recommend retreat as the fittest
setting for a virtuous life. He fully acknowledged that the principles

61. Boyle, "Aretology," 73–74. This and similar passages in Boyle's early writings
strongly resonate with Stoical sentiments; see, for example, strikingly similar phraseology
in Epictetus, *Epictetus His Manuell* (trans. 1616), 91.
62. Boyle, "Dayly Reflection," 215–16.
63. Boyle, "Aretology," 56.
64. Boyle, "Doctrine of Thinking," 187, 195.

of moral virtue included "Naturall Courtesy or Humanity, consisting in an Esiness of Accesse and an Obliging Behauior." His injunction to take up a civic calling was justified in part by the accepted Renaissance gentlemanly obligation to contribute "to the Good of the Common-wealth."[65] Moreover, Boyle deemed it necessary to prove virtue by exposing it to all the temptations offered by the quotidian patterns of gentle society. It was good, on occasion, "to let our Youth haue a siht of the Riotous Courses of Euil Company" so that, when he necessarily came among them he might "not be a Nouice." Since it was not possible for someone of his condition wholly to reject civil conversation, tempta-tion must be turned into a test of self-command: "Temptations in this life cannot possibly be auoided, and to go out of the reach of Temta-tion is to go out of the World. Wherefor since yow cannot fly them, ouer com them."[66] Boyle did not, therefore, take a straightforwardly polar position in the debates over engagement and solitude as did many other early modern social commentators. Rather, he endeavored to attach his emerging conception of a happy and virtuous life to the merits associated with each of the repertoires. Acknowledging the irre-ducible civic obligations associated with anyone of his condition, he nevertheless sought ways of warranting disengagement as a civically virtuous state. Elements of both repertoires were, therefore, made available to construct and present an identity as Christian, gentleman, and philosopher. And, as I shall later note, Boyle's presentation did indeed become a prize for those extolling *both* activity and contempla-tion, a public and a private life.

The most superficial aspect of presentation of self is, paradoxically, one of the least visible to historical scrutiny. Lay assessments of identity in general and trustworthiness in particular have always proceeded partly upon the basis of physical presentation: physiognomy, costume, gesture, posture, patterns of speech, and facial expression. Erving Goffman distinguishes between impressions that individuals "give" and those they "give off" in face-to-face interaction.[67] Of course, in an age when sumptuary codes had not entirely disappeared, aristocratic standing might, in the absence of other information, be read off cos-tume and carriage, while Boyle's life also spanned periods in which the wearing of the wig or one's own hair, the manner and matter of eating and drinking, the exact form of a bow, the fabric out of which stockings were made, and the color of coats might signal precise reli-

65. Boyle, "Aretology," 49, 85.
66. Ibid., 79, 117.
67. Goffman, *Presentation of Self*, esp. 2–4. The former includes verbal and nonverbal communication in the usual narrow sense, and assumed to be intentional, while the latter involves a "wide range of action that others can treat as symptomatic of the actor," including actions presumed to be nonintentional.

gious and political allegiances. The physical body was thus a text on which basic social identity might be inscribed and which might be written upon to secure other identities.[68] Needless to say, the retrieval of Boyle's given-off impressions is, in almost all respects, a highly speculative exercise. Yet historians do have access to a reasonable amount of information about the state of his physical body and the way in which that bore upon his presentation of self. And, although it may appear at first glance that anatomical and physiological condition have little connection with the questions of identity, legitimacy, and credibility with which I am concerned, the ways in which those states were represented, perceived, and used in the local culture do indeed speak to these questions.

Throughout his life Boyle's purposefully disengaged posture was partially explained and excused by the understood poor state of his bodily health. At the same time, cultural resources were available which assisted an understanding of physical frailty as a badge of spirituality. As a boy and adolescent, Boyle seems to have had no more than the normal share of "agues" and other minor illness.[69] While at age sixteen he pointed to his "weakness" as a reason to avoid a military adventure, nothing then reported by his various tutors and governors gives reason to suspect an unusually frail constitution. The earliest evidence we have of Boyle's health problems coincides with his first Stalbridge period, a time at which he was, in any case, looking about for justifications to retreat from the full obligations of country sociability.[70] As early as 1647, he began to experience the first of many painful bouts with the stone that lasted throughout his life.[71] In summer 1649, he complained to Katherine of "a quotidian ague" which had then lasted several weeks and for which he had sought medical assistance. The condition was evidently so disabling that Boyle had to eschew horseback riding and was conveyed about in a litter, but not so disabling that it kept him away from his laboratory: "The nature of my disease forbids all

68. For general arguments linking body-as-text to early modern social and political action, see A. Bryson, "Rhetoric of Status."

69. His skepticism about the value of physicians and the efficacy of traditional therapeutics did, however, date from his Eton days: Boyle, "Philaretus," 17–18; see also Maddison, *Boyle,* 219–22. Aubrey (*Brief Lives,* 37) said that Boyle was "verie sickly and pale" at Eton, though more contemporary testimony tells against that. For accounts of how chronic and minor illnesses were understood and practically managed in seventeenth-century England, see Beier, *Sufferers and Healers;* idem, "Experience and Experiment."

70. Boyle to second earl of Cork, 14 July 1646, in Boyle, *Works,* VI, 44.

71. Boyle's condition was probably kidney rather than bladder stone: Birch, "Life of Boyle," cxxix. Samuel Hartlib also suffered from stone and his end of their correspondence through the late 1650s is a vivid record of the agonies of that condition: Boyle, *Works,* VI, 92–127; see also Burnet, "Character of a Christian Philosopher," 362.

Figure 1. Portrait of Robert Boyle at age sixty-two, after Johann Kerseboom, *ca.* 1689. (Courtesy of The National Portrait Gallery, London.)

strains."[72] Texts from the 1660s invoked "cramps" and "an odd quartianary distemper" to excuse not only delay in publication but stylistic imperfection, experimental incompleteness, and conceptual inconsistency.[73]

Gilbert Burnet reckoned that Boyle suffered from "feebleness of body" and "lowness of strength and spirits" for the last forty years of his life.[74] He do not *look* well: six feet tall and thin, visitors and friends tended to comment on his emaciated frame and valetudinary manner.[75] John Evelyn identified his fragility as a form of refinement and

72. Boyle to Lady Ranelagh, 2 and 31 August 1649, in Boyle, *Works,* VI, 48–50; Birch, "Life of Boyle," xliv–xlv; Maddison, *Boyle,* 75.

73. Among many examples, see Boyle, "Continuation of New Experiments," 276.

74. Burnet, "Character of a Christian Philosopher," 361–62; see also Birch, "Life of Boyle," cxxxvi–cxxxvii.

75. Aubrey, *Brief Lives,* 37; Maddison, *Boyle,* 222.

even of strength: "[His body was] so delicate that I have frequently compared him to a chrystal, or Venice glass; which, though wrought never so thin and fine, being carefully set up, would outlast the hardier metals of daily use."[76] Chapter 3 noted Walter Charleton's Hippocratic association of wit and bodily delicacy. The "finest wits," he wrote, are rarely committed to "the custody of gross and robust bodies; but for the most part [are lodged] in delicate and tender Constitutions."[77] It cannot be said that Boyle bore his illnesses with Stoic silence, and all his acquaintances were constantly kept apprised of the state of his health.

The early modern gentlemanly gaze was trained to discern humoral temperament from complexion and bodily form, and in Boyle many saw a man tending to melancholy, the scholar's occupational disease. Indeed, while friends rejected imputations of melancholia, the young Boyle liked to describe himself as well as his Stalbridge circumstances as "melancholy."[78] In Boyle's early formulation, a melancholic presentation might be allusively associated with virtue, even if, within the codes of civil conversation, melancholic patterns of conduct could not be justified: "Men oftentimes in the Vertuus mistake seriousness, and employednes of Mind for Melancholy humors, as if the hart cud not be merry within without hanging out the flag of lafter at the Mouth. . . . The Vertuus ar melancholy, not because they ar Vertuus, but because they ar not Vertuus enuf."[79]

While one has little reason to doubt that Boyle's early illnesses were both genuine and distressing, his own friends and relations occasionally expressed their opinion that they were marks of a melancholic temperament or the price to be paid for a withdrawn and studious form of life. In the early 1650s, William Petty tried to dissuade Boyle from the "continual reading" which he and other friends thought was ruining Boyle's health. Petty delicately suggested possible hypochon-

76. Evelyn to William Wotton, 30 March 1696, in Evelyn, *Diary and Correspondence*, III, 351.

77. [Charleton], *Discourse Concerning the Different Wits of Men* (1669), 104–05. This text developed from a paper originally presented to the Royal Society.

78. E.g., Boyle to Lady Ranelagh, 13 May 1648, in Boyle, *Works*, VI, 45. The key sources here for scholarly melancholy are Ficino, *Three Books on Life* (1489), and Burton, *Anatomy of Melancholy* (1628), esp. 259–82 (cf. Heyd, "Burton's Sources on Enthusiasm and Melancholy"), and, for surveys of the attributed relationship between scholarly solitude and melancholy, see Klibansky, Panofsky, and Saxl, *Saturn and Melancholy*; Babb, *The Elizabethan Malady*, 9–10, 21–30; Shapin, "'The Mind Is Its Own Place,'" esp. 192–203; idem, "'A Scholar and a Gentleman,'" esp. 289–95.

79. Boyle, "Aretology," 68–69. Michael MacDonald (*Mystical Bedlam*, 151) notes a consequential association between melancholy presentation and gentility in seventeenth-century England: "Melancholy and gentility became boon companions."

driasis, speculating that the root-ailment was "your apprehension of many diseases, and a continual fear, that you are always inclining or falling into one or the other. . . . This distemper is incident to all that begin the study of diseases." Petty sought unsuccessfully to warn Boyle off excessive self-medication and to remind him of the properly manly disregard with which illness ought to be borne.[80] Boyle himself recognized that friends thought his condition was either psychologically caused or was induced by excessive study, but he favored the view that complications deriving from a childhood fall from a horse, combined with a weak inherited constitution, were at the roots of all his problems.[81]

Like many devout seventeenth-century Protestants, Boyle persistently set his illness within a providential framework.[82] Convinced that orthodox physicians were unlikely to do him much good, Boyle raised self-treatment to the level of high art, reporting that he had cured himself of a "violent quotidian" by applying to his wrists a mush of salt, hops, and currants, of cramp by wearing a ring made of elk's horn, and of an attack of stone by drinking several ounces of quite rancid walnut oil.[83] Complaints about his poor eyesight, necessitating the use of amanuenses throughout the rest of his life, began to surface while Boyle was still in his twenties.[84] By the time that Boyle's philosophical identity was taking shape in the 1650s and 1660s, it was widely understood that he wore the badges of a "hard student," liable to constitutionally and habitually induced distempers that might excuse normal gentlemanly obligations to civil conversation. In July 1670, Boyle suffered a stroke, and, although he made a relatively full recovery over the following year, he was left with a tremor in his hands, and his last twenty years were marked by an even more withdrawn

80. William Petty to Boyle, 15 April 1653, in Boyle, *Works*, VI, 137–39. Cf. G. W. Jones, "Boyle as a Medical Man," 143; Hunter and Macalpine, "Harvey and Boyle," 117; L. S. King, "Boyle as Amateur Physician."

81. Boyle, "Medicinal Experiments," 315–16; idem, "Some Considerations Touching the Usefulness of Experimental Natural Philosophy," 200.

82. See, for example, Macfarlane, *Family Life of Ralph Josselin*, 163–82; Wear, "Puritan Perceptions of Illness," 70–78.

83. Boyle, "Some Considerations Touching the Usefulness of Experimental Natural Philosophy," 157–58; idem, "Reconcileableness of Specific Medicines," esp. 104–05, 115.

84. E.g., Boyle to John Mallet, 5 September 1655, quoted in Maddison, *Boyle*, 85; Boyle, "Some Motives to the Love of God" (1659), 243; idem, "Defence against Linus" (1662), 122; Boyle to Henry Oldenburg, *ca.* 1660s, in Boyle, *Works*, VI, 37–38. In "A Proëmial Essay" (1661), 317, Boyle importantly excused his tendency not to cite other authors' views by pointing to the "weakness of my eyes" which "this long time kept me from reading almost any books, save the Scripture." See also Burnet, "Character of a Christian Philosopher," 352, 361–62; Maddison, *Boyle*, 180–81, 187, 219; M. B. Hall, "Boyle's Method of Work," 111–14.

posture.[85] Thus, the state of his body was available to be read both as an expression of the state of his mind and as a justification for a disengaged and spiritual form of life. Physiology supported culture even as cultural expectations were discerned in physiological states.

A Christian and a Gentleman

Boyle's presentation of self as a Christian virtuoso was central both to his public identity and to the utility of that identity for the program of experimental knowledge-making. I have already indicated that such a presentation was constructed out of standard cultural materials, even though the character and the potency of Boyle's presentation were specific. This section needs to explore Boyle's identity as *Christian* gentleman in more detail. I want especially to address those aspects of Boyle's religious identity which bore most powerfully upon the perceived legitimacy and integrity of the philosophical practice cultivated by himself and others from midcentury. How were valued features of Christian religiosity made over into a fit identity for a gentleman-virtuoso?

Robert Boyle was by no means the first publicly recognized Christian gentleman of seventeenth-century England, yet he was one of the most influential. His life and deeds were widely known and remarked upon, even among those who had little interest in natural philosophy. His birth and standing made his example particularly prized for those arguing the case for Christian gentility, not least in the learned community, where Boyle's "honourable" standing shed honor on the experimental enterprise. It was an immensely *useful* life. Patterns of Christian and virtuous gentility were widely available to Boyle: from the late Tudor productions of the Philip Sidney circle to Sir Thomas Browne's *Christian Morals* (comp. *ca.* 1650) to Richard Brathwait's *The English Gentleman* of 1630. By the Restoration the pattern was being further consolidated, against uncongenial court trends, in Christian courtesy and ethical texts produced by such writers as Clement Ellis, Sir George Mackenzie, Richard Allestree, William Ramesey, and many others.

I do not profess to know *why* Robert Boyle chose a publicly visible life of Christian virtue. A self-inventory of his native temperament and disposition—such as was widely recommended by contemporary courtesy writers and educationalists—may have had something to do with it.[86] A decision to celebrate the Cork-ideal—as was made by sisters

85. For his 1670 illness, see Maddison, *Boyle*, 145–47; Boyle to John Mallet, 23 May 1671, in Boyle, *Works*, I, xcix–c. Health was occasionally, but not always, offered as the major excuse for retirement; see, for example, Boyle Papers, Vol. 35, ff. 194, 203; Birch, "Life of Boyle," cxxviii–cxxix; Maddison, *Boyle*, 177–78, 188.

86. For Boyle's sense of the importance of such self-assessment in choice of vocation, see his "Aretology," 86–90.

Katherine and Mary—may also be germane: it was a wholly plausible, though in no way necessary, thing for a younger son of such a father to do. Boyle himself set great store upon the months immediately following his return to England and residence with the Ranelagh family, "where he heard many pious discourses, & saw great store pious examples," seeing the hand of "a gracious Providence" in this experience.[87] Whatever the idiosyncratic reasons for Boyle's decision, one needs to note both that such a choice was not without relevant precedents and that the serious and systematic embrace of a reflectively religious life was relatively rare for someone of Boyle's condition and degree. This made him a great prize for the party of virtue, and a greater prize for the community of authors concerned to inscribe the inducements to virtue in the formal record of literate culture. I want to discuss some features of Boyle's religiosity in a way that connects them to the perceived legitimacy and credibility of philosophical goods.

Personal providentialism of various forms was not uncommon among seventeenth-century English Protestants of various social conditions. The God who inspected individual hearts could also take action to reward or punish what He found there. Nor was it rare for devout Protestants periodically to study the texts of their own lives for indications of divine intercession. For the young Boyle the most accessible model of a highly personal providentialism was, of course, his own father. Boyle endorsed his father's view of God's personal superintendence; he incorporated it into his own way of accounting for events in his life; and he made providentialism publicly available as an understanding of who he was and why his practice ought to be accounted sincere and legitimate. The autobiographical "Philaretus" repeatedly argued that divine intercession alone could account for remarkable events in his childhood and adolescence, and then used that evidence of providence to construct a narrative which made his own life visible as divinely shaped.

Proof that from an early age he was a special "Obiect of Heu'ns Care" was readily available: when seven years old he was saved from drowning in an Irish stream; a storm that delayed his departure for Eton was accounted "not only a Tast but an Omen (& an Earnest) of his future Fortune"; at Eton a bedroom wall collapsed and would have crushed him "had not his Bed been curtain'd by a watchfull Prouidence." These and "diuers other . . . Deliuerances" he "wud not ascribe . . . vnto Chance, but would be still industrious to perceiue the hand of Heu'n in all these Accidents: & indeed he would professe that in the Passages of his Life he had obseru'd so gratious & so peculiar a Conduct of Prouidence, that he should be equally blind & vngreatfull,

87. British Museum Sloane MSS 4229, f. 68 (quoted in Maddison, *Boyle*, 53–54).

shud he not both Discerne & Acknowledge it."[88] Boyle's record of his
conversion experiences while on the grand tour, though not exceptional for devout Protestants, likewise implicated a deity who specially
laid on "Claps of Thunder" and "Flashes of lightning" to stimulate his
religious awakening.[89] His early essay on sin urged men to take special
note of "the Dispensations of Prouidence in particular Familys and
Persons," and, for these, Boyle said, one would not have to burrow in
the "Ancient Chronicles."[90]

Boyle's claim that particular persons were specially touched by divine
providence bears an important resemblance to his specification of the
natural philosopher's identity as he helped forge it through the 1650s
and 1660s. In the mid-1640s he had used familiar humanist resources
in identifying what he called "Heroicke Spirits." These were individuals endowed with an extraordinary degree of virtue or intellect, and,
although such qualities might be differentially excited by varying social
and political environments, Boyle expressed himself convinced that
heroic goodness or intellect might be reliably read as a sign of divine
intercession.[91] God picked just a few individuals as instruments to work
His will: "thes Heroicke Spirits are not excited euery Yeare: but perhaps one or 2 in an age: when it pleases God to reforme Arts or Mores:
or make some great reuolution in Commonwealths." Such heroic spirits appeared not just in moral and theological domains but also in
philosophy (Plato, Aquinas, Pico della Mirandola), medicine (Aesculap-
ius, Hippocrates, Galen, Paracelsus), astronomy (Copernicus, Tycho,
Galileo), and the mechanical arts (Dürer, Stevin).[92]

Boyle's conception of the natural philosopher as "priest of nature"
has now been well documented.[93] The roles of the natural philosopher

88. Boyle, "Philaretus," 5, 7, 15–16; see also idem, "Some Motives to the Love of
God," 289–90; idem, "Christian Virtuoso," 519–22; Harwood, *Early Essays*, xxxvi. Boyle
also saw strong evidence for the hand of providence in "the strange revolutions" afflicting Ireland: Boyle to Lady Ranelagh, 27 February 1647, in Boyle, *Works*, I, xxxvi.
For sister Mary's parallel uses of personal providentialism, see Rich, *Autobiography*, e.g.,
1, 3, 17–21.
89. Boyle, "Philaretus," 32 (also 34–35); and Hunter, "Casuistry in Action," 95–97
(for Boyle's continuing anxieties about the purity of his religious belief). For Pyrrhonian
crises as a topic in seventeenth-century religious development, see Trevor-Roper, "The
Great Tew Circle," 201–04.
90. Boyle, "Of Sin," 148; cf. Boyle to Alice Barrymore, 21 December 1649, quoted
in Maddison, *Boyle*, 75.
91. Boyle, "Aretology," 130–32.
92. Boyle Papers, Vol. 192, ff. 123–24 (quoted in Harwood, *Early Essays*, xxx). There
is a clear resemblance between Boyle's views and the *prisca* tradition mobilized by Isaac
Newton: McGuire and Rattansi, "Newton and the 'Pipes of Pan.'"
93. Fisch, "The Scientist as Priest"; Jacob, *Boyle*, 96–118; Schaffer, "Godly Men and
Mechanical Philosophers."

and the priest were anciently allied. Those who systematically contemplated nature were bound to become pious: "the noblest and most intelligent praises, that have been paid Him by the priests of nature, have been occasioned and indited by the transcending admiration, which the attentive contemplation of the fabric of the universe . . . justly produced in them."[94] As the only rational and verbal of God's creatures, all men, in Boyle's view, possessed a general obligation and fitness for performing the offices of nature's priests: "reason is a natural dignity, and knowledge a prerogative, that can confer priesthood without unction or imposition of hands." Thus, every man was "born the priest of nature" and labored under the consequent obligation "to return thanks and praises to his Maker, not only for himself, but for the whole creation."[95] Every man, fulfilling his nature as human being, possessed the duty to be "Spokesman for the Commonwealth of Nature."[96]

Boyle also took a view about the differential distribution of *special* philosophical skills. *Certain* men were more fit than others to serve as priests in the divine temple. Those who had labored to acquire greater and more detailed knowledgeability of nature or superior manipulative skill in displaying natural objects were better able to perform priestly-philosophical functions: "such persons have such piercing eyes."[97] Boyle also advanced a remarkable providentialist theory of the distribution of philosophical gifts. Rejecting the Paracelsian and Helmontian view that the mysteries of chemistry were disclosed to some men "by good angels, or by nocturnal visions," Boyle announced himself nonetheless persuaded that "the favour of God does (much more than most men are aware of) vouchsafe to promote some men's proficiency in the study of nature." God guided certain philosophers' efforts in two specific and important ways: by "protecting their attempts from those unlucky accidents, which often make ingenuous and industrious endeavours miscarry," and, more important, by steering their philosophical intuitions, "directing them to those happy and pregnant hints, which an ordinary skill and industry may so improve, as to do such things, and make such discoveries by virtue of them, as both others, and the person himself, whose knowledge is thus increased, would

94. Boyle, "Disquisition about Final Causes," 401; see also idem, "Some Considerations Touching the Usefulness of Experimental Natural Philosophy," 32, 55, 57. For his early characterization of contemplative men as "Priuy Counsellors of Nature," see idem, "Aretology," 29.

95. Boyle, "Some Considerations Touching the Usefulness of Experimental Natural Philosophy," 8, 32.

96. Boyle Papers, Vol. 8, f. 138r.

97. Boyle, "Some Considerations Touching the Usefulness of Experimental Natural Philosophy," 63; see also Fisch, "The Scientist as Priest," 259.

scarce have imagined to be possible." God Himself is the "dispenser of the chief mysteries of nature," and God chooses to which individuals He will so reveal His mysteries.[98] Boyle's readers were thus invited to identify the farseeing and ingenious natural philosopher (Boyle) as God's instrument, doing God's work, reading God's Book and speaking by divine guidance.[99]

Personal providentialism was also put to work in presenting an especially powerful version of a sincere and morally integrated self. A God who so invigilated the individual was not to be fobbed off with mere external acts of devotion. Such a God, in such a relationship with His chosen people, demanded purity of mind and heart. Here as elsewhere, there is no reason to insist on the novelty of the cultural materials with which Boyle worked in developing his identity. Conceptions of an invigilating God and requirements for an invigilating interior dialogue between 'me and myself' were, of course, widely distributed in Protestant culture. The significant originality consisted in Boyle's adaptation of familiar resources to particular circumstances and, eventually, in the plausible presentation of a life combining aristocracy and pious virtue. Boyle's early ethical essays experimented with conceptions of God's relationship to the virtuous man and what that relationship required. The resulting picture of how one ought to live contrasted the life of "heroic virtue" with chivalric conceptions of gentility. It imposed upon the virtuous man a system of discipline and mental management that shaped the visible quotidian patterns of his life. And it made those practices of discipline available as a public warrant for the sincerity and integrity of him who imposed them upon himself.

Boyle's early ethical writings identified the properties of moral virtue as "Syncerity, Integrity, and Perseuerance." All of these required the

98. Boyle, "Some Considerations Touching the Usefulness of Experimental Natural Philosophy," 61–62. Boyle's anonymous first publication claimed that extraordinary discoveries in physick were "rather inspired than acquired": "Epistolical Discourse" (composed *ca.* 1648, published 1655), 384. And into the 1660s he professed sympathy with those "ancient heathens" who referred extraordinary skill in healing "to the gods, or godlike persons" ("Some Considerations Touching the Usefulness of Experimental Natural Philosophy," 200). Later, Boyle pointed to ancient practices by which even heathen philosophers acknowledged divine inspiration: "Christian Virtuoso, Second Part," 763.

99. There are clear signs that Boyle maintained a providential view of discovery throughout his career and that this was widely known. The Somerset virtuoso John Beale repeatedly ascribed Boyle's inventiveness to providence, claiming "that (confining to the philosophical affair) never was man so deeply indebted to God as you are" (Beale to Boyle, 18 April 1666, in Boyle, *Works*, VI, 398–400, quoting 400; cf. Beale to Boyle, 25 January 1667 and 16 February 1680, in ibid., 423–24, 441–43 [on 442]). Certainly, his friend Gilbert Burnet pointedly referred to this sort of providentialism in his funeral sermon for Boyle. Scientific success, Burnet said, is so variably distributed among individuals "that the difference can be resolved into nothing, but a secret direction and blessing of Providence": Burnet, "Character of a Christian Philosopher," 343–44.

virtuous man not only to do virtuous deeds but to do them for virtuous reasons and to think virtuously in doing them. Integrity demanded that one "embrace all Vertus, and detest all Vices without any exception or reserue." One had to be perfect and entire in pursuit of virtue. There was no such thing as a private sin—not in the commission nor indeed in the intention, "for the Conscience . . . is more then 1000 Witnesses, and God more than a 1000 Consciences." An invigilating God respected no private places, not even, nor especially, the privacy of one's own heart.[100] Sincerity is "that Affection of Vertu that makes all it's Actions be don willingly, and for a Riht end." One could not do good while thinking ill: "Performances without Syncerity being but the Carcases of Vertu." A reliable sign of sincerity was the doing of good when there were no human witnesses and there was nothing to be gained from the act. The opposite temper to sincerity was hypocrisy, and this, as Boyle agreed with Christian courtesy writers, was one of the characteristic sins of the age. Hypocrisy is that "real Equivocation, which is A Simulation of Moral Vertu; or, if yow wil, the Putting on of a seeming Vertu, for the more easy attainment of a man's owne By-Ends." What was done out of "Desire of Aduantage and Desire of Applause" could not be done with sincerity and could not be virtuous. The prostitution of the noblest qualities of the soul to secure advantage was not only vicious, it was a mark of "a Base and Meane Spirit."[101]

Nobility of spirit was expressed in commitment to truth-telling. Boyle early remarked upon his innate disposition towards truthfulness. It was a quality which was said to have especially endeared him to his father

> who vs'd (highly) to commend him [for] his Veracity: of which . . . he would often giue him this Testimony; that he neuer found him in a Lye in all his Life time. And indeed Lying was a Vice both so contrary to his nature & so inconsistent with his Principles, that as there was scarce any thing he more greedily desir'd then to know the Truth, so was there scarce any thing he more perfectly detested; then not to speake it. . . . So perfect an Enemy was he to a Ly, that he had rather accuse himselfe of another fault, then be guilty of that.[102]

100. Boyle, "Aretology," 101, 104. For parallel early discussions of sincerity and integrity, see idem, "Dayly Reflection," esp. 203–04.

101. Boyle, "Aretology," 105, 108–09, 112–13. Among the "most vsual Symptoms of a Dissembler" were "Extolling his own Goodness: as Mountebanks boast more the Excellency of their Receits, then the most able Fisitians" (ibid., 111).

102. Boyle, "Philaretus," 5–6; see also idem, "Some Motives to the Love of God," 244. Boyle related this particular story because, in common with a host of Tudor and Stuart moralists and educationalists, he reckoned that "men's natiue Dispositions" were seen most clearly when they were very young and when they were dying.

Like many Christian moralists of the period, Boyle identified a religious basis for truthfulness: the devil was "the Father of Lys."[103] Finally, perserverance was the property that enabled the virtuous man "to persist in the ways of vertu to the very End . . . notwithstanding all Discouragements and Oppositions."[104] It was the moral technology that informed and facilitated the disciplining of self which fitted the virtuous man to withstand divine invigilation.

Lionel Trilling has identified an early modern moment at which an arguably new element entered the moral life of Europe, the "quality of the self which we call sincerity." When Polonius instructed Laertes (I, iii) "to thine own self be true," he simultaneously pointed to the condition in which one could "not then be false to any man." Trilling brilliantly observed that sincerity was at once an attributed state of personal existence, a moral relationship between individuals, and a product of "the most arduous effort." Sincerity and the avoidance of falsehood to God and man was the "fulfillment of a public role."[105] When you observed a man doing good, you could not conclude that he did it with sincerity. As sincerity was a state of mind accessible only to God, you had to find outward signs of inward states of virtue. What you saw, and what you might take as the emblem of a man's sincerity, was the quotidian pattern of discipline which he imposed upon himself and which alone warranted that good acts were virtuously done. Boyle's religiosity was thus a strand in the development of practical presentations of early modern notions of the self. Like many early seventeenth-century Protestant moralists, Boyle laid great stress upon the development and celebration of moral technologies for disciplining the mind.[106] Those techniques could be described, and, indeed, much of Boyle's early writing was concerned with their description. But they might also be made visible in the quotidian routines of an individual life. A disciplined mind was understood to be signified by a disciplined life. Those who knew Boyle were presumed to be able to read the structure of his day as testimony to the quality of his mind: one who was true to his own self and who could not be false to any man.

Boyle followed the general drift of late Tudor and Stuart Christian moralism in arguing for the necessity of discipline and vocation. All men required a calling: it is a "souueraigne Preseruatiue agenst Idle-

103. Boyle, "Doctrine of Thinking," 198; idem, "Occasional Reflections," 345; see also idem, "Aretology," 6, 49.
104. Boyle, "Aretology," 114.
105. Trilling, *Sincerity and Authenticity*, 2–6. Trilling plausibly speculated (12–16) that concern for sincerity was a situated response to the contemporary theatrical and court cultures of feigning, pretence, and personation, and to the vastly increased social mobility that made such theatricality expedient.
106. See, e.g., Weintraub, *Value of the Individual*, ch. 10; Taylor, *Sources of the Self*, chs 8–9.

ness, (that mother of Vices) and an excellent preuention [against] a world of Idle, melancholick and exorbitant thouhts, and vn-warrantable Actions. . . . An honest Calling is a School of Vertu."[107] The avoidance of idleness was both a divine obligation and a way of achieving virtue. The precise form of labor thus enjoined ought to vary according to individual constitution—"euery man is not bound to labor with his hands: there is a Sweat of the Braines, perhaps no less Toylsom then the Sweat of the Brow"—though Boyle said he occasion-ally found advantage in doing bits of physical work, "digging, sawing of Wood, and such other ways." Indeed, every man ought to "lern som indifferent skill . . . or som manuall Vocation"—"not that I wud haue a Gentleman make a Trade his Bisness"[108] And some ways of ex-pending time were clearly more capable of forming virtue than others. The young Boyle reckoned accordingly that there was no virtue to be had in the quotidian life of the fashionable country gentleman, a potentially "vseful Instrument of the Publick Good," who elected to "spend his whole stock of ‹precius› time in Carding, Dicing, Hunting, reuelling, Seeing of Plays, Reading of Romances, Powdring his haire, Staring vpon looking-glasses, courting of Ladys that he means not to marry (not to mention what is worse) and in Sum make Vacation his only Vocation."[109]

During his Stalbridge period, Boyle made the practice of disciplined meditation and self-examination into one of the structuring compo-nents of his daily life. A characteristically Protestant interrogation of self was developed into a solution to the mundane problem of idleness and the moral problem of avoiding vice and encouraging virtue. "A tru and searching Self-examination" was labor—"a very difficult peece of Bisnes."[110] Self-contemplation was more "noble" and "worthy" than

107. Boyle, "Aretology," 85; see also idem, "Of Time and Idleness," esp. 237; idem, "Of Sin," 151; idem, "Occasional Reflections," 336–37; cf. Brathwait, *English Gentleman*, 46, 103–64 (which was possibly a major source of Boyle's treatment); and, for typical later English injunctions to gentle industry and vocation, Barrow, "Of Industry, in Our Particular Calling, as *Gentlemen*," in idem, *Works*, III, 334–44; [Allestree], *Gentleman's Calling*, 1–7, 72–88.

108. Boyle, "Aretology," 87–88; idem, "Of Time and Idleness," 244–46; see also Jacob, *Boyle*, 69–70.

109. Boyle, "Aretology," 88. For general Christian humanist condemnation of idle-ness, see, e.g., Todd, *Christian Humanism*, 32–33, ch. 5. Boyle was not above a little hawking, hunting, and fishing himself: Boyle, "A Proëmial Essay," 316; idem, "Occa-sional Reflections," 390–93, 399–405, 410–11, 418–19.

110. Boyle, "Aretology," 90; also idem, "Of Sin," 166–67; see also Browne, "Christian Morals" (*ca.* 1650), 270–71 (on the virtues of self-conversation); Lewalski, *Protestant Poetics*, chs 5–6; Todd, *Christian Humanism*, 27–30 (for general Protestant meditational techniques and Christian humanist approval of self-examination); and Weintraub, *Value of the Individual*, esp. 231–32 (for self-examination and the form of English Protestant autobiography).

any other intellectual employment.[111] An early essay on "Self-Conversation" argued that "we ouht to be as much concern'd in the Knowledg of our selves, as we ar in it's object: & he wil hardly deserve the Esteem of a Wise-man, that must always travel out of himself for a Companion; that wants Company whensoever he is without it."[112] Self-examination makes a man "both the Teacher, the Scholler and the Booke of his owne selfe."[113] In order to habituate and discipline the self to purity and sincerity, self-examination had to be done regularly and built into the fabric of daily life. The life of virtue was *work:* thought had to be controlled by arduous labor; a sincere self had to be laboriously constructed, inspected, and maintained. That disciplined labor was publicly visible to be taken as a token of inner sincerity and integrity.[114]

One of the notable marks of Boyle's Christian piety was his chastity. At age fifteen, Cork arranged a marriage for him, but, as he was then on the grand tour, it could not be executed until his return. He escaped marriage through his father's death, even though, as a minor, he might still have been cajoled into the match by his eldest brother. When the young lady married another, Robert was not, apparently, desolate, and sister Katherine, who knew him best, wrote to congratulate him on being set "at liberty from all appearances you have put on of being a lover; which though they cost you some pains and use of art, were easier, because they were but appearances."[115] In 1648 he acknowledged, and curtly dismissed, rumors that he was courting the beautiful and intelligent daughter of the earl of Monmouth, even though John Evelyn continued to credit the story.[116] In 1669 some of his Oxford friends canvassed the idea that Boyle marry Lady Mary Hastings, daughter of the earl of Huntingdon, but that plan too met with no enthusiasm.[117] In the event, Boyle lived contentedly either alone or,

111. Boyle, "Doctrine of Thinking," 185; see also idem, "Dayly Reflections." For Boyle's published views on thought-control and self-examination, see, e.g., idem, "Occasional Reflections."

112. Boyle Papers, Vol. 7, f. 291; see also idem, "Aretology," 52, 73–74; idem, "Occasional Reflections," 336–37. The pervasiveness of this trope in classical and early modern ethical writing is noted in Shapin, "'The Mind Is Its Own Place,'" 198, 210–11.

113. Boyle, "Dayly Reflections," 208.

114. As early as 1653 acquaintances seemed to be well aware of the basic structure of Boyle's meditational practices., e.g., William Petty to Boyle, 15 April 1653, in Boyle, *Works*, VI, 137–38.

115. Lady Ranelagh to Boyle, *ca.* 1645–46, in Boyle, *Works*, VI, 534; also Maddison, *Boyle*, 55–56; cf. Lady Ranelagh to Boyle, 3 June [1648?], in Boyle, *Works*, VI, 522.

116. Boyle to Lady Elizabeth Hussey, 6 June 1648, in Boyle, *Works*, VI, 46–47; Birch, "Life of Boyle," cxxxvii; Maddison, *Boyle*, 73n.; Evelyn to William Wotton, 30 March 1696, in Evelyn, *Diary and Correspondence*, III, 349–50.

117. Birch, "Life of Boyle," cxxxviii; John Wallis to Boyle, 17 July 1669, in Boyle, *Works*, VI, 459–60.

from 1668, with his pious sister Lady Ranelagh, undisturbed in their affection for one another after the death of Katherine's drunkard rake of a husband in 1670. There is nothing to contradict the idea that Boyle died a virgin. I have already noted that there was little unusual in a younger son of an aristocratic family remaining unmarried, and celibacy was recognized as a common condition for scholars and philosophers.[118] Nevertheless, Boyle publicly advertised his chastity and sensual disengagement, and he did so as signs of his personal integrity and as guarantees of an authentically Christian philosophy. As John Evelyn rhetorically asked, "What are we not to expect from so timely a consecration of your excellent abilities?"[119]

Boyle's early ethical experiments were preoccupied with the control of passion and carnality.[120] Meditational techniques were designed to effect the strictest mental discipline: "To make a man put a Bridle upon his thoughts."[121] The young Boyle debated love's proper object both as a speculative and as a practical matter. Did carnal love, even of a legitimate nature, compromise Christian piety and moral integrity? Could the passions fueling carnality be disciplined and redirected towards higher goals? His autobiography announced that he too felt the sexual passion of "boyling Youth" even as he gloried in his ability heroically to control those passions.[122] Papers from his Stalbridge period indicate his gradual identification with a celibate life and the cultural resources contingently linked with celibacy. The "Aretology" tried out a dubious derivation of an argument for celibacy from the cherished principle of the virtuous mean.[123] There are drafts of apparent love-letters, directed to no named person, and possibly representing experiments in assessing the strength of whatever carnal inclina-

118. Newton and Henry More were celibate; John Locke and Thomas Hobbes lived single lives; and Robert Hooke was unmarried, though notably unchaste.

119. Evelyn to Boyle, 29 September 1659, in Evelyn, *Diary and Correspondence*, III, 121–26: "It was an extraordinary grace, that at so early years, and amidst the ardours of youth, you should be able to discern so maturely, and determine so happily: avoid the Syren, and escape the tempest. . . . You, Sir, found . . . that men then ceased to be wise when they began to be in love, unless, with you, they could turn nature into grace." Evelyn nevertheless regretted "that such a person as Mr. Boyle be so indifferent, [as to] decline a virtuous love."

120. For Boyle's autobiographical worries about uncontrollable thoughts (or what he called "raving"), especially as triggered by the reading of romances, see "Philaretus," e.g., 15, 17–18, 24; also idem, "Aretology," 18, 24, 90, 96, 117; idem, "The Doctrine of Thinking," 188–89, 192–95; Jacob, *Boyle*, 83-86; Harwood, *Early Essays*, xlviii–li.

121. Boyle Papers, Vol. 7, f. 291 ("Self-conversation").

122. Boyle, "Philaretus," 33; see also Jacob, *Boyle*, 39.

123. Boyle, "Aretology," 96: "If the Principal Act (or duty) of the Vertu be placed in Abstaining: then that Vice (generally) that Sins in the Defect, is less vnlike the Vertu, then that which is faulty in the Excesse: For the like Reason Whence to ouer-Abstaine from the Vse of Women (tho lawfull) is neere of kin to Chastity then Whoring is."

tions he had. By age twenty-one, however, he had evidently resolved never to marry: "I am constant to love but not to Women; or Constant to the Passion, not to the Persons. . . . Marriage is a Lottery: he that gets a Written Scroule gets much: but for one of those there are 100 blankes."[124] Although he professed himself formally no "enemy to matrimony," he acknowledged that he was widely considered to be one.[125] In later life he confided to Gilbert Burnet that "he abstained from purposes of marriage, at first out of policy, afterwards more philosophically."[126]

Boyle's disciplined control and redirection of carnality were developed into a further public token of his religiosity. In 1648, writing his essay on *Seraphic Love* from the former Augustinian priory occupied by his sister Mary Rich, Boyle elaborated a conception of platonic love appropriate to himself as Christian philosopher and suitable as a public moral statement.[127] He acknowledged that he had "never known the infelicities of [sensual] love" himself, and counseled those suffering from its effects to reconsider love's proper nature and object. The highest and purest form of love should be directed towards God: the practice of this seraphic love makes man tranquil, compared to "the disquiets, and the torments" of "sensual love." Those who genuinely wished to commit themselves to piety had to learn to renounce "the unmanly sensualities and trifling vanities" of the world, and to "undergo chearfully all the hardships and dangers, that are wont to attend a holy life."[128] Boyle's life *was* widely recognized as a holy one, spreading a holy aura over his practice of philosophy.

The virtuous identity Boyle recommended to others and proposed for himself was carefully qualified. Like the Christian courtesy writers of the early to mid-seventeenth century, Boyle was well aware of the widely acknowledged conflict between the codes of gentlemanly society

124. Boyle Papers, Vol. 44, ff. 94–112 ("Divrnall Observations, Thoughts & Collections. Begun at Stalbridge April 25th 1647"), esp. ff. 94v–97; see also Boyle to Alice Barrymore (his sister), 21 December 1649, in Boyle, *Works*, VI, 51–52; Fell-Smith, *Mary Rich*, 132.

125. Boyle, "Some Motives to the Love of God" (1659), 260. See also Boyle to Lady Barrymore (his niece), *ca.* 1645–50, quoted in Birch, "Life of Boyle," cxxxvii.

126. Quoted in Birch, "Life of Boyle," cxxxviii.

127. Boyle, "Some Motives to the Love of God." The lovesick "Lindamore" to whom the essay was addressed was possibly his brother Francis. That brother was never stably reunited with his wife, the vain and flighty court companion Elizabeth Killigrew, and her daughter Charlotte was sired by the future Charles II, who at the Restoration conferred the title of Viscount Shannon on Francis as apparent compensation (Fell-Smith, *Mary Rich*, 157). Brother Orrery was one of many Restoration wits who made fun of a cult of platonic love which was fashionable at the court of Charles I.

128. Boyle, "Some Motives to the Love of God," 246, 248–49, 259, 281, 290, 293; see also idem, "Of Piety," 173–74.

and the customary presentations of religious identity. It was indeed said of the virtuous that they were "Dul and Melancholick," that they were poor and addicted to poverty, earnest and serious, lacking in gallantry and civility. The "Aretology" acknowledged the legitimacy of some of these characterizations: "For certinly the mopish retiredness of the greatest part of the religius, I can no way either Deny or Approue: it being extremely iniurius To themselves, vpon whom they pul down such an vnnecessary drooping."[129] His early ethical writings mobilized familiar cultural resources in arguing not only the compatibility of gentlemanly and Christian codes but the advantages of Christian devotional practices in enhancing gentle virtues. It was, Boyle argued, not only *possible* to be a gentleman and a Christian, Christian devotion was *necessary* for the achievement of a properly grounded gentlemanly character. Sullenness and retreat were only contingently associated with virtuous character; a fortune built up through virtuous actions might take longer to achieve but was more securely held; true virtue prohibited no lawful pleasures nor the observance of legitimate civil codes.[130]

More fundamentally, Christian devotion promoted the virtues most intimately associated with a gentle nature and gentle conduct. "The virtues or qualifications, which, as so many constitutent parts, make up greatness of mind . . . , are peculiarly befriended by Christianity"—valor, constancy, liberality, humility, civility, "a contempt of all that is base." Greatness of mind was by another name magnanimity, a central gentlemanly virtue. And, while the inwardly virtuous man did virtuous deeds, one could not gauge his quality by the measures of "vulgar" repute. The only positive effect of worldly applause was to confirm the approbation of conscience. While, as I note below, Boyle importantly recruited the codes of gentlemanly civility to specify proper philosophical deportment, he also acknowledged that Christian heroes might be obliged intermittently to stand against current codes. The forms of civility might be an occasional casualty of heroic virtue: "For interest, bashfulness, and that very complaisance and civility, that is so usually found in well-bred or good-natured persons, makes them very unwilling to offend or disoblige the company they live with, and whom they have several inducements rather to please and gratify by imitation and compliance, than tacitly to reproach by non-conformity to their sentiments and practices." Religion stiffens the sinews, if necessary, "to disobey custom and example." The Christian hero was a man

---

129. Boyle, "Aretology," 67. On Boyle and religious melancholy, see Hunter, "Casuistry in Action," 91–92.
130. Boyle, "Aretology," 69–72.

of courage and fortitude, too brave to be injured by the censure or ridicule of the base or the fashionable.[131] Christian gentility, Boyle argued, might well draw its champions into conflict with polite codes. For that reason alone it was a more effective discriminator between those who possessed genuine internal honor and those who made their honor the plaything of vulgar repute.

Why was the "priest of nature" not then a "priest"? The question was pertinent for the experiments in vocation and identity Boyle was conducting in the 1640s and 1650s. He repeatedly professed himself not merely concerned to establish his own virtue but to give men inducements to behave virtuously themselves. How better to shape the forms of public conduct than to preach from the pulpits of the established church? The acceptance of high Anglican office would not have been unusual for an aristocratic younger son, though not as common for one so well off as Boyle. In fact, early manuscripts give some indication that he was mulling over the possibility of taking holy orders.[132] However, at least as early as 1660 he had firmly decided against a priestly vocation, and the reasons he publicly offered, then and later, for that decision are significant in understanding his identity and the credibility of the culture he produced.

In 1660 Boyle was evidently offered high ecclesiastical office in the restored church. His friend Gilbert Burnet explained Boyle's reasons for declining. On the one hand, Boyle reported that he had not experienced a divine vocation, "not having felt, within himself, an inward motion to it." To take holy orders, therefore, he would have been obliged to "have lied to the Holy Ghost." Being seen to decline the priesthood on those grounds thus buttressed his reputation for integrity. Within a sincerely Protestant culture, the lack of vocation was understandable as an entirely sufficient reason. On the other hand, Boyle justified his course of action by claiming that to become a priest would be to compromise the public *credibility* of his religious professions. The greater the integrity and perceived disinterestedness of the actor, the greater the credibility of his claims. Burnet reported Boyle's sentiments

131. Boyle, "Greatness of Mind Promoted by Christianity" (1690), 551–52, 555, 559, 562; see also idem, "Some Motives to the Love of God," 244 ("I never swore allegiance to custom"); idem, "Of Valour," Boyle Papers, Vol. 196, ff. 63–69, esp. 65 ("An excessive feare of Dishonor it self is Dishonorable"); and Jacob, *Boyle,* 63. Boyle systematically pointed out the deleterious moral effects of bad company and the codes that endorsed fashionable behavior; see, esp., idem, "Free Discourse against Customary Swearing"; idem, "Aretology." 78–79. For contemporary portraits of moral gallantry and Christian Stoicism, see, e.g., Mackenzie, *Religio Stoici;* idem, *Moral Gallantry.*

132. Boyle Papers, Vol. 44, f. 95.

that his having no other interests with relation to religion, besides those of saving his own soul, gave him, as he thought, a more unsuspected authority, in writing or acting on that side; he knew the profane crew fortified themselves, against all that was said by men of our profession, with this, 'that it was their trade, and that they were paid for it'.[133]

Burnet reported his friend's sentiments accurately, and Boyle intermittently published similar reasoning concerning the relationship between perceived professional interest and credibility. In *The Christian Virtuoso* (composed *ca.* 1650, published 1690) Boyle acknowledged that his was a scoffing age in which the cynical would always evaluate moral arguments according to the imputed interest of the source. This circumstance made Boyle's *independent* authorial posture all the more valuable. There are, he said, "too many persons, that are like to be found more indisposed to be impressed on by arguments, in favour of religion, from professed divines, how worthy soever, than from such as I, who am a layman."[134] *The Excellency of Theology* (composed 1665, published 1674) was prefaced by a general argument about the link between role and credibility. So far as religious books were concerned, Boyle reckoned "that those penned by lay-men, and especially gentlemen, have (*cæteris paribus*) been better entertained, and more effectual, than those of ecclesiasticks." Advice to forgo the pleasures of vice was more credible when it came from those with the leisure and means systematically to indulge in vicious behavior. The recommendation of *any* study proceeded more effectively from those who were not socially or remuneratively identified with its practice. Thus, all circumstances being equal, "he is the fittest to commend divinity, whose profession it is not." Gentlemanly leisure and integrity might therefore appear as positive resources in achieving credibility and authority. Reputation was enhanced by the participation of men

> whose condition and course of life exempt them from the usual temptations to partiality to this or that study, which others may be engaged to magnify, because it is their trade or their interest, or because it is

133. Burnet, "Character of a Christian Philosopher," 357–58; see also Birch, "Life of Boyle," lx. It is also *possible* that Boyle's well-known "tenderness" in the matter of oath-taking masked doubts over items in the Test Acts which would have acted as a dissuasive to taking holy orders. He may have been, as Maddison suggests (*Boyle*, 146), "a dissenter at heart"; cf. Hunter, "Alchemy, Magic and Moralism," esp. 393; idem, "Casuistry in Action," 90–93; and Trevor-Roper, "The Great Tew Circle," 186–92 (for the Socinianism of the Great Tew circle with which Lady Ranelagh was closely associated). Nevertheless, as Burnet says, Boyle supported all the institutions and forms of the established church, and there is no evidence that his religious *identity* was in any way suspect.

134. Boyle, "Christian Virtuoso," 509.

expected from them; whereas these gentlemen are obliged to commend it, only because they really love and value it.[135]

A gentleman's word effectively secured the propagation of divine testimony.

A Scholar and a Gentleman

In the early years of Boyle's Stalbridge residence, he experimented
with philosophical as well as religious identities. Indeed, the essays
written during his late adolescence and early adulthood argued (following Francis Bacon, Thomas Browne, and other Protestant moralists) that a properly constituted philosophy contributed to right religion. Having acquired a taste for chemistry and useful learning from
members of the Hartlib circle, Boyle gradually grafted particular moral
and theological justifications for the philosophical study of *nature* onto
the stock of general justifications for the pursuit of a properly conducted philosophy.[136] Nevertheless, nothing then written in defense
of philosophy need be equated with the outcome that Boyle take on
the identity of a philosopher, still less that of a philosopher of nature.

That a Jacobean Englishman of birth and wealth should *study* philosophy was, of course, nothing extraordinary. From the first third of
the sixteenth century English humanist writers (e.g., Thomas Elyot,
Thomas More, Roger Ascham) had been condemning the practical
equation between English gentility and ignorance and urging gentlemen to take to their studies and to the universities. Courtesy writers
like Henry Peacham advertised Italian patterns of gentle connoisseur-
ship and aestheticism. Book-learning was recommended as an avenue
to virtue, polish, and political influence in the expanding Tudor and
early Stuart court. The relative success of the humanist case has been
measured by the influx of gentlemen into the new public schools and
the universities in the period from *ca.* 1558 to *ca.* 1642.[137] While Puritan thinkers held ambivalent views of educational goods, the dominant

135. Boyle, "Excellency of Theology," 2–3. Boyle's "Some Considerations about the
Reconcileableness of Reason and Religion" (1675) was published anonymously, but tellingly, "By [Rober]T. [Boyl]E. a Lay-Man" (see p. 153 for the advantage of secular standing). When his pious *Occasional Reflections* appeared in 1665, Boyle had already secured
an identity as a philosopher, and the text was apparently criticized by several writers
who thought such work would be better coming from a theologian's than a philosopher's
pen. His sister Katherine was, however, sufficiently familiar with the argument from
integrity to credibility to remind Boyle not to worry: Boyle to Richard Baxter, *ca.* late
June 1665, in Boyle, *Works*, VI, 520–21; and Lady Ranelagh to Boyle, 29 July 1665, in
ibid., 525–26.

136. E.g., Boyle, "Aretology," 55–57; idem, "Occasional Reflections"; idem, "Christian
Virtuoso."

137. Shapin, "'A Scholar and a Gentleman,'" 282–86.

thrust of Christian humanist writing commended learning as it contributed to virtue, the knowledge of God's works, and the alleviation of man's estate. As I noted in the previous chapter, by the time Boyle was composing his early ethical essays, there were several cultural repertoires circulating in England which specified the proper constitution of the gentleman. One repertoire (understandably underrepresented in literate culture) defiantly identified gentility with "pleasure," recognizing a gentleman by his birth, wealth, repute, and quarrelsomeness, and the traditional avocations (hunting, hawking, gambling, visiting) structuring his day. Another repertoire celebrated knowledge and its presumed product, virtue.

If the acquisition of learning was, therefore, unexceptional for at least a portion of English gentlemen, what remained extraordinary was an aristocratic *identification* with the pursuit of knowledge, an aristocratic presentation of self *as philosopher*. Early modern English culture traced an important contrast between the character of a gentleman and that of a scholar. Standard portrayals of the professional scholar depicted him as impoverished, otherworldly, melancholic, disputatious, pedantic, lacking in civility and sense of decorum. All the civic virtues that made gentlemen agreeable to one another were widely deemed deficient in "gown-men." Thus, while the acquisition of a degree of learning came to be considered a desirable gentlemanly accomplishment, the acquisition of a scholarly identity was not. The contrast between the perceived attributes of the gentleman and the scholar became more credible as the gentleman became greater. It is not easy to enumerate more than a handful of seventeenth-century aristocrats who presented themselves in the *identity* of scholar or philosopher.[138] The problems of such presentation were very considerable. They had to do with the concrete circumstances in which scholars and gentlemen lived their lives, the cultural resources which identified scholars and gentlemen, and the body of culture manipulated by scholars. Problems also arose from the contrast between the social forms in which that scholarly culture was produced and transmitted, on the one hand, and the conventions of gentlemanly conversation, on the other.

During his Stalbridge period, Boyle gradually embraced philosophy as a vehicle of virtue. The "Aretology," for example, dismissed "contemplative knowledge" as a source of happiness and treated education mainly as one of the "acquired secondary causes of morall vertu." Phys-

138. Ibid., esp. 287–92. Among individuals who *identified themselves* with a philosophical enterprise, there were few who equaled or outranked Boyle socially, and arguably none of these identified themselves so closely with the *practice* of natural philosophy: e.g., Henry Percy, eighth duke of Northumberland ("The Wizard Earl"), Sir Kenelm Digby, the Cavendishes (William and Charles), Sir Robert Moray, and Viscount William Brouncker.

ics, metaphysics, and mathematics were recommended as auxiliaries to an ethical project. Such studies were, of course, distractions from temptation and antidotes to idleness, and they also instructed "vs in many things, whose Knoledg is to the Ethickes if not Necessary, at least vsefull: as the Doctrine of principles, Causes and Ends; that of the Soule with it's Faculty and Immortality, and the like." Moreover, the "Aretology" approved the study of nature as an accessible reservoir of moral emblems: "How . . . can [man] consider the Ruf Draughts and Images of vertu in the Very Brutes, without a Noble Scorn, that he shud make himself inferiour to them by his Actions, that God made so much superior to them by his Birth."[139] Certainly, as early as the middle of 1646, Boyle announced that he was applying himself to "natural philosophy, the mechanics, and husbandry."[140]

Manuscripts from the same period show Boyle deploying the repertoires of philosophical and eremitic identity warrantably to justify withdrawal from the normal duties of gentle sociability. An anguished early paper pleaded with "deare Philosophy" to "come quickly & releeve Your Distressed Client" of his trivial social obligations: "Delay not one Short moment if You would rescue Your incens'd Votary from some strange hasty, Anchoritish Vow."[141] The drawing room of fashionable Dorset society was a madhouse to young Boyle: "Had my Eares lodg'd all my Senses, I should have beleev'd my Selfe in Bedlam . . . There sat a couple of Female's flattering & envying the Fashion of a Third's Patches: & disputing with greater nicety & Concernednesse, of the Præheminence of the Square or round Figure for them; then ever your Daughter Geometry made me do about the Quadrature of the Circle."

Philosophy was identified as a safe and virtuous refuge from the venality, the tedium, and the superficiality of polite society. She was "my deare Mistris," more agreeable and pleasing than any mortal woman: "enuf to keepe me from seeking (I might have say'd Accepting) many . . . fashionable Mistresses, & Constant beyond the very thought of Diminution." He said that solitary philosophical conversation "makes me disrellish all others," and he was jealous of time spent

139. Boyle, "Aretology," 8, 50, 55–56 (quotation from p. 56). Jacob (*Boyle*, ch. 2) has laid great stress on just these passages in this manuscript. Unlike Jacob, however, I cannot see that the "Aretology" expresses any very pronounced recommendation of natural knowledge or personal identification with the role of natural philosopher. Those expressions become more significant in the *Occasional Reflections* (composed 1646–49) and definitive in *The Usefulness of Experimental Natural Philosophy* (composed 1652–58).

140. Boyle to Marcombes, 22 October 1646, in Boyle, *Works*, I, xxx–xxxiv, quoting xxxiv.

141. Boyle Papers, Vol. 37, ff. 166–67 ("Come Deare Philosophy"). All quotations here and in the following paragraph are from this manuscript.

in human society, for it was wasted time, time spent away from his mistress:

> How dull a Thing it is, to come from the Company of Plato, Aristotle, Seneca, & those other ornaments of Mankind, . . . who teach me to vanquish Fraylty, Fortune, Nature & master my owne Passions; and whose Company I never leave but Wiser & Better, to prate with those, who shall squander away a whole afternoone in tatling of this Lady's Face. . . . You can Your Selfe, Philosophy, beare me witnesse, how frequently & Studiously I have declin'd all other Companys, to enjoy the Blessing of Yours.

Indeed, both Boyle's lack of enthusiasm for the conversational obligations of gentle society and his philosophical warrant for shunning them were widely advertised and acknowledged in his circle of acquaintance.[142] In 1649 he used sacred tropes to tell sister Katherine how blissfully happy retreat into his Stalbridge laboratory made him: "*Vulcan* has so transported and bewitched me, that as the delights I taste in it make me fancy my laboratory a kind of *Elysium*, so as if the threshold of it possessed the quality the poets ascribe to *Lethe,* their fictions made men taste of before their entrance into those seats of bliss." He said that it was fit that laboratory work be performed, like divine service, on Sundays.[143] By 1650 he was telling Hartlib that "if my Irish fortune" would permit it, he would "build a pretty house in *Athens,* where I may live to philosophy."[144]

For all that, Boyle (like many English humanist writers before him) was well aware of the distempers of existing forms of academic philosophy and the defects of the traditional philosophical character. Neither current school-philosophy nor the school-philosopher was any good to the goals of gentlemanly virtue, harmony, and technical control. Bacon had offered a systematic diagnosis of the delicate, fantastic, and contentious forms of existing academic philosophy, and Boyle took that general picture of the unreformed philosophical temperament and practice as understood.[145] Philosophers would be both civically and

142. Among many letters complaining about social demands upon his time and yearning to be free of them, see, e.g., Boyle to Lady Ranelagh, 30 March 1646, in Boyle, *Works,* I, xxvii–xxx.

143. Boyle to Lady Ranelagh, 31 August 1649, in Boyle, *Works,* VI, 49–50; see also Boyle Papers, Vol. 8, f. 128. For extended treatment of holy and laboratory solitude, see Shapin, "House of Experiment," 383–88; idem, "'The Mind Is Its Own Place,'" 201–08.

144. Boyle to Hartlib, 1 May 1650, in Boyle, *Works,* I, xlvi.

145. Esp. Bacon, "Advancement of Learning." The role of the Hartlib circle in these respects was doubtless important for Boyle's early thinking, but his emerging project for the reform of philosophy resonated more strongly in Restoration public culture with Baconian themes.

morally disabled until they remedied their egoism and contentiousness. Philosophy would continue culturally crippled until it found right objects, right epistemic goals, and right methods for yielding knowledge of those objects and achieving those goals.

Boyle's critique of academic pedantry was as pervasive in his writings as it was unsystematic. The early "Aretology" propagated a common early modern trope in dissociating existing scholarly learning from either morality or civically useful common sense. So many of "your great learned men . . . haue whole Oceans of Science, but scarce Drops of Conscience." They teach well, but they live badly, and thus "Confute their Doctrine by their Practice, and Condemn their Practice by their Doctrine."[146] One could and should identify rightly constituted knowledge by its effects in the world: first, by the moral examples of those who purveyed it, since all genuine knowledge tended to the virtue of its possessors, and, second, by its extension of man's dominion, since genuine knowledge of God's nature would be signified by its utility in restoring man's rightful estate.

Boyle's early essays and correspondence were saturated with references to the civic disabilities of school-philosophers and to the virtues of alternative presentations. His autobiography claimed that at Eton "he was so addicted to more reall Parts of Knowledge, that he hated the study of Bare words, naturally; as something that relish't too much of Pedantry to consort with his Disposition & Desseins." Boyle celebrated his tutor Isaac Marcombes as someone who "hated Pedantry as much as any of the seauen Deadly sins."[147] The early "Doctrine of Thinking" rejected "the Nice and Perplext speculations" of "leasurd [school] hermits" in favor of "the Practicall Part" of learning.[148] His first correspondence with Hartlib testifies to Boyle's impatience with "the prattling of our book-philosophers," and letters to Francis Tallents, then a Magdalene, Cambridge, fellow, cheekily advertised members of his "invisible college" as "men of so capacious and searching spirits, that school-philosophy is but the lowest region of their knowledge."[149]

The decision to leave Stalbridge for Oxford was taken against the background of Boyle's ambivalent attitude towards academic forms. The relative tranquillity of academic society was attractive, and the particular company of the Wilkins-Wallis-Ward circle "exactly suited

146. Boyle, "Aretology," 54. For the spread of this trope, see Shapin, "'A Scholar and a Gentleman,'" 291.
147. Boyle, "Philaretus," 19, 22.
148. Boyle, "Doctrine of Thinking," 185.
149. Boyle to Hartlib, 19 March 1647, in Boyle, *Works*, I, xxxvii–xxxviii; Boyle to Tallents, February 1647, in ibid., xxxiv–xxxv.

[his] inclinations."[150] But it was that particular group which tempted him away from Stalbridge, not university society in general, for Boyle's tracts written in the mid- to late 1650s continued to characterize traditional academic philosophy as pedantic, dogmatic, and disputatious, as Wilkins acknowledged when he wrote to Boyle in 1653 that in coming to Oxford he could not "expect to learn anything amongst pedants."[151] Yet by 1655 Boyle told Hartlib that this group alone disproved "much of what you & I had been inform'd of concerning the servileness of & disaffection to real learning of that university."[152]

The experimental practice that Boyle described and recommended in texts of the early 1660s was said to both require and reinforce civic virtue.[153] The unwarranted "confidence" and quarrelsomeness of the school-philosopher were juxtaposed to the humility and modesty of the experimentalist. "Diffidence" in asserting truths and the professed willingness to alter one's views were mobilized into emblems of disinterestedness. The presentation of claims as certain and exact, by contrast, was identified as the mark of a scoundrel.[154] One was invited to recognize the genuine experimental philosopher by his civility, decorum, and display of the Christian virtues. And, even as Boyle wrote about how the experimental philosopher ought to behave, so he exemplified that behavior. The authority of his person was to give authority to the practice.

Texts, Property, and the Presentation of an Authorial Self

Boyle's first (albeit anonymous) publication identified a "costive humor" afflicting certain strands of cultural practice. Composed in 1647 and published eight years later, Boyle's letter invited "all true lovers of Vertue & Mankind, to a free and generous Communication of their Secrets and Receits in Physick." Boyle condemned "the avarice" of those "secretists" who secured profit through the practice of intellectual privacy. Both Christian charity and civic virtue demanded that useful knowledge circulate in the public domain, for the public benefit. If the physician and the chemist behaved as did the merchant, then they too would acquire the merchant's character, violate common no-

---

150. Birch, "Life of Boyle," lv.

151. Wilkins to Boyle, 6 September 1653, in Boyle, *Works*, VI, 633–34.

152. Boyle to Hartlib, 14 September 1655, quoted in Maddison, *Boyle*, 85.

153. Detailed accounts of the temperament and manners of the ideal experimental practitioner are in Shapin, "Pump and Circumstance"; idem, "'A Scholar and a Gentleman'"; Shapin and Schaffer, *Leviathan and the Air-Pump*, chs 2, 4–5.

154. E.g., Boyle, "A Proëmial Essay," 307, 311–12; idem, "Some Considerations Touching the Usefulness of Experimental Natural Philosophy," 45; idem, "Sceptical Chymist," 462; idem, "Christian Virtuoso," 522–23, 536. For the identification of proper and improper expectations of mathematical exactness and certainty, see chapter 7 below.

tions of justice, and merit the condemnation of civil society: "How universally should [he] be execrated, that in a scarcity would keep his Barns cram'd, while he beholds his pining neighbours starving for want of bread?"[155]

In general terms, Boyle's recommendation of intellectual openness—continued and elaborated in such texts as *Sceptical Chymist* and *Certain Physiological Essays* of 1661—amounted to a specification of the proper moral posture of a genuine producer of philosophical knowledge. He should not seek egoistically to celebrate himself or to secure property rights in knowledge but modestly to detach knowledge from the self that produced it.[156] The point was to persuade men to behave more *generously* than traditional scholars—"to mind more the advancement of natural philosophy than their own reputations."[157] Proper knowledge neither proceeded from nor belonged to individuals: it derived from nature and was owned by the commonwealth. Such a posture was, of course, easier to achieve, maintain, and make credible if one's circumstances permitted it, while the easy forgoing of property rights in knowledge was a more fraught strategy for those who owned no other property. In his old age Boyle himself recognized the link between his economic ease and the presentation of his disinterestedness: "Being a bachelor, and through God's bounty furnished with a competent estate for a younger brother, and freed from any ambition to leave my heirs rich, I had no need to pursue lucriferous experiments, to which I so much preferred luciferous ones, that I had a kind of ambition . . . of being able to say, that I cultivated chemistry with a disinterested mind."[158] Boyle's early texts thus drew a picture of a

155. Boyle, "Epistolical Discourse," 381; see also Golinski, "Boyle: Scepticism and Authority," esp. 66–71. This specific example of the violation of natural justice is discussed in Thompson, "Moral Economy of the Crowd." There are now very many excellent treatments of the themes of secrecy, openness, and civility in early modern science, by, for example, Biagioli, Dear, Eamon, Findlen, Golinski, Iliffe, Johns, Long, and Tribby (see bibliography).

156. For fine accounts of the historical development of conceptions of authorial property, see Long, "Invention, Authorship, 'Intellectual Property,'" and, especially, Johns, "Wisdom in the Concourse." Cf. Lawrence Principe ("The Gold Process," 204; "Boyle's Alchemical Secrecy"), who has recently cited some passages of Boyle's alchemical work ostensibly as decisive evidence against his overall commitment to "the ideal of open scientific communication."

157. Boyle, "A Proëmial Essay," 302.

158. Boyle to [?], *ca.* 1689, in Boyle, *Works*, I, cxxx–cxxxi. Eighteenth-century debates over authorial property rights continued importantly to identify the *disinterestedness* of legitimate knowledge-producers. In 1774 Lord Camden judged that "Glory is the Reward of Science, and those who deserve it scorn all meaner Views. . . . It was not for Gain, that *Bacon, Newton, Milton, Locke,* instructed and delighted the World; it would be unworthy [of] such Men to traffic with a dirty Bookseller for so much as a Sheet of Letter-press" (quoted in Rose, "Author as Proprietor," 54).

philosophical self whose production of credible knowledge depended upon the publicly recognized material bases of integrity.

One can track Boyle's identification with a philosophical role through both stable and changing elements in his presentation of an authorial and proprietary self.[159] A remarkably constant feature of that presentation was the character in which Boyle displayed himself as author of his texts. Throughout his authorial career Boyle deployed a restricted repertoire of practices which worked to disengage his self from his texts. Several of the texts published from the early 1660s were advertised as printed forms of letters written to specific individuals, intended originally solely to encourage that individual to the pursuit of virtue or experimental philosophy. Thus, the *New Experiments Physico-mechanical* of 1660 was identified as a version of letters written to his nephew Lord Dungarvan—eldest son of the second earl of Cork—who had ostensibly entreated his uncle to send him more detail about the new air-pump experiments. *Certain Physiological Essays* of the following year was said to be addressed to another nephew Richard Jones ("Pyrophilus")—Katherine Ranelagh's only son—to persuade him to take up physiological inquiries, as were the *Experiments Touching Colours*, bits of *The Usefulness of Experimental Natural Philosophy* (both 1663), and *Experimenta & Observationes* (1691).[160]

Prefaces to these and other texts pervasively sought to *justify* publication. There was never an assumption of the naturalness of Boyle appearing in the person of an author of printed texts, and, indeed, Boyle invariably portrayed himself as being dragged unwillingly into that role. Why, for example, were personal letters suffered to be published? The basic program of the air-pump experiments had, Boyle replied, already "made some noise among the Virtuosi" and "I could not, without quite tiring more than one amanuensis," supply all the copies that were being requested. Various "intelligent persons . . . persuaded" him that publication would be a service to the world of learning, and it was "to gratify ingenious men" that Boyle permitted publication.[161]

159. Accordingly, I am concerned here with exactly those questions about "the socio-historical analysis of the author as an individual" which Foucault set aside in his "What Is an Author?" (esp. p. 115): how the author was individualized, how the author was embedded within systems of value.

160. The use of the addressee "Pyrophilus" eventually became wholly dissociated from its original designation of Richard Jones. It has not been previously noted how disastrously those early avuncular encouragements turned out. There is no evidence that young Jones *did* take up the pursuit of either experimental philosophy or virtue. In adult life Jones was, as Fell-Smith notes, "a terrible spendthrift of moneys acquired by falsification, on a huge scale, of accounts in the public offices he held," and, for that reason, was later expelled from the House of Commons: Fell-Smith, *Mary Rich*, 356–57.

161. Boyle, "New Experiments Physico-mechanical," 1, 4; idem, "Origin of Forms," 4.

There is scarcely a single text by Boyle that did not excuse its imperfect, disorganized, preliminary, or unfinished character on the grounds that publication was implored by others to whom Boyle had an obligation. Tracts were printed "to gratify other men's curiosity"; because "divers persons" were "soliciting me for composures"; because of the printer's or publisher's "importunity"; because "I was induced . . . to give some satisfaction to a friend" and "to please an ingenious person"; because he acknowledged a Christian duty speedily to make materially useful knowledge public.[162] Indeed, the presentation of reluctant authorship by individuals who were (or hoped to be accounted) gentle was a standard trope of early modern culture. Among very many examples, Sir Thomas Browne's *Religio Medici* protested unwilling and disengaged authorship in terms strikingly similar to those used by his admirer Boyle: the composition had been undertaken "for my private exercise and satisfaction" and not with a view to publication. But "broken and imperfect" copies were circulating; "the importunity of friends" was great; allegiance was owed to the truth; he did not necessarily own and acknowledge early conceptions contained in the text. William Harvey's *On the Motion of the Blood* (1628) explained publication as "yielding to the requests of my friends" and ensuring that his views not be publicly "traduced." And William Gilbert's *De Magnete* (1600) justified publication by expressing an insouciant disregard for fame or public reaction: "We care naught, for that, as we have held that philosophy is for the few."[163]

Boyle's *New Experiments Touching Cold* and *Hydrostatical Paradoxes* were both identified as coming into existence by "the command" of the Royal Society.[164] His published response to Hobbes's criticisms of his air-pump experiments was justified not on the grounds of defending personal reputation or honor but because Boyle owed an obligation to truth and to others in the experimental community.[165] And if there was a legitimate philosophical obligation to one's reputa-

162. Among very many examples, see Boyle's "A Proëmial Essay," 298; "Sceptical Chymist," 458; "Experiments and Considerations Touching Colours," 663; "Some Considerations Touching the Usefulness of Experimental Natural Philosophy," 202–03; "Excellency of Theology," 2; Disquisition about Final Causes," 393; "Christian Virtuoso," 508; "Experimenta & Observationes," 564–65; "General History of the Air," 611; "Memoirs for the Natural History of Human Blood," 595.
163. Browne, *Religio Medici,* "To the Reader," 1–2; Harvey, "On the Motion of the Blood," in idem, *Works,* 19–20; Gilbert, *De Magnete,* xlix. For treatment of Copernicus's celebrated fame-denying, and audience-restricting, preface to *De Revolutionibus* (1543), see Westman, "Proof, Poetics, and Patronage," esp. 179–82.
164. Boyle, "New Experiments Touching Cold," 469; idem, "'Hydrostatical Paradoxes," 738.
165. Boyle, "Defence against Linus," 119.

tion, it was to the accurate representation of what one believed. Thus, Boyle kept *Seraphic Love* (written as letters to Mary Rich) back for eleven years, resisting all solicitation to publication, and printing was agreed to only because an imperfect copy had fallen into the hands of someone who threatened to have it published without Boyle's consent.[166] Because Boyle's published texts were cobbled together from bits and pieces of different dates, it was, he said, not to be expected that he should now own or approve all the sentiments expressed therein.[167] He would not even vouch for the technical accuracy of his texts. Since the distemper of his eyes made him rely upon amanuenses, he had no way of reliably checking over their work or that of Henry Oldenburg, who acted as Boyle's "publisher" and saw Boyle's work through the press.[168]

The presentation of self as *modest* and *humble* was, indeed, part of Boyle's disengaged posture *vis-à-vis* his authorial person. Humility was, after all, a Christian virtue, a manifestation of authentic "greatness of mind." Yet in the early modern context, such a presentation by such a person might effectively elicit other understandings. Boyle was reminding readers that he was not the *kind of person* to whom authorship was normal. Those who presented themselves naturally in the person of an author were seekers after fame and celebrity, individuals of compromised integrity who sought personal identification with the claims and systems presented under their names because, so to speak, *it was their trade.*[169] Authorship as a taken-for-granted posture was accounted normal for priests, physicians, philosophers, chemists, and mathematicians—and this despite their intermittent protestations to the contrary—but *not* for free and independent gentlemen. The presentation of nonreluctant authorship was a handicap to credibility since interest might be plausibly attached to the published claims. For Boyle, a

166. Boyle, "Some Motives to the Love of God," 243; cf. idem, "Some Considerations Touching the Usefulness of Experimental Natural Philosophy," 3–4. For excellent accounts of complex attitudes to authorship and the problems scientific authors, including Boyle, experienced with the Restoration book trade, see Johns, "History, Science and the History of the Book"; idem, "Wisdom in the Concourse," ch. 4, esp. 166–70, 180–81.

167. E.g., Boyle, "Some Considerations Touching the Usefulness of Experimental Natural Philosophy," 4; idem, "Medicina Hydrostatica," 454.

168. E.g., Boyle, "New Experiments Physico-mechanical," 3; idem, "A Proëmial Essay," 298; idem, "Some Considerations Touching the Style of the Holy Scriptures," 252; see also M. B. Hall, "Boyle's Method of Work," 111–15, and, for a brief account of the slapdash publication of a particular text, see Fulton, *Bibliography of Boyle,* 70–71. I discuss the extent of Boyle's reliance upon support personnel in chapter 8.

169. Sprat (*History of the Royal Society,* 74) sarcastically invoked *"ostentation"* and the "desire of glory, and to be counted *Authors*" as a practical obstacle to medical and alchemical secrecy.

disengaged and nonproprietary presentation of authorial self was, on the one hand, a way of reminding readers (including philosophical readers who might not know who he was) that he was *not* someone professionally committed to the claims contained in his texts and, on the other, a valuable resource in securing a disinterested appearance for his knowledge-claims. He was the sort of man who had no reason to misrepresent how matters stood in nature.

I have already noted that Boyle persistently dissociated his religious commitments from those of professional divines. This was a specific manifestation of a general disavowal of professional expert interest in knowledge. Thus, Boyle denied that he came to his experimental work "prepossessed" with philosophical theories, or, indeed, that he had even systematically read the works of the grand theorists of natural philosophy. He owed allegiance to no philosophical sect or party.[170] The "rudeness" of his literary style was excused by noting that he was a person "that professes not rhetorick."[171] His medical writings were pervasively identified as coming from one who was free of physicians' professional interests and commitments: "neither physick nor chymistry [are] my profession," and he wrote "less like a physician than a naturalist."[172] As his publisher Robert Sharrock reminded readers of Boyle's *Usefulness*, the author wrote *in* medicine and pretended to competence in it, even though "it might be looked upon as unbecoming for him to meddle with the physician's art, of which he never did (*nor could, by reason of his native honour*) make any profession."[173] He acknowledged physicians' proprietary interests and, while he was proud of his contributions to materia medica and therapeutics, he "was

170. E.g., Boyle, "New Experiments Physico-mechanical," 2; idem, "Some Specimens of an Attempt to Make Chymical Experiments Useful to Illustrate the Corpuscular Philosophy" (1661), 355.

171. Boyle, "Some Considerations Touching the Style of the Holy Scriptures," 254. Harwood (*Early Essays*, lvii–lxii) strongly argues Boyle's rhetorical self-consciousness, as, indeed, I have done elsewhere (Shapin, "Pump and Circumstance"). But I want to insist that Boyle's visible departure from rhetorical practices *standard among schoolmen and sectors of fashionable society* was a means he used to warrant his intellectual integrity.

172. Boyle, "Medicinal Experiments," 314, 316; idem, "Reconcileableness of Specific Medicines to the Corpuscular Philosophy," 74.

173. Sharrock, "The Publisher to the Reader" (introduction to Boyle, "Some Considerations Touching the Usefulness of Experimental Natural Philosophy," 2 [italics added]); see also Cook, *Decline of the Old Medical Regime*, esp. 56–60 (for treatment of the medical profession and ideas of gentility in Stuart London); idem, "Physicians and the New Philosophy" (for tension between the medical corporations and the new virtuosic practice, quoting [p. 263] an anonymous 1660s manuscript, possibly by Henry Stubbe, accusing Boyle of mercenary motives in his medical writing); Cunningham, "Sydenham and the 'Good Old Cause,'" esp. 179–84 (for Boyle's influence upon strands of medical practice).

careful to decline the occasions of entrenching upon their profession."[174]

Boyle repeatedly maintained that he was not a mathematician and
insisted on the relatively poor state of his mathematical competences.[175]
His early *Sceptical Chymist* came "from a person altogether a stranger
to chymical affairs," while, at the end of his life, Boyle assured readers
that he "aimed not to appear a chemist" but only to write of chemical
subjects.[176] The materially useful knowledge freely presented in his
more utilitarian texts was generated for the advantage of the commonwealth and in free compliance "with the dictates of philanthropy," not,
as with tradesmen and artisans, for personal gain.[177] His portrayal of
the Christian virtuoso contrasted that person with the "vulgar scholar"
and "mere school-men."[178] He persistently protested that he was
"never a professor of philosophy, nor so much as a gown-man," and,
for that reason, could be relied upon to set down experimental findings
as they were actually produced, "without fraudulently concealing any
part of them, for fear they should make against [me]."[179] In *Style of the
Holy Scriptures* (1661), he recognized that many now saw him as "a
naturalist," yet he insisted upon the fact (which "all that do know me"
knew) that he did not share the irreligious characteristics widely attributed to the role of naturalist.[180] *Not being* a professional philosopher
was a condition for "philosophical freedom."[181]

As a great gentleman, Boyle's plausible dissociation from the corporate commitments of all professional experts meant that he could tactically move at liberty between identification and disengagement.[182]

174. Boyle, "Memoirs for the Natural History of Human Blood" (1684), 637–38, 641;
and idem, "Experimenta & Observationes" (1691), 583, where Boyle recorded physicians' displeasure at his "meddling"; see also G. W. Jones, "Boyle as Medical Man,"
142–43. Nevertheless, English quacks later traded on "the ever-honoured Esquire"
Boyle's name as the inventor of "Effectual Pills" (quoted in R. Porter, "Language of
Quackery," 85).

175. E.g., Boyle, "Some Considerations Touching the Usefulness of Experimental
Natural Philosophy. Second Tome," 425; idem, "Excellency of Theology," 22; and, for
detailed treatment of this point, see chapter 7 below.

176. Boyle, "Sceptical Chymist," 459; idem, "Experimenta & Observationes," 598.

177. E.g., Boyle, "Medicinal Experiments," 315.

178. Boyle, "Christian Virtuoso, Second Part," 763.

179. E.g., Boyle, "Experimenta & Observationes," 566; also idem, "Hydrostatical Discourse," 596.

180. Boyle, "Some Considerations Touching the Style of the Holy Scriptures," 253;
cf. idem, "Christian Virtuoso," 508–09.

181. Boyle, "Free Inquiry," 158.

182. For treatment of "the production of identity through negation" among early
modern authors, see Stallybrass and White, *Politics and Poetics of Transgression*, ch. 2, esp.
88–89.

Thus, *A Free Inquiry* announced that he wrote "as a Physiologer, not as a Christian," whereas in communications to the Reverend Richard Baxter he complained that readers of *Occasional Reflections* identified him as a philosopher, lacking competence to publish divine speculations.[183] He asserted legitimate *competence* in chemistry, medicine, philosophy, and theology, while noting that he was not a chemist, a physician, a philosopher, or a theologian. Writing of general obstacles to the apprehension of truth, Boyle pointed to the masses of men "whom their prejudices do so forestall, or their interest bias."[184] Professionals were thus handicapped. Tied to no one profession, Boyle might credibly contribute to any of them. The Christian virtuoso was situated everywhere and nowhere in professional space. This was a presentation fundamental to Boyle's perceived integrity, and it was made plausible both by shared background knowledge about him in the local culture and by his own literary specifications of who he was. Having no commitments to corporations of experts and institutionalized bodies of culture, he was free to commit himself to truth. A selfless self was a free actor in the world of knowledge; all others counted as constrained.

Boyle's disengaged presentation persisted to the end of his publishing career. Despite that persistence, however, there was marked change over time in Boyle's practical actions *vis-à-vis* proprietary interests in knowledge-claims. The condemnation of intellectual secrecy and "costiveness" in medical receipts that constituted Boyle's first published work was, indeed, echoed and extended through the essays of the early 1660s. Yet by that time it was becoming clear that Boyle was not content that knowledge he viewed as rightfully his should be appropriated and owned by another author. That is to say, his presentation of self began to include elements associated with the character of professional scholars. In 1663, for example, he excused the possible lack of novelty in some of the matters of fact related in *Usefulness of Experimental Natural Philosophy* on the grounds that his manuscript reports had been in free circulation and had been illegitimately presented by others as their own.[185] A few years later Boyle publicly worried that his growing repu-

183. Boyle, "Free Inquiry," 159; Boyle to Richard Baxter, *ca.* early June 1665, in Boyle, *Works*, VI, 520–21; see also Lady Ranelagh to Boyle, 29 July 1665, in ibid., 525–26. Boyle did not object when Baxter volunteered the opinion that his philosophy was theologically driven: "I read your theology as the life of your philosophy, and your philosophy as animated and dignified by your theology, yea indeed as its first part" (Baxter to Boyle, 14 June 1665, in ibid., 516–20, quoting 516).

184. Boyle, "Christian Virtuoso," 509–10. Cf. Boyle's tabular manuscript outlining the "Remoras [Hindrances] of Truth": Boyle Papers, Vol. 14, f. 24 (printed in Harwood, *Early Essays*, xl). The resonance here with Bacon's idols is clear.

185. Boyle, "Some Considerations Touching the Usefulness of Experimental Natural Philosophy," 3; also ibid., "The Second Tome" (1671), 395–96.

tation for reliability and veracity was tempting other writers to appropriate his experimental testimonies without acknowledgment of their source.[186] Soon Oldenburg was publishing, on Boyle's behalf, specific allegations of plagiarism: "about fifty experiments [were] taken out of our author's book of colours, without owning any of them to him, or so much as naming him or his book."[187]

In 1665, Boyle took his full part in establishing recording practices that aimed to secure to members of the Royal Society (including himself) proprietary and priority rights in reports of transfusion experiments: "jealousy" that such reports might be stolen and published under others' names was "not altogether groundlesse."[188] Boyle encouraged Oldenburg to make up a catalog of his writings, expressing fear that the circulation of loose sheets risked intellectual theft, "having found by experience, that if a man proceed not cautiously in these matters, he may hereafter be thought to have stolen from others, what indeed they owe . . . to his communication." Oldenburg was now instructed to date exactly when letters from Boyle were received, the more effectively to secure Boyle's proprietary rights in knowledge.[189] Boyle had thought that his practice of writing down his experiments in loose and scattered sheets might preserve him from theft, but he now concluded that he had nevertheless been the victim of straightforward "fraud."[190] The ownership of philosophical goods was acknowledged as a form of credit, the accumulation of which made reputation, and reputation was a powerful instrument in making knowledge. By 1674, Boyle was keeping back from publication details

186. Boyle, "New Experiments Touching Cold," 470–71.
187. [Oldenburg], "Publisher to the Reader," in Boyle, "Experiments, Notes, &c. about the Mechanical Origin of Divers Qualities," 230–31; see also Boyle to Oldenburg, 29 December 1667, in Boyle, *Works*, VI, 71–72; Fulton, *Bibliography of Boyle*, 148–49.
188. Boyle to Oldenburg, 27 August 1665, and Oldenburg to Boyle, 29 August 1665, in Oldenburg, *Correspondence*, II, 483–87, quoting 484. Oldenburg (485) offered to "register" all reports by Boyle and his colleagues so as to establish the identity of "the first authors of experiments"; see also Boyle to Oldenburg, 20 June 1665, in ibid., 408–10, for Boyle's anxieties about unauthorized printings. Johns, "Wisdom in the Concourse," ch. 4, esp. 166–67, includes much relevant material on Boyle's developing attitudes to philosophical proprietorship and originality; and see Iliffe, "'Idols of the Temple,'" esp. 161–266, for parallel materials relating to Newton.
189. Boyle to Oldenburg, 17 October 1667, in Oldenburg, *Correspondence*, III, 532–34, quoting 533; Boyle to Oldenburg, 26 October 1667, in ibid., 539–41. For Boyle's concern that unauthorized Latin translations of his works printed in Holland might give the impression that his discoveries were made later than they really were, see Boyle to Oldenburg, 29 December 1667, in ibid., IV, 93–95.
190. Boyle to Oldenburg, *ca.* late 1667, in Oldenburg, *Correspondence*, IV, 98–99; cf. Boyle, "Advertisement about the Loss of His Writings," in Birch, "Life of Boyle," cxxv–cxxviii.

of medicinal preparations, even those he deemed publicly valuable, for the sake of maintaining cordial relations with other chemists, and he expressed increasing concern about the effects of letting loose "marvellous" experiences, such as the phosphorus, into a nonphilosophical community.[191]

By the end of his life, Boyle left little doubt in the public mind that he wished acknowledgment and proprietorship of his own intellectual goods. In 1688 he published a broadsheet advertisement vigorously complaining of intellectual fraud and theft. Here Boyle protested that the credibility he had accumulated by virtue of his selflessness had made him invisible as the author of some of his own works:

> I think it necessary to advertise equitable readers, that he [Boyle] has been the worse dealt with by several writers, upon the very account of that candour and faithfulness he has exercised in delivering matters of fact. For whereas when experiments and observations are related by men whose faithfulness is dubious, the more cautious sort of plagiaries think themselves obliged to mention the names of their authors, lest an experiment not proving true, its falsity should be (as it justly may be) imputed to them, they think they may safely rely on the truth of what our author relates, that their reputation runs no venture in making any experiment that he delivers, pass for their own. . . . And this hath been done by some of them, without so much as naming the true author.[192]

Plagiarism was the compliment scoundrels paid to the creditworthy. But it was a compliment that Boyle the philosopher rejected. Throughout his career he manipulated a set of repertoires by which he presented his self in different settings and for different purposes. A presentation as selfless public benefactor underwrote a display of disinterestedness and the achievement of trustworthiness. Yet the very success of that presentation generated its successor-problem: the dissolution of the author into his transparent narratives about the world. Boyle was not content that this should happen. Reputation, after all, counted for something. He evidently worried that his narratives had become *too* transparent for the maintenance of a philosophical identity. If reputation were to assist the production of true and legitimate knowledge, then an honorable man had to remain visible as the author of that knowledge.

---

191. Boyle, "Account of the Helmontian Laudanum," 149–50; Golinski, "A Noble Spectacle," esp. 24, 27, 29–30.

192. Boyle, "An Advertisement about the Loss of His Writings," in Birch, "Life of Boyle," cxxvi.

A Usable Honor

The local potency of Boyle's presentation of self is beyond dispute.[193] Until the public emergence of Isaac Newton as the paladin of a newly mathematized natural philosophical enterprise, no single individual life was so widely pointed to as the pattern of what it meant to be an English philosopher of nature. Boyle's presentation was put to practical moral use even before he began appearing in the person of a philosophical author; it was intensively appropriated and celebrated by the early Royal Society; and it persisted long after his death. From the mid-1650s through the early 1690s, it was Boyle's example—more than that of any other practitioner—which was mobilized to give legitimacy to the experimental philosophy. (Thomas Sprat's influential *History of the Royal Society* [1667] was, in large part, the validation of pictures of the experimental philosopher and experimental social practices developed earlier by Robert Boyle.) Patterns which Boyle recommended and exemplified offered practical solutions to problems of managing belief and assent within the Restoration experimental community.[194]

At his death, the funeral sermon preached by his friend Gilbert Burnet celebrated Boyle's life as a template not just for Christian virtuosity but for Christian life in general: it was a life which might be considered as an almost perfect "pattern of living."[195] The sermon identified and endorsed almost every major feature of Boyle's presentation of self from the 1650s to the end of his life. Burnet dilated upon Boyle's personal holiness and the piety of his philosophical practice— "nature seemed entirely sanctified in him"—and, as an intimate acquaintance, confirmed that private devotion corresponded exactly to

193. I say "local" in order to point to the circulation and appropriation of Boyle's pattern in the experimental community and among many Anglican theologians. I have, however, argued elsewhere that Boyle's ambition to persuade English gentlemen in general to adopt Christian virtuosity was not substantially successful. Indeed, to many Restoration court wits and satirists Boyle was a figure of fun; see, e.g., Shapin, "'A Scholar and a Gentleman,'" 304–12.

194. These patterns are treated in Shapin and Schaffer, *Leviathan and the Air-Pump*, esp. chs 2, 4–5.

195. Burnet, "Character of a Christian Philosopher," 348. (This text was liberally drawn upon by eighteenth-century biographers Peter Shaw and Thomas Birch, and remained in print through the nineteenth century. When William Wotton solicited John Evelyn's views on a possible biography of Boyle, Evelyn's comments closely followed Burnet's sermon: Evelyn to Wotton, 30 March 1696, in Evelyn, *Diary and Correspondence*, III, 346–52; and, for Evelyn's attendance at Burnet's sermon, see ibid., II, 316–17.) It has to be emphasized that Boyle enjoyed a significant reputation as a *moralist* through the seventeenth and eighteenth centuries, and that this reputation *might be* founded on grounds quite independent of his experimental and natural historical work. Burnet recognized Boyle's philosophical work but did not give it any more stress than his theological, casuistical, and charitable activities.

public profession.[196] The quest for "heroic virtue" which informed the "Aretology" was, in Burnet's view, fully realized in Boyle's conduct of life. Stoical self-command was traced to Christian foundations. Even as a youth he was "wholly the master of himself"; he "bore all his infirmities, and some sharp pains, with the decency and submission, that became a christian and philosopher"; he neglected all display of "pomp in clothes, lodging, furniture, and equipage." He subjected his very body to the ascetic discipline imposed upon his mind: over a course of more than thirty years "he neither ate nor drank, to gratify the varieties of appetite, but merely to support nature."[197]

The civic world that whipped up other men's passions and interests held no attractions for Boyle. He was a man of such complete integrity that there was nothing worldly he wanted, nothing worldly that could move or compromise him—"His mind was . . . entirely disengaged from all the projects and concerns of this world"; "he had neither designs nor passions"; "he withdrew himself early from affairs and courts," resisting the temptations of fame and civic power that might have been his for the asking. He was unmoved even by the defense of his own being: "as to life itself, he had the just indifference to it, and the weariness of it, that became so true a christian."[198] Chemistry was his "peculiar and favourite study," but he practiced it disinterestedly, "with none of those ravenous and ambitious designs" that animated vulgar practitioners.[199] He possessed absolute integrity, and he reveled in that possession: "The sense of his own integrity . . . afforded him the truest of all pleasures."[200]

196. Burnet, "Character of a Christian Philosopher," 352, 354. For the intimate relationship between Boyle and Burnet, and the extent to which Burnet's sermon reflected Boyle's preferred presentation, see Hunter, "Alchemy, Magic and Moralism," 387–88; idem, "Casuistry in Action," 86–87.

197. Burnet, "Character of a Christian Philosopher," 351, 361–62. (This appropriates the proverbial abstemiousness attributed to Socrates and, by extension, to philosophers in general: "Other men live to eat, but he eats to live.") Cf. Evelyn, *Diary and Correspondence*, III, 351; Frank, *Harvey and the Oxford Physiologists*, 226 (for John Ward's testimony to Boyle's abstemiousness); Aubrey, *Brief Lives*, 37 (who noted that, while Boyle was "very temperate, and vertuose, and frugall," he nevertheless "keepes a Coach"). For a range of later parallel neo-Stoical attributions to French academicians, see Paul, *Science and Immortality*, 86–109; Outram, "Language of Natural Power"; idem, *Cuvier*, esp. 53, 64, 94, 100, 117.

198. Burnet, "Character of a Christian Philosopher," 358, 362, 368, 371; cf. Evelyn, *Diary and Correspondence*, III, 351: "Nor could I discern in him the least passion, transport, or censoriousness."

199. Burnet, "Character of a Christian Philosopher," 370. Burnet here included Boyle's pharmaceutical work within "chymistry," and stressed his (and Lady Ranelagh's) charitable dispensing of medical receipts and drugs.

200. Ibid., 371.

The humor he displayed to other men exactly fitted his disengagement from worldly concerns:

> He had . . . nothing of frolic and levity in him: he had no relish for the idle and extravagant madness, of the men of pleasure; he did not waste his time, nor dissipate his spirits, into foolish mirth; but he possessed his own soul in patience, full of that solid joy, which his goodness, as well as his knowledge afforded him.[201]

For all that, it was not to be thought that he displayed the character of a melancholic hermit or philosopher. Boyle knew what was owed to other men and what civic obligations were laid upon him by the law of God and the code of a gentleman. "To a depth of knowledge, which often makes men morose; and to a height of piety, which too often makes them severe, [Boyle] added all the softness of humanity, and all the tenderness of charity, and obliging civility. . . . He had nothing of the moroseness, to which philosophers think they have some right."[202] He "lived in the due methods of civility"; he was "exactly civil, rather to ceremony"; he never "offended any one person, in his whole life, by any part of his deportment."[203] A great and wealthy aristocrat, Boyle had power to do hurt but would do none. Because he would "never assume the authority, which all the world was ready to pay him," his authority was all the greater.[204]

Burnet thus described Boyle as a man who had successfully created an identity that recombined and respecified in one person the valued characteristics of the gentleman, the Christian, and the scholar. He was "the purest, the wisest, and the noblest creature."[205] It was a presentation that lasted. In 1692, an anonymous necrological sheet eulogized "Great BOYLE by Birth, Greater by *Knowledge* far,/*Natures* chief Fav'rite, and the brightest *Star*/That *Heav'ns* ere shew'd to guide the *Learned World*/Th[r]o' tumbling Seas of *Trials*, Waves that hurl'd/The tender *Bark*, in quest of *Truth*."[206] In the 1720s, Daniel Defoe pointed to Boyle as a paragon of the gentleman-scholar, and used his career as a stick with which to beat the stupid squires of the English shires.[207] In 1796, the editor of an edition of Izaak Walton's *Lives* celebrated Boyle's memory: "To the accomplishments of a scholar and a gentle-

201. Ibid.
202. Ibid., 332, 367.
203. Ibid., 360–61, 366–67; cf. Evelyn, *Diary and Correspondence*, III, 350: "He was affable and civil rather to excess."
204. Burnet, "Character of a Christian Philosopher," 367.
205. Ibid., 333.
206. Anon., *On the Death of the Honourable Robert Boyle* (1692), reproduced in Fulton, *Bibliography of Boyle*, fig. 24 (facing p. 173).
207. Defoe, *Compleat English Gentleman*, 69.

man, he added the most exalted piety, [and] the purest sanctity of manners."[208]

Burnet's account of Boyle's pattern was both powerful and persistent. There was, however, little in it that had not been, repeatedly if less systematically, said before. John Evelyn told Boyle in 1659 that his *Seraphic Love* displayed such "divine inclinations, as are only competent to angels and to yourself."[209] Some years later an Oxford natural historian confided to Boyle that God had "(visibly) stamped his image upon you, in knowledge, wisdom, and holiness."[210] In 1665 the physician Richard Lower dedicated his *Vindicatio* to Boyle, announcing that the author embraced "a free and independent philosophy, and surrender[ing] my hands in bondage to truth alone and thus to you, her holiest priest and fiercest champion."[211] Aubrey declared that Boyle was a "profound Philosopher, accomplished Humanist, and excellent Divine, I had almost sayd Lay-Bishop."[212] And in 1668 Joseph Glanvill described him as combining "the *gentilest smoothness*, the most *generous* knowledge, and the *sweetest* Modesty" with "the most *devout, affectionate* Sense of *God* and of *Religion*," suggesting that in other ages Boyle might have been regarded as a "deified Mortal."[213] John Wilkins portrayed him as "a great master of civilities as well as learning," and Sir Robert Southwell endorsed the form, telling the grand duke of Tuscany that Boyle "was as much a master of civility as knowledge."[214]

In the mid-1660s there was a brief exchange of pamphlets between two British authors representing themselves respectively as exponents of solitude and public engagement. In 1665, Sir George Mackenzie, Scottish judge and moralist, propounded the superior claim of solitude over "publick employment, and all it's Appanages; such as Fame, Command, Riches, Pleasures, Conversation, &c." Two years later, John Evelyn, F.R.S., replied, arguing the other side of the old case, that "Publick Employment and an Active Life" are to be preferred to solitude.[215] Mackenzie commended retirement because it was a setting which enhanced pious contemplation and protected gentlemanly integrity. Evelyn applauded a civic life on the grounds of man's natural sociability.

208. Zouch, *Lives*, 480n–81n.

209. Evelyn to Boyle, 29 September 1659, in Evelyn, *Diary and Correspondence*, III, 121.

210. Ralph Austen to Boyle, 14 January 1664, in Boyle, *Works*, VI, 645.

211. Lower, *Vindicatio*, 198.

212. Aubrey, *Brief Lives*, 36.

213. Glanvill, *Plus Ultra*, 93.

214. Wilkins to Boyle, 6 September 1653, and Southwell to Boyle, 10 October 1660, in Boyle, *Works*, VI, 633, 297.

215. Mackenzie, *Moral Essay Preferring Solitude*, and Evelyn, *Publick Employment;* see also Vickers, "Public and Private Life."

Christian charity required social engagement, and even philosophical contemplation proceeded most effectively in a collegial setting.

Each writer sought to justify his preferred way of life by citing one, and just one, living individual whose conduct shed legitimacy on the form. For Mackenzie this individual was Robert Boyle:

> And if . . . ye will not conclude a solitary Life to be more noble, then publick Employment, yet, at least, ye will, with seraphick Mr. *Boyl*,[216] confess, that, there is such a kind of difference betwixt virtue, shaded by a private, and shining in a publick life, as there is betwixt a candle carryed aloft in the open air, and inclosed in a lantern; In the former of which situations, it gives more light, But in the latter, it is in less danger to be blown out.[217]

And for John Evelyn the paragonic individual was also Robert Boyle:

> And if after *all this* yet, [Mackenzie] admit not an *Active life* to be by infinite degrees more *noble;* let the *Gentleman* whose first *Contemplative* piece he produces to establish his Discourse, *confute* him by his *Example;* since I am confident, there lives not a *Person* in the *World,* whose *moments* are more *employ'd* then Mr *Boyles,* and that more confirms his *contemplations* by his *actions* and *experience:* And if it be objected, that his employments are not *publick,* I can assure him, there is nothing more *publick,* than the *good* he's always *doing.*[218]

Boyle had evidently succeeded in establishing himself as a potent pattern for two historically distinct repertoires of gentlemanly legitimacy. Whatever his form of life, the rights to its interpretation was a prize worth contesting.

I have argued that one of Boyle's greatest achievements was the creative respecification of gentlemanly identity and its extension into cultural terrain then occupied by the philosopher and the devout Christian. The *achieved* identity of this person was made into a valuable resource in securing legitimacy for the experimental enterprise and credibility for empirical knowledge-claims. Nevertheless, contemporary acknowledgment of the value of these moves depended largely upon the basic social identity with which Boyle was equipped at birth. The potency of the particular patterns of action Boyle recommended proceeded from recognition of *what sort of person* made and exemplified those patterns. When Boyle advertised his own humility and the modesty of experimental practice, it was understood as the humility and the modesty of *noblesse oblige* and legitimate condescension.[219] It was

216. The allusion was to Boyle's recently published "Some Motives to the Love of God," whose running title was *Seraphic Love.*
217. Mackenzie, *Moral Essay Preferring Solitude,* 111.
218. Evelyn, *Publick Employment,* 118–19.
219. E.g., Boyle, "A Proëmial Essay," 301–03, 307–12.

the fact of birth and wealth and the value placed upon them that might give dignity to the laborious pursuit of natural-philosophical knowledge. The traditionally perceived meanness of a scholar's identity and the baseness of manual occupations might be repaired by the systematic participation of persons who *were* neither mean nor base.

The early Royal Society fully appreciated the significance of having aristocrats as its most visible members. During an early move to elect Boyle president, Oldenburg explained that the society thought "it very important to choose persons into that chair, in whom birth and ability are in conjunction."[220] Honorable men honored cultural practices by affiliation. As early as 1651, the physician Nathaniel Highmore celebrated Boyle's identity as a resolution of the evaluative conflict between gentility and labor: "You stand both a pattern and wonder to our Nobility and Gentry. . . . You have not thought your blood and descent debased, because married to the Arts."[221] In 1666 Thomas Sydenham applauded Boyle for accompanying him in visiting the sick, "descending to offices, which . . . are little recognized by the spirit of the age we live in."[222] These were sentiments whose significance Boyle understood and worked to propagate. I have already noted his early endorsement of physical labor as a Protestant antidote to dangerous idleness. His *Usefulness of Experimental Natural Philosophy* urged the nobility of inquiries even into nature's most "vile" and "despicable" creations, and, more pertinently, the manly nobility of manual work in that cause. Even the handling of excrement might be dignified by the purpose for which it was handled and by the identity of him who took it into his hands: "I have been so far from that effeminate squeamishness, that one of the philosophical treatises, for which I have been gathering experiments, is of the nature and use of dungs. . . . Nor when I am in my laboratory, do I scruple with [my own hands] naked to handle lute and charcoal. . . . I think my actions fit to be examples."[223]

220. Oldenburg to Boyle, 24 February 1666, in Boyle, *Works*, VI, 217.

221. Highmore, *History of Generation*, "Dedication" (quoted in Birch, "Life of Boyle," xlvii, and Maddison, *Boyle*, 78). And see Fulton, *Bibliography of Boyle*, 155–170, for almost fifty dedications to Boyle from 1651 to his death and beyond, esp. identifications of Boyle as a perfect pattern of nobility, honor, virtue, and learning by Robert Sanderson, Robert Sharrock, John Evelyn ("It is from You alone, that I might describe the Character of an accomplish'd Genius, great, and worthy our Emulation"), Ralph Austen ("The Worthy Patron and Example Of all Virtue"), Thomas Sydenham, Henry Oldenburg, Thomas Smith, and Sir George Mackenzie.

222. Sydenham, "Epistle Dedicatory to First Edition" (1666), *Medical Observations*, in idem, *Works*, I, 10.

223. Boyle, "Some Considerations Touching the Usefulness of Experimental Natural Philosophy," 14. (Lute is a claylike cement.) For the continuing late-seventeenth- and eighteenth-century opinion that inquiries into nature's vile and despicable creations were unsuitable for gentlemanly participation, see Shapin, "'A Scholar and a Gentleman,'" 304–12.

The rejection of the rule of Aristotle, and the consequent opening up of nature's possibilities, precipitated enormous problems of practical authority for the new experimental enterprise, and I will treat these in the next chapter. The experimental credo professed to rely upon "no man's word" and to accept only the testimony of nature itself. In fact, such a prescription was, and is, impossible to act upon. The prescription is best taken as a normative disengagement from certain institutionalized practices and sources of authority in favor of others. Some spokesmen for reality were to be replaced by others. But where was that new authority and who were the new spokesmen? I argue that the new authority was constituted by and through the creative respecification of existing practical solutions to the problem of credibility. Chapter 3 showed that the word of a gentleman was such an existing solution, and that the civil conversation by which gentlemen traditionally managed the daily practices of assenting, modifying, believing, and disbelieving was a resource which might be redeployed as a practical solution to the problem of authority in the new experimental practice. The norms of everyday civil conversation specified that gentlemen *were to count* as transparent spokesmen for reality. The conventions of civil conversation put a cost upon the denial that they were so, and the same civil conversation embedded rich resources for performing dissent without disaster.

The Honourable Robert Boyle made for himself, and was assisted by others in making, a very particular identity—one which had not previously existed in early modern culture. In making "the experimental philosopher" and "the Christian virtuoso," Boyle achieved the artful respecification of the existing characters of the philosopher, the Christian, and the gentleman. Yet of these three the identity of gentleman was the one with which he was born and the one he had to do least to secure. And while he was a vigorous participant in the contemporary argument over the legitimate grounds of gentility, Boyle could draw upon the cultural capital which recognized gentlemanly integrity and the truthfulness which was understood to flow from that integrity. Evaluations of Boyle's special personal integrity could be laid on top of the general integrity attributed to gentlemen. He was a truthful man in a community of truth-tellers. Burnet noted that he did not "act a part, or put on a mask." He was incapable of deceit. If necessary he could keep silent when to speak the truth would wound others or himself, but "he could neither lie, nor equivocate."[224] The apothecary John Warr warranted the potency of Boyle's medical receipts by insisting upon their source: "What comes forth in the name of Mr. Boyle, and is genuinely his, needs no farther recommendation. His *ipse dixit*

224. Burnet, "Character of a Christian Philosopher," 334, 368.

is sufficient."[225] And John Evelyn's vivid likening of Boyle's physical person to fine glass or crystal drew out the moral implications of the metaphor: "he was withal clear and candid; not a blemish or spot to tarnish his reputation."[226] Such a man might truly be a transparent spokesman for reality.

225. Warr, preface to 1692 edition of Boyle, "Medicinal Experiments," 374.
226. Evelyn, *Diary and Correspondence,* III, 351.

CHAPTER FIVE

Epistemological Decorum:
The Practical Management
of Factual Testimony

Every truth is true in its place.
—Michael Oakeshott, *Experience and Its Modes*

Two major tasks have been taken up thus far. First, I have pointed (chapter 1) to the ineradicable role of trust in constituting systems of both social order and empirical knowledge. There have to be working answers to the questions 'whom to trust?' and 'who tells the truth?' if there is to be shared knowledge and shared social order. Second, I have pointed (chapters 2 through 4) to some major resources available in early modern English society for the identification of truth-tellers, laying particular stress upon the role of truthfulness in gentlemanly social relations and the cultural practices attending the practical handling of gentlemanly testimony. Now I need to pick up the problem of truth from the other end. I have to display truth-making practices in action. Here and in the next chapter I discuss the trajectory traced by empirical knowledge-claims in seventeenth-century English science, noting how their practical management mobilized the truth-making culture treated earlier as well as other related practices which bore upon assessment of whether or not particular claims were veridical.

Accordingly, this chapter is in three parts. First, I examine early modern changes in systems of *plausibility* which rendered a range of existing systems dubious, in whole or in part. What were the new *problems* in the constitution of natural knowledge which prompted a body of systematic reflection about empirical matters-that-might-be-the-case? Second, I sketch the properties of a number of formal schemes proposed in the seventeenth-century English context better to make up the stock of empirical knowledge, to police its legitimate boundaries, and to evaluate testimony of candidate knowledge-claims. Third, I show what was taken for granted in such schemes, and how certain

entrenched, and largely tacit, elements associated with these knowl-
edge-evaluating frameworks assisted the resolution in practice of problems which were insoluble in principle. This done, I prepare the
ground for the next chapter, which traces the career of some candidate
empirical knowledge-claims from the Royal Society setting, showing
how they were practically engaged with and assessed, and how both
formal and informal elements were brought to bear to resolve their
standing as possible knowledge-about-the-world.

"The Compass of the World"

When Hamlet told Horatio that there were "more things in heaven
and earth than are dreamt of in your philosophy," he was adopting a
widespread early modern ontological posture. Traditional inventories
of things-that-existed-in-the-world were deemed to be illegitimately
impoverished. What grounds were there for crediting anciently established limits on the stock of factual matters? Every day presented new
phenomena about which the ancient texts were silent. Travelers from
the New Worlds to east and west brought back plants, animals, and
minerals of which there were no counterparts in European experience,
and tales of still more. Sir Walter Raleigh protested to stay-at-home
skeptics that "there are stranger things to be seen in the world than are
contained between London and Staines."[1] From the early seventeenth
century, observers using telescopes and microscopes claimed to reveal
the limits of unassisted human senses and suggested that even more
details and more marvels awaited only instrumental improvements to
be discovered. New and altered intellectual practices probed back in
natural time and human history and advanced claims to reliable knowledge about phenomena no living person had witnessed. Newly observed entities which posed uncomfortable problems for existing philosophical systems were seized upon by those concerned to discomfit
orthodox theorists. Who could confidently say what did and did not
exist in the world when tomorrow might reveal as yet undreamed
inhabitants in the domains of the very distant and very small?

Moreover, changes in the foci of intellectual interest and in the
boundaries of cultural participation brought new experiences to the
attention of those who had previously not cared or not known. Who,
among the philosophizing classes, had previously known the extent of
factual knowledge informally circulating among miners, potters, and

---

1. Quoted in Williams, *Raleigh*, 150; see also Doran, "On Elizabethan 'Credulity,'"
esp. 156–58. For valuable insistence that European experience of the New World was
mediated through textual traditions, see Grafton, *New Worlds, Ancient Texts*.

chemists?[2] New ontological possibilities impressed receptive minds. In principle, there was no reason why new knowledge-claims could not have been rejected or ignored, and, indeed, some practitioners did both. In practice, groups concerned to erode the authority of the 'ancients' and their contemporary spokesmen validated the new knowledge-claims in the process of invalidating the old schemes and undermining the legitimacy of their spokesmen. The work of prying open the inherited box of plausibility and restocking it with new things and phenomena was fundamental to the emergence of new intellectual practices. In the process, new and modified forms for the making and warranting of empirical truth had to be proposed and put in place. The 'modern' critique of the adequacy, and, especially, the exhaustiveness, of traditionally established stocks of empirical knowledge is wholly familiar to many historians.[3] I need here to document some widely distributed features of that critique which indicate just how it was proposed to constitute reliable empirical knowledge through the apparent systematic rejection of reliance upon authority and trust. Then I will go on to show how in practice trust was not rejected but *managed.*

Montaigne's skeptical posture towards the stock of knowledge fastened upon people's illegitimate confidence in the adequacy of their own reason and experience. Why ever should these be treated as the gauge of what might or might not exist in the world?[4] Intellectuals were particularly drawn to the "foolish presumption" to "go around disdaining or condemning as false whatever does not seem likely to us." Even if we cannot establish implausible claims as true, neither can we confidently dismiss them as false: "How many things of slight probability there are, testified to by trustworthy people, which, if we cannot be convinced of them, we should at least leave them in suspense! For to condemn them as impossible is to pretend, with rash presumption, to know the limits of possibility." A man who had never seen a river thought the first one he came across was the ocean. The scale of local experience may be limited, just as the scale of human knowledge cannot reach to the possibilities of God's productive power. People are accustomed to call "prodigies or miracles" whatever is presently beyond their knowledge or reason: "Habituation puts to sleep the eye of our judgment," and what we designate as miracles arise "from our ignorance of nature, not from the essence of nature." The

2. See, notably, Webster, "Paracelsus and Demons" (for validation of miners' knowledge); also Rossi, *Philosophy, Technology, and the Arts,* ch. 1.
3. Traditional sources include: R. F. Jones, *Ancients and Moderns,* ch. 6, and Butterfield, *Origins of Modern Science,* chs 4–7.
4. For Montaigne as fideist Catholic and Pyrrhonist skeptic, see Popkin, *History of Scepticism,* ch. 3.

first step in rectifying our knowledge was to open up our apprehension of the world, to keep our confidence in plausibility assessments under check.[5] Montaigne did not regard *any* system of knowledge—ancient or modern—as inspiring much legitimate confidence, but his skepticism was nevertheless powerfully brought to bear upon the presumption that traditionally constituted inventories of nature's existents were adequate.[6]

If early modern skeptical voices warned against closing nature's box too firmly or too soon, writers seeking to guarantee knowledge upon new foundations also had reason to expand the domain of nature's possibilities. Francis Bacon's enumeration of the minor distempers (or "peccant humours") of learning notably included the tendency to distrust novel claims. While people were prepared to credit—even to a fault—the empirical reports of the ancients, they were distrustful of new knowledge-claims and reports of new natural phenomena. Antiquity deserved "reverence" but not obedience. Too servile an attitude to the ancients induced epistemic error: "a distrust that any thing should be now to be found out, which the world should have missed or passed over so long time. . . . So it seemeth men doubt lest time is become past children and generation; wherein contrariwise we see commonly the levity and unconstancy of men's judgments, which, till a matter be done, wonder that it can be done; and as soon as it is done, wonder again that it was no sooner done." As in acts so in knowledge: "most of the propositions of Euclid, which till they be demonstrate, they seem strange to our assent; but being demonstrate, our mind accepteth of them by a kind of relation . . . as if we had known them before."[7]

It was an error to gauge new factual knowledge-claims solely through past experience and its ancient inscription. Truth was "the daughter of time, not of authority," and, if truth emerged over time, then moderns must hold open the possibility that new matters may warrantably come into their awareness of which the ancients knew nothing, and whose existence they may even have explicitly rejected.[8] Recent voyages of discovery proved the point: "By the distant voyages and travels which have become frequent in our times, many things have been laid open and discovered which may let in new light upon

5. Montaigne, "Of Custom" and "It Is Folly to Measure the True and False by Our Own Capacity," in idem, *Essays*, 80, 132–33.

6. E.g., Montaigne, "Apology for Raymond Sebond," in ibid., 391, 430.

7. Bacon, "Advancement of Learning," 291. Here Bacon alluded to a legal analogy for his general epistemological point.

8. Bacon, "New Organon," 82; see also Wilkins, *Discourse Concerning a New Planet* (1640), 138.

philosophy. And surely it would be disgraceful if, while the regions of the material globe . . . have been in our time laid widely open and revealed, the intellectual globe should remain shut up within the narrow limits of old discoveries."[9]

> The world is not to be narrowed till it will go into the understanding . . . , but the understanding to be expanded and opened till it can take in the image of the world, as it is in fact. . . . And then shall we be no longer kept dancing within little rings, like persons bewitched, but our range and circuit will be as wide as the compass of the world.[10]

As fine historical work by Lorraine J. Daston and others has now established, Bacon sought to loosen the cultural ties that bound knowledge of entities in the natural world to philosophical frames they might be said to confirm or to fit.[11] Anomalies, marvels, and the "Heteroclites or Irregulars of nature" were to be searched for, collected together, and deliberated upon. They were philosophically needed "to correct the partiality of axioms and opinions, which are commonly framed only upon common and familiar examples."[12] There was every reason to suppose that our currently recognized stock of knowledge of natural entities and phenomena had been illegitimately restricted by traditional philosophical enterprises which rejected those items which could not be encompassed within the relevant theoretical frameworks. The work of disengaging fact from theory, and of reconstituting natural philosophy, could therefore be powerfully assisted by attention to new and strange facts. Important recent essays by Peter Dear have shown that the English 'moderns' rejected Aristotelian relations of experience as 'things that happen in the world' in favor of historically specific accounts of 'what happened at a particular time and place.' On that

---

9. Bacon, "New Organon," 82; see also ibid., 73, 75, 91–92. For the relationship between new discoveries and attacks on Aristotle, see Ingegno, "New Philosophy of Nature," esp. 244–47. The role of travelers in the constitution of natural-historical knowledge is treated in chapter 6 below.

10. Bacon, "Preparative towards a Natural and Experimental History," 255–56.

11. Park and Daston, "Unnatural Conceptions," 43–51; Daston, "Factual Sensibility," 465–66; idem, "Marvelous Facts," esp. 110–13; idem, "Baconian Facts"; see also Dear, "*Totius in Verba*," 148–49. Daston is largely concerned with the functional interpretation of what she has aptly called this "pointillistic vision of reality" ("Factual Sensibility," 467): wonders and marvels were resources for breaking down existing intellectual systems, for rearranging cultural boundaries (as between art and nature), and for stimulating religious sentiments. In contrast, my interest is mainly directed towards the consequences of Baconian openness for the *reconstitution of the very practices* through which factual knowledge might be had and warranted.

12. Bacon, "Advancement of Learning," 330–32; see also idem, "Preparative towards a Natural and Experimental History," 255–56.

score alone, the whole inventory of Scholastic 'experience' might be deemed inadequately constituted.[13]

Such modern practitioners as William Gilbert instructed doubting readers not to distrust experimental relations simply because they went against common experience or traditional textual authority: "Men are deplorably ignorant with respect to natural things, and modern philosophers, as though dreaming in the darkness, must be aroused."[14] There was no more characteristic 'modern' English philosophical move than the inversion of authority relations between word and world. Legitimate new experience must not be rejected because it conflicted with existing plausibility schemes; instead, those plausibility schemes must be set aside or rejected because they conflicted with legitimate new experience. The self-evident view that testimony and authority were to be resorted to only when we cannot have individual experiential access is, as Ian Hacking has argued, a creation of just this culture: "The Renaissance had it the other way about. Testimony and authority were primary, and things could count as evidence only insofar as they resembled the witness of observers and the authority of books." Hacking documents the shift in seventeenth-century usage from the "probable" as opinion warranted by authoritative and respected sources (as in "probity") to the "probable" as a quality of uncertain knowledge apportioned to the evidence available.[15]

By 1638 the young John Wilkins endorsed and refined Baconian ontological openness. Arguing the probable case for the existence of an inhabited world in the moon, Wilkins offered a considered account of the forces which illegitimately stabilized knowledge and which rendered people too suspicious of novel claims. While our divinely gifted primitive nature was to hunger after the new, the devil's work was to pervert that God-given disposition and to make us doubting and suspicious. Satan had been so successful that people now equated the new and singular with the false: "Any truth doth now seem distasteful for that very reason, for which error is entertained; novelty. . . . Solitary truth cannot anywhere find so ready entertainment; but the same novelty which is esteemed the commendation of error, and makes that acceptable, is counted the fault of truth and causes that to be rejected."

13. Dear, *"Totius in Verba,"* esp. 148–54; idem, "Jesuit Mathematical Science"; idem, "Miracles, Experiments, and the Ordinary Course of Nature"; idem, "Narratives, Anecdotes, and Experiments." Cf. Shapin, "Pump and Circumstance," 490–97; Shapin and Schaffer, *Leviathan and the Air-Pump,* 60–69; and Golinski, "Boyle: Scepticism and Authority" (for detailed accounts of circumstantiality in English experimental reporting).
14. Gilbert, *De Magnete* (1600), xlix, 47, 77, 171–72, 265, quoting 47.
15. Hacking, *Emergence of Probability,* 18–33 (quotation from 33) and chs 1–5 in general, for excellent treatment of early modern concepts of evidence and authority; see also Daston, *Classical Probability,* ch. 1, for cautious criticism of Hacking's thesis.

We are distrustful of the new and odd in just the way that we are distrustful of strangers. Yet truth is often solitary and derided: "It is not common opinion that can either add or detract from the truth." Proper philosophy, Wilkins argued, simply required a greater openness and willingness to entertain superficially implausible knowledge-claims: "A new truth may seem absurd and impossible not only to the vulgar, but to those also who are otherwise wise men and excellent scholars: and hence it will follow, that every new thing which seems to oppose common principles, is not presently to be rejected, but rather to be pryed into with a diligent enquiry, since there are many things which are yet hid from us." Columbus was mocked when he promised a New World; authorities mocked at the idea of the antipodes: "though all truth be eternal, yet in respect of men's opinions, there is scarce any so ancient but had a beginning, and was once counted a novelty."[16]

A degree of ontological openness was the mark of the free man as well as the wise man: "It behoves every one in the search of truth, always to preserve a philosophical liberty; not to be so enslaved to the opinion of any man, as to think whatever he says to be infallible."[17] Into the 1660s and beyond, scientific practitioners in the Royal Society and their cultural allies repeatedly insisted upon the epistemic and moral merit of loosening the grip of traditionally constituted schemes of plausibility. Boyle, for example, judged that the commonwealth is not "much beholden to those, that too rigidly, or narrowly, circumscribe, or confine the operations of nature." Recent history abundantly testified to the ease with which "improbable truths" passed into philosophical probability or even matter of fact.[18] Moreover, it was the particular skill of a "Christian virtuoso" who knows how experimentally "to put nature to her plunges" to "see such things performed by her, as make him think the vulgar catalogue of impossible or incredible things to be far greater than it ought to be."[19] In the same vein Thomas Sprat rebutted any charge that the Royal Society dabbled in "incredulous stories" by claiming that "many things, which now seem *miraculous*" will not be so when we come to be more fully and philosophically acquainted "with their *compositions*, and *operations*."[20]

16. Wilkins, "Discovery of a New World" (1638), 3–5, 10–11; idem, "Discourse Concerning a New Planet," 136–37.

17. Wilkins, "Discourse Concerning a New Planet," 136; see also Dear, "*Totius in Verba*," 150.

18. Boyle, "Some Considerations Touching the Usefulness of Experimental Natural Philosophy," 188, 194; also idem, "Men's Great Ignorance," 471–73.

19. Boyle, "Christian Virtuoso. Appendix to the First Part," 679.

20. Sprat, *History of the Royal Society*, 214; and, for the New World and the newly visible worlds as gushing sources of novel objects, ibid., 381–85; Hooke, *Micrographia*, "Preface" and 242; and Glanvill, "Modern Improvements of Useful Knowledge," in idem, *Essays*, 16–25.

Policing Possible Worlds

The opening up of ontological possibility was therefore central to the
very idea of what it was to be a 'modern.' Public statements that the
world demonstrably contained more things than were dreamt of in
established inventories were resources employed to display the inadequacy of traditional philosophies. For such critiques to be effective,
the constitution of those surprising matters of fact which had been
naturally found or artificially produced had to be seen as legitimate.
If this were not so, then there simply would be no new matters whose
existence could confute the authority of Aristotle and the schoolmen.
Of course, the ontological opening proposed by the moderns could
never be more than partial. Despite even the most radical rhetoric,
changes took place on the margins of existing institutionalized practices, and chapter 1 offered a general argument why skepticism can
never be total. If, *per impossibile,* the whole of the inherited stock of
knowledge were to be rejected, then one would have no way of sorting out experiences as between normal and abnormal, expected and
surprising.[21]

Even those seventeenth-century English commentators who most
vigorously urged ontological openness expressed concern that not just
any empirical reports should find their way into the stock of certified
knowledge. If, indeed, the natural world was a great treasure trove of
hitherto unimagined marvels and singularities, the legitimate scientific
practitioner was by no means obliged to credit *all* pertinent knowledge-
claims. Marvels indubitably existed, but they had to be authenticated
as such: *this* marvel-report had to be verified. Just as the authority of
the ancients was insufficient, so the mere say-so of just any modern
reporter was deemed inadequate for the constitution of empirical
knowledge. The moderns proposed to be as skeptical about contemporaneous knowledge-sources as they were about ancient authority.

As Bacon said, traditional bodies of knowledge—historical and
philosophical—had been damaged by a "facility of credit, and accepting or admitting things weakly authorized or warranted." Religious
culture, for example, had too readily accepted reports of miracles
"wrought by martyrs, hermits, or monks of the desert," which, after
time had worked its winnowing effects, had been revealed as but "old
wives' fables, impostures of the clergy, illusions of spirits, and badges of
antichrist, to the great scandal and detriment of religion." A reformed
history of nature had to learn that lesson. Existing registers of natural
facts had been corrupted by credulity: "There hath not been that
choice and judgment used as ought to have been." Authoritatively

---

21. See Hacking, *Emergence of Probability,* 82–84, for Wilkins's mixed reliance upon
individual experience and ancient authority.

accepted narrations of Pliny, Cardano, and other ancient and Renaissance natural historians were "fraught with much fabulous matter, a
great part not only untried but notoriously untrue, to the great derogation of the credit of natural philosophy with the great and sober kind
of wits."[22] A reformed natural history needed to set aside "all supersti-
tious stories": "For I would not have the infancy of philosophy, to
which natural history is as a nursing-mother, accustomed to old wives'
fables."[23] Neither ancient authority nor modern testimony was deemed
adequate to serve as the gauge and guard of empirical knowledge.

No historian of early modern empirical science neglects this
theme. The rejection of authority and testimony in favor of individual
sense-experience is just what stands behind our recognition of seventeenth-century practitioners as 'moderns,' as 'like us,' and, indeed, as
producers of the thing we can warrant as 'science.'[24] Thomas Browne's
identification of the radical scope of 'modern' philosophical free action
belongs to the genus we find most easy to recognize: "Nor is only a
resolved prostration unto Antiquity a powerfull enemy unto knowledge, but also a confident adherence unto any Authority, or resigna-
tion of our judgements upon the testimony of any Age or Author
whatsoever."[25] We are wholly familiar with the rhetoric of individualistic empiricism produced by Royal Society publicists (e.g., Sprat, Oldenburg, and Glanvill) and leading practitioners (e.g., Boyle, Hooke,
and Wilkins), all of whom repeatedly insisted upon the insufficiency
of authoritative texts and upon the careful inspection of testimony.
The Royal Society's motto—*Nullius in verba* (On no man's word)—
crystallized members' insistence upon the problematic status of testimony and the epistemic virtues of direct individual experience and
individual reason in the constitution of genuine knowledge.

A few examples suffice to illustrate the topic and highlight the presumed relationship between individualism and epistemic virtue. William Harvey's *On the Generation of Animals* directed readers "to strive
after personal experience, not to rely on the experience of others,"
even urging them "to take nothing on trust from me."[26] John Evelyn's
Sylva condemned writers "who receiving all that came to hand on *trust*,
to swell their monstrous *Volumes*, have hitherto impos'd upon the
credulous *World*, without *conscience* or *honesty*." It was "base" and "servile" to subject our divinely given sensing faculties to the "blind Tradi-

22. Bacon, "Advancement of Learning," 228; see also Evelyn, *Sylva* (1664), sig. B2v;
Doran, "On Elizabethan 'Credulity.'"
23. Bacon, "Preparative towards a Natural and Experimental History," 255.
24. See Welbourne, *Community of Knowledge*, ch. 3, for philosophical remarks on the
neglect of the topic of testimony.
25. Browne, *Pseudodoxia Epidemica* (1646), 25.
26. Harvey, "On the Generation of Animals," in idem, *Works*, 157.

tions" of authority.[27] A manuscript note by Boyle on the "Use of Reason in Natural Philosophy" asserted that "the great Reverence men usually give to humane Authority is undeserved" and that "Humane Testimony ought not to be of force against either right Reason or Experience." It was, Boyle wrote, "improper" to "urge and relye on Testimonys for matters, whose Truth or Falshood may be proved by manifest Reason or easy Experiment."[28] Boyle urged practitioners to follow his example in scrupulously distinguishing "betwixt the matters of fact, they deliver as upon their own knowledge, and those, which they have but upon trust from others."[29] John Ray's preface to Francis Willughby's *Ornithology* assured readers that they had not relied upon "other mens descriptions, but we our selves did carefully describe each Bird from the view and inspection of it lying before us." They had rectified the mistakes of earlier writers who had themselves erred because they accepted correspondents' accounts.[30] Chapter 1 briefly quoted John Locke's systematic critique of reliance upon others' opinions, and further rhetorical expressions of seventeenth-century English empiricist individualism will be cited throughout the remainder of this book. It was a rhetoric which insisted that no source of factual information possessed greater reliability or inspired greater confidence than the direct experience of an individual. The legitimate springs of empirical knowledge were located in the individual's sensory confrontation with the world.

Epistemological Decorum

This sort of individualistic rhetoric, taken by itself and at face value, would count as a massive misrepresentation of scientific practice. In fact, seventeenth-century English natural historians and natural philosophers, writing in other moods and for other purposes, showed themselves well aware that it was. Many of the same practitioners who produced some of the most vigorous individualistic methodological pronouncements also displayed keen appreciation that there was a proper, valuable, and ineradicable role for testimony and trust within legitimate empirical practices. There were three broadly overlapping reasons for this recognition: pragmatic considerations, more or less formal epistemological justifications, and moral arguments having to do with the contingent cultural value placed upon bodies of knowledge undeniably founded wholly or mainly upon testimony.

First, it was widely acknowledged that the category of "experience"

---

27. Evelyn, *Sylva*, sig. B2v.
28. Boyle Papers, Vol. 9, f. 25v.
29. Boyle, "New Experiments Touching Cold," 476.
30. Willughby, *Ornithology* (1678), sig. A2 2v.

customarily and justifiably encompassed not just what individuals had by way of their own senses but also the reliable testimony they had of others' sensory engagements with the world. In the case of phenomena removed from one in space and time, it was freely conceded that one's knowledge had to be indirectly secured. There was nothing necessarily faulty about knowledge which came to one through these routes, and to say that such knowledge was not part of an individual's "experience" was either pedantic or solipsistic.[31] Boyle was one among many commentators who noted that it was through testimony that we come securely and warrantably to have such factual historical knowledge as that Caesar existed and that a new star appeared in the heavens in 1572.[32]

In the same manuscript in which Boyle sought to limit the force of testimony where individual reason or direct experience were available, he also wrote that "Humane Testimony is of great and almost necessary use in natural Philosophy."[33] John Wilkins concurred: there are "several things which we cannot otherwise know, but as others do inform us of them. As namely *matters of fact,* together with the account of *persons* and *places* at a distance."[34] According to the former Cromwellian courtier Sir Charles Wolseley, to deny credit to testimony is

> to deny our selves the benefit of any part of the World, or of any thing done in any part of the World, at any time in the World; but just what we our *selves saw* in the times and places wherein we lived. No one Age can be of any use to another, in any Record of it; nor any one Man of use to another, by his Credit . . . For, the same reason, that will make a Man not to believe others, will be as good to them, not to believe him: and so, all Mankind must *live upon their eye-sight.*

The members of each generation would have to seek independent warrant for each item of knowledge transmitted to them. Each genera-

---

31. There were, to be sure, a few English writers concerned radically to devalue the status of testified experience. Hobbes (*Leviathan,* 132) notably argued that when one's knowledge arises from "some saying of another, of whose ability to know the truth, and of whose honesty in not deceiving, he doubteth not," then "the Discourse is not so much concerning the Thing, as the Person; And the Resolution is called Beleefe, and Faith: *Faith, in* the man; *Beleefe,* both *of* the man, and *of* the truth of what he says."

32. Boyle, "Christian Virtuoso," 525–29; cf. Glanvill, *Essays,* 49. Boyle then distinguished (p. 525) between "personal experience, which a man acquires immediately by himself, and accrues to him by his own sensations," and "historical experience," which, "though it were personal in some other man, is but by his relation or testimony, whether immediately or mediately, conveyed to us." I intend no implication here that such arguments were particular to English 'moderns': similar material is in seventeenth-century Scholastic textbooks.

33. Boyle Papers, Vol. 9, f. 25v.

34. Wilkins, *Principles and Duties of Natural Religion* (1678), 4.

tion would have to (if it could) build its culture anew.[35] But this was understood to be absurd and impossible. In matters transacted, for example, "before he was born, and such as he never saw," a man had no practical option but to rely upon "the credible Testimony of others . . . 'tis not possible to know them any other way."[36]

Theologians as well as natural philosophers identified as madmen those skeptical of all knowledge derived from testimony. Ask of such a skeptic "whether he doth question everything in the world, which he was not present at the doing of himself": "If he peremptorily resolved to *believe* nothing but *what* he *sees*, he is fit for nothing but . . . to be soundly *purged* with *Hellebore* to free him from those *cloudy humours* that make him suspect the whole world to be an *imposture*." In fact, we cannot even imagine any man "so destitute of reason, as to question the truth of every matter of fact which he doth not see himself." The "most *concerning* and *weighty actions* of mens *lives*, are built on no other *foundation*" than testimony. A gentleman's title to his land derives from testimony. So does a trader's knowledge of the existence of such a place as the Indies, and, indeed, all persons' knowledge of their own natural parents. What would it be to question one's own mother's honesty?[37]

Gilbert Burnet identified the libertine earl of Rochester as just that kind of person who cynically rejected legitimate testimony: "I answered to all this, that, believing a thing upon the testimony of another . . . where there was no reason to suspect the testimony . . . was not only a reasonable thing, but it was the hinge on which all the government and justice in the world depended."[38] A person who would not take information on the same bases as others would not know what others knew, and, accordingly, would not be accounted a competent and reasonable member of society. Wolseley said that a man who "would believed nothing but what he has seen" was an idiot, and Wilkins said that he would be "a fantastical incredulous fool."[39] Anyone who, therefore, wished to belong to the relevant polity was practically obliged not to be skeptical about the testimonial sources of 'whatever everyone knows.'

The pragmatic recommendation of testimonial sources of proper

35. Wolseley, *Unreasonableness of Atheism* (1675), 145–48.

36. Ibid., 23–24, 125; see also Wilkins, *Principles and Duties of Natural Religion*, 10.

37. Stillingfleet, *Origines Sacræ* (1662), 111–12. (Hellebore was a botanical drug used in treating the mentally ill.) The invitation to consider disbelief in one's own parentage was a standard trope in early modern apologies for testimony, its force deriving largely from the honor culture in which impugning legitimate birth reliably elicited the *mentita;* see also Wolseley, *Unreasonableness of Atheism*, 146; Wilkins, *Principles and Duties of Natural Religion*, 27.

38. Burnet, "Life and Death of the Earl of Rochester," 210–11.

39. Wolseley, *Unreasonableness of Atheism*, 24–25; Wilkins, *Principles and Duties of Natural Religion*, 10; see also Shapiro, *Wilkins*, 230–31.

factual knowledge was recognized to apply to those specialized experiences of concern to scientific practitioners. Bacon's projected experimental history of monsters necessitated trust in testimony, as such later practitioners as Boyle were well aware: "All those that happened in other times and places than we have lived in (and those will be incomparably more than any of us has personally observed) we must take upon the credit of others." Experience which was in principle available to all living persons might in practice be accessible only to a few, as was, for example, telescopic experience of sunspots or Saturn's rings. Those modern natural philosophers who had not the good fortune to see such things for themselves "must take these phænomena upon the credit of those that have observed them."[40] The thrust of Boyle's, and the Royal Society's, early program was to build a solid factual foundation for a reformed natural philosophy by soliciting more and more testimony and extending networks of justified trust further and further.

Here the English experimentalists were markedly less skeptical, and more sociable, than Descartes, who reckoned that even if one man were not equal to the job of making the necessary experiments or observations, yet "he could not, to good advantage, employ other hands than his own, excepting those of artisans or persons of that kind whom he could pay, and whom the hope of gain—which is a very effectual incentive—might cause to perform with exactitude all the things they were directed to accomplish." As for experimental communications from others, it was probably not worth the philosopher's time soliciting and evaluating them: they were generally so biased and so clogged with "many circumstances or superfluous matter, that it would be very difficult for him to disentangle the truth."[41] Cartesian rationalism could tolerate—even require—that degree and quality of skeptical individualism.

Yet so far as seventeenth-century English writers were concerned, it was not at all evident that knowledge derived through reliance on others was necessarily less sound than that based upon more direct individual means. Wolseley reckoned that an Englishman who had never been to London might be as certain of the existence of such a place "as he can be of any *Mathematical* proposition." Anyone who sought to persuade Wolseley that adequately testified knowledge was insecure was himself vulnerable:

> I may, with as good reason, trouble him with objections, and provoke him to doubt of what he himself sees; and tell him; either his *eye sight* may fail, or mis-inform him; or else, the object may be such as may

40. Boyle, "Christian Virtuoso," 528.
41. Descartes, "Discourse on Method" (1637), 126–27.

be purposely disposed to couzen and delude his sight; In the one, a man hath nothing but the single testimony of his *own eyes;* In the other, the testimony of thousands transferred to him upon unquestionable credit.

Wolseley noted how commonly rational men accept that their senses are mistaken. We 'see' the sun as a disk a few inches wide, yet we 'know' that it is immensely large.[42]

Galileo famously applauded Aristarchus and Copernicus for making "reason so conquer sense that, in defiance of the latter, the former became the mistress of their belief."[43] Just because categories of people varied in their ability to master and discipline sense, Galileo recommended teaching different things about the motion of the earth to the learned and to the vulgar.[44] Wilkins agreed that it was a characteristic vulgar error to accord primacy and privilege to immediate sense impressions: "You may as soon persuade some country peasants that the moon is made of green-cheese, (as we say) as that it is bigger than his cart-wheel, since both seem equally to contradict his sight, and he has not reason enough to lead him farther than his senses."[45] Descartes linked the persistence of Scholastic philosophy to the childhood error of supposing that what the senses apprehended is what really exists.[46] Joseph Glanvill noted that "in many particular cases, we are not assured of the report of our Senses," needing knowledge to "correct their Informations."[47] Boyle argued that the judgment of "the undiscerning multitude . . . seems rather lodged in the eye than in the brain," and that was the major basis for vulgar error.[48] The philosopher might be distinguished from the vulgar man precisely because the latter was a slave to his senses while the former was at liberty to disbelieve the immediate impressions of eyes and ears when his rational knowledge

42. Wolseley, *Unreasonableness of Atheism,* 24, 127.

43. Galileo, *Dialogue Concerning the Two Chief World Systems* (1632), 328; cf. Kepler's *Defence of Tycho against Ursus* (1600), in Jardine, *The Birth of the History and Philosophy of Science,* 155–56.

44. E.g., Galileo, "Letter to Christina" (1615), 182, 196, 220–01. For treatment of this position in the context of important early modern "exoteric/esoteric" distinctions, see Bagley, "On the Practice of Esotericism," esp. 234–35.

45. Wilkins, *Discovery of a New World,* 11; see also Browne, *Pseudodoxia Epidemica,* 8. For the argumentative context of Wilkins's remarks, see Johns, "Wisdom in the Concourse," 16–18; idem, "Ross versus Wilkins and the Meanings of Copernicanism."

46. Descartes, "Principles of Philosophy," 247, 249–50; see also Garber, *Descartes' Metaphysical Physics,* 100–02.

47. Glanvill, "Of Scepticism and Certainty," in idem, *Essays* (1676), 48–49.

48. Boyle, "Greatness of Mind," 551. For a systematic account of the unreliability of temperature sensation, see idem, "New Experiments Touching Cold," 481–84.

of the nature of things informed him of sensory error. The rational knowledge which corrected sense might come from adequate testimony.

Second, reliance upon legitimate testimony was treated and condoned in the context of formal discussions of the natures of different kinds of knowledges. Seventeenth-century English philosophers were in substantial agreement with Aristotle that one could legitimately demand of an item of knowledge only that kind of justification and that quality of certainty of which it was in its nature capable.[49] Various accounts rested absolute certainty and binding assent in mathematical demonstration and in direct eyewitness, while developing the notion of a lesser, but still wholly adequate, quality of certainty and basis of assent in the *probable* knowledge of, for example, physical cause or historical fact. John Tillotson explicitly cited Aristotelian warrant in condemning those who would unreasonably "expect the same kind of proof and evidence for every thing, which we have for some things."[50] John Wilkins said that men should be satisfied by the "best evidence . . . which [each] kind of thing will bear."[51] It was "the more natural way, and should be observed in all controversies, to apply unto every thing the proper proofs of it."[52]

Stillingfleet cautioned that "all things are not capable of the like way of proof": it was "most unreasonable for any to seek for further *evidence* and *demonstration* . . . , then the *matter* to be proved is *capable* of. . . . Whoever yet undertook to bring *matters* of *fact* into *Mathematical demonstrations*, or thought he had ground to question the certainty of any thing that was not proved in a *Mathematical* way to him?"[53] Glanvill recommended that "a Man proportion the degree of his Assent, to the degree of Evidence."[54] Boyle influentially argued that "it is not just to require other proofs of a thing, than such as, in case it be true, the nature of it will bear."[55] And John Locke systematically reflected upon the varieties of knowledges and the "degrees of assent" appropriate to

---

49. Aristotle, *Nicomachean Ethics*, I. 1094^b 24–27; idem, *Metaphysics*, II. 995^a 15–16; idem, *Posterior Analytics*, I. 88^a 31–88^b 29; see also Van Leeuwen, *Problem of Certainty*, 22–25, 38–41, 67.
50. Tillotson, "Sermon I. The Wisdom of Being Religious," in idem, *Works*, I, 16.
51. Wilkins, *Principles and Duties of Natural Religion*, 23–25. For details of schemes used by English writers to discriminate varieties of knowledge, see Shapiro, *Probability and Certainty*, esp. 27–37, 83–88, and Van Leeuwen, *Problem of Certainty*, esp. chs 3–5.
52. Wilkins, *Discovery of a New World*, 65.
53. Stillingfleet, *Origines Sacræ*, 111, 380; also 383.
54. Glanvill, "Of Scepticism and Certainty," in idem, *Essays*, 46; see also Van Leeuwen, *Problem of Certainty*, 71–89.
55. Boyle, "Christian Virtuoso. Appendix to First Part," 681; see also idem, "Excellency of Theology," 41–43.

each. It would be "vain," Locke said, for one "to expect demonstration and certainty in things not capable of it" and to "refuse assent to very rational propositions . . . because they cannot be made out so evident, as to surmount every the least . . . pretence of doubting." Pragmatic considerations supported formal epistemological classification:

> He that, in the ordinary affairs of life, would admit of nothing but direct plain demonstration, would be sure of nothing in this world, but of perishing quickly. The wholesomeness of his meat or drink would not give him reason to venture on it: and I would fain know what it is he could do upon such grounds as are capable of no doubt, no objection.[56]

It was neither proper nor expedient to demand absolute certainty of the knowledge upon which we carry out everyday actions: "The conduct of our lives, and the management of our great concerns, will not bear delay." In matters where judgments may legitimately differ, it would "become all men to maintain peace, and the common offices of humanity, and friendship in the diversity of opinions."[57] Boyle argued similarly. The moral order of everyday action had to rest upon a quality of knowledge that was in principle insecure but in practice fully answerable to the demands placed upon it. In seventeenth-century English usage, this quality was referred to as "moral certainty."[58] Provided that we supposed "the truth of the most received rules of prudence and principles of practical philosophy," a moral certainty is the "surest, that men aspire to, not only in the conduct of private men's affairs, but in the government of states, and even of the greatest monarchies and empires."[59]

Tillotson pointed out that this kind of assurance was deemed sufficient by hardheaded merchants "who never were at the East or West Indies, or in Turkey or Spain, yet do venture their whole estate in traffic thither, though they have no mathematical demonstration . . . that there are such places."[60] For Wilkins moral certainty did not, as

56. Locke, *Essay Concerning Human Understanding*, Bk. IV, ch. 11, sect. 10.

57. Ibid., ch. 16, sects. 3–4.

58. The nature and grounds of moral certainty have been well and extensively treated by, among others, Shapiro, *Probability and Certainty*, chs 2–3; idem, "'To a Moral Certainty'"; Van Leeuwen, *Problem of Certainty*, ch. 2; Daston, *Classical Probability*, 191–94; Gigerenzer et al., *Empire of Chance*, 6–10; see also Shapin and Schaffer, *Leviathan and the Air-Pump*, e.g., 24, 107, 316, 327.

59. Boyle, "Some Considerations about the Reconcileableness of Reason and Religion" (1675), 182; cf. Descartes, "Principles of Philosophy" (1644), 301: "Moral certainty [is that] which suffices for the conduct of life." Boyle went on to cite judicial practices, though, again, it should be noted that he did so by way of generally recognized maxims of prudence.

60. Tillotson, "Sermon I. The Wisdom of Being Religious," in idem, *Works*, I, 23.

mathematical certainty did, "necessitate every man's Assent," yet its proofs may "be so plain, that every man whose judgment is free from prejudice will consent unto them."[61] Knowledge we had by way of testimony might be only probable, but there were degrees of probability which effectively mimicked the certainty of demonstration and eyewitness and which were wholly adequate as bases for conducting the affairs of everyday life. To expect more of knowledge which was not capable of more was to sever oneself from the common grounds of common action. Assent to legitimate testimony was grounded in "the common principles of reason."[62] To recognize the legitimate boundaries of demonstration and eyewitness as well as the legitimate calls of testimony was to behave with *decorum:* ways of behaving and judging were adapted to circumstances. The fine judgments of epistemological decorum were anchored in, and justified by, the value placed in the civil conversations of everyday life.

Third, explicitly moral justifications for testimony shaded into pragmatic and formal epistemological apologies. How one was counseled to act upon testimonial sources of knowledge drew upon repertoires instructing people how to lead a successful, a happy, and a virtuous life. The moral "bottoming" of these justifications is evident in reflectively philosophical genres and in the practical ethical texts treated in chapter 3.[63] However, the most obviously moral context for the legitimization of testimonial grounds of knowledge is found in seventeenth-century English accounts of *religious* knowledge. Much religious knowledge manifestly had a historical character. The truth of beliefs concerning, for example, the existence of Christ, his divinity, the miracles he performed, and his crucifixion and resurrection could be neither demonstrated nor confirmed by direct personal experience. There was no denying that such matters of fact *could in principle be untrue,* just as it could be untrue that a man's parentage was what his mother said it was, that such a person as Caesar ever existed, or that a new star had appeared in the heavens in 1572. Nevertheless, it was a central concern of Christian apologetics to warrant scriptural testimony as reliable and to show that people might as securely give their assent to it as to formally more certain types of knowledge. This meant that it had to be shown that the probable quality of properly testified matters substantially and practically overlapped with the quality of both demonstrable matters and the facts accessible to personal witness.

61. Wilkins, *Principles and Duties of Natural Religion,* 7–8; cf. [Ward], *Philosophicall Essay* (1652), 95.

62. [Ward], *Philosophicall Essay,* 119.

63. The term *bottoming* is tellingly used in Locke, *Essay Concerning Human Understanding,* Bk. IV, ch. 16, sect. 4. I have already begun to show the use of such considerations in handling scientific testimony, and the next chapter will further develop the theme.

As Stillingfleet put it, "a *moral certainty* is a *sufficient foundation* for an *undoubted assent.*"[64]

The development of the category of moral certainty was the business of practitioners in law, science, theology, and history, as well as everyday actors in English civil society. The notion did important work in all these contexts, securing a legitimate role for testimony while policing its proper usage. Its moral charge was most evident in the writings of those concerned to show the adequacy of religious testimony, while almost all commentators, whatever their specialized practices, acknowledged that scriptural truths were the foundations of moral order and, for that reason, required justification and protection. Many English theologians elaborated a generally applicable model for validating testimony through a particular defense of the reliability of biblical factual narrative.

Wolseley drew out the sweeping consequences of mistrusting scriptural relations: "He that upon no terms will admit us to be *morally certain*" of scriptural events, even as handed on through a chain of testifiers,

> must (with great absurdity, and without the least colour of Reason, or certain knowledge of his own to contradict it,) put the *Fool* and the *Lye* upon all Men of all sorts, in an Age: and of necessity, render them so *foolishly* weak, as not to be able to judge whether a thing be done, or not done; or else, so *maliciously false* to all Mankind, as to agree together to convey a *Lye* down to them, and impose an eminent Cheat upon them.

Were these truths to be undone, and, consequently, were religious authority to be undermined, there could be no such thing as a binding oath or promise, no source of obligation, no civil order.[65] Wilkins argued a related case for the religious merit of belief in what could not be demonstrated. Three plus three equals six, necessarily, but there is no religious virtue in giving assent to matters which command assent: "Rewards and Punishments do properly belong to *free* Actions . . . , not to such as are *necessary.*" Jesus said to doubting Thomas: "Blessed are they that have not seen and yet have believed" (John 20:29).[66]

Scientific practitioners in the English setting were no less concerned to secure religious testimony, yet the way of arguing sketched above was equally valuable within their specialized culture. This was the set-

---

64. Stillingfleet, *Origines Sacræ*, 112.

65. Wolseley, *Unreasonableness of Atheism*, 139–40, 154–55.

66. Wilkins, *Principles and Duties of Natural Religion*, 30–32; see also ibid., 7. The verse is cited to the same effect in Tillotson, "Sermon I. The Wisdom of Being Religious," in idem, *Works*, I, 23.

ting in which Thomas Sprat, while publicizing Royal Society advocacy of personal witness, argued against those who would not "consent to any mans *Opinions,* unless he sees the *operations* of his hands agree with them."[67] Boyle spoke for both religion and empirical science in elaborating a working sensibility of moral certainty:

> It is manifest, that there are many truths . . . that, by the nature of the things, are not capable of mathematical or metaphysical demonstrations, and yet, being really truths, have a just title to our assent; it must be acknowledged, that a rational assent may be founded upon proofs, that reach not to rigid demonstrations, it being sufficient, that they are strong enough to deserve a wise man's acquiescence in them.[68]

For these commentators the practical test of what were "really truths" and of "rational assent" was, indeed, the fact of "a wise man's acquiescence."

The Prudential Maxims of Testimony

Testimony was therefore understood to be necessary to the constitution of practical knowledge and to the performance of collective practical actions. Yet a wide range of practitioners and commentators expressed deep concern that testimony be properly evaluated and rigorously controlled. On the one hand, testimony was fully recognized as an invaluable resource for the making of knowledge and the ordering of society; on the other, there was acute anxiety that *undisciplined* reliance upon testimony would destroy both knowledge and social order. For Bacon, a philosophical practice that did not duly investigate and assess its sources of information would be just as insecure as a "kingdom or state" that directed "its counsels and affairs, not by letters and reports from ambassadors and trustworthy messengers, but by the gossip of the streets."[69] How was one to discern testimony that might be safely relied upon to build one's knowledge and to conduct one's affairs? Seventeenth-century English writers vigorously engaged with this question in formal treatments of right conduct and proper knowledge even as practitioners reached working solutions inscribed in their everyday social practice. John Locke's discussion of probability and testimony in Book IV, chapter 15 of the *Essay Concerning Human Understanding* is perhaps the most widely known reflection on this, but the problem was also handled with varying degrees of systematicity by,

67. Sprat, *History of the Royal Society,* 352.
68. Boyle, "Discourse of Things above Reason," 450.
69. Bacon, "New Organon," 94.

inter alia, Bacon, Boyle, Glanvill, Hooke, Sprat, Stillingfleet, Tillotson, Wilkins, and Wolseley, while in the eighteenth century David Hume's treatment of miracles turned upside down the preferred solution arrived at by most of these authors.[70] I want here briefly to offer a schematic summary of some seventeenth-century prescriptive engagements with the problem of testimony. I will then notice some little-recognized features of these prescriptions which make their status as 'rules' or 'norms' of conduct problematic. That will prepare the ground for the next chapter's treatment of a number of cases of practical action in the assessment of knowledge-claims, showing how assessments were managed in concrete instances and what bearing formal justifications had in the everyday reasoning of scientific practitioners.

I discern seven maxims for the evaluation of testimony canvassed in the seventeenth-century literature:[71] (i) assent to testimony which is plausible; (ii) assent to testimony which is multiple; (iii) assent to testimony which is consistent; (iv) assent to testimony which is immediate; (v) assent to testimony from knowledgeable or skilled sources; (vi) assent to testimony given in a manner which inspires a just confidence; and (vii) assent to testimony from sources of acknowledged integrity and disinterestedness.

(i) Since we customarily assent to testimony which corresponds to our overall knowledge of the world, few formal schemes for the evaluation of testimony devoted much space to elucidating a *principle* of plausibility. It was for the most part simply assumed that plausibility judgments rightly figured in shaping assent. Nevertheless, Locke's formal account of the "inducements" to receive testimony as true commenced with "the conformity of anything with our own knowledge, observation, and experience."[72] We may evaluate new probable knowledge-sources, not by inquiring into the circumstances and quality of that

70. Leibniz's commentary in the 1690s closely followed Locke's treatment of testimony and the inducements to assent: Leibniz, *New Essays Concerning Human Understanding,* Bk. IV, chs 11, 16. For accounts of Locke's scheme, see, e.g., Daston, *Classical Probability,* 193–96; Van Leeuwen, *Problem of Certainty,* 132–35.

71. This list is assembled from a wide range of sources, though in its content and philosophically systematic character it is closest to Locke's account. Most seventeenth-century treatments of testimony were, however, neither as formal nor as systematic as this listing might imply. So, to some extent, my purpose here is implicitly to contest the impression given by more modern philosophers that maxims of this sort could, as it were, stand alone or that their application could be clear-cut and unproblematic: see, e.g., Hempel, *Philosophy of Natural Science,* ch. 4. I use *maxim* in the Aristotelian sense: "a statement, not about a particular fact . . . , but of a general kind; nor is it about any and every subject . . . but only about questions of practical conduct" (*Rhetoric,* II. 1394[a] 20–25; see also Jonsen and Toulmin, *Abuse of Casuistry,* 73–74, 252–53).

72. Locke, *Essay Concerning Human Understanding,* Bk. IV, ch. 15, sect. 4.

testimony, and not by assessing the relationship between different sources of testimony, but simply by deploying a criterion of likelihood, by juxtaposing a given claim with what we already *know*.[73]

Plausibility assessments normally appear so routine and mechanical that, in everyday practice, it is unclear whether they ought strictly to be regarded as judgments at all. If we hear tell that it was wet in Edinburgh yesterday, or that swans in Australia are white, we tend simply to take such testimony in and to act upon it as if it were the case. If, as Locke put it, "another tells me he saw a man in England, in the midst of a sharp winter, walk upon water hardened with cold, this has so great conformity with what is usually observed to happen, that I am disposed by the nature of the thing itself to assent to it." Most of what we are told about the world is likely to stand in broad agreement with what we already know, and, indeed, it is hard to imagine a stable situation in which *very much* testimony amazed or astounded. Of course, if the testimony were of dubious plausibility, or if "some manifest suspicion attend the relation" even of an otherwise highly plausible matter of fact, then other maxims might have to be brought to bear upon its assessment.[74] Plausibility as a gauge of the credibility of relations was, of course, a thoroughly well-understood, and even reflected upon, feature of everyday civil conversation. It was on this basis that early modern gentlemen were practically advised (see chapter 3) to avoid acquiring an untrustworthy reputation, if necessary by refraining from relating implausible matters—even if these matters were believed to be true and even if they had been witnessed by the potential testifier.[75]

(ii) Locke went on to recommend that in considering the testimony of others we ought to take account of the *number* of such sources. This maxim might be stated thus: 'As the number of testifiers increases, so it becomes more likely that what they testify is true.'[76] Matthew Hale noted that "that which is reported by many Eye-witnesses hath greater

73. Sometimes seventeenth-century writers referred to this consideration as the "credibility of a thing" (see, e.g., Burnet, "Life and Death of the Earl of Rochester," 210), though for the sake of consistency I mean to reserve that term for the *outcome* of assessments of knowledge-claims in which plausibility is one element.

74. Locke, *Essay Concerning Human Understanding*, Bk. IV, ch. 15, sect. 5. Note that Locke matter-of-factly assimilated the scheme against which testimony is compared to "the thing itself," thus eliding the role of testimony in the constitution of base knowledge. Cf. my treatment of plausibility in chapter 1 above.

75. E.g., Brathwait, *English Gentleman*, 83–84; Guazzo, *Civile Conversation*, I, 153–54; Castiglione, *The Courtier*, 139–40. Ronald Westrum's work on the "social intelligence system" of modern science (e.g., "Science and Social Intelligence about Anomalies") is a notable locus for discussion of implausibility judgments and reluctance to testify.

76. Locke, *Essay Concerning Human Understanding*, Bk. IV, ch. 15, sect. 5.

motives of credibility than that which is reported by few."[77] And Wilkins cited Aristotelian license for the "proper way of Reasoning from *Authority*":

> That which seems true to some wise men, may upon that account be esteemed somewhat probable; what is believed by most wise men, hath a further degree of probability; what *most men*, both wise and unwise, do assent unto, is yet more probable: But what all men have generally consented to, hath for it the highest degree of Evidence of this kind, that any thing is capable of: And it must be monstrous arrogance and folly for any single Persons to prefer their own judgments before the general suffrage of Mankind.[78]

Here again writers sometimes traced analogies with formal legal procedures. Sprat noted that people were generally content that the law condemn persons on the agreeing testimony of "two, or three witnesses," and urged that they be equally content in assenting to knowledge-claims "if they have the concurring Testimonies of *threescore or an hundred*" fellows of the Royal Society.[79] Boyle fleshed out his apology for moral certainty by drawing attention to "the practice of our courts of justice here in *England*" in cases of murder "and some other criminal causes": "For, though the testimony of a single witness shall not suffice to prove the accused party guilty of murder; yet the testimony of two witnesses, though but of equal credit, that is, a second testimony added to the first, though of itself never a whit more credible than the former, shall ordinarily suffice to prove a man guilty." Boyle assimilated legal practice to quite widely distributed appreciations of what it was "thought reasonable to suppose," namely "that, though each testimony single be but probable, yet a concurrence of such probabilities, (which ought in reason to be attributed to the truth of what they jointly tend to prove) may well amount to a moral certainty." Just as everyday actors understood that multiple testimony provided a surer warrant for assent than a single relation, so conviction of a capital crime and the sentence of death were reasonably considered to be adequately grounded in multiple testimony against the indicted person.[80] The

77. M. Hale, *Primitive Origination of Mankind* (1677), 129 (quoted in Shapiro, "'To a Moral Certainty,'" 162).

78. Wilkins, *Principles and Duties of Natural Religion*, 41; see also Doran, "On Elizabethan 'Credulity,'" 155.

79. Sprat, *History of the Royal Society*, 100. The original requirement for "two or three witnesses" to justify capital punishment is biblical, e.g., "At the mouth of two witnesses, or three witnesses, shall he that is worthy of death be put to death; but at the mouth of one witness he shall not be put to death" (Deuteronomy 17:6).

80. Boyle, "Some Considerations about the Reconcileableness of Reason and Religion," 182. For systematic treatment of multiple witnesses in legal proceedings, see Shapiro, *Probability and Certainty*, 174, 184, 187. In his treason trial of 1603, Sir Walter Raleigh argued that he could not be convicted upon the (subsequently withdrawn) "pa-

reasonableness of legal practices was securely grounded in everyday understandings of how reasonable men proceeded.

Similarly, historical testimony multiply attested at the time the events were said to occur was identified as more secure than that for which there was only one witness and one direct testifier. To be sure, a man might lie or be deceived about an event, yet, as the relevant eyewitness testimony multiplied, so it became *obviously* unreasonable to assume that all such testimony was corrupt.[81] The same held for *categories* of phenomena. While testimony of specific "extraordinary effects which have been in nature" might singly be doubtful, yet "multitudes" of *similar* happenings have been related, and here the multiplicity of testimony could be recruited to establish the probability of the genus 'miracle' even where single events might in principle be open to doubt.[82]

(iii) Locke further advised that testimony be assessed according to "the consistency of the parts, and circumstances of the relation."[83] Here the maxim might be formulated: 'Inspect for contradiction or inconsistency the internal and external relations of testimony, and, if you find any such problems, take these as an indication that the testimony may be untrue.' Little more needed to be said to explain or justify this maxim since it too was a widely distributed resource in everyday practical reasoning. Chapter 3 noted Montaigne's pragmatic counsel against lying: the truth was one, lies were many, and he who lied might reliably be found out through discrepancies in his utterances. A man might say that he had seen a mermaid near Newfoundland and on another occasion say that he had seen it near Iceland. Credibility might be enhanced by adding circumstances to the claim, creating that verisimilitude which would be hard to reproduce had he not seen a mermaid. Or he might offer circumstantial information which was potentially checkable, and hence make a moral display of confidence such as no liar would risk presenting: he had seen it together with a named acquaintance, known to the auditors of his tale. These were the schemes used by theologians to validate scriptural testimony. Stillingfleet, for example, argued that the apostles delivered their "testimony with the greatest particularity as to all circumstances."[84] Boyle's celebrated prolix and circumstantial experimental

per accusation" of a single man, but his judges denied that such corroboration was necessary, or, indeed, that his accuser needed to be brought to confront him: Williams, *Raleigh*, 196–201.

81. E.g., Wolseley, *Unreasonableness of Atheism*, 129–40.

82. E.g., Stillingfleet, *Origines Sacræ*, 419–20. For systematic treatment of seventeenth-century English attitudes towards the credibility of miracle-testimony, see Burns, *Great Debate on Miracles*, esp. ch. 3; Reedy, *The Bible and Reason*, esp. ch. 3.

83. Locke, *Essay Concerning Human Understanding*, Bk. IV, ch. 15, sect. 4.

84. Stillingfleet, *Origines Sacræ*, 297; see also 419–20.

reporting traded upon the same moral-epistemic scheme linking moral risk, consistency, and veracity.[85]

Consistency, in this sense, referred to the perceived internal and external relations of a given narration: did it fit together and did it fit with what else one knew? Yet consistency judgments were also deemed pertinent to assessing the credibility of multiple sources, and were, accordingly, directed towards the relations *between* testimonial sources. Indeed, the very idea of multiple sources which might warrantably induce assent presupposed a judgment that these were reports *of the same thing*. When Locke commended assent to "the concurrent reports of all that mention it," he was making such a presupposition.[86] A decision that reports significantly varied might, at the same time, count as a decision that they were reports of *different* things and therefore could not legitimately sum. On the other hand, there is nothing inherent in the nature of varying reports dictating a judgment that they differently refer, and chapter 7 examines Boyle's ontological repair of varying measurements of physical qualities.

Nevertheless, given an expectation that the world-to-be-reported-upon possesses a determinate structure which reliably generates in competent human beings determinate perceptions and reports, then the same pragmatic moral resource explaining internal inconsistency as a sign of untruthfulness might also identify the inconsistency of collective reports as a serious trouble: the sources were not all direct witnesses; they agreed to deceive and were betrayed by the multiple faces of untruth. By contrast, where multiple reports were deemed to agree, there was on that basis a legitimately strong presumption that all reporters had experience of the matter and that no lie was being perpetrated or delusion propagated. It was, as Wolseley said, "wholly Incredible to believe" that globally agreeing assent was founded in a universal conspiracy to deceive and effectiveness in carrying out that deception—"that no body . . . should contradict the Fact . . . and discover the Cheat." When "very many together agree to witness to the fact of a thing they saw, it must needs give all the cumulative advantage to the Certainty of it that possibly we can expect."[87]

(iv) The reliability of testimony was formally deemed to vary in pro-

---

85. For the rhetoric of historicity in seventeenth-century science, see Shapin, "Pump and Circumstance"; Dear, "Miracles, Experiments, and the Ordinary Course of Nature"; idem, "Narratives, Anecdotes, and Experiments"; Bazerman, *Shaping Written Knowledge*, chs 3–4; and for the classical rhetorical tradition of *enargheia* (or the ability to communicate an illusion of reality), see Ginzburg, "Checking the Evidence," 80, and Wintroub, "The Looking Glass of Facts."

86. Locke, *Essay Concerning Human Understanding*, Bk. IV, ch. 16, sect. 6.

87. Wolseley, *Unreasonableness of Atheism*, 128–29, 138; see also Stillingfleet, *Origines Sacræ*, 289–97.

portion to the closeness of its connection with the matter upon which it reported. Locke noted that "no probability can rise higher than its first original." The veracity of the factual records of antiquity were, on this basis, only as good as the testimony provided by those who witnessed the relevant matters: no matter whether that testimony was subsequently cited and re-cited by swarms of others who were not there. The matter, "so far from receiving any strength thereby, . . . is only the weaker." Any number of considerations could induce one man to quote another wrongly, and the length of a testifying chain might be taken as an indication of the uncertainty of what was claimed. An original testimony of great probability might be undermined by repeated retellings and reinscriptions but could never be more judged more probable than it originally was.[88]

William Gilbert repeatedly cast doubt upon ancient authority by aligning himself with humanist sensibilities about the corruption of texts: the errors cumulatively introduced into ancient texts by "mere copyists" might be corrected by insisting upon direct experience.[89] Boyle wrote that "I dare not trust" every author's quotations from others: many times, on inspection, the quotation was incorrect, and sometimes it had been willfully fabricated.[90] Locke drew attention to a "rule observed in the law of England" and "so generally approved of as reasonable . . . that I never yet heard of any one that blames it," namely "that though the attested copy of a record be good proof, yet the copy of a copy, ever so well attested . . . will not be admitted as a proof in judicature."[91] Understandably, this maxim was not forcefully recruited in practices which aimed to secure a central role for testimony of great antiquity. Theologians, for example, did not dwell upon the maxim of directness, while Bacon elaborated it in the context of a skeptical treatment of religious fables.[92] But even religious writers were comfortable enough with it to argue that the orginal sources of biblical testimony were to be believed because they "were *eye-witnesses* at the first [and] had as much certain assurance of [the matter], as of any thing we now see. And therefore, their report of it then cannot be false, unless they designed it should be so."[93]

In more practical contexts, Bacon prescribed a reporting regime for natural history in which practitioners were to mention whether a

88. Locke, *Essay Concerning Human Understanding*, Bk. IV, ch. 16, sect. 11.

89. Gilbert, *De Magnete*, e.g., 170–72, 265; see also Browne, *Pseudodoxia Epidemica*, 22; Hobbes, *Leviathan*, 105–06; and, for humanist inspiration to direct observation in botany, Reeds, "Renaissance Humanism and Botany."

90. Boyle, "New Experiments Touching Cold," 476–77.

91. Locke, *Essay Concerning Human Understanding*, Bk. IV, ch. 16, sect. 10.

92. E.g., Bacon, "Advancement of Learning," 287.

93. Wolseley, *Unreasonableness of Atheism*, 126; see also Stillingfleet, *Origines Sacræ*, 132.

source took a matter "from report, oral or written . . . , or rather affirmed it of his own knowledge; also whether it was a thing which happened in his own time or earlier."[94] Boyle famously averred of alchemical phenomena "that they that have seen them can much more reasonably believe them, than they that have not," and, accordingly, that eyewitnesses offered more reliable testimony than indirect sources.[95] Time and again Boyle's narratives specified the closeness of the link between himself as author and his sources of information. Matters were vouchsafed on the basis of his own direct experience or upon the testimony of those whom Boyle reliably believed to have had the relevant quality of witness.[96] More minutely, Hooke advised that great care be given to record experiments promptly, insisting that testimony received likewise be inspected for the immediacy of its inscription—"because of the Frailty of the Memory."[97]

(v) Formal schemes prescribing the proper evaluation of testimony recommended that one take into account the knowledgeability or competence of the source. Locke, for example, urged that one consider "the skill of the witnesses." He gave as an example the epistemic distinction between one who worked through the demonstrative proof that the three angles of a triangle were equal to two right angles and one who received this information as testimony from "a mathematician, a man of credit." In the former case, the knowledge is demonstrative; in the latter, it is but probable, its precise quality hinging upon the source's mathematical competence as well as probity.[98] The pertinent maxim might thus be expressed: 'Assent to those who know whereof they speak.'

This was a maxim of everyday conduct thoroughly familiar to early modern actors, most especially to those who recognized as legitimate institutionalized distributions of expertise and knowledgeability. In or-

94. Bacon, "Preparative towards a Natural and Experimental History," 259–60.
95. Boyle, "Two Essays, Concerning the Unsuccessfulness of Experiments," 343.
96. Among very many examples, see Boyle, "Experimenta & Observationes," 569; idem, "Of the Temperature of the Submarine Regions," 342; idem, "General History of the Air," 712. But cf. the discussion of Boyle's technicians in chapter 8 below.
97. Hooke, "General Scheme of the Present State of Natural Philosophy," 63.
98. Locke, *Essay Concerning Human Understanding,* Bk. IV, ch. 15, sects. 1, 4; see also ibid., ch. 18, sect. 4. A parallel argument holds for factual knowledge. Note also that geometrical or logical knowledge, in this sensibility, can only properly be characterized as demonstrative if an individual works through the relevant demonstrations and has the relevant psychological experiences. For all those who do not pass through the proper psychological states, including those who come to hold logical truths by testimony, formally demonstrative knowledge is probable and, therefore, equivalent to historical knowledge. Presumably, logical knowledge is also probable for those who, having worked through the proofs, can no longer summon up from their memory the pertinent psychological states. If this line of reasoning is followed, then knowledge of greater than probable status retreats into a domain radically circumscribed by time.

der to assent to knowledgeable sources, one had to recognize these sources, and, in order reliably to do so as part of a communicative exercise, one had to agree with others as to the identity of the sources. What was knowledge and who was in a posture testifying to its possession? That question might be satisfactorily answered by pointing to the expertise presumed to be located in existing professional or craft roles. Thus, Boyle wrote that there were cases in which it was right for one to subject direct experience to others' expertise:

> Discreet men will oftentimes consult skilfull Jewelers, about the Luster & Beauty (as they speak) even of such Diamonds and other precious Stones, as they do not suspect to be Counterfeit. Epicures themselves in the choice of Wines, do oftentimes desire the Skilfull to Tast these Liquors for them, and relye more on the Palates of Others than their own.[99]

Chapter 3 briefly noted how 'vulgar errors' of perception and reporting were traced to 'vulgar ignorance.' Thomas Browne referred "the Erroneous Disposition of the People" to their "unqualified intellectuals," rendering them "unable to umpire the difficulty of its dissentions." In one mood, early modern commentators vigorously endorsed direct sensory experience over preconception and theoretical prepossession, while in another, as I have already indicated, they were quite able to identify the fallibility of uninstructed sense. Unreliable perceptions and untrustworthy reports were likely to emerge from sources unable to discipline sense through the judicious use of reason and experience:

> For the assured truth of things is derived from the principles of knowledge, and causes, which determine their verities; whereof their uncultivated understandings, scarce holding any theory, [the common people] are but bad discerners of verity. . . . Their understanding is so feeble in the discernment of falsities, and averting the errors of reason, that it submitteth unto the fallacies of sence, and is unable to rectifie the error of its sensations.[100]

Such sensibilities were as common within the practice of early modern natural philosophy as they were in the civil conversations of everyday life. I have noted how such moderns as William Gilbert insinuated the corrupt status of multiply copied ancient texts and approved direct experience as the means for purifying natural knowledge. Accordingly, magnetic testimony by "illustrious navigators and by many intelligent seamen" was recommended over that offered by existing plau-

---

99. Boyle Papers, Vol. 38, f. 154. Boyle here was offering an apology for trusting others' experiments in certain cases rather than making them oneself.

100. Browne, *Pseudodoxia Epidemica*, 8.

sibility schemes and the testimony of the schoolmen. Among these navigators there were those highly skilled in observing the variation of the compass and those of inferior skill. Even on dry land, measurement may not "be made with exactitude save by experts," skilled in the use of instruments and knowledgeable about possible biasing influences.[101] Wilkins similarly argued the case for special expertise in rendering astronomical judgment. The "common people" were to be excluded because they "judge by their senses, and therefore their voices are altogether unfit to decide any philosophical doubt, which cannot well be examined or explained without discourse and reason." General theological and moral knowledgeability, otherwise accounted very valuable, gave insufficient qualification to judge in astronomical matters:

> The ancient fathers, though they were men very eminent for their holy lives, and extraordinary skill in divinity, yet they were most of them very ignorant in that part of learning which concerns [the Copernican theory] . . . and therefore it is not their opinion neither, in this business, that to an indifferent seeker of truth will be of any strong authority.

The maxim which prescribed assent to knowledgeable speakers could be effectively brought to bear in deciding whose observations and whose theoretical conclusions were to be credited. Copernicus "was a man very exact and diligent in these studies for above thirty years," and those who endorsed his views included "most of the best astronomers" and "many of the best skill."[102] Wilkins advised those considering their assent to inspect, as it were, the track record of the adherents of various facts and theories: that which the most knowledgeable believed was most likely to be true.[103] The experimental narratives of such Royal Society practitioners as Boyle pervasively endorsed the likelihood that testimony was sound by noting the expertise, skill, or knowledgeability of the source. Information came from "a very ingenious physician," "a very experienced mason," "an intelligent gentleman," "an adeptus," and so on.[104] By contrast, while he welcomed the opportunity to learn of chemical operations "from illiterate persons," he was not bound on

101. Gilbert, *De Magnete*, 181, 265, 317.

102. Wilkins, *Discourse Concerning a New Planet*, 138, 143; see also ibid., 148.

103. At the same time, Wilkins (*Discourse Concerning a New Planet*, 141–42) cautioned that track record should not be too strongly linked with the reliability or unreliability of a particular claim: "If a man's error in some particulars should take away his credit for every thing else, this would abolish the force of all human authority; for *humanum est errare*."

104. These examples come from Boyle, "General History of the Air," 714–23, and idem, "Strange Reports," 605–09, though practically any Boylean text relating matters of fact not personally witnessed or produced is a rich source of similar locutions.

their "credit" to "take up any opinion about them."[105] Elsewhere, Boyle elaborated the sensibility which allowed him to credit expert reports of phenomena which were perceptually available to the vulgar as well: "If these stories were related by ordinary persons . . . , the oddness of them might well tempt a wary man to suspend his judgment; but the judiciousness of the writers, and the profession [medical] they were of . . . may well be permitted to bring credit to their assertions."[106]

(vi) While few formal pronouncements on the assessment of testimony made much mention of the *manner* in which testimony was offered, maxims recommending attention to the style of presentation and the moral posture of sources were pervasive in the early modern practical ethical literature. In advising attention to "the circumstances of the relation," Locke was evidently referring to consistency features treated in (iii). Yet courtesy texts repeatedly counseled gentle readers, if they wished to be credible, to perform their relations without boasting, passion, or pedantry. I have already noted that gentlemen were cautioned against acquiring the reputation of "wonder-mongers" and, accordingly, the character of a boaster. It was uncivil to put too great demands upon auditors' belief: truth might be made subservient to civility.[107] Early modern gentlemen were highly skilled in decoding and manipulating manners and gestures in order to assess and enhance the veracity of communication. When communication was in written form, attention might be focused on the rhetoric and style in which relations and the authorial self were presented, and, when communication took place orally in a face-to-face forum, fine details of gesture, posture, manner of speech, and auditors' response were also available for inspection and exploitation. Here the relevant maxim, pervasive in the civil conversations of early modern gentlemanly society, was 'believe those whose manner inspires confidence.'

One repertoire for the decoding of speech held it to be natural that a man should seek to secure celebrity, power, interest, and advantage. Accordingly, speakers were instructed to disguise their ends in order better to achieve them, and auditors learned to inspect manner for signs of spontaneity and sincerity or design and deceit. Bacon repeated ancient wisdom recognizing that public words, gestures, and manners were routinely under tight control, and advising auditors that "more trust be given to countenances and deeds than to words; and in words, rather to sudden passages and surprised words, than to set and pur-

---

105. Boyle, "Sceptical Chymist," 462–63; idem, "New Experiments Touching Cold," 652 (for distinctions between chemists' trustworthiness).

106. Boyle, "Systematical or Cosmical Qualities of Things," 317.

107. E.g., Brathwait, *English Gentleman*, 83–84; Guazzo, *Civile Conversation*, I, 153–54; Castiglione, *The Courtier*, 139–40.

posed words."[108] This was the sensibility that informed barristers' attempts to get the truth out of unfriendly witnesses by browbeating and disorienting them: lying was assumed to require composure and unsettled witnesses might be made to betray themselves.[109] The game could take as many turns as players' minds could track. If one knew that one's manner was being monitored as controlled, then one might use artfully designed outbursts in order to encourage belief. In the main, however, the gentlemanly game was usually considered to take place at no more than one level of disguise. The presentation of self as modest, sober, restrained, tolerant, and unconcerned for fame was considered effectively to enhance the credibility of what one claimed.

Much civil and theological advice in seventeenth-century England identified the desirability of avoiding the appearance of passionate attempts to persuade and of letting truth find its own argument. Rhetoric was to be eschewed, or, more properly, made invisible as a persuasive resource; fluency and prettiness of speech or prose might be taken as signs that the matter could not itself carry the argument; vehement demands that one was to be believed were to be replaced by straightforward presentations of the grounds for free belief; proud insistence upon the scope and originality of one's claims was to be transformed into the modesty and diffidence that marked a man concerned not for celebrity but for truth. 'Modern' preferences for a 'plain' rhetorical style occasionally pointed towards its capacity for engendering trust. Izaak Walton, for example, used his unembroidered ways of writing to support his claims to biographical truth: "The beholder . . . shall here see the Authors Picture in a natural dress, which ought to beget faith in what is spoken: for, he that wants skill to deceive, may safely be trusted."[110]

Bacon's rules for registering natural-historical testimony specified that one was to set down "whether the author was a vain-speaking and light person, or sober and severe."[111] Boyle's unpublished scheme for the "Use of Reason in Natural Philosophy" dictated "that cited Testimonies ought to be considerately and candidly deliver'd."[112] He repeatedly expressed skepticism about reports delivered in a "dogmatical," "violent," or "confident" manner, and, conversely, commended "warily" given testimony.[113] This is the scheme which so powerfully

108. Bacon, "Advancement of Learning," 457.
109. See, e.g., C. P. Harvey, *The Advocate's Devil*, ch. 7, esp. 141, 147. (I owe this reference to Michael Lynch.)
110. Quoted in Anderson, *Biographical Truth*, 16.
111. Bacon, "Preparative towards a Natural and Experimental History," 260.
112. Boyle Papers, Vol. 9, f. 25v.
113. E.g., Boyle, "New Experiments Touching Cold," 588, 594; idem, "Remoras of Truth," No. 4.3, Boyle Papers, Vol. 14, f. 24 (printed in Harwood, *Early Essays*, xl); and,

informed Boyle's presentation of himself as an under-laboring spokesman for nature and which, in conjunction with widely distributed knowledge of his identity, underwrote the assent which others gave to his relations. This author of experimental narrative constituted himself as an antiauthor, playing upon, and negating, the egotistical and fame-seeking manner ascribed to the dominant tribe of philosophical authors. The antiauthor secured credibility by confessing his own (excusable) faults, by identifying (limited) troubles in the matters he claimed, by giving readers and auditors (inadequate) grounds freely to withhold their assent, and, hence, permitting them freely to constitute the basis of the assent they ultimately had to give.[114] He who did not *demand* assent might be taken to be speaking truth. Good manners might be recognized as a sign of good intellectual matter. The civility and decorum of tale-tellers testified to their truthfulness, even as it acknowledged the free action of auditors in giving their assent.

(vii) Finally, both formal and informal schemes for the assessment of testimony powerfully advised that one assent to testimony from sources possessing integrity and disinterestedness: 'Believe people who have no reason to misrepresent how things are; believe people who are not subject to delusion and who have a reputation for truth-telling.' Locke's framework advised one always to consider "the integrity of the source," to find "fair witnesses," to assent to testimony from those "of more credit, and [who] have no interest to speak contrary to the truth."[115] Seth Ward urged one to consider "whether there be sufficient reason to beleeve, that [a relator] would not voluntarily deliver a falshood, in stead of truth." There was no reason to believe "that men will lye, unlesse they either be known to be corrupt or some end be visible of gain to them from their lying." Ward acknowledged that this invigilation of interest was, indeed, common usage.[116] Wilkins recommended that "as for evidence from *Testimony* which depends upon the credit and authority of the Witnesses, these may be qualified as to their *ability* and *fidelity*."[117]

---

for Boyle's condemnation of Hobbes's "confident way of writing," see idem, "Examen of Hobbes," 186, 190, and Shapin and Schaffer, *Leviathan and the Air-Pump*, 175–76.

114. Boyle's presentation of a modest authorial self, and his insistence upon communicating experimental troubles, are now very well documented in, e.g., Golinski, "Boyle: Scepticism and Authority"; Shapin, "Pump and Circumstance"; and chapter 4 above. Yet the general form of that modest presentation was prevalent in English seventeenth-century gentlemanly and theological culture; see, e.g., Shapin, "'A Scholar and a Gentleman.'"

115. Locke, *Essay Concerning Human Understanding*, Bk. IV, ch. 15, sects. 4–5; ibid., ch. 16, sect. 6.

116. [Ward], *Philosophicall Essay* (1652), 92–93.

117. Wilkins, *Principles and Duties of Natural Religion*, 10; see also Shapiro, *Wilkins*, 231.

Conversely, one was counseled to inspect for possible bias the relationship between what was said and who said it, and, if such interests
were found, to discount the truth of the matter accordingly. Hobbes
pointed to the wisdom of common ancient usage in asking, *cui bono?*:
"For amongst Præsumptions, there is none that so evidently declareth
the Author, as doth the Benefit of the Action." That is why, in Hobbes's
view, the testimony of those subjected to torture was paradigmatic of
unreliability: "What is in that case confessed, tendeth to the ease of
him that is Tortured; not to the informing of the Torturers: and therefore ought not to have the credit of sufficient Testimony: for whether
he deliver himselfe by true, or false Accusation, he does it by the
Right of preserving his own life."[118] Truth could not be generated by
interested perception, inquiry, or representation. Stillingfleet said that
the major source of error was the "*partiality* and *preoccupation* of *Judgement:* which makes men enquire more diligently after the *dowry* then
the *beauty* of Truth, its *correspondency* to their *Interests,* then its *evidence*
to their *understandings.*"[119] Locke identified a major cause of "wrong
assent" as an endemic tendency to see and credit what suits intellectual
or material interest rather than what is:

> Let ever so much probability hang on one side of a covetous man's
> reasoning, and money on the other; it is easy to see what will out-
> weigh. Earthly minds, like mud walls, resist the strongest batteries:
> and though, perhaps, sometimes the force of a clear argument may
> make some impression, yet they nevertheless stand firm, and keep
> out the enemy, truth.[120]

Hobbes famously claimed that the only reason geometrical truths
had escaped dissension was that "men care not, in that subject, what
be truth, as a thing that crosses no mans ambition, profit, or lust," and
this radical extension of the potential truth-corroding force of interest
was debated by the theologians, some agreeing, some protecting the
purity of the distinction between necessary and probable truths.[121]
Love of theory worked as powerfully to distort as love of lucre: Bacon's
"Idols of the Theatre" actively projected theoretical dispositions onto
reality and the "Idols of the Cave" disturbed the perception of truth

118. Hobbes, *Leviathan,* 199–200, 704. On the culture of credibility surrounding English judicial torture, see Hanson, "Torture and Truth."

119. Stillingfleet, *Origines Sacræ,* 7.

120. Locke, *Essay Concerning Human Understanding,* Bk. IV, ch. 20, sect. 12; see also
Wilkins, *Principles and Duties of Natural Religion,* 36; Stillingfleet, *Origines Sacræ,* 136.

121. Hobbes, *Leviathan,* 166; Wolseley, *Unreasonableness of Atheism,* 70–71; Stillingfleet,
Origines Sacræ, 228–29; Tillotson, "Sermon I. The Wisdom of Being Religious," in idem,
Works, I, 24; cf. Shapin and Schaffer, *Leviathan and the Air-Pump,* 323–24, 328–29,
333–34.

through attachment to previously achieved individual investments.[122] The diagnosis of mundane material interest as a circumstance arguing against the veracity of relations was a standard trope of early modern gentlemanly society. Legal proceedings, for example, routinely gauged the likely truth of witnesses' testimony according to their general integrity and their imputed interest in the outcome, and in so doing the law effectively played on maxims of common sense.[123] Sir Walter Raleigh's prosecutors noted that "a denial of the defendant must not move the jury [for he] doth it *in propria causa* [in his own cause]."[124] The privileged credibility of deathbed testimony likewise proceeded from presumptions that persons facing death had no inducement to lie and every reason to tell the truth: "For then masks are usually laid aside, or pulled off, and men make . . . more sincere confessions and declarations of their judgment."[125] Chapters 2 and 3 described the rich moral repertoires available to everyday gentlemanly actors wanting to inspect persons for interest and to identify those whom interest could not sway.

Bacon analyzed "the facility of credit, and accepting or admitting things too weakly authorized or warranted" in terms of systematic interests. Take the example of religious history, where predisposing interests that such things existed illegitimately assisted the credibility of miracle reports by "hermits, or monks of the desert," who themselves were predisposed to see and to warrant as true "such illusions of spirits."[126] Defenders of scriptural truth, contrarily, commonly argued that biblical sources had no reason to lie and that some of them, indeed, had an interest that miraculous events *not* be reported and credited. Ward defended the honor of both secular and sacred historians: Caesar's histories were delivered by "a man of honour that would not write a lye"; Sallust's histories were true because "he was a man of knowledge and could not gain any thing that he hath delivered if it were untrue"; and the persecution of the apostles established that they had nothing to gain, and everything to lose, by preaching the Gospel.[127] Stillingfleet asserted the "fidelity" of Moses who had "no intent to deceive." God chose the recorders of His deeds to be men of probity, "it being impos-

---

122. Bacon, "New Organon," 55–60; cf. Hooke, "General Scheme of Natural Philosophy," 9–11; see also Van Leeuwen, *Problem of Certainty*, 6–12; Martin, *Francis Bacon, the State, and the Reform of Natural Philosophy*, 148–50.

123. See, e.g., Shapiro, *Probability and Certainty*, 174–93; idem, *'Beyond Reasonable Doubt,'* ch. 1; Martin, *Francis Bacon, the State, and the Reform of Natural Philosophy*, 78; Gigerenzer et al., *Empire of Chance*, 7: "For example, the testimony of a relative of the accused might count only one-third as much as that of an unimpeachable witness."

124. Quoted in Williams, *Raleigh*, 210.

125. Boyle, "Christian Virtuoso. Appendix to First Part," 792.

126. Bacon, "Advancement of Learning," 287.

127. [Ward], *Philosophicall Essay*, 94–95, 112–14.

sible that persons employed by a *God* of *truth* should make it their
design to impose upon the world; which gives us a *rational account,* why
the *wise God* . . . made choice of such a *person* to record it, who gave
abundant evidence to the world that he acted [upon] no private design."[128] Far from having an interest in propagating stories of divine
intervention, many of those testifying to their reality were Jews, who
were a fractious and suspicious people and who, in the case of Christ's
miracles, had a presumptive interest in keeping silent or exposing
them as fraudulent.[129]

Even where multiply testifying sources were all marred by interest
it might be claimed that the very disparity in those interests might yet
warrant the truth of what was claimed: the corrosive effect of a single
interest was considered canceled by that of others working in different
directions. Wolseley argued just this warrant for scriptural testimony,
which was proffered by "men of all Interests, though never so different
in themselves, all concurring in a matter of Fact."[130] Concurrence
counted as a practical argument against interest, as Ward indicated:
"It is possible that all men may combine together to say that they have
seen such things as they have not seen, because every man is a lyar:
but how they should come to doe it, or to what end, is so invisible
and inconceivable, that the matter, taken in the grosse, is altogether
incredible." Disbelief in historians' relations had a moral cost. Impugning integrity was a serious act, any instance of which had to be
carefully considered. Cautioning against facile dissent, Ward precisely
mobilized the ritual codes of the honor culture:

> Whosoever challengeth or questions the Integrity of an Historian,
> and upon that cause refuseth to receive his Testimony, it is requisite
> that he produce the reasons of his supposition, that he charge the
> Authors of corruption, and prove the charge which he hath objected;
> or that he discover and manifest the ends, which he might propound
> to himself, as the reward of his imposture; that he shew the gain that
> might accrue, or the losse, avoid; and manifest that his accusation
> hath not proceeded from malice, but from judgement, from some
> grounds of reason, and not from perversenesse, or spight, or any
> inhumanity.[131]

Practical evaluation of scientific testimony pervasively relied upon
the recognition of integrity and disinterestedness in the source. Narra-

128. Stillingfleet, *Origines Sacræ,* 109, 135.
129. Wolseley, *Unreasonableness of Atheism,* 131–32; Stillingfleet, *Origines Sacræ,* 113–15, 132.
130. Wolseley, *Unreasonableness of Atheism,* 129.
131. [Ward], *Philosophicall Essay,* 95–96, 104; see also ibid., 110, 121.

tives of empirical evidence received through testimony repeatedly specified the integrity of sources: "a gentleman," "a person of quality," "a person of honour."[132] The following chapter will describe ways in which those whose integrity might be doubted by Royal Society practitioners could obtain moral vouchers for their testimony. And, of course, Royal Society fellows often named their sources, trusting readers to recognize the integrity of specific individuals. I shall develop this point below, and for the present I need note only some general features of these assessments. Wilkins accounted for the erroneous modern opposition to Copernicanism by drawing upon the sensibility which informed Bacon's scheme of idols and Locke's identification of the distorting effect of self-love. These false judgments proceeded from

> an over-fond and partial conceit of their own proper inventions. Every man is naturally more affected to his own brood, than to that of which another is the author; though perhaps it may be more agreeable to reason. It is very difficult for any one, in the search of truth, to find in himself such an indifferency, as that his judgment is not at all swayed by an over-weaning affection unto that which is proper unto himself.[133]

Even so, the ascription of interest might allow one to sift out true from false claims. So truth could be imputed to telescopic observations precisely because their reality was testified even by "such as were come with a great deal of prejudice, and an intent of contradiction."[134] Boyle deployed the scheme which allowed one to cancel varying interests and to reject the possibility of collusion when he specified the *independence* of testifying sources. Similar information about the temperature of subterranean regions derived "from the credible relations of several eye-witnesses differing in nation, and for the most part unacquainted with each other," and testimony concerning phenomena to be observed in extreme cold came from "several persons, both of them scholars, and strangers to one another."[135] Truth might be found by the calibration of claim and interest, but the recipe for finding reliably veridical testimony was the identification of those men who mastered self-interest and who freely submitted themselves solely to truth.

---

132. These examples come from Boyle, "New Experiments Touching Cold," 635; idem, "Temperature of Submarine Regions," 345; idem, "General History of the Air," 635.

133. Wilkins, *Discourse Concerning a New Planet*, 146.

134. Wilkins, *Discovery of a New World*, 49.

135. Boyle, "Temperature of Subterraneal Regions," 327; idem, "New Experiments Touching Cold," 534; see also Glanvill, "Of Scepticism and Certainty," in idem, *Essays*, 49.

Maxims and Systems

These maxims for the evaluation of testimony were sometimes presented in the form of a *list* of counsels, or, at any rate, in a manner
indicating that they were ultimately to be considered together. The
results of plausibility judgments, for example, were to be weighed together with the results of multiplicity findings, and so on. Yet even in
such formal presentations as Locke's there was no definitive or detailed
instruction about how one was to go about securing a final judgment
and how one was to collate the results of these assays. Nor was it
specified *ceteris paribus* how much multiplicity justified assent, how direct testimony needed to be, how consistent testimonies had to be, and
how assessments on each scale were to be brought to bear on each
other. Locke invited readers to imagine some sort of summing or balancing exercise. One was advised to assemble the results of the assays
and reflect whether a just confidence was induced:

> The mind, if it will proceed rationally, ought to examine all the
> grounds of probability, and see how they make more or less for or
> against any proposition, before it assents to or dissents from it; and,
> upon a due balancing the whole, reject or receive it, with a more or
> less firm assent, proportionably to the preponderancy of the greater
> grounds of probability on one side or the other.[136]

The assumption or explicit invocation of "balancing" or "weighing"
practices had been prevalent before Locke, both in reflective and everyday usages.[137] King James I counseled his son how to "discern wisely
betwixt true and false reports" of human actions: first, one was to
consider "the nature of the person" reporting; second, "what entresse
hee can haue in the weale or euill of him, of whom hee maketh the
report"; third, "the likelie-hoode of the purpose itselfe; and last, the
nature and by-past life of the dilated person."[138] Assessing the results
of the individual assays was a matter of simple prudence. Boyle wrote
to Henry Stubbe in 1666 that he was "very backward to believe any
strange thing . . . unless the testimonies that recommend it be propor-
tionable to the extraordinariness of the thing proposed."[139] Seth Ward
recommended that those receiving testimony, "however difficult or

136. Locke, *Essay Concerning Human Understanding*, Bk. IV, ch. 15, sect. 5; see also
ibid., ch. 15, sect. 6; ibid., ch. 16, sects. 3–4, 6, 9–10; and Burns, *Great Debate on Miracles*,
59–61.
137. A similar matter-of-fact balancing procedure was even invoked as a commonplace in Aristotle, e.g., *Rhetoric* I. 1371ᵃ 8–14.
138. James I, *Basilikon Doron* (1603), 99–100. Examples of advice of this general sort
in the early modern ethical literature could be multiplied *ad libitum*.
139. Boyle to Stubbe, 9 March 1666, in Birch, "Life of Boyle," lxxvi.

strange it be," should consider "the qualities of the relators, and the manner of the relation, and [whether] there is not any improbability proceeding from the difficulty or rarity of the accidents, which may not be outweighed by the known disposition and properties of the Relators." Indeed, such an exercise corresponded to the "inward discourses" men ordinarily used upon receiving "any relations whatever." If all factors concurred, there was no reason to doubt; if some failed, belief was weaker, since "the belief of the conclusion can never exceed the force and evidence of the premises."[140] And in the eighteenth century, Locke's "balancing" act was famously elaborated in David Hume's treatment of miracles: "We frequently hesitate concerning the reports of others. We balance the opposite circumstances which cause any doubt or uncertainty; and when we discover a superiority on any side, we incline to it; but still with a diminution of assurance, in proportion to the force of its antagonist."[141] Philosophical "balancing" of inducements to assent here represented the soundest everyday practical reasoning.

Locke illustrated how the mind might either mistake or, by following his rules, "proceed rationally" in a particular instance of natural-historical testimony. The Dutch ambassador was (apocryphally) entertaining the king of Siam with particulars of the envoy's native country. In Holland, the king was told, water sometimes froze so hard that men walked upon it "and that it would bear an elephant if he were there." A rational mind, in these circumstances, would, Locke suggested, weigh the local implausibility against the directness, knowledgeability, and integrity of the source, and would seek out corroboration from other trustworthy sources. Once the rational balancing had been accomplished, thick and hard icy rivers would become part of the monarch's picture of the world. But, proceeding on defective grounds, the king came to an erroneous conclusion: "Hitherto," he told the ambassador, "I have believed the strange things you have told me, because I look upon you as a sober fair man, but now I am sure you lie."[142]

To ensure rational practice with respect to testimony, Locke offered his balancing exercise while more practical counsels such as Boyle's noted the specific external dependencies between assays: "That many

140. [Ward], *Philosophicall Essay*, 90–91, 93.

141. Hume, *Enquiry Concerning Human Understanding*, 112.

142. Locke, *Essay Concerning Human Understanding*, Bk. IV, ch. 15, sect. 5; cf. Daston, *Classical Probability*, 195. The same story was later worked through by Leibniz, *New Essays Concerning Human Understanding*, 530, and Hume, *Enquiry Concerning Human Understanding*, 113–14, and I shall note Boylean precedents (e.g., "New Experiments Touching Cold," 477, 573) in the next chapter.

Testimonies are insufficient for want of moral Qualifications in him that gives them"; "That even of honest and sincere Witnesses, the Testimony may be insufficient if the matters of fact require Skill in the Relator."[143] The advertised power of these methods of evaluating testimony relied heavily upon the perceived independence of assays. What was the point of comparing assay 1 to assay 2 and balancing their results if the assessments were not independent? Commonsensically, such assays often do appear to be independent: plausibility judgments seem quite different things from directness judgments, and so on. Nevertheless, I want to argue that these maxims are systematically linked in a deeper way than is suggested by Locke's exercises. Accordingly, the appearance that testimony can be evaluated by Locke's balancing-rationality is illusory, and the real power of that illusion itself testifies to the processes by which the role of trust is excised from formal epistemologies.

There are too many dependencies among these assays to permit individual treatment. I must, therefore, make my case schematically in the main, developing the systematic association between assays in several perspicuous instances. The dependencies I am alluding to are *internal* to the presumptively independent assays. That is to say, the exercise of scanning testimony for one feature, such as multiplicity, implicates supposedly independent features, such as plausibility; consistency implicates integrity; and so on. The supposedly independent assays are in fact linked in a network in which the ability to scan testimony for one feature depends upon the outcome of other assays. I want to offer some general ways of recognizing these systematic dependencies; then I will go on to show how these systematic dependencies lead to potential troubles with testimony which were insoluble in principle but manageable in practice.

According to popular seventeenth-century schemes, testimony ought to come from knowledgeable sources, and advice of that general sort was readily understood and found sensible by a wide range of actors. Indeed, as I have indicated, this was a maxim of everyday conduct. In these connections, the emergence of 'modern' positions rendered problematic the identification of 'knowledge,' and, consequently, the identity of its institutionalized possessors. If the schoolmen were accused of claiming that they were the expert and knowledgeable spokesmen for nature by virtue of their guardianship of ancient classic texts, their opponents disputed such entitlement by contesting whether traditional practices did reliably produce knowledge. So ability to identify a knowledgeable source flowed from large-scale decisions about plausibility—what knowledge was—and how it was to be obtained, as

143. Boyle Papers, Vol. 9, f. 25v.

well as from more mundane notions of experiential immediacy and instrumental skill.[144] Similarly, to note that a practitioner had a good track record in producing true testimony depended systematically upon a view of what the world was like, upon a notion of consistency between what he said and what the world was like, and, in most cases, upon the knowledgeability and integrity of those who assured one that the individual did indeed have a good track record, since this presumed reliability can rarely, if ever, be independently inspected and checked.

Formal and informal schemes for the evaluation of testimony repeatedly stipulated that multiple testimones were superior to solitary relations. Yet the idea of multiple testimony embeds the presumption that the narrations in question refer *to the same thing* or event. Given endemic variation in reporting and representation, judgments that testimony has 'the same referent' contain decisions about the nature of the phenomenon. Chapter 7 will treat some late experimental work by Robert Boyle on the specific gravity of various minerals. His own reiterated measurements varied and he acknowledged discrepancies between his measurements and those performed at other times and places by different practitioners. Nor did he find anything remarkable in that circumstance, having throughout his career offered technical and moral instructions about how to regard such variation. Nevertheless, any particular conclusion about the nature of that variation, including the judgment that such discrepant findings testified to the same reality, involved practical decisions about, for example, plausibility, skill, and integrity. The range of reported variation that accurately testified to real variation in nature (either impurities in materials or constitutive variation in 'the same' substances) needed to be decided, as did that portion of variation which arose from excusable or culpable experimental inaccuracy (including variation in measuring standards), and from the theoretical or material interests of testifying sources. Judgments that these testimonies were or were not multiple therefore embedded judgments about what the distribution of skill was like, about what the material world was like, and about the moral characteristics of certain people. Knowing how to evaluate testimony was, therefore, *knowing one's way around a cultural system,* knowing how to go on in specific circumstances whose characteristics and exigencies no rulebook could possibly envisage. Scientific practitioners, as well as everyday actors, generally showed great facility in knowing how to go on in

144. This is a macrocultural transposition of the "experimenter's regress" identified in H. M. Collins's microsociology of modern scientific practice: *Changing Order,* chs 4–5. The "regress" arises when judgments of whether or not an experiment has been skillfully performed can be made only by knowing what counts as an outcome truly reflecting reality.

assessing specific testimony, yet that facility ultimately derived not from formal epistemological rules but from the deployment of uncodified skills.

Maxims and Countermaxims

I have noted some problems for formal accounts of the application and interrelationship of testimonial assays. Now I want to identify some fundamental problems with the assays themselves. It was commonsensical to advise actors to assent to testimony which was plausible, multiple, direct, from a knowledgeable source, and so on. Yet the same seventeenth-century scientific culture which elaborated those rules also proffered advice which, in specific circumstances, ran in the opposite direction. That is to say, the commonsensical rules pointing in one direction were all shadowed by rules pointing in the other, which, when articulated in the context of practical action, seemed equally mundane and rational.[145] How to select which rule to follow? There were, in fact, no explicitly formulated rules for doing so, nor, indeed, was there any formal recognition of the potential problem. Yet actors evidently knew when, where, and how to adduce the relevant rule. Here is yet another constitutive reason why the evaluation of testimony is a skill-like capacity.

The multiplicity of testimony was routinely held rightly to induce assent, yet that multiplicity could also count as an argument against the truthfulness of what was claimed. 'Modern' practitioners were highly skilled in condemning opinion by noting that it was "commonly" held. I have already indicated how seventeenth-century natural philosophers invalidated the widely distributed perceptual reports of the "vulgar," pointing to the necessity of expert knowledge in correcting errors of sense. Indeed, nothing was deemed so likely to be in error as common opinion, and a variety of early modern commentators elaborated schemes justifying the rhetorical equation between error and the beliefs of the multitude. Richard Hooker influentially argued that shared opinion was *usually* insecurely founded:

> It fareth many times with men's opinions as with rumours and reports. That which a credible person telleth is easily thought probable by such as are well persuadeth of him. But if two, or three, or four, agree all in the same tale, they judge it then to be out of controversy, and so are many times overtaken for want of due consideration; either some common cause leading them all into error, or one man's oversight deceiving many through their too much credulity and easiness

---

145. For the identification of Mertonian "norms of science" and their accompanying "counter-norms," see Mitroff, *Subjective Side of Science,* esp. 73–79, though I will reject the framework which treats such a situation as a sign of "ambivalence."

of belief. . . . Though ten persons be brought to give testimony in any cause, yet if the knowledge they have of the thing whereunto they come as witnesses, appear to have grown from some one amongst them, and to have spread itself from hand to hand, they all are in force but as one testimony.[146]

William Gilbert was one of many 'moderns' who argued that error had crept into ancient systems of knowledge by the process of adapting them "to the capacity of the vulgar herd," by which he meant not the common people but the schoolmen.[147] The ways of securing genuine knowledge were as arduous as the path to error was easy. Accordingly, the truth-speaker was always likely to be recognized by the fact that a confederacy of dunces was leagued against him, and truth itself was apt to be more solitary than sociable. Even Hobbes, elsewhere suspicious of special expertise, acknowledged that "commonly truth is on the side of the few rather than the multitude."[148] Cartesian methodology identified publicly held beliefs as sources of error and sought to secure indubitable knowledge by throwing the solitary knower back upon himself. The multiplicity of opinion and testimony did not in itself, therefore, count as an inducement to assent. Multiplicity needed the systematic discipline of the results of other assays to weigh for or against assent.

Similarly, there was nothing about the consistency of testimony that rendered it necessarily an argument for assent. Too great a display of internal consistency was routinely used in both lay and philosophical contexts as an argument of insincerity and as a sign that a polished performance had been prepared. It was on these grounds that writers like Stillingfleet gauged the sincerity of testimony from errors and imperfections let slip, and Boyle urged that experimental writers wishing to gain credit should communicate troubles and failures as well as successes. Incoherently circumstantial narrative offered a moral voucher of the historicity of the phenomena whose existence was being claimed.[149] Claims which corresponded too neatly to anticipation, like experimental results which too accurately fit theoretical expectation, might attract suspicions of interest and be discounted accordingly, and

146. Hooker, *Laws of the Ecclesiastical Polity* (1593–97), I, 113. Hooker was here glossing sentiments attributed to Galen.
147. Gilbert, *De Magnete*, 318, 335.
148. Hobbes, "Human Nature," 71.
149. E.g., Stillingfleet, *Origines Sacræ*, 137; Boyle, "Two Essays, Concerning the Unsuccessfulness of Experiments," esp. 349. As early as the 1650s the relation of experimental troubles was recognized as a voucher of *English* sincerity. In communicating alchemical procedures to Boyle, George Starkey added: "Now to show yr Honor yt I am an English man I shal adde a disaster" (Starkey to Boyle, [April/May 1651], in Boyle Papers, Vol. 6, ff. 99r–100v, transcribed in Newman, "Newton's *Clavis* as Starkey's *Key*," 570).

chapter 7 will deal in detail with Boylean skepticism about mathematical canons of accuracy. Furthermore, the external consistency of multiple testimonies could, as Hooker and others suggested, be taken as a sign that collusion had occurred or that the opinion of one man was being falsely represented as that of many. Again, consistency among testimonies in itself counted neither for nor against assent. One might, in specific circumstances, as warrantably cite testimonial consistency as an incentive or as a dissuasive to belief.

The directness and immediacy of testimony were widely identified as inducements to assent. However, a range of early modern commentators expressed intermittent suspicion of direct testimony and showed how very highly mediated testimony could be identified as possessing special marks of truth. Time put knowledge-claims to repeated test. Given sufficient time, the truth would out and error would be discovered. Error might impose itself upon one group of people and upon one generation, but it could not easily survive the winnowing effects of repeated investigation or experience. This was a powerful argument for Christian apologists who defended the veracity of biblical relations by mobilizing this counter to the maxim of directness. Stillingfleet and Wolseley, on the one hand, identified scriptural sources as having firsthand experience of what they related, and, on the other, pointed to the antiquity of these relations as evidence that no error or imposture had been discovered. False religious claims had been reliably found out by time—they said that Islam had been exposed as a lie— but no such falsehood had been detected in the canons of Judaism and Christianity.[150] In fact, 'modern' natural philosophers routinely supported the 'direct' evidence of firsthand observation with the authoritative arguments of antiquity—when, in their view, ancient knowledge had survived uncorrupted.[151] Bacon cautioned that "the sincerity" of historical relations "published near the time of the actions themselves" must "be taken with reservation," since such accounts were typically engaged and biased—"being commonly written either in favour or in spite." Better to rely upon more indirect testimony, produced "after party heat has cooled down."[152] So there was nothing

150. Stillingfleet, *Origines Sacræ*, 113–15, 132, 301; Wolseley, *Unreasonableness of Atheism*, 138, 141. The reason that Muslims continued in their professed beliefs was due, according to Stillingfleet, to the coercion exerted upon them by their societies' authorities. Christianity, like science, was identified as the belief of free men, and free action was the condition for truth to out.

151. See, e.g., Gilbert, *De Magnete*, 54, 78; Wilkins, *Discovery of a New World*, 55–62; idem, *Discourse Concerning a New Planet*, 141–42; Harvey, "On the Circulation of the Blood," in idem, *Works*, 91–92.

152. Bacon, "The Dignity and Advancement of Learning" (1623), 305; see also Anderson, *Biographical Truth*, 160.

inherent in the immediacy of testimony which commended it to belief: both directness and indirectness could be cited in favor of assent.

Testimony from knowledgeable sources was commonly recommended over that from the unlearned or unskilled. Yet the countermaxim to this was by no means uncommon in early modern science. Indeed, the notion that those who possessed institutionalized knowledge were handicapped with respect to securing truth was a set piece of 'modern' rhetoric. And here, as I have indicated, the notion of genuine knowledgeability was split off from that which was institutionally recognized as knowledge. Paracelsus vigorously juxtaposed the direct sympathetic engagement of the unlettered to the corrupt authority-mongering of the schoolmen and incorporated physicians, and he was followed in this by many Puritan critics of the universities during the civil wars and Interregnum.[153] Montaigne commended the testimony of "a simple, crude fellow" as "a character fit to bear true witness; for clever people observe more things and more curiously, but they interpret them; and to lend weight and conviction to their interpretation, they cannot help altering history a little."[154]

Boyle urged that a piece of natural-historical testimony concerning the nature of ambergris be viewed as "very sincere, and, on that score, credible," just because the report "was not written by a philosopher, to broach a paradox, or serve an hypothesis, but by a merchant, or factor, for his superiors, to give them an account of a matter of fact."[155] Hooke argued that directly skilled sources were sometimes less reliable, especially in noting the routine and detailed features of familiar phenomena, than "one who that is altogether ignorant and a Stranger" to them, and, indeed, this was a popular Royal Society tactic in arguing that trade practices ought to be checked over by gentlemen.[156] The disabilities of the knowledgeable in providing truthful testimony were not only pointed out by those who wished to condemn their knowledge. I have noted how Bacon and Locke cautioned against everyman's love of his own theory and the resulting intellectual bias this attachment introduced. And Boyle's repeated insistence that he had no theoretical investments and prepossessions—that, indeed, he had not even read the works of major philosophical system-builders—was a major resource in warranting that he testified to truth alone.

In treating the *manner* in which testimony was given I have already

153. E.g., Webster, "Paracelsus and Demons."
154. Montaigne, "Of Cannibals," in idem, *Essays*, 151–52; see also M. McKeon, *Origins of the English Novel*, 104–05. I take up the gauging role of knowledgeability once more in chapter 6.
155. Boyle, "Letter Concerning Ambergris" (1673), 732; see also Dear, *"Totius in Verba,"* 156; idem, "From Truth to Disinterestedness," 627.
156. Hooke, "General Scheme of Natural Philosophy," 62.

introduced the notion of a countermaxim. For it if were to be said that one was to believe testimony proffered in a smooth and confident manner, then it is apparent that practitioners in the early Royal Society circle overwhelmingly endorsed the countermaxim commending narrative which was imperfect, hesitant, diffident, halting, and visibly lacking in the rhetorical arts of persuasion. Indeed, so complex and subtle were the linguistic games which rhetorically denied rhetoric, and so artful were the gestures by which a sincere self was publicly presented and monitored, that it is difficult to say what was an early modern manner-assessing maxim and what its countermaxim. For all Boyle's reiterated recommendations that the experimental truth-teller adopt a modest manner of presentation, he intermittently vouched for factual testimony on the grounds of the passionate commitment displayed by its source.[157] Harvey chastised critics of his doctrines for their hesitancy, urging them to speak out "heartily . . . as becomes a philosopher."[158] Did diffidence, rhetorical coarseness, and the jumbled confession of faults enhance the credibility of testimony or did it diminish it? In the eighteenth century, Hume cautioned auditors to reserve assent when claimants "deliver their testimony with hesitation, or, on the contrary, with too violent asseverations."[159] Early modern commentators varied in the advice they gave, but all were confident that the monitoring of verbal, gestural, and physiognomic manner was an invaluable assay.[160]

The plausibility of testimony admits of degrees. Hence, the maxim advising assent to plausible claims worked on a finely graded scale. Presumably, at one end of the scale was factual testimony whose content could not be conceived as otherwise, while at the other were claims whose truth could not be imagined. Just in that sense, it might be said that there is no countermaxim to the advice to assent to plausible testimony. Yet the whole of the factual testimony with which early modern practitioners were concerned—including the stopping of the sun, the multiplication of loaves and fishes, and the existence of 'men whose heads do grow beneath their shoulders'—fell somewhere short of absolute plausibility. Such things might be so, and both Christian apologists and early modern natural philosophers devoted much energy to arguing that there were adequate grounds for assenting to highly implausible claims.

The 'modern' critique of Scholastic ontology, as I have noted, specified the insufficiency of its plausibility schemes. The implausibility

157. E.g., Boyle, "Strange Reports," 609.
158. Harvey, "On the Circulation of the Blood," in idem, *Works*, 101.
159. Hume, *Enquiry Concerning Human Understanding*, 113.
160. I briefly take up the question of face-to-face interaction in chapter 6 and again in the epilogue.

of an empirical claim—as assessed by traditional schemes—was no longer to count as evidence that it was false, and, indeed, those claims which most discomfited Scholastic doctrines were most highly celebrated by 'modern' practitioners. Accordingly, Aristotelian ontology was mobilized to function, in part, as an antiplausibility scheme, and the implausibility of testimony within its rubric was identified as one inducement towards assent. The fable of the king of Siam, and widely distributed stories like it, were always available to show the foolishness of framing judgments upon too narrow an empirical base: the king was as much wrong to reject the reality of icy Dutch rivers on the grounds of his own limited experience of the world as he was not to find the Dutch ambassador a source reliable enough to justify assent.

I have noted how early modern ethical literature cautioned gentlemanly readers against telling marvelous tales—even if true—lest their reputations be endangered and the company be unduly put upon. It was therefore understood that he who told implausible stories was taking upon himself a substantial risk. Accordingly, practical advice was occasionally formulated to credit marvelous stories *just because of their implausibility* and the attendant moral risk taken by their teller. Anyone making this move was not merely rejecting some institutionalized plausibility scheme; he was in fact being skeptical of his own. Thus, Obadiah Walker influentially urged gentlemen to experiment with inverting the usual relationship between plausibility and assent: "When news comes from an uncertain Author, though probable and expected, yet suspend your belief; because men easily report what they desire or expect; but rather give heed to certain extravagant and unexpected Relations, as unlikelier to be invented."[161] Here the countermaxim was the paradoxical but proverbial 'Strange, therefore true.'[162]

There is, however, one inducement to assent to which I cannot find, nor indeed have I been able to imagine, a counter: this is the maxim which counseled assent to testimony from people characterized by their integrity and disinterestedness. To say that people were disinterested was to identify the adequate grounds of their truthfulness: there was nothing that worked on such people to induce them to represent matters otherwise than they were (see chapters 2 and 3). Truth-speaking then emerged unmotivated, simply as an attribute of persons so circumstanced that the passions and the interests could not wreak their distorting effects. The maxim thus had an apparently tautologous character. In practice, as I note shortly, its most common manifestation

161. Walker, *Of Education*, 248–49.
162. See, in this connection, M. McKeon, *Origins of the English Novel*, 111 ("this most daring, and most dangerous, claim to historicity"), 433 n. 73.

was as a justificatory gesture at 'a credible person' as the source of testimony. 'A credible person' was a source of testimony that might be believed. Integrity was not, like 'a confident manner' or 'knowledge-ability,' a feature of the source whose inverse might also be cited as an inducement to assent, for the opposite of saying that people were possessed of integrity and disinterestedness was just to say that they were not credible sources. Therefore, the maxim advising assent to trustworthy, credible, or disinterested sources had the ability, like geometrical axioms, to "bottom" an argument, locating "those necessary maxims or axioms which stop wrangling."[163] It practically closed a hermeneutic circle which remained open in principle. In certain sorts of people credibility was *embodied*.

The recognizable integrity of sources remained, of course, a property of a cultural system, and, although for reasons treated in chapter 3 it was a circumstance very powerfully inducing assent, it might be weighed against other properties of the system, as Boyle illustrated when he specified that even "honest and sincere Witnesses" might be deficient in necessary skill.[164] The ascribed credibility of a source could not, that is, determine assent by itself. Nevertheless, the integrity of sources was the one inducement to assent which did not generate a countermaxim, and this integrity of its own was the basis of its justificatory power. On the condition that participants could together locate credible persons, they might, by pointing at those sources, "stop wrangling" and bring to a practical close deliberations about the veracity of testimony.

Credible Persons and Credible Knowledge

In characterizing relatively formal treatments of the problem of testimony I have intermittently referred to inducements as 'rules,' endeavoring thereby to capture something of the philosopher's engagement with the admitted contingencies and uncertainties of the domain of the probable. For my own part, I prefer, however, to speak of these inducements as 'maxims of prudence,' and this is a usage I want now briefly to justify.[165] If a rule is understood to be a procedural direction sufficient in itself to guide conduct reliably towards the desired end,

163. Quoting Alexander Campbell Fraser's editorial note to Locke, *Essay Concerning Human Understanding*, 373 n. 1.

164. Boyle Papers, Vol. 9, f. 25v.

165. *Prudence*, in common early modern usage, signified condensed practical knowledge, guiding one's actions in this instance on the basis of accumulated past experience: as, for example, Hobbes, *Leviathan*, 97–98, 115, 117, 138, 682. Alternative terms included *foresight* and *wisdom*. Hobbes, like many rationalist thinkers, devalued the quality of prudential knowledge, while practical ethical writers celebrated its everyday worth compared to the results of more reflective exercises.

then the inducements discussed here certainly appear inadequately qualified. First, the correct application of such a rule depends upon a stock of background knowledge which is not specified in the rule itself, for example, how consistent must consistent testimonies be? Second, each rule is a member of a system whose manipulation is likewise not specified in any formulated rule nor in the instructions for juxtaposing a set of rules: where is the rule for balancing multiplicity and knowledgeability, and how, indeed, does one constitute the inducements to be weighed against each other without using the others to compound each assay? Finally, where are the rules for knowing when to deploy a rule and when to use its counter?[166] In Michael Oakeshott's formulation, "A belief is never guaranteed by a 'series of reasons' or a 'number of witnesses', for these (and the testimony they offer) must themselves be believed before they can influence our belief. . . ." We have to find the inducement to believe not in an isolated rule or set of rules but in the relatively stabilized practices that thwart dissent and check distrust in our overall ways of living: "what actually guarantees our beliefs for us is always present."[167]

The notion of the prudential maxim is therefore more apposite here than that of the rule. The rationalist construal of rules for regulating assent would suggest that, in the absence of the appropriate additional rules, actors would display massive uncertainty or even anomie in evaluating testimony. In fact, as I shall detail in the next chapter, there was little such sense of uncertainty, even in light of the ontological opening to which 'modern' practitioners were committed. Practitioners showed every indication that they knew how to go on in specific instances of considering testimony, and they knew how, if required, locally to justify their actions. Whereas the rationalist engagement with the management of testimony might expect such competences to be the result of a well-ordered structure of rules, it appears that practitioners got by with something far more informal and diffuse, something mobilizing prudential wisdom and embedded in streams of practical activity.

I use the term *maxim* to indicate both a practical guide to what to do 'now and here,' and a practical justification of the done thing. Moreover, unlike the rationalist conception of a rule, the maxim is recognized to depend utterly upon taken-for-granted background knowledge and to vary in its sense and force according to the scene and purpose of practical activity. It has a local rather than a global sense

166. Here I allude to Wittgenstein's antirationalist account of what it is to follow a rule. See, notably, explications by Collins, *Changing Order*, 12–16; Bloor, *Wittgenstein*, esp. 17, 88–89, 112–19; idem, "Left and Right Wittgensteinians," esp. 268–69; Lynch, "Extending Wittgenstein," esp. 220–24.

167. Oakeshott, *Experience and Its Modes*, 115.

and potency. The speaker and hearer of a maxim take it as a prudential guide to specific actions in specific settings. It requires the normal
interpretative unfolding of a normally competent member, granting
that there are maxims pointing in different directions whose apposite-
ness in different settings is likewise granted. The interpretation of each
maxim incorporates within itself a presumption that it will be honored
for all practical purposes, *ceteris paribus*, in light of relevant features of
the scene and action proposed. The art of doing the right thing *here*
and finding the right warrant for action *here* is indeed the exercise of
the skill of decorum.[168] As Castiglione indicated, it was difficult "to
give any rule in this": judgment of what to do in any given setting was
reliably honed through practical experience.[169] Decorum was the skill
of making both knowledge and moral order, and, indeed, of making
them together. The ethical resonance here is with the casuistical tradition which pays attention to the specific locally varying requirements
of particular cases of action rather than with that more philosophically
popular framework seeking eternal, universal, and unchanging principles of right action.[170] Understood this way, the philosophers' rules
have the character as rationalizations of action rather than as the adequate grounds of action.

Diffuse and philosophically untidy these maxims may appear, yet
their invocation was a potent means of managing uncertainty and arriving at epistemic conclusions. Uncertainty was well controlled. And
management of testimony was accomplished by mobilizing prudential
maxims whose force and reference were well understood in the local
culture—maxims of wise action whose challenge carried with them
known costs. I refer here, of course, to the references of 'truth-teller,'
'trustworthy or credible person' in everyday conversational contexts.
What was epistemically expected of those assessing philosophical testimony was what was morally expected of participants in gentlemanly
civil conversation: the exercise of *decorum*, the prudential adaptation
of means to ends, displaying due regard to the continuance of that
conversation as a good in itself.

Here one is struck with the contrast between the absolutely pervasive
practical use of the notion of the 'credible person' and the virtual

168. For the technical early modern English use of maxims in common law, see Martin, *Francis Bacon, the State, and the Reform of Natural Philosophy*, 88–90; see also in this
connection Obelkevich's interesting treatment of proverbs and their local contextual
meanings ("Proverbs and Social History," esp. 48–55), and Geertz, "Common Sense as
a Cultural System," 90–91 (for the "immethodicalness" of commonsense use of maxims).
169. Castiglione, *The Courtier*, 109, 139; see also Shapin, "'A Scholar and a Gentleman,'" 289.
170. See Jonsen and Toulmin, *Abuse of Casuistry*, for an excellent resuscitation of the
seventeenth-century casuistical tradition, and Toulmin, *Uses of Argument*, for systematic
defence of epistemological localism.

absence of early modern exercises aimed at specifying and defining who, indeed, a credible person was. Shapiro and Martin have noted that early modern English judicial proceedings saw a change in the constitution of a juror's identity, from one who had firsthand knowledge of the matters under investigation to one who possessed general 'credibility' and who could assess credibility in others. The separation of roles between the juror and the witness proceeded together with the mobilization of means for recognizing credibility.[171] Yet, despite this heightened technical concern for standards of credibility, and despite the increased injunction by legal thinkers to consider witness credibility, there is little evidence of systematic attempts to spell out what this credibility consisted in and how it might be recognized.

The same situation obtained in other English contexts wherein the assessment of testimony was a matter of practical importance. The texts of seventeenth-century English natural history and natural philosophy were, as I have indicated, replete with justificatory gestures at testimonial sources as 'credible persons.' Here are a few randomly chosen locutions used by seventeenth-century scientific practitioners to commend scientific testimony, though a diligent compilation of similar usages would certainly produce a list hundreds of items long: "It is reported of one of very good credit"; "[Experiments] were received from persons of very good credit" and from "men worthy of credit"; "A credible person assured me"; "[A person] very well worthy of credit assured me"; and on and on.[172] Often the identification of a 'credible person' was conjoined with other inducements to assent—especially knowledgeability—but often it was not. The ascription of credibility to a knowledge-source was evidently taken—unmodified and unsupplemented—to count as an understood voucher of the thing claimed.

The reason that neither legal nor scientific practitioners spelled out the grounds of credibility or the identity of a credible person was that they had no need to do so. The power of the 'credible person' as a resource to end 'wrangling' and to close the interpretative circle resided in local understandings and local practices. Cultural silence about the identification of the credible person was not a sign of ignorance but of immense knowledgeability. Participants 'just knew' who a credible person was. They belonged to a culture that pointed to gentlemen as among their society's most reliable truth-tellers, a culture that asso-

171. E.g., Shapiro, 'Beyond Reasonable Doubt,' ch. 1, esp. 5–12; Martin, Francis Bacon, the State, and the Reform of Natural Philosophy, 77, 154, 164–67.

172. Sources include Bacon, "Sylva Sylvarum," 372, 462; Boyle, "New Experiments Touching Cold," 529–31, 573, 603, 618, 630; idem, "Medicinal Experiments," 313; idem, "General History of the Air," 721; idem, "Strange Reports," 605; idem, "Temperature of the Subterraneal Regions," 326; Sprat, History of the Royal Society, 200; Birch, History of the Royal Society, I, 273, 402.

ciated gentility, integrity, and credibility. They understood and appreciated the local consequences of disputing that culture and those entitlements. It was not, to be sure, that dispute could not be done. Indeed, I will indicate in the next chapter how it could be done, with difficulty and at cost. Yet the shared knowledge of the relationship between truth and power pointed to major resistances to skepticism even as it offered a major resource in managing testimony and making truth.

CHAPTER SIX

Knowing about People and Knowing about Things: A Moral History of Scientific Credibility

> In Beleefe are two opinions;
> one of the saying of the man;
> the other of his vertue.
>
> —Hobbes, *Leviathan*

John Locke's king of Siam did not accept factual testimony when there were adequate inducements to believe. Old wives and country idiots believed when inducements were inadequate. The wise man was, accordingly, ideally poised somewhere between the credulous idiot and the incredulous king of Siam. How to secure that position? How to know that one was there? The preceding chapter outlined some properties of schemes which aimed at achieving and warranting a just assent to factual testimony. I need now to display these schemes in practical action in the scientific culture of seventeenth-century England. To that end, I describe some general characteristics of the predicament in which practitioners were placed *vis-à-vis* the sources of factual knowledge, laying special stress upon some spatial features of the relationship between those who gave and those who received testimony. I then work through four examples of the assessment of factual scientific testimony, following their trajectories through time, space, and cultural systems, and drawing attention to the fine-grained practical reasoning processes through which the status of claims as true or untrue, 'the case' or 'not the case,' was decided. Throughout, I note the constitutive role of knowledge about persons in securing knowledge about things.

Travelers' Tales

The king of Siam and the Dutch ambassador were asymmetrically placed in relation to experience of the world and in relation to the readers of texts in which such parables appeared. First, the Dutchman had been both in Holland and in Siam. He had firsthand experience of a range of natural conditions of which the king had only a restricted experience. Second, the parable works its hortatory effect through knowledge held in common between ambassador, author, and reader: all these *know* that rivers freeze rock-hard in Dutch winters (though, as I pointed out in chapter 1, not all of those who unshakably know this fact know it through direct personal experience). The king of Siam is, by contrast, doubly foreign: he is not 'one of us' by race and nationality and he is not 'one of us' by knowledge. He makes a mistake such as foreigners and those of restricted experience tend to do. That, indeed, is one way we recognize 'the other.'

The problem for those concerned to secure reliable knowledge of the world was, in part, how not to wind up like the king of Siam. With respect to the properties of river water in Dutch winters, the king's incredulity appears self-evidently unreasonable, but that is just because of the security of the knowledge we already bring to the story. Suppose, however, that we and the king are alike in *not already knowing* that the testimony in question is true. Then the practical task of assessment appears in higher relief, and the illegitimacy of the king's inductive inference seems less clear-cut. What is it that the king is supposed to do, with regard to this instance, which will yield reliable knowledge across the board? This was, indeed, the practical task confronted by the scientific practitioners of seventeenth-century England.

Both the king of Siam and the fellows of the Royal Society were told things about the world which were—in practice, and sometimes in principle—beyond their own experience. Some of these things were surprising, stretching the seams of existing plausibility schemes. If one reposed utter confidence in one's present picture of the world—such naive confidence as might be widely ascribed to oriental potentates—then the conclusion was clear: whatever one was told that was beyond one's ken was false. But if, like the 'moderns' of seventeenth-century English philosophy, one was committed to prying open the traditionally stocked box of plausibility, then one's course of action was rarely obvious. As Locke and others suggested, some sort of deliberative processing exercise, some weighing and balancing of 'factors,' was indicated. Although much seventeenth-century rhetoric pointed to a golden mean between radical skepticism and naive credulity, the local politics of the 'modern' English scientific community pitched it forcefully against Scholastic ontological restrictions, while, as the preceding chapter has shown, the critique of skepticism flowed from predicaments and interests shared between scientific practitioners, theologians, and everyday actors. I hazard an impressionistic guess that, for these reasons, early Royal Society members were marginally *more* worried by illegitimate skepticism than by illegitimate credulity.

In early modern England, surprising things about the natural world were very commonly conveyed back to centers of judgment by travelers. Long-distance travel was hazardous, time-consuming, and expensive, while persuasive means of reliably representing what had been experienced in alien places were largely restricted to the traveler's narrative. Nevertheless, travel across the globe was a major means for extending experience and for testing the adequacy of scientific generalizations, and all versions of scientific culture came to practical terms with travelers' tales, finding adequate means to take some portion of them into the stock of warranted natural knowledge. Indeed, it is difficult to imagine what early modern natural history or natural philosophy would look like without that component contributed by travelers, navigators, merchant-traders, soldiers, and adventurers. The relationship between these categories of people and the scientific-practitioner-at-home was significantly shaped by the culture of credibility discussed at length in preceding chapters, and I will have more to say here about the ascribed trustworthiness of travelers. Yet aspects of the traveler-philosopher relationship obtain more diffusely in the making of factual knowledge. I mean to use the predicament posed by the traveler's tale to open up awareness of fully general problems of trust and the making of empirical knowledge. Whenever, and for whatever reasons, those who judge observation-claims cannot be at the place and time where the phenomena are on display, then judgment has to be made 'at a distance.' The trust relationship is, in that sense, inscribed in space. Those who cannot directly witness a phenomenon must either reject its existence or take it on trust from those who have, or from testimony still more indirect.[1] And that judgment has, as the Hobbesian epigraph to this chapter notes, an apparently dual character: there is judgment of matters and judgment of the people who testify to these matters.[2]

Early modern practical ethical literature displayed great sensitivity to the epistemic predicament of both travelers and those who stayed at home and received their testimony. A general problem was widely acknowledged to attend the giving and receiving of travelers' narratives.[3] I have noted that a number of courtesy texts cautioned against telling fabulous and wonderful stories concerning what one had seen on one's travels. Such narrations taxed one's listeners' credulity, in

1. The spatial significance of the trust relationship is developed in Shapin, "House of Experiment," and Ophir and Shapin, "The Place of Knowledge."
2. I mean this dualism to describe actors' schemes. Analytic problems with the distinction between the trustworthiness of people and the plausibility of claims have been described in chapters 1 and 5.
3. When travelers were not *English*, special disabilities arising from imputations of national unreliability (as treated in chapter 3) might come into play.

many cases could not be supported by others' testimony, and ultimately might cast doubt on one's own reliability or sobriety. That counsel meshed with practical advice to those who had to listen to travelers' tales. Richard Brathwait warned that it was a "great indiscretion" to give credence to "whatsoever is related" from abroad: "Neither are any sort of men more subject to the garbe of strange and novell relations than Travellers: who may arrogate to themselves a libertie of invention in this kinde, by authoritie. Whence it is said, that Travellers, Poets and Lyers, are three words all of one signification."[4]

If listeners' assent were not secured, then one's own reputation for veracity could only suffer, since resources were freely available to default travelers' tales by ascribing them to an illegitimate desire to cause amazement and wonder. The traveler was another sort of "juggler" or "wonder-monger" whose unreliability was pervasively pointed to in much modern English philosophical literature. Michael McKeon has splendidly documented "an ancient and habitual association of travel narratives with tall tales and of travelers with liars," and an early seventeenth-century proverb observed "that Travellers may tell Romances or untruths by authority."[5] The Hartlibian reformer Gabriel Plattes structured his utopian *Macaria* of 1641 as a dialogue between a traveler and a scholar. The traveler commenced his narration about his marvelous island, whereupon the scholar interrupted him and said that he regarded the tale as incredible: "You Travellers must take heed of two things principally in your relations; first, that you say nothing that is generally deemed impossible. Secondly, that your relation hath no contradiction in it, or else all men will think that you make use of the Travellers privilege, to wit, to lie by authority."[6] In the Restoration, Samuel Butler pointed to the general predicament in which an auditor was placed by those who had been where one had not: "If Travellers are allowed to Lye in Recompense of the great Pains they have taken to bring home strange Stories from foreign Parts, there is no Reason why *Antiquaries* should not be allow'd that Priviledge, who are but Travellers *in Time*."[7]

The problem with crediting travelers' tales was twofold. First, if the tales were regarded as worth telling, they frequently, and naturally, conflicted with what was already securely known about the world; hence, they possessed inherent credibility-handicaps. Second, they

4. Brathwait, *The English Gentleman* (1630), 137.
5. M. McKeon, *Origins of the English Novel*, 100; see also Adams, *Travelers and Travel Liars,* esp. ch. 12. After this chapter was written, Robert Iliffe kindly gave me a typescript of his important study ("Foreign Bodies") of the position of the foreigner in Restoration natural philosophy.
6. [Plattes], *Macaria* (1641), 2–3.
7. Butler, *Characters*, 270.

were commonly told by people about whom one knew little or nothing, by people to whom one might legitimately impute an interest—to entertain, to sell books or peddle projects—in fabricating testimony or embroidering the truth, or by people whose reliability was accounted suspect or compromised in the general culture which related integrity and truth-telling. Accordingly, there was very widespread early modern sensitivity to the predicament in which the traveler placed those who wished to know about the wide world. Travel narratives appeared as a necessary source of knowledge, and also as an endemic trouble for the knower. How could one effectively secure this sort of knowledge, and could one know when it was secure?

Coming In from the Cold

The experimental program commended by Bacon stressed the importance of subjecting nature to *analysis*. The application of extreme heat was one way of analyzing substances and discerning their constituent parts, and chemists were highly skilled in the construction and use of suitable furnaces. But practitioners were differently placed with respect to extreme cold, that other "great instrument of operation."[8] As Bacon said, "heat and cold are nature's two hands, whereby she chiefly worketh,"[9] but "man's power is clearly lame on one side":

> We have the heat of fire, which is infinitely more potent and intense than the heat of the sun as it reaches us, or the warmth of animals. But we have no cold save such as is to be got in winter time, or in caverns, or by application of snow and ice. . . . But they are nothing to be compared to the heat of a burning furnace, or with any cold corresponding to it in intensity.

In consequence, natural philosophers' knowledge was for instrumental reasons unsatisfactorily skewed: "All things with us tend to rarefaction, and desiccation, and consumption; nothing hardly to condensation and inteneration. . . . Instances of cold therefore should be collected with all diligence."[10]

In the early 1660s, urged on by his colleagues in the Royal Society, this is just what Boyle set out to do.[11] He took up the task of documenting the effects of cold, displaying the analytic work cold performed on

8. Bacon, "New Organon," 237.
9. Bacon, "Sylva Sylvarum," 370.
10. Bacon, "New Organon," 237. Inteneration was the process of making things soft or tender; see also idem, "Sylva Sylvarum," 370–71; idem, "Calor et Frigus," 648–52; idem, "History of Dense and Rare," 370.
11. Boyle quoted Bacon's *Sylva Sylvarum* as inspiration for a large but unsystematic collection of the phenomena of extreme cold: Boyle, "New Experiments Touching Cold," 468.

natural bodies, devising instrumental means to measure the degrees of cold, and offering hypotheses which assimilated the nature and effects of cold to the basic principles of mechanical philosophy. Here he found little sound existing work, among either ancient or modern natural philosophers, to assist his inquiries, and much in the way of "vulgar" lore that was evidently "untrue" or "uncertain."[12] A proper natural history of cold had to be begun anew, conducted through reliable procedures for sorting out the true from the fabulous. His text pervasively acknowledged the epistemic limits upon his knowledge of cold constituted by the constraints of place and time: even the English winters of the 'little Ice Age' were not cold enough to produce the frigid extremes corresponding to the violent heat of an efficient chemical furnace, and, while artificial means were known which would produce more cold than was naturally available, no such instrumentalities could replicate the natural cold of the most northerly regions of the globe.[13] Nor did Boyle indicate that he had ever thought of making a personal journey to the coldest regions: his delicate health and press of business precluded even considering that. He started out possessed of general layman's knowledge that there were degrees of cold to be experienced in Russia, Greenland, Newfoundland, and Iceland incomparably greater than any naturally or artificially available in England. Now he wanted more, more precise, and more reliable information about the extremes of cold to be encountered there. That is, he required distant phenomena to be brought home.

Those phenomena of cold that could not be laid on in Boyle's house and laboratory had to be secured by way of travelers' testimony. *New Experiments Touching Cold* was, accordingly, a mixed performance, such as was typical of Boylean texts, containing "those particulars, that I myself have tried or observed, or at least have received upon credible testimony." Given the temperateness of even the coldest English winter, Boyle recognized that he "must either make use of other men's testimony, or leave some of the remarkablest phænomena of cold unmentioned."[14] To leave testimonial phenomena unmentioned, and *a fortiori* to omit them from one's picture of the world, was unexcusably to commit the error of Locke's Siamese king. Even so, Boyle announced that he was tempted to leave out of his account a range of apparently implausible phenomena,

12. Ibid., 468–69, 475–76.
13. Ibid., 476, 479, 508–09, 530.
14. Ibid., 471, 476–77. Boyle's own experiments and observations were largely made from his Chelsea residence and accommodation at Stanton St. John's, near Oxford. Several winters in the early 1660s were, indeed, unusually severe.

were it not, that many of the relations, that may appear so wonderful, seem not to me to be repugnant to the nature of things, but only suppose a far greater degree of cold, than we have in these parts; and yet the familiar effects of the cold we have here, would, perhaps, be looked on as incredible, by one, that was born and bred in the kingdom of *Congo*. . . . Some, that have been in the *East-Indies*, inform us, that in some parts of those countries they were looked upon as great liars, for affirming, that in *Europe* the fluid body of water was often without any artifice or endeavor of man turned in a few hours into a solid and compact body, such as ice.[15]

That the phenomena of extreme cold presented themselves as inherently implausible flowed from the contingent fact that practitioners and laymen had built up plausibility schemes upon a restricted empirical base. Boyle thus reckoned himself already so reliably possessed of sufficient background knowledge about frigid regions that he could competently assess particular new claims. This was the testimonial base from which new specific testimony might be judged: "I can by very credible testimony make it appear, that an intense cold may have a greater operation upon the texture even of solid and durable bodies, than we in this temperate climate are commonly aware of."[16] Boyle already knew enough to avoid Siamese skepticism.

Boyle displayed far more sensitivity than Bacon to the potential troubles involved in reposing trust in such testimony. Cognizant of the tradition of "vulgar errors" and "jejune" philosophizing upon the phenomena of cold, Boyle needed to decide upon whom he could safely rely. Here he matter-of-factly deployed the system of maxims described in the last chapter: direct testimony was to be preferred to hearsay testimony; multiple testimony to single; knowledgeable sources to vulgar; and so on. These were the maxims to be generally deployed in evaluating textual evidence. Moreover, Boyle looked for vouching-practices which might assure him, and others, that he had indeed relied upon "credible travellers."[17] For his information about extreme cold, Boyle relied significantly upon travelers' texts: Dutch, Swedish, and English accounts of voyages to Novaya Zemlya, Arctic Scandinavia, and Canada. Justifying his use of such texts, Boyle assured readers that he was properly positioned between skepticism and credulity. One text, he acknowledged, was by an author of "very suspected credit, [who] delivers some things upon hear-say" which Boyle himself would be reluctant to accept. Nevertheless, Boyle noted, the author bore the undeniable marks of general trustworthiness: he was archbishop of

15. Ibid., 477, 573; see also idem, "Men's Great Ignorance," 473.
16. Boyle, "New Experiments Touching Cold," 534.
17. Ibid., 573.

Uppsala "and appears to have more learning, than many, that never read his books, imagine."[18]

The travel-book which, Boyle said, provided him more observations than any other was Captain Thomas James's (1633) *Strange and Dangerous Voyage* to Hudson Bay in search of a northwest passage to the South Seas. Here was a source which carried with it special warrants of reliability. First, Boyle knew that James had acquired a record for reliability and skill from those in a position to judge: he was chosen for the voyage by "the inquisitive merchants of *Bristol*," and, more important, was commanded on his return to publish his travel journals by the king himself. These were major circumstances arguing that "this gentleman's relations may well be represented to us, as likely to deserve our consideration and credit." Second, James was marked out from the general run of seamen and navigators by evident signs of knowledgeability: "So, by his breeding in the university, and his acquaintance with the mathematicks, he was enabled to make far better use than an ordinary seaman would have done, [of] the opportunity he had to observe the phænomena of cold."[19]

Nevertheless, both the manner and the matter of his travel-narrative make it evident what, apart from his standing and reputation, constituted the special marks of reliability that Boyle recognized, for James's text was distinguished from the general run of exotic wonder-mongering as much by its precision as its providentialism. When God's mercy was not being acknowledged, God's nature was being subjected to exact measurement. An appendix to the *Voyage* lists a particularly impressive range of mathematical instruments for establishing position, as well as "a *chest* full of the best and choicest *Mathematicall bookes* that could be got for money in *England*." A further appendix by Henry Gellibrand, Gresham College professor of astronomy, vouched for

18. Ibid., 478. The text concerned was Olaus Magnus, *A Compendious History of the Goths, Swedes, & Vandals, and Other Northern Nations* (London, 1658). In this connection Boyle also prominently cited Gerrit de Veer's narratives of Dutch voyages to the Arctic, translated into English in 1609 as *The True and Perfect Description of Three Voyages* (reprinted by the Hakluyt Society in the nineteenth century as de Veer, *Three Voyages of William Barents*).

19. Boyle, "New Experiments Touching Cold," 478, and, for another example of Boyle acknowledging a mariner's "reputation" for skill and accuracy, see idem, "Relations about the Bottom of the Sea," 350–51. A fine treatment of the contemporary credibility of mariners' reports of magnetic variation is Pumfrey, "'O Tempora, O Magnes,'" esp. 185–87, 204–06. It is not, in fact, certain that Captain James (1593?–1635?) did attend university, while one source refers to him as a barrister of the Inner Temple: Christy, introduction to idem, ed., *Voyages of Foxe and James*, I, cxxxi–clxxxix. Thomas Nash's preface to James's *Strange and Dangerous Voyage*, 451, referred to James as "my fellow-Templar."

James's "Iudgement, Circumspection, and Exactnes."[20] And, while there was apparently no weatherglass available to James for the standard numerical registering of the degrees of cold, the effects of extreme cold and its perception by captain and crew were circumstantially and minutely detailed, as were a range of other natural-historical, meteorological, and astronomical observables. Where standard measures were available to James—as in reports of latitude and compass bearing, time, dimension, and hydrographic soundings—these were related in due form:

> A North-west, a North-west by North, and a North-North-west winde (if it blew a storme) would raise the Tydes extraordinarily; and, in briefe, from the West North-west to the North North-east, would raise the tydes in proportion, as they did blow from the middle point. . . . The sixth [of January 1632], I observed the latitude with what exactness I could (it being very clear Sunshine weather), which I found to be 51.52. . . . The one and twentieth, I *obserued* the Sunne to rise like an *Ouall* alongst the *Horizon*. I cald three or foure to see it, the better to confirme my Iudgement, and we all agreed that it was twice as long as it was broad. We plainly perceiued withall that, by degrees, as it got vp higher, it also recouered his roundnesse.[21]

Finally, James was personally known, esteemed, and vouched for to Boyle "by some friends of mine, who were well acquainted with him."[22] That is, he was accounted a trustworthy source by those whom Boyle *knew* to be trustworthy sources. As in the natural history of things, so in the moral history of men. Wherever practical, Boyle attempted to interview travelers directly and look them in the eye when they told their tales. To that end—"for better gaining of such informations"— Boyle ultimately took a financial interest in voyages of discovery and trade to the Arctic regions, becoming one of the "adventurers" in the Hudson's Bay Company.[23]

The second of Boyle's two most important sources of testimony concerning extreme cold was a physician named Samuel Collins (1619– 1670). He was the son of an Essex vicar—possibly a celebrated Braintree Puritan of the same name—and was a scholar at Corpus Christi

20. James, *Strange and Dangerous Voyage*, 604–06, 613–14, 619. For remarks on the significance of James's voyage for the Gresham College mathematical circle, see Bennett, "Practical Challenge of Mathematics," 188–89.

21. James, *Strange and Dangerous Voyage*, 532; see especially 535–36 for attempts to calibrate the human experiences of extreme cold.

22. Boyle, "New Experiments Touching Cold," 478.

23. "The Publisher to the Reader," in ibid., 463; Maddison, *Boyle*, 119, 134. Boyle was also involved with the East India Company and the Turkey Company, again at least partly for the purpose of securing effective direct access to testimonial sources.

College, Cambridge, leaving without a degree, and proceeding to an M.D. at Padua. Between 1660 and 1669, Collins was physician to the czar in Moscow, and his book on Russia was published posthumously.[24] Boyle acquired Collins's factual knowledge more directly than James's. He had known Collins before he went to Russia, conversing with him about witchcraft at sister Mary's house at Leese.[25] Boyle had supplied Collins with some of his favorite "chymical medicines," which, proving "very well liked" by the czar, induced Boyle to request a *quid pro quo:* Boyle would write out a list of inquiries—largely concerning "the divers effects of cold"—and the ingenious physician would supply detailed responses.[26] Only a few letters from Collins to Boyle survive— and none in the other direction—though scores of references to Collins's information in *New Experiments Touching Cold* testify to his importance in Boyle's building up of an overall picture of the phenomena of extreme cold.[27] Collins was for Boyle a credible person; his testimony was in general better than that even of a good text. He was someone who had broken bread with Boyle, with whom Boyle had established civil conversation, into whose face Boyle had looked and seen trustworthiness, and who, accordingly, could now function as an extension of Boyle's own senses.

James and Collins, in their different ways, bore the recognizable signs of credibility. That meant that they could supply factual testimony whose competence and sincerity Boyle saw no adequate reason to doubt. It was in that sense privileged testimony. This is not the same thing as saying that Boyle simply validated whatever it was they claimed about the world of extreme cold. For one thing, their testimonies might not concur with each other, with other credible sources, or with the facts of Boyle's own artificially produced frigid phenomena. Judgment that a relation is sincere and competent need not itself count as judgment that the relation is adequate and sufficient to constitute knowledge of what is the case. I have indicated how Boyle warranted James

24. [Collins], *The Present State of Russia* (1671).

25. Collins to Boyle, 1 September and 20 November 1663, in Boyle, *Works*, VI, 639–42. Since Collins was an Essex man, there was a possible prior social connection with Boyle via Mary Rich's local circle of acquaintance, and, indeed, Collins's letters did request Boyle to convey his personal greetings to Mary. In an undated letter to Boyle, Collins referred to "my Lady of Warwicke" as "a noble patronesse to my deceased father": Boyle Letters, Vol. 2, f. 33. Boyle also directly secured knowledge of Russian cold via the ambassador extraordinary, the earl of Carlisle (Boyle, "New Experiments Touching Cold," 685n.).

26. Boyle, "New Experiments Touching Cold," 463–64, 685n; see also ibid. 515.

27. For Boyle's warranting, and use of, Collins's testimony, see, especially, Boyle, "New Experiments Touching Cold," 515, 729–30; idem, "General History of the Air," 697–98, 711–12, 725. Unpublished letters from Collins to Boyle are in the Boyle Letters, Vol. 2, ff. 31, 33–34.

and Collins as credible persons. I need now briefly to show how he wove their credible testimony into an ontological and moral fabric.

Archimedes and the Icebergs

Boyle was a participant in seventeenth-century debates over the physical causes of ice floating in a body of water. That this was due to its expansion was not in question, but the physical cause of that expansion was contested. Boyle was in the mainstream of modern natural-philosophical opinion in claiming that the expansion of ice, and hence its levity in water, was owing largely to the bubbles produced in it, which "make the water, when congealed, take up more room than when fluid." The content of these bubbles remained uncertain, and debates over whether they contained atmospheric air, an ethereal fraction of "pure air," or, possibly, nothing at all, roughly paralleled contemporary debates over the nature of the Torricellian space at the top of an inverted tube of mercury, and, indeed, in this connection Boyle offered criticisms of Thomas Hobbes's plenist philosophy of nature.[28] Whatever the provenance of these bubbles which were the cause of levity, Boyle was one of a number of practitioners concerned to make accurate measurements of the extent of that levity, and thus to produce a precise quantitative experimental hydrostatics. Boyle did not doubt Archimedean principles, and accepted them as "proved, after the manner of mathematicians." His research program was, however, concerned with investigating a range of geometries and physical compositions, "to manifest the physical reason, why [they] must be true."[29]

For practical reasons Boyle reckoned that the levity of ice was best studied in ice-masses of great size: with small pieces of ice so small a portion was above water level that measurements were evidently imprecise. But if one could encounter, or obtain reliable information of, very large naturally occurring bodies of ice,

> it would not be difficult for any, that understands hydrostaticks, to give a pretty near guess at the height of the extant part by the help of what we lately observed of the measures of water's expansion, and by the knowledge of the immersed part; which supposing, that the ice

28. Boyle, "New Experiments Touching Cold," 543. For later work on establishing the specific gravity of ice and the nature of bubbles contained therein, see, e.g., Hooke, *Philosophical Experiments and Observations*, 134–42. For a 1660s program of research on bubbles and porosity, see Shapin and Schaffer, *Leviathan and the Air-Pump*, ch. 6, esp. 238–56.

29. Boyle, "Hydrostatical Paradoxes," 763; cf. his better-known resistance to discovering physical causes of natural regularities, as, for example, expressed in "New Experiments Physico-mechanical," 11–12; see also Shapin and Schaffer, *Leviathan and the Air-Pump*, 49–53. Boyle's views on the contrast between mathematical and physical investigations are treated in chapter 7 below.

were of a prismatical figure, and floated in an erect position, would, in fresh water, amount to about eight or nine times the length of the part of the prism superiour to the surface of the water.[30]

Or, as we all know, nine-tenths of an (ideal) iceberg is below the surface of (ideal) water. A problem, however, appeared at the intersection of experiment and testified experience, for credible travelers to "gelid" parts of the world related iceberg dimensions conflicting with Boyle's experimentally obtained inferences. Whether and how to reconcile credible testimony from the Arctic and that directly secured in a cold laboratory during an Oxford winter?

Travelers told of icebergs looming taller than they ought to, given their underwater extent, an assumption of prismatic shape, and the known principles of hydrostatics. Captain James made several mentions of enormous icebergs, some "twice as high as our top-mast head" (perhaps 60–70 feet), though he did not seek to establish precise underwater dimensions.[31] Dutch travelers offered more exact reports of icebergs in the Siberian Arctic which measured sixteen fathoms above the water and thirty-six fathoms below, and Danish expeditions to Greenland yielded reports of icebergs measuring twenty fathoms above water and forty below.[32] This should not be. The reported depths "of these stupendous pieces of ice seem not at all answerable to what [they] may be supposed to be" according to Boyle's own work on the expansion of ice "and that grand hydrostatical theorem demonstrated by *Archimedes* and *Stevinus*."[33] How to repair the inconsistencies? I will follow the course of Boyle's practical reasoning in some detail,

30. Boyle, "New Experiments Touching Cold," 542. Boyle's major text in this area was his *Hydrostatical Paradoxes* of 1666, where he took Pascal to task for proceeding more demonstratively than experimentally or historically in establishing hydrostatic regularities (esp. 745–46). I have no very satisfactory idea why Boyle supposed icebergs to be prismatically shaped. Possibly, this was a simplifying assumption, allowing him to make certain calculations and certain analogies between laboratory and sea; possibly too Boyle had seen few or no drawings of icebergs, while travelers' accounts had little to say about their shape.

31. James, *Strange and Dangerous Voyage*, 472 (cf. 465), as referred to in Boyle, "New Experiments Touching Cold," 552.

32. E.g., De Veer, *Three Voyages of William Barents (1594–1596)*, 97–98; also White, *Collection of Documents on Spitzbergen & Greenland*, 37; Frobisher, *Three Voyages 1576–8*, 68–69, 126.

33. Boyle, "New Experiments Touching Cold," 552; see also idem, "Hydrostatical Paradoxes," 763; Stevin, "Fourth Book of Statics" (1634), esp. 143–46; De Waard, *L'expérience barométrique*, 72–73 (for Stevin's hydrostatics). Sounding techniques for determining the depth of the water were, of course, standardized and unproblematic. Since sounding devices also brought up a sample of the bottom, this *might* explain how contemporary measurements of icebergs' underwater extent were made. Whatever techniques were used, Boyle apparently saw little to question about their reliability.

Figure 2. Engraving of William Barents's encounter with floating ice near Spitzbergen or Novaya Zemlya ("How the ice heaved up the fore part of our ship"). From Gerrit de Veer, *The Three Voyages of William Barents to the Arctic Regions (1594, 1595, and 1596)*, 2d ed. (London: Hakluyt Society, 1876; orig. publ. in English translation 1609), between pp. 100 and 101. This illustration *could* have been seen by Boyle. (By permission of the Syndics of Cambridge University Library.)

showing how he found his way around a system of maxims which spoke of what nature was like and what people were like.

Two possible ways of repairing this recognized trouble which were available in principle were not evidently even considered: the reliability of these travelers' testimony could simply have been rejected (they were liars or gross incompetents), and the order of nature could have been identified as radically different as between Oxford and the Arctic, or between the 1630s and the 1660s. I am not concerned here to explain just why such specific courses of action were not taken in this instance.[34] Suffice it to note that both the wholesale rejection of the sincerity and competence of testimony and the splitting of nature's

34. It is, however, relevant to note that, while the credibility of sea captains like James proceeded partly from their knowledgeability, there was no reason to suspect that formally theoretical presuppositions—e.g. a concern to discredit Archimedes or Simon Stevin—might lead them to misrepresent real dimensions. Here the identity of a knowledgeable sea captain might be contrasted to that of a knowledgeable natural philosopher.

characteristics *were* tactics adopted in other assessments, and, indeed, such cases will be treated later in this chapter. Nevertheless, both such tactics present substantial costs to those who engage in them: on the one hand, one is unlikely to be able to use any other testimony from sources so massively discredited, or to be able in future to 'look them in the face' and engage them in civil conversation; on the other, insofar as one is concerned to develop an overall picture of how nature behaves in a range of circumstances, the willy-nilly splitting of nature into differently constituted and differently behaving space-time regions is potentially destructive of any such generalizing enterprise.

Boyle, however, repaired these recognized troubles in such a way as to preserve both the in-principle reliability of testimonial sources and the in-principle reliability of hydrostatical rules supposed to obtain— *ceteris paribus*—for all samples of water and ice. Granting the truthfulness of these testified iceberg dimensions, perhaps it was the case that the ice was not free-floating but grounded? Indeed, when Captain James reported his icebergs "twice as high" as his mast, he also specified that these "great pieces of ice . . . were a-ground in 40 [fathoms of water]."[35] Was not Captain James known to be an honorable man, and was it not possible that the Dutch and Danish observers simply neglected to check whether their icebergs were similarly grounded? Foreign travelers sincerely and competently reported what was there to be witnessed, but not *everything* that was there to be witnessed. Had these icebergs not been resting on the seabed, they would have presented different above- and below-water dimensions, and the reports of these sincere and competent observers would, no doubt, have differed accordingly. So, adding the circumstance of icebergs-on-the-seabed to these relations and to the principles of hydrostatics helps to repair apparent trouble, turning apparent inconsistency into real consistency.

Nevertheless, it was possible, Boyle considered, that *some* testified dimensions pertained to genuinely free-floating icebergs. What could then be said to repair trouble and restore consistency? Perhaps there were some local variables which explained why so much of the icebergs was above water, some features of the scene witnessed by Arctic travelers which did not obtain in an Oxford laboratory. Boyle's calculations about what ought to be observed in the Arctic were largely informed by freshwater experiments, but, of course, the seas were salty. Maybe, because of the greater heaviness of salt water, the "ice will not sink so deep into that, as into [fresh water]."[36] Certainly, that possibility

35. James, *Strange and Dangerous Voyage,* 472, and referred to in Boyle, "New Experiments Touching Cold," 554.
36. Boyle was presumably aware that icebergs were largely freshwater (although he did not know that they were broken-off bits of glaciers) and that sheet-ice was salty,

corresponded to much local practical experience, including some of Boyle's own laboratory manipulations. But while the great saltiness of the sea might go some way to restore consistency between travelers' observations and hydrostatical knowledge, the same supposition introduced a possible inconsistency with other well-testified knowledge, in this case the observation of "some modern geographers" that the polar seas are not very salty. If one decided to preserve the truthfulness of *this* testimony, then the testimony of the iceberg witnesses might be difficult to recuperate. As it happened, while the great saltiness of northern seas might not be available to repair testimony of iceberg dimensions, its great coldness might help do the trick. Boyle had experimentally noted some covariation of coldness and levity in his Oxford laboratory. Perhaps seawater, being far more reluctant to freeze, "may, by so vehement a cold as reigns in the winter-season in those gelid climates, be far more intensely refrigerated, and thereby more condensed than common water is here."[37]

Finally, Boyle deemed it possible that the troubling testified dimensions of icebergs might be owing partly to the manner of their concretion. Hydrostatical calculations of what ought to be observed presupposed coherent and homogeneous bodies, but there was no certainty that naturally occurring large masses of ice were so composed. Perhaps icebergs were "vast piles or lumps, and masses of ice, casually and rudely heaped up and cemented by the excessive cold"; perhaps they were concretions of distinct icy masses with great interspersed air-filled cavities; perhaps also portions which appeared to be ice, or which were hidden from view, were actually uncompacted, or slightly compacted, snow.[38] If any one of these plausible states of affairs obtained, then, again, both the dimensions reported by credible travelers and the principles of Archimedean hydrostatics might be preserved and rendered practically consistent.

So far as this particular inquiry was concerned, that was where the matter was left. Additional information about the dimensions of icebergs would be welcome. Indeed, any traveler now going out to Arctic

while travelers' reports indicated that icebergs might acquire a salty surface-glaze: White, *Collection of Documents on Spitzbergen & Greenland*, 37; Frobisher, *Three Voyages*, 126.

37. Boyle, "New Experiments Touching Cold," 553; see also idem, "Temperature of the Submarine Regions," 349. For Boyle's understanding of salinity, see idem, "Observations and Experiments about the Saltness of the Sea," especially 775–76 (for the differential saltiness of polar and tropical oceans); idem, "Hydrostatical Paradoxes," 794; and idem, "New Experiments about Differing Pressure," 646–47 (for swimming in the Dead Sea).

38. Boyle, "New Experiments Touching Cold," 552–54; and, for Boyle's receipt of information on this point, see Oldenburg to Boyle, 24 November 1664, in Oldenburg, *Correspondence*, II, 321; see also White, *Collection of Documents on Spitzbergen & Greenland*, 19.

regions could be asked carefully to check the saltiness of water, the makeup of icebergs, and, as soon as reliably transportable thermometers were available, the exact degrees of cold.[39] For the present, however, Boyle's ingenious mundane reasoning produced a world-picture which contained sincere and competent sea captains, true Archimedean hydrostatical principles, icebergs with too much of their mass above the sea which might be resting on the seabed, which might contain great air-cavities, and which might be floating free in very cold or very salty water. Civil conversation about these matters might continue.[40] The condition of securing knowledge about the nature of nature was the possession of knowledge about the nature of people. Having knowledge about the nature of people allowed experience to be brought back from distant times and places and transformed into public knowledge.

Divers' Reports

Captain James and Dr. Collins were credible persons, providing Boyle with trustworthy testimony. What Boyle knew about James and Collins permitted them to act as extensions of his own senses, to colonize his own mind and the minds of the public for whom Boyle was himself a credible person. I want now to work through an example in which potentially troubling testimony came from persons who might *not* be regarded as creditworthy. How might physical and moral *disqualifications* to perceive and reliably to report upon reality be used in systematic processes of deciding nature's constitution?

Boyle's early program of air-pump experimentation served locally to establish the claim that the air had a weight and a pressure. We lived at the bottom of a vast ocean of air; it pressed down upon us; and that pressure could experimentally be made manifest and subject to measurement. Variation in the height of mercury in a barometer

39. Thermometers of various types were in the course of development from the early to mid-seventeenth century by, among others, Galileo, Santorio Santorre, Robert Fludd, Cornelius Drebbel, J. B. Van Helmont, Jean Rey, Boyle, and Hooke, but they were not available to the travelers whose testimony Boyle used in the 1665 text: see Middleton, *History of the Thermometer*, chs 1–3. For detailed inquiries supplied by Royal Society members to Arctic travelers, see, e.g., Hooke, *Philosophical Experiments and Observations*, 18–22; see also "Directions for Sea-men, Bound for Far Voyages," *Philosophical Transactions* 8 (8 January 1666), 140–43 (prepared by Laurence Rooke); "An *Appendix* to the *Directions* for Seamen," ibid., 9 (12 February 1666); and Thomas Mackrith to Boyle, 5 February 1666, in Boyle, *Works*, VI, 664–67 (for a specimen response).

40. By the 1680s credible reports about iceberg dimensions by Arctic travelers had evidently been brought into line with Archimedean principles; see Hooke, *Philosophical Experiments and Observations*, 136–37, which, nevertheless, rehearsed Boyle's repertoire of reasons why too much of the ice might still be observed to extend above the water surface.

could be pointed to as a reliable sign of variation in the pressure of atmospheric air. Yet we do not *experience* any such pressure; we have no sensation of being oppressed by the great columns of air under which we live. Indeed, that absence of such sensation was a potential trouble for Boyle's doctrines about the air, and he was concerned to reconcile positive ontological claims about pressure and weight with negative phenomenological evidence of 'how it felt.' Place your hand over the hole at the top of the glass receiver of an air-pump, and then have the operator exhaust the pump. You will feel a strong, even a painful, suction on the bottom of your hand. That experience of suction, Boyle argued, was properly to be interpreted as experience of the air's pressure acting upon the upper surface of the hand. Air normally exerted its pressure *isotropically.* Accordingly, the sensation experienced in this experiment was that of the pressure of the air *when pressure was not being exerted from below.* Here was direct experiential evidence for the reality of the pressure of the air: you could be made to feel it. Under artificially arranged conditions, phenomenology could be brought into line with ontological claims and made powerfully to support them.[41]

Whatever the local persuasiveness of this demonstration, neither it nor the series of related experiments Boyle later reported proffered a definitive explanation of why *normally* we do not experience the pressure of the air. Hints, and the general form of an explanation, were indeed offered: presumably this had something to do with the disposition of the fluid and solid portions of our bodies; perhaps our embryological development in a pressurized medium guaranteed that we would withstand that pressure and not even experience it as such; perhaps it was a matter of sensory or physical habituation, such that people accustomed to living in a less-pressurized environment might experience as crushing a force we do not even notice.[42] These were, in Boyle's view, hypothetical debates: men-in-the-moon were not about to come to earth and tell us what they felt, and it was not considered that men who had climbed even the highest earthly mountains had freed themselves from a sufficient portion of the air's pressure reliably to generate an experience of rarefaction or levity. By contrast, statical debates concerning the pressure of *water* crucially pointed to the experience of those who dove to great depths. How did they *feel*? And how were reports of their experience to be balanced with other sorts of information?

41. Boyle, "New Experiments Physico-mechanical" (1660), 15–16; idem, "Hydrostatical Paradoxes," 795. For an account of Boyle's work on, and presentation of, air-pressure, as well as local resistances to his claims, see Shapin and Schaffer, *Leviathan and the Air-Pump*, esp. chs 2 and 4.

42. See, e.g., Boyle, "New Experiments about Differing Pressure," 643–44.

Here again the problem of testimony was recognized as central to the constitution of reliable knowledge. Boyle himself "never pretended to be a diver": "I do not pretend to have visited the bottom of the sea; [and] none of the naturalists whose writings I have yet met with, have been there any more than I."[43] The natural philosopher would, accordingly, have to rely mainly upon the reports of those who had dived, or, at least, of those credible persons who had spoken with divers. Boyle himself sought reliable testimony wherever he could: "purposely conversing with persons that have dived, some without, and some by the help of [diving] engines"; by inquiring of "a person of quality" who knew African divers and who had dived a bit himself; by interviewing persons who were familiar with diving practices in the East Indies; by quizzing a "man that gets his living by fetching up goods out of wrecked ships."[44]

The overall thrust of divers' reports was that they experienced no crushing pressure, no matter how deep they dived or how long they remained submerged. This was not, as the aerostatic example shows, necessarily a decisive argument against the reality of water-pressure. In the event, however, divers' reports were available to be importantly mobilized as reliable and decisive negative evidence by natural philosophers who argued, in the Peripatetic manner, that neither air nor water "gravitated" or pressed upon itself "in its proper place." Even the experimental philosopher Henry Power distinguished between the gravitation of air, which he was happy to accept upon Boylean experimental grounds, and that of water, which was said not to weigh upon itself, on the evidence of divers' testimony.[45] By the mid-1660s and early 1670s, Boyle found himself in conflict with a range of practitioners who condemned the general principles of his mechanical phi-

43. Boyle, "Temperature of the Submarine Regions," 342; idem, "Relations about the Bottom of the Sea," 349.

44. E.g., Boyle, "Temperature of the Submarine Regions," 342, 345; idem, "Relations about the Bottom of the Sea," 349; Boyle Papers, Vol. 18, f. 60; also idem, "Hydrostatical Discourse," 621; idem, "New Experiments about Differing Pressure," 646–48. There was much early Royal Society practical interest in diving-engines and the pressure of water: see, e.g., Birch, *History of the Royal Society*, I, 180–82, 392, 399; Hooke, *Philosophical Experiments and Observations*, 14–18; also Hunter, *Science and Society*, 95; 'Espinasse, *Hooke*, 52–53, 73.

45. Power, *Experimental Philosophy* (1664), 106: "Water we experimentally know (which is a fluid and dissipable Body, as Ayr is) does not gravitate in its own proper place; for if we dive never so deep, it's so far from depressing of them lower, or weighing on them, that it is readier to buoy them up again." Hobbes related it as "well enough known" that divers "feel no weight of water resting on them," while offering a mechanical account of why that feeling was reliable: Hobbes, *White's 'De Mundo' Examined* (ca. 1643), 224.

losophy by *inter alia* crediting divers' reports and valorizing them as reliable testimony of the nongravitation of water.[46]

In his 1666 *Hydrostatical Paradoxes* (composed 1664), Boyle vigorously defended the reality of water-pressure while appearing to accept the authenticity of divers' reports. Those reports were adduced by opponents as evidence against water-pressure, and this was, in Boyle's judgment, "so noble" an objection to mechanical hydrostatics that it demanded systematic investigation. He took up the challenge of either explaining divers' reports in accordance with properly mechanical principles or explaining them away by discrediting their reliability. Boyle here adopted the first course, arguing that water, like air, exerted its pressure isotropically, pressing bodies submerged in it from all directions. The body of a diver did not, accordingly, sustain the full weight of the water column above him, since the water below his body pressed upwards with sufficient strength "not only to support the weight of the incumbent water, but so far to exceed it, that it would not only support the immersed body, and the incumbent water, but buoy up the body, if it were never so little lighter *in specie* than water." In this connection Boyle recruited experimental work with the air-pump as specific evidence for the pressure of *water*.[47]

Nevertheless, divers' reports continued to trouble Boyle as much as they continued to be validated by opponents of his mechanical philosophy. Given that water pressed upon a submerged body in all directions and towards the center of that body, it was by no means clear why divers should report what they did. Something concerning the structure of human bodies might have to be added to the isotropic pressure of water: "It seems [that] the texture of the bodies of animals is better able to resist the pressure of an every way ambient fluid, than, if we were not taught by experience, we should imagine." The internal structure and relative firmness of bodies might also need to be adduced to explain divers' testimony. Experiments were performed 'compressing' water in which tadpoles were placed, and they showed no signs of injury nor were they "sensibly hurt." Boyle concluded from this "that the texture of animals is so strong, that, though water be allowed to weigh upon water, yet a diver ought not to be oppressed by it."[48] By the mid-1660s, therefore, Boyle had reached a position where he and his opponents both credited divers' reports but embedded them within

46. For Boyle versus Henry More on related subjects, see Shapin and Schaffer, *Leviathan and the Air-Pump*, 212–24.
47. Boyle, "Hydrostatical Paradoxes," 795. Boyle was here glossing the explanation previously offered by Simon Stevin: "Fourth Book of Statics," 146–47 (Theorem VIII, Proposition X); idem, "Fifth Book of Statics," 157–58 (Proposition III).
48. Boyle, "Hydrostatical Paradoxes," 796–97.

different physical frameworks. For antimechanists, phenomenology was aligned with ontology; for Boylean mechanists it was not. This mismatch was contingently, if not necessarily, a trouble for Boyle. It was a difficulty he might persistently be asked to account for.

Over the next five to ten years Boyle periodically returned to the status of divers' testimony, exploring ways of repairing the mismatch between testimony and theorized physical reality. Perhaps divers' reports need not be accepted as wholly reliable indications of underwater realities. He announced "that I am not entirely satisfied about the matter of fact." Boyle continued to interview divers and credible men who knew about the business. He started to express skepticism about "vulgar reports about diving" and to make distinctions between the settings from which reports emerged and between characters and constitutions of different sorts of diver: "I do not yet know, whether it fares alike with the divers in all depths of water." Maybe the experience of pressure was available at greater depths than those from which he had previously secured his testimony. Maybe also there was something about the *business* of diving which militated against philosophically reliable self-evidence. Those who dove without engines "usually make such haste, or are so confounded, or have their minds so intent upon their work, that they take not notice of such lesser alterations, as else they might observe." These were, after all, not philosophers but laborers—"persons void of curiosity and skill to make such observations."[49] There *were*, Boyle now suggested, real pressure experiences there to be had, but not everyone in fact had them. A distinction was thus introduced between the realities which made themselves available for competent experience and the experiences actually had by different sorts of persons. Having an experience was here to be accounted an entitlement.

Testimony now might be sorted into reliable and unreliable according to the knowledgeability or skill of those who provided it. Boyle interrogated several especially experienced divers. One man who got his living by retrieving goods from shipwrecks "complained to me" that if he dove very deep, even with the aid of his diving bell, "and made some stay there, he found himself incommodated." The professional diver imputed the discomfort to cold, but Boyle "was inclined to suspect that the pressure . . . might have an interest in the troublesome effect."[50] Divers were generally "ignorant and heedless," but, when

49. Boyle, "Hydrostatical Discourse," 621; idem, "New Experiments about Differing Pressure," 647.

50. Boyle, "New Experiments about Differing Pressure," 647; also idem, "Hydrostatical Discourse," 618. One of the diving "engineers" in question was possibly the "Mr. Roachford" (or "Roquefort") mentioned in these connections by Robert Hooke: *Philosophical Experiments and Observations*, 137; see also Hunter, *Science and Society*, 95.

one came across a rather more knowledgeable diver, he was even more likely to ascribe "a new sensation, that really proceeds from pressure, to other causes," since he might be informed of learned men's opinion about the nongravitation of water.[51] And even if the common run of divers said they felt no pressure, the evidence of their bodies might testify to its reality. Boyle asked "an ingenious Chirurgeon" experienced in the retrieval of treasure from Spanish wrecks what he knew about divers' experience. The surgeon told Boyle that divers varied in their skill and stamina, but "that when they div'd deep, they found, (as I suspected) their Chests & Bellys considerably prest against by the incompassing water, wch especially prest against their Ears, to their great trouble, & in some of them did much affect the Eyes; producing a kind of *Ophthalmia* in them; and in others had this more dangerous Effect, that it made them spit blood." That the divers displaying these signs had indeed descended to at least eight fathoms could be vouched for by the surgeon: the water was so clear that he could see them at work, "even the black Dyvers."[52] Women divers in Japan were reliably reported to suffer bleeding of the eyes that "you may know a diving woman from all other women," and this effect Boyle also ascribed to pressure.[53]

If vulgar divers' bodies spoke more truthfully than their tongues, then it might be possible securely to establish the reality of pressure effects by relying not upon the testimony of persons but upon the testimony of things. In the early 1670s Boyle extended his early experimental work in hydrostatics by attempting to obtain testimony from those who could give informed reports about what happened to submerged vessels. He announced that testified experience of this sort strongly spoke in favor of water-pressure. "Discoursing one day with an engineer of my acquaintance that had been often at sea, and loved to try conclusions," Boyle was told that new experimental trials to prove the point were unnecessary:

[The engineer] assured me, that having divers times opportunity to sail near the streights mouth over a place where the sea was observed to be of a notable depth, he had found, that if he had let down, with a weight into the sea, not a strong round glass bottle, but a phial, such as the seamen use to carry their brandy and strong waters in; such a vessel, which might contain a pint or quart of water, would,

51. Boyle, "Hydrostatical Discourse," 618–19.

52. Boyle Papers, Vol. 18, f. 60. This paper is undated, but seems to have been prepared for the 1672 "New Experiments about Differing Pressure" (see esp. p. 647) or "Hydrostatical Discourse" (esp. pp. 621, 626). (The manuscript names the surgeon as a "Mr. Handyside," but there is no such attribution in the published tract.) For further reports of bleeding divers, see Birch, *History of the Royal Society*, I, 392, 399.

53. Boyle, "Hydrostatical Discourse," 618.

when it come to be sunk 40 fathoms under water, if not sooner, be
so oppressed by the pressure of the incumbent and lateral water, as
to be thereby broken to pieces.[54]

Sir Robert Moray, a former president of the Royal Society, told Boyle
that "a mathematical friend of his" let down "in a deep sea" a weighted
pewter-bottle, and when he pulled it up "he was much surprized to
find the sides of his pewter-bottle very much compressed, and, as it
were, squeezed inward by the water." Boyle inquired of "an observing
acquaintance of mine" what happened to bottles let down into tropical
seas to be cooled. He was told by the "amazed" friend that the corks
were driven in so tightly that they could not be removed, and similar
testimony came from a colonial physician (probably the notorious
Henry Stubbe).[55]

The redistribution of credibility between vulgar divers and pewter-
bottles was meant to secure assent to a picture of the world which
contained the empirical fact of water-pressure. This fact, in turn, was
testified by Robert Boyle, who thus sought to secure the rights to speak
for things, for other people, and for the appropriate distribution of
credibility within and between the sets of things and people. In the
case of divers' reports, this was accomplished by opening up a gap
between the categories of reality, experience, and reliable report. Since
the experience of pressure evidently depended upon the relative texture of bodies, the firmness or tenderness of human bodies might also
be pointed to as a relevant circumstance. I noted in chapter 3 that
Galenic and Hippocratic thought about human natures identified significant differences flowing from birth and way of life. It was a commonplace of early modern culture that those who engaged in manual
labor were "coarsened" thereby and, conversely, that the contemplative
life "softened" and "refined." Within that scheme, it might be plausibly
reckoned that divers' bodies were firmer than those of gentlemen and
scholars. Boyle repeatedly alluded in this connection to "bodies of so
firm a texture as those of lusty men" and to the relative firmness of
human "membranes and fibres." The fibers of "porters, carriers, and
other lusty men" were accustomed to hard labor and, accordingly,
such men experienced little compression and pain. Vulgar men were,
literally, thick. Scholars and gentlemen were not wont to dive, but, if
they did, they would experience what the "illiterate vulgar" did not:
"If observations about diving were made by philosophers and mathematicians, or, at least, intelligent men . . . , we should perhaps have an
account of what happens to men under water, differing enough from

54. Boyle, "Relations about the Bottom of the Sea," 352.
55. Boyle, "Hydrostatical Discourse," 624–25.

the common reports."[56] The common reports of common people might be *perceptually insensitive or incompetent.*

Divers' testimony might be credited if there were other grounds for it apart from their own say-so, for example, if what they reported was contained within recipients' plausibility schemes. However, gentlemanly-philosophical culture offered a range of costlessly deployable resources to discredit their experience and their testimony. Greed, ignorance, and bias could be reliably assigned to people like divers, transforming direct experience into deceit or delusion. Vulgar divers went down solely to bring up "shipwrecked goods." Their attention fastened upon sordid interest and gain, they minded neither the state of their bodies nor the philosophical curiosities to be observed underwater. Like other men who labored under material necessity, any testimony which bore upon such interest might be judged unreliable for that reason. And, when such persons acquired any notion about the pressure of water, they were liable to take on the "vulgar opinion" of its nongravitation, thus adding theoretical "prepossession" to other credibility handicaps. That was the framework within which it might be possible and plausible to assent to the testimony of things rather than to that of certain sorts of people:

> The pressure of the water in our recited experiment having manifest effects upon inanimate bodies, which are not capable of prepossessions, or giving us partial informations, will have much more weight with unprejudiced persons, than the suspicious, and sometimes disagreeing accounts of ignorant divers, whom prejudicate opinions may much sway, and whose very sensations, as those of other vulgar men, may be influenced by predispositions, and so many other circumstances, that they may easily give occasion to mistakes.[57]

The things whose testimony Boyle wanted credited were *his* things. He gave them voice and he wrote their scripts. They spoke either through the mouths of men he knew to be trustworthy, or in texts emerging from experimental scenes over which he presided and the meaning of which he had the undeniable rights to set. Giving assent to pressure-gauges and pewter-bottles was giving assent to their spokesman.[58] Not to believe what these things 'said' was not to believe

56. Ibid., 618, 621; also idem, "New Experiments about Differing Pressure," 648.

57. Boyle, "Hydrostatical Discourse," 626. The significance of this passage in connection with Boyle's disputes with Henry More is briefly noted in Shapin and Schaffer, *Leviathan and the Air-Pump,* 218; see also Schaffer, "Making Certain," 145.

58. Here I acknowledge the importance of Bruno Latour's stress on the role of scientists as "spokesmen for nature" while declining his apparent invitation to treat things and human beings as ontologically equivalent (Latour, *Science in Action;* Callon and Latour, "Don't Throw the Baby Out," esp. 352–57). These pewter-bottles spoke *only* through Boyle's mouth.

Boyle. By contrast, there might be no cost in disbelieving divers' testimony. One might discredit divers' perceptual competence, disinterestedness, knowledgeability, or moral integrity, and, if one were a person like Boyle and his Royal Society associates, one might do so with impunity.[59] Indeed, as chapter 3 documented, there was an enormous institutionalized body of early modern gentlemanly culture available to anyone who wished to discredit vulgar testimony.

To be sure, divers' disqualification from contributing to Boyle's phenomenal world was not absolute but conditional. A diver whose testimony about water-pressure was discredited was still, presumably, in a position to have his testimony about air-pressure (and many other things) accepted. Vulgar divers did not inhabit the same social worlds as Boyle, and, by withholding his assent from their testimony, Boyle ensured that, in certain respects and for certain conditions, they did not inhabit his phenomenal world. Divers possessed no acknowledged moral right to be believed by Boyle, and there was nothing of consequence they could do about it if their testimony was gainsaid in places inhabited by scholars and gentlemen.

Manners, Mundanity, and Moral Uncertainty in Cometary Astronomy

Histories of astronomy note the appearance of two theoretically important and widely observed comets in 1664 and 1665.[60] The so-called "comet of 1664" (hereafter C1) was first sighted in Spain on 7/17 November 1664 and continued to be followed there until 10/20 March 1665.[61] In Holland it was seen by Christiaan Huygens from 23 Novem-

---

59. For important accounts of the Royal Society's roughly contemporary research on transfusing sheep's blood into a man, and their general procedures for handling testimony about one's own bodily condition, see Schaffer, "Self-Evidence," and idem, "Experimental Subjects in the 1660s."

60. This account relies extensively upon Yeomans, *Comets*, ch. 4, the three-page account in Hetherington, "Hevelius-Auzout Controversy," and a range of sources including Thorndike, *History of Magic and Experimental Science*, VIII, 325–28; P. L. Brown, *Comets, Meteorites and Men*, 236; Guerlac, *Newton on the Continent*, 29–40; McGuire and Tamny, *Certain Philosophical Questions*, 296–304; idem, "Newton's Astronomical Apprenticeship," 349–54; Bennett, "Hooke and Wren and the System of the World"; idem, "Magnetical Philosophy and Astronomy," 226–27; Wilson, "Predictive Astronomy in the Century after Kepler," 204–05; and, especially, Ruffner, "Background and Early Development of Newton's Theory of Comets," ch. 6, and idem, "The Curved and the Straight," 187–91; see also some brief remarks on these comets in connection with Oldenburg's role as scientific intelligencer: Shapin, "O Henry," 421–22. Simon Schaffer's detailed comments on an early version of this section have been invaluable.

61. See explanatory remarks on conventions of date-giving in the prefatory notes to this book.

ber / 3 December; in Danzig (now Gdansk in Poland) by Johannes Hevelius from 4/14 December; at Cambridge by Isaac Newton from 10/20 December; and at various other times at the turn of the year by eminent astronomers in England and the Continent (Robert Hooke, Giovanni Domenico Cassini, Gilles François Gottigniez, Adrien Auzout, Pierre Petit, Giovanni Alfonso Borelli) and even in Massachusetts (Samuel Danforth). Reaching its maximum brightness on 19/29 December 1664, and with a tail about 40° long, this brilliant comet was at certain times visually accessible to almost anyone observing the sky on a clear night, and, like other recent comets, was widely available for appropriation as a moral and political portent.

Although C1 was readily visible to the naked eye in mid- to late December, it was evidently only marginally so by late January and February. Just as the 1664 comet was fading from view in March of 1665, a striking second comet (C2) was discovered in the south of France, and it too was widely followed by the same professional observers until it disappeared on 10/20 April. These two comets were of special importance because they were among the first comets to be subject to significant, geographically widespread, and relatively coordinated telescopic study and because their apparent paths were plotted in deliberate attempts to establish the general features of comets' place in the cosmos, composition, and proper motions.[62] They were philosophically interesting objects whose interpretation was closely associated with questions of the earth's motion, the legitimacy of Aristotelian cosmology, the accuracy and adequacy of a range of mathematical instruments, the cultural identity of astronomy, and the relative cultural and social standing of the practitioners of astronomy and astrology.[63]

Thus far, this is a textbook account of the comets of November 1664 to April 1665, and, indeed, it closely follows a version which consensually emerged from the astronomical community by *ca.* February 1667. I want, however, to retrieve a situation of uncertainty obtaining before that consensus developed. I want to display the techniques of moral management which figured in the assessment of

62. Technical usage distinguishes between a comet's true physical trajectory through the cosmos (its *proper motion*) and the path across the skies plotted by terrestrial observers (its *apparent motion*), though the latter is, of course, a technical resource used to establish the former. Henry Guerlac notes (*Newton on the Continent,* 35–36) that C1 "chose to arrive at a time when precision astronomy had made remarkable advances, and when scientists of England and Europe were beginning to enjoy that regular communication which the newly founded Academies made possible." Accordingly, C1 "led to the first concerted attempts since the time of Kepler not only to determine the parallax of a comet and its distance from the earth . . . but to work out its true path."

63. A sensitive recent study of these dimensions to an Italian controversy about the comets of 1618 is Biagioli, *Galileo, Courtier,* ch. 5.

apparently discrepant testimony and to show how knowledge about the heavens and knowledge about people-reporting-about-the-heavens were juxtaposed and evaluated so as to produce new knowledge of both comets and cometary observers.[64] Here I mean to highlight a contrast between the management of testimony from ignorant divers and that from skillful astronomers. Reports from the vulgar might be costlessly negated in order to build up or hold stable some valued representation of nature whereas representations of nature might be adjusted in order to hold stable the moral order of skillful and sincere colleagues.

Determining the observed path of a comet through the skies—its apparent motion—was a collective enterprise. From the first moment at which the Royal Society circle was made aware of C1 in December 1664, practitioners concerned to locate and plot the comet worked with observations from a variety of sources. Accordingly, for those reports to count as reports-about-this-comet, decisions had to be made about the general reliability of testimonial sources and about the particular reliability of these reports. On 15/25 December 1664 Hooke wrote to Boyle (then in Oxford) about the first reports received and discussed at the preceding day's Royal Society meeting. Accounts of "the appearance of a very great comet in the south south-east, with a very long tail, extended towards the north-west" had been received from unnamed sources in various parts of England, including Yorkshire, Cheshire, and Hampshire. Hooke himself immediately set about attempting to observe the comet, but weather conditions were poor and he did not see it until 23 December 1664 / 2 January 1665.[65] Boyle then told Oxford colleagues, including Savilian professor of geometry John Wallis, and further collective telescopic attempts were made to witness the comet, but conditions continued unsuitable. On the night of 23 December / 2 January, Wallis, looking for C1 according to Hooke's directions, reported success in seeing "another comet" in Orion (call this

64. Although the apparent motion of these comets was highly significant to the development of theories of their proper motion, I shall not touch significantly upon the latter, save when contemporaries' knowledge of others' theoretical attachments bore upon the moral management of discrepant observation-reports. Here I shall focus almost wholly upon the situation as it appeared, so to speak, from Henry Oldenburg's desk and from the point of view of the Royal Society colleagues for whom he spoke. Consequently, this is not offered as an exhaustive account, and more ought to be written about why different participants produced the observations they did.

65. Hooke to Boyle, 15/25 December 1664, in Boyle, *Works,* VI, 501; Hooke, "Cometa" (1678), 223. At Cambridge, Newton also saw C1 on 17/27 December and then not again until 23 December / 2 January, though there is no evidence that his early observations—uncertain and technically insecure—were communicated to the London and Oxford circle: McGuire and Tamny, *Certain Philosophical Questions,* 299; idem, "Newton's Astronomical Apprenticeship," 350–54.

C1a), apparently convinced that the positions he had been given from London were so different from what he saw that distinct entities were involved.[66] C1a enjoyed only a brief life. By 21/31 January 1665 at the latest, Wallis and his colleagues Christopher Wren and Viscount Brouncker were sufficiently assured that what they had seen on 23 December / 2 January *was* C1, and they produced a plot of its path across the heavens based partly on intermittent Oxford observations including that of 23 December / 2 January and extending to 10/20 January.[67]

Several days before 21/31 January, the Royal Society had received and distributed to Oxford a printed paper on C1 by Adrien Auzout (1622–1691), a well-respected natural philosopher at Paris, a former Rouen colleague of Pascal, and a member of the Montmor Academy.[68] This was a document of great boldness, for Auzout had produced a *search ephemerides*—a table of position *predictions*—of C1's future path across the heavens. Traditional opinion was that "the motions of *Comets* were so irregular, that they could not be reduced to any known Laws, and men . . . contented themselves, to observe exactly the places, through which they *did* pass; but no man, that [Auzout] knows, [has] been so bold as to venture to foretell the places, through which they *should* pass, and where they should cease to appear." To the English, Auzout thus appeared as "this *Philosophical Prophet.*" He claimed that the ephemerides had been projected from no more than five of his own observations, which, as Christiaan Huygens "& several French Gentlemen" were called to witness, he had not altered before publication in light of subsequent observations; and he invited the English to confirm or disconfirm his hypothesis.[69]

66. Wallis to [Oldenburg?], 24 December 1664 / 3 January 1665, in Oldenburg, *Correspondence,* II, 339–40. For uncertainties about Wallis's observation, see McGuire and Tamny, *Certain Philosophical Questions,* 302–03.

67. Wallis to Oldenburg, 21/31 January 1665, in Oldenburg, *Correspondence,* II, 353–56. Bennett ("Hooke and Wren and the System of the World," 49–60; "Magnetical Philosophy and Astronomy," 226–27) documents Royal Society interest in the comets of 1664–1665 as part of a contemporary research project on planetary motion and physical forces.

68. Auzout, *L'ephémérides du comète.* Although the paper is dated 2 January 1665 (23 December 1664 old style), it may have been printed up to ten days later. Auzout was especially well-known for his instrumental skills, becoming a member of the Paris Académie royale des sciences on its foundation, but an ill-judged quarrel drove him to Italy in 1668. For details of Auzout's life and work, see R. E. McKeon, "Auzout, Adrien," and H. Brown, *Scientific Organizations in Seventeenth Century France,* esp. 138–44.

69. "The Motion of the Late Comet Prædicted," *Philosophical Transactions* 1 (6/16 March 1665), 3–8; see also Oldenburg, *Correspondence,* II, 341–42n.; and Auzout to [?], 3/13 March 1665, ibid., 375, where Auzout claimed that he had used only *three* observations, those of 12/22, 16/26, and 21/31 December. For an account of the techniques Auzout used to produce his ephemerides, see Yeomans, *Comets,* 72.

Oldenburg's précis of Auzout's paper briefly alluded to, and dismissed, the possibility that *two* comets (C1 and C1b) were involved, perhaps owing to discrepancies between English and French observations, but there seems little doubt that from this point on English and French observations were treated as basically the same, and referring to the same comet C1. Variation between these series of reports was treated as instrumentally 'normal,' requiring no particular techniques of redress or resolution. Further confirmation of both the identity of C1 and of Auzout's predictive accuracy came in a letter of 4/14 February 1665 from Giovanni Domenico Cassini in Rome. He marveled at "the strange agreement" between Auzout's and his own tables and discovered the physical presuppositions upon which the Frenchman had produced his tables.[70] C1 was beginning to be well stabilized as a discrete celestial object: observations were being received from other astronomers (including Huygens and Borelli) which, when collated and compared in such scientific centers as London, Oxford, and Paris, were taken as broadly confirming the Auzout-Cassini plot and, therefore, the identity of C1 as a persistent and discrete natural object.

Certainly by May 1665, after C1 had disappeared from view, a solid consensus—among perhaps as many as ten or twenty skilled astronomers and a somewhat larger number of relevant mathematical colleagues—had developed about its identity and apparent motion. That consensus involved trust in other practitioners' skill and integrity, since all paths were collective compositions, and since some of those involved in warranting C1's path never observed it themselves while others observed only some of the positions which were linked up and smoothed out to yield a path. The consensus also involved trust in the reliability of some portions of existing knowledge. I have noted that there was little agreement about the proper motions which gave rise to observations of apparent motion, but there was sufficient confidence to reject certain observed positions as incompatible with plausible proper motions. Finally, the consensus was predicated upon agreement to *ignore*

70. Cassini to [?], 4/14 February 1665, in Oldenburg, *Correspondence*, II, 359–62; see also "Extract of a Letter, Lately Written from *Rome*, Touching the Late Comet, and a New One," *Philosophical Transactions* 2 (3/13 April 1665), 17–18. For reasons stated above, I will not detail those presuppositions here, save to note that apparent cometary motion could be made out in a variety of ways, depending upon whether one assumed circular, conical, or rectilinear motion; whether one allowed motion to the earth (this was a connection in which parallax measurements were considered to bear upon the Copernican hypothesis); and where in the heavens comets were presumed to be (Aristotelian meteorology put comets, with other 'changeable' things, below the moon, whereas the consensus of opinion of C1 interpreters, again using parallax measurements, was that it was well above the moon). For accounts of the significance of cometary observations in the Copernican revolution, see Westman, "The Comet and the Cosmos"; Barker and Goldstein, "The Role of Comets," esp. 303–05.

or set aside certain sorts of discrepancy as endemic to skilled and sincere observation of *the same comet.*

Discrepancies in observed position and path were widely recognized, but they were deemed manageable within a one-comet framework and were not considered a threat to the stable identity of C1. Indeed, a view on the nature of 'normal' error was part of the constitution of C1, such that *these* reports might be ascribed to the distorting effects of endemic error-factors on the observation of a real entity while *those* reports were spurious.[71] Hooke was evidently one of the most skeptical of this group, arguing that pervasive and significant variation among observational reports made most of them useless, but even Hooke reckoned that he had access to enough reliable observations to construct a collective cometary plot across the heavens.[72] Moreover, many, if not all, contemporary theories of proper motion asserted the possible deviation of comets from any smoothly plottable path due to all sorts of uncomputable factors, such as magnetic attractions, solar forces, the resistance of ether, gravitational influences, and the like.[73]

Cassini's 4/14 February letter also announced the discovery of a "new comet" (C2), first observed at "about the 24° of Aries" on 1/11 February, though bad weather had prevented observations over the next several days. At the time, C1 was also in Aries, and, while both comets were retrograde in motion (seeming to travel from east to west, opposite to the direction of planets), other features of the new comet, presumably including its slower velocity, greater brightness, and more distinct shape, permitted Cassini and, later, other skilled observers confidently to distinguish the two.[74] Auzout and his Parisian colleagues were unable to verify Cassini's new comet until 23 March / 2 April, though they continued to follow C1 through and out of Aries, but by 27 March / 6 April, Auzout had completed a search ephemerides for C2, and shortly dispatched it to the Royal Society. This time he was rather less confident: C2 was not as happily positioned for precise

71. For a study of nineteenth-century astronomers' awareness of, and attempts to quantify, personal sources of certain sorts of observational variation, see Schaffer, "Astronomers Mark Time."

72. E.g., Hooke, "Discourse of Comets," 150–53; idem, "Cometa," 236–38.

73. Hooke, for example, reckoned either that some observations of C1 "are false" or that any supposition of rectilinear motion needed to be supplemented by the curving effects of the sun's attractive power: see, e.g., Bennett, "Magnetical Philosophy and Astronomy," 226–27; idem, "Hooke and Wren and the System of the World," 59; Wilson, "Predictive Astronomy in the Century after Kepler," 204–05.

74. Cassini to [?], 4/14 February 1665, in Oldenburg, *Correspondence,* II, 359–62; see also "Extract of a Letter, Lately Written from *Rome,* Touching the Late Comet, and a New One," *Philosophical Transactions* 2 (3/13 April 1665), 17–18. Newton lost track of C1 on 23 January / 2 February and first saw C2 on 1/11 April (McGuire and Tamny, *Certain Philosophical Questions,* 416–17).

observation as C1, and he had been obliged to "trust to the Observations of others, whereof [I] know not the exactness."[75] The English too were soon satisfied with the identification of two distinct comets though there were some early suspicions that they *might* be the same object. In April 1665 Wren wrote to Moray requesting Hooke's observations of this new comet, since they had a substantial bearing upon the theory of proper motion he was then attempting:

> I have a great desire to find whither this be not yet the same. For who knowes what disposition of the matter makes the various intention or remission of Light in Comets, & though this last appearance were brighter & more silver coloured then ever the first was, yet as long as I see it in the same path & Retrograde when the other should be retrograde, I have some suspicions it may be the same.[76]

Soon another major player entered the game: Johann Hövel, better known as Johannes Hevelius (1611–1687), a wealthy brewer and senator (*Rathsherr*) of Danzig, a long-time valued correspondent of Henry Oldenburg, and one of the most eminent and instrumentally skilled astronomers of the time. His study of the moon—the sumptuously printed and self-illustrated *Selenographia* of 1647—was well known and well respected by the English astronomers, and he was made a fellow of the Royal Society in 1664. His father's death in 1649—and two judicious marriages—freed up funds to construct in his own house what became for a short period "the world's leading astronomical observatory," where he received visits from many of Europe's most eminent astronomers.[77] Moreover, from 1663 Hevelius was receiving a pension of twelve hundred livres a year—approximately £400—from Louis XIV of France, and later astronomical texts were dedicated to Colbert and Louis, whose patronage was an important material and moral resource for doing his astronomical work and securing credibility for it.[78]

Hevelius had written a long astronomical letter to Oldenburg on 22 May / 1 June 1665, though, owing to typically poor communications between London and Danzig, the letter was delayed and did not arrive until September or October. He had observed C1 from 4/14 December 1664 until 8/18 February, when he lost it, and C2 from 27 March / 6

75. Auzout to [?], 3/13 March 1665, in Oldenburg, *Correspondence*, II, 377; "The Motion of the *Second* Comet Predicted, by the Same Gentleman, Who Predicted That of the *Former*," *Philosophical Transactions* 3 (8/18 May 1665), 36–40.

76. Wren to Moray, 11/21 April [1665], Royal Society MS. EL. W. 3, no. 5, quoted in Bennett, "Hooke and Wren and the System of the World," 54–55.

77. Details from MacPike, *Hevelius, Flamsteed and Halley*, 1–16; A. R. and M. B. Hall's editorial note in Oldenburg, *Correspondence*, II, 29n.; and North, "Hevelius, Johannes."

78. Targosz, "Hevelius et ses démarches." This very large sum was equal to the annual stipend of the Paris academicians. It ceased being paid by the early 1670s.

April until 10/20 April. His massive *Cometographia* (1668) was then in the process of going through the press, and Hevelius was reluctant to disturb it in order to encompass the new observations, but, "at the insistence of important friends," he decided to print off a pamphlet describing C1—the *Prodromus Cometicus*—copies of which for his Oxford friends John Wallis and Seth Ward accompanied the letter to Oldenburg, and he promised a further little treatise on C2.[79] By 7/17 June at the latest, Auzout had obtained a copy of Hevelius's plot for C1. The French astronomer spotted a major "mathematical error" in Hevelius's plot and "interest in the truth" impelled him immediately to print a rebuttal in the form of a letter to his colleague Pierre Petit.[80]

The "error" that disturbed Auzout and others about Hevelius's plot for C1 was its position on the night of 8/18 February. Hevelius placed it near the first star of Aries while Auzout put it 1° 17' away from that star. Hevelius himself expressed his surprise in finding C1—after a long search—"in a place where I by no means expected it to be visible, namely, near the first star of Aries."[81] In terms of the precision expected of skilled astronomical observers in the 1660s, this counted as a massive discrepancy. When John Wallis told Oldenburg that he did not consider his December-January observations to be "very exact," he specified that they might be off by a quarter of a degree; Hooke claimed an accuracy using telescopic sights of nearly a second of arc; and Hevelius himself maintained that he had achieved an accuracy, without telescopic sights, of 15 to 30 seconds of arc.[82] Hevelius was a member of the soon-to-be-obsolete Tychonic tradition of using naked-eye sighted instruments—quadrant and sextant—to establish position, while the telescope was used to examine the appearance of comets' heads and tails. Within the Tychonic mode of practice, Hevelius was considered to be extremely accurate, and he was also understood to have remarkably good eyesight.[83]

79. Hevelius to Oldenburg, 22 May / 1 June 1665, in Oldenburg, *Correspondence*, II, 398; also "An Account of *Hevelius* His *Prodromus Cometicus*, Together with Some Animadversions Made upon It by a *French* Philosopher," *Philosophical Transactions* 6 (6/16 November 1665), 104–08.

80. Auzout to Oldenburg, 22 June / 2 July 1665, in Oldenburg, *Correspondence*, II, 425–26. Auzout's pamphlet is *Lettre de Monsieur Auzout du 17 juin [1665] à Monsieur Petit.*

81. Hevelius, *Prodromus Cometicus*, 18–19 (translation courtesy of Simon Schaffer).

82. Wallis to Oldenburg, 21/31 January 1665, in Oldenburg, *Correspondence*, II, 356; Hevelius to Oldenburg, 18/28 October and 1/11 December 1668, in ibid., V, 115, 244; Hetherington, *Science and Objectivity*, 20; Pannekoek, *History of Astronomy*, 259–60. By the end of the sixteenth century, Tycho was routinely achieving accuracies of one minute, occasionally attaining 20 to 25 seconds: Thoren, *Lord of Uraniborg*, 190–91.

83. Chapman, *Dividing the Circle*, 31–33. We have no certain way of establishing the cause of Hevelius's 'error,' nor, as I shall indicate below, did contemporaries other than Hooke publicly offer explanations. Certainly, C1 was then growing increasingly dim and observation must have been more than usually difficult: see, e.g., Ruffner, "The Curved

Tabula Longitudines & Latitudines

Cometæ exhibens; ad eos scilicet dies, qui-
bus ab Autore Sidus istud Crinitum
observatum est.

Anno 1664		Hora.	Longitud. Com. Gr. Min. Sig.			Latitud. Com. Grad. Min.		
Die	14 Decemb.	5 mane	8	0	♎	22	0	Aust.
	15	5	7	20	♎	22	20	A.
	18	4	3	45	♎	25	30	
	21	4	28	0	♍	30	0	
	23 Decemb.	4	22	0	♍	34	30	A.
	28	2 mane	4	0	♌	49	30	
	29	9 vesp.	28	40	♊	47	0	fere.
	30	9	12	40	♊	40	10	
	31 Decemb.	9 vesp.	2	40	♊	34	0	A.
1665	1 Januarii	9	24	20	♉	27	45	
	3	9	14	20	♉	19	0	
	4	9	11	0	♉	15	20	
	5	7 vesp.	8	40	♉	13	0	
	6	7	7	0		10	36	
	7	7	5	30		8	36	
	9	7	2	50		5	40	
	10	7 vesp.	2	0	♉	4	40	
	11	7	1	20		3	30	A.
	17	7	28	20	♈	1	0	Bor.
	19	7	27	40		1	45	
	20	8 vesp.	27	25	♈	2	12	Bor.
	21	7	27	20		2	36	
	23	7	27	0		3	0	
	28	7	26	30		4	12	
	2 Febr.	7 vesp..	26	20	♈	5	8	Bor.
	3	7	26	19		5	13	
	4	7	26	19		5	16	Stat.
	10	7	26	40 .		6	20	
	12	7 vesp.	27	0	♈	6	30	B.
	13	7	27	13		6	35	
	14	7	27	27		6	40	
	18	7	28	37		7	10	

Figure 3. Table of positions for C1, from Hevelius, *Prodromus Cometicus* (1665), facing p. 20. The troubled observation is the last one. (By permission of the Syndics of Cambridge University Library.)

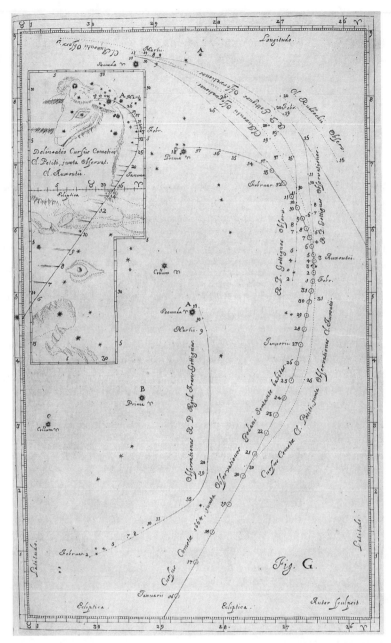

Figure 4. Plots of C1, as observed by Hevelius and other astronomers, from
Hevelius, *Mantissa Prodromi Cometici* (1666), figure G, facing p. 128. Hevelius's
disputed path is that bending sharply to the left from the observations for 12
and 13 February. Observational conditions were not suitable on 15, 16, and 17
February and these positions are, therefore, Hevelius's inferences, given the
terminal 18 February position. The solid line forking off from 12 February and
leading towards the second star of Aries is, presumably, Hevelius's conception
of where C1 would have gone had it carried on in its course up to 12 February.
(By permission of the Syndics of Cambridge University Library.)

No party to the ensuing quarrel seems to have considered that discrepancies of this order might be the outcome of 'normal' instrumental or human error juxtaposed to 'the same' real cometary object. Participants knew what precision might be expected of skilled observers, and they knew that these discrepancies were well outside the 'normal limit.' (Thus, the discrepancies between Hevelius's and Auzout's plots up to 3/13 February [see figure 4] amounted to seconds of arc—and were therefore deemed inconsequential—while discrepancies of a degree or two could not by any available means by thus set aside.) Auzout immediately drew out the physical absurdity of validating Hevelius's testimony: "This Comet could not, on that day of *February,* be there where M. *Hevelius* placeth it, *viz* in *Prima Arietis;* unless it be said. That it visited that Star of *Aries* on the 18th, and returned thence the 19th, into its ordinary course."[84] In other words, there was no way of saving that portion of the path upon which Auzout and Hevelius agreed (ignoring the manageable discrepancies between the two plots until 3/13 February), without imagining that C1, as Moray said, "made a crooked motion in the 18. totally unlyke any part of its former motion," that is, a detour from Auzout's plot between his observations of 7/17 and 9/19 February.[85] As it happened, Auzout and his colleagues had *not* made any observations on the night of 8/18 February, and there was no directly comparable observation-point on Auzout's curve to juxtapose with Hevelius's. It was logically possible that C1 had made its Hevelian detour, but, despite the notorious known intractability of construing comets' proper motions, no participant considered it physically possible that any comet should move in such a way as to save the truthfulness of both sets of testimony. Given the state of the relevant culture, that option was simply not available.

Auzout charged Hevelius with an "error" and Hevelius rejected the charge, referring the discrepancies for resolution to the Royal Society, "to whom as they are all skilled in these matters and impartial judges, I commit the whole business; and I will willingly acquiesce in their judgment whatever it may be."[86] A group of "some of the ablest *Philosophers* and *Astronomers* of *England*"—including Boyle, Brouncker, Hooke, Moray, Wallis, Ward, and Wren—had already taken up the

and the Straight," 188; idem, "Background and Early Development of Newton's Theory of Comets," 149, 155.

84. "An Account of *Hevelius* His *Prodromus,*" *Philosophical Transactions* 6 (6/16 November 1665), 108.

85. Moray to Oldenburg, 16/26 November 1665, in Oldenburg, *Correspondence,* II, 609.

86. Hevelius to Oldenburg, 6/16 January 1666, in Oldenburg, *Correspondence,* III, 6.

examination of "this important Difference between two very Learned, and very deserving Persons." They expressed collective confidence that they were "very likely to discern where the mistake lies; and having discern'd it, will certainly be found highly impartial and ingenious in giving their sense of the same."[87] Leading fellows of the Royal Society had removed to Oxford while the plague raged in London. Meeting informally, they nevertheless constituted the society's institutional voice. Hevelius's observations of C1 had generated concern from the first moment they were seen in England. In September Moray told Oldenburg that "as yet I want not some apprehension that Auzoust may have some advantage of [Hevelius], at leaste in the business of the motion of the Comet," and that Wallis too was worried how to resolve such massive discrepancies.[88]

For months the Oxford group cast about for a solution that would acquit the requirements of both astronomical plausibility and philosophical civility. Boyle wrote that he and his colleagues "cannot but Wonder to find yt either yor Ingenious Monsr. should soe much misrender Hevelius's Affirmations, or yt Hevelius should soe widely mistake in affirming yt, wch disagrees soe strangely."[89] Brouncker was reported to worry and vacillate—"hee inclines to think Hevelius not mistaken"—while Moray was "not a little affrayed Auzout is in the right."[90] Weeks later, Moray said that the Oxford group could not hope to decide the issue without comparing the Auzout and Hevelius observations "with other mens." Perhaps the matter might yet be resolved through deploying the maxim of multiplicity, validating the more numerous competent observations over the less. As Brouncker put it, "ye difference depending principally upon matter of fact, 'tis ye authority, number and reputation of other Observers, yt must cast the Ballance."[91]

However, despite Boyle's early expectation that there were relevant English observations, it now began to appear that there were not: "and unless Hook or some other have observed precisely (as I am affrayed none here away hath) the place of the Comet the 18. of feb. as Hevel.

87. "An Account of *Hevelius* His *Prodromus*," *Philosophical Transactions* 6 (6/16 November 1665), 108.

88. Moray to Oldenburg, 28 September / 8 October 1665, in Oldenburg, *Correspondence*, II, 528–31.

89. Boyle to Oldenburg, 14/24 October 1665, in Oldenburg, *Correspondence*, II, 569.

90. Moray to Oldenburg, 29–30 October / 8–9 November 1665, in Oldenburg, *Correspondence*, II, 582.

91. Oldenburg to Boyle (quoting Brouncker), 30 December 1665 / 9 January 1666, in Oldenburg, *Correspondence*, II, 653. Oldenburg very much liked this formula, and I note him below repeating it in the *Philosophical Transactions*.

Figure 5. Title page vignette from Hevelius, *Prodromus Cometicus* (1665). Note the comet—probably C1—in line with the telescopic observers (lower right). As a Tychonic practitioner, Hevelius used quadrant and sextant (lower left) to take cometary positions and the telescope to observe their internal appearance. It is possible that Hevelius's 8/18 February 'error' occurred in the course of moving between observational modes. (By permission of the Syndics of Cambridge University Library.)

sayes hee did, & Auzout nor his friend [Petit?] did not how can the controversy be decided?" The hope developed that Hooke would have made and registered a decisive observation for 8/18 February, but the ensuing proceedings give no solid indication that he did.[92] Indeed, the path for C1 published in Hooke's 1678 *Cometa* shows observations for 7/17 February and 22 February / 4 March and nothing in between.[93] The judgment produced by the Royal Society in February 1666 referred to "the observations made with *Telescopes* at home" and consultations with "some of the most intelligent Astronomers amongst them," but the relevant correspondence establishes that the English did not have their own C1 observation for 8/18 February 1665.[94] What

92. Moray to Oldenburg, 16/26 November 1665, and Oldenburg to Boyle, 30 December 1665 / 9 January 1666, in Oldenburg, *Correspondence*, II, 609, 653; see also Boyle to Oldenburg, 14/24 October 1665, in ibid., 569 (where he tried to remember whether or not he, Brouncker, and Moray had made the appropriate observation while in London).

93. Hooke, "Cometa," figure 4. This plot shows C1 very far from the first star of Aries on 7/17 February.

94. "Of the Judgement of Some of the *English* Astronomers, Touching the Difference between Two Learned Men, about an Observation Made of the First of the Two Late Comets," *Philosophical Transactions* 9 (12/22 February 1666), 150; Oldenburg to Hevelius,

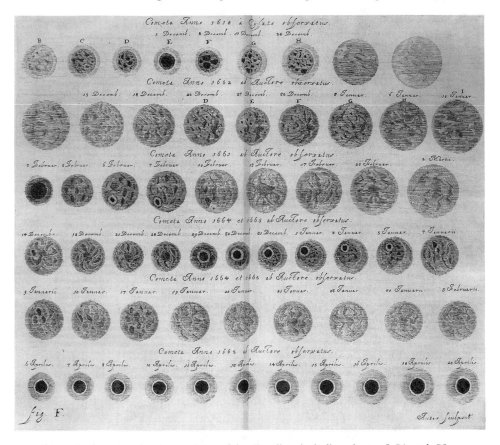

Figure 6. Cometary heads, as observed by Hevelius, including those of C1 and C2 (lower two rows). Ruffner ("The Curved and the Straight," 190–91) notes a relationship between Hevelius's view that comets had disklike nucleated magnetic heads and the possibility that they might experience radical anomalies (or "lurches") in their motion, especially as they approached the sun. If so, this might account for Hevelius's contentment with his plot for 3/13 through 8/18 February, although even he rejected a "detour" back to Auzout's path. From Hevelius, *Cometographia* (1668), figure F, pp. 414–415. (By permission of the Syndics of Cambridge University Library.)

they did have was evidence of broad agreement between Auzout, Petit, Borelli, and Huygens, and a vigorously expressed representation from Auzout—speaking for himself and others—that Hevelius's position was not true.

That was the array of testimony which "cast the Ballance" against

24 January / 3 February 1666, in Oldenburg, *Correspondence*, III, 30 (where the relevant English observations were said to be those of 6/16 and 15/25 February).

Hevelius. The Royal Society's judgment of February 1666 contained not only its conclusion about the path of C1 but also its sense of proper means for managing divergent factual testimony:

> Whatever that Appearance was, which was seen near the *First star* of *Aries*, by *Monsieur Hevelius* (the truth of whose relation concerning the same, they do in no wise question) the said *Comet* did not come neer that *Star* in the left *Ear* of *Aries*, where the said M. *Hevelius* supposes it to have passed, but took its course neer the *Bright Star* in its *Left Horn* . . . And since that the Observations of judicious both *French, Italian, & Dutch* Astronomers (as many of them, as are come to the knowledge of the *English*) do in the main fully agree with theirs, they do not at all doubt, but that, there being such an unanimous consent in what has just been declared, & the Controversie being about *Matter of fact*, wherein Authority, Number, and Reputation must cast the Ballance, Mons. *Hevelius*, who is well known for his Ingenuity, as Learning, will joyn and acquiesce in that sentiment.[95]

A philosopher was one who loved truth more than reputation and celebrity, and the Royal Society was giving Hevelius his opportunity to display that self-denying love. Privately, Oldenburg wrote to Hevelius that the English astronomers were "unanimous" in their opinion that Hevelius's 8/18 February position was wrong but expressing confidence "that you will fall in with this consensus of opinion."[96] Belief in Auzout's plot for C1 and its position on 8/18 February 1665 was thus identified as a collective possession, a mark that defined the civic state of skilled astronomers. Hevelius was very welcome to continue a respected member of that community, so long as he acknowledged that C1 had never been near the first star of Aries.

There was, however, a massive cost involved in a straightforward admission on Hevelius's part that his 8/18 February observation was untrue. And, unless the discrediting of Hevelius's testimony was tactfully managed, that cost might be paid not just by Hevelius but by the community of which he was a valued member.[97] Among the ways available to account for Hevelius's 8/18 February observation, some of the most obvious were incompatible with his continued membership in the moral-technical community or, indeed, with the community's continued use of his observations *apart from that of 8/18 February*. That

95. "Of the Judgement of Some of the *English* Astronomers," *Philosophical Transactions* 9 (12/22 February 1666), 150–51.

96. Oldenburg to Hevelius, 24 January / 3 February 1666, in Oldenburg, *Correspondence*, III, 30.

97. For his part, Auzout expressed annoyance that "yr Phil. Transact. [of 6/16 November 1665] did speake wth so much caution and reservation of ye Controversy: there being no person either here or elsewhere, that harbored ye least doubt of it" (Auzout to Oldenburg, 2/12 February 1666, in Oldenburg, *Correspondence*, III, 38).

is to say, just as his 8/18 February observation constituted a serious trouble for agreeing on a C1 path, so his observations prior to that date formed a valuable resource for astronomical practice in general. Moreover, the same English astronomical group which was assembled to discredit Hevelius's 8/18 February observation of C1 had been important users and beneficiaries of his previous work on the moon and the planets. In fact, there had been, and continued to be, significant criticism of other aspects of Hevelius's cometary observations. The ever-critical Hooke was continually in dispute with Hevelius on instrumental matters, and denied the accuracy of his representations of the appearance of cometary nuclei and blazes.[98] Yet both in connection with C1 and C2, and in later astronomical exchanges into the late 1670s, Hooke never ceased to use Hevelius's observations and publicly to credit them as "diligent," "accurate," and "skilful." Even for Hooke, Hevelius was, and remained, one of the very few exact and reliable observers.[99]

It *could* have been said that Hevelius's C1 position arose from gross incompetence, delusion, or mendacity. Both Hevelius and his English judges were arguably as aware of these possibilities as they were reluctant to see any of them publicly expressed. As early as 6/16 January 1666—before Hevelius was told about the Royal Society's judgment— he assured Oldenburg that he had "dreamed nothing and feigned nothing in the appearance of the comet. What I depicted with great care and reproduced was only that which I had plainly seen, together with other notable persons."[100] On 30 March / 9 April, Oldenburg attempted further to smooth possibly ruffled feathers by assuring Hevelius that the society "will be favorably disposed towards whatever you can produce to show that the agreement among observations militating against you does not detract from that observation of yours which is in dispute"—in other words, to suggest a way of saving *both* Auzout's path as a collective achievement and resource *and* the validity of Hevelius's 8/18 February observation.[101] The English philosophers clearly meant that the controversy should stop there, none of them expressing significant interest in probing the controverted discrepant observations

98. E.g., Hooke, "Cometa," figures 2 and 3.
99. E.g., Hooke, "Discourse of Comets," 151–53; idem, "Cometa," 219, 222, 238–39 (where Hooke suggested [p. 236] that "strange errors and mistakes" may be made in producing tables of comets' positions, not because of astronomers' want of "care and accurateness," but because of "the carelessness and neglect of the [En]graver"). The likely sense of this remark is illuminated by the widely known fact that Hevelius made his own engravings.
100. Hevelius to Oldenburg, 6/16 January 1666, in Oldenburg, *Correspondence*, III, 6.
101. Oldenburg to Hevelius, 30 March / 9 April 1666, in Oldenburg, *Correspondence*, III, 75.

for a definitive explanation. Their view of Auzout's "knowledge and honesty" was signaled in May 1666, when Oldenburg successfully proposed him for fellowship in the Royal Society.[102] Other astronomical matters were now occupying Auzout and the English—including telescopic observations of Saturn's rings and spots on Mars—and C1's identity had for all practical purposes been registered and established. However, Hevelius was far from best pleased when he belatedly became aware of the Royal Society's decision. He refused to let the matter drop, and, in pressing the issue, he at once raised the stakes of any direct gainsaying of his testimony and responded to Oldenburg's emollient invitation to think up some morally and epistemically suitable way of accounting for the 8/18 February observation.[103]

Hevelius claimed that he had been "condemned without a hearing" by the Royal Society astronomers and that he had been given inadequate notice and time to prepare a proper defense: "truth and equity" demanded no less. Now Hevelius published an extended response to Auzout's charges—the *Mantissa* to the *Prodromus Cometicus*—which he submitted to the judgment of "those Fellows who are learned in these matters, being free from prejudice and self-interest." He repeated his insistence that neither his instruments, his dedication to accuracy, nor his integrity could be faulted. The self-contained nature of the dispute had to be recognized: "I do not maintain (as you seem to hold) that I wish to reject all those observations made by so many famous men in England, France, and Italy which show (it is said) that some phenomenon was seen near the second star in Aries during March. But, I say, the question to be investigated is this: was that phenomenon the selfsame comet seen before?"[104]

Hevelius thus responded to Oldenburg's invitation to consider a way of accounting for discrepancies without impugning integrity or skill. Auzout and others had, indeed, reliably and honestly seen "some phe-

102. Oldenburg to Auzout, 24 May / 3 June 1666, in Oldenburg, *Correspondence*, III, 141.

103. I am not here concerned to explain *why* Hevelius was so stubbornly attached to his deviant observation. Simon Schaffer has suggested to me (personal communication) that patronage from the French court may have been at issue (see Targosz, "Hevelius et ses démarches"), and this would assimilate the Hevelius-Auzout dispute to a characteristic early modern patronage-contest of the sort documented by Biagioli and Westman, though whether any such considerations were *known to the English* is uncertain. Hevelius had been involved in an earlier credibility contest with Huygens over observational accuracy, and he may well have become unusually sensitized to imputations of insincerity or incompetence: see Van Helden, "'Annulo Cingitur'"; idem, "Saturn and His Anses"; idem, "Telescopes and Authority."

104. Hevelius to Oldenburg, 23 June / 3 July 1666, in Oldenburg, *Correspondence*, III, 171–72.

nomenon" near the second star of Aries. This was *not* C1 but, in all probability, *some other comet.* C1 had proceeded, as Hevelius had claimed, by way of the first star of Aries before disappearing from view. In fact, the rudiments of this strategy of ontological splitting can be retrieved from proceedings early in the history of C1. Recall the brief careers of C1a and C1b as well as the fact that C2 had not evidently been widely traced between Cassini's discovery on 1/11 February and Auzout's verification on 23 March / 2 April. There were enough comets in the skies during 1664 and 1665, and enough endemic uncertainty about the paths comets might follow, to warrant a range of ontologically consequential stipulations about the discrepant observations in questions.[105] In October 1665 Oldenburg had written to Spinoza about the Hevelius-Auzout quarrel, indicating that a 'two-comet' hypothesis was then being considered, and Spinoza replied that he was "eager to know whether all astronomers conclude that there were two comets because of their motion or rather to save Kepler's hypothesis [that comets move in straight lines]."[106]

To be sure, it is not absolutely clear from the context whether Oldenburg was here suggesting that Hevelius's 8/18 February observation might come to be seen as a reliable position for a comet other than C1, possibly C2. I have already noted that Wren was actively considering the identity of C1 and C2 as early as April 1665.[107] Recall also the terms of the Royal Society's formal judgment of January 1666— "whatever that Appearance was, which was seen near the *First star* of *Aries,* by *Monsieur Hevelius* (the truth of whose relation concerning the same, they do in no wise question)." There *was* an entity where and when Hevelius placed it, and Hevelius was invited, if he wished, to say what that entity was, so long as it was *not* C1 as Auzout construed it. Similarly, Hevelius was willing to grant that Auzout and other astronomers had reliably witnessed *something* near the second star of Aries in early March, so long as *this* was not identified with C1 as Hevelius construed it. The quarrel might be morally managed if only partici-

105. For references to a number of other current comets, see "An Account of Several Books Lately Published [including Hevelius's *Descriptio Cometæ*]," *Philosophical Transactions* 17 (9/19 September 1666), 302–03; Oldenburg to Boyle, 29 August / 8 September 1665, in Boyle, *Works,* VI, 193; "Extract of a Letter from Ballasore, Jan. 6. 1665/6. From Mr. Henry Powell, to His Father," in Hooke, *Philosophical Experiments and Observations,* 29; Stanislas Lubienietzki to Oldenburg, 26 January / 5 February 1667, in Oldenburg, *Correspondence,* III, 327–29. Westfall (*Never at Rest,* 391–92, 433–34) recounts similar expert uncertainty about cometary appearances in 1680–1681: Flamsteed distinguished two comets while other astronomers maintained that only one was involved.
106. Oldenburg to Spinoza, 12/22 October 1665, and Spinoza to Oldenburg, 10/20 November 1665, in Oldenburg, *Correspondence,* II, 568, 602.
107. Bennett, "Hooke and Wren and the System of the World," 54–55.

pants could be encouraged to make low evidential claims for the disputed observations: not a sighting of C1 but of 'something.'[108]

Oldenburg attempted to reassure Hevelius that the society's judgment ought not to be taken as "condemnation," merely as a recital of the balance of testimony and a reminder of generally accepted impersonal maxims for the management of factual testimony. He informed Hevelius that Auzout was now a colleague in the Royal Society: "Since this has been done, it will be only fair for us to respect the good name of each of you as much as we can and, setting aside personal prejudice, we meanwhile declare our opinion for truth's sake alone."[109] Auzout expressed reluctance to have another go at Hevelius, while sardonically conceding the duty put upon him by his adversary's public display of civility: "The interest of truth and ye obliging manner, he has treated me wth, doe engage me to answer him." Perhaps the issue could be confined to "the simple question of fact," leaving aside more intractable considerations to do with the real physical motion of comets. But Auzout warned Oldenburg that Hevelius's offer of ontological splitting was not much liked by the Parisians: "I can assure, yt his invention of two comets is not relisht here by any, and is only lookt upon as an evasion."[110] If the French did not relish two comets, the irenically inclined English found the idea quite palatable.

Oldenburg referred the affair back to Oxford, where John Wallis squirmed in apparent discomfort. He had given Hevelius's response to Auzout "a cursory reading" and was impressed by his "pains" and "accurateness":

> I must trust his ingenuity for ye triall of the Calculation (for it were too long a task to examine it all over:) But supposing it were true (as I have no reason to doubt:) & that ye result answeres ye account hee had formerly given us of ye place & motion [of C1 on 8/18 February 1665], I see not why wee should disbelieve him in matter of Fact.

Wallis deferred to the evident instrumental skill Hevelius had deployed to establish C1's position—"I must needs assent to him" for that—but was perplexed how such a conflict of competent testimony could be resolved so as to save valued representations of celestial phenomena and the valued relationships by which such representations were assembled. There did not appear to be sufficient degrees of interpreta-

108. See, in this connection, Trevor Pinch's important sociological study of the systematic linkage between credibility and the claimed theoretical significance of the observation-claims of modern physics: "Towards an Analysis of Scientific Observation."

109. Oldenburg to Hevelius, 24 August / 3 September 1666, in Oldenburg, *Correspondence*, III, 219.

110. Auzout to Oldenburg, 18/28 December 1666, in Oldenburg, *Correspondence*, III, 298.

tive freedom to make reconciliation possible. Auzout's ephemerides was a prized achievement, abundantly supported by credible testimony, but Hevelius was an equally valued colleague who had produced other prized achievements and whose sincerity could not be doubted: "The great controversy Between him & Mons. Auzout (whether ye Comet came to ye first or second star of Aries,) I know not how to reconcile. I have no reason to suspect that either would willingly falsify an Observation: And yet how both can be solved, without allowing two Phaenomena, I cannot tell." Indeed, "two Phaenomena" might yet be an answer which the relevant community could technically sustain and morally live with: "That there should be two [comets], seems somewhat odde; yet it is not impossible." After all, was not C2 lurking in the general neighborhood and at roughly the same time?—"for we see, presently after, yet another (undoubtedly) near ye same place (viz: ye latter Comet.)." It would, of course, be best for Hevelius to sacrifice his one contested observation; then "I see noe reason why all ye rest should not bee admitted."[111]

There were some observational discrepancies between Hevelius and others prior to 8/18 February, but Hevelius's positions "do not differ so much from ye place of ye Comet observed from others, but that the Error may, with as much probability at lest, be cast on their part as on his. Especially his Instruments being much better; & himself a diligent & long experienced observer." Wallis shared his English colleagues' opinion about the path of C1—"they being disinterested persons, & having no temptation to be biassed"—but the two-comet notion came to seem increasingly attractive: "If Mons. Hevelius did, notwithstanding, observe any thing of that nature near ye first of Aries, on ye 18th of Febr: I must take that to be somewhat else than this Comet [C1]." After all, "no body else did then & there look for it, & the thing in itself be nothing impossible; I had rather suspend judgment, than determine anything concerning it."[112] If the directly contested observation could not be definitively explained, or explained away, maybe it would be best to find a way of excluding it from the processes by which formal examination and explanation occurred, bracketing it, leaving it alone for the time being: "And what shall become of this doubtfull appearance must for ought I see, be left undetermined."[113] The astronomical conversation could continue without

111. Wallis to Oldenburg, 19/29 January 1667, in Oldenburg, *Correspondence*, III, 313.

112. Wallis to Oldenburg, 31 January / 10 February 1667, in Oldenburg, *Correspondence*, III, 330–31. *Suspend judgment* translates the Greek απεχειν.

113. Wallis to Oldenburg, 19/29 January 1667, in Oldenburg, *Correspondence*, III, 313.

resolving this matter. In fact, it might only continue if the matter was sheltered from definitive resolution.

Over the next several months the matter slowly drifted out of the arena of deliberation and reflective decision. The two-comet hypothesis remained registered but undeveloped.[114] Oldenburg promised Hevelius a final judgment by "a certain skilled astronomer of the Royal Society."[115] This was probably Hooke, but he was then stretched by his work in the rebuilding of London after the Great Fire, and did not get around to resuming his general contest of skill and accuracy with Hevelius until 1674. Auzout likewise promised a response to Hevelius, but his time and energies were taken up with the founding of the Paris Royal Academy, and, by 1668, with a more personally serious local quarrel. Hevelius from time to time over the next year or so expressed his continuing sense of injustice, suggesting that Auzout was content that the matter should be left as it was because the Royal Society's original judgment "yields honor to him [and] will prejudice me in the eyes of some people." The credibility of the whole of Hevelius's work on comets, he argued, hung in the balance: let genuine mistakes be identified and corrected, "for nothing is dearer to me, than that Truth should stand forth."[116]

But the Royal Society was reluctant to let matters be brought to issue, and Hevelius was intermittently informed that the dispute might be taken up again only when Auzout or Hooke published their responses. So far as I can tell, neither report ever materialized, and participants' references to the original quarrel became rarer and rarer.[117] The astronomical conversation carried on, generating further ontological disputes and extruding further areas of factual agreement. Auzout and Hevelius continued as members of an astronomical community whose knowledge of the number, trajectories, and identities of comets

114. Wallis to Oldenburg, 12/22 February 1667, in Oldenburg, *Correspondence*, III, 342.

115. Oldenburg to Hevelius, 27 February / 9 March 1667, in Oldenburg, *Correspondence*, III, 354.

116. Hevelius to Oldenburg, 3/13 June 1668, in Oldenburg, *Correspondence*, IV, 448.

117. E.g., Lubienietzki to Oldenburg, 13/23 April 1667; Henri Justel to Oldenburg, 25 September / 5 October 1667; Oldenburg to Hevelius, 11/21 October 1667; Hevelius to Oldenburg, 11/21 October 1667; Auzout to Oldenburg, 19/29 December 1667; Oldenburg to Hevelius, 31 January / 10 February 1668, in Oldenburg, *Correspondence*, III, 391, 486, 516, 519, and IV, 66–68, 137. Hooke's published engagements with Hevelius in the 1670s and 1680s referred to C1 and C2, but nothing in these texts counted as the promised resolution of the Hevelius-Auzout quarrel: e.g., Hooke, "Animadversions on the *Machina Coelestis* of Mr. *Hevelius*" (1674); idem, "Cometa" (1678); idem, "Discourse of Comets" (1682). In 1695 Edmond Halley's correspondence with Newton alluded to, and attempted to repair, the faultiness of some of Hevelius's observations of C1: Halley to Newton, 7/17 September, 28 September / 8 October, and 15/25 October 1695: Halley, *Correspondence and Papers*, 91–92, 95.

traversing the skies in the late winter and spring of 1665 was, importantly, *morally uncertain*.[118] Book XI of Hevelius's *Cometographia* appeared in 1668, even as he was continuing to pursue his credibility-contest with Auzout. Here Hevelius simply dropped his controverted 8/18 February observation (see figure 7). He did not admit that he was wrong; indeed, the accompanying text insisted upon the accuracy of all his observations.[119] He gave no reason for this omission nor, to my knowledge, was it ever publicly pointed out by his English interlocutors.

(An epilogue: modern readers keen to know which parties to this dispute, after all, had truth on their side are free to take their choice, according to their own maxims of credibility. Neither the comet of 1664 nor that of 1665 has yet returned to permit a recalculation of its proper motions. Current astronomical knowledge has apparently incorporated corroborating observations from all the major players, while setting aside Hevelius's disputed 8/18 February position. The two comets are treated as distinct. Both are now named after Hevelius.)[120]

Here I briefly note several features of this dispute, returning to develop them more fully at the end of this chapter.

(i) I want to draw attention to the reference and formal structure of this controversy. It was, to be sure, a dispute about *things*. Where in the heavens was a comet at a certain time? What course did this comet, and comets in general, take through the skies? Yet it was also—at the same time, and in the same sense—a dispute about *people*, their virtues and capacities. Who was an adequately skilled and sincere teller of factual truths about comets? Whose testimony might be trusted to constitute others' stock of factual knowledge? The proceedings did not, as it were, *alternate* between knowledge of people and knowledge of things. Rather, knowledge of people was constitutively used to make and unmake knowledge of things. There was no point at which participants could help themselves to a pure form of 'thing-knowledge' since, as I have repeatedly argued, schemes of plausibility are built up through prior decisions about who, and in what connections, counts as a trustworthy source.

118. Despite Hooke's intermittent attempts to impugn his instrumental skill, Hevelius remained a valued source of astronomical testimony for the English into the 1680s. Although Auzout continued to contribute through the 1680s, his career rather foundered after his withdrawal from the Paris Academy, and he sought employment in several Italian courts before finally drifting into obscurity.

119. Hevelius, *Cometographia*, Bk. XI, 755–57; see Ruffner, "Background and Early Development of Newton's Theory of Comets," 154.

120. P. L. Brown, *Comets, Meteorites and Men*, 26 and Appendix IV; also Yeomans, *Comets*, 84.

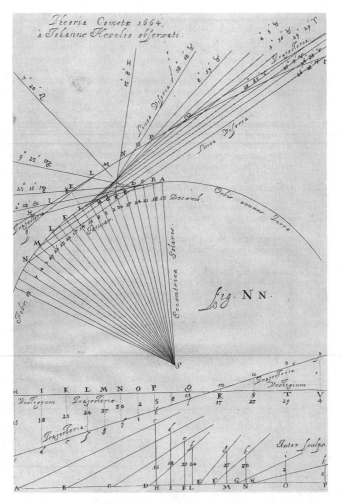

Figure 7. Hevelius's projection of C1's trajectory. Note that the last observation used is that of 3/13 February. From Hevelius, *Cometographia* (1668), figure NN, facing p. 760. (By permission of the Syndics of Cambridge University Library.)

(ii) One can imagine the Hevelius-Auzout dispute handled, and even resolved, in a number of ways: Hevelius's factual testimony could have been credited and Auzout's denied; Auzout's could have been accepted and Hevelius's rejected; differences could have been split; both claims could have been thrown out; and the discrediting of specific observations could have spread like a cancer over the field of other observations from the discredited source. These and other courses of action were available in principle. In practice, something happened which was at once much more subtle and more radical than these possibilities. The quality and character of participants' knowledge-about-things-in-the-world were adjusted so as to protect the credibility and the ascribed moral integrity of *both* contested sources. A controversy whose terminal ritual form demanded truth to be allocated to one or the other contestant was practically managed by distributing truth between them. That *mundane reasoning*—introduced in chapter 1 and alluded to intermittently—was deployed to adjust knowledge-about-things-in-the-world *as a moral act*. The participants' map of the world might have come, as a matter of certainty, to contain a discrete comet C1, not conflatable with any other well- or ill-understood celestial or atmospheric existent. As it came to pass, however, those entrusted with judgment elaborated a picture of the world which contained cometary objects whose number, trajectories, and identities were indefinite and uncertain. That uncertainty was as much moral as epistemic. Adjustments in the heavenly economy enabled the continuance of conversation in the moral economy of those who made astronomical knowledge.

(iii) Neither Hevelius nor Auzout was an ignorant diver. Each man stood in the relationship of colleague to the English practitioners asked to judge their quarrel. I have noted that Hevelius had been a fellow since 1664 and that Auzout was elected to fellowship during the course of the controversy. Each man had already offered the philosophical community gifts of knowledge which were required for the collective construction of astronomical representations, and each had available scarce skills and facilities which would be needed for the making of future knowledge.[121] To impugn the integrity of either would not only be to risk losing his participation in collective astronomical work, it would also be potentially to discredit the competence and sincerity of past achievements already integrated into a developing picture of the heavens. Consequently, a solution which retained both Auzout and Hevelius as members of the astronomical polity appealed on epistemically pragmatic as well as disinterestedly moral grounds. A judgment that either was incompetent or lying would have generated a corollary reinspection of their previous contributions to knowledge, a withholding of future rights to contribute, and a possible reconsideration of the informal criteria used to recognize credible persons in this domain.

While Auzout and Hevelius were not ignorant divers, neither did they clearly exhibit marks of entitlement to gentle standing. Auzout was the son of a clerk of court, and Hevelius was a brewer and a son of a brewer. The modest, self-effacing, and fame-denying presentation recommended and exemplified by Boyle was no part of either man's

---

121. For fine treatment of the significance of gift relations in early modern Italian science, see Findlen, "Economy of Scientific Exchange."

identity. Both Auzout and Hevelius repeatedly insisted upon their property rights in astronomical knowledge, and both were content in so doing to bring their quarrel to issue. Hevelius insisted that his credibility demanded direct vindication, and Auzout had a prior history of quarrels precipitated by his exposures of rivals' mistakes. To both men, imputations of inaccuracy, want of skill, and failures of diligence were clearly as insupportable as suggestions of mendacity. In early modern society such patterns of behavior were identified more with the traditional role of the quarrelsome scholar than with the civic gentleman.

These protagonists were not gentlemen nor did they obviously pattern their behavior upon the Boylean program for civic philosophy then being disseminated by the Royal Society. Yet several of the men who judged their dispute *were* gentlemen-philosophers, and all were members of a society which had pledged itself to producing reliable knowledge in and through a moral economy patterned upon the conventions of gentlemanly conversation. Moreover, Auzout and Hevelius, while foreigners not engaged in daily face-to-face interaction with each other or with the English community, were effectively linked to English practitioners by a network of face-to-face recognitions and vouchings. Auzout was well known to the English by virtue of his membership in the respected Montmor Academy, whose meeting-place had been visited by Oldenburg and members of Boyle's own family. During part of the controversy Christopher Wren was in Paris and in close contact with Auzout. Hevelius was perhaps even better integrated into the philosophical system of recognitions, having been to Holland, England, and France in the early 1630s (where he made the acquaintance of Mersenne, Gassendi, Boulliaud, Kircher, and, perhaps, Dury and Hartlib). From the late 1640s through the 1680s, his Danzig observatory was a place of continual pilgrimage for English astronomers, notably including Edmond Halley. There is also some evidence of long-standing friendship relations between Hevelius and English practitioners. In 1686 John Flamsteed wrote to Richard Towneley explaining John Wallis's puff of a new book by Hevelius: "Hee is onely minding to gratifie his old friend."[122] If the skill or sincerity of either man were to be publicly impugned, the effects would reverberate throughout a system of recognitions, impinging upon the integrity of those who recognized them and vouched for them. Ignorant divers

<hr/>

122. Turnbull, *Hartlib, Dury and Comenius*, 268, 417; Flamsteed to Towneley, 15 March 1686, quoted in MacPike, *Hevelius, Flamsteed and Halley*, 95. Hooke's war with Hevelius concerning telescopic sights was still continuing, and Wallis was said to be sensible of the damaging effects of "Hookes intolerable boastes." See, however, *private* aspersions of Hevelius's character and technical reliability by Edmond Halley: Halley to William Molyneux, 27 March / 6 April and 27 May / 6 June 1686, in Halley, *Correspondence and Papers*, 60, 65.

could do nothing about the gainsaying of their testimony, while Auzout and Hevelius had friends.

Master Narratives: The Testimony of Robert Boyle

I have used episodes of contested testimony as windows into the early modern system of cultural practices by which credibility was accomplished. The processes by which claims are disputed draw matters of principle into justificatory practice, and it is for that reason that the study of controversy enjoys its special place in the understanding of cultural action. Yet there would be something systematically misleading about any suggestion that controversy over factual testimony was endemic. Episodes of skepticism and controversy are not difficult to identify, but neither are they the norm. I shall note below that the overwhelming majority of factual testimonies arriving at the Royal Society were not subject to dispute or even to processes of deliberative assessment. Skepticism, like formal reflective appraisal, was something that happened on the margins of a well-working, routinely trusting system. I need now briefly to display that trusting system working at its greatest efficiency, to identify a testimonial source which the relevant community placed at the opposite extreme from vulgar divers.

From 1660 until his death in 1691 Robert Boyle was, without doubt, the Royal Society's most prolific source of experimental and natural-historical testimony. Moreover, both his presentation of self and his formal methodological writings provided the society—at least until the dominance of Isaac Newton later in the century—with its preferred posture for the reception and evaluation of others' testimony. *This* was how the authentic Christian virtuoso ought to behave with respect to the provision and reception of factual claims. How did Boyle advertise his solution to the problem of Siamese skepticism, and how did the community handle the flow of factual testimony from him?

Boyle was a master of credibility. He had solved the problem of becoming a transparent spokesman for natural reality, and chapter 4 described the role of his ascribed identity and public behavior in achieving that solution. A remarkable feature of his relations with the Royal Society, and with the philosophical community in general, was the easy passage enjoyed by his factual testimony from personal claim to collective assent. With some qualifications to be noted below, one might even say that his factual testimony was *never* negated by the Royal Society or by those whom it recognized as competent practitioners.[123] For all that, I need now to deal with some apparent excep-

123. Here I may need to repeat that my subject is testimony of what was regarded as *fact* rather than of *interpretation*. I have already noted that the cultural boundary between factual and interpretative items enshrined in probabilistic natural philosophy

tions to such a generalization, for they 'prove the rule' in a strong and perspicuous sense.

There were, to be sure, a number of instances in which Boyle's factual testimony was met with degrees of skepticism. Thomas Hobbes's important gainsaying of the testimony delivered from Boyle's air-pump has been detailed elsewhere.[124] Hobbes denied the experimentalists' epistemic boundary between fact and theory, while his adversary's response invited him to observe those very boundaries and the moral practices that supported them: "Mr. *Hobbes* does not," Boyle wrote, "deny the truth of any of the matters of fact I have delivered."[125] Whether or not Hobbes did dispute Boyle's factual testimony is, and was, an interpretative matter. In response to his adversary's qualified assertion that the air-pump was almost empty of atmospheric air, Hobbes claimed that it was full of rapidly circling "pure air." The act of negation depends upon the identity of the claim that might be subject to denial, and that identity is notoriously flexible and difficult to establish in this context. Boyle's preferred judgment was that Hobbes had *not* negated his factual testimony, and, in so doing, Boyle sought to recruit his adversary's criticism to support the standing of the very factual category which Hobbes's natural philosophy sought to erode.

In the early 1660s another opponent of experimental and probabilistic conceptions of natural philosophy expressed more gentle skepticism about some of Boyle's experimental testimony. The bulk of Benedict Spinoza's criticisms disputed the interpretative significance Boyle put on his experimentally generated matters of fact. Occasionally, however, he appeared to question the facts themselves. In 1663 he told Oldenburg that he suspected the diligence or skill with which Boyle had carried out some measurements on niter, doubting "whether the very illustrious Mr. Boyle could have observed with sufficient care what he says he discovered with the aid of the balance." The philosophical love of truth, no less than intellectual brotherhood, demanded that one avoid "sheer flattery, which I consider most dangerous and pernicious in friendship." One could not count oneself as a philosophical brother if one were not more a friend of truth than a friend of the "very noble Mr. Boyle."[126] A few years later, Adrien Auzout expressed disappointment about the unsatisfactorily piecemeal nature of Boyle's experimental testimony, broaching, then veering away from, a sugges-

---

lowered the moral cost of disputing interpretations while it raised the cost of controverting factual claims.

124. Shapin and Schaffer, *Leviathan and the Air-Pump*, esp. chs 4–5.

125. Boyle, "Examen of Hobbes" (1662), 197.

126. Spinoza to Oldenburg (for Boyle), 17 July 1663, in Oldenburg, *Correspondence*, II, 95–96. Boyle's response simply passed over the possible denial of his care or sincerity: Oldenburg (from Boyle) to Spinoza, 4 August 1663, in ibid., 103–04.

tion of insincerity. He had just read through Boyle's new *Origin of Forms and Qualities:*

> I came across many fine experiments but it is annoying that nearly always some mishap prevented their being carried to a conclusion; although I am certain of the author's sincerity this kind of mishap is so common among chemists (since it is always the end of all their fine promises) that I am sorry Mr. Boyle should have recourse to it in presenting his work historically.[127]

In 1669 Boyle added an essay on absolute rest in solid bodies to a new edition of his *Certain Physiological Essays.* Boyle narrated observations he had made himself and had received "from the credible relations of masons" and "an ingenious gentleman of my acquaintance." Boyle was here concerned to present credible evidence of internal motion in apparently solid and quiescent bodies. Marcasites spontaneously broke apart when left to sit on Boyle's windowsill, and a "turquois-stone" had colored spots which "seemed, though very slowly, to move from one part of the stone to the other." Boyle was skeptical when told of this stone by the "ingenious gentleman" who owned it, so he asked to borrow it and "employed an ingenious youth, that then lived with me" to keep "a watchful eye upon it" and, from time to time, to draw pictures of the moving spots over a period of weeks. It was "unanimously concluded" that the spots did indeed move.[128] Christiaan Huygens found this testimony hard to swallow. While he accepted the basic corpuscular principles which made such phenomena possible and interesting, Huygens told Oldenburg that he did "not dare entirely to credit what he says about the changing of spots in certain hard stones, and I should require some very authentic and carefully verified attestations to it."[129] In reply, Oldenburg blandly repeated Boyle's assurance that he had made these observations "in good faith," that the phenomena had been adequately witnessed, and that Boyle was benignly indifferent as to Huygens's judgment, "leav[ing] it to the reader's discretion to believe it or not."[130]

At about the same time, Boyle had reported the successful performance of an experiment on cohesion whose earlier failure had much troubled him and his colleagues: cohered smooth marbles were supposed to separate in a vacuum and Boyle was worried when he could not obtain that result.[131] Several years later, Huygens was still appar-

---

127. Auzout to Oldenburg, 28 December 1666, in Oldenburg, *Correspondence*, III, 294.

128. Boyle, "Essay of the Intestine Motions of Quiescent Solids," 450–51.

129. Huygens to Oldenburg, 12 January 1670, in Oldenburg, *Correspondence*, VI, 426.

130. Oldenburg to Huygens, 31 January 1670, in Oldenburg, *Correspondence*, VI, 460.

131. For these experiments and their significance in the Hobbes-Boyle exchanges, see Shapin and Schaffer, *Leviathan and the Air-Pump*, esp. 46–49, 185–201.

ently unaware of Boyle's claimed success, and he published reports in which the actual outcome was identified with Boyle's previous failure. Reading Huygens's account, the young Leibniz wrote to Boyle via Oldenburg: "I have forgotten to ask Mr. Boyle what he thinks of Huygens' experiment . . . , which [result] I nevertheless recalled as being contrary to what Boyle says in his most recent [tract]." Oldenburg's response was simply to reiterate the substance of Boyle's factual testimony and sharply to remind Leibniz with whom he was dealing: "Boyle says that that experiment of his . . . was related by himself in good faith; he cannot answer for the experiments of others."[132]

Next to Hobbes, the Royal Society's most vigorous and irritating Restoration critic was the physician Henry Stubbe (1632–1678).[133] Responding to Glanvill's and Sprat's celebrations of the society's early work, Stubbe targeted the credibility of the fellows' experimental and natural-historical relations. Of Glanvill, Stubbe said that his history "is very *false*," that his "credit is now irrecoverably lost," and that "I have no mind to believe this *Virtuoso* in any thing he says"; Glanvill's "great and admired friend Mr. *Sprat* relates general Encounters false" and was an unreliable source of historical fact; Oldenburg's *Philosophical Transactions* "report an *Untruth*" about the notorious human-sheep transfusion experiment.[134] Sprat had assured readers that the Royal Society's histories, collected "by the plainest Method, and from the plainest Information," were almost as strongly supported as scriptural truth, and Glanvill had said that "the relations of your Tryals may be received as undoubted Records of certain events, and as securely depended on, as the Propositions of Euclide."[135] However, Stubbe identified a series of material mistakes in the society's register of fact: "I am confident there is less credit to be placed in the Narrations of some of our *Virtuosi*, who have been so mistaken in their Accounts . . . ; what man will give himself the trouble to inform *them*, either at home, or abroad? with what *negligence* and *imperfectness* will they register things? how *un-philosophical* will their memories be?" Ironically, the society was accused of sloppiness and credulity in circulating "*Narratives* picked up from *negligent*, or *un-accurate Merchants* and *Seamen*": "What judgement have these *men of no reading*, whereby to *rectify* or

132. Leibniz to Oldenburg, 26 February 1673, and Oldenburg to Leibniz, 26 May 1673, in Oldenburg, *Correspondence*, IX, 494, 668.

133. See Jacob, *Stubbe*, for a provocative interpretation of Stubbe's war with the Royal Society as expression of covert radicalism.

134. Stubbe, *Legends No Histories* (1670), 19–21, 133; Stubbe to Boyle, 17 December 1669, in Birch, "Life of Boyle," xci.

135. Sprat, *History of the Royal Society*, 99–100, 257; Glanvill, *Scepsis Scientifica*, "Preface," sig. c1r; cf. "Dr. *Hook*'s Method of Making Experiments," in Hooke, *Philosophical Experiments and Observations*, 27–28.

enlarge their *Enquiries?*" Denying the priority and value of the Royal Society's research program on transfusion, Stubbe made it clear what he thought of their collective integrity: "Least I should seem to deal too *severely* and *maliciously* with them, rather then it shall be said *that they invented nothing*, I grant, that *they* invented a LYE."[136]

Here was a critic who did not scruple publicly to give Royal Society virtuosi the 'lie direct,' and, accordingly, to undermine the moral and epistemic bases of the factual knowledge upon which the experimental program depended. Boyle was indeed implicated in Stubbe's attack upon the society's reliability. *Legends No Histories* disputed Boyle's priority in the invention of the air-pump and the notion of the air's spring, declaring "that Mr. *Boyle* is very much mistaken" with respect to certain pharmaceutical claims.[137] At the same time, Stubbe distinguished between the integrity of Boyle and the rest. Publicly, Stubbe never identified Boyle's practices with those of his mendacious colleagues; privately, Stubbe kept up a remarkable correspondence with the man whose friends and associates he accused of lying.[138] Glanvill told Oldenburg that Stubbe's Bath "vapourings" against the Royal Society had indeed targeted Boyle. Stubbe was alleged to have followed his accusations against Glanvill, Sprat, and Henshaw by saying "that Mr Boyles relations no where hold true, [but] that he will spare him because he hath obliged him; kindly suffering him to hide himself among ye heard."[139]

Whether or not Stubbe gave Boyle the lie-direct orally and behind his back, he neither published such a charge nor pressed it privately. Writing personally to Boyle on the publication of *Legends No Histories*, Stubbe added a bland postscript suggesting that Parliament might find Thomas Sprat, as the author of the Royal Society's *History*, "chargeable with high-treason." Several months later Stubbe assured Boyle that he

136. Stubbe, *Legends No Histories*, 21, 120. For Glanvill's account of Stubbe's oral "railing" against the Royal Society at Bath, see Glanvill to Oldenburg, 19 July 1669, in Oldenburg, *Correspondence*, VI, 137–40. Here Stubbe was alleged to have said that Sprat's dedication to the king "hath a great lye in every sentence of it," and that Nathaniel Henshaw (a member of the Royal Society and the author of a tract on saltpeter included in Sprat's *History*) "is so noted a Lyar yt no one believes one word he sayes."

137. Stubbe, *Legends No Histories*, 9, 29, 129.

138. Stubbe had been, and remained, a significant source of natural-historical testimony for Boyle (see, e.g., Boyle, "General History of the Air," 645–46, 692, 694, 713, 718). I have already noted Boyle's probable use of Stubbe's relations from Jamaica in the 1672 *Hydrostatical Discourse*. At least some of Boyle's frequent references to a "learned," "ingenious," or "judicious physician" in the West Indies point to Stubbe, who had been there between 1662 and 1665, and there is also evidence that Stubbe had been an early recipient of Boyle's patronage: Jacob, *Stubbe*, 44–49, 58.

139. Glanvill to Oldenburg, 19 July 1669, in Oldenburg, *Correspondence*, VI, 138. Oldenburg, who most certainly would have told Boyle, did not rise to the bait, and his next letter to Glanvill made no mention of Stubbe's alleged charge.

had "never doubted, but that Mr. *Boyle* would never swerve from the
rules of honour and strict virtue, whatever the other virtuosi might
do. You are still constant to yourself and worth, but so are not they."
Stubbe associated Boyle's honor with his epistemic modesty. He noted
a distinction between such dogmatical advocates of the Royal Society
program as Glanvill, "who says it is *concluded* to be so," and "you, who
make no such positive conclusion." Boyle was celebrated for the sincerity of his commitment to probabilism and the genuineness of his philosophical humility which his baser colleagues had merely simulated. It
was "a great unhappiness, that several persons of honour like yourself
should ever mix with such insignificant talkers, as the generality [of
fellows] are; for you could get no credit by them, and their arrogance
and folly would unavoidably run you all into quarrels, if not contempt."[140] Like Spinoza, Stubbe reckoned that proper philosophical
friendship prized truth-telling over oily adulation. All the physicians,
he confided to Boyle, condemn "your experimental philosophy" as a
fraud, though none dare, "as the mode is, tell you to your face." He
told Boyle that his association with the Royal Society was endangering
his good name and integrity: "It will be impossible for you to preserve
your esteem, but by a seasonable relinquishing of these impertinents.
I tender you this testimony of my sincere respects, that I am thus free
with you; and whilst others flatter you, there is an old servant of yours
informs you of the truth."[141] I have found no record of Boyle's response to these accusations and assurances.

Some of Boyle's experimentally produced factual testimony was rejected by a philosophically more substantial source. In 1662 and again
in 1671 the Cambridge Platonist Henry More wrote against the technical adequacy and theological safety of Boyle's mechanical accounts of
the air-pump trials.[142] More conceived that he and Boyle shared moral
and epistemic aims, but that Boyle had misinterpreted the results of
his pneumatic trials in a way that encouraged atheists, enthusiasts, and
scoffers. Boylean mechanism needed to be supplemented by a directive
nonmechanical and immaterial principle. Having read Boyle's *New Experiments Physico-mechanical*, More responded in 1662 to the author's
repeated invitations to treat matters of fact as interpretatively open,

140. Stubbe to Boyle, 17 December 1669 and 18 May 1670, in Birch, "Life of Boyle,"
xc–xciv. For important earlier exchanges between Boyle and Stubbe over the 'stroking
cure,' and the nature of miracles, see ibid., lxxv–lxxxv; Jacob, *Stubbe*, 50–63, 164–74;
Steneck, "Greatrakes the Stroker"; Kaplan, "Greatrakes the Stroker."
141. Stubbe to Boyle, 4 June 1670, in Birch, "Life of Boyle," xcv–xcvi.
142. More, *Antidote against Atheisme*, 3d ed. (1662); idem, *Enchiridion Metaphysicum*
(1671). For Boyle's parallel response to George Sinclair's criticism of his hydrostatics,
see Boyle, "An Hydrostatical Letter." These disputes are recounted at length in Shapin
and Schaffer, *Leviathan and the Air-Pump*, 207–24, and the theological context is treated
in Henry, "More versus Boyle."

and he explicated the air-pump trials as evidence of a nonmaterial "hylarchic principle" rather than of mechanical spring. More here accepted the status of Boyle's experimental testimonies as matters of fact, as, indeed, he did in writing to Boyle several years later about his *New Experiments Touching Cold:* "Sir, you will infinitely oblige posterity, by the records of your so faithful and multifarious experiments. . . . [Your] repute with posterity must have no such firm foundation, than the constancy of nature, of which your writings will now find so true a copy, as that future appeals will be made to them amongst the learned, as to the judicature of nature herself."[143]

More acknowledged Boyle as a transparent spokesman for natural reality, but Boyle refused to countenance what he saw as an illegitimate appropriation of what he so faithfully delivered about that reality. In so doing, Boyle raised the moral and epistemic stakes of the disagreements he was conducting with More. The 1671 *Enchiridion Metaphysicum* offered further reinterpretations of Boyle's hydrostatic and pneumatic experiments, and Boyle responded in his 1672 *Hydrostatical Discourse.* He suggested that More had endeavored to make his own opinions appear "not only untrue, but irrational and absurd," and he was concerned that More's confident manner and reputation for learning would undermine the status of "that what I judge to be true." He impugned More's competence to perform and interpret the relevant experiments and implied that his adversary was subject to "hallucinations."[144] More contended that his hylarchic principle was experimentally evinced; Boyle countered that it was a hypothesis for which he had no need if the factual status of his experimental testimony was credited: the power of the air's spring was, in this view, a fact whose *cause* might be freely and civilly debated.

It was therefore open to Boyle, if he chose, to represent his quarrel with More as a dispute over the competence and sincerity of his experimental testimony. This is what he elected to do. One issue in dispute between More and Boyle concerned the question of water-pressure dealt with in Boyle's 1666 *Hydrostatical Paradoxes* and summarized earlier in this chapter. Boyle consulted with Royal Society colleagues, one of whom (probably Sir Robert Moray) he identified as More's "particular friend." This friend carefully read over the criticism of Boyle's hydrostatical testimony in More's *Enchiridion Metaphysicum* and, Boyle wrote, judged that More was flirting with the 'lie-direct': "[He] told me, that what seemed most probable to him, was, that though the doctor was too civil to give me, *in terminus* the lye; yet he did indeed deny the matter of fact to be true." If so, it would not only be Boyle

143. More to Boyle, 5 June 1665, in Boyle, *Works,* VI, 512–13.
144. Boyle, "Hydrostatical Discourse," 597, 628.

who was injured. Resentment might be justly taken on behalf of the
king himself. Boyle wrote that he could not "easily think" that his
testified matter of fact was untrue, "the experiment having been tried
both before our whole society, and very critically, by its royal founder,
his majesty himself."[145]

More was appalled that he now stood publicly accused of showing
Boyle and his friends such terminal disrespect. A mutual friend came
to his rooms at Christ's College and "acquaint[ed] me so explicitly how
you have taken offence at what concerns you in my *Enchiridion Metaphysicum*." More groveled, withdrawing any imputation of mendacity
and begging Boyle's forgiveness. When he had last met Boyle, he
formed the impression that Boyle was not concerned for his own reputation but for Descartes's. He was sorry that in opposing Cartesian
mechanism he had swept up positions defended and owned to be true
by Boyle. He had hoped "that all, whose hearts are seriously set upon
God and religion, would give me hearty thanks for my pains," and was
dismayed that he "had the ill hap to give offence to that incomparable
person Mr. *Boyle*." That could not have been foreseen, since More
reckoned that his behavior was in accord with "the royal law of equity."
He acknowledged Boyle's superior skill and experience in making experiments, and repeated that his intention was not to deny authentic
matters of fact but rationally to appropriate them for a safer philosophy of nature. Yet offense had been given, and he labored to
assure Boyle that it was not meant and would not, in any case, be
repeated:

> If I be mistaken in my inference from [Boyle's experiments], I am
> so grossly and unexpectedly disappointed by my reason, that I shall
> never hereafter trust mine own, or any one's else subtil reasonings in
> philosophy. . . . But I was so transported and warmed with the light
> and clarity of my reasonings in this discourse, that I hope, if in so
> full a career of heat and zeal for the main points I labour for, any
> thing has happened, that may seem less discreet, your great candour
> and Christianity will easily pardon it; and that so great and virtuous a
> soul, that is acquainted with such sentiments of the mind, as infinitely
> surpass all notions and speculations, that are not subservient to that
> end, will not think himself damnified, if other conceptions, that make
> nothing to that noble end, be assaulted by any one; especially, if they
> appear sound after the assault; and if they do not, yet there is the
> gain of a new truth if one will, or the loss of such a victory: so little
> hurt is there in philosophical oppositions amongst the free and in-
> genuous![146]

145. Ibid., 615.
146. More to Boyle, 4 December [1671], in Boyle, *Works*, VI, 513–15.

I have not located any additional significant gainsayings of Boyle's factual testimony, though it would, of course, be foolish to claim that none existed. I want, nevertheless, to note the extreme rarity of such episodes. Even my sketchy treatments have, I fear, given these episodes a weight and importance they did not historically possess. Given the torrents of testimony flooding out of Boyle's laboratory, such passages are remarkably infrequent. Boyle was the acknowledged master of scientific credibility. Moreover, I can note several features of these incidents which help to refine the rule to which they are indeed exceptions. First, it is not absolutely clear that any of these episodes *do* involve direct negations of Boyle's factual testimony. Whether or not direct negation occurs is, as I have indicated, the purposeful bringing of a matter to that 'issue': Auzout's, Spinoza's, and Huygens's engagements were too oblique for that to occur; Stubbe's texts exempted Boyle from Royal Society mendacity, while knowledge of his private remarks is too uncertain to permit judgment; Boyle declined to read Hobbes as denying his matters of fact; and he raised the possibility that More had indeed done so as a powerful way of increasing the quarrel's stakes and chasing his adversary from the field. Moreover, the very cultural boundary between 'fact' and 'theory' that differentially costed denial was, as Schaffer and I have elsewhere argued, conventionally located. For example, was the spring of the air a fact (which could only be doubted by impugning competence and sincerity) or was it a hypothesis (about which practitioners might legitimately entertain contrary imaginations)?[147] For a quarrel to *be about* matters of fact, participants had to *agree* that it was and thus to constitute it as such. Resources were widely available to identify 'the same' quarrel as about fact or about the interpretation of fact.

Second, none of these episodes clearly originated from critics who were in dense social interaction with Boyle and his friends. Stubbe, More, and Huygens certainly had met Boyle on at least several occasions, and they belonged to a social system in which Boyle's identity and personal reputation were widely distributed.[148] Auzout, Spinoza, and Hobbes had almost certainly never met him. Auzout, Huygens, and More were fellows of the Royal Society. Auzout did not come to England until 1682; Huygens had visited on several occasions in the 1660s and had a prior history of criticism from Boyle; and I have seen no evidence establishing that More ever attended the Royal Society. Hobbes and Stubbe embodied the type of person the society

147. Shapin and Schaffer, *Leviathan and the Air-Pump*, 49–55.

148. John Henry writes ("More versus Boyle," 55) that More and Boyle were "close friends," and, while he offers a fine analysis of shared (as well as divergent) theological concerns, I have not been able to find evidence suggesting "close friendship," nor does the tenor of their exchanges seem to support it.

wished to exclude. A group of critics of such great diversity and small size does not license glib generalization. Nevertheless, one is not dealing here with any individuals who had significant face-to-face interaction with either Boyle or his colleagues in the Royal Society. They tended towards the margins of Boyle's circle, and several, by their criticisms, assuredly placed themselves beyond expectation of ever belonging, if, in fact, that was what was wanted. While the generalization seems sustainable, I would not wish to press it too hard: one must always allow for the possibility that individuals are badly advised or poorly socialized, become deranged, or make genuine mistakes in expression or in judgment of what reaction might be elicited from a criticized individual. Nevertheless, this patchy evidence tends to support a link between comembership and ascribed credibility. If one wishes, or wishes to continue, to share a moral order with others, the price is granting others' basic veracity and competence in their factual testimony.

Boyle liked to be seen to ignore critics, responding to Hobbes and More, he said, not to protect personal honor, but from a concern that their reputations for wit and learning might endanger the credibility of the experimental community to which he acknowledged obligations. In the event, neither Boyle nor his friends considered that he had ever been discredited. Chapter 4 described how rapidly Boyle's reputation for truthful and reliable testimony spread. By the mid-1660s, indeed, Boyle drew public attention to the troubles caused him by his acknowledged status as a master of credibility. In 1665 his *New Experiments Touching Cold* complained of the "inconvenience" to which he had been put by his reputation for "strict fidelity to truth." His rights of authorship had been disputed by those practitioners who felt they could help themselves to Boyle's factual testimony without acknowledgment, without fear, and without moral risk:

> Some men, who probably would not mention the experiments of most others, without vouching their authors, for fear of losing their own credit, in case the thing related should not prove true, have, without taking the least notice of me, made use of such experiments of mine, as I have strong motives to think they never made nor saw, only because they had been related by one, after whom they thought they might without a hazard of their credit deliver any matter of fact.[149]

Those troubles continued to afflict him, and chapter 4 quoted a broadsheet advertisement Boyle released towards the end of his life complaining of fraud and identifying his own reputation for truthful-

149. Boyle, "New Experiments Touching Cold," 470–71; see also idem, "Experimenta & Observationes," 566 (for Boyle's awareness of his universal reputation for "sincerity").

ness as the reason why others stole his work: "For whereas when experiments and observations are related by men whose faithfulness is dubious, the more cautious sort of plagiaries think themselves obliged to
mention the names of their authors, . . . they think they may safely
rely on the truth of what our author relates, that their reputation runs
no venture in making any experiment that he delivers, pass for their
own."[150] His very transparency as a spokesman for nature made difficult the right assigning of his authorship. Yet how could the community know that it might rely upon *this* claim unless it knew also that
Boyle was its author? That apparent paradox was both Boyle's predicament and the most powerful sign that he was *an embodied solution* to
the problem of testimony.

That solution was a collectively prized achievement. Boyle's identity
locally checked the spread of skepticism and powerfully propelled individual experience into public knowledge. Chapter 4 introduced Boyle's
contemporary reputation for veracity and reliability. Throughout his
life there was a chorus of voices agreeing with Henry More that Boyle's
testimony was a "true copy" of nature, and with Ralph Cudworth that
"your pieces of natural history are unconfutable."[151] On his death,
commentators took stock of Boyle's resolution of the problem of Siamese skepticism and how that solution had become institutionalized in
the English natural-philosophical community. It was a life finely, and
morally, poised between skepticism and credulity. Gilbert Burnet wrote
that Boyle delivered his factual testimony "with so scrupulous a truth,
that all who have examined them, have found how safely the world
may depend upon them."[152] A Boyle family historian expressed some
worry that Boyle had acquired a partially justified reputation for "believing many things too easily upon the Credit of other People." A
moderate credulity was perhaps an outward mark of an inner noble
nature: "It is probable, that as he abhorred to affirm what was false
himself, he could not readily believe others capable of so mean a
Practice."[153]

The chemist Peter Shaw wrote of Boyle's "candour" and "fidelity"
as adequate grounds for belief, even in the most philosophically implausible claims: "We may certainly depend upon this, that what Mr.
Boyle delivers as an experiment or observation of his own, is related in
the precise manner wherein it appear'd to him: no one ever yet deny'd,
that he was a man of punctual veracity." It should not be concluded

150. Boyle, "An Advertisement [of Mr. Boyle] about the Loss of His Writings" (1688),
in Birch, "Life of Boyle," cxxvi.

151. More to Boyle, 5 June 1665, and Cudworth to Boyle, 16 October 1684, in Boyle,
Works, VI, 513, 511.

152. Burnet, "Character of a Christian Philosopher," 369–70.

153. Budgell, *Memoirs of the Earl of Orrery* (1732), 125.

from Boyle's relations of "extraordinary things" that he was credulous. In his laboratory he had produced phenomena which "the vulgar, or persons unacquainted with experimental philosophy" found "incredible." If so, then it was the vulgar who suffered from an illegitimately and immorally restricted sense of the possible, not Boyle from credulity: "Mr. *Boyle* was so happy, as to have seen, with his own eyes, much more of the powers of nature and art, than can easily be imagin'd." "Wherever our author believes more than other men, it is because he had more reason than they." Most philosophers and chemists, for example, do not believe that Boyle possessed a liquor "wherewith he cou'd convert gold into silver," just because they never saw such a thing done and "had tied themselves down to a narrow strait-laced philosophy":

> But if Mr. *Boyle* has actually done the thing; and others, men of veracity, have assured him they had done it too; is he credulous for believing it? Those rather were so, who, without sufficient evidence, rashly concluded the thing impracticable. Since Mr. *Boyle* assures us, and gives us sufficient grounds to believe, that he has render'd silver, gold, fixed alkalies, &c. volatile . . . and perform'd numberless other surprizing things, that appear as so many contradictions among the unskilful; may he not, with good reason, speak of them as feasible . . . ? or may he not, upon the strength of human testimony; upon the relation of his friends and acquaintance, believe that other men have done the same, or even greater things than these; tho' himself was not an eye witness of them?

Boyle had solved problems of skepticism as a moral matter. It was just because he was "open, candid, generous, and communicative," because he was far above "selfish pleasure," that he was in a position to pursue truth himself and to recognize it in others' testimony. "Here was a noble soul! This the desirable character!"[154]

Registrations, Recognitions, Reservations

I have argued here that knowledge about people was constitutively implicated in knowledge of things. One cannot have thing-knowledge without bringing to bear people-knowledge. That implication is arguably both generic (knowledge of people is a condition for having knowledge of things) and specific (what comes to be known about particular sorts of things is shaped by knowledge of particular sorts of people). What counts as thing-knowledge and what as people-knowledge has first to be segregated by actors as different epistemic

154. Shaw, "General Preface" to *Boyle's Philosophical Works* (1725), ix–xv. Note that this sort of testimony was a major vehicle for others coming to know of Boyle's 'track record.'

sorts and then recombined to evaluate new claims. The practical actions involved in doing so are infinitely complex and infinitely finely adjusted to case and setting. *That is the art of decorum.* It would be visionary to seek to specify the 'rules' of such actions, but not, perhaps, to trace some 'rules of thumb' by which assessment got done by particular sorts of people in a particular cultural context. It is only by having a go at that sort of generalization that one can hope to use detailed historical studies to open a window on more widely distributed features of cognitive action.

First, I want to draw attention to some general features of how factual knowledge-claims reached the threshold of assessment. I have already noted that the overwhelming majority of such knowledge-claims arriving at the Royal Society were *not* subjected to deliberative processes of judgment. Acts of formal assessment, such as I have described above, were *not* typical of how information was received. Moreover, it is impossible to understand how actors proceeded in deliberation without recognizing a broad background of nonassessed knowledge. In early modern England there was a particular term-of-art used to indicate the passage of claims into a cultural space from which some few might be selected for reflective assessment: they were *registered.* Originally, the Royal Society had a member (Dr. William Croone) who functioned as the "register" of phenomena described by letter, testified by members *viva voce,* or produced and witnessed at its meetings. Shortly afterwards, a *Register-Book* was instituted, into which a selection, but not all, of such claims were copied.[155] That *Register* then served as an institutional memory. It was a place to which members might go, if they wished, to retrieve past claims, to revive their assessment in a new situation, or to bring them to bear upon a new claim. The perceived reliability of what was registered depended upon individuals' short-term memory, both that of the person who served as register and that of the members asked promptly to check the *Register-Book* for accuracy. But, after that, it stood independent of individuals' medium- or long-term memory, and the reliability attributed to it flowed from that independence. Properly managed, the *Register* would, as Hooke maintained, "prove undoubted Testimony to Posterity of the whole History" of experimental acts and outcomes.[156]

Registering a claim was an act of civility: it displayed the fact that receipt was acknowledged and that the matter was worthy of being

155. See, e.g., Birch, *History of the Royal Society,* I, 7, 83; Sprat, *History of the Royal Society,* 94, 148; Lyons, *Royal Society,* 21, 25; Johns, "Wisdom in the Concourse," 152–60, 167, 171–73; and, for detailed accounts of the form of the society's meetings, M. B. Hall, *Promoting Experimental Learning,* chs 3–5.

156. "Dr. *Hook*'s Method of Making Experiments," in Hooke, *Philosophical Experiments and Observations,* 27–28.

placed into medium- or long-term institutional memory. Individuals whose claims were registered received a sign that others judged them potentially able to colonize their minds. Some process of this form is probably a quite general feature of social interaction. All practical actors are presumably indifferent to most of what they are told about the social and natural worlds. What 'engages their current interest' is a vanishingly small portion of what they are told. Yet there are reasons why they are impelled to find some way of 'marking' this information: first, because it may be useful to retrieve information in some unforeseeable future circumstance; second, because 'marking'—as opposed to deliberation—frees up today's practical action for other things; and third, because if we are to expect further communications from that source, some moral token must be given that the communicative system is in order, that the message is welcome and has been received. Just as dubiety takes place on the margins of trusting systems, so deliberation floats on a sea of routine registrations. Goffman and the conversational analysts have treated just such features of everyday face-to-face interaction: the 'uh-huhs' and 'mmms' that are our part as conversational receivers, the omission of which reliably elicits our partner's request to know whether we are 'there' and whether 'everything is all right.'[157] A refusal to register, mark, or acknowledge communications is both a reliable indicator of moral orders not shared and an effective way of breaching one previously shared. Registration is therefore best viewed not as failed or imperfect deliberation but as a positive moral and epistemic action. It is a pervasively distributed epistemic and moral buffer, a morally warrantable posture in which to receive information from others and to get on with today's business. Imagine all claims being treated to deliberative assessment; imagine a significant number being totally ignored.

Second, factual knowledge-claims came to individuals and centers of assessment through *systems of recognition*. Typically, recipients already knew quite a lot about testifying sources when they received their testimony, or, if they did not, they knew quite a lot about those who knew the sources, and so on. That knowledge encompassed individuals' standing, ascribed virtues, reputation for skill and sincerity, and, crucially, the likely consequences of granting or withholding assent. The relative cost of gainsaying vulgar divers, skilled mathematical practitioners, and the Honourable Robert Boyle was important social knowledge. Nor was this knowledge static, since awareness of the cost and consequences of assent was also a matter of *decorum*, finely adjusted to cultural and social circumstances. In their most concrete forms these

157. Goffman, *Strategic Interaction*, 104–13; idem, "Replies and Responses," in idem, *Forms of Talk*, 5–77.

recognitions occurred in face-to-face interaction, where the knowledge of the speakers' physical individuality was at the same time recognition of their circumstances and identity. As one heard Boyle speak, one recognized who he was and what was his authority for speaking. Both the society of seventeenth-century English gentlemen and that of the learned were intensely face-to-face societies with highly developed public spheres of interaction. Members typically brought much shared knowledge of standing and reputation to interaction; they monitored current interaction for the visible signs of credibility; and they assumed that networks of communication would effectively convey sentiments expressed in one public forum to relevant others.[158]

Moreover, members who did not directly recognize a visitor or an epistolary source looked for, and expected to obtain, vouchers for others' standing and virtues from those they did recognize. Receipt of these vouchers often counted as the price of admission to gentlemanly and learned spaces, both for individuals and for their knowledge-claims. Such a voucher might be no more than an individual's plausible presentation of self as someone whose legitimate reputation preceded him, just as exclusion might effectively arise, for example, from gentlemanly members' recognition of a woman, a servant, a Jew, or a known troublemaker. Travelers arriving at cultural spaces to which they wished access frequently carried with them letters of introduction from individuals already directly known to members, and factual communications were often covered by a letter introducing the unknown testifier to recipients.[159]

Introduction of the candidate to the system of recognitions was in itself an act of vouching. The individual who introduced others thereby warranted those persons and their testimony as fit to be received. Just as one might rely upon the voucher's factual testimony, so one might rely upon that of those he vouched for. Some people might speak for things in their own voice; other people had to have their rights to speak validated or to speak through others' voices. The moral texture of the social relations involved determined the nature of the vouching. At one extreme, vouching was not deemed necessary, and any demand for the provision of bona fides would be grounds for resentment. A gentleman's word was his bond, and I have indicated how Oldenburg responded to rare expressions of skepticism about Boyle's experimental testimony simply by repeating the findings and reminding the skeptic of Boyle's identity.

At the other extreme, testimony might only be put into circulation

158. E.g., Laslett, "The Face to Face Society"; A. Bryson, "The Rhetoric of Status." For the persisting importance of face-to-face modes of interaction in English science, see, e.g., Rudwick, *Great Devonian Controversy*, 34–37.
159. Shapin, "House of Experiment," 388–90.

if it or its source was vouched for by others of known standing, sincerity, or skill. I have already noted several examples of the proffering of or demand for vouchers, and the records of the Royal Society circle offer very many more. In 1671 such a request was cautiously made of some medical testimony from a cleric and founding fellow who had sent Seth Ward an exceptionally large kidney stone allegedly passed in the urine of a patient in Exeter. Medical fellows had never seen such a big one and wanted its provenance validated. Oldenburg complied: "Since you are pleased to offer to ye Society, yt you will procure a Testimony under ye Patients own hand, [the fellows] kindly accept of it, to be thereby ye better enabled to assure others of ye truth of ye thing, though they be sufficiently assured of it them selves by wt you have related thereof."[160] In 1670 a nonconformist preacher in Cheshire wrote to Oldenburg about a remarkable mineral specimen. Expecting skepticism, the preacher volunteered a voucher: "If it be the credibilitie of my reports you stick at, because altogether unacquainted with me My Lord Delamer (Now at the Parliament) or any of his servants can give you a character of me."[161] In 1678 a Newcastle practical chemist wanting his metallurgical testimony acknowledged by the Royal Society provided "certificates from persons of good credit" vouching for the historicity of the event, and these were forwarded in due course to Robert Boyle.[162] A few years later Nehemiah Grew requested and received a signed affidavit from a London apothecary assuring him of his care and honesty in preparing pure chemicals for experimental purposes.[163]

The first microscopical observations of the Delft draper Antoni van Leeuwenhoek were communicated to the Royal Society in 1673 with a covering letter from the well-known physician and anatomist Reginald de Graaf introducing his fellow townsman as "a certain very ingenious person" of great instrumental skill.[164] Two years later Leeuwenhoek made claims for the existence of vast numbers of little animals in pondwater, smaller and more numerous than any microscopist had ever previously observed. Earlier microscopical testimony from Leeuwenhoek had already encountered some Royal Society skepticism and this claim engendered much more. Leeuwenhoek was proud of his instrumental ability but he knew the drill. His claim to have seen hosts of little swimming animals was duly vouched for by eight local worthies—

160. Oldenburg to Edward Cotton, 19 January 1671, in Oldenburg, *Correspondence,* VII, 400; for the testimonials, see ibid., 420–22.

161. Adam Martindale to Oldenburg, 4 November 1670, in Oldenburg, *Correspondence,* VII, 238.

162. Luke Hodgson to Boyle, *ca.* April 1678, in Boyle, *Works,* VI, 655–56.

163. Grew, *Anatomy of Plants* (1682), 268.

164. De Graaf to Oldenburg, 18 April 1673, in Oldenburg, *Correspondence,* IX, 603.

mainly clerics and lawyers—none of whom possessed any relevant technical expertise. Leeuwenhoek was neither a philosopher, a medical man, nor a gentleman. At the time of his emergence he was known by no one in the English philosophical community to which he addressed his testimony. He had been to no university, knew no Latin, French, or English, and little relevant natural history or philosophy. The rough and vulgarly styled letters through which he communicated his testimony gave visible signs of his problematic and compromised identity. His claims strained existing schemes of plausibility, and his identity was of no help in securing credibility for those claims. The Delft worthies he mobilized vouched for his probity as well as his skill.[165]

Finally, I want to draw attention to some epistemic correlates of the system of exchanges and recognitions in which credibility was assessed. The system was recognized to have a reciprocal character. That is, insofar as members took themselves to be dealing with equals or near-equals, how they handled others' testimony might have a future bearing on how one's own testimony was treated. The Golden Rule might then appear in a pragmatic guise. Too much skepticism of others' testimony might, for that reason alone, engender skeptical treatment of one's own. This was a matter of such commonsensical prudence that it rarely needed to be articulated. Oldenburg typically took it upon himself to remind fellows of brisker spirits or ungenerous dispositions that publicly expressed distrust might be consequential.[166] In 1667 he specifically cautioned fellows not to deny within the society's rooms experimental testimony deriving from foreign practitioners. He took an offending fellow aside after such an incident and asked him "how he would resent it, if he should communicate upon his own knowledge an unusual experiment to [those foreign philosophers], and they brand it in public with the mark of falsehood: that such expressions in so public a place, and in so mixed a company, would certainly prove very destructive to all philosophical commerce."[167]

For related reasons it was widely recommended that dubiety or skepticism which might be construed as impugning honesty or competence should be hidden or masked from public forums. Ways ought to be

165. Dobell, *Leeuwenhoek*, 172–77. Leeuwenhoek's mobilization of local worthies as vouchers was repeated in 1688: Leeuwenhoek, *Collected Letters*, VIII, 57; Palm, "Leeuwenhoek and Other Dutch Correspondents," 191. Chapter 8 below describes the structure of vouching in which *technicians'* work and word was embedded.

166. For remarks on Oldenburg's work as moral buffer, see Shapin, "O Henry," esp. 421–24.

167. Oldenburg to Boyle, 10 December 1667, in Oldenburg, *Correspondence*, IV, 26–28; cf. Oldenburg to Boyle, 6 October 1664, in ibid., II, 248 (for Oldenburg upbraiding a similar act of public distrust by Hooke); see also Shapin, "House of Experiment," 398–99. The 1667 episode concerned reports about transfusion from physicians in Danzig.

found by which conflict might be managed without bringing the contest to issue. Thus, Boyle expressed concern about a dispute between Hooke and the physician Walter Needham. He hoped that as they were "both members of the *Royal Society*, . . . if it were possible, they may be brought to agree, without making their opposition éclater." And Oldenburg encouraged Huygens to keep his mathematical dispute with James Gregory out of the public arena.[168] It was generally recognized that the intensity of face-to-face interaction made it easier to resolve quarrels while, at the same time, negating another's testimony to his face was a uniquely costly act. Hevelius told Oldenburg that he was confident he could resolve his technical controversy with Hooke if only "I could discuss the question face to face," while Oldenburg told Wallis about Hobbes's impudent slur on Wallis's geometrical competence delivered in front of the king: "He ought to be soundly lash't for it; and I was very sorry, yt none of our Mathematicall Society men, yt know both you and him, were present, to tell him, yt he durst not say such words to yr face."[169]

Probabilistic discourse lowered the moral and epistemic cost of disputing causal notions; failures of instruments and assistants might be warrantably cited as excuses for factual error; and the processes of mundane reasoning offered rich resources for finding and sustaining a civically appropriate account of reality. Representations of reality might be elaborated so as to preserve the in-principle reliability of accounts which might otherwise be judged seriously discrepant. Icebergs with air pockets, like skies with two comets, were accounts which saved both locally adequate interests in natural reality and the moral comembership of different sources of information. Finally, the civil order of a knowledge-producing community might be protected by lowering the standards of certainty, accuracy, and exactness legitimately to be expected of claims about the world. I have already observed how conventions of gentlemanly discourse worked against expectations of too much accuracy or precision. To value truth above good manners was not decorous; it was to disrupt civil conversation; it was the mark of a pedant. In 1669 the Belgian mathematician René François de Sluse wrote to Oldenburg about a geometrical quarrel between Fermat and James Gregory. He hoped that their dispute would keep within civil bounds: "For in my opinion learning is not so great a thing that one should be forgetful of good manners on its

168. Boyle to Oldenburg, 3 April 1668, and Oldenburg to Huygens, 4 February 1669, in Oldenburg, *Correspondence*, IV, 301, and V, 374.

169. Hevelius to Oldenburg, 19 November 1668, and Oldenburg to Wallis, 5 August 1671, in Oldenburg, *Correspondence*, V, 186, and VIII, 185; see also Shapin, "House of Experiment," 397–98.

account."[170] Gentlemanly conversation worked with and enshrined a conception of truth as adequate to the practical task. And that task was not the attainment of more, more exact, or more powerful truth, but the continuance of the conversation itself. Insofar as the English experimental community had relocated gentlemanly codes into the practice of natural philosophy, that conception of conversation was available for the practices by which adequate truth was itself recognized and produced.[171]

It was common in early modern society to contrast the society of gentlemen with that of scholars according to the different values they respectively placed upon truth and good manners. Polite writers condemned traditional scholars because they would sacrifice the good order of conversation to the imperious demands of truth and accuracy, while the scholar might justify himself through variants of the ancient trope used to identify oneself as 'a friend of Aristotle but more a friend of truth.' Yet changed conceptions of the nature of scholarly practice in the seventeenth century—especially in England but also elsewhere—increasingly reordered and respecified the characters of the scholar and the gentleman. It was now urged that the end of philosophy—the search for truth—might best be acquitted by deploying features of conversational practices that had traditionally belonged to gentlemanly and not to scholarly society. Lowered expectations of philosophical accuracy, a more reserved way of speaking, a less passionate attempt to claim exact truth for one's claims were justified on explicitly epistemic as well as explicitly moral grounds. It might be *reality itself* which demanded a more decorous and reserved way of speaking about it. The world might be such a storehouse of experiences which sustained *as competent and sincere* a range of differing accounts that practitioners offered of it. The next chapter offers a detailed examination of a philosophical practice which embedded such a view of reality, of representation, and of a morally sustainable civil conversation about the world.

170. Sluse to Oldenburg, 25 February 1669, in Oldenburg, *Correspondence*, V, 419.
171. Materials richly documenting the persistence of gentlemanly codes in English scientific practice into the nineteenth century are in Rudwick, *Great Devonian Controversy*, passim, but especially ch. 5.

CHAPTER SEVEN

Certainty and Civility: Mathematics and Boyle's Experimental Conversation

What scientists seek in numerical tables
is not usually "agreement" at all, but what they often call
"reasonable agreement."
Furthermore, if we now ask for a criterion of
"reasonable agreement," we are literally forced
to look in the tables themselves.

—T. S. Kuhn, "Function of Measurement"

When we assess the truth of a claim to factual knowledge, we typically take a view on whether or not it is a representation that corresponds to the world. That assessment embeds some notion of adequate precision: How exact is that correspondence supposed to be? How much variation is to be expected in independent reports about 'the same' reality beyond which we conclude that they do not reliably report upon the same world at all or that one or the other is untrue? That is to say, a decision that a representation is true—that it corresponds to reality— incorporates some notion of legitimate variation. Sometimes practitioners produce reflective accounts of the nature and source of variation, but always they have practical ways of identifying and managing it. As Kuhn has argued, in order to say that experimental results 'fit' or 'confirm' a hypothesis, one has to implement some procedure for identifying when fit is good enough. One could, of course, endeavor explicitly to formulate a rule for 'good enough fitting,' only to find oneself in need of a further rule to determine how the fitting rule ought to be applied. In practice, as the epigraph to this chapter indicates, adequate fit is characterized through its instantiation by a relevant community of reasonable people.[1]

I want here to argue that practical decisions about precision and

1. Kuhn, "Function of Measurement"; also idem, "Function for Thought Experiments," 261–62.

variation in factual reports are moral judgments and that they too have a social history. They are, of course, judgments about what the world is like such that *this range* of reports accurately corresponds to it.[2] But they are also judgments about the probity and skill of the practitioners who produce these reports, and, accordingly, they embed norms about the degree of exactness and certainty *it is right* to expect of competent and sincere human reports. How do we recognize trustworthy testimony about the world? What accuracy and certainty *ought* we to demand of each other? With what confidence *ought* we to advance our claims about the world? What warrant *ought* those claims to have? Precision judgments, consequently, always have a normative character. They are consequential decisions about the moral economy of those who testify about nature.

The case I want to work through is central to the probabilistic, observational and experimental English tradition which has been the focus of this book. It concerns Robert Boyle's view of the proper place of mathematics, and the proper expectation of mathematical exactness and certainty, within the practice of experimental natural philosophy. Like many other English and Continental natural philosophers of the seventeenth century, Boyle clearly identified mathematical techniques as valuable resources in securing and representing natural knowledge. Galileo famously claimed that the Book of Nature was "written in the language of mathematics," and Boyle found occasion to quote Plato, saying that "the world was God's epistle written to mankind" and that "it was written in mathematical letters."[3] Nevertheless, Boyle also repeatedly expressed uneasiness about certain conceptions of mathematics, and certain views of precision and epistemic confidence associated with mathematics, within experimental practice. Notions of truth traditionally connected with mathematical culture were deemed out of place in experimental natural philosophy. They counted as violations of epistemological *decorum*.

I will argue that Boyle judged the appropriate place and role of mathematics in experimental philosophy as matters pertinent to the *civility* of that practice. How did he regard mathematical expectations and procedures as bearing upon the possibility and stability of a civil

2. Lorraine J. Daston ("Problems of Early Modern Quantification") has urged the seventeenth-century significance of distinguishing between *precision* (construed as the clarity and distinctness of concepts) and *accuracy* (taken as the fit of numbers to some part of the natural world). In ordinary, or dictionary, usage, however, *precision* and *accuracy* are widely taken as interchangeable, and my concern with Boylean practice spans Daston's otherwise useful distinction.

3. Galileo, "The Assayer," 237–38; Boyle, "Excellency and Grounds of the Mechanical Hypothesis," 77; also idem, "Some Considerations Touching the Usefulness of Experimental Natural Philosophy," 29.

experimental conversation? The character and scope of such an argument need to be carefully specified. First, I do not mean to argue that questions about the place of mathematics in natural philosophy were shaped by civil considerations *versus* philosophical judgments. Indeed, the value of mathematics in early to mid-seventeenth-century natural philosophy was being extensively debated by non-gentle scholarly practitioners, and sentiments against grand claims for mathematical methods were strong. I focus here on Boyle's views, and I try to show how his assessments of different philosophical traditions *were* evaluations of their potential for the form of civil conversation called experimental natural philosophy. This is a description of the constitutive role of considerations of social order in an individual's evaluation of philosophical propriety and epistemic merit. I mean to show how this gentleman, with the cultural equipment, identity, and values of a seventeenth-century English gentleman, judged among philosophical traditions. Second, it will become apparent that Boyle's worries about the experimental propriety of mathematical canons were of a limited nature. Boyle clearly reckoned that there was much about the physical world that was amenable to mathematical treatment. Third, the argument is about an individual, and, while I indicate that his evaluations had local antecedents and resonance, the Royal Society's later adaptation to a Newtonian program of mathematical natural philosophy is proof enough that Boyle's views were not without rivals even in the community whose codes he did so much to shape. Boyle's judgments were neither idiosyncratic nor Royal Society dogma, and questions to do with the 'influence' of Boyle's assessments are to one side of this chapter's main concerns.

Insofar as the scientific revolution is identified with mathematical natural philosophy, and its central achievements with the mathematicization of physics, arguments *against* mathematics may seem odd or even retrograde.[4] Nevertheless, I want to indicate how limitations on the place of mathematics figured in describing, warranting, and maintaining the moral order of the English experimental community, even as these same limitations configured what was recognized as knowledge and the domain to which knowledge rightly referred. In Boyle's view,

---

4. Kuhn, for example, has argued ("Mathematical versus Experimental Traditions") that the revolutionary achievements of seventeenth-century science belonged not to the new experimental but to the older mathematical traditions of work. Crombie (*Augustine to Galileo,* 278) maintained that "it was precisely those branches of science which were most amenable to measurement that showed the most spectacular developments [in the sixteenth and seventeenth centuries]," and Koyré (e.g., "Experiment in Measurement," 89–91; see also idem, "Galileo and Plato," 19–20, 38–39) famously saw the "essence and structure" of modern science in "substituting for the world of the more-or-less of our daily life a universe of measurement and precision."

neither the physical world reported upon by competent and sincere practitioners, nor the desired moral order of the experimental community, could sustain dominant mathematical conceptions of truth, precision, and certainty. Accordingly, notions of the quality of factual knowledge implicated decisions about what the physical world was like and what the moral order of those who testified about it ought to be.

Boyle as Mathematician

Boyle himself never produced a mathematical chemistry or physics. Geometrical diagrams and symbolic notations are very rarely encountered in his works. It is, as I shall show, ironic that Boyle is now best known for a mathematically expressed physical 'law' which he never expressed in mathematical terms or indeed ever characterized as a law. A straightforward answer to the question why Boyle did not do mathematical natural philosophy already exists in the historical literature, and it is an answer of satisfying simplicity: Boyle did not speak the language of mathematics because he was not able to do so; he was, it is said, mathematically incompetent at the relevant level, if not mathematically illiterate. According to one of his biographers, Boyle himself "admitted he was so deficient he could not use mathematical analysis in his work."[5] Indeed, his essay *Of the Usefulness of Mathematicks to Natural Philosophy* confessed that he had "often wished, that I had been employed about the speculative part of geometry, and the cultivating of the specious Algebra I had been taught very young, a good part of that time and industry, that I spent about surveying and fortification . . . and other practick parts of mathematicks. . . . I do not pretend to have taken that pains, which else I might have done, to become a speculative geometrician."[6] In his original reports of experiments with the air-pump, Boyle excused his eschewal of physical generalization in part because this would have "require[d] more skills in mathematics than I pretend to."[7] Chapter 4 discussed the significance of a range of Boylean disavowals of professional standing, among which was a description of himself as one "who pretend[s] not to be a mathematician."[8]

Other historians, citing other evidence, have sprung (as they sup-

5. More, *Boyle*, 64.

6. This essay is included in Boyle, "Some Considerations Touching the Usefulness of Experimental Natural Philosophy. Second Tome" (1671), 425; see also Maddison, *Boyle*, 31n., and the sketch of Boyle's education in chapter 4 above.

7. Boyle, "New Experiments Physico-mechanical," 36.

8. Boyle, "Excellency of Theology," 22; cf. idem, "Defence against Linus," 122, where Boyle gave his poor eyesight as a reason for avoiding the study of texts containing "mathematical schemes," i.e., diagrams.

posed) to Boyle's defense. Marie Boas Hall claimed that Boyle was in fact "well-educated in the mathematical sciences"; he was "by no means ignorant either of mathematics or of the mathematical sciences."[9] Writing to his father while on the grand tour of the Continent with his tutor Isaac Marcombes in 1642, Boyle noted that "we continue our Study in the Mathematickes which is (as I thinke) the bravest Science in the world (after Divinity), and I hope to become a good proficient therein."[10] In 1647, having reached his majority, Boyle wrote to Samuel Hartlib that he was reading Oughtred's *Clavis Mathematica,* which "does much content me," and that he was seriously engaged in a program of mathematical studies. Five years later Boyle referred to "those excellent sciences, the mathematics, having been the first I addicted myself to."[11] By 1654, according to Thomas Birch, Boyle "had laid in a great stock of mathematical knowledge," and was evidently recognized as sufficiently adept for John Wallis to dedicate his 1659 tract on cycloids to him, extolling Boyle's mathematical abilities.[12] Gilbert Burnet judged that Boyle had run "the whole compass of mathematical sciences; and, though he did not set himself to spring new game, yet, he knew even the abstrusest parts of geometry."[13] The available evidence indicates that the mathematical scope and intensity of Boyle's education at Eton and by his tutor was impressive, although not too far out of the ordinary for Tudor-Stuart English gentlemen. As Boyle noted, the stress was upon the practical aspects of mathematics, especially those having to do with surveying and fortification, and it fed into the gentry's current infatuation with mechanical devices as "artificial miracles" and with experimental displays valued "for their novelty or prettiness."[14] Of course, much—and probably most—of the mathematics Boyle knew in his mature years was derived from self-study, and was mediated by his colleagues at Oxford from the mid-1650s.

Nothing I want to say about these episodes depends upon deciding the real state of Boyle's mathematical skills. I am concerned with the deployment of mathematics in Boyle's experimental practice and writing, and also with explicit public arguments he proffered concerning the proper place of mathematical notions of certainty and precision in the practice of the emerging community of experimentalists. One can

9. M. B. Hall, *Boyle and Seventeenth-Century Chemistry,* 13, 36.
10. Boyle to earl of Cork, 15 May 1642, quoted in Jacob, *Boyle,* 10.
11. Boyle to Hartlib, 8 May 1647, in Birch, "Life of Boyle," xli; excerpts from Boyle, "Considerations on the Style of Scripture," in ibid., xlix.
12. Birch, "Life of Boyle," lv, lix; Wallis, "Tractatus Duo. Prior, De Cycloide," in idem, *Opera Mathematica,* I, 491.
13. Burnet, "Character of a Christian Philosopher," 369.
14. Feingold, *Mathematicians' Apprenticeship,* ch. 6, esp. 193–95; A. J. Turner, "Mathematical Instruments and the Education of Gentlemen"; Johnston "Mathematical Practitioners and Instruments."

imagine a situation in which those arguments were rationalizations for genuine mathematical incompetence, and one can, with equal plausibility, suppose that Boyle set aside real mathematical abilities in favor of alternative practices, the superiority of which he deeply felt.[15] Whatever Boyle could or could not do, he was certainly concerned publicly to give reasons why mathematics ought to be viewed with some suspicion in the proper conduct of experimental philosophy. These reasons were not unique to him—indeed, I shall show that certain relevant ontological considerations were widely distributed in relevant sectors of early modern culture. But the repertoires of reasons which Boyle assembled, and which he brought to bear upon the moral economy of the experimental community, were both specific and consequential. They enjoyed substantial, though not universal, credibility within the English experimental community. As ever, Boyle simultaneously *did* experimental philosophy and set a pattern of how an experimental community *ought* to conduct its affairs in the search for natural knowledge.

In the cause of my own standards of precision I start by confronting evidence which seems to show Boyle's positive evaluation of mathematics, or of its legitimate place in experimental philosophy, or which appears to establish crucial incorporations of mathematical conceptions into Boyle's experimental practice. Some of this evidence does, as I shall note, illustrate ways in which Boyle did applaud mathematics and its uses in specific contexts. In other instances, however, the evidence that Boyle approved of a central role for mathematics in experimental philosophy is weak or illusory, and is counterbalanced by strong and reiterated arguments as to why the role of mathematical standards and expectations should be limited. Boyle, to repeat, was not arguing against mathematics; his arguments were directed towards the *unseemliness* of a range of mathematical conceptions within experimental practice.

In early modern culture the terms *mathematics, the mathematics,* and *the mathematical sciences* were far more inclusive than present-day understandings of mathematics. The legacy of mathematical sciences inherited from antiquity included, in addition to the 'pure mathematics' (geometry and arithmetic), such forms of physical inquiry as astronomy, optics, statics, and musical theory. All of these had traditionally been closely associated with the use of arithmetic or geometrical concepts and modes of proof, and, as Kuhn says, "might better be de-

---

15. The latter possibility has appealed to such historians as Marie Boas Hall (*Boyle and Seventeenth-Century Chemistry,* 34): Boyle, she theorizes, "notoriously avoided mathematical language. But this . . . was a pose more than a fact, a deliberate adoption of a manner, designed to aid him in debate."

scribed as a single field, mathematics."[16] Within that broad span of cultural activity so designated, distinctions were made between 'pure' (or 'speculative' or 'abstract') and 'mixed' mathematics, according to whether the inquiries were formalistic or contained a physical dimension. Moreover, early modern senses of the boundaries of mathematics often encompassed practices whose *methods* were deemed to be characteristic of pure mathematics, and, especially, of geometry. Thus, studies which applied the methods of logic, including the syllogistic mode of demonstration, and which aimed at securing demonstrative grades of certainty, were routinely referred to as 'mathematical.' Boyle's arguments about the decorousness of mathematics dealt with all these aspects of mathematical culture.

Finally, a note about the roles of those whom early moderns designated as 'mathematicians' or 'mathematical practitioners.' There was a widespread and consequential early modern distinction in cultural and social standing between 'mathematicians' and 'philosophers.' Throughout the European context, mathematicians were widely considered to be predominantly practically orientated individuals, who sought to apply number to the arts or to establish certain quantitatively expressed regularities in the natural world without attempting to ascertain what the real physical causes of those regularities actually were.[17] This was the conception of the mathematician's role which informed John Wallis's often-quoted (if somewhat exaggerated) comments on the low esteem in which mathematical studies were held in the early seventeenth-century English universities: "*Mathematicks* (at that time, with us) were scarce looked upon as *Accademical* Studies, but rather *Mechanical;* as the business of *Traders, Merchants, Seamen, Carpenters, Surveyors of Lands,* or the like."[18]

While Biagioli richly documents changing Continental roles, niches, and evaluations of mathematical practitioners from the late sixteenth century, there remained significant evaluative distinctions between mathematical and philosophical practice. There was a difference in social roles, as well as in epistemic goals, between advancing the Copernican hypothesis as a piece of mathematics or of natural philosophy.[19] Moreover, English commentators repeatedly expressed worry about

16. Kuhn, "Mathematical versus Experimental Traditions," 36–37.

17. This despite strenuous efforts of several noted astronomers to argue the propriety of making philosophical claims, e.g., Westman, "The Astronomer's Role"; Jardine, *The Birth of History and Philosophy of Science,* 144–46, 156, 225–57.

18. Scriba, "Autobiography of Wallis," 27; also 29–30.

19. Biagioli, "Social Standing of Mathematicians." And see Johnston, "Thomas Digges," for a study of a wellborn Elizabethan English mathematical practitioner who sought, in broadly 'Baconian' fashion, to revalue mathematical skills by showing their worth to the Tudor state.

the effects of mathematical or logical 'pedantry' on gentlemanly behavior, and the place of mathematical study in polite education was closely monitored.[20] The humanist Roger Ascham, for example, observed that "all Mathematicall heades, which be onely and wholy bent to those sciences" were "unfit to liue with others" and "unapt to serue in the world." As mathematical studies "sharpen mens wittes over much, so they change mens maners over sore."[21] Thus, while mathematical inquiries might be esteemed as producing a high degree of precision and certainty, and having, so to speak, a high truth-content, it was not necessarily the case that such pursuit of precision and certainty was attached to a very highly valued social role. From the point of view of gentlemanly culture, the mathematician undoubtedly appeared as a useful sort of person, just as the practical parts of mathematics were useful components of gentlemanly education, while the mathematician's quest for precision and certainty might also seem to lack philosophical point, purpose, and decorum.

The Case for Mathematics

I can distinguish six senses in which Boyle either deployed mathematics in his experimental practice, explicitly approved of its role in the overall culture, or apparently commended it formally as having a central place in natural philosophy. The first possibly ought not to be dignified with the term *mathematics* at all, even if it was an important usage for Boyle. He significantly deployed *number* in the vocabulary of his experimental language. While in very many instances he was content to report that a particular experiment had been tried "divers time," or that a certain piece of glassware was "divers feet" in length, in others Boyle was at pains to specify exactly how many times an experiment had been tried, just how many movements of the air-pump piston had been required to achieve a given effect. This presentation was, as I have shown elsewhere, an aspect of Boyle's deliberately *circumstantial* style of narrating experimental performances as really occurring, historically specific events.[22] That style was offered as a morally effective means of assuring readers of experimental texts that the described experiments had really been performed and that, on this occasion, nature had behaved in just the way recounted. A reader

20. E.g., Shapin, "'A Scholar and a Gentleman,'" esp. 291–95, 301; and, for a notable example of the scurrility of exchanges between early modern mathematicians, see Jardine, *The Birth of History and Philosophy of Science*, esp. Pt. I.

21. Ascham, *The Scholemaster* (1570), 5v. On injunctions against too deep an engagement with mathematics for gentlemen, see Feingold, *Mathematicians' Apprenticeship*, 29–30, 190–93.

22. Shapin, "Pump and Circumstance"; Shapin and Schaffer, *Leviathan and the Air-Pump*, esp. ch. 2.

who believed in the reportorial reliability of these dense prose pictures would come to count as an effective member of the witnessing community and assist in the transformation of individual testimony into collective knowledge.

A second, and related, usage involved the employment of number as a scalar measure of physical qualities investigated in Boyle's experimental practice. There were many contexts in which Boyle's concern for the exact numerical specification of physical qualities emerged. His first experimental publication lamented national variations in spatial measures and one of his last tracts complained about the lack of adequate universal standards for weight.[23] How could a program for extending experimental knowledge by replication be effective if practitioners did not report their results as accurately as possible? And how, even if accuracy were diligently pursued, could experimental knowledge circulate as a stable object if practitioners were unable to translate each others' numerical language? Experimental practitioners, however competent and honest, would not be able to tell whether or not they had successfully replicated a trial reported by others living in a different metrological culture.[24] Numerical precision, and the ability, if necessary, reliably to translate from one numerical language into another, was deemed essential to the extension of experimental practice and to the stabilization of the factual knowledge reported from experimental performances. Here Boyle arguably took the lead in articulating sentiments about number and precision which circulated very widely in the experimental community.

Third, Boyle approved of mathematics as a tool appropriate in principle for investigating and explicating the properties of a physical world considered as corpuscular and mechanical. A world whose ultimate constituents were geometrically figured particles, arranged into various geometrical "textures" and subject to determinate states of motion, was such a reality as lent itself to mathematical construal and representation.[25] Historians of science routinely see the link between the mechanical philosophy and mathematical techniques as a matter 'of course': the "mathematical view of nature involves, of course, a mechanical conception of its operations."[26] Boyle himself occasionally pointed to the co-dependence of mathematics and physical inquiry. His 1671 essay on the *Usefulness of Mathematicks to Natural Philosophy*

23. Boyle, "New Experiments Physico-mechanical," 38; idem, "Medicina Hydrostatica" (1690), 487.

24. For important recent sociological engagement with problems of metrology, see Latour, *Science in Action*, ch. 6; O'Connell, "Metrology."

25. E.g., Kuhn, "Boyle and Structural Chemistry"; M. B. Hall, *Boyle and Seventeenth-Century Chemistry*, ch. 3; Alexander, *Ideas, Qualities and Corpuscles*, 58–66, 74–79.

26. Burtt, *Metaphysical Foundations of Modern Science*, 173.

opposed views that would confine mathematics to the domain of "abstracted quantity and figure" and that argued against its application to the realm of real physical processes and existents. Mathematical notions and skills were, Boyle urged, supremely useful to the physical inquiries of experimental, corpuscular, and mechanical philosophers:

> It is true, that matter, or body, is the subject of the naturalist's speculations; but if it be also true, that most, if not all the operations of the parcels of that matter (that is, of natural bodies) one upon another, depend upon those modifications, which their local motion receives from their magnitude and their figure, as the chief mechanical affections of the parts of matter; it can scarce be denied, that the knowledge of what figures are, for instance, more or less capacious, and advantaged and disadvantaged, for motion or for rest, or for penetrating or resisting penetration, or the being fastened to another, &c. must be of considerable use in explicating many of the phænomena of nature.[27]

Such 'modern' natural philosophers as Galileo and Torricelli had demonstrated that the trajectory of projectiles could be geometrically explicated. Mathematical knowledge aided the naturalist in framing and evaluating physical hypotheses. Here Boyle underlined the natural philosophical place of the debate over Copernicanism: "How without the knowledge of the doctrine of the sphere will the naturalist be able to make any sober and well grounded judgment in that grand and noble problem, which is the true system of the world?" The mathematical study of optics was essential to explicating the physical structure of the eye, just as the principles of statics were requisite to making specific gravity measurements. And Galileo's work on the pendulum was cited to show the physiological utility of the doctrine of proportions—"the soul of the mathematicks themselves."[28] Accordingly, a repertoire of geometrical and arithmetical concepts could be applied, if only by rough analogy, to the understanding of a corpuscular and mechanical universe. While the traditional sphere of application of geometry and arithmetic was to an ideal, matterless world, Boyle was one of a number of 'modern' natural philosophers who argued that the ideal geometrical world might—in some way yet to be specified—correspond to the world of real physical entities. For that reason alone, there was in principle a legitimate role for arithmetic and geometric procedures in physical studies. The experimental philosopher, it was said, might therefore legitimately be required to equip himself with a "competent," if not a "profound," knowledge of mathematics.[29]

27. Boyle, "Some Considerations Touching the Usefulness of Experimental Natural Philosophy. Second Tome," 426–27.
28. Ibid., 429–31, 433–34.
29. Ibid., 426.

Fourth, Boyle was again not alone in commending mathematics, and especially pure mathematics, as a valuable training and discipline for the mind. The theme was handed down from antiquity: for Plato the "greatest recommendation" of the theory of numbers was "that it rouses the naturally drowsy and dull, and makes him quick, retentive, and shrewd."[30] In his early ethical writings Boyle said that mathematics, along with other "Contemplatiue Sciences," "greatly conduce[d] to the Practice of Vertu." Several times he announced that he had successfully controlled his "raving" tendencies and "fix[ed]" his thoughts through "Geometricall Speculations" and "the Extractions of the Square and Cubick Roots, with those other more Difficult and laborious Operations of Arithmetick and Algebra."[31] A mind concentrated upon a rigorous and abstracted realm did not wander into unwholesome paths. In a more mature formulation Boyle noted that the "modern Algebra" was "one of the clearest exercises of reason that I ever yet met with."[32] Thus, pure mathematics was recommended not just to the service of experimental philosophy, but to educationalists and to all those concerned to set culture on a more moral and rational footing.[33]

Fifth, Boyle identified specific contributions that mathematics might make to protecting right religion and rational methods of evaluating testimony and experience. His 1681 *Discourse of Things above Reason* displayed the proper place in religious belief of matters inaccessible to human reason. It was, for example, right to believe in the existence of God and incorporeal spirits even though these are entities the nature of which we cannot comprehend. It was likewise right to believe both in human free will and in God's perfect foreknowledge, even though these two truths were, in Boyle's terminology, "unsociable," that is, "we see not how to reconcile [the one] with some other thing, that we are perswaded to be a truth."[34] There were wholly legitimate limits to the coherence and consistency that might be demanded of our body of beliefs. Even so, it was necessary to specify sufficient causes for as-

---

30. Plato, *Laws*, VI. 747b; also VII. 819c.

31. Boyle, "Doctrine of Thinking," 195; see also parallel wording in idem, "Philaretus," 17–18.

32. Boyle, "Some Considerations Touching the Usefulness of Experimental Natural Philosophy. Second Tome," 426.

33. Bacon's approval of pure mathematics as training for the mind was typical of much English (as well as Continental) humanist writing, although, as I have indicated, the courtesy literature set limits upon the depth of mathematical engrossment prudent for gentlemen: see Bacon, "Advancement of Learning," 360; cf. Descartes, "Rules for the Direction of the Mind," 5, 11, 31.

34. Boyle, "Discourse of Things above Reason," 407.

senting to that which appeared to be above reason, to have a rational warrant for a belief that seemed to conflict with reasonable belief in general or with another specific reasonable belief. These sufficient causes were of three kinds: experience, reliable testimony (including divine testimony), and mathematical demonstration.

Boyle adduced mathematical instances to display the general propriety of belief in that which the mind could not rationally conceive. We render necessary assent to the propositions that the diagonal of a square is incommensurable with its sides and that finite lengths are infinitely divisible. Yet our assent, however necessary and binding, does not imply our ability rationally to conceive how such things might be the case:

> Though mathematical demonstrations assure us, that these things are so, yet those, that have strained their brains, have not been able clearly to conceive how it should be possible, that a line (for instance) of not a quarter of an inch long should still be divisible into lesser and lesser portions, without ever coming to an end of these sub-divisions.[35]

Mathematical demonstration indeed supplied practitioners with a species of "positive proof," offering a model of obligatory assent to

> those consequences, that are clearly and legitimately inferred from any manifest acknowledged, or already demonstrated truth. To this sort [of positive proof] belong divers mathematical propositions and corollaries, which though being nakedly proposed they seem incredible to the generality of learned men, and sometimes to mathematicians themselves, are yet fully assented to, because they clearly follow from either manifested or demonstrated truths.[36]

Certain Euclidean propositions were, therefore, necessarily true—our assent to them is obligatory—even though they remained inconceivable and incomprehensible. Just as it was no derogation of the Christian religion that the truth of scriptural history could not be demonstrated, so it was not to count against mathematics that it contained inconceivability at its core.[37] Here was a domain where the legitimate production and recognition of truth did *not* require knowers' intellectual free action.

The discussion of epistemological decorum in chapter 5 dwelt upon English probabilistic appropriations and reworkings of Aristotelian

35. Ibid., 408. For the incommensurability of the diagonal, see idem, "Christian Virtuoso. Appendix to First Part," 688–89; idem, "Christian Virtuoso. Second Part," 754–55.
36. Boyle, "Discourse of Things above Reason," 456.
37. For a fine study of Bishop Berkeley's identification of, and preference for, mystery in mathematics and religion, see Cantor, "Berkeley's *The Analyst* Revisited."

views that different practices were legitimately characterized by different degrees of certainty and methods for warranting items of knowledge. Leading members of the English experimental community wholly accepted the rightness of that classification, and Boyle underscored its significance for the cultures of pure mathematics and physics: "In pure mathematicks, he, that can demonstrate well, may be sure of the truth of a conclusion, without consulting experience about it."[38] Accordingly, if the aim were uncontroverted certainty and confidence in one's knowledge, the culture of pure mathematics possessed the means to satisfy that goal. It was, in just that sense, the highest grade of knowledge.[39]

Finally, I come to an apparent usage of mathematics in Boyle's experimental practice with which everyone is familiar even if they know nothing else about Boyle's life and work. That is the use of mathematical representation to express experimentally discerned natural regularities. The eponymous 'Boyle's law,' after all, symbolically frames a relationship between the pressure and volume of gases. Here, it seems, is clear evidence for an absolutely central deployment of mathematical language in Boyle's program of experimental philosophy—the statement of a mathematically formulated law of nature which holds universally and precisely and which expresses in mathematical language the real underlying structure of the physical world.

I have now briefly pointed to a series of real or apparent Boylean uses of mathematics, of laudatory remarks about mathematics in relation to the overall culture, religion, or natural philosophy in general. I want now to focus specifically upon his experimental practice, drawing attention to the strict limits which Boyle imposed upon the deployment of mathematics in that practice. These limitations and restrictions were expressed in explicit arguments which Boyle enunciated throughout his working life. Taken together, they amount to an identification of the indecorousness of aspects of mathematics in physical inquiries and the unseemliness of mathematical expectations of precision with respect to the assessment of experimental testimony. It would, Boyle argued, be *wrong* to demand mathematical precision of genuine experimental practitioners. That epistemic judgment bound together an ontology and a practical social theory. On the one hand, sectors of physical reality might not be such as to license expectations of precision and certainty; on the other, mathematical means of communication were embedded within, and protected, an improper moral order.

38. Boyle, "Hydrostatical Paradoxes," 742.

39. For influential seventeenth-century Jesuit stress upon the certainty of mathematics, see, e.g., Dear, *Mersenne and the Learning of the Schools*, chs 3–4, esp. 37–38, 41–42, 66–70.

Did Boyle Discover 'Boyle's Law'?

Boyle did not write Boyle's law. The claim that he did not do so has an apparent character of trivial truth. He did not write down any representation of that law taking the symbolic form $P_1V_1 = P_2V_2$ (where temperature is constant), nor did he write $PV = k$, nor $P_1/P_2 = V_2/V_1$.[40] The scientific culture of the middle of the seventeenth century probably contained only three mathematically expressed laws of nature in terrestrial physics: the law of reflection (known in antiquity), Snell's and Descartes's law of refraction, and Galileo's law of free fall. All of these were expressed in geometrical rather than algebraic form.[41] That much is, perhaps, obvious: a basic historicist sensibility may legitimately draw attention to the specific forms in which historical actors represented their conceptions, even if translation from seventeenth-century to more modern language appears unproblematic. However, the historicist sensibility can be taken into more difficult terrain. When modern scientists employ Boyle's law they typically mean to note some regularities obtaining among the set of natural kinds called 'ideal gases.' Yet the natural philosophical culture Boyle and his colleagues manipulated did not contain ideal gases. The natural kinds designated 'gases,' including, for example, nitrous oxide, oxygen, and the mixture of gases referred to as 'atmospheric air,' did not come into the English natural philosopher's vocabulary until long after Boyle's time.[42] The relationship between pressure and volume noted by Boyle pertained not to the set of gases but to the unique and variable substance atmospheric air, and I shall have more to say later about prevalent early modern conceptions of what kind of thing atmospheric air was. Accordingly, any translation of what Boyle did into more modern language—whether performed by historians or by historical actors—consists not simply in modes of representation but in that which is represented, that is, a translation of *reference*. In order to explicate what significance was attached to measurements of a natural kind one

40. For historical background to Boyle's law and its transformation over time, see, e.g., Webster, "The Discovery of Boyle's Law"; Agassi, "Who Discovered Boyle's Law?"; and, for fine sensitivity to the historical referent of Boyle's work in this area, see Ravetz, *Scientific Knowledge and Its Social Problems*, 204n. Cf. A. R. Hall, *The Scientific Revolution*, 227: "[Boyle's experiment] gave quantitative results which *could be simply interpreted* to yield 'Boyle's Law' ($pv = k$)" (my emphasis).

41. E.g., Cohen, *Newtonian Revolution*, 33–34. A case might also be made for statical laws and musical rules.

42. The word *gas* was first used—albeit in an alchemically specific sense of an occult vital principle—by J. B. Van Helmont in the early seventeenth century. Its first English usage to designate any aeriform or elastic fluid dates from the late eighteenth or early nineteenth century: see, for example, Partington, "Van Helmont," 370–75; Leicester, *Historical Background of Chemistry*, 106.

has to understand how the natural kind subjected to measurement was conceived.[43]

If Boyle did not produce a mathematically formulated universal relationship between the pressure and volume of gases, what did he actually do? The procedures which generated his expressed findings were exceptional enough, both in terms of his own normal practice and that of the contemporary English natural philosophical community. He set out in 1661 to test a hypothesis about the behavior of a physical entity under artificial conditions and did so by producing and juxtaposing two sets of numbers (figure 8).[44] He had a J-shaped glass tube constructed, sealed at the top of the short arm and open at the top of the long arm. As mercury was poured in, measurements were serially taken of the increasing height of the mercury column in the long arm and that of the decreasing height of the enclosed air in the short arm. Linear measures of height stood for both the volume of the air and the weight or pressure exerted by the mercury.[45] The second right column in figure 8 is the sum (in inches) of the height of the mercury column in the long arm and the height of mercury sustained by the atmosphere, taken here to be 29½ inches.[46] The right-hand column in figure 8 is captioned (in its printed form): "What that pressure ought to be according to the *Hypothesis,* that supposes the pressures and expansions to be in reciprocal proportion." Note that no corresponding values in these two columns agreed exactly, although one reading in the following table of rarefactions did so agree.[47]

The right-hand column of this well-known table consists, therefore, of results expected on theory, and the second right column testifies to actual experimental findings. The validity of the hypothesis was to be assessed by the goodness of fit between the two columns—theory and

43. See a parallel argument with respect to Boyle and "elements" in Kuhn, *Structure of Scientific Revolutions,* 140–41.

44. Boyle was aware in 1661–1662 of relevant data by Henry Power and Richard Towneley which appeared a few years later: Power, *Experimental Philosophy* (1664), 121–30. For a similar table by Hooke, see *Micrographia* (1665), 226; and for Boyle's table of rarefaction, see his "Defence against Linus," 160.

45. For a standard account of this experiment, see, e.g., Conant, "Boyle's Experiments in Pneumatics."

46. A typographical error in the 1772 edition of Boyle's *Works* gives 22½ inches.

47. The table was printed in Boyle's "Defence against Linus," p. 158. Boyle did not say whether his table represented the results of one continuous trial or whether it was a combination or averaging of a series of trials. From my own familiarity with the circumstances of Boyle's experimental work I would speculate that this table represented work done discontinuously over a period of days or even weeks and that, insofar as the second right column combined a series of results, there was no strict protocol for doing so.

An Experimentall
Account of ȳ
Compression
of Aire.

Made by Mr. Boyle.

Inches of Aire to bee compressed			Weight of mercury to compresse that Aire			What ought to have been according to Hypothesis
48	12	29 1/8	00	29 1/8		29 1/8
46	11 1/2	29 1/8	1 3/16	30 5/16		30 3/8
44	11	29 1/8	2 8/16	31 7/16		31 5/16
42	10 1/2	29 1/8	4 3/8	33 4/16		33 1/2
40	10	29 1/8	6 3/16	35 5/16		35
38	9 1/2	29 1/8	7 7/8	37		36 15/19
36	9	29 1/8	10 7/16	39 3/8		38 7/8
34	8 1/2	29 1/8	12 8/16	41 5/8		41 2/17
32	8	29 1/8	15 1/16	44 3/16		43 11/16
30	7 1/2	29 1/8	17 15/16	47 1/16		46 3/5
28	7	29 1/8	21 3/16	50 5/16		50
26	6 1/2	29 1/8	25 3/16	54 5/16		53 10/13
24	6	29 1/8	29 11/16	58 13/16		58 2/8
23	5 3/4	29 1/8	32 3/16	61 5/16		60 18/23
22	5 1/2	29 1/8	34 15/16	64 1/16		63 6/11
21	5 1/4	29 1/8	37 15/16	67 1/16		66 4/7
20	5	29 1/8	41 9/16	70 11/16		70
19	4 3/4	29 1/8	45	74 1/8		73 11/19
18	4 1/2	29 1/8	48 12/16	77 7/8		77 2/3
17	4 1/4	29 1/8	53 11/16	82 6/16		82 2/17
16	4	29 1/8	58 2/16	87 3/16		87 3/8
15	3 3/4	29 1/8	63 15/16	93 1/16		93 1/5
14	3 1/2	29 1/8	71 5/16	100 3/16		99 6/7
13	3 1/4	29 1/8	78 11/16	107 6/16		107 7/13
12	3	29 1/8	88 7/16	117 9/16		116 3/8

29 1/8

Enterd October the [?] 1661.

Figure 8. Manuscript table (1661) of the compression of air (Boyle's law). Royal Society Register Book Original, Vol. I, p. 103. (Courtesy of Royal Society of London.)

experimental reality. While comparisons of the actual with the theoretically expected were common in astronomy (see, for example, the cometary work treated in the preceding chapter), the use of tabular forms to produce numerical comparisons in terrestrial natural philosophy was rare at the time. Galileo, we know, did systematically compare predicted and observed values, but he did not *publish* these forms.[48] Boyle did, and he presented this juxtaposition in the context of a persuasive exercise: here is an expectation, here is how matters actually turned out when put to a specific test, here is reasonable agreement—the adequate grounds for regarding the hypothesis tested as true.

With respect to Boyle's own experimental practice, such numerical comparisons were never to be repeated. They were, however, a notable feature of the way in which two of his assistants—Robert Hooke and Denis Papin—represented their work, and material in the following chapter could serve to strengthen the case that Boyle's law, as historically presented, owed much to assistants' intellectual labor. Thus, a 1680 text under Boyle's name contains a much more schematic representation of the law than the 1662 original—"The remaining space : the total space :: the first pressure : the total pressure" (that is, the ratio of the remaining space to the total space is proportional to the ratio of the first pressure to the total pressure)—as well as the diagram reproduced here as figure 9.[49] However, as the next chapter will show, it is virtually certain that this material was composed by Boyle's then paid assistant Papin. There is also a strikingly parallel instance of a contemporary theory-data table in a 1664 letter from Hooke to Boyle, in which Hooke included a table of the refractive capacities of water, brine, and oil of turpentine, systematically juxtaposing observed and hypothesized angles.[50] Although I am not concerned in the present context with reattributing authorship of Boyle's law, nothing in this discussion counts against the contention that Hooke, who was then in Boyle's employ, had substantial responsibility for the way it was represented in Boyle's text.[51]

It is quite well known that Boyle did the pertinent research and prepared the relevant table in the context of an argument he was then having over the power and scope of mechanical explanations in natural

48. Drake, "Galileo's Accuracy," 5–6.

49. Boyle, "Continuation of New Experiments. The Second Part," 512.

50. Hooke to Boyle, 29 October 1664, in Boyle, *Works*, VI, 496–97; see also Hooke, *Micrographia*, "Preface," sig. f. Hooke's version of the elasticity theory-hypothesis table is in ibid., 226.

51. See, in this connection, Centore, *Hooke's Contributions to Mechanics*, 52–60; Pugliese, "The Scientific Achievement of Hooke," esp. 146–201.

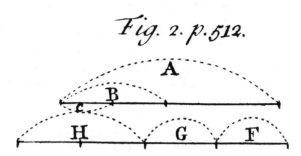

Figure 9. Schematic representation of Boyle's law, from Boyle, *Continuation of New Experiments. The Second Part* (1680, 1682), Plate 2, figure 2. *A* represents the space occupied by a certain quantity of air when the compressing force is *F*. If that force is increased by the addition of *G*, then the space occupied is reduced to *B* (which equals *A*/2. If force *H* is added, so that *F* is ¼ the total pressure *F* + *G* + *H*, the air then occupies space *C*, which is ¼ total space *A*. (Courtesy of Edinburgh University Library.)

philosophy. Shortly after the publication of Boyle's 1660 *New Experiments Physico-mechanical,* the Jesuit natural philosopher Franciscus Linus disputed Boyle's mechanical interpretations, specifically impugning the competence of the spring of the air.[52] An Aristotelian antimechanist, Linus claimed that the air's spring was not powerful enough to counterpoise a mercury column 29 inches high (that is, under normal atmospheric conditions), and that it was necessary to adduce a threadlike "funiculus" (probably composed of rarefied mercury) which pulled the column up. Boyle was moved to perform further experiments, notably including those in the specially designed J-tube, to generate pressures much greater than those obtaining in normal atmospheric conditions. He would refute Linus by showing how very much *more* powerful spring was than he had previously claimed: "So that here our adversary may plainly see, that the spring of the air, which he makes so light of, may not only be able to resist the weight of 29 inches, but in some cases of above a hundred inches of quicksilver, and that without the assistance of his Funiculus."[53] Numerical measures expressed the real power of mechanical causes in nature and of mechanical explanations in natural philosophy. They

52. Linus's criticisms are detailed in Shapin and Schaffer, *Leviathan and the Air-Pump,* 156–69.
53. Boyle, "Defence against Linus," 159.

counted as potent arguments against those who would deny mechanism.

At this point, those resistant to historicist sensibilities will probably want to point to figure 8 and argue that little 'essential' is lost in the translation from mid-seventeenth-century to present-day scientific language and what is now understood as Boyle's law. Is it not just historical pedantry to insist upon differences between the theory Boyle was testing and modern formulations? Indeed, Boyle did say that the "hypothesis" he set out to assess, and that generated the numbers in the right-hand column, was that "the greater the weight that leans upon the air, the more forcible is its endeavour of dilatation, and consequently its power of resistance."[54] And isn't that just a stylistic variant of $P_1V_1 = P_2V_2$? The programmatic defense of historicism is not my task in this book, nor do I believe that historicism is without its problems and proper limitations.[55] Historicist resistance to allowing the proposed translation can be further justified, yet for present purposes I will let it pass and concede what should elsewhere be disputed: that the modern eponymous law counts as an unproblematic translation of Boyle's "hypothesis."[56] The question remains: did Boyle conclude that experimental evidence confirmed theory, that this theory was true, that it legitimately stood as a law of nature?

Some of what Boyle wrote looks very much like an argument that evidence confirmed theory:

> Now although we deny not, but that in our table some particulars do not so exactly answer to what our formerly mentioned hypothesis might perchance invite the reader to expect; yet the variations are not so considerable, but that they may probably enough be ascribed to some such want of exactness as in such nice experiments is scarce avoidable.[57]

The table displays 'reasonable agreement' between theory and evidence; theory is confirmed; and, consequently, 'reasonable disagree-

---

54. Ibid., 156.

55. Some virtues and vices of historicism in the history of science are discussed in Shapin, "Discipline and Bounding," 352–55.

56. It would be very desirable to have a detailed study tracing changes in representation and reference of Boyle's law from the seventeenth to the twentieth century. Historicists are now highly skilled at displaying the past as different from the present, and condemning writers who conflate past and present. They might now apply the same sensibilities to understanding the ways in which *historical actors* transform past into present.

57. Boyle, "Defence against Linus," 159.

ment' or 'error' is instantiated.[58] There is an evident invitation to forget about, ignore, or let pass variation from theoretical expectation. Yet a view on the nature of that very "want of exactness" is just what permits readers to see theory being confirmed here. Boyle was offering up a model of standards of precision it was proper to expect of those performing real physical investigations.

Later sections of this chapter will treat the significance of how "want of exactness" was interpreted and, especially, its moral and ontological dimensions. For the present, however, I want to draw attention to some little-remarked passages in which Boyle himself assessed the standing of his evidentially confirmed hypothesis. As it happens, Boyle had reservations about the lawlike status of his theory: "But for all that, till further trial hath more clearly informed me, I shall not venture to determine, whether or no the intimated theory will hold universally and precisely."[59] The "further trial" Boyle alluded to was, so far as I can find out, never made, and, accordingly, Boyle never concluded that he had experimentally established a law of nature. He did not claim confirmation of a law; he did not refer to his "hypothesis" or "theory" as a law, even one whose proper entitlement to that standing was still to be determined. Peter Dear has noted that when the French philosopher Edmé Mariotte produced his version of the 'law' in 1676 his procedure was very different from Boyle's. Mariotte gives a postulate; he gives the results; he announces that it is now "sufficiently evident that one can take for a certain rule or law of nature, that air condenses in proportion to the weight by which it is loaded."[60] Dijksterhuis wrote that "Boyle did not assign to the law afterwards called 'Boyle's Law' its true significance as the first quantitative relation in the field of the physics of gases."[61] Putting the epistemic evaluation to one side, one might say that Dijksterhuis was quite right.

It might be objected here that historicism is again being taken to pedantic extremes. I must, therefore, display the nature of the reservations that Boyle himself held about his theory as a precisely and universally applicable law of nature. These include: (i) his conception of natural law and its proper status in natural philosophy; (ii) his notion of

58. Hooke's corresponding table (*Micrographia*, 226–27) displays comparable discrepancies between hypothesis and experimental measurements, as well as comparable sensibility towards 'reasonable agreement': "From [these] Experiments . . . we may safely conclude, that the Elater of the Air is reciprocal to its extension, or at least very neer."

59. Boyle, "Defence against Linus," 159.

60. Mariotte "Discours de la nature de l'air," in *Oeuvres de Mr. Mariotte* (Leiden, 1717), 152, quoted in Dear, "Miracles, Experiments, and the Ordinary Course of Nature," 668. Cf. Pascal *Physical Treatises*, 30 and note. For recent concurrence with this section's claims about Boyle's law, see MacIntosh, "Boyle's Epistemology," 109–12.

61. Dijksterhuis, *Mechanization of the World Picture*, 457.

the human and instrumental limits on experimental precision and his view of the techniques appropriate to the reporting of genuine experimental results; and (iii) his view of natural reality as the physical referent of possible precise, certain, universal, or lawlike propositions.

The Status of Natural Law

Boyle intermittently expressed uneasiness about the legitimacy within experimental natural philosophy of certain prevalent conceptions of natural law. While he acknowledged that such laws did exist, it was vital for right philosophy and right religion that they be correctly conceived. First, he cautioned against the "vulgar" notion of natural law as a "notional rule of acting according to the declared will of a superior." It was potentially dangerous as well as incorrect to say that matter obeyed natural law in the same sense that intelligent agents acted in accordance with civil law. While Boyle himself from time to time used the category of "natural law," he insisted upon a rigorous dissociation between his usage and any connotation of sentient matter:

> And if I sometimes scruple not to speak of the laws of motion and rest, that God has established among other things corporeal, and now and then, (for brevity's sake, or out of custom) to call them, as men are wont to do, the laws of nature; [I have] in due place declared, in what sense I understand and employ these expressions.[62]

Later in the same tract Boyle helped himself to that same vulgar analogy between natural and civil law, informally distinguishing between "the laws of nature, more properly so called, and the custom of nature, or, if you please, between the fundamental and general constitutions among bodily things, and the municipal laws (if I may so call them) that belong to this or that particular sort of bodies." So when water falls to the ground, as it usually does, we should refer its behavior to "the custom of nature," and when it ascends in a suction-pump, "that motion, being contrary to that which is wonted, is made in virtue of a more catholic law of nature, by which it is provided that a greater pressure . . . should surmount a lesser."[63]

While it would be unwarranted to attribute to Boyle too coherent a view of the laws of nature, it seems clear (i) that Boyle reckoned they existed as a quite fundamental set of principles of order in systems of

---

62. Boyle, "Free Inquiry," 170; see also Ruby, "Origins of Scientific 'Law.'" I have not been able to locate the systematic treatment of natural law to which Boyle here alluded. Boyle's "Excellency and Grounds of the Mechanical Hypothesis" (1674), 68–69, acknowledged that divinely instituted and upheld "rules of motion" might by custom be called "the laws of nature," but he resisted any further specification of how laws of nature might *rightly* be conceived.

63. Boyle, "Free Inquiry," 219–20.

matter and motion; (ii) that even in those rare instances when his own philosophical practice touched upon such principles—as his work on the pressure and volume of air undoubtedly did—he was reluctant to characterize an experimentally confirmed hypothesis as a law; and (iii) that he was anxious about illegitimate philosophical and theological appropriations of the notion of natural law, especially with respect to vulgar views of the capacities to be ascribed to "nature" instead of nature's Creator.[64] *Natural law* was not a term lightly to be bandied about. It was attended with technical and theological awkwardness, and, in any case, an experimental program could proceed without systematically engaging with it as a central concept.

Boyle was, however, quite comfortable with the notions of the "ordinary course of nature" and nature's "settled phenomena." That there were patterns of regularity in the natural world and that the human mind was capable of apprehending them were not in question. But whatever we were able to know about these patterns belonged to the class of contingent rather than necessary truths. This kind of knowledge was generally reliable, but it was endemically subject to inexactness and uncertainty. We ought not to claim too much for it. Investigations into real physical bodies and processes were, as I shall note, subject to instrumental and human error. However, there were other considerations which might possibly have borne upon Boyle's reluctance to advertise items as universally and precisely holding laws of nature.

Boyle acknowledged that the exactness of our knowledge of the behavior of physical bodies might be limited by the scope of divine power. If investigation of the "ordinary course of nature" was the basis of natural-law claims, then any instances of divine intervention might produce variation, not naturally but supernaturally caused. Much has rightly been written of the dominant orthodox Anglican preference for confining the age of miracles to the apostolic past. Unlike the Roman Catholic church, the Church of England had no current need for miracles, and leading Anglican theologians saw themselves in a continuing battle against popular eruptions of miracle-claims which threatened to erode their moral authority. Consequently, it is said, the issue of current miracles posed no serious problem among English natural philosophers for the constitution of natural laws while Catholic philosophers and theologians positively required the notion of natural law to generate cultural space for miracles.[65]

64. For interpretation of Boyle's *Free Inquiry* as a political response to hylozoist radical sectaries, see Jacob, *Boyle*, 159–64; idem, "Boyle's Atomism"; Shapin, "Social Uses of Science," 99–102, 134–37.

65. See in these connections McGuire, "Boyle's Conception of Nature"; Shanahan, "God and Nature in the Thought of Boyle"; Osler, "Intellectual Sources of Boyle's

It is perhaps best not to make too absolute a claim with regard to Anglican 'beliefs' about current miracles. Argumentative contexts in which the status and currency of miracles were assessed varied, and, as they varied, so did actors' professions about whether or not one might now expect to encounter miracles, who might reliably testify to miracles, and how credible miracle-testimony might be recognized and authenticated. Stillingfleet's *Origines Sacræ* (1662) is a standard source for establishing Anglican rejection of current miracles, yet that same text offered a *general* argument that God's power of creation is the same as His power to alter the course of nature. It is, Stillingfleet said, an "immutable *Law* of *Nature*" that physical things remain in their course, but this only holds until some creative power otherwise disposes things. It would be theologically improper to restrict God's power to do what He liked with the settled course of nature. It was, therefore, at most an empirical, and hence uncertain, claim that the age of miracles was past. One could be as confident of that as one was of any empirical generalization, and no more.[66]

Boyle himself explicitly addressed the relationship between miracles and physical knowledge. If the miracles attested to in Scripture were true (which they were), and if these involved a suspension or alteration of the oridinary course of nature (which they did), then there were real and general limitations upon the character and quality of our physical knowledge. From the acknowledgment of miracles it followed that "it cannot well be denied, but that physical propositions are but limited, and such as I called collected truths, being gathered from the settled phænomena of nature, and are liable to this limitation or exception, that they are true, where the irresistible power of God, or some other supernatural agent, is not interposed to alter the course of nature."[67] Generalizations about natural regularities *ought* to be expressed with that due reservation or condition, whether or not any

---

Philosophy of Nature," 185–88; Burns, *Great Debate on Miracles*, chs 2–5; and, especially, Dear, "Miracles, Experiments, and the Ordinary Course of Nature," 669–74. Dear's excellent paper quite rightly corrected (p. 675 and n. 37) an earlier impression I had apparently given (Shapin, "Boyle and Mathematics," 37–39) that *a priori* or absolute necessity was essentially attached to the notion of natural law and that the theological implications of this were the basis of Boyle's dislike. What I should have said is that Boyle opposed any notion of natural necessity, that he shared concern that *some people* were conceiving of natural laws inappropriately, and that this made the use of the concept troublesome.

66. Stillingfleet, *Origines Sacræ*, 253–56.

67. Boyle, "Discourse of Things above Reason," 462–63; see also similar sentiments in idem, "Christian Virtuoso. Appendix," 679–80; idem, "High Veneration Man's Intellect Owes to God," 140 (for criticism of Descartes's laws of motion proceeding from unwarranted stress upon divine immutability). J. J. MacIntosh ("Locke and Boyle on Miracles," 12) notes that Boyle reckoned it possible that "many apparent deviations from (accepted) laws of nature may be instances of long term regularities."

current miracle-claim bearing on the regularities was at issue. In fact, whatever the dominant tendency of Anglican thought, and whatever he said elsewhere, Boyle was on occasion emphatic in his claim that the age of miracles might *not* be past. Writing to Henry Stubbe in connection with Valentine Greatrakes's stroking cures, Boyle proclaimed that he was properly poised between credulity and skepticism:

> For my part, though I be very backward to believe any strange thing in particular, though but purely natural, unless the testimonies that recommend it be proportionable to the extraordinariness of the thing proposed; yet I remember not, that I have hitherto met with (no more than you have done) any, at least any cogent proof, that miracles were to cease with the age of the apostles.[68]

For these and other reasons, Boyle argued that it was not right to be overconfident in the quality of our knowledge of natural regularities, or to frame natural laws advertised to "hold universally and precisely."[69]

Mechanism and Mathematics

Boyle propagated a mechanical conception of nature, and he identified himself as a mechanical philosopher. This mechanism was the scheme which, historians claim, *implied* a mathematical view and which was itself implied by a mathematical investigation of nature, and I have already noted some of Boyle's in-principle arguments for the compatibility between mathematics and mechanical philosophy. Yet nowhere in Boyle's experimental practice was this merger between mechanism and mathematics realized. What was in principle possible (and, according to some writers, logically entailed) was in practice avoided. There is some oddness about Boyle's disinclination to integrate mechanism and mathematics, and not just to modern sensibilities trained to applaud the merger and to identify it as the 'essence' of the scientific revolution. First in *The Sceptical Chymist* (1661) and later in *The Origin of Forms and Qualities* (1666), Boyle elaborated a matter-theory couched in mathematical concepts. In the earlier text Boyle described the cosmogonical marriage of matter and geometry. He reckoned it "not absurd to conceive" that the original creation divided a homogeneous "universal matter" into "little particles, of several sizes and shapes, variously moved." These particles were then "associated into minute

68. Boyle to Stubbe, 9 March 1666, in Birch, "Life of Boyle," lxxvi. In this case, Boyle decided not to credit Greatrakes's cures as miracles. He assented to Stubbe's testimony of matters of fact, but not to his explication of those facts (ibid., lxxxi); see also Burns, *Great Debate on Miracles,* 51–57; MacIntosh, "Locke and Boyle on Miracles," 21.

69. A fine recent account of Boyle's voluntarism is Henry, "More versus Boyle," see esp. 66–67.

masses or clusters" differentiated by the arrangement of their constituent parts.[70] Boyle then expanded this theory, arguing that the qualities or properties of things are achieved "by virtue of the motion,
size, figure, and contrivance of their own parts." New qualities are
produced by "changing the texture [i.e., structure or arrangement] or
motion" of bodies' constituent corpuscles.[71]

No view of the material world was, it would seem, better suited to
producing physical explanations which were mathematical in form.
One could specify the shapes of different corpuscles, identify their
geometrical arrangements, quantify their states of motion. In practice,
while other mechanical philosophers sought to do just that, Boyle
never attempted any such mathematical specification. Indeed, if one
wished to claim that doing so is definitive of mechanical explanation,
then one would have to conclude that Boyle never gave a mechanical
explanation in his life. As Dijksterhuis rightly said, Boyle's was "a program for the interpretation of nature rather than the interpretation
itself. In fact, Boyle never attempts to determine what is the texture
or the mixture of particular elements . . . or compounds."[72] Boyle
intermittently gestured at a range of plausible mechanical explanations, all the while taking care not to claim that such accounts were
physically true. A late tract sought typically to display the "reconcileableness" of specific medicines (i.e., those that were effective only
in particular diseases) with corpuscularianism. Here Boyle helped himself to elaborate speculations about shape, size, texture, and states of
motion, and about how different dispositions of these might account
for acidic and alkaline properties, precipitation, organic sympathy, fer-
mentation, temperature changes, and the like. However, those speculations were never carried through or embedded within a mathematical
idiom, nor did Boyle permit them to be read as identifications of true
cause: "I did not assert, that the ways I pitched upon were the true
and genuine ones, by which the medicine does act, but only propounded them, as ways, by which it may act."[73]

This studied reluctance to push mechanical accounts into a mathe-

70. Boyle, "Sceptical Chymist," 474–75.
71. Boyle, "Origin of Forms and Qualities," 13; see also idem, "Some Considerations
Touching the Usefulness of Experimental Natural Philosophy. Second Tome," 427;
Kuhn, "Boyle and Structural Chemistry," 17–18, 21–24.
72. Dijksterhuis, *Mechanization of the World Picture*, 437 (cf. 440); see also Mandelbaum,
"Newton and Boyle and 'Transdiction,'" esp. 90, 97–99.
73. Boyle, "Reconcileableness of Specific Medicines to the Corpuscular Philosophy,"
108; see also G. W. Jones, "Boyle as Medical Man," 146–48. For relevant Boylean views
of "good" and "excellent hypotheses," see McMullin, "Conceptions of Science," 54–56.
Here the pertinent contrast is with the specificity of Cartesian philosophizing about the
shape and motion of ultimate particles, as, for example, in Descartes, "Principles of
Philosophy," Part III.

matically specific form was a pervasive feature of Boyle's practice and of the posture he recommended for the Christian virtuoso. His central concept of the air's spring was identified as a physically and culturally powerful mechanical cause, but Boyle declined, even when pressed by mechanical adversaries like Hobbes, to specify those textures or states of motion of the corpuscles that accounted for elasticity. His "business," Boyle insisted, "is not . . . to assign the adequate cause of the spring of the air, but only to manifest, that the air hath a spring, and to relate some of its effects."[74] In this way, Boyle stipulated and exemplified the terms in which experimental philosophers ought to frame accounts, while pointing out the proper limits of those accounts. Mathematical as well as physical dogmatism, pride, and pedantry were contrasted to experimental modesty. Experimental practice was shown the limits of epistemic decorum.

An exact mathematical account of the corpuscular realities beneath the appearances of physical things was deemed neither necessary to the business of experimental philosophy nor desirable for its continuance. In principle, explanations which reduced effects to "bulk, shape and motion" were to be accounted "the most satisfactory to the understanding," but at the same time Boyle warned experimentalists not to "despise" those explanations deduced from such secondary qualities as "heat, cold, weight, fluidity, hardness," and the like. The experimental philosopher, accordingly, was not only allowed but encouraged to trade in explanations which mobilized qualities expressed by unanalyzed language circulating in the public culture. There was to be a legitimate overlap between the public categories and those permissible in giving philosophical accounts. The job of deducing secondary from primary qualities in particular instances was assigned, significantly, to another community of practitioners—"speculative wits, well versed in mathematical principles."[75] Different communities terminated their explanatory chains at different conventionally agreed points, and it was right and proper that they do so.

Mathematics and Access to the Experimental Community

The mathematician might speak to other mathematicians but experimental philosophers pitched their accounts where they could speak to everyday actors. In Boyle's version, the proper language of mechanical philosophy was bound to everyday language in just the same way, and for the same reason, that a mechanical and corpuscular ontology was bound to the everyday world of sensible objects. The world upon which

74. Boyle, "New Experiments Physico-mechanical," 12; Shapin and Schaffer, *Leviathan and the Air-Pump*, 178–85.
75. Boyle, "A Proëmial Essay," 308.

the experimental philosopher was considered in principle to operate, and the world which was held to mandate his proper referential talk, was one whose basic processes and ultimate constituents were treated as *corresponding to* the everyday world of sensible medium-sized objects. Little parcels of matter, shaped as triangles, circles, and squares, arranged into patterns, moving fast and slow, banging into each other, sticking or bouncing apart—these were said in principle to be adequate accounts of the invisible world, just as they were thoroughly familiar features of everyday experience and talk about it. An experimental program which was organized around historically specific, witnessed manipulations of sensible matter, whose permissible discourse was limited to sensible matters, was taken to *refer* to an invisible world which was *like* the sensible world of machines and billiard-balls. One could and should subject the visible world to *analysis,* but the results of that analysis *resembled* the visible world from which one started.[76] That was just what, in Boyle's view, made the corpuscular and mechanical philosophy "intelligible" and what recommended it over the Scholastic doctrine of "forms." Mechanical philosophers were to operate in a visible realm, their work open to view, their discourse referring to an invisible world which was warrantably *like* the world in which they could be seen operating. They did not need to offer specific and precise accounts of the invisible makeup of particular bodies, and indeed those who did so ran the risk of subjecting the visible to the invisible, the accessible to the inaccessible, the concrete to the abstract. Intelligibility was defined by the public character of philosophical language, just as unintelligibility was identified with linguistic privacy. An intelligible philosophy was therefore bound to a civic life. To conceive the world through the languages of other communities was simultaneously to leave intelligibility and civic culture.[77]

Boyle understood mathematics to encompass an abstract, esoteric, and private form of culture. That was a major reason why he worried about its place within experimental natural philosophy. If experimental philosophy was to secure legitimacy and truth by implementing a public language, then the incorporation of mathematical culture might threaten a new privacy. In specifying that mathematics was written for mathematicians, Copernicus had only given prominent voice to widespread understandings of the place of mathematics in the overall literate culture. As Kuhn has observed, it was only the nonexperimen-

76. Mandelbaum, "Newton and Boyle and 'Transdiction.'"
77. I argue here that the civic grip of experimental natural philosophy counted as a widely shared *aspiration* among practitioners and that civic codes counted as practical solutions to local problems of order. Elsewhere, I have assessed the limited success of extending experimental philosophy into gentle culture: Shapin, "'A Scholar and a Gentleman,'" esp. 304–12.

tal mathematical sciences that were characterized, even in antiquity, "by vocabularies and techniques inaccessible to laymen and thus by bodies of literature directed exclusively to practitioners."[78] Boyle repeatedly remarked upon the relative inaccessibility of mathematics. To go on as mathematicians did was, in his view, to restrict the size of the practicing community. Such restriction risked its very capacity to produce physical truth. To be sure, mathematical culture possessed very powerful means of securing *belief* in the truth of its propositions, while the proportion of those *believers* whose assent was freely and competently given was small. In contrast, members of a properly constituted experimental community freely gave their assent on the bases of witness and the trustworthy testimony of other witnesses.

The significance Boyle attached to his densely circumstantial prose style has been noted above and treated in detail elsewhere. Boyle sought to make historically specific experimental performances vivid in readers' minds and to make it morally warrantable that these things had actually been done as, when, and where described. This type of narrative was also reckoned to be more *intelligible* than alternative styles of communication. His *Hydrostatical Paradoxes* specified that he *could have* reported findings in more stylized and mathematical form, but had *chosen* not to do so: "Those who are not used to read mathematical books, are wont to be so indisposed to apprehend things, that must be explicated by schemes [diagrams]; and I have found the generality of learned men, and even of these new philosophers, that are not skilled in mathematicks," so unacquainted with hydrostatical theorems that a more expansive and inclusive exposition was indicated. Notions of this sort could not "be thoroughly understood without such a clear explication of [these] theorems, as, to a person not versed in mathematical writings, could scarce be satisfactorily delivered in a few words." Many words had to be used. It was, Boyle confided, "out of choice, that I declin'd that close and concise way of writing." He was writing not "to credit myself, but to instruct others," and, for that reason, "I had rather geometricians should not commend the shortness of my proofs, than that those other readers, whom I chiefly designed to gratify, should not thoroughly apprehend the meaning of them."[79] The relevant contrast here was probably with the mathematical formalism of Mersenne's and Stevin's, as well as Pascal's, hydrostatics. Boyle wrote that Mersenne, "affecting brevity, hath made himself obscure; so what he writes can scarce be understood, but by mathematical persons."[80] There is evidence of Boyle's success in resisting mathematical exclu-

78. Kuhn, "Mathematical versus Experimental Traditions," 36, 39.
79. Boyle, "Hydrostatical Paradoxes," 740–41.
80. Boyle, "Medicina Hydrostatica," 473.

siveness. In 1725, Peter Shaw wrote that Boyle "endeavours to make
all the things he treats of, plain, easy, and familiar. There is no deep
knowledge in mathematics, or algebra, previously required to understand him fully."[81]

Throughout his career, Boyle insisted that his eschewal of mathematical formalism and conciseness was a matter of choice. The logical
"niceties" of Scholastic texts had the effect, Boyle said, of making it
"very difficult for any reader of but an ordinary capacity to understand
what they mean."[82] In late medical hydrostatical work, Boyle maintained that "I have not cast a treatise, about a subject wherein mechanics are so much employed, into the form of propositions, and given it
a more mathematical dress." Doing so would have run the risk of
"discouraging those many, who, when they meet with a book, or writing, wherein the titles of theorem, problem, and other terms of art,
are conspicuously placed, use to be frighted at them; and, thinking
them to be written only for mathematical readers, despair of understanding it; and therefore lay it aside, as not meant for the use of such
as they."[83] This was no *mere* concern for 'popularization,' as a modern
idiom might have it: the circulation of knowledge in public space was
deemed vital for securing its veracity and legitimacy. Languages of
exclusion were, therefore, out of place in the public forums of truth-
making.

Reason, Reality, and Experimental Precision

English experimental inquiries were supposed to investigate real physical entities and processes. Experimental testimony was supposed to
report upon the historically specific results of those investigations.[84]
Boyle led the English rejection of what are now termed 'thought experiments.' Reliable knowledge could not be secured by mere reason. Real
work had to be done if real physical knowledge was to be secured.
How did one recognize testimony as authentically arising from actually
occurring engagements between an honest experimenter and concrete
physical reality? Previous work has drawn attention to the narrative
technologies by which readers were assured of authorial sincerity.[85] I
want here to show how differing patterns of engagement with the

81. Shaw, "General Preface," i–v.
82. Boyle, "Origin of Forms and Qualities," 4–5.
83. Boyle, "Medicina Hydrostatica," 454.
84. Peter Dear's recent work is the best source for the Englishness of stress upon
experience pertaining to historically specific events, e.g., "*Totius in Verba*"; idem, "Jesuit
Mathematical Science and the Reconstitution of Experience"; idem, "Narratives, Anecdotes, and Experiments."
85. Shapin, "Pump and Circumstance"; Shapin and Schaffer, *Leviathan and the Air-
Pump*, esp. 60–79.

physical world were reckoned to produce different patterns of precision, and, accordingly, how certain kinds of variation in and among experimental testimonies could also be taken as signs that real physical inquiries had been conducted.

During the 1660s Boyle developed a strongly supported English critique of thought experiments and the culture in which such practices were accounted legitimate and valuable. His specific targets included Hobbes, Spinoza, and Pascal. None of these writers found a philosophically important place for historically specific experience and each of them, in varying ways, maintained the superiority of mathematical and logical techniques over Boyle's concrete experimental program. In 1664 the Royal Society requested Boyle to report upon a series of hydrostatical experiments communicated by Pascal. Boyle expressed skepticism that Pascal "actually made" some of the experiments he reported. He famously doubted the historical specificity of a Pascalian experiment that required "that a man should sit [fifteen or twenty feet under water] with the end of a tube leaning upon his thigh; but he neither teaches us, how a man shall be enabled to continue under water, nor how, in a great cistern full of water, twenty foot deep, the experimenter shall be able to discern the alterations, that happen to mercury, and other bodies at the bottom" (see figure 10). In Boyle's opinion, Pascal "thought he might safely set [this experimental result] down, it being very consequent to those principles of whose truth he was already persuaded." For the Frenchman it seemed to be sufficient that he had a "just confidence" that he was not "mistaken in his ratiocination." Pascal's practice thus offered a vivid example of moral and epistemic impropriety. It was the kind of thing that *would not do* in Boylean experimental philosophy. And Pascal's reports ought not to be credited as reliable testimony of real physical inquiry: "experiments, that are but speculatively true . . . may oftentimes fail in practice." What was *necessarily* true in one practice might be deemed not true at all in another.[86] One might therefore recognize merely speculative claims to truth by the precision and certainty with which they were testified. Such precision might constitute an adequate basis for discrediting them.

Considerations of epistemological decorum bore upon mathematical and logical practice, on the one hand, and real physical inquiry, on the other. Each practice embedded its proper means of securing assent, proper grade of certainty, and proper expectation of precision.

86. Boyle, "Hydrostatical Paradoxes," 745–46, 758–59; Pascal, *Physical Treatises*, 20–21. For modern treatment of these passages, see, e.g., Kuhn, "Mathematical versus Experimental Traditions," 44–45; Koyré, "Pascal Savant," 148–52; and, especially, Dear, "Miracles, Experiments, and the Ordinary Course of Nature," 675–76; cf. Naylor, "Galileo's Experimental Discourse," 124–27.

Figure 10. Depiction of Pascalian hydrostatic experiment about whose actual performance Boyle expressed pointed skepticism. From Pascal, *Traitez de l'equilibre* (1663), figure 17. (By permission of the Syndics of Cambridge University Library.)

Each had legitimacy within its own domain. It was, however, both wrong and unseemly to intrude the one upon the other or to misrepresent the one as the other. Reliable knowledge of real physical bodies and processes was to be secured by experimental inquiry, not by mathematical speculation. The mathematician's "just confidence" was unwarranted within experimental practice. One could not, and ought not, expect of real physical experiment what one might legitimately expect of geometry or logic.

The relative seemliness of mathematical versus experimental procedures and expectations flowed from their respective engagements with the material world. It was undeniably *possible* to conceive the world abstractly, to construct idealizations of the world, and then to construct mathematical representations of such abstractions and idealizations. It was also possible to interrogate the world of physical particulars. One might expect great certainty and precision of the former, but greater physical truth of the latter. It was, Boyle said, the "privilege and glory [of] mathematical writers" to "affirm nothing, but what they can prove by no less than demonstration." Yet such mathematicians were apt to err when they moved from their abstract domain to the world of physical particulars:

> The certainty and accurateness, which is attributed to what they deliver, must be restrained to what they teach concerning those purely mathematical disciplines, arithmetic and geometry, where the affections of quantity are abstractedly considered: but we must not expect from mathematicians the same accurateness, when they deliver observations concerning such things, wherein, it is not only quantity and figure, but matter and its other affections that must be considered.[87]

This is, of course, an Aristotelian theme: the *Metaphysics* noted that "the minute accuracy of mathematics is not to be demanded in all cases, but only in the case of things which have no matter."[88] And the Aristotelian Simplicio of Galileo's *Dialogue Concerning the Two Chief World Systems* claimed that "in physical matters one need not always require a mathematical demonstration"; "these mathematical subtleties do very well in the abstract, but they do not work out when applied to sensible and physical matter."[89]

Boyle recognized that some of his readers "will not like, that I should offer for proofs such physical experiments, as do not always demonstrate the things, they would evince, with a mathematical certainty and accurateness." Yet he insisted that "in physical enquiries it is often sufficient, that our determinations come very near the matter, though they fall short of a mathematical exactness." Mathematicians might well view such imprecise reports as faulty—"not positive and determinate enough to be employed about matters, to which mathematical demonstrations are thought applicable."[90] But such reports were not for that reason defective, only seeming so to those who presumed a different experiential warrant for them than the one proper to experimental practice.

How should the imprecision of genuine experimental testimony be

87. Boyle, "Two Essays, Concerning the Unsuccessfulness of Experiments" (1661), 347; cf. A. R. Hall, *The Scientific Revolution,* 224–34, for an argument that the application of mathematical analysis to physics was limited by "purely mathematical difficulties," by "the nature of mathematics itself."

88. Aristotle, *Metaphysics,* II. 995ª 15–16.

89. Galileo, *Dialogue Concerning Two Chief World Systems* (1632), 14, 203; see also Koyré, "Galileo and Plato," 37.

90. Boyle, "Hydrostatical Paradoxes," 741.

accounted for? First, real experimental measurements were *contingently* imprecise because of the inadequacies of currently available measuring instruments. Actual, as opposed to ideal, experiments were endemically liable to instrument-caused variations. In late work on mineral waters, Boyle sought very precise specific-gravity measurements, freely acknowledging that instruments adequate to this task were extremely hard to come by. Practitioners were warned that legitimate confidence in such measurements was limited by the accuracy of which the instruments were capable.[91] In a similar experimental context, Boyle said that he did not "pretend (and indeed it is not necessary) that the proportion, obtainable by our method, should have a mathematical preciseness. For in experiments where we are to deal with gross matter, and to employ about it mathematical instruments, it is sufficient to have a physical, and almost impossible to obtain (unless sometimes by accident) a mathematical exactness."[92] Boyle did seek precision and his reports circulated within cultures that valued precise measurements. Yet the very contingent inexactness that Boyle worked to reduce was turned into a resource for securing credibility for specific claims and legitimacy for the experimental enterprise. Once practitioners recognized what degrees of precision were actually appropriate, they would not expect from physical inquiry what was unreasonable, and they would be able properly to target skepticism. Reports of measurements which concurred—externally, with theoretical expectation, or, internally, with reiterations of the same sort of measurement—*too* much or which were *too* exact might rightly be suspected. Contrarily, one should not rush to reject metrological testimony which deviated somewhat from expectation. Instrumental imperfections might offer a warrantable excuse for failure and for what was to count as 'reasonable agreement' between expectation and outcome. A degree of imprecision might be pointed to as a moral voucher that real physical inquiries had been performed and reported by honest practitioners. Reasonable agreement, and permissible imprecision, were not defined; they were instantiated in the practice of a competent and trustworthy source.

There was a second major reason why the mathematician's precision was not to be expected from real physical inquiries. The physical materials upon which the experimentalist operated might be, indeed typically were, heterogeneous and impure. For Boyle and other experimentalists, both the natural impurity of chemical materials and their intentional adulteration (or "sophistication") were endemic troubles in experimental performance and communication. These were im-

91. Boyle, "Short Memoirs for the Natural Experimental History of Mineral Waters," 810; see also idem, "General History of the Air," 652–53.
92. Boyle, "Medicina Hydrostatica," 480.

mensely important practical as well as philosophical problems. How could one know that chemical materials were what they were supposed to be? That they were pure? And, if impure, what their actual composition was? So far as the experimental program was concerned, impurity might, on the one hand, account for variation and imprecision in experimental results, and, on the other, excuse and explain away apparent failures of replication. How could replicators know that they had repeated 'the same' experiment, that their results were properly comparable with those of others, if they could not be sure that they had employed 'the same' materials?[93]

Moreover, much of the point of Boyle's later work on specific gravities was supplied by a constituency for *independent* means of determining the purity of substances, free from reliance upon the dubious testimony of those who supplied them. Here the elaboration of metrological technique might follow the power relations of English imperialism. Boyle noted that once a man had determined "the true specific gravity" of a sample of gold, that number might be used as "a standard, with relation to which he may make his estimates of the fineness of other parcels of . . . gold, that he is concerned to buy or to examine." Hydrostatic technique could discipline savage testimony:

> And, by this means, he may oftentimes prevent that chief fraud of the negroes, whereof several traders to the golden coast are not a little apprehensive, as being in danger to be much damnified by it. For they complain, that though the blacks be, otherwise, for the most part, but a dull sort of people; yet they have often made a shift to cheat the traders, by clandestinely mixing with the right sand-gold, filings of copper, or rather of brass, whose colour do so resemble that of gold, that the fraud is not easily discerned.[94]

The numerical reading of a set of scales would expose and control the mendacity of blacks.

Impurity was, therefore, quite an important reason why investigations into real physical entities might yield imprecise and varying results, why there might be less-than-perfect fit between theoretical expectations and experimental outcomes. Yet it was not the most fundamental reason Boyle advanced for rejecting mathematical exact-

---

93. For Boyle's views of the problems attending "sophisticated" and variable materials, see, e.g., idem, "Two Essays, Concerning the Unsuccessfulness of Experiments," 319–33; and for a practical use of such variation to account for failure to replicate, see, e.g., Francisco Travagino to Oldenburg, 11 October 1675, in Oldenburg, *Correspondence*, XII, 10.

94. Boyle, "Previous Hydrostatical Way of Estimating Ores," 498–99; cf. idem, "Two Essays, Concerning the Unsuccessfulness of Experiments," 322–23.

ness as a legitimate anticipation in physical inquiries. At issue here, in Koyré's words, was no less than "the structure of science, and therefore the structure of Being."[95] Boyle reckoned that substances about whose purity and identity one was otherwise justifiably satisfied might and did vary in their physical properties.[96] For this reason, measurements made upon them were *inherently* likely to be varying and imprecise. Here it was not our instruments' fault, nor the fault of human frailties, nor even, in a strict sense, the fault of the complexities of real physical situations which accounted for experimental inexactness. Imprecision was construed as a feature of competent and accurate reports about natural kinds *as they actually were*. A reality so structured was one that spoke against the propriety of mathematical canons of precision and exactness.

Boyle shared with many other practitioners the view that such substances as air and water varied in their physical properties from one time and place to another. Though the ancients considered air as an element, nevertheless Aristotle described the array of "exhalations" received by the atmosphere, and the Hippocratic corpus vividly described variations in atmospheric *airs*.[97] Galileo parenthetically noted that the air was "a mixture of various terrestrial vapors and exhalations."[98] William Gilbert wrote that "air is but exhalation and the effluvium of the earth given out in every direction."[99] Bacon's *History of the Winds* collected evidence that the air contained effluvia from the bowels of the earth, and that different winds bore differently constituted air. Following Aristotle, Bacon understood earthquakes as violent releases into the atmosphere of noxious subterranean airs.[100] The Somerset virtuoso John Beale told Samuel Hartlib that he had "long conceived this ambient air to consist of as many & different ingredients, as our earth and seas."[101] Henry Stubbe picked out the heterogeneity of the air as a potential trouble for Boyle's pneumatic researches, while

95. Koyré, "Galileo and Plato," 37.

96. This was very briefly noted some time ago by Marie Boas Hall (*Boyle and Seventeenth-Century Chemistry*, 216), though she judged this an "unfortunate conviction," a defect in Boyle's otherwise praiseworthy experimental practice.

97. E.g., [Pseudo-]Aristotle, *On the Universe*, 394^a 8–22; idem, *Problems*, I. 862^a 3–9.

98. Galileo, *Dialogue Concerning Two Chief World Systems*, 142.

99. Gilbert, *De Magnete*, 338.

100. Bacon, "History of the Winds," e.g. 158–62; Aristotle, *Meteorology*, II. 365^b 23–24, 366^b 14–21. Yet Bacon also insisted (presumably gesturing at some notion of 'pure air') that "water and air are very homogeneous bodies": "History of the Winds," 168.

101. Beale to Hartlib, *ca.* August 1661, quoted in Hartlib to John Worthington, 26 August 1661, in Worthington, *Diary and Correspondence*, I, 368. Beale went on in this letter to praise Boyle's *New Experiments Physico-mechanical*.

Boyle's colleague Robert Hooke treated the varying constitution of the
air at length in the context of his work on earthquakes and refraction.[102] Early modern medical men were skilled in linking the momentarily varying makeup of the air to individual or epidemic disease.

For Boyle atmospheric (or common) air was *inter alia* the referent
of his work on the relationship between pressure and volume. Boyle
studied air experimentally from the late 1650s until the end of his life.
Throughout, he took pains to say what kind of body he considered air
to be and to set his conception against those of other practitioners:
"By air I understand not, (as the Peripateticks are wont to do) a mere
elementary body. . . . There is scarce a more heterogeneous body in
the world." The air was "that great receptacle or rendesvous of celestial
and terrestrial effluviums," of "innumerable seminal corpuscles, and
other analogous particles." "Steams" and "exhalations" fed into the air
from the bowels of the earth; "emanations" from the sun and planets
very probably enriched the atmospheric stew from above.[103] When
Boyle addressed the matter systematically, he said that it was "not improbable" that this "great rendesvous" of common or atmospheric air
contained three general sorts of corpuscles: the first consisted of a
great variety of particles thrown up by earthy exhalations; the second
consisted of more subtle species making up "the magnetical steams of
our terrestrial globe" or emitted in the form of light by the sun, stars,
and other celestial bodies; and the third, properly deserving the name
of air, he referred to variously as "pure," "true," or "perennial air."[104]
To be sure, he never reckoned that he had held a sample of pure air
in his hands, nor did he ever seek to isolate such a thing. Nevertheless,
it was this pure air to which he uniquely ascribed the property of
spring: "I have not observed any one attribute, that I think to be so
much the property of air, and so fit to distinguish its true particles
from aqueous vapours, earthy exhalations, and the effluvia of other
bodies, as a durable elasticity or springiness."[105] The properties of pure
air were theorized, while the experimentally manifested properties of

102. Stubbe, *Legends No Histories*, 8, 162; Hooke, "Discourse of Earthquakes," 363–70,
428–33; idem, *Micrographia*, 219; see also Birch, *History of the Royal Society*, III, 365,
370–71.

103. Boyle, "Suspicions about Some Hidden Qualities in the Air," 85, 91, 95; see also
idem, "Examen of Hobbes," 196; idem, "General History of the Air," 612–15. For
disputes between Boyle and Hobbes dealing with the constitution of the air, see Shapin
and Schaffer, *Leviathan and the Air-Pump*, 178–85; for the astrological context of Boyle's
views on air, see Curry, *Prophecy and Power*, 62–63, 148.

104. Boyle's most extensive account of the composition of common air was "General
History of the Air," 613–14.

105. Ibid., 618; see also Boyle, "New Experiments Touching Cold," 545; idem, "Suspicions about Some Hidden Qualities in the Air," 90.

the substance contained in Boyle's air-pump and J-tube were, in Boylean usage, matters of fact.

Experimental investigations were conducted not with "pure" but with "common air." Its precise constitution at any given time and place depended upon the effluvia it was receiving from the earth and celestial bodies, and, correspondingly, its physical properties, including its elasticity, varied according to its momentary makeup. So, while Boyle accounted it probable that it was to the properties of pure air that "most of the phænomena of our engine, and many other pneumatical experiments seem to be due," he was also content to acknowledge that imprecision and variation in such physical investigations might proceed from the variation in the real physical substance contained in his pumps and tubes.[106] As early as 1660, for example, Boyle speculated that discrepancies in experimental results emerging from France and Italy, as opposed to England, might be due to the relative "grossness" of English air.[107] Thus, when Boyle said that he was unwilling to determine whether his theory about the pressure and volume of air "will hold universally and precisely," he was pointing not just to experimental error but to correct canons of experimental exactness *when reliably brought to bear upon the world of real matter.*

It was only to be expected that different samples of common air would exhibit different elasticities. Mixtures, of their nature, did not manifest the pure properties of individual constituents. Perhaps, it might be thought, a sample of the pure air (which Boyle did not consider was ever contained in any of his tubes) would have yielded experimental results of the homogeneity and precision allowing Boyle to announce a law of nature holding "universally and precisely." These are speculations. Boyle repeatedly expressed his satisfaction that a program of real experimentation should operate upon substances as uncontrollably heterogeneous as common air. Moreover, he identified a certain sort of imprecision as a moral voucher that sincerely testifying experimenters had conducted real investigations of real matter in all its concrete particularities. Here Boyle's sensibility has important modern echoes. In the early years of the twentieth century, Pierre Duhem expressed skepticism about the reference of the laws of physics:

> Let us take one of these laws, Mariotte's law [English translator's note: [Boyle's law]. . . . At a constant temperature, the volumes occupied by a constant mass of gas are in inverse ratio to the pressures they

106. Boyle, "General History of the Air," 614.
107. Boyle, "New Experiments Physico-mechanical," 38. Boyle's formulas for managing variation in experimental testimony appealed to the Yorkshire natural philosopher Henry Power, who also recognized that French air was "more thin and hot then ours": Power, *Experimental Philosophy* (1664), 94.

support. . . . Let us put ourselves in front of a real, concrete gas to which we wish to apply Mariotte's law; we shall not be dealing with a certain concrete temperature embodying the general idea of temperature, but with some more or less warm gas; we shall not be facing a certain particular pressure embodying the general idea of pressure, but a certain pump on which a weight is brought to bear in a certain manner.[108]

Boyle insisted upon the supremacy of the concrete and particular over the abstract and the general, even to the extent of sacrificing the experimental identification of a 'law of nature.'[109]

Yet the ontological warrant for expectations of experimental variation and imprecision was even more fundamental than the case of atmospheric air suggests. Towards the end of his life Boyle worked up methods for determining with great accuracy the specific gravities of a wide range of substances. Here he encountered practical problems in securing the same results when using various samples of given substances. In measuring the specific gravity of rock crystal (which he made into something of a standard), Boyle got differing values. He concluded that "it was not improbable, that different pieces of rockcrystal itself, though of equal bulk, may not be precisely equal in ponderosity." Lodestones from different countries also differed in their specific gravities; "Spanish mercury," which is "counted the richest," differed from "common quicksilver"; and Boyle "did not find that all running mercuries, *though they did not appear adulterated,* to be precisely the same weight."[110]

A related tract assembled a large number of specific gravity values in tabular form (excerpted in table 1). For some substances Boyle gave a range of numerical results. Thus, the table contains four specific gravity values for bezoar stone (a medically useful calculus found in the guts of ruminants), three for lapis manati (probably a stone associated with the cetacean), three for marcasites (copper or iron pyrites), and two for talc. In some cases it is evident that Boyle ascribed such differences in physical properties to impurity: that indeed was what

108. Duhem, *Aim and Structure of Physical Theory* (1906), 166.

109. See discussion of the abstract and concrete in the construal of natural laws in Cartwright, *Nature's Capacities and Their Measurement,* esp. ch. 5. Cartwright's work is vital to the historical understanding of the practices and references of scientific laws. I do not engage with her important work here because I mean to insist upon Boyle's explicit reservations about natural law. Nevertheless, her Aristotelian sensibility towards "capacities" as the reference of natural laws is potentially directly applicable to Boyle's work on spring and its manifestation.

110. Boyle, "Medicina Hydrostatica," 467–68 (emphasis added); see also idem, "Two Essays, Concerning the Unsuccessfulness of Experiments" (1661), 322–27, for early recognition of variation between samples of such common substances as gold, lead, tin, antimony, talc, vitriol, common salt, and saltpeter.

Table 1
Excerpt from table of specific gravities, in Boyle,
A Previous Hydrostatical Way of Estimating Ores (1690),
pp. 505–07

Substance	Specific Gravity
Bezoar-stone	1.48
A piece of the same	1.64
A fine oriental one	1.53
Another	1.34
Lapis manati	2.86
Another of the same	2.29
Another from Jamaica	2.27
Marcasites	4.45
Another from Stalbridge	4.5
Another more shining than ordinary	4.78
Talc { Venetian	2.73
Jamaican	3

recommended hydrostatical methods to practitioners concerned to establish the richness of ores or to decide whether materials proffered for sale had been adulterated. Yet in other instances variation in the physical property of weight (or the relative weight inscribed in specific gravity) was *not* taken as a measure of impurity but was ascribed to natural variation in what were *rightly* called 'the same' substances. Imprecision and variation in measured qualities were here construed as the right outcome of metrological techniques reliably brought to bear upon a particularistic physical reality. Boyle made this plain in commenting upon discrepancies between his values and those obtained by other competent and sincere practitioners. Such variation may "very probably be imputed to that variety of texture and compactness, that may be found in several bodies *of the same kind of denomination, neither nature nor art being wont to give all the productions, that bear the same name, a mathematical preciseness, either in gravity or in other qualities.*"[111]

Boyle here fell in with Baconian attitudes towards measurement and the physical world of things to be measured. Bacon had studied the relative density of substances, producing a numerical table of relative weights (taking pure gold as a standard), and, while the table did not

111. Boyle, "Previous Hydrostatical Way of Estimating Ores," 505 (emphasis added). For Boyle's manuscript notes on these measurements, see Boyle Papers, Vol. 189, ff. 151–52. Boyle did not evidently consider that *all* substances manifested such variation, only that *many* did so, and the full table of specific gravities printed in this text shows variation as pervasive.

register varying values for 'the same' substances, Bacon made it plain that such variation, and resulting imprecision of measurements, were wholly to be expected:

> No doubt but many of the bodies set down in the Table admit of more or less, as to gravity and bulk, in their own species. . . . Therefore with respect to nice calculation there is some uncertainty. And moreover those individuals with which my experiment deals may not represent exactly the nature of their species, nor perhaps agree to a nicety with the experiments of others.[112]

Boyle was well aware of this work, one of his commonplace books noting with evident approval Bacon's views on the limits to mathematical precision in physical inquiries.[113] Neither Bacon nor Boyle elaborated detailed theories of matter, nor is it clear what ontology Bacon gestured at when referring to "the nature of their species," nor, indeed, what views informed Boyle's invocation of the varying "texture and compactness" to be found in "bodies of the same kind." Nevertheless, both Bacon and Boyle evidently belong within a long tradition of nominalist sentiment about the relationship between ontology and cultural classifications.[114] Both philosophers set themselves against tendencies towards abstraction and idealization associated, on the one hand, with mathematical practice, and, on the other, with Scholastic doctrines of forms: "In nature nothing really exists beside individual bodies."[115] Bacon had also expressed general approval of mixed mathematical practices and of diligent measurement in the new philosophy, while eschewing mathematical idealization and making sure that a proper ontology submitted itself to the discipline of physics rather than of mathematics:

> So highly did the ancients esteem the power of figures and numbers, that . . . Pythagoras asserted that the nature of things consisted of numbers. In the meantime it is true that of all natural forms (such as I understand them) Quantity is the most abstracted and separable from matter; which has likewise been the cause why it has been more carefully laboured and more acutely inquired into than any of the other forms, which are more immersed in matter. For it [is] plainly the nature of the human mind, certainly to the extreme prejudice of

112. Bacon, "History of Dense and Rare," 343 (table at pp. 341–42). For a summary of the metaphysical context of this work, see Urbach, *Bacon's Philosophy of Science*, 79–81, 139–40.

113. Boyle Papers, Vol. 189, ff. 3–4.

114. See here, especially, McGuire, "Boyle's Conception of Nature," and, for an interpretation of Bacon's undeveloped notions of matter, see Rees, "Bacon's Semi-Paracelsian Cosmology," esp. 168–71.

115. Bacon, "New Organon," 120.

knowledge, to delight in the open plains (as it were) of generalities rather than in the woods and inclosures of particulars.

Just because of mathematicians' "daintiness and pride" and their insistence upon abstraction, idealization, and absolute certainty, mathematics might be allowed a valued auxiliary role in philosophy but must never be permitted to "domineer over Physic."[116] Mathematical expectations, canons, and forms of discourse were judged unseemly within the conversation of an experimental community. These were sentiments which Boyle endorsed and extended.

The Voice of Conversation in the Practice of Precision

In treating the precision and certainty legitimately to be expected of experimental inquiries, I have dealt with responses to a number of apparently distinct questions: What were the inspectable characteristics of competent and sincere testimony deriving from real physical investigations? With what precision and certainty ought experimentalists to present their testimony? With what expectations of precision and certainty ought experimentalists to evaluate others' testimony? What was the world like such that testimony offered with particular degrees of precision and certainty might be taken as reliable accounts of it? These questions were not, however, discrete in practice: in order to answer one, practitioners had to be satisfied about answers to others. One is dealing here, as with the maxims discussed in chapter 5, with a cultural *system.* Practitioners knew that certain kinds of imprecision might be taken as signs of reliable testimony about the world only insofar as they took a view about what the world was like, while their evidence about what the world was like derived from the testimony of investigators recognized as competent and sincere. Note also how the naturalistic and the normative were systematically bound together. Practitioners recognized others as honest and competent, and they told each other how they ought to behave, only in respect of a shared view of the world which they investigated. Experimental culture shared norms insofar as its members shared a view of reality. It was this ontology which was the ultimate sanction on members' conduct. If you are a genuine investigator of the natural world, then *this* is how your reports ought to look and *this* is the epistemic status you ought to claim for them.

Reality is a potent normative resource, and its normativity becomes invisible as such. That is the condition of its power. Reality cannot serve its justificatory function unless the relevant culture recognizes

116. Bacon, "Advancement of Learning," 369–70; cf. idem, "Preparative towards a Natural and Experimental History," 259. For an informed, if historically unconvincing, philosophical attempt to 'save' Bacon from the judgment that he "undervalued" mathematics, see Urbach, *Bacon's Philosophy of Science,* 134–43.

it as separate from, and set above, the behavior of those who report about it and constitute our knowledge of it. That is why, as I noted at the outset of this book, there is such intense resistance to the very idea of a social history or sociology of truth. But consider the judgments of the historical actors involved in these passages. They too recruited reality as the ultimate sanction upon investigators' behavior, yet they had to judge, among alternative accounts of reality, the nature of the reality relevant to specific interventions and inquiries. It was no part of Boyle's case, for example, that mathematical certainty and precision were globally impossible or illegitimate. Mathematical idealizations *might* be constructed, and operations upon such constructs *might* be conducted. It was, therefore, entirely possible to *abstract* from nature qualities whose cultural manipulation might yield the certainty and precision which were the subject of mathematicians' "daintiness and pride." Boyle evidently never doubted that such moves and expectations were possible. What he claimed was that they might be *improper* and *out of place* within a practice which expected of members a different posture *vis-à-vis* the world-to-be-known-and-reported-about and *vis-à-vis* each other. If, in the context of mathematical practice, absolute certainty and precision were the goals of inquiry, in experimental practice they presented themselves as potential troubles for the development and continuance of an investigative *conversation*.

Previous chapters dwelt upon early modern appreciations of the practice known as civil conversation. Thus construed, conversation was the assemblage of means by which people lived with each other, and by which they ensured that they might continue to do so. The goal of conversation was not understood as instrumental, save in the sense that the maintenance of public discourse, and one's continuing participation in it, offered members the possibility of future instrumental actions in which they might require the assistance of others. Knowledge, of course, figured in the practice of conversation, as did judgments of the legitimate content and character of knowledge. Yet a consequential distinction was commonly made between the scholar's goal of rigorously attaining and securing formal knowledge and the gentleman's more disengaged and pragmatic attitude towards the truth and certainty of knowledge. Courtesy texts, as I have indicated, continually urged gentlemen not to be too dictatorial, proud, or demanding in their claims to knowledge. To require very great rigor, precision, and certainty might be to put too great a strain upon conversation; it was to endanger its continuance. Certain conceptions of truth and precision were not worth that price. They ought to be civically bounded.

Several twentieth-century commentators have resurrected early modern appreciations of the conversational mode and the implied dis-

tinction between conversation and inquiry, and chapter 3 introduced
Niklas Luhmann's contrast between early modern conversation and a
Cartesian conception of scientific inquiry. Among Anglo-American
moral philosophers, the most powerful spokesman for the "voice of
conversation" in cultural practice has been Michael Oakeshott. For
Oakeshott, the practice of conversation was to be highly valued; it was
to be seen as constitutive of the civic condition; and its conduct was to
be juxtaposed to that of "inquiry," and, particularly, of logical and
scientific inquiry: "In a conversation the participants are not engaged
in an inquiry or a debate; there is no 'truth' to be discovered, no
proposition to be proved, no conclusion sought."[117] Chapter 5 noted
Locke's acceptance that the world of everyday life was a realm of practical reasoning, to be distinguished from that of science and philosophy,
and even Descartes acknowledged that philosophical canons of truth
and reason stopped at the threshold of practical affairs.[118] There is
much historical evidence to support a contrast between scientific or
philosophical inquiry and civil conversation *as a significant actors' distinction*. Oakeshott's views of science are important and subtle, yet I draw
attention to his conception of conversation precisely to argue that it is
most useful not as a *contrast* with science but as a way of illuminating
the nature of scientific practice.

Boyle's attitudes towards mathematical rigor and precision offer unusually perspicuous materials in this connection. Mathematical expectations and practices were seen as potential troubles for the conversation of experimental philosophers. Within this practice, the way that
mathematicians customarily went on was both morally and epistemically wrong. If the reliability of experimental practice was seen to be
founded upon the free action of its testifying members, then mathematical canons of proof and demonstration threatened to bind assent
in iron chains of logic. If the progress of experimental philosophy was
seen to proceed from the growth of the experimental community and
the multiplication of experimental actors, then mathematical language
was exclusive and restrictive. Experimental practice might use elements
of everyday language, while mathematical language was accessible only
to mathematicians. Moreover, mathematical expectations of precision
identified variation in testimony as a potential civic disaster.

Take three measurements of the specific gravity of talc, none agree-

117. Oakeshott, "Voice of Poetry in the Conversation of Mankind" (1959), 198. Oakeshott's views of conversation are now perhaps best known (though not best represented)
through Richard Rorty's argument that philosophy is properly to be regarded as a
conversational activity: Rorty, *Philosophy and the Mirror of Nature*, esp. 389–94; see also
Franco, *Political Philosophy of Oakeshott*, esp. 133–34; Grant, *Oakeshott*, 65–70.
118. Descartes, "Principles of Philosophy," 219–20.

ing exactly with the others. What resources were available to account for this variation? For the mathematician, there were instrumental error, impurity, incompetence, and insincerity. The first three might be morally consequential within a culture that highly valued skill; the last was morally consequential in general. Needless to say, even within mathematical practice there were moral techniques by which variation in testimony might be innocuously accounted for and repaired. Yet the risk of dispute, division, and disaster was always considerable. For the experimentalist of Baconian or Boylean persuasion, however, there was a far more powerful resource available to ensure that variation in testimony—even within a practice that sought and valued precision— did not have to precipitate civic disaster. Varying testimonies might be, locally and within conventionally agreed limits, equally competent and sincere *because that was what this bit of the world was like.*

In Oakeshott's terms, then, Boylean specific-gravity measurements smack not of scientific inquiry but of civil conversation. Yet that is not the conclusion I want to support. Boyle's program was undoubtedly scientific inquiry. Its stipulated goal was knowledge; indeed it sought knowledge of great precision, valued for itself. But that knowledge could not be secured and extended if the community of inquirers could not itself be sustained, if its members could not count upon others' trustworthiness, reliability, and assistance in future actions. In other words, Boyle's precision-science had the characteristics of conversation as well as of inquiry. Its conversational character was what enabled it to seek the precision-knowledge it aimed at and to recognize when *sufficient precision* had been attained. There is no doubt that there were, and, of course, are, scientific practices discontented with Boylean canons of precision and committed to far stricter standards of exactness and certainty.[119] I will resist the temptation here specifically to extend this sensibility to more modern practices aiming at great precision.[120] But I will not resist the temptation to speculate that *every* practice, however committed to the production of precise and rigorous truth about the world, possesses institutionalized means of telling members when 'reasonable agreement' or 'adequate precision' has been achieved, when 'enough is enough,' when to 'let it pass,' when to invoke idiopathic 'error factors' and not to inquire too diligently into the

119. Indeed, Shapin and Schaffer, *Leviathan and the Air-Pump*, is a study of the confrontation with Hobbesian conceptions of certainty and precision.

120. But see in these connections Beller, "Experimental Accuracy, Operationalism, and Limits of Knowledge"; Ben-Menahem, "Models of Science"; Olesko, *Physics as a Calling*, chs 7–10; and, especially, Schaffer, "Astronomers Mark Time"; idem, "Measuring Virtue"; idem, "Accurate Measurement"; idem, "Late Victorian Metrology."

sources of variation in testimony.[121] The toleration of a degree of moral uncertainty is a condition for the collective production of *any future moral certainty*. This toleration allows truth-producing conversations to be continued tomorrow, by a community of practitioners able and willing to work with and to rely upon each other.

121. For suggestive examples of the treatment of endemic uncertainty in modern physical science, see Pinch, "The Sun-Set: The Presentation of Certainty in Scientific Life," esp. 138–45; cf. Sir Karl Popper's modern endorsement (*Unended Quest,* 24) of epistemological decorum: "One should never try to be more precise than the problem situation demands."

CHAPTER EIGHT

Invisible Technicians:
Masters, Servants, and the Making
of Experimental Knowledge

Great persons must necessarily hear and see with other mens ears and eyes;
and whom can they trust so well as their own servants?

—Obadiah Walker, *Of Education*

In 1680, Robert Boyle published the *Second Part* of his *Continuation of
New Experiments Physico-mechanical, Touching the Spring and Weight of the
Air*. This text was an extension of a series of experimental narratives
concerning the physical, chemical, and physiological properties of the
air, commenced in 1660 and continued in 1669. Like earlier members
of the set, the second part was a *seriatim* narrative of a large number
of experiments performed in a version of the air-pump which Boyle
and Hooke had originally devised in the late 1650s: "a loose heap (or
rather chaos) of particulars belonging to the air."[1] The 1680 text was,
however, more utilitarian in focus, being largely concerned with processes of organic decay *in vacuo*: examinations into the rate at which
various foods putrefied in an exhausted air-pump, and attempts to
develop a gauge reliably measuring the extent of evacuation. Interpretative glosses and theoretical extensions of experimental findings
were even more sparse than in the earlier members of the series: the
spring and weight of the air were here treated as securely established
matters of fact.

Despite these differences from previous publications, the 1680 text
was a wholly unremarkable articulation of conceptual and technical
innovation achieved earlier—late Restoration 'applied' as well as 'normal science.' Nevertheless, there is something quite unusual about how

---

1. Boyle, "Continuation of New Experiments. The Second Part," 508. Unusually for
Boyle, the text was printed first in Latin, and then, two years later, in English (see note
5 below).

this text was presented. According to Boyle's preface, the experimental work upon which this tract reported was mainly done by a remunerated technician whom he named as Denis Papin.[2] The air-pump with which the experiments were performed was, Boyle said, of Papin's own design, one which differed materially from those Boyle previously employed.[3] "I gave him," Boyle announced, "the freedom to use his own [pump], because he best knew how to ply it alone, and . . . how to repair it more easily."[4] Moreover, the measurement and registration of experimentally produced phenomena were given over to the technician's charge: "The calculation of the degrees of the rarefaction and condensation of the air, included in our mercurial gage, was intrusted to his care." At least some, and perhaps the greatest part, of the design of the experimental project was also owing to the technician. Boyle said that he would indicate with an asterisk those experiments Papin "himself propounded as if they had been formed in his own brain," but, in fact, this was not done in either the original or in subsequent editions. It seems also that the technician was partly, if not mainly, responsible for the composition of the experimental narratives.[5] Boyle explained that because of another painful attack of the stone "it was judged meet, that monsieur *Papin* should set down in writing all the experiments and phænomena arising therefrom, as if they had been made and observed by his own skill." "I was not," Boyle acknowledged, "very sollicitous about the style, because, being infirm in point of health, and besides, surrounded with many businesses, I was enforced to leave the choice of words to monsieur *Papin*." Finally, Boyle indi-

2. Papin worked for Boyle from 1675 to 1679, having previously been employed in Christiaan Huygens's Paris laboratory. From 1679 to 1681 he was hired by the Royal Society to assist Robert Hooke with his secretarial duties, and after spending some time as an experimental curator in Venice, returned again to London, where he was temporary curator with the Royal Society for several years in the mid-1680s: Robinson, "Papin"; MacLachlan, "Papin, Denis"; M. B. Hall, *Promoting Experimental Learning,* 79–87, and see 181 n. 10 (where Hall incorrectly states that Papin "is not named directly" in Boyle's "Continuation of New Experiments. The Second Part").

3. The major improvement was Papin's development of a double-barreled mechanism obviating the existing necessity for reiterated manual settings of stopcocks and plugs. For a description, see Boyle, "Continuation of New Experiments. The Second Part," 510–11, and, for a diagram, see Boyle, *Works,* IV, Plate I, fig. 1. It was also in this context that Papin developed his celebrated pressure cooker, or "digester" (see figure 11), later described in his own text *A New Digester* (1681), preface.

4. Boyle, "Continuation of New Experiments. The Second Part," 506. Nevertheless, Boyle insisted upon the continuing adequacy of his own contrivance with which his "domestics were better acquainted," and which, "because of its more solid structure," was said to be more reliable.

5. At the time, Papin was not fluent in English; his French laboratory notes were translated into Latin for the 1680 text; see ibid., 507–10. As usual, Boyle's "publisher" did extensive editorial work in rendering these experimental notes into more or less coherent sequential form.

Figure 11. Denis Papin (1647– *ca.* 1712), holding a diagram of his "digester." Papin worked for Boyle for several years in the mid- to late 1670s and was one of the few remunerated assistants Boyle mentioned by name. Lithograph, from anonymous portrait at University of Marburg. (Courtesy of Wellcome Institute Library, London.)

cated that certain types of *interpretation* contained in the text were also the product of his technician's labor: "Some few of those inferences owe themselves more to my assistant than to me."[6] So, according to his employer's own testimony, the paid assistant was at least partly, and probably mainly, responsible for providing the necessary experimental apparatus, some of which, Boyle specified, was made with Papin's "own hands." The technician performed the skilled manipulations which produced experimental phenomena; he recorded the phenomena that his skilled work made manifest; he embedded these records in literary form, adding occasional inferential corollaries which were likewise the product of his own thinking.

What did his master contribute to the enterprise? Boyle said that he, or at least "his domestics" (for there were evidently still other assistants involved whose names were not given), did perform certain of the experiments (we do not know which), that he was physically "always present at the making of the chief experiments, and also at some of those of an inferior sort" (again, there is no way of telling which), that he instructed Papin to "acquaint me with [relevant] alterations" during longer experiments performed durng Boyle's absence from his Pall Mall laboratory, that he read (or, more accurately, had read to him by an amanuensis) "the whole work" composed by his technician, "that so no mistake might pass by unobserved about the experiments themselves."[7] And, of course, he composed the brief preface which is historians' only substantial testimony to the circumstances I have just related. In short, Boyle took overall responsibility for what was claimed as matter of fact and its legitimate interpretation in this text. He was, and insisted that he was, in charge of the scene and the operations that took place in his laboratory. Indeed, the laboratory was part of Boyle's own house.[8] Boyle hired the technician to do work Boyle considered was worth doing and when it was worth doing. Boyle was intermittently physically present in order "to observe whether all things were done according to my mind," but he accepted that this physical supervision and limited participation was, by itself, insufficient to guarantee that everything was done as Boyle would have wished it done. In the end, he *trusted* the technician, and he assured readers that he had adequate grounds for so doing: "I had cause enough to trust his skill and diligence."[9]

6. Ibid., 506–07. I have alluded to Papin's likely role in representing Boyle's law in the preceding chapter; see figure 9.
7. Boyle, "Continuation of New Experiments. The Second Part," 506–07.
8. Or, strictly speaking, his sister's house, though that was not a distinction which would have affected Boyle's relations with his technicians: Shapin, "House of Experiment," 379–82.
9. Boyle, "Continuation of New Experiments. The Second Part," 506–07.

I use this example to open up a window on the political and moral economy of scientific work in seventeenth-century England. I intend it to introduce an account of the collective nature of experimental knowledge-making, and, specifically, to point to the epistemic role of support personnel. I am concerned with problems of trust that are engendered by and through the collective character of empirical knowledge-making and knowledge-holding. Just as the role of trust is rendered invisible by positing a solitary knower as the sufficient maker and possessor of scientific knowledge, so the importance of its practical management becomes evident once one acknowledges that scientific knowledge is produced by and in a *network* of actors. I document the collective nature of knowledge-making work in order to revert to questions about authority and authorship raised in chapter 4. How were skill and knowledgeability distributed between different actors, and how, indeed, were the respective categories recognized and valued? How was authority exercised and authorship established within this economy of collective work? If knowledge was made by many, how did it come to be vouched for by the testimony of one? Here the study of assistants' roles offers a counterpoint to the investigation of authorial identity and its truth-making potency. Assistants can be conceived as 'antiauthors,' knowledge of whose work has the potential to erode the epistemic standing of authored knowledge. How were dependence and authority practically managed and how did that management square with local presumptions about characteristics, like free will and spiritual equality, that might be attributed to all actors alike? What was the practical political theory in terms of which one man spoke for others? How was that spokesmanship constituted as a warrant for the truth of what was spoken? That is, how is social theory made manifest as epistemology?

The 1680 story has the virtues of vividness and relative circumstantiality. Nevertheless, there is something about this story which ruins its status as typical evidence of the work-world of seventeenth-century English science: we know the technician's name. We know it because it was explicitly and repeatedly given by Boyle as employer-author, together with reports of the technician's specific activities and views. As I shall show, it was exceptional in the extreme for a seventeenth-century technician to be so identified by those who engaged his services. Anonymity is almost a defining characteristic of the technician in that setting. The philosopher has a name and an individual identity; the technician does not. One might even plausibly say of those who were so individually identified that they were not then functioning wholly in the technician's role, and there are, as I indicate below, reasons to find the status of Papin ambiguous between assistant and associate.

Technicians are triply invisible. First, they have traditionally been invisible to historians and sociologists of science. Until quite recently, there was no single piece of work in the literature systematically dealing with technicians, their work, and their role in making scientific knowledge.[10] Second, they have been largely, if not entirely, invisible in the formal documentary record produced by scientific practitioners. Even when one is committed to doing so, it is extremely difficult to retrieve information about who they were and what they did. Third, technicians have arguably been invisible as relevant actors to those persons in control of the workplaces in which scientific knowledge is produced. Thus, their anonymity in the documentary record plausibly proceeds from their employers' sense that what they did was not important, or even from their employers not noticing what it was they did. Technicians have been 'not there' in roughly the same sense that servants were, and were supposed to be, 'not there' with respect to the conversations of Victorian domestic employers.

Consequently, any systematic inquiry into technicians' role in knowledge-making has to take up a dual task. I want here to make technicians' work in the production of seventeenth-century scientific knowledge as visible as I can. For the reasons I have just indicated, this is not an easy task. There are times when I must proceed from patchy evidence to inferences that more cautious historians will doubtless find unsound.[11] On the other hand, I want to understand why technicians

10. The gradual emergence of interest in technicians has been associated, on the one hand, with attention to experimental practice, technique, and skill among sociologists of scientific knowledge, and, on the other, with the extension of the sociology of work and organization into the study of science. See, among many examples, my semipopular sketch ("The Invisible Technician") of this chapter's argument; Schaffer, "Astronomers Mark Time"; Mukerji, *A Fragile Power*, ch. 7; and, for general discussion of the invisibility of work, see Star, "Sociology of the Invisible"; Daniels, "Invisible Work." Of course, technicians and other support personnel have been mentioned *en passant* in a variety of science studies exercises: e.g., Hagstrom, *The Scientific Community*, 149–51; Cole and Cole, "The Ortega Hypothesis," 373; Latour and Woolgar, *Laboratory Life*, 245, 255; Hacking, *Representing and Intervening*, 179; Rudwick, *Great Devonian Controversy*, 425. Polanyi (*Personal Knowledge*), Ravetz (*Scientific Knowledge and Its Social Problems*), and Collins (*Changing Order*) have all pressed conceptions of science as craftwork that make attention to the technician's role potentially interesting to sociological and philosophical enterprises.

11. While the documentary evidence with which I deal is undeniably patchy, it displays recurrent patterns, which, together with independent evidence about the cultural and social setting, give me some confidence in my inferences. I intend to cite no more than a few instances for each characterization of technicians' work, though references could, in most cases, be multiplied *ad libitum*, and to no useful purpose. In the event, historians should appreciate that this is an inquiry in which the alternative to vulnerable inference is to continue in silence.

were indeed invisible in the seventeenth-century scientific economy.[12] Going back to the introductory example, the relevant question might be phrased this way: 'Why was Boyle the author of Papin's text?' That question, and the inquiry which follows, is naturalistically conceived. I have no intention here to redistribute 'credit' between Boyle and his technicians, though some readers may well wish to use these materials to do so. As it happens, I have no evidence that this right of authorship was privately resented by Papin or publicly contested by the relevant community.[13] Rather, I am interested in the cultural scheme in terms of which Boyle's authorship was considered legitimate and in terms of which the work of some persons was effectively subsumed into the voice of another.

Technicians' Identity

Some methodological and etymological ground has first to be cleared. In my working definition, technicians are persons in a setting dedicated to the production of scientific knowledge who are remuneratively engaged to deploy their labor or skill at an employer's behest. While the contractual aspect of the definition is apparently straightforward (in principle, contracts could be located and their terms inspected), the notions of labor and, especially, of skill, are not. Labor clearly involved observable notions of muscular and manipulative activity, but the recognition of certain activities *as* labor depended upon such moral and political considerations as the source of direction and control and the cultural value placed upon the action in question. I do not offer to define what skill is in this connection, save to identify it as a species of manipulative work and its associated capacities which was *defined by relevant actors* in practical opposition to notions like knowledgeability. While skill might encompass the category of manual labor, and might be treated as an elevated form of labor, it also sat at one end of an evaluative opposition at the other pole of which was some notion of *knowledge,* conceived not as work but as thought. So the knowledge-skill distinction is a particular version of such pervasive cultural divides as theory-practice, contemplation-action, and head-hand. For historical purposes, therefore, we have to see how notions like skill functioned

12. Inevitably, an inquiry so framed creates persuasive problems for itself: to the extent that I succeed in building up a picture of who technicians were and what they did, I precipitate doubt about that invisibility which is also my topic. I will do what I can to keep the two exercises in tension.

13. Papin's later account of his *New Digester,* Preface (see also p. 49), discussed the earlier experimental series made "for Mr. *Boyle*" without making any claim for Papin's ownership.

as attributions and how such attributions were related to distributions of social value. Technicians and knowlegeable agents defined each other and their respective capacities in the course of mundane interaction and within institutionalized systems of cultural practice.

The term *technician* was not, in fact, a seventeenth-century English usage, and definitely not as a designation for someone working in a natural-scientific context. I have yet to encounter it in the course of my own research into this setting. The examples provided by the *Oxford English Dictionary* date from the nineteenth century and point to a relatively distinct usage, namely "a person conversant with the technicalities of a particular subject"; or "one skilled in the technique or mechanical part of an art, as music or painting."[14] Well into this century, *OED* usage failed to specify a natural-scientific setting. Arguably, that reference for the *technician* developed through the late nineteenth and early twentieth centuries in close association with the designation *scientist* and the accompanying social-structural realities.[15]

In seventeenth-century England a variety of terms was used to designate individuals engaged to exert their labor and skill in natural-scientific settings at the behest of philosopher-employers. Individuals employed in specialized chemical (and alchemical) venues were commonly referred to as *laborants* or, more rarely, as *laborators*. For example, Hartlib told Boyle in 1654 that he was waiting upon the arrival of his son-in-law's "laborant," and that Kenelm Digby was summoning an unnamed "expert ancient old laborant." At the same time, the chemists Thomas Vaughan and Thomas Henshaw were employing a German "laborator" in their Kensington rooms, and Aubrey alluded to a "Laborator" kept by the Countess of Pembroke. Boyle's *A Chymical Paradox* of 1682 referred to a "laborant" then managing distillations for him. Experimental tracts about explosions in the mid-1670s gave some details about chemical operations performed by his "laborant." And one of Boyle's last publications referred to pneumatic work being undertaken by his "laborant."[16] A range of texts testify to employers' jaun-

14. The adjective *mere* precedes two of the four *OED* examples: for example, "the mere technician can never interest; the literary man, even if deficient in stage *technique*, may do so in a high degree" (1895).

15. As late as 1959 the *Webster's New World Dictionary* echoed the *OED* definition ("specifically an artist, writer, or musician") while still omitting mention of laboratory work; cf. *Chambers 20th Century Dictionary* (1983) (sense 2): "someone who does the practical work in a laboratory, etc."

16. Hartlib to Boyle, 8 May 1654, in Boyle, *Works*, VI, 87, 90; Wilkinson, "Hartlib Papers. Part II," 89; Aubrey, *Brief Lives*, 139; Boyle, "Chymical Paradox," 498, 500, 502; idem, "New Experiments about Explosions," 593, 595; idem, "General History of the Air," 619; see also idem, "Some Considerations Touching the Usefulness of Experimental Natural Philosophy," 139, 141; idem, "Aerial Noctiluca," 396; idem, "New Experiments and Observations made upon the Icy Noctiluca," 489.

diced view of laborants' moral character and cognitive competences. Boyle's *The Sceptical Chymist* distinguished "betwixt those chymists, that are either cheats, or but laborants, and the true *adepti*," and Hartlib related that Benjamin Worsley had "laid all considerations in chemistry aside, as things not reaching much above common laborants, or strong-water distillers."[17] In employers' apparent view, laborants possessed *mere* skill. The skilled assistance designated by the term laborant was evidently both hard to secure and hard to trust. In *The Sceptical Chymist*'s usage, for example, laborants were chemical mercenaries, undeniably possessing skill but not genuine knowledge or the moral makeup that might make their claims straightforwardly credible.[18]

In scientific settings where mechanical contrivances or optical devices were used, skilled employees were customarily called "operators," though the term was intermittently also applied to anatomical and chemical workers. In 1645 the London experimental science group met at Dr. Jonathan Goddard's lodgings in Wood Street, because, as Wallis later wrote, he kept "an Operator in his house, for grinding Glasses for Telescopes and Microscopes."[19] In 1655 Boyle's "Philosophicall Diary" mentioned a Mr. Smart, "operator" at Dorchester House in London.[20] Anthony Wood wrote of a Merton College scholar who "spent much labour and money in the art of chymistry [and] kept an operator."[21] After the founding of the Royal Society, it retained the services of an "operator" to conduct its experiments: the first was probably the chemist Peter Stahl, succeeded in 1663 by Richard Shortgrave, and in 1676 by Henry Hunt. The "operator" was a role distinct from that of the society's "curator of experiments" (Robert Hooke from 1663 to 1677), who supervised the operator's labor, as well as performing experiments himself.[22] In 1669 the Royal Society was soliciting applications for an "Anatomical Operator"; John Mayow's medical pneumatic tract of 1674 contained several references to the role of an unnamed "operator"; and Ambrose Godfrey Hanck-

17. Boyle, "Sceptical Chymist," 462–63 (cf. idem, "New Experiments Touching Cold," 652); Worsley to Hartlib, as related in Hartlib to Boyle, 28 February 1654, in Boyle, *Works*, VI, 79.

18. Arguably, the most relevant example was the alchemist George Starkey, who worked in association with Boyle *ca.* 1651 on the *ens veneris*, but by 1653 was described by Hartlib as morally "altogether degenerated": Hartlib to Boyle, 28 February 1654, in Boyle, *Works*, VI, 79–80; Wilkinson, "George Starkey." Forthcoming work by William Newman treats the role of George Starkey as supplier of chemical skill and materials to Boyle in the early 1650s.

19. Scriba, "Autobiography of Wallis," 39; Gunther, *Early Science in Oxford*, I, 9.

20. Quoted in Maddison, *Boyle*, 86.

21. Wood, *Athenae Oxoniensis*, IV, 477; Frank, *Harvey and the Oxford Physiologists*, 50.

22. M. B. Hall, *Promoting Experimental Learning*, 24–27; Turnbull, "Peter Stahl"; Frank, *Harvey and the Oxford Physiologists*, 51.

witz became Boyle's "operator," *ca.* 1683–1684, having previously been "Master of the *Laboratory* or Operator" at Apothecaries' Hall.[23] In other mechanical connections there are references to the work of casually employed "artificers,"[24] although D. T. Whiteside's translation of Newton's Latin *artifex* as "technician" is, for reasons I have indicated, anachronistic.[25]

There were also apparently generic terms widely used to indicate persons performing the technician's role. I have already quoted Boyle's reference to Papin as "my assistant," and it seems possible that this term (in Boyle's usage) pointed to a degree of collegiality in the relationship even if remuneration was involved, while John Flamsteed's corps of paid "assistants" at the Greenwich Observatory came largely from trade and mercantile families.[26] And, of course, those employed to supply technical skill might be referred to by a large number of other generic or oblique forms: "workmen," "those persons whom I

23. Wallis to Oldenburg, 15 April 1669, in Oldenburg, *Correspondence*, V, 494; Mayow, *Medico-physical Works*, 70, 95; Maddison, "Studies in the Life of Boyle. Part V," 165; idem, *Boyle*, 164–66; Golinski, "A Noble Spectacle," esp. 20; see also E. Bernard to John Collins, 3 April 1671, in Rigaud, *Correspondence of Scientific Men*, I, 159; Christopher Wren to Oldenburg, 7 June 1668, in Oldenburg, *Correspondence*, IV, 455; and, for references to operators in Boyle's texts, see, e.g., "New Experiments about Flame and Air," 564, 580; "New Experiments about Explosions," 594–95. For the "operatory" as a place where mechanical and optical instruments were used, see, e.g., Hooke, *Diary*, 191; Hooke to Boyle, 3 March 1666, in Boyle, *Works*, VI, 505; Oldenburg to Boyle, 24 February 1666, in Oldenburg, *Correspondence*, III, 45.

24. E.g., Boyle, "New Experiments Physico-mechanical," 64; idem, "Continuation of New Experiments," 236, 246, 259, 275; and see idem, "New Experiments Touching Cold," 631, 637, for comments on the reliability of the work of an occasionally employed "smith."

25. Newton, *Mathematical Papers*, VII, 288–89. The text is the 1693 *Geometry* in which Newton referred to geometrical objects as mechanically fabricated: "Any plane figures executed by God, nature or any technician [*artifice*] you will are measured by *geometry*. . . . A technician [*artifex*] is required and postulated to have learnt how to describe straight lines and circles before he may begin to be a geometer." See also Garrison, "Newton and the Relation of Mathematics to Natural Philosophy," 611–13.

26. E.g., Stubbe, *Legends No Histories* (1670), 3 (for alchemical "assistants"); Birch, "Life of Boyle," lv; Aubrey, *Brief Lives*, 165; and Wood, *Athenae Oxoniensis*, IV, 623–31 (for Hooke as "assistant" to Willis and Boyle); Boyle to Oldenburg, 29 October 1663, in Oldenburg, *Correspondence*, II, 124 (for presumption that Oldenburg knew an "assistant's" identity); Boyle, "Historical Account of a Degradation of Gold," 371 (for a "learned and experienced physician" as "assistant" to Boyle); Webster, "Richard Towneley," 70 (for a prominent recusant gentleman as astronomical "assistant"); Birch, *History of the Royal Society*, III, 277, 293 (entry for 20 January 1676) (for Newton's use of an assistant in his prism experiments); cf. Flamsteed to Oldenburg, 18 February 1671, in Oldenburg, *Correspondence*, VII, 464–65 (for "ye help of any vulgar assistant" in astronomical work). Murdin, *Under Newton's Shadow*, esp. 25–26, 30–31, 40, 52–53, 64, 68, collates much suggestive material on Flamsteed's workshop and late seventeenth- and early eighteenth-century astronomical assistants.

employ," "a dextrous hand," "a boy," "a youth," etc. But perhaps the most common terms found in this connection are the related series: "domestic," "domestic servant" or, simply, "servant."[27] There are intermittent indications that individuals serving Boyle as general domestic servants might be put to work in his laboratory, to make natural-historical observations, or to fetch and carry papers and experimental items, and Boyle's various amanuenses might also be designated generically as "servants."[28] I have already documented Boyle's reference to his "domestics" working the air-pump.[29] Aubrey's description of Boyle's Pall Mall "noble Laboratory" reported that he had "severall servants . . . to looke to it," and, when an ecclesiastical relation proposed visiting, he requested Boyle "to order some servant of yours to shew me your laboratory."[30] From the mid-1650s there are references to an unnamed, but apparently specific, individual serving as Boyle's "chymical servant."[31]

The term *servant* might well designate individuals serving Boyle in a domestic role who were regarded as possessing no knowledgeability and little skill. Domestic and scientific service were, to an extent, interchangeable. "Servants" carried mail and goods for Boyle, and they performed generic observational and manipulative tasks in connection with pneumatic and chemical experimentation. In 1665, for example, Boyle referred to a "servant" plying the air-pump, and, in 1672, to an observation of luminescence made "by one of the Servants of the house."[32] We do know something about the identity, terms, and conditions of domestic servants in seventeenth-century England, and, to the extent that domestics were employed in technical capacities, about at least one category of scientific support personnel. While the sons of aristocrats routinely passed through the status of 'servant' in noble houses before coming into their inheritance and independence, there was a large cadre of urban domestic servants who had little expectation

27. For parallel discussion of the varieties and designations of servitude in old-regime France, see Fairchilds, *Domestic Enemies,* esp. ch. 1.

28. E.g., Oldenburg to Boyle, 22 September 1657, in Oldenburg, *Correspondence,* I, 137.

29. E.g., Boyle, "Continuation of New Experiments. The Second Part," 506; also idem, "New Experiments Touching Cold," 529, 632, 640, 655; idem, "General History of the Air," 620.

30. Aubrey, *Brief Lives,* 37; bishop of Cork to Boyle, 12 June 1683, in Boyle, *Works,* VI, 615.

31. Hartlib, *Ephemerides* (1654), ff. WW-WW7-8 (quoted in Dewhurst, *Willis's Oxford Casebook,* 163); Turnbull, "Hartlib's Influence on the Royal Society," 115.

32. Boyle, "New Experiments Touching Cold," 565; idem, "Some Observations about Shining Flesh," 651; idem, "General History of the Air," 623. The term *servant* was by no means restricted to the unlettered. The usage *domestic servant* or *domestic,* however, designated a more specifically undignified category.

of ever emerging from servitude and were understood to be permanently in that condition. (In common seventeenth-century English usage, "*servants* (or [those who] lead a servile life" referred to "all those who get their living by their daily labour."[33] Cissie Fairchilds's study of servitude in old-regime France notes that domestic service was considered an *état* rather than a *métier*, and this is a sensibility which seems adequately to describe English attitudes as well. A "domestic" was defined not by the type of work he did, but "by the fact that he lived in a household not his own in a state of dependency on its master.")[34]

Domestic servants of the sort mentioned by Boyle were probably usually engaged by annual contracts, though they might develop long-term relationships with the household and become literally part of the family. Typically such servants would be unmarried, have only one master, and live in their employer's house.[35] Peter Earle reckons the average number of domestic servants per seventeenth-century London household at about two, though the 3 percent that employed six or more would certainly have included Lady Ranelagh's Pall Mall establishment. Servants' annual wages, not including bed and board, ranged from 30 shillings to £8 or more.[36] At the highest levels, educated men serving as superior secretaries, tutors, or amanuenses in aristocratic households might be much more highly remunerated. The natural philosopher Walter Warner, who assisted the "Wizard Earl" of Northumberland in his chemical experiments, commanded £20 a year in 1595, rising to £40 in 1607, and, after a quarter century of faithful service, was elevated to "pensioner" status. And Thomas Hariot, who entered Sir Walter Raleigh's service as a mathematical tutor in 1580, wound up with an annual pension of £100.[37]

The search for seventeenth-century technicians' identity and role inevitably leads to Robert Boyle and his workplaces. On the one hand,

33. [Wetenhall], *Enter into Thy Closet* (1684), 33; see also Macpherson, *Political Theory of Possessive Individualism*, 282–86; MacDonald, *Mystical Bedlam*, 85–88.

34. Fairchilds, *Domestic Enemies*, 3.

35. The Latin *familia* meant "servant." Hecht (*Domestic Servant Class*, 82) estimates three to four years as the average length of London domestic service with one master. For servants as prescriptively unmarried during their time of service, see, e.g., Gouge, *Of Domesticall Duties*, 605; for the early modern family encompassing kin and servants, see Gailhard, *Two Discourses*, 15–18; Kussmaul, *Servants in Husbandry*, 7–8; and for the economics, politics and cultural understanding of servitude, ibid., ch. 1 and appendix 1; Hecht, *Domestic Servant Class*, ch. 3; Fairchilds, *Domestic Enemies*, 2–20.

36. P. Earle, *Making of the English Middle Class*, 218–29; see also Heal, *Hospitality in Early Modern England*, 44–48, 149–50, 155–67. The figures quoted derive from two wealthy City parishes. Females predominated in households with only a few servants, the proportion of males rising as the number of servants increased.

37. Shirley, "The Scientific Experiments of Ralegh," 56–59.

Boyle's great wealth meant that he could afford far more assistance than the average experimental philosopher. On the other, Boyle's mountains of highly circumstantial experimental narrative offer historians' their best chance to develop an overall appreciation of the seventeenth-century laboratory as collective workshop. Much of the evidence I have unearthed does derive from Boylean settings, and its preferential use permits the construction of a relatively coherent picture of seventeenth-century laboratory life. While it may well be objected that Boyle's Pall Mall laboratory was an atypical instance of seventeenth-century 'big science,' my major concern is with the moral texture of knowledge-making relations, and, in that respect, I see little significant difference between the evidence from Boyle's laboratories and that coming from the (perhaps less densely populated) workplaces of other gentlemen-practitioners.[38]

In this connection I am mainly concerned with individuals whom Boyle remuneratively engaged to do technical work on his behalf. Had I been more systematically interested in the role of support personnel, I would have needed to treat the role of several other classes of actors. For example, in Boyle's case I might have discussed the important assistance offered by instrument-makers and apothecaries, such as the apothecaries John Crosse (with whom he lived in Oxford for some years) and Thomas Smith (who lived in Boyle's Pall Mall house for many years and who was one of the beneficiaries of his will). I might also have dealt with the crucial role played by his employee, agent, and friend Henry Oldenburg as editor and publisher over a period of almost two decades. Oldenburg collated his master's scattered sheets of experimental narrative into more or less coherent texts, advised and consulted with Boyle about matters of style and presentation, translated his texts into Latin, supervised and chided printers, conveyed scientific, religious, and political news to Boyle, responded to his requests for information, and solicited the opinions of Continental philosophers, mobilizing their approval and stipulating the correct interpretation of Boyle's writings. Oldenburg acted as a buffer between Boyle and a potentially disturbing or disagreeable world. More than any other individual, Oldenburg was the man who helped Boyle present his self to the international community. The condition for the

38. The atypical status of Boyle's laboratories was pressed on me by John Heilbron (personal communication). For other early modern scientific settings engaging the labor of large numbers of assistants, see, for example, Tycho's Uraniborg and other astronomical observatories (Thoren, *Lord of Uraniborg*, esp. chs 5–6; idem, "Tycho as the Dean of a Renaissance Research Institute"), Rudolph II's alchemical laboratory at Prague, and the corporate workplaces of scientific societies in Florence, London, Paris, etc.

effective representation of Boyle was Oldenburg's own intellectual transparency.[39]

Extending the inquiry, I might have tried to assess the significance of Boyle's various amanuenses. Largely, though not entirely, because of his poor eyesight, Boyle employed a series of amanuenses throughout his life. After the mid-1650s very little of 'Boyle's' writing survives in his own hand. Amanuenses not only took down Boyle's dictation, they also read to Boyle from their notes, his texts, letters to him, and the books of other authors. They were responsible for keeping his papers in their customary disorder, and for conveying selected boxes of narrative bits and pieces to Oldenburg for him to cobble together. They transcribed extensively from other amanuenses' notes, and, in so doing, were obliged to make sense, and sensible English narrative, out of often intractable materials. At times amanuenses were enlisted in technical work, making and registering observations or handling apparatus.[40] As Marie Boas Hall has observed, not all of Boyle's amanuenses were notably well educated, and they apparently "often misunderstood or misheard" Boyle's words, thus introducing not only the possibility of error but also perhaps their own conceptions of sensibleness into 'Boyle's' manuscripts.[41] More generally, the network of support personnel about which one could (and in principle should) speak is potentially infinite: the suppliers of the chemicals he used and the paper on which he wrote, the butchers who kept him in meat and the Irish farm workers whose labor kept him in cash to give to servants to buy and cook the meat. Without the work of all such people,

39. Shapin, "O Henry"; Bazerman, *Shaping Written Knowledge*, 129–34; Hunter, "Promoting the New Science"; Henry, "Origins of Modern Science"; M. B. Hall, "Boyle's Method of Work," 114–15; idem, *Promoting Experimental Learning*, 59–65. For the role and identity of the seventeenth-century editor (with special reference to Oldenburg), see Iliffe, "Author-Mongering," and for treatment of the editor's role as central to understanding the collective nature of authorship, see Becker, *Art Worlds*, ch. 7. For Oldenburg's Pall Mall house as an alternative experimental workplace for Boyle, see, e.g., Boyle, "New Experiments about the Preservation of Bodies," 149; for Oldenburg as experimental witness, see idem, "New Experiments about the Weakened Spring of the Air," 217; and for Oldenburg as experimental performer, see idem, "Experimental Discourse of Quicksilver Growing Hot with Gold," 225.

40. See, e.g., Boyle, "Some Observations about Shining Flesh," 651 ("an amanuensis of mine, accustomed to make observations . . ."); idem, "New Experiments Touching Flame and Air," 581; idem, "New Experiments Touching Cold," 467, 522. And see Birch, *History of the Royal Society*, I, 17–21, 33–34, 46–47, 75–80, for early examples of the society's amanuensis (possibly Michael Wicks) doing experimental work. In 1661 the amanuensis was made into an experimental subject, being directed to stay in the society's "diving engine" for almost half an hour (ibid., 35). For attempted identifications of Boyle's amanuenses, see Hunter, *Letters and Papers of Boyle*, xxx–xxxix.

41. M. B. Hall, "Boyle's Method of Work," 113; cf. Bacon's well-known criticism of his amanuenses, and approval of Hobbes's accurate performance of that role, in Aubrey, *Brief Lives*, 9, 149–50.

'Boyle's' science could not have happened or, in any event, not in the form it did. The limits I draw in treating support personnel proceed partly from pragmatic considerations and partly from a concern to focus closely upon activities as proximal as possible to experimental knowledge-making scenes.

Invisible Women

While we know that the domestic servant who made the luminescence observation was female, there is little reason to think that women were involved on anything but a casual basis in Boyle's program of technical labor: I know of no female laborant, operator, or chemical servant in Boyle's employ, nor is there even indirect evidence to suggest that women might have worked for him in these capacities. Boyle's laboratory was in all probability a male preserve, though there is indeed some evidence of female technical assistance in other seventeenth-century scientific workplaces.[42] Nevertheless, I can briefly treat both the presence of women in various stages of Boyle's knowledge-making, as well as their substantial absence as authorial voices in contemporary scientific culture. Chapter 4 has already addressed Boyle's chastity as well as his portrayal of chattering painted women as distractions from philosophical commitment. While the rejection of carnal love and female society was a standard gesture among early modern intellectuals, Boyle's disengagement from women was only one aspect of the posture he adopted to keep the demands of polite society at arm's length. He was quite capable of recognizing and acknowledging female intellectual ability when he encountered it. On the one hand, Boyle participated fully in the institutionalized systems of exclusion that effectively prevented the vast majority of women from having a significant voice in formal culture or even from proposing the possibility of speaking in those forums; on the other, he seems not to have had manifested any particular personal investment in justifying that exclusion or bringing it to bear upon any particular women in his acquaintance.

It therefore seems to require little special explanation that women feature so infrequently in Boyle's accounts of empirical knowledge-making scenes: their invisibility, unlike that of male technicians, arises from the fact that they were, in all probability, physically not there.

42. Aubrey (*Brief Lives*, 49–50) related an anecdote of the physician William Butler's maid who was ordered to tend his chemical apparatus: "That he was chymical I know by this token, that his mayd came running in to him one time like a slutt and a Furie; with her haire about her eares, and cries, Butler! come and looke to your Devilles your selfe, and you will; the stills are all blowne up! She tended them, and it seems gave them too great a heate." Both John Flamsteed and Johannes Hevelius importantly used their highly talented wives as astronomical assistants: for material on the assistance of astronomers' wives, see Murdin, *Under Newton's Shadow*, 62–68.

Nevertheless, as I shall indicate, the very intimacy of Boyle's intellectual relations with his sisters Katherine and Mary does make the natural-philosophical invisibility of women rather more interesting than the 'exclusion' of numerous other social groups. And when on rare occasions female presences were circumstantially referred to, the systems of exclusion became slightly more visible. When one of "two very fair ladies" first showed Boyle the "experiment" of hair being attracted to her skin (through static electricity), Boyle at first did not credit the report, turning "it into a complemental raillery, as suspecting there might be some trick in it." This woman was, however, "no ordinary virtuosa" and she allayed Boyle's skepticism by reproducing the experiment in his presence with her own wig. Women knew the phenomenon very well, while Boyle, not much frequenting female society, thought it initially incredible. Yet he soon found the experiment easy enough to replicate, and even turned it into a small-scale research project about the conditions in which static electricity manifested itself. He made inquiries "among some other young ladies," getting little useful information, "except from one of them eminent for being ingenious," but she turned out to be a poor informant about the circumstances in which the phenomenon appeared.[43] Even women of his own condition, testifying about experiences intimately known to them, seem to have been treated as less than wholly reliable sources.[44]

Female intellectual ability, and even virtuosity, was, of course, available for Boyle's appreciation closer to home. I have already noted that his sister Lady Ranelagh, who watched over him so solicitously from the mid-1640s and with whom he lived from 1668, was a major figure in Interregnum political and religious culture. Although she published no philosophical or theological text, we have much testimony from contemporaries that she was a considerable intellectual presence. Her brother attributed her nonappearance as a theological author solely to disinclination and modesty, rather than to individual- or gender-based incapacity.[45] There is no doubt that intellectuals of the quality of Viscount Falkland, Milton, Oldenburg, and Hartlib found her conversation informed, formidable, and valuable. Their letters testify to the respect in which she was held and no sense of female intellectual incapacity was, to my knowledge, attached to her by members of that circle. One can therefore say that it was not she who was invisible in the production of culture but only the ephemeral scenes of salon and

43. Boyle, "Experiments and Notes about the Mechanical Origin of Electricity," 351–52.
44. Cf. Schaffer, "Self-Evidence"; idem, "Experimental Subjects in the 1660s," for the management of testimony about bodily experiences.
45. Boyle, "Occasional Reflections," 324.

dining-table conversation, which the solidity of bound volumes obscure from historians' awareness.

Boyle was deeply appreciative of Lady Ranelagh's intellectual abilities, as, indeed, he was of his other devout sister, Mary Rich, countess of Warwick. Though evidence to establish the claim is patchy, I have little doubt that Lady Ranelagh provided her brother with important and continuing intellectual, as well as material and emotional, support. She introduced him to people he ought to meet and she guarded him against the intrusions of those he did not wish to meet. She fed his friends and associates at her table. She owned the house in which he lived and put her domestic servants at his disposal. In 1668 she ordered part of her house to be made into a chemical laboratory, oversaw its renovation in 1677, and tolerated the sporadic explosions and the stench of luminescent rotten fish which many an elder sister would have taken a dim view of. She held pious discourses with him and nursed him when he was ill. There was no one in the world to whom Boyle owed more, or to whom he was closer. Indeed, his death only a week after Lady Ranalagh's was widely understood as the ultimate gesture of intimacy and respect. She was, in a loose but important sense, Boyle's greatest technician.

For all that, it is difficult to retrieve her role from Boyle's texts. She appears, to the extent that she does, refracted through her brother's concerns and expository conventions. There is no evidence that Lady Ranelagh was a physical presence in Boyle's laboratory, or, indeed, that she was at all concerned with the quotidian processes of chemical and pneumatic work that went on there. Nor is there any substantial evidence that she took a view on matters belonging to the practice of experimental natural philosophy: the cause of porosity, the correct mechanical explanation of colors or cold, or the specific gravity of talc. In quite general terms, it is evident that she approved the 'modern' critique of school philosophy and actively concurred with her brother and his friends about the potential religious benefits of a mechanical philosophy of nature.[46] Like many seventeenth-century gentlewomen, Lady Ranelagh thought it right that the woman of the house be able to practice elementary medicine, and she kept a collection of medical 'receipts' which her brother intermittently acknowledged in his publications and which, indeed, may have been an important source of his own work on medicinal 'specifics.'[47]

46. See, especially, Lady Ranelagh to Boyle, 29 July [1665], in Boyle, *Works,* VI, 525.
47. See, e.g., Boyle, "Some Considerations Touching the Usefulness of Experimental Natural Philosophy," esp. 242–45; idem, "Medicinal Experiments"; Lady Ranelagh to Boyle, 29 July [1665], in Boyle, *Works,* VI, 526; see also Pollock, *With Faith and Physic;* Fraser, *The Weaker Vessel,* 133; Hole, *English Housewife,* ch. 4 (for women's role in the "stillroom" and the preparation of medicines generally); Mendelson, *Mental World of*

Lady Ranelagh's invisibility in experimental natural philosophy
therefore stems substantially from her apparent lack of interest in the
details of what was going on in her brother's laboratory at the back of
her house and in the particular knowledge-claims which flowed out of
it. It was Katherine, not her brother, who alluded to a gender-based
distinction between her abilities in theological matters and her alleged
incompetencies in other cultural practices.[48] And neither she nor Mary
Rich was invisible as moral and theological interlocutor in Boyle's letters and texts. While strands of English Protestant culture very generally insisted upon the spiritual equality of all men and women, Boyle
clearly regarded both Mary and Katherine as particularly competent
discussants in religious matters. Throughout their lives these three
Boyle siblings conducted "holy discourses" together and treated each
other as the most qualified religious interlocutors. Several of Boyle's
most influential religious tracts were dedicated to these sisters. *Seraphic
Love* was written at Mary's Leese Priory and shown to her for her
inspection "almost sheet by sheet." The *Occasional Reflections* were dedicated to Katherine ("Sophronia"), celebrated as a great "mistress of wit
and eloquence."[49]

The Ghost and the Machine

The Boylean material is, however, only *relatively* rich in evidence about
support personnel. In the whole corpus of his experimental reporting,
extending from 1660 to posthumous publications of 1692, perhaps
only two currently employed skilled assistants were ever fully named.
These were Denis Papin (in the example already discussed) and Robert
Hooke, and whether either of these was then functioning strictly in
the technician's role is moot. At the time Papin's name was given he

Stuart Women, 35 (for Margaret Cavendish's typification of female "Receit" writing); and
Harwood, *Early Essays*, xvi n. 3 (for relatives' contributions to Boyle's collections of medical receipts) and lxii n. 90 (for discussion of Lady Ranelagh's household and medical
receipts preserved at the Wellcome Institute and British Library). Budgell (*Memoirs of
the Life of the Earl of Orrery*, 147) confirmed that Katherine "distributed *gratis* . . . all the
noble Medicines [Boyle] compounded in his Laboratory."

48. Lady Ranelagh to Boyle, 14 November [1665], in Boyle, *Works*, VI, 528. After
professing great keenness to be permitted to read a secret parcel of her brother's religious writings, Katherine reminded him that "I am of a sex, that has long been allowed
for an excuse of the frailties of those who are of it; and, considering how much you
believe of those, I must not fear but you will consider them as tenderly as they require
to be considered, and then you will not stick to afford me such a pardon. I am very
much pleased with the assurance my experience of God's goodness to you gives me . . .
but I should be more pleased in having a share in what you are about, that exceeds not
my capacity of understanding."

49. Boyle, "Some Motives to the Love of God" (dedicated to Mary Rich), quoting 244;
idem, "Occasional Reflections," 324.

was already an author of a scientific text, and had been introduced to the Royal Society as "a gentleman," which usage, even in loose late Restoration practice, meant something.[50] Hooke was named just once (in 1660) during his period of formal engagement by Boyle, and by the time he was named again (in 1668 and 1669) he was also a considerable author, a colleague of Boyle in the Royal Society, and had been professor of geometry at Gresham College for five years.[51] There is no certain evidence that there were significant pecuniary considerations in Hooke's dealings after 1662 with his former employer. In addition to Hooke and Papin, who were identified by surname, Boyle referred (in 1660) to a "Mr. G." (the instrument-maker Ralph Greatorex) and (in 1669) to "J. M." (the Oxford medical graduate John Mayow) as "this ingenious young man (whom I often employ about pneumatical experiments)."[52] Apart from these sorts of references, technicians are anonymous presences in the texts reporting what went on in Boyle's workplaces, subsumed into the authorial first person, the plural form of which might either be conventional or an informal indication of the presence of collegial helpers and witnesses.[53]

50. Birch, *History of the Royal Society*, III, 486 (entry for 22 May 1679). Papin's book was *Nouvelles expériences du vuide* (1674). Among other assistants, Frederic Slare—who worked for Boyle together with Papin and who was a cousin of Theodore Haak, F.R.S.—was also university educated and, after leaving Boyle's employ, developed a medical practice while serving as remunerated curator of experiments for the Royal Society: M. B. Hall, "Slare," 25–27; and, for Slare's work on phosphorus, Golinski, "A Noble Spectacle," esp. 20, 25, 33–34.

51. Boyle, "New Experiments Physico-mechanical," 7; idem, "New Experiments Concerning Light and Air," 160 (originally communicated in *Philosophical Transactions* for 6 January 1668); idem, "Continuation of New Experiments," 180. Boyle's "New Experiments Touching Cold" (1665), 705, 707, 709, referred to Hooke as colleague and fellow practitioner; see also idem, "General History of the Air," 650. Hooke's identity, and the moral texture of his relations with Boyle, have been treated in detail in Shapin, "Who Was Robert Hooke?" Hooke is, arguably, the most scientifically notable early fellow of the Royal Society for whom no portrait exists.

52. Boyle, "New Experiments Physico-mechanical," 7; idem, "Continuation of New Experiments," 187–88; see also ibid., 208, 221. Mayow was the son of a Cornish gentleman, and in the 1660s he was a fellow of All Souls. It is unclear in his case whether "employment" by Boyle was remunerative: see Frank, *Harvey and the Oxford Physiologists*, 224–27; idem, "John Ward Diaries," 170; Shapin and Schaffer, *Leviathan and the Air-Pump*, 232 (for Mayow's work with Boyle).

53. For treatment of witnessing in Boyle's texts, see Shapin, "Pump and Circumstance"; Shapin and Schaffer, *Leviathan and the Air-Pump*, esp. ch. 2. Marie Boas Hall (*Boyle and Seventeenth-Century Chemistry*, 45; cf. 208–09) is more confident than I can persuade myself to be that Boyle's assistants were made wholly visible: "[Boyle] kept a close watch on what was going on in his laboratory. It was his ideas that the laborant carried out, and when an idea was contributed by one of these assistants Boyle was always careful to say so." It is also noteworthy to compare the invisibility of technical assistants in Boyle's writing with their much greater presence in Hooke's *Diary* and other narratives. I have argued elsewhere that Hooke's relations with his technicians, unlike

Nevertheless, his own testimony, a variety of independent reports, and plausible inference establish that Boyle engaged a large number of assistants throughout his career and that they performed a great range of tasks on his behalf. Indeed, one can probably go further than this and say that there is reason to believe that relatively little of the manipulative and representational work involved in Boyle's experiments was done by Boyle himself.[54] Such a claim appears to fly in the face of one of the most characteristic tropes of the English experimental philosophy. From Bacon onwards, advocates of empirical and experimental methods argued the case for a revaluation of practice *vis-à-vis* theory, of the ways of the hand *vis-à-vis* those of the head. The traditional ethos that deprecated the mechanical arts was tactically transformed to display the fitness of laborious mechanical means in the gentlemanly pursuit of proper natural knowledge. Sprat, for example, described it as the Royal Society's "Fundamental Law" that "whenever they could possibly get to handle the subject, the Experiment was still perform'd by some of the Members themselves."[55] It was said of Prince Rupert that he "actually perform[ed] the most difficult and laborious [chemical] Operations himself; not disdaining the most sooty and unpleasant labour of the meanest Mechanick."[56] And in 1683 Boyle was gratified to note in connection with experiments on salinity that the king himself "for greater certainty, was pleased to employ his own hands."[57] The social innocuousness as well as the moral and epistemic value of direct experience and instrumental manipulation were repeatedly asserted. Boyle's early essay condemning idleness recommended occasional manual labor, even though he acknowledged that "this will be spurn'd at by all our Gallants as a Proposition fit to be made rather to blue Aprons then to skarlet Cloakes."[58] I have already noted that Boyle was one of many moderns who rejected the acceptance of "unverified reports or vulgar traditions, being careful," he insisted, "that

---

Boyle's, were shaped by collegial and craft patterns: Shapin, "Who Was Robert Hooke?" 267–69.

54. Thoren's work on Tycho Brahe's Uraniborg observatory (*Lord of Uraniborg*, 201–02, 212) treats the decreasing proportion of his observations that were made by his own eyes and hands.

55. Sprat, *History of the Royal Society*, 83. Recent work by Oster ("Scholar and Craftsman Revisited," esp. 270) insists upon a "genuine realignment" of *attitudes* towards the gentility of work while offering little evidence that such attitudes were realized in Boylean or Royal Society practice.

56. *Historical Memoires of Prince Rupert* (1683), 73–74 (quoted in Morrah, *Prince Rupert*, 391).

57. Boyle, "General History of the Air," 744. Charles II evidently liked spending time in his Whitehall laboratory, working with, *inter alia*, Nicholas Le Fevre and Sir Robert Moray.

58. Boyle, "Of Time and Idleness," 244.

the bulk of the matters of fact I deliver should consist of things, whereof I was myself an actor, or an eye-witness."[59] Boyle's associate John Locke—who indeed supplied much natural-historical evidence for Boyle's texts—gave the most systematic form to modern epistemological individualism and distrust of trust: "We may as rationally hope to see with other men's eyes, as to know by other men's understandings."[60]

Chapter 4 described how Boyle himself recruited Protestant sentiments to show the real moral value of even physical labor in securing direct natural knowledge. The early *Usefulness of Experimental Natural Philosophy* declared that even so great an aristocrat as himself did not disdain "with my own hands" to dissect animals and handle filthy laboratory materials. Yet that same passage affirmed that his "condition" enabled Boyle "to make experiments by others hands."[61] If, indeed, Boyle was making a significant proportion of his experiments with his own hands in the Stalbridge laboratory, during the rest of his life personal circumstances very probably increased his reliance upon others' hands, eyes, and minds. First, his move to Oxford in 1655, and then to London in 1668, almost certainly increased the accessible supply of skilled technical assistants. Second, his deteriorating health—poor eyesight, headaches, stone, and, after 1670, stroke and palsy—constituted additional reasons to rely upon the manipulative, observational, and representational skills of paid assistants. Despite Boyle's employment of a rhetoric of solitude, it is likely that his laboratories were among the most densely populated workplaces of seventeenth-century experimental science: my crude estimate is that on a busy day from two to six paid assistants might have been working there, quite apart from occasional visits from instrument-makers and suppliers of experimental materials.

Moreover, as a general matter, rhetoric stressing the importance of direct experience deserves close reinspection. When seventeenth-century experimentalists said that they had done experiments 'themselves' or even 'with their own hands,' it *did not necessarily mean* that all the skilled and unskilled physical labor involved in any given perfor-

59. Boyle, "Experimenta & Observationes," 569. Here Boyle insisted upon his practice as an advance on Bacon's.

60. Locke, *Essay Concerning Human Understanding*, Bk. I, ch. 3, sect. 24. For Locke's assistance in Boyle's pneumatic and chemical work, see Stewart, "Locke's Professional Contacts with Boyle" and Dewhurst, "Locke's Contribution to Boyle's Researches."

61. Boyle, "Some Considerations Touching the Usefulness of Experimental Natural Philosophy," 14 (published 1663, though there are indications that this section dates from 1647–1648); and see idem, "New Experiments Physico-mechanical," 7 (for claims that Boyle had done pre-air-pump experiments *de vacuo* "with my own hands"); idem, "Experimental Discourse of Quicksilver Growing Hot with Gold" (1676), 223–24 (where Boyle insisted that he did certain disputed trials "when I was all alone").

mance was solely their own, that all the reported experiments and attendant observations in a series were done by themselves or even in their presence, that they possessed all the relevant bits of technical, conceptual, and representational competences embedded in the workings of instruments, the registering and reporting of outcomes, and the fitting of findings to interpretative traditions. Indeed, we already know this much from the (admittedly exceptional) case of Papin's assistantship, since these experiments were regarded as no less 'Boyle's' for all the work that was done for him by Papin and the domestics. And the case for Boyle's reliance upon Hooke's conceptual as well as instrumental skill is now widely appreciated.[62]

Authority—even in a practice that stressed the value of work and direct experience—clearly had other sources than the individual manipulative labor-content of scientific claims, and, as I shall note later, Royal Society experimentalists were quite able to make important moral and epistemic distinctions between the value of gentlemanly and mechanic labor. A plausible interpretation of what was intended and understood by the seventeenth-century claim that one had 'done experiments oneself' is that the experimental work had been instigated by oneself, that the historical events reported in the resulting experimental narrative did actually occur and occurred when and as described, that they occurred in a place over which one exercised authority, that one had indeed taken responsibility for what happened, and that one now vouched for the truthfulness of what was textually related. While Boyle, to be sure, had particular reasons to rely upon paid assistants and enjoyed particular advantages in being able to afford them, it is likely that when he referred to 'his experiments,' he meant, and was understood to mean, much the same as any other seventeenth-century gentleman-philosopher using a similar locution. Despite new rhetoric stressing the laying on of experimental hands, the traditional gentlemanly culture condemning manual work had by no means disappeared, even in Royal Society circles.

Remunerated assistants were thus an important feature of experimental scenes, yet their employers almost never accorded them an identity as relevant or authoritative presences in those scenes. How then did texts betray these anonymous presences? At times Boyle's narratives made reference to the work being done by generically designated agents. Consider the series of experiments involving the air-pump, originally constructed and probably largely designed for Boyle by his then assistant Robert Hooke. The work of exhausting the large glass receiver was arduous, requiring considerable muscular energy

---

62. E.g., Hesse, "Hooke's Vibration Theory," 434–37; Shapin, "Who Was Robert Hooke?" 263–65.

exerted over many minutes. In the original *New Experiments Physico-mechanical,* and later experimental series, the skilled assisting agent who actually performed these manipulations was invoked only obliquely: "he that manageth the pump," "he that draweth down the sucker [piston]," "him that managed it," "the pumper," "a dextrous hand we imployed," "those we appointed to attend it." It was, however, more common for Boyle to avoid reference to a separate manipulative presence and simply to record that "we pumped," "I caused the pump to be plied," or to use the passive voice: "the pump being set on work."[63] In later pneumatic trials requiring more extended exertions than usual, Boyle mentioned the special employment of "a strong man that was used to exercise his hands and arms in mechanical labours," an unnamed locksmith "that was a lusty and dexterous fellow."[64]

Apart from those few whom Boyle himself designated, it has proved very difficult to discover the name of any individual who "managed the pump" and related apparatus for Boyle through the 1660s and 1670s. I think I may have identified one, though the uncertainty of this identification is indicative of the endemic invisibility of support personnel. In 1667, when Boyle's sister Lady Ranelagh was urging him to leave Oxford and come to live with her at her London house in Pall Mall, she mentioned that she had ordered one of her domestic servants *"Thomas* to look out for charcoal, and should gladly receive your order to put my back-house in posture to be employed" as Boyle's laboratory.[65] Other family letters of the period referred to "Thomas" as someone available to run errands for Boyle.[66] This "Thomas" was possibly a long-term family retainer and may, indeed, have served Boyle during part of his residence at Oxford. In 1665, Sir Robert Moray, chemist and Royal Society colleague of Boyle, mentioned experimental work performed by "Mr Boiles man" whom he elsewhere named as "Thom."[67] This Thom is possibly also the unnamed amanuensis-assistant mentioned by Boyle early in 1666 as "one, that you know, whose hand is employed in this paper, and begins to be a diligent observer of natural things," and about whom Robert Sharrock wrote to Boyle concerning "your lad's improvement in chemistry"[68] Boyle did finally remove to Pall Mall in 1668, and the period from then to

63. E.g., Boyle, "New Experiments Physico-mechanical," 17, 27, 34, 56–57; idem, "Continuation of New Experiments," 215; idem, "Hydrostatical Paradoxes," 790.

64. Boyle, "Continuation of New Experiments," 265–66.

65. Lady Ranelagh to Boyle, 13 November [1667], in Boyle, *Works,* VI, 531. (Birch provisionally assigned this letter to 1666, but other evidence makes 1667 more likely.)

66. E.g., Lady Ranelagh to Boyle, 12 and 18 September [1666], in ibid., 529–30.

67. Moray to Oldenburg, 12 and 16 November 1665, in Oldenburg, *Correspondence,* II, 606, 610.

68. Boyle, "Confirmation of the Former Account Touching the Late Earthquake near Oxford," 797–98; Sharrock to Boyle, [*ca.* 1663], in Boyle, *Works,* VI, 321.

1672 was one of the most active phases of his pneumatic experimental program. In September 1672, Henry Oldenburg wrote on Boyle's behalf to Isaac Newton at Cambridge. He wanted to know whether Newton knew of any employment at Cambridge open to "a young Chymist, that hath lived many years wth Mr Boyle, and attained to a good skill in that Art." Oldenburg named the young man as "Mr Thom Huyck," possibly, but not certainly, the same "Thomas" earlier mentioned by Lady Ranelagh or the "Thom" mentioned by Sir Robert Moray.[69] In view of the lengths to which Oldenburg went in trying to secure Thom's future employment (Oldenburg had just begun his difficult correspondence with Newton), Huyck was clearly viewed by his employer as a valuable experimental asset. For all that, I cannot locate any mention of Thom by name in Boyle's publications or even in his letters.[70]

Technicians' Work: Individuality, Knowledgeability, and Value

The assessment of technicians' work is plagued by the same practical difficulties as those attending the establishment of their identity. If a named agent was reported to have been responsible for a specific piece

69. Oldenburg to Newton, 24 September 1672, in Newton, *Correspondence*, I, 242–43. Both the editors of the Oldenburg *Correspondence* (IX, 256) and Michael Hunter (personal communication; *Science and Society*, 75) seem satisfied that "Huyck" is the same individual as the "Tom Hewk" frequently mentioned in Hooke's *Diary*. I am not at all sure of that identification, partly because Hooke's man seems to have been married and not living with Boyle. For a "Hewke" as apothecary to the London College of Physicians from 1673 to 1679, see Cook, *Decline of the Old Medical Regime*, 184 n. 5. (I thank Dr. Hunter and Prof. Cook for their replies to my queries.) I have considered, and dismissed, the possibility that the "Thomas" referred to by Lady Ranelagh was the apothecary Thomas Smith, who, Birch said ("Life of Boyle," ii), "lived seventeen years with Mr. *Boyle*, and was with him at his death," though Smith may well have provided important technical assistance to Boyle. Boyle's will named Smith as "my servant," and other "servants" receiving small bequests included his secretary John Warr (or Warre) the younger, his Stalbridge bailiff Nicholas Watts, technical assistants Hugh Gregg, Christopher White, and Frederick Schloer [= Slare], Robert St. Clair, John Dwight, John Milne, and John Whittacre (about the last four of whom nothing significant is known): for the will, see Maddison, *Boyle*, 257–82, and, for partial identification of Boyle's technicians, ibid., 136, and idem, "Studies in the Life of Boyle. Part V. Boyle's Operator," 159.

70. There is no record of a reply from Newton to Oldenburg's request, nor (unless Huyck *is* Hooke's Tom Hewk) have I traced any record of his doings subsequent to 1672. An undated letter included by the editor in Boyle's posthumously published "General History of the Air," 685, refers intriguingly to "an industrious young man, that, whilst he was my domestic, I bred up to chemistry, (of which he now teaches courses)," and who then lived in Oxford. On balance, however, it is more likely that the reference here is not to Huyck but to Peter Stahl (or Sthael): see Maddison, *Boyle*, 98. I speculate below about the reason for Huyck seeking to leave Boyle's employ. (We also know the name of one long-time amanuensis to Boyle—Robin Bacon: see, e.g., Harwood, *Early Essays*, xvi n. 3, xlix, 194 n. 21.)

of work, that individual was unlikely to have been functioning solely in the technician's role: during the periods Boyle engaged them, Hooke, Papin, Slare, and Mayow all had entitlements to a degree of collegiality. More commonly, the identification of technicians' work means that fragmentary evidence needs to be patched together by plausible inference. Thus, a text which reports the work of no agent save the authorial first person need not be taken as the product of an isolated individual, and evidence of assisting agents from other texts may plausibly be brought to bear on the understanding of the work-scene in question. In principle, the range of technicians' work was very large. At one extreme, there was Denis Papin, who we know, through Boyle's own testimony, was responsible for every aspect of experimental labor save its ownership. At the other, there were the ghostly inferred hosts of unnamed actors who shifted instruments about and exerted their muscular labor in making them yield phenomena that authors presented as philosophical knowledge.[71] I want to understand what technical support personnel did and how that work was regarded within the knowledge-making culture. How was work of different kinds related to the identity, the legitimacy, and the credibility of knowledge? I argue that the relationships between work and authority were embedded within systematic attributions of value, that these attributions belonged to the culture of gentlemen-masters, and that their effective implementation proceeded from the exercise of power in the workplace and the wider society. In particular, the value set on different types of work mobilized attributions of individuality and knowledgeability.

I have already hinted at the probability that Boyle himself was involved only in a very limited way in 'his' experimental manipulations. The device which became known as the *machina Boyleana* was almost certainly constructed for him by remunerated assistants Ralph Greatorex and Robert Hooke, and even the extent of Boyle's role in its evolving design remains unclear.[72] The glass J-shaped tube that yielded 'his' law of pressures and volumes was again almost certainly made for him and had to be manipulated by him in collaboration with assistants, if not solely by them.[73] The furnaces in his laboratory, and the alembics in which long-term distillations were performed, were probably tended by assistants. Experimental materials were fetched

71. Cf. M. B. Hall, *Boyle and Seventeenth-Century Chemistry*, 208: "The names of most of Boyle's . . . assistants have been lost, because they were not men of independent scientific merit."

72. E.g., Boyle, "Continuation of New Experiments," 180, where Boyle shared credit with "the ingenious Mr. *Hook*" for improvements to the original air-pump. For a concise account of Hooke's contribution to Boyle's work, see Fulton, *Bibliography of Boyle*, 10–12.

73. For details of how these experiments were performed, see Boyle, "Defence against Linus," 161.

and carried by assistants: buckets of snow, blood from the butcher's shop, lenses from the instrument-maker's. This is the sort of work which is evaluated similarly by both seventeenth-century philosophers and present-day scientists: it is not 'significant' or 'important'; 'anyone could do it.' Interchangeability and authority were taken to stand in inverse relationship: if one individual were not available to shift the instruments about, then it was considered that another could take his place without material consequence. Though experimental-philosophical knowledge could not be made if this work were not competently done, the knowledge was not thought to be marked by the individual signature of those who did it. During the Great Plague of 1665–1666 Hooke reassured Boyle (then at Oxford): "I do not hear of the death of any of your workmen save Mr. *Thompson* and Mr. *Shaw* the founder; and here are others of the same trade good workmen."[74]

Of course, both the skill-content of this sort of work and the relative availability of relevant personnel on the labor-market were matters of judgment, and those who judged good founders and reliable servants to be thick on the ground in Restoration London may well have been expressing a particular sense of cultural value as much as describing socioeconomic realities.[75] It was, for all that, widely acknowledged that certain kinds of assistance involved a very high degree of manual skill. Lens-grinding, metal-boring, glass-blowing, and certain types of chemical operations were all intermittently recognized as requiring considerable skill and dexterity. It was *not* considered that 'anybody could do' work of this sort, and the dependence of experimental philosophy upon a limited supply of such skilled personnel was occasionally expressed. I have already noted Boyle's complaints that he was unable to do chemical experiments when in Ireland, and experimentalists even criticized Oxford for its scarcity of appropriate skilled labor. Edward Bernard wrote to John Collins that everything was well suited for experimental work in Oxford except for the skill shortage: "We lack a corporation, a set of grinders of glasses, instrument-makers, operators, and the like, that experiments may be well managed in this place, which otherwise, by reason of our living all, as it were, together . . . is most convenient for such a design."[76] When Boyle re-

74. Hooke to Boyle, 21 March 1666, in Boyle, *Works*, VI, 505–06.
75. P. Earle (*Making of the English Middle Class*, 220) points to increasing wages and a significant shortage in the market for domestic servants in late seventeenth-century London, certainly exacerbated by the plague. Indeed, the contemporary practical literature on household management continually lamented that one couldn't get decent servants anymore.
76. Bernard to Collins, 3 April 1671, in Rigaud, *Correspondence of Scientific Men*, I, 159; cf. Boyle, "Continuation of New Experiments," 245, for the lack of "dexterous artificers" in Oxford hampering pneumatic work.

treated in the early 1660s from Oxford to a village several miles away, he justified a more speculative experimental style because he had to write "of experimental matters, in places where I cannot have workmen, nor instruments fit for my turn."[77] In 1688, when some of Boyle's loose sheets of experimental narrative were accidentally destroyed, he explained to his secretary John Warr that it would be impossible to repeat such experiments: in the past, Boyle said, he had better access to "exact instruments and skilful workmen" than he now enjoyed.[78] And, while Boyle never reflected systematically on this fact in print or in letter, the pace of his program of pneumatic experimentation slowed down markedly when Hooke left his service in 1662 and then again in 1673 when, presumably, Thom Huyck also departed.[79]

Insofar as technicians did manipulative and observational work for their masters, it was, strictly speaking, they, rather than those who gave them directions, who enjoyed that direct and unmediated access to the complex flux of experience which was so highly commended by seventeenth-century empiricists. Nevertheless, that directness of experience did not in itself confer epistemic value on technicians' understandings. Was technicians' experience taken to be relevant, consequential, and reliable? Was it to count as *knowledge,* or merely as skill, or, indeed, not *even* as skill? Could the technician who made the machine work make truth in his own name? The value put upon technicians' experience, and even the possibility of it finding a voice in experimental workplaces and narratives, depended upon decisions taken by employers. Since technicians were so intimately involved with the flux of experimental experience, they were *potentially* in a consequential position of judgment. For instance, technicians had routine experience of how reiterated experimental operations tended to go, as well as unverbalized, or unverbalizable, understandings of how they might best be conducted and what outcomes might be expected in a range of circumstances. Whether such direct and tacit experience was recognized by employers, how it was valued, whether it was encouraged or allowed to speak, and whether its voice was then represented, all depended upon the moral texture of social relations obtaining in the workplace. If, as I have argued, identity was a resource in making credible knowledge, then the political relationship of mastery and servitude was inscribed within the body of knowledge.

This is, of course, a general argument about the master-servant relationship in knowledge-making enterprises, and evidence from Boylean

77. Boyle, "New Experiments Touching Cold," 473.

78. Boyle, "An Advertisement about the Loss of His Writings," in Birch, "Life of Boyle," ccxxiii.

79. For some Boylean sensibility about this problem, see "Continuation of New Experiments," 176–77.

workplaces is sparse. In a series of air-pump experiments undertaken in the 1670s, Boyle several times related instances in which experimental design arose at least partly from his operator's judgment of the time it would take to exhaust a particular receiver, something about which the assistant was evidently acknowledged to have a relevant understanding.[80] Yet later in the same text a report of his assistant's judgment was embedded within a little moral and epistemic homily. Boyle was here interested in the general relationship between flammability and the presence of air, and particularly in whether a particle of ignited gunpowder in *vacuo Boyliano* could ignite other particles. He was trying to ignite the powder in the exhausted glass receiver by focusing sunlight on it with a lens. He was having little success, and related that "the operator, though versed in such experiments, would not allow that it would signify any thing to continue the trial any longer." Boyle reported that he refused to be guided by the operator's judgment. Boyle was "obstinate to prosecute it" further and demanded that the operator persist. A receiver with thinner glass was found and the powder on which the light was focused was successfully ignited.[81] The moral of this tale was that the merely experienced agent was rightly subservient to the reasoning agent. Or, as Boyle elsewhere observed, "Experience is but an assistant to reason."[82]

The rational knowledgeability which historians recognize that Boyle possessed, which he attributed to himself, and which he contrasted to his assistants' mere experience, was both a justification of his authority over the scene and an attribution of value. Of course, in a quite obvious sense, Boyle must have possessed knowledgeability far greater than that of the general run of assistants he employed. Let us say simply say that 'he knew more philosophy.' Yet the grounds upon which that knowledgeability was constituted can still be queried and explicated. It is unlikely, despite seventeenth-century rhetoric valorizing experience, that Boyle's knowledgeability was grounded in direct observational familiarity of all that was going on in his laboratory during all working hours. His assistants, presumably, possessed *that* sort of knowledgeability and passed it on to Boyle, just as Boyle was hugely dependent upon amanuenses' labor for the acquisition and arrangement of his bookish philosophical knowledge. So Boyle's knowledgeability probably consisted in his capacity to 'make sense' of what was going on in his laboratory. It was a philosophical sense, constituted by the capacity to say

80. Boyle, "New Experiments Touching Flame and Air," 569, 576.
81. Ibid., 582; see also idem, "Continuation of New Experiments," 245. And, for parallel instances of a laborant's defective judgment, see idem, "New Experiments and Observations Made upon the Icy Noctiluca," 489; and idem, "New Experiments Touching Cold," 560.
82. Boyle, "Christian Virtuoso," 539.

what was the 'point,' within a given cultural context, of certain laboriously produced phenomena. Yet the capacity to identify the philosophical point of laboratory work was also a right and privilege, an exercise of authority.

While for the historian the audibility of diverse voices in Boyle's laboratory is virtually nil, one cannot deny that they existed. Even in the cases of Hooke's and Papin's labor, it was Boyle who 'got to say' what the point of their work was. The attribution of knowledgeability is, therefore, an expression of the capacity of certain individuals to define the action of the work scene. Boyle's understanding and definition of experimental labor were superior to those of his assistants. Assistants' hands were subsumed in his head. And this circumstance of subsumption massively expressed as well as constituted the political order of early modern England.

Trusting Others' Eyes: Technicians and Testimony

Just as technicians were dependent upon Boyle for their directions and for the definition of laboratory work, so Boyle was dependent upon them for the empirical foundations of his knowledge. The moral order of the laboratory was an economy of trust and power relations. Precisely because assistants prepared, tended, and worked the instruments, Boyle was dependent upon them for his avowal that his experiments were really done, were done as he directed, and yielded the results that he would credibly relate to others. While the authorial voice was Boyle's, his narratives largely spoke for, and vouched for, what others had done, observed, and represented. Their labor and testimony became largely transparent in Boyle's accounts, and that transparency powerfully assisted the establishment of Boyle's narratives as true. What was said in Boyle's voice was the testimony of a free and independent gentleman, and what might be said in his assistants' voices was the potentially unreliable testimony of the dependent, the vulgar, and the interested. The early modern literature on practical household management made much of gentlemen's dependence upon their servants, and I want now to show the significance of that trust-dependency for the moral economy of knowledge-making. I need to establish in some detail how collective scientific work mobilized a trust relationship, and how the production of scientific truth rendered that relationship invisible. I then go on to describe some moral and epistemic circumstances in which this relationship might become spectacularly visible.

Boyle's narratives offer much evidence that his various unnamed assistants acted as important primitive observers and recorders of natural historical and experimental phenomena. Boyle was frequently away from his laboratory for extended periods, during which assistants might be entrusted with the entire performance and recording of experimental trials. Even when he was in residence, the press of other business, his various indispositions, and his sense of the reliability of his employees meant that, in all probability, supervision was restricted.

Some mention of his assistants' work as primitive observers and recorders appears in connection with fine perceptual discriminations, especially (though not exclusively) in marginal cases where acute eyesight was needed to establish the existence of phenomena. In such cases Boyle intermittently mentioned the concurring testimony of his assistants. Respiration experiments investigating the quantity of air dissolved in water required careful readings of water levels in glass tubes. Here the "chief operator" was said to have confirmed Boyle's visual judgment.[83] Microscopical studies of mineral waters were similarly left to an assistant "that had young eyes, and was accustomed to make use of" the relevant instruments.[84] Inquiries into the effects of cold or a vacuum upon luminescent bodies also needed precise visual discernment: was a piece of luminescent rotten fish getting brighter or dimmer? at what moment did luminescence disappear? Here Boyle related trials in which "he that had the youngest eyes in the company could not at all discern [any luminescence]," and that "neither I, nor a youth that I employed to look on [the fish], could perceive . . . that it retained any light."[85]

The moral and epistemic adequacy of assistants' independent observations might also be glancingly referred to as an incidental feature of densely circumstantial experimental narrative. Readers' presumption that the authorial first person signified physical performance or direct

83. Boyle, "New Pneumatical Experiments about Respiration," 362–63. (These experiments were communicated at about the time of Boyle's stroke in summer 1670.) Throughout his experimental career, Boyle sought to develop instrumental gauges which might discipline human testimony and reliably certify natural states of affairs (e.g., scalar height gauges for degrees of vacuum or pressure). Nevertheless, few experimental series dispensed with assistants' judgments about how matters stood, and the extent of a Boylean vacuum was persistently assessed by the testimony of an operator about the piston's resistance to muscular effort; see, for example, Boyle, "New Experiments Touching Flame and Air," 569, 576. For Boyle's work on gauges to be used in pneumatic experimentation, see Shapin and Schaffer, *Leviathan and the Air-Pump,* ch. 6, esp. 263–64.

84. Boyle, "Short Memoirs for the Natural Experimental History of Mineral Waters," 812.

85. Boyle, "New Experiments Concerning the Relation between Light and Air," 159; idem, "Observations and Trials about Burning Coal and Shining Wood," 172. And for nice perceptual judgments of phosphorescence, see Golinski, "A Noble Spectacle," 32–34.

witness by Boyle might be reinforced by occasional reference to his morally or practically warrantable absence from the observational scene. Knowledgeable colleagues occasionally observed work in Boyle's laboratory during his absence, but more commonly he seems to have delegated this to remunerated assistants.[86] In a version of Pascal's celebrated Puy-de-Dôme experiments, Boyle related assistants' role as observational delegates: "And though when I came to try the experiment I happened to have an indisposition that forbid me to do it all myself . . . , I committed our instrument to a couple of servants that I had often employed about pneumatical and mercurial experiments, giving them particular instructions what to do." Within hours the servants had returned, bringing back a precise report of barometric levels which Boyle accepted, related, and vouched for.[87] Servants were sent to the butcher's shop to report upon the temperature of blood issuing from a just-slaughtered cow: a "scal'd and gag'd weather-glass" would provide an objective measure of heat, but that measure was constituted through trust in the servant's report of what the weather-glass said.[88] In the 1670s Boyle related an important observation which he credited to one of his assistants, giving the circumstances which prevented him from vouching for the matter of fact upon his own witness: "[I] chanced to be then in an inconvenient posture for seeing [an experiment concerning the flammability of camphor in a vacuum]. . . . But my amanuensis that happened to be on the best side of the receiver, affirmed, he plainly saw the flame of the brimstone reach the [camphor], without being able to make it flame."[89] Boyle's narratives also offer some evidence about technicians as systematic recorders of experimental phenomena. A tract concerning distillations specified the role of a laborant who "kept a kind of journal" of the processes; results were here vouched for on the basis of "my own memory and the laborant's."[90] And the preface to the text on which Papin worked related the assistant's representational, as well as manipulative, labor in some detail.

86. E.g., Boyle, "Account of the Helmontian Laudanum" (1674), 150 (where Boyle noted that pharmaceutical preparations were "often watched in my absence by a very learned and industrious London doctor," possibly his neighbor Thomas Sydenham).

87. Boyle, "Continuation of New Experiments," 224. And, for dependence upon miners' barometric readings, see idem, "General History of the Air," 686–87 (as related by John Locke).

88. Boyle Papers, Vol. 18, f. 21 (see also f. 36 for reliance upon servants' reports of the color and weight of blood samples).

89. Boyle, "New Experiments Touching Flame and Air," 581.

90. Boyle, "A Chymical Paradox," 498, 502. A number of laboratory notebooks in assistants' handwriting are preserved in the Boyle Papers; see, e.g., the commonplace book in Boyle Papers, Vol. 190.

Sometimes Boyle alluded to assisting eyes and judgments in a routine and matter-of-fact fashion. The claimed findings were as expected; Boyle himself might have been present to supervise, confirm, and vouch for them; the testifying assistants were of a probity and skill sufficiently known to the reader of Boyle's narrative.[91] More pervasively, one can speculate, insofar as the experimental outcome conformed to Boyle's sense of normalcy, that technicians' observational and representational labor was transparently subsumed into the workings of the instrument without attribution of assisting human agency: 'it was found.'[92] Technicians' testimony could be assessed using the same maxims outlined in chapter 5 for testimony generally. The plausibility of assistants' testimony might be set against any credibility handicaps they might possess. Yet on other occasions there was textual recognition that reliance upon others' hands, eyes, and judgments could constitute troubles for authored knowledge-claims. Could these specific assistants be trusted? In this particular case, was their skill sufficient, their perceptual competence reliable enough, their integrity satisfactory? Should the views of an ancient authority, or of a modern colleague, be put in doubt without the most direct possible involvement by the author himself? What surety was there *in this case* for assistants' testimony?

Boyle's texts never handled such questions explicitly and reflectively but only as matters of situated practice. Problems of trust in technicians' testimony arose in specific practical settings and were dealt with as seemed expedient to the matter in hand. Consider how Boyle weighed his own and his assistants' judgments in the experiments on flame and air done in the early 1670s. Here again fine visual discriminations were involved. Since the materials under study apparently ignited only partially, judgments about the fleeting production of a spark or two, made in daytime conditions, were critical. Boyle was at pains in these trials to affirm the experimental phenomena on the basis of his own eyewitness: "In another trial," he reported, "two of the assistants plainly saw a spark or two fly out . . . though I, that chanced to stand in an inconvenient place, did not then perceive it." In this case, assistants' testimony was credible enough to be circumstantially related, but not credible enough to be accepted, and still less to become narratively transparent. "Afterwards, having caused the experiment for my

91. Recall that very many of Boyle's experimental texts took the form of a letter to a particular person who was assumed to be familiar with his workplace and its procedures and personnel.

92. I do not want in this connection to take issue with the claim that Boyle did his experimental work without formal theoretical predispositions, but I need to point out that *some* expectation about how matters would turn out was a precondition for Boyle's insistence that experiments could yield surprises.

fuller satisfaction to be repeated, I freed myself from the need of trusting others eyes."[93]

Nevertheless, Boyle trusted others' eyes, hands, and judgments pervasively, and one can scarcely conceive what his experimental career would have looked like had he declined to do so or if his trust in assistants' skill, reliability, and sincerity had been significantly less than it was. The dimensions and consequences of that trust need now to be drawn out. Narratives about experiments on the circumstances and effects of cold provided a setting in which Boyle elected (possibly not wanting to imitate Francis Bacon's fate) to delegate to his technicians even more observational and manipulative work than usual. Boyle was *inter alia* interested in testing popular claims about the relative ability of certain chilled materials to generate ice when immersed in cold water. The general philosophical question animating this work concerned the mechanisms of freezing and thawing, with special reference to the porosity of bodies.[94] One of Boyle's domestics related that water had turned to ice when poured into some newly purchased glasses that had been lying outside the laboratory door. As previous such attempts with glass had not produced ice, Boyle "suspected [that] the ice might have come from, or rather with the water, that was poured into the glass." Asking the servant whether that had been the case, Boyle was "assured of the contrary," and so the matter of fact was recorded. The effects of cold on the brittleness of iron had to be calibrated against the known skill and sincerity of "an expert smith I then used to imploy." The observation that certain iron springs broke in extreme cold might mean either that the smith "*gratis* deceive[d] me in the [quality of] irons I imployed" or that such a degree of cold might have such an effect on iron of good quality.[95]

Like many natural philosophers from antiquity to the present, Boyle was interested in the claim that hot water would freeze more quickly than cold. (In Boyle's understanding, the claim concerned the relative speed at which two samples *at the same temperature* would freeze, one of which had been previously heated.)[96] This was the sort of authoritative 'tradition,' going back to antiquity, about which the 'modern' natural philosophers liked to express vigorous skepticism: *Nullius in verba.* Ar-

93. Boyle, "New Experiments Touching Flame and Air," 572; see also ibid., 573, where Boyle again rejected what "by-standers affirmed" and "caused the experiment to be made once more, to ground my narrative upon my own observations."

94. See parallel experiments on freezing carried out by the Accademia del Cimento from 1657 to 1662, and published in 1667: Middleton, *The Experimenters,* 166–215, 380. The Florentines addressed their experiments on freezing more explicitly to assessing Scholastic doctrines, particularly concerning the *horror vacui.*

95. Boyle, "New Experiments Touching Cold," 529, 637.

96. See treatment of recent research into a related claim (the so-called Mpemba effect) in Barnes, *About Science,* 59–62.

istotle noted as a matter of fact that previously warmed water cooled faster, and that "many people" acted upon this knowledge.[97] Even Bacon mentioned as a matter of course that "water slightly warm is more easily frozen than quite cold."[98] As a good 'modern' should, Boyle proposed to discipline ancient authority through artificially contrived direct experience. Painstaking experimental testing was morally enjoined to "express a civility to so famous a philosopher as *Aristotle.*" Boyle said that he had made repeated trials of the matter, none of which found "any truth in the assertion"—"at least with our water, and in our climate." He specified that his ill health rendered him unable "to have so immediate an inspection" of these experiments as he would have liked, and "I was fain to trust the watchfulness of my servants (whom I was careful to send out often) to bring me word." Relays of domestics were appointed to prepare and watch the vessels. Special care was taken that the water in each vessel was at the same temperature at the moment of exposure, and one servant, "whose care I had no reason to distrust, [was appointed] to examine the tempers of these several waters, with a more than ordinarily sensible weather-glass." The same servant was instructed to stand out in the "sharp air"—Boyle being "unable to support such weather my self"—and to report what transpired. The servant observed both vessels begin to freeze at the same time, bringing them in to his master for confirmation. On that basis, Boyle judged the traditionally accepted truth "to be but chimerical."[99]

These episodes allow not one but two stories to be told about the proper relationship between authority and experience. The first story was the one normatively enjoined by the text, and, plausibly, read in this text by both seventeenth- and late twentieth-century 'moderns': tradition had avowed a state of affairs in nature which nature itself would not admit; tradition had been enforced by authority and assisted by credulity; a free and unconstrained practitioner had, however, confuted authority by interrogating *nature itself.* The Honourable Robert Boyle, deploying right method, had refuted Aristotle. The second story seems equally supported by the text in question, yet the conflict between it and the modernist moral is evident: trust in tradition was

97. Aristotle, *Meteorology,* I. 348ᵇ 31–33. For the medieval career of this doctrine of "antiperistasis," see Clagett, *Giovanni Marliani,* 92–100.

98. Bacon, "New Organon," 238. This reference was notably cited by Kuhn (*Structure of Scientific Revolutions,* 16) as representative of the uncritical preparadigm stage of science.

99. Boyle, "New Experiments Touching Cold," 638–40. (Precise time measurements of the freezing process were provided, all, presumably, as recorded by servants.) It was not related whether or not this particularly trusted servant was aware of his master's skepticism about tradition.

not simply supplanted by individual experience; Boyle's scientific work was done collectively, and much of the direct experience involved in rejecting tradition was had by his assistants and became his by virtue of their trusted performances and relations; trust in ancient authority was replaced by trust in assistants' experience. Aristotle was refuted by some anonymous technicians.

Noises Off: Technicians' Work as Excuse

If Boyle's technicians were typically transparent with respect to normal experimental practice, they became notably visible when troubles arose. From the outset of his career as an experimental author, Boyle urged that the faithful practitioner acknowledge an obligation circumstantially to report not just successes but failures and miscarriages.[100] Indeed, the richest seams of evidence of technicians' doings in the seventeenth-century literature are to be found in sporadic reports of experimental trouble. Here technicians' work came to constitute a morally and practically understood resource for explaining and excusing experimental failure. Experimental failure need not imply the refutation of the supposed order of nature the trial was designed to interrogate. It could, instead, be concluded that this was how such a natural order responded when it was badly interrogated *in just this way*.

The journal-books of the early Royal Society record constant dissatisfaction with the skill and reliability of its employees, including Robert Hooke. Hooke himself was periodically enraged by the fecklessness and incompetence of his assistants, and, most notably, Boyle's texts are replete with explanations for experimental failures which pointed to technicians' ineptitude and unreliability, their unwillingness or inability to follow what Boyle regarded as clear and simple orders. Boyle's domestic servants were, for example, constantly blamed for mislaying his papers, for losing his post, and for neglect in its prompt delivery. Towards the end of his life, Boyle explained the more-than-usual patchiness of his forthcoming experimental narratives: an assistant had poured sulfuric acid over an accumulated store of irreplaceable manuscripts.[101] Boyle's artificers continually failed to construct instruments according to his specifications, causing experiments to miscarry or to

100. E.g., Boyle, "Two Essays, Concerning the Unsuccessfulness of Experiments" (1661), esp. 339–40, 353; see also Shapin, "Pump and Circumstance," 494; Shapin and Schaffer, *Leviathan and the Air-Pump*, 64–65, 185–201.

101. Boyle, "An Advertisement about the Loss of His Writings," in Birch, "Life of Boyle," ccxxiii; Maddison, *Boyle*, 176; see also Boyle to Oldenburg, 29 August 1664; Oldenburg to Boyle, 3 November 1664; Oldenburg to Boyle, 10 December 1667, in Oldenburg, *Correspondence*, II, 211, 283; IV, 27; Boyle to Narcissus Marsh, 1 August 1682, in Boyle, *Works*, VI, 604. For pertinent modern sociological treatment of shoddiness and dependence, see Roth, "Hired Hand Research."

yield potentially misleading results.[102] Laborants misinterpreted the genuine outcomes of experiments with which they had been entrusted.[103] Technicians' free will was apt to erupt at any moment, turning laboratory good order into carnival, with disastrous results for competent experimental inquiry.

Boyle was once unable to judge whether violet leaves had lost their odor after an extended period in a vacuum "because he that included them had, for his own ease, contrary to my express direction crushed many of them together in thrusting them down."[104] Manometric gauge readings were rendered dubious because "a boy [had] unknown to me removed the tube from its wonted station, to place somewhat else there, without doing it heedfully enough," and quantitative investigations of freezing were ruined by "the negligence or mistake of an *Amanuensis*" who had committed "a manifest oversight . . . in the setting down the numbers which my memory does not now enable me to repair."[105] Boyle's researches on the composition of human blood were subverted by ignorant assistants who mistook laboriously obtained chemical substances for rubbish.[106] When Boyle laid his own hand upon experimental apparatus, he was apt to be put at risk "through the mistake of him that managed the pump, who, unawares to me, set it on work" and injured his master's hand.[107] And even so collegial an assistant as John Mayow was mentioned in Boyle's air-pump narratives in the context of a mistake which had catastrophic consequences:

> I had one day invited Dr. *Wallis* to see such an experiment. . . . After this learned person and I had continued spectators as long as we thought fit, we withdrew into another room, where we had not sat long by the fire before we were surprized by a sudden noise, which the person that occasioned it presently came running in to give us an account of, by which it appeared that this ingenious young man (whom I often employ about pneumatical experiments, and whom I mentioned to your Lordship because *J. M.* has the honour to be somewhat known to you) . . . plyed the pump so obstinately, that at length [the receiver broke], render[ing] it unserviceable for the future.[108]

102. E.g., Boyle, "New Experiments Physico-mechanical," 64; idem, "Continuation of New Experiments," 176, 246.

103. E.g., Boyle, "A Chymical Paradox," 500.

104. Boyle, "New Experiments about the Preservation of Bodies," 146.

105. Boyle, "General History of the Air," 619; idem, "New Experiments Touching Cold," 522 (see also 629 n.).

106. Boyle Papers, Vol. 18, f. 18.

107. Boyle, "Continuation of New Experiments," 215.

108. Ibid., 187–88. For other accounts of assistant-caused damage to experimental apparatus, see, e.g., idem, "New Experiments Physico-mechanical," 83; idem, "New Experiments Touching Cold," 561–62; idem, "General History of the Air," 620.

Explosive 'noises off' the room where Boyle sat form a staccato counterpoint to the flow of his experimental narratives. He reported a number of experimental disasters in some detail, invariably caused by the failings of his assistants, and, equally invariably, taking place when Boyle was both out of harm's way and out of direct control of the scene. Probably the most dangerous experimental trials Boyle conducted concerned the conditions for and nature of explosions. Early in this research he had become aware of the potentially violent outcome of mixing nitric acid and alcohol. In one instance the mixing caused so violent an explosion that, as Boyle related, some of the liquid "flew out of the glass, and hit against the ceiling of the room," then, dripping down, fell "upon his face that held the glass [and] made him think (as he told me) that fire had fallen upon it, and made him run down the stairs like a madman, to quench the heat at the [water] pump." Boyle's response was to bid "the laborant proceed more warily." Now fully cognizant of the risks of these experiments, Boyle gave the assistant even more detailed instructions and ensured that related trials now be made in a room big enough so that any spectators would not be endangered "and that even the operator, that shook the vessel, should stand at a convenient distance from the mixture," in this case of sal ammoniac and sulfuric acid. Unfortunately, if typically, the technician did not do as he was ordered and, as Boyle gruesomely related,

> whilst I was withdrawn to a neighbouring place to write a letter, the operator . . . rashly inverted the instrument, without taking care to get away; when it happened, that as soon as ever the contained liquor . . . was poured out . . . there was so surprizing and vehement an expansion or explosion made, that with a great noise (which as the laborant affirmed, much exceeded the report of a pistol) the glasses were broken into a multitude of pieces, many of which I saw presently after, and a pretty deal of the mixture was thrown up with violence against the operator's doublet and his hat, which it struck off, and his face; especially about his eyes, where immediately were produced extremely painful tumors, which might also have been very dangerous, had I not come timely in.[109]

These experiments were published in 1672. In September of that year Boyle's long-term chemical servant Thom Huyck—possibly now horribly disfigured—was seeking alternative, and perhaps safer, employment with Isaac Newton.

109. Boyle, "New Experiments about Explosions," 593–95. The violently exothermic character of chemical reactions of this type later fascinated Isaac Newton: *Opticks*, 377–79.

Technicians and the Moral Economy of the Scientific Workplace

The social and moral distance between masters and servants laid conditions upon the terms in which technicians might contribute to the making of philosophers' knowledge. It was *not* the case that technicians were simply distrusted—I have shown the very great extent to which Boyle relied upon them for making his knowledge—rather, it was that they *might* be distrusted, costlessly and consequentially. The scientific testimony of even so great, so skilled, and so (ambiguously) collegial a servant as Robert Hooke might have conditions laid upon it by his corporate paymasters, particularly when that testimony conflicted with the expectations of knowledgeable colleagues. Early in 1663, the Royal Society's *Journal-Book* recorded that Hooke, as remunerated curator of experiments, "made the experiment of condensing air by the pressure of water; but the trial agreeing not with the hypothesis, it was ordered to be repeated at the next meeting."[110] In 1672 the society considered the question whether air was generated or consumed by burning. Success or failure in these experiments had to be gauged in relation to some expectation about what the resulting measurement should be. Hooke's colleagues reserved the right to define whether or not his experimental work counted as success or failure. Indeed, when Hooke eventually reported "success," the *Journal-Book* referred guardedly to the experiment "he said, he had made," and members of the society were delegated to act as direct witnesses to a repetition.[111] Repeatedly, Hooke's masters and philosophical colleagues assumed the right to identify when Hooke had or had not performed experiments competently. On failure, Hooke was directed to take the experiment away until it worked properly, and only then bring it back to be shown in public.[112] Hooke was frequently obliged to make good his testimony about experimental trials performed in his own rooms by displaying the processes in public. In the 1680s, as Pumfrey has shown, Hooke was sharply taken to task "for not performing his experiments publicly."[113]

As with all commands he received from those he recognized as his masters, Hooke tended to accept such orders without significant demurral. Yet there are occasional signs of resentment at the conditions placed upon his veracity and skill. In 1667 Hooke was one of the major

110. Birch, *History of the Royal Society*, I, 177 (meeting of 14 January 1663). Hooke's 'incredibility' is treated in detail in Shapin, "Who Was Robert Hooke?" 282–85.

111. Birch, *History of the Royal Society*, III, 61, 77–78 (20 November 1672, 19 March 1673).

112. For the significance of the Royal Society distinction between "trying" and "showing" experiments, see Shapin, "House of Experiment," 400–04.

113. Birch, *History of the Royal Society*, IV, 261–62 (27 February 1684); Pumfrey, "Mechanizing Magnetism," 13.

experimenters in the society's vivisectional work on respiration. He was clearly irritated that his testimony of experimental success had not been credited by philosophical colleagues:

> I did heretofore give this *Illustrious Society* an account of an Experiment I formerly tryed of keeping a Dog alive after his *Thorax* was all display'd by the cutting away of the *Ribs* and *Diaphragme;* and after the *Pericardium* of the Heart also was taken off. But divers persons seeming to doubt of the certainty of the Experiment (by reason that some Tryals of this matter, made by some other hands, failed of success) I caus'd at the last Meeting the same Experiment to be shewn in the presence of this *Noble Company,* and that with the same success, as it had been made by me at first. . . . This I say, having been done . . . the Judicious Spectators [were] fully satisfied of the reality of the former Experiment.[114]

Hooke thus insisted upon his sincerity and skill, and also reminded his masters of their dependence upon him and of the potential costs of unbridled distrust. Indeed, Royal Society distrust of its curator's testimony was *not* routine, and one could hardly imagine how the society could have arranged its affairs if Hooke's testimony had not been generally accepted. The point is that even Hooke's experimental testimony might have conditions laid upon it, and that the authority to do so flowed from his standing as (ambiguous) servant.

Chapter 3 described how early modern gentlemanly culture construed the unreliability of servants' utterances. Servants were among the categories of persons who were thought to have reasons to tell untruths by virtue of their dependent and compromised standing. Their lack of integrity meant that they *might* be suspected of doing so, and there were few social costs attached publicly to contesting their narrations. The philosopher-master relied very substantially upon assistants' experience for the constitution of his own knowledge, yet early modern ethical literature constantly cautioned against the foolishness of trusting servants without adequate check or control. Gouge's popular *Of Domesticall Duties* (1622) prescribed the proper submission of servants' will to that of their masters, while lamenting what was widely seen as the growing unruliness of the servant class and urging the repair of the sumptuary codes in which master and man might be readily distinguished by dress.[115] Brathwait's *English Gentleman* (1630) warned that "as a *good servant* is a precious jewell, tendring the profit and credit of him he serveth; so an *evill servant* . . . , is a scatterer of

---

114. "An Account of an Experiment Made by Mr. *Hook,* of Preserving Animals Alive by Blowing through Their Lungs with Bellows," *Philosophical Transactions* 3 (1667), 539–40.

115. Gouge, *Of Domesticall Duties,* 602–03.

his substance whom he serveth; aiming only at his owne private profit, without least respect had to his *Masters* benefit."[116]

The potential unreliability of servants was a theme that continued into the eighteenth century and beyond. The golden age in which servants knew their place, did their duties, and reliably functioned as their masters' delegates was always in the past. Darrell's *Gentleman Instructed* (1704) echoed much common prudence in counseling gentlemen to keep a careful eye on their servants and not automatically to rely upon what they said: temptation compromised whatever native honesty servants possessed.[117] In the 1720s Defoe warned masters not to give over too much authority to their servants and apprentices: "Such a servant is well, when he is visibly an assistant to the master, but is ruinous when he is taken for the master." Accordingly, the master must be "as diligent as the servant" and must be "as much at the shop as the man."[118] Obadiah Walker challenged John Locke's epistemological individualism on a practical level, recognizing that as a general matter *"great persons* must necessarily hear and see with other mens ears and eyes; and whom can they trust so well as their own servants?" Yet he also advised masters to lay a consequential condition upon that trust: "It falls out many times, that [servants] inform for their own interest, not their Patrons. Wherefore a wise man believes little, but keeps himself in suspense till the truth be manifest."[119]

A man who trusted his servants too blindly made himself dependent upon their judgments and interests when they should be dependent upon his. As a practical matter, a man who kept servants made them the guardians of his reputation: servants "are Eare, and Eyewitnesses of your Words, Deeds, and Cariage."[120] Just because their tongues might be looser than they should be, there were mundane pragmatic reasons for making oneself a pattern of proper conduct. Practical arguments for mistrusting servants prevailed in the secular ethical litera-

---

116. Brathwait, *English Gentleman*, 160.

117. [Darrell], *Gentleman Instructed*, 17.

118. Defoe, *Complete English Tradesman*, 179–91 (quoting 179–80). Defoe was here treating a specifically mercantile setting, but similar sentiments were widely expressed throughout the seventeenth and eighteenth centuries about the proper supervision of servants in the houses of the gentry.

119. Walker, *Of Education*, 261 (cf. Locke, *Essay Concerning Human Understanding*, Bk. I, ch. 4, sect. 23). Walker was one of several English ethical writers who insisted upon the wholly contractual basis of servitude: "None can compell another to serve him against his will; nor can I contract with him for his *service*, but at the same time he will bargain with me for his *salary*." Yet, just because *"service* is nothing but a *compact betwixt the rich and poor,* for their mutual advantage," the servant-in-service serves his own interests by serving his master's (ibid.; see also Osborne, *Advice to a Son*, 31). Thus, even relatively egalitarian commentators on servitude came to the conclusion that the servant was properly his master's instrument.

120. Stafford, *Guide of Honour* (1634), 56; see also Gouge, *Of Domesticall Duties*, 628–29.

ture, while religious justifications dominated the literature pushing Christian conceptions of gentility. Gentlemen were God's stewards over their families' behavior. The subordination of servant to master "is but the wise *Oeconomie* of their Lord."[121]

The laboratory economy was also shaped by these understandings of master-servant relations. Seventeenth-century rhetoric valorizing the tacit knowledge of the unlettered is well known to historians. Those who were closest to natural and mechanical processes were said to be in a privileged position *vis-à-vis* the making of proper empirical knowledge and the detection of illegitimate accounts. Experimentalists were encouraged to take craft and artisanal knowledge seriously, to extract that empirical and factual knowledge from those who possessed it, to give it systematic form, and not to stint in that enterprise because of false notions of social pride and prejudice.[122] Such rhetoric figured largely in the developing critique of arid school-philosophy.

For all that, traditional gentlemanly disdain for the mechanical arts and contempt for those who remuneratively practiced them were not expunged but only tempered in seventeenth-century English culture, even among some of those most closely associated with the new rhetoric. Thus, Boyle said that he spent much of his spare time at Stalbridge in "catechis[ing] my gardener and our ploughmen, concerning the fundamentals of their profession," and told the Hartlibians that he had indeed found their conversation both illuminating and productive.[123] Yet Boyle's early endorsement of philosophical openness was soon compromised by, as he put it, the sordid requirements of trading with those who "need to make a pecuniary advantage" of secret knowledge.[124] By 1674 Boyle made no scruples about his distaste for necessary philosophical dealings with the artisan and trading classes, warning the neophyte that the experimental philosopher would need to apply

> himself to such a variety of mechanick people, (as distillers, druggists, smiths, turners, &c.) that a great part of his time, and perhaps all his patience, shall be spent in waiting upon tradesmen, and repairing the losses he sustains by their disappointments, which is a drudgery greater than any, who has not tried it, will imagine, and which yet being as inevitable as unwelcome, does very much counter-balance

121. [Allestree], *Gentleman's Calling*, 89–93; see also Brathwait, *English Gentleman*, 154–64; [Ramesy], *Gentlemans Companion*, 88–91; Mackenzie, *Moral Essay Preferring Solitude*, 104; Petrie, *Rules of Good Deportment*, 32–33.

122. Among very many examples of these injunctions, see Boyle, "Some Considerations Touching the Usefulness of Experimental Natural Philosophy," 162, 167; see also Rossi, *Philosophy, Technology, and the Arts*, ch. 1.

123. Boyle to Benjamin Worsley, *ca.* mid-1640s, in Boyle, *Works*, VI, 40.

124. Boyle, "A Proëmial Essay" (1661), 315.

and allay the delightfulness of [experimental philosophy]. In which so great a part of a man's care and time must be laid out in providing the apparatus's necessary for the trying of experiments.[125]

While the mechanic classes might indeed be the bearers of valuable empirical knowledge, that knowledge needed to be drawn out, freely and disinterestedly reflected upon, and codified for its value to be realized. It had to be rendered into something fit for *philosophy*. Only when it had been so rendered did newly systematized knowledge acquire the capacity to *improve* the arts. By the early 1660s, Boyle himself was describing the great benefits that practical chemists and instrument-makers had already enjoyed by receiving back from philosophical gentlemen their own trade knowledge, digested, objectified, and enriched.[126] Much hinged upon whether the Royal Society circle had successfully achieved the translation of craft ingenuity into free philosophy. Its advocates announced that the mechanical philosophy was the more genuinely philosophical for its mechanic content and means of production, while contemporary detractors scored a palpable moral hit by insisting upon the demarcation between proper philosophy and whatever could be achieved by *mere* ingenuity.[127] Hobbes's criticisms of Royal Society experimentalism voiced quite traditional conceptions of the relations between the liberal and mechanical arts, as well as the relative propriety of each for gentlemanly pursuit: "Not every one that brings from beyond seas a new gin, or other jaunty device, is therefore a philosopher. For if you reckon that way, not only apothecaries and gardeners, but many other sorts of workmen, will put in for, and get the prize." Fiddling with the air-pump was as undignified as it was unphilosophical.[128]

Thomas Sprat articulated the Royal Society's official approval of mechanic pursuits, while acknowledging that there was something about the mechanic mind and its habitual employment that made it

125. Boyle, "Excellency of Theology," 35–36; cf. idem, "Some Considerations Touching the Usefulness of Experimental Natural Philosophy. Second Tome," 396–99. His friend John Evelyn similarly found insupportable "the many subjections . . . of conversing with mechanical capricious persons": Evelyn to Boyle, 9 August 1659, in Boyle, *Works*, VI, 288.

126. E.g., Boyle, "Some Considerations Touching the Usefulness of Experimental Natural Philosophy," 138, 144, 146; ibid., "Second Tome," 398–99, 401, 403–04; Simpson, "Hooke and Practical Optics," 36.

127. Bennett, "The Mechanics' Philosophy and the Mechanical Philosophy"; also idem, "Hooke as Mechanic and Natural Philosopher."

128. Hobbes, "Considerations on the Reputation of Hobbes," 436–37. For treatment of Hobbes versus Boyle on "engines" and "ingenuity," see Shapin and Schaffer, *Leviathan and the Air-Pump*, 125–39; and, for continuing late seventeenth-century polite views that mechanical means were inappropriate for the constitution of genuine knowledge, see Shapin, "'A Scholar and a Gentleman,'" 304–12.

unsuitable for participation in a genuinely philosophical enterprise. Artificers, Sprat said, take their work as a matter of habitual remunerative routine. While such men undeniably possessed detailed, exact, and expert knowledge, they oriented to that knowledge in a meretricious and philosophically barren way. By contrast, gentlemen-philosophers—"men of freer lives"—approached mechanic matters in a posture quite distinct from that of mechanics themselves. Gentlemen made up in moral and epistemic capacity for what they lacked in expertise: "They do not approach those *Trades*, as their dull, and unavoidable, and perpetual *employments*, but as their *Diversions*." Just because of their lack of expert knowledge, gentlemen were apt to make mistakes when they took up the mechanical arts. Yet those literally amateur mistakes were the source of genuine philosophical illumination: "[Their] very faults, and wandrings will often guid them into new *light*, and new *Conceptions*." The gentleman-philosopher was a free spirit, set upon an intellectual quest to which traditional chivalric rhetoric might legitimately be applied:

> There is also some privilege to be allow'd to the *generosity* of their *spirits*, which have not bin subdu'd, and clogg'd by any constant *toyl*, as the others. *Invention* is an *Heroic* thing, and plac'd above the reach of a low, and vulgar *Genius*. It requires an *active*, a bold, a nimble, a restless *mind:* a thousand difficulties must be contemn'd, with which a mean heart would be broken; many *attempts* must be made to no purpose; much *Treasure* must sometimes be scatter'd without any return; much violence, and vigor of thoughts must attend it . . . which may persuade us, that a large, and an unbounded mind is likely to be the *Author* of greater *Productions*, then the calm, obscure, and fetter'd indeavors of the *Mechanics* themselves.[129]

The ability to make knowledge was therefore considered importantly to flow from the mental and moral qualities of those who confronted the phenomena. Epistemic capacity was expressed in the same idiom used to describe and justify social order.

The moral distance between masters and servants was made manifest in the practical procedures of command, control, and supervision. Like all servants, technicians' labor was contractually engaged for a period of time on terms which specified the nature and extent of their obligations. We know most about the contractual terms of those few rather grand technicians who uneasily mixed the roles of servant and colleague, and recent work on Robert Hooke fastens upon the language used by his Royal Society masters to direct his labors. Some technicians functioned in the role of *apprentices*, having entered into a contractual relationship in which they provided their labor in exchange for train-

129. Sprat, *History of the Royal Society*, 392.

ing. This pattern was certainly evident in Hooke's relations with his own technicians, at least some of whom had formally apprenticed themselves to him.[130] Yet the Hookean pattern was not the norm in the materials under discussion: gentlemen-philosophers were rarely in a position to offer servants marketable training in craft skills, and Aubrey's description of Boyle's chemical servants as "Prentices to him" was simply careless.[131] Boyle was not training his assistants to do what he did, not least because they could not become what he was.

The apprentice pattern aside, seventeenth-century relations between technical assistants and philosopher-employers were not standardized. Even within a remunerative relationship, some assistants might be treated in a manner verging on the collegial, some as menials, and some in any manner in between. Ingenious young university graduates were occasionally employed by gentlemen-philosophers—as technical assistants, clerks, or amanuenses—on their way to permanent professional careers. Thus, traditional professional patterns may have informed Boyle's engagement of Hooke, Mayow, Slare, and possibly even Locke.[132] Here the assistant's presentation of himself might materially shape the eventual form of the master-servant relationship. Almost the whole of Hooke's career was strongly marked by confrontation between his stipulations about his identity and the identity ascribed to him by his masters. In the early 1650s, the alchemist, and Harvard graduate, George Starkey tried to stipulate the terms of his relationship with Boyle, insisting that he was *not* to be treated as a mere laborant.[133] Like family tutors and secretaries, educated young men called upon in scientific capacities commonly resided with their employers and might be regarded as valued, if obviously subordinate, family members.[134]

One thinks in this connection of the Walter Warner and Thomas Hariot examples mentioned earlier, and especially of Thomas

130. Shapin, "Who Was Robert Hooke?" 262–69; Pumfrey, "Ideas above His Station."

131. Aubrey, *Brief Lives,* 37.

132. For the possibility that Locke assisted Boyle in 1666–1667, see Dewhurst, "Locke's Contribution to Boyle's Researches," 201. In 1677 Locke was urging Boyle from Paris to give him some scientific "employment," although this most probably consisted in nonremunerated news-gathering: Locke to Boyle, 25 May 1677, in Locke, *Correspondence,* I, 484. And, as is well known, Locke saw Boyle's posthumously published *General History of the Air* through the press, adding meteorological records he had collected at Boyle's behest.

133. Starkey to Boyle, [April–May 1651], in Boyle Letters, Vol. 6, ff. 99r–100v, transcribed in Newman, "Newton's *Clavis* as Starkey's *Key,*" 572; and forthcoming work on Starkey kindly shown me in typescript by Prof. Newman.

134. For prescriptions about the role of secretary in a seventeenth-century aristocratic household, see Brathwait, *Some Rules and Orders for the Government of the House of an Earle,* 17–18.

Hobbes's lifelong relationship with the Cavendish family—as tutor, secretary, and house scholar—though the Cavendishes were ultimately as keen to establish Hobbes's independence as Hobbes was not to appear a "domestique."[135] Hooke notably shared living quarters with Boyle at Oxford and appears to have had dining and domiciliary rights at Lady Ranelagh's house until he secured his rooms at Gresham College.[136] Henry Oldenburg, while almost certainly not a skilled experimental agent, seems to have worked on a retainer from the Boyle family, and later from Boyle himself, from the mid-1650s to the end of his life, moving from his early role as family tutor to that of Boyle's publisher and philosophical intelligencer. Oldenburg's second, and advantageous, marriage made him a distant relation of his employer. Although Oldenburg undeniably worked at Boyle's behest, their relationship had a significantly collegial basis, even if it was inevitable that Boyle decided the extent of permissible collegiality. However, most of Boyle's technical assistants were probably engaged on the same basis, and on the same understanding, as his domestic servants. Servitude was their lot in life, not a transient stage on a path leading to a professional career or the life of a leisured gentleman.

Decisions about the fine structure of a relationship between master and servant flowed from decisions about the identity of the persons employed and the purposes for which they were employed. There is particularly illuminating material about such decisions in an interchange between Oldenburg and John Wallis in 1669. The Royal Society's secretary had approached the Oxford professor for a recommendation of "an Anatomical Operator," although it was unclear to Wallis whether this person was to work for the Royal Society or for some individual associated with it. Oldenburg had evidently told Wallis that the person to be engaged was to have the substantial annual pay of "20 lb & diet [i.e. board and lodging]." The operator was to be both skilled and honest: "to have a good hand at it, diligent, & humble." Wallis, in reply, wanted as precisely as possible to pin down Oldenburg's terms of engagement, for upon their construal would depend the sort of individual to be recommended, and how that person might expect to be dealt with. "I suppose," Wallis returned, "by a good hand, you mean onely one dextrous & intelligent," presuming that in this instance knowledgeability might be required as well as mere skill—someone "who by experience may come to be more knowing." An already knowledgeable person ("experienced & perfect" at the busi-

135. Rogow, *Hobbes*, 110–13, 208–09, 229–31. So generous were the Cavendishes that Hobbes was receiving a pension/salary of £80 per annum towards the end of his life and died worth nearly £1,000; cf. Shirley, "The Scientific Experiments of Ralegh," 56–59 (for Warner and Hariot).

136. Birch, "Life of Boyle," lv; 'Espinasse, *Hooke*, 111.

ness) "will either hardly be found" or would be looking for a permanent professional position. Most important, in Wallis's view, was the
exact construal of Oldenburg's requirement that the operator be
"humble." In Wallis's view this concerned the vital distinction between
the condition of servitude and that of a free colleague:

> By humble; if it be meant meerly in ye condition of a servaunt: it will
> be ye lesse inviting to ingenious persons & scholars of any standing,
> who will scarce be willing to go from ye University to such a condi-
> tion. . . . If it be intended of one to goe in an ingenious way, as a
> gentleman, but of no proud or peevish nature: it will be proper to
> propose it to some M[aste]r of Arts or Bachelour of Arts, who studied
> Anatomy & have some competent skill in it. If to be in a meaner
> servile imployment; it must be some servitour (for others will hardly
> condescend to it) & wee shall hardly find one, in that condition, very
> fit for it; but possibly such as may bee in a capacity of being taught.[137]

This exchange between Wallis and Oldenburg, a rare instance of explicit discussion of the terms on which technical assistants were to be
engaged, highlights the two defining characteristics of the technician's
role: the dependency relationship and the distinction between knowledgeability and skill that was considered to be embedded in the ideal-
type of that relationship. The philosopher was both free and knowledgeable; his technician dependent and merely skilled.

Despite important variation in philosopher-assistant relations, I have
observed that the term *servant* might be used to designate all remunerated assistants, and there are some basic moral features of the general
master-servant relationship which figure importantly in the early modern knowledge-making economy. I have already noted that Christian
ethical writers stressed masters' moral responsibility for their servants,
and Boyle obviously embraced it with respect to his technicians. As a
young man he argued against swearing partly on the grounds that
it would corrupt servants as well as diminishing the master's moral
authority.[138] And in 1668 he refused to persist in a promising line of
investigation, "it being *Sunday* night [and] I was unwilling to scandalize
any, by putting my servants upon a laborious and not necessary
work."[139] Furthermore, the honesty and moral attributes of individual
servants had to be *vouched for,* and that vouching was an integral part
of the processes by which technicians were engaged. Technical assis-

137. Wallis to Oldenburg, 15 April 1669, in Oldenburg, *Correspondence,* V, 494 (Oldenburg's letter to Wallis has not survived). The editors of the Oldenburg *Correspondence*
(ibid., 495 n. 5) think that discussions about a suitable appointee involved the physicians
Walter Needham, John Ray, and Richard Lower.

138. Boyle, "Free Discourse against Customary Swearing," 11 (written *ca.* 1647; posthumously publ. 1695).

139. Boyle, "New Experiments Concerning the Relation between Light and Air," 168.

tants were passed on from one gentleman-philosopher to another, the previous employer offering some token that he staked a part of his own reputation upon the "character" he gave his former servant. Cascades of gentlemanly credibility were thus inscribed in the institution of the letter of reference. Such letters vouched for the probity as well as the technical skill of a prospective employee. In 1653 John Wilkins wrote a recommendation to Boyle, to be delivered by the "young man"—probably not Hooke—in question: "I am apt to believe, that upon trial you will approve of him. But if it should happen otherwise, it is my desire he may be returned, it being not my aim so much to prefer him, as to serve you."[140] The following year Hartlib was telling Boyle about the possibility of hiring a laborant "very much commended for his mineral skill."[141] Boyle took on Hooke upon the recommendation of his previous employer, Thomas Willis, and afterwards recommended Hooke for technical service with his colleagues in the Royal Society.[142]

The society's first salaried employee was probably Michael Wicks (or Weeks), engaged as a clerk in 1663 on the recommendation of Dr. Jonathan Goddard, who had previously employed him to look after his stills at Gresham College.[143] I have just mentioned Oldenburg's solicitation of Wallis's recommendation of an anatomical operator for the Royal Society; the technician Henry Hunt was recommended to the society in 1673 by Hooke, having been Hooke's personal apprentice. Hunt became Hooke's experimental assistant in Royal Society matters, sharing quarters with him, and in 1676, after the council "heard several good testimonies given him of his ability and honesty," Hunt was appointed experimental "Operator."[144] It was Christiaan Huygens who recommended Denis Papin to the service of the Royal Society philosophers. He wrote to Oldenburg requesting him to grant his former assistant "your favour and protection" and to arrange introductions to Boyle and Viscount Brouncker. Huygens vouched for Papin's experimental skill: he was "ingenious"; his mechanical contrivances worked effectively; he "understands everything in mechanics very well and also knows geometry." But Huygens also vouched for Papin's moral probity: "He has lived with me for two years [and] . . . as to his

140. Wilkins to Boyle, 6 September 1653, in Boyle, *Works*, VI, 633–34; see also More, *Boyle*, 79–80.

141. Hartlib to Boyle, *ca.* 1654, in Boyle, *Works*, VI, 87.

142. Gunther, *Early Science in Oxford*, VI, 5.

143. Birch, *History of the Royal Society*, I, 236; Robinson, "Administrative Staff of the Royal Society," 194; Lyons, *Royal Society*, 37–38; M. B. Hall, *Promoting Experimental Learning*, 26–27 (for the possibility that Wicks had been serving as the society's amanuensis since 1661).

144. Birch, *History of the Royal Society*, III, 322 (20 November 1676).

being prudent and modest, I can reply by the experience I have had of him all the time that he has been with me, and he is of too honest parents to fail in that respect."[145]

Once engaged, there seems to have been little confusion in technicians' minds about their standing *vis-à-vis* employers. Even so eminent an assistant as Hooke tellingly referred to himself as "belonging" to Boyle. So long as his labor was remuneratively engaged, Hooke appears in the main to have accepted his employers' right to tell him what to do and even, on occasion, their right to lay conditions upon the acceptance of his experimental testimony.[146] And, as I noted above, Papin also accepted authorial subsumption as he accepted Boyle's money. What went for technicians who had presumptive intellectual claims to collegiality went more forcefully for those who lacked them. Although the servant's role in seventeenth-century England might be rejected, modified, or imaginatively turned upside down, it was a role whose justifications and patterns of conduct were nevertheless well understood. However knowledgeable or skilled the servant, the acceptance of money in exchange for labor tended effectively to elicit relatively stable sensibilities towards the master's rights and the servant's duties. The demarcation between the state of servitude and that of the independent free agent was basic both to practical social theory and to practical decisions about the knowledge-making economy.

Finally, the texture of moral relations between master and technical servant was made manifest in practical procedures for assigning and managing the ownership of knowledge. Chapter 4 discussed Boyle's well-known advocacy of openness in physic, chemistry, and natural philosophy, while also noting a growing proprietary attitude towards the intellectual goods produced in his laboratory. Chemical servants, like servants generally, were frequently placed in a position of trust *vis-à-vis* their masters' secrets. Gouge's *Of Domesticall Duties* was one of many similar texts to comment on the moral consequences of the fact that "seruants come to know many of their masters secrets." On the one hand, this meant that the prudent master maintained a careful watch on them; on the other, the servant accepted a moral obligation to avoid "blabbing abroad all such things as seruants know concerning their masters." "*Faithfulnesse*" required servants to keep masters' secrets close, while Sprat's *History of the Royal Society* matter-of-factly noted the "*Treachery* of servants" as a major vehicle for the publication of their

145. Huygens to Oldenburg, 1 July 1675, in Oldenburg, *Correspondence*, XI, 380; see also Robinson, "Papin," 48; Birch, *History of the Royal Society*, III, 486 (for the introduction of Papin to the Royal Society by Hooke, for whom Papin worked 1679–81).

146. Shapin, "Who Was Robert Hooke?" 262–67, 280–85.

masters' secrets.[147] That moral obligation occasionally took documentary form. One of Boyle's late commonplace books contains a remarkable document, a draft of an oath evidently to be taken and signed by technicians entering his service. While Boyle himself was notably "tender in point of oaths" and reckoned that it was sufficient that his 'yea be yea and nay be nay,' such sensitivity was not extended to technicians, men whose circumstances might well induce them to break faith.

> Whereas I _____ being now in ye service of Mr. _____ he is pleas'd to imploy me about ye making of divers Expts yt he would not haue to be divulg'd; I do hereby solemnly & faithfully promise & ingage myself yt I wil be true to ye trust repos'd by my sayd master in me, yt I wil not knowingly discouer to any p[er]son w[ha]tsoever, whether directly or indirectly, any process, medicine, or other Expt, wch he shal injoin me to keep secret & not impart; wthout his consent first obtain'd to communicate it. And this I promise in ye faith of a Xtian, witnes my hand this _____ day of _____.[148]

If a gentleman's word was his bond, the servant required double-bonding.

Servitude and Subsumption

The identity of the author of a claim offers a warrant for the truth of what is claimed. But who is the author, and what are the bases upon which authorship is assigned? These are questions whose salience to the study of knowledge-making practices emerges only through a display of the collective nature of those practices. In the case of early modern science one must systematically discredit the validity of individualistic epistemic assumptions before one is entitled to make deep claims about the political character of knowledge. This chapter has attempted *inter alia* to display the inadequacy of an individualistic picture of seventeenth-century knowledge-making scenes.

Who gets to speak? Whose speech may be accounted truth? These are political matters. Arguably, they are the most fundamental matters to be settled in any polity, and as they are resolved so political order

147. Gouge, *Of Domesticall Duties*, 622–35 (quoting 628); Sprat, *History of the Royal Society*, 74.

148. Boyle Papers, Commonplace Book 189, f. 13r. There is residual uncertainty about the Boylean usage of this oath since his proper name is not actually given here. On the other hand, there cannot have been very many other contemporary figures specifically requiring *experimental* secrecy. For Boyle's sensitivity about oaths and obligations, see Hunter, "Casuistry in Action," esp. 82–85, 89–90; idem, "The Conscience of Boyle."

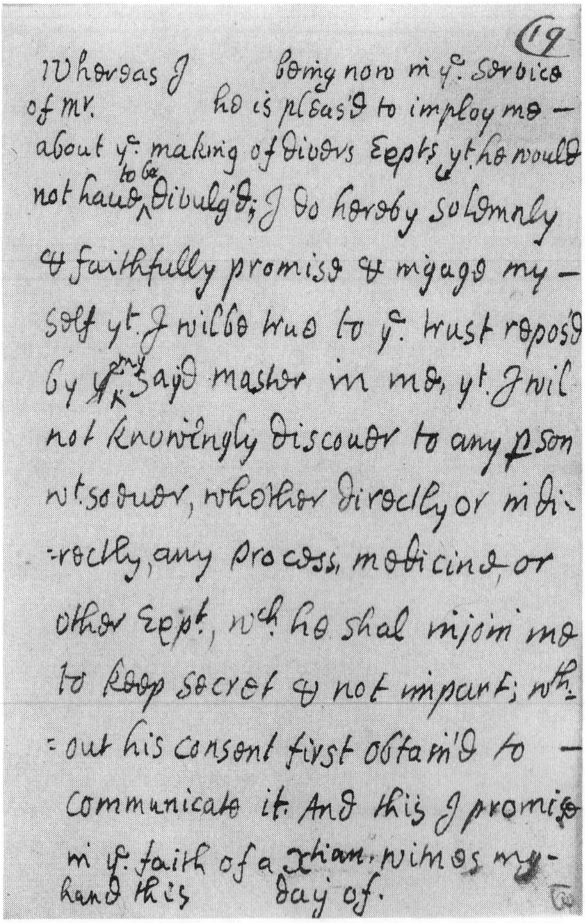

Figure 12. Draft of an oath, probably to be taken and signed by Boyle's technicians. (Boyle Papers, Commonplace Book 189, f. 13r.) This draft is thought to be in the hand of the amanuensis Robin Bacon, who worked for Boyle from the 1670s until Boyle's death (see Hunter, *Letters and Papers of Boyle,* xxxi, 81). There is reason to believe that such documentary oaths were commonly enforced upon servants, although this one was clearly designed specifically for experimental servants. (Courtesy of Royal Society of London.)

is constituted, both in the house of knowledge and in the state. I have already noted the broad seventeenth-century English understanding of the 'servant's' identity. The term *servant* was routinely used to designate all individuals who worked for an employer for wages and who were, accordingly, dependent upon that master for their way of living.

In Locke's formulation "a Free-man makes himself a Servant to another, by selling to him for a certain time, the Service he undertakes
to do, in exchange for Wages he is to receive."[149] Scientific technicians
were thus unambiguously servants in this sensibility, and what was
understood of the condition of servants generally was understood of
them as well.

In the late 1640s the Putney Debates over the nature and extent of
the franchise made explicit much of what had been taken for granted
about the nature and bounds of the English polity.[150] Both the Levellers (on the 'left') and Cromwell and Ireton (on the 'right') were agreed
that the franchise—the right to speak and consequentially to be heard
in civil society—ought to be greatly extended. Its bounds ought now
to include "all inhabitants that have not lost their birthright," that is,
their native freedom. On these grounds, servants—all those who sold
their labor to another—were excluded. They were considered to have
"lost their birthright" by contractually reassigning their rights of free
action.[151] The contemporary understanding and justification of that
exclusion are thoroughly familiar from the early modern gentle culture interpreting the relations between free action, truth, and power.

In the opinion of the Leveller Maximilian Petty, "the reason why we
would exclude apprentices, or servants, or those that take alms, is because they depend upon the will of other men and should be afraid
to displease (them)." It was not that servants were therefore unrepre-
sented in the polity. As they were "included in their masters," so they
were spoken for by their masters.[152] And the same presumption about
free action and political speech that excluded servants also underlay
the—scarcely considered—exclusion of women: they too were dependent upon their masters/husbands/fathers, and might be presumed
"afraid to displease them." In this culture there was no legitimacy in
giving political voice to those who could not be presumed to speak
truth, and who were, in the event, spoken for by others. Free action
warranted truth, and free action licensed political speech. Only those
who were free could have a political voice; only those who were free
deserved to be listened to, because free action was the condition for
speaking truth. Those who could not speak truth in their own right

149. Locke, *Two Treatises of Government*, Bk. II, sect. 85.

150. Macpherson, *Political Theory of Possessive Individualism*, esp. 54, 107–08, 120–48,
282–86; Hill, "Pottage for Free-born Englishmen," 223–34.

151. Macpherson (*Political Theory of Possessive Individualism*, 118 n. 2) notes just one
Leveller document including servants in the franchise.

152. Ibid., 123, 146; also idem, "Harrington's 'Opportunity State,'" 43. For criticism
of Macpherson's specific interpretation of Leveller views on servitude and the franchise,
see, for example, Davis, "Levellers and Democracy," and Howell and Brewster, "Reconsidering the Levellers."

either could not be relied upon to speak the truth, or were spoken for by those free actors who commanded their labors. This was the same political theory which subsumed the identity of Boyle's technicians into that of their master. As a free acting gentleman he was the author of their work. He spoke for them and transformed their labor into his truth.

All workshops contain diverse points of view. The modern hospital, for example, contains technicians, nurses, physicians, accountants, and administrators. The sociologist can choose to hear diverse voices speaking about hospital realities and the 'point' of hospital work. Nevertheless, there is little difficulty in identifying the 'official' story and the officially constituted spokesman for the institution. As Howard Becker notes, spokesmen make assertions on the behalf of subordinates "and are held responsible for the truth of those assertions." The institution constitutes a "hierarchy of credibility."[153] I have focused here upon the official story of scientific truth-making, yet in order to write that story I have felt it necessary to trace the bounds of inclusion and the grounds of exclusion that distinguished between actors.

Because my interest has been in the constitution of scientific knowledge—the sort which eventually got written up and put into books—I have attended to a gentlemanly culture. That was the culture which, with scholarly associates and minions, overwhelmingly produced and consumed books. Just as this chapter may be taken as a token of my belief in the significance of the nongentle within gentlemanly practices, so there is nothing whatsoever here that should be read as a claim that other economies of truth did not coexist with the gentle versions I have treated. I do not know enough to tackle the problem of relevant early modern cultural diversity in anything but an airily speculative way. Did servants, women, and the nongentle generally believe that they were untruthful? Again, I do not know, but I suspect not. I suspect that as servants dealt with servants, and women with women, they were able to warrant their collective reliability and to sort out truthful from untruthful individuals in their midst. One could hardly imagine how their everyday relations could be otherwise conducted. Similarly, there is little reason to doubt that within nongentle and nonmale culture, a jaundiced eye was intermittently cast at gentlemanly arrogations of virtue and truth: every Don Giovanni has his Leporello as well as his Donna Elvira.

At the same time, I see no reason to dispute the *authority*, and, therefore, the spread, of gentlemanly codes across the early modern social

153. Becker, "Whose Side Are We On?" 129. This perspective on institutions and authority has also been pressed forcefully by such Chicago-school sociologists as Everett Hughes, Anselm Strauss, and their students; see, for example, Mukerji, "Having the Authority to Know."

landscape. The point is not that gentlemanly honor, virtue, and truth-fulness were everywhere credited. Subversive eruptions establish that they were not, even if it would be wrong to conclude on *a priori* grounds that the nongentle *must* have been continuously seething in skeptical resentment. Yet in this connection it is pertinent to note that the same culture which warranted gentlemanly veracity could prove useful to those who wished to contest the fact that gentlemen spoke the truth. For example, the culture of chivalry that was 'owned' by seventeenth-century English gentlemen was also notably appropriated by London apprentices and merchants during the civil wars. Honor was here said to consist of honorable conduct; the gentry were debased and had lost their legitimate claims to deference; the mercantile classes were the genuinely honorable and truthful ones.[154]

The mark of authoritative cultural practices is, therefore, not neces-sarily universal slavish assent to those who arrogate to themselves the practices and attendant evaluations. Authority is also signed by contests for the ownership of that culture. It follows, however, that the gentle-manly culture of honor and truth must have been very widely viewed as relatively well working and legitimate. If it had not been so consid-ered, there would have been no point in contending for its ownership, or in extending its practices as resolutions of problems of dissent and disorder elsewhere in the culture.[155] And that gentlemanly culture could hardly have been seen as relatively well working and legitimate if it did not, on the whole and in general, effectively regulate relations between gentlemen and others, if it did not, on the whole and in gen-eral, justify hierarchy. Insofar as one can identify gentlemen as power-ful agents in early modern society, thus far one has said that they solved the problem of being recognized as truth-speakers. Their ways of going on could be appropriated for the job of finding and war-ranting truth in other domains.

154. Hunt, "Civic Chivalry and the English Civil War," esp. 205–06. And recall the sketch of Gellner's treatment of such concepts as "nobility" ("Concepts and Society") at the beginning of chapter 3 above.

155. This general judgment is not 'owned' by historians of any particular political disposition: the 'left-wing' E. P. Thompson (e.g., *Customs in Common,* ch. 2) here occupies broadly the same terrain as the 'right-wing' J. C. D. Clark (e.g., *English Society*), although, of course, the conclusions each draws from the observation of customs in common vary enormously.

Epilogue:
The Way We Live Now

That which is not able to be performed
in a private house
will much less be brought to pass
in a commonwealth or kingdom.

—William Harrison, *The Description of England*

In early modern society people tended to live where they worked. The miller lived at the mill, and when you paid a call on the miller you visited the place where water-power turned the wheels that transformed corn into flour. One of the distinguishing marks of modern society is the radical disjunction of residences and workplaces.[1] The place of work is set aside from home. People leave where they live to go to where they work. Typically, corn is now ground in large mills, and when we visit the people who do that work we no longer see the process in action. Workplaces thus take on a double specialization: they are set apart in space and in knowledge. Many people who go to work in mills, but few who do not, now know how flour gets made.

The analogy with the making of scientific knowledge is both appropriate and pertinent to the case at hand. In seventeenth-century England, for example, such practitioners as Robert Boyle lived where their laboratories were. When you paid a call on Boyle, you visited the place where technicians cranked the piston of the air-pump up and down and where knowledge of the physical properties of the air was produced. And, although for practical reasons the seventeenth-century laboratory might be round the back of the house, discussions about scientific findings and theories typically took place in the public rooms of the residences occupied by public persons.[2] In modern society, however, despite various characterizations of science as 'public knowledge,'

1. See esp. Weber, *The Protestant Ethic and the Spirit of Capitalism*, 21–22. For a fine account of work and residence in the seventeenth-century English printing-house, see Johns, "Wisdom in the Concourse," 31–71.
2. Shapin, "House of Experiment," 376–80.

it is made and evaluated in some of our most private places. If you want to pay a call on a friend or neighbor who happens to be a high-energy physicist, you do *not* wander into CERN or SLAC. We typically now enter the places where scientific knowledge is made only by special arrangement and on a special basis: we come as visitors, as guests in a house where nobody lives.[3]

This same modern separation of house and workplace can be identified as sign and cause of a fundamental shift in the nature of trust and in the practical means by which the credibility of knowledge is secured. Here, then, is one quite plausible and compelling story about long-term change in these matters. Premodern society managed its affairs in a face-to-face mode. When people assessed the credibility of what they were told, they were able to draw upon the resources of *familiarity*. The persons who told one stories about the natural world beyond one's own experience were known to one, or, if they were not, they were known to those who were known to one. Knowledge circulated within a system of everyday recognitions, just as the crediting or gainsaying of relations formed the fabric of everyday interaction. Premodern society looked truth in the face.

Veracity was understood to be underwritten by *virtue*. Gentlemen insisted upon the truthfulness of their relations as a mark of their condition and their honor. The acknowledgment of gentlemanly truthfulness was the acknowledgment of gentlemanly identity. Free action and integrity were seen as the conditions for truth-telling, while constraint and need were recognized as the grounds of mendacity. Accordingly, the moral economy of premodern society located truth within the practical performances of everyday social order. Truth flowed along the same personal channels as civil conversation. Knowledge was secured by trusting people with whom one was familiar, and familiarity could be used to gauge the truth of what they said.

Seventeenth-century commentators felt secure in guaranteeing the truthfulness of narratives by pointing to the integrity of those special sorts of men who proffered them. Seth Ward was one of many writers who defended the veracity of historical narratives by noting that they were delivered by "a man of honour that would not write a lye."[4] Understandings of how certain sorts of persons were placed in socioeconomic circumstance, as well as notions of virtue, were available to identify *types of persons* who would not, could not, lie. The gentleman was that special sort of person, and, just as early modern culture of-

3. For splendid treatment of the 'privatization' of modern science from the point of view of political theory, see Ezrahi, *Descent of Icarus,* esp. ch. 11. For the significance of modern scientific privacy in relation to appropriate forms of popular education, see Shapin, "Why the Public Ought to Understand Science-in-the-Making."

4. [Ward], *Philosophicall Essay* (1652), 94–95, 112–14.

fered understandings of why he was truthful, so early modern social practices protected him from imputations that he was not.

By the eighteenth century there were signs that aspects of that culture and those practices were beginning to erode. David Hume's argument against the credibility of miracle-reports crucially relied upon just such an erosion. Hume offered as a "general maxim" that "no testimony is sufficient to establish a miracle, unless the testimony be of such a kind, that its falsehood would be more miraculous, than the fact, which it endeavours to establish." Men may be deluded or may lie: not some men, nor most men, but men.

> There is not to be found, in all history, any miracle attested by a sufficient number of men of such unquestioned good-sense, education, and learning as to secure us against all delusion in themselves; of such undoubted integrity as to place them beyond all suspicion of any design to deceive others.

It is the very absence of a crucial discrimination between sorts of men—in their different conditions and with their different virtues—which marks a considerable shift from early modern ethical theory.[5] The modern sensibility has no difficulty accepting the social theory of Hume's epistemic argument: Hume was right.

By contrast, so the same story continues, the modern condition permits no such effective resort to familiarity and personal virtue in deciding upon the truth or falsity of knowledge-claims. Now we are told things about the world by people whom we do not know, working in places we have not been. Trust is no longer bestowed on familiar individuals; it is accorded to institutions and abstract capacities thought to reside in certain institutions.[6] The village has given way to the anonymous city, relative simplicity of social structure to relative complexity. We trust the reliability of airplanes without knowing those who make, service, or fly them; we trust the veracity of diagnostic medical tests without knowing the people who carry them out; and we trust the truth of specialized and esoteric scientific knowledge without knowing the scientists who are the authors of its claims. Abstracted from systems of familiarity, trust is differently reposed but vastly extended.[7] While traditional warrants for assent are hard to find, the cost of practical skepticism is great. If we do not give practical assent to the institutions

5. Hume, *Enquiry Concerning Human Understanding*, 115–16. For a summary of the historical background to Hume's argument, see Burns, *Great Debate on Miracles*, chs 6–7.
6. Here I summarize well-known views on trust and modernity associated with Niklas Luhmann and Anthony Giddens, and introduced in chapter 1 above: Luhmann, *Trust and Power*, Pt. I, esp. chs 3, 6–7; Giddens, *Consequences of Modernity*, esp. 26–36.
7. Max Weber ("Science as a Vocation," 138–39) addressed just these aspects of techno-scientific specialization as part of his identification of modern 'disenchantment.'

of modern society, it is the everyday course of our lives which is made difficult or impossible. Practical skepticism about airplanes, medical diagnosis, and bodies of specialized scientific knowledge makes modern life deeply troublesome *for us*. It is this character of modern trusting that Niklas Luhmann has termed "system trust"—trust without familiarity and without effective possibility of mistrusting.[8]

What stands behind this kind of trust? What is the nature of the warrant for truth that is offered in the modern condition? What do we say when asked to justify our trust in the knowledge emerging from the specialized institutions of modern society? A popular response is that we now live in a 'postvirtuous' culture. Modernity guarantees knowledge not by reference to virtue but to *expertise*. When we give our trust to—'have faith in'—modern systems of technology and knowledge, our faith is now widely said not to be in the moral character of the individuals concerned but in the genuine expertise attributed to the institutions. The expertise of individuals is itself considered to be vouched for by the institutions from which they speak and which are the ultimate sources of that expertise.[9]

Max Weber's 1918 essay on "Science as a Vocation" marked a transitional point between traditional notions of intellectuals' virtue as a guarantor of objectivity and emerging appreciations of the peculiar social structure in which they found themselves.[10] Scarcely twenty years later, one of the most influential American sociologists presented it as a matter *of course* that scientists 'were as other men,' and that the production of objective knowledge could not possibly be underwritten by the dispositions and temperaments of individual practitioners. Disinterested and objective knowledge was produced by interested and, occasionally, irrationally acting individuals: "A passion for knowledge, idle curiosity, altruistic concern with the benefit to humanity, and a host of other special motives have been attributed to the scientist. The quest for distinctive motives appears to have been misdirected." There is "no satisfactory evidence" that scientists are "recruited from the

8. Luhmann, *Trust and Power*, 1–22; idem, "Familiarity, Confidence, Trust," 102–03.

9. For speculations about the nineteenth-century English transition from virtue to expertise, see Shapin, "'A Scholar and a Gentleman,'" 312–15, and, for detailed materials relating to that setting, see Heyck, *Transformation of Intellectual Life in Victorian Britain*, esp. chs 3–5.

10. Weber, "Science as a Vocation," esp. 131–35. For identifications of eighteenth- and nineteenth-century natural philosophers as morally exceptional persons, see, e.g., Paul, *Science and Immortality*, 86–109; Outram, *Cuvier*, e.g. 79, 94; and for twentieth-century residues, see Rosenberg, *No Other Gods*, 123–31 (for Sinclair Lewis's Martin Arrowsmith as scientist-hero), and Nieburg, *In the Name of Science*, ch. 7. Note also the transitional moment between conceptions of 'vocation' as a divine calling and as a 'job.' Cf. Temkin, "Historical Reflections on a Scientist's Virtue." In another context, one might want to dwell upon national differences in appreciations of intellectuals' virtue.

ranks of those who exhibit an unusual degree of moral integrity" or that the objectivity of scientific knowledge proceeds from "the personal qualities of scientists." Rather, what underpins scientific truthfulness is said to be an elaborated system of institutional norms, whose internalization guarantees that transgressions will generate psychic pain and whose implementation by the community guarantees that transgressors will be found out and punished. So by the middle of the twentieth century it appears that the causal link posited by gentlemanly culture between truth-telling and free action had been turned upside down. Objective knowledge is not now thought to be underwritten by the participation of "gentlemen, free and unconfin'd," but by institutions which most vigilantly constrain the free action of their members. Robert Merton was, accordingly, well aware of apparent *lèse-majesté* in declaring that "the activities of scientists are subject to rigorous policing, to a degree perhaps unparalleled in any other field of activity."[11] The modern place of knowledge here appears not as a gentleman's drawing room but as a great Panopticon of Truth.

Insofar as recipients of scientific knowledge-claims credit this story about the community from which those claims emerge, they will accept it as a basis of further disengagement between truth and personal virtue. The resulting assent takes an impersonal form, since, unlike the traditional condition, the relations by which credibility is accomplished have been, as Giddens says, "disembedded" from the immediacies of the contexts of personal interaction. How do we tell that particular scientists are speaking the truth about the world? We inspect them for the recognized insignia of affiliation with the institutions in which expertise lives. How do we tell that the institutions harbor genuine knowledge? We inspect them for signs of internal "rigorous policing" or are otherwise assured that institutional control has been exerted against the passions and interests of their members. Who would not misrepresent the truth for advantage if they get away with it?[12]

11. Merton, "The Normative Structure of Science" (1942), 275–76; see also idem, "Science and the Social Order" (1938), 259; idem, "Priorities in Scientific Discovery" (1957), 290–91; idem, *Sociological Ambivalence,* 34–35; cf. Nowotny, "Does It Only Need Good Men to Do Good Science?"

12. It is not, of course, the *existence* of an appreciation of truth-through-the-policing-of-interest which is new in the twentieth century, just its extension and dominance. In the seventeenth century, Johannes Kepler warranted the truthfulness of astronomical testimony by his young assistant Benjamin Ursinus by describing him as "a student of astronomy who, because he loves the art and has determined to cultivate philosophy, would never consider undermining, right at the beginning, the credibility necessary to a future astronomer by false evidence": quoted in Van Helden, "Telescopes and Authority." There were always knowledge-producing jobs—notably in mathematical practices— where falsehood was reckoned 'more than the job was worth.'

That is one story about long-term change in the nature of trust and in the recognition of truth-speaking about the natural world. The great divide between traditional and modern social forms—the 'way we lived then' and the 'way we live now'—generates a corresponding great divide in the means by which truth is accomplished and recognized. The gentleman has been replaced by the scientific expert, personal virtue by the possession of specialized knowledge, a calling by a job, a nexus of face-to-face interaction by faceless institutions, individual free action by institutional surveillance. It is a story with great intuitive—and emotional—appeal: there are few sentiments more characteristic of modernity than the view that modern social life is a disaster and that its anonymity is the most telling sign of its ruined state.[13]

Nevertheless, this account of modern conditions for living and knowing is adequate only in a carefully qualified sense. The question to which this story was a response was one loosely to do with how the modern 'we' come to believe the sayings of 'scientists-them.' Accordingly, I encouraged readers to consider the nature of the assent *they* give to unfamiliar expert-others, while the unfamiliarity obtaining between laity and scientific experts is undeniable. Suppose, however, one specifically invites reflection upon the assent given *within* communities of practitioners, for example within the communities of scientific knowledge-producers. Here it is far from obvious that the world of familiarity, face-to-face interaction, and virtue is indeed lost. It seems quite likely that small specialized communities of knowledge-makers share many of the resources for establishing and protecting truth that were current in the pre- and early modern society of gentlemen. And, while modern sociological studies of science are notably silent about the face-to-face domain in the making of scientific knowledge, there are impressionistic bases for speculation about the local persistence of a world of truth-making which our first story tells us has been definitively lost.

While outsiders—including many philosophers and sociologists—tend happily to refer to vast numbers of practitioners called 'scientists,' insiders function within specialist groups of remarkably small size. One may be 'a scientist' for passport or survey purposes, but one spends one's working day studying the role of childhood poliomyelitis in the epidemiology of motor neuron disease, establishing the timing of phosphorylase enzymatic induction in the development of *Drosophila* embryos, or investigating the possible use of animal behavior patterns in predicting seismicity. The group of people mutually judged capable of participating in each of these specialized practices—what has been

13. E.g., Sennett, *The Fall of Public Man.*

called the core-set—may be very small.[14] There is hardly any systematically collected information on the subject, but I would not be surprised if, across a range of practices, core-sets were as small as ten or twenty individuals—about the size of an army platoon or mess-group.[15]

It may be that some of these individuals 'live with each other' in the same laboratory, although it is probably more common in modern science for members of a core-set to be widely distributed across the globe. Nevertheless, the lives of core-set members are bound together over time in ways which flow from their high degree of interdependence. Members of scientific core-sets arguably 'know each other' in roughly the same way, and along roughly the same dimensions, that the society of early modern English gentlemen 'knew each other.' They probably 'look each other in the eye' with about the same frequency that members of the seventeenth-century English gentry did, with the international scientific conference taking the place of the court or the London 'season.' They function within broadly comparable systems of recognition, and 'know each other's people' in ways comparable to the culture manipulated by traditional gentlemen, where patterns of institutional training and theoretical or practical affiliation do the work done for gentlemen by family and kin. And for present-day members of scientific core-sets, the consequences of radical distrust are arguably just as consequential as they were for the early modern gentry. Core-set members are utterly dependent upon each other—for data, techniques, and materials, and, most importantly, for credibility—because it is predominantly members of this small group of familiar others who hold the immediate fate of one's knowledge-claims in their hands.[16]

So one story about the modern condition points to anonymity and system-trust in abstract capacities, while the other identifies persisting patterns of traditional familiarity and trust in known persons. The first captures something important about our lived experience as we move away from the familiar places of work, family, and neighborhood; the second reminds us of the texture of relations within familiar places. One can then characterize the modern condition through the serial applicability of both stories. There are now so many settings through

14. Collins, "The Role of the Core-Set in Modern Science" (although Collins's precise usage restricts the core-set to infrequent passages of 'extraordinary science' in which the existence or nonexistence of relevant phenomena is contested).

15. Here I allude to studies of military small-group dynamics which are suggestive of parallel processes of social solidarity and conflict management in scientific core-sets: e.g., Keegan, Face of Battle, 47–48, 52–53, 74; R. Holmes, Firing Line, esp. ch. 2 ("Mysterious Fraternity").

16. Suggestive remarks on familiarity among scientists and its consequences are in Mitroff, "Norms and Counter-norms," 585–86; Collins, "The Seven Sexes," 212–16; idem, "Son of Seven Sexes," 47–48; Woolf, "The Second Messenger."

which we move, so many institutions with which our lives bring us in contact, and so few of these evidently offer us the warrants of familiarity. The very elaboration of unfamiliar places, however, seems to blind us to the residual significance of face-to-face interaction.

It is in this connection that Giddens briefly identifies the role of "access points" in the specialized institutions of modernity, points at which 'faceless institutions' present a particular human face to those who encounter and pass through them. Traveling on an airplane experiencing severe turbulence, we inspect the faces of cabin-crew for signs of 'normality,' and they, in turn, are trained to supply the appropriate signs of reassurance. More consequentially, our primary access to the specialized knowledges of modern science is via teachers, just as specialized medicine is literally embodied in the doctors whom we consult in their offices and in the surgeons who visit at our bedside. No doubt such access points are hard to locate for many modern institutions whose esoteric workings and products we are obliged to trust, but, where they are available, they provide significant opportunities to live and to know in the modes of a world some commentators have assured us is lost: "The access points of abstract systems are the meeting ground of face-work and faceless commitments."[17] Such access points exist for many modern institutions, while the social forms in which those institutions' specialized knowledges are produced are, as I have argued, shot through with the patterns of interdependent trust-in-familiar-people.

I have not taken on the task of explaining why persisting patterns of familiarity have become so difficult for commentators to recognize, although perhaps this has something to do with the social distance between those who theorize about modernity and the lived-experience of modern techno-scientific knowledge-makers. In any event, my suggestions about the understanding of credibility-management in modern scientific core-sets are of a frankly speculative nature and may well be wrong. However, I am much more concerned about the invisibility of trust-relationships in modern science, for here I suspect that difficulty in recognizing and acknowledging their role arises from a massively important *evaluation*. Modern culture inherits from antiquity a consequential symbolic association between the worth of knowledge and the disengagement of its producers and places of production. In its seventeenth-century 'modern' rhetorical form, this association explicitly identified reliance upon trust and authority as a major source of epistemic error. And so we are widely accustomed to regard knowledge as true to the extent that we may identify the agent of its production as a solitary.

17. Giddens, *Consequences of Modernity*, 83.

I began by arguing that science is a system of knowledge by virtue of its being a system of trusting persons. I have sought to show the ineradicable role of trust in the constitution even of empirical forms of scientific knowledge, where resort to trust has seemed most unlikely. While I have showed how a particular past culture managed its solution to the problem of trust, I have also advanced a fully general case that every culture must put in place *some* solution to the problem of whom to trust and on what bases. Accordingly, this book has argued against dominant philosophies and sociologies of science which celebrate science solely as a nexus of skepticism. Far from being less trusting than everyday action, I want to suggest that there is a legitimate sense in which modern science is much *more* trusting. The role of core-set trust-in-familiar-persons has been noted above. Yet the potency of trust extends to every aspect of the day-to-day processes by which scientific knowledge is held and extended. As I indicated in chapter 1, a mundane biochemical assay can only proceed through trusting the integrity of materials and those who supply them, trusting textual tables of spectroscopic absorption and biological activity, trusting the honesty and competence of colleagues and technicians. Nor does such trust have only a static or conservative character. For scientists' practical capacity to advance knowledge, even skeptically to check over another's claim with a view to falsifying it, depends upon their ability to trust *almost everything else* about the scene in which they do skepticism and the resources which permit skeptical activities to be carried through. The very power of science to hold knowledge as collective property *and* to focus doubt on bits of currently accepted knowledge is founded upon a degree and a quality of trust which are arguably unparalleled elsewhere in our culture.

Just as ancient and early modern theorists pointed to the importance of trust in effecting any coordinated civil enterprise, so the notable success of modern science in upholding consensual knowledge indicates that it too takes place on a field of trust. Nor is it the case that scientists have, as it were, *first* to be instructed in the principles of social order and civility and *then* in the knowledge and techniques of their discipline, for they learn about social order *as* they learn about the natural world. Correspondingly, trust and the moral economy of science are protected through scientists' investment in the knowledge they have and the changes they may wish to work on existing knowledge.[18] Scientists know so much about the natural world by knowing so much about whom they can trust.

18. This formulation is a plausible précis of central arguments in Kuhn's *Structure of Scientific Revolutions*.

Bibliography

Full references to manuscript sources (papers of Robert Boyle and related materials) in the Royal Society of London are given in the notes, as are full bibliographic details of items in the *Philosophical Transactions* of the Royal Society, and these are not repeated in the bibliography.

Writings of Robert Boyle

Essays Cited

All citations of Boyle's published writings are from *The Works of the Honourable Robert Boyle,* ed. Thomas Birch, 2d ed., 6 vols. London: J. & F. Rivington, 1772. Individual essays cited are listed below alphabetically (by first substantive word in title), with location in Birch edition and date of original publication. My practice is to cite individual tractate titles rather than the overall title of collected items (e.g., *Certain Physiological Essays*).

"An Account of the Two Sorts of the Helmontian Laudanum," IV, 149–150 (1674).

"The Aerial Noctiluca: or, Some New Phænomena, and a Process of a Factitious Self-shining Substance," IV, 379–404 (1680).

The Christian Virtuoso," V, 508–540 (1690); "Appendix to the First Part, and the Second Part," VI, 673–796 (1744).

"A Chymical Paradox," IV, 496–505 (1682).

"A Confirmation of the Former Account Touching the Late Earthquake near Oxford," II, 797–798 (1666).

"A Continuation of New Experiments Physico-mechanical, Touching the Spring and Weight of the Air, and Their Effects," III, 175–276 (1669); ". . . The Second Part," IV, 505–593 (1680 in Latin; 1682 in English translation).

"A Defence of the Doctrine Touching the Spring and Weight of the Air . . . against the Objections of Franciscus Linus," I, 118–185 (1662).

"A Discourse of Things above Reason," IV, 406–469 (1681).

"A Disquisition about the Final Causes of Natural Things," V, 392–444 (1688).

"An Essay of the Intestine Motions of the Particles of Quiescent Solids," I, 444–457 (1669).

"An Examen of Mr. T. Hobbes His Dialogus Physicus de Natura Aëris," I, 186–242 (1662).

"About the Excellency and Grounds of the Mechanical Hypothesis," IV, 67–78 (1674).

"The Excellency of Theology Compared with Natural Philosophy," IV, 1–66 (1674).

"Experimenta & Observationes Physicæ," V, 564–603 (1691).

"An Experimental Discourse of Quicksilver Growing Hot with Gold," IV, 219–230 (1676).

"Experiments and Considerations Touching Colours," I, 662–788 (1663).

"Experiments and Notes about the Mechanical Origin of Electricity," IV, 345–354 (1675).

"Experiments, Notes & c. about the Mechanical Origin or Production of Divers Particular Qualities," IV, 230–236 (1675).

"A Free Discourse against Customary Swearing," VI, 1–32 (1695).

"A Free Inquiry into the Vulgarly Received Notion of Nature," V, 158–254 (1686).

"The General History of the Air," V, 609–750 (1692).

"Greatness of Mind Promoted by Christianity," V, 550–563 (1690).

"Of the High Veneration Man's Intellect Owes to God, Peculiarly for His Wisdom and Power," V, 130–157 (1685).

"An Historical Account of a Degradation of Gold, Made by an Anti-elixir," IV, 371–379 (1678).

"An Hydrostatical Discourse, Occasioned by the Objections of the Learned Dr. Henry More," III, 596–628 (1672).

"An Hydrostatical Letter," III, 629–634 (1674).

"Hydrostatical Paradoxes, Made Out by New Experiments," II, 738–797 (1666).

"A Letter Concerning Ambergris," III, 731–732 (1673).

"Of the Mechanical Origin of Heat and Cold," IV, 236–259 (1675).

"Medicina Hydrostatica: or, Hydrostatics Applied to the Materia Medica," V, 453–489 (1690).

"Medicinal Experiments: or, a Collection of Choice and Safe Remedies," V, 312–391 (1688).

"Memoirs for the Natural History of Human Blood," IV, 595–759 (1684).

"Of Men's Great Ignorance of the Uses of Natural Things," III, 470–494 (1671).

"New Experiments about the Differing Pressure of Heavy Solids and Fluids," III, 643–651 (1672).

"New Experiments about Explosions," III, 592–595 (1672).

"New Experiments and Observations Touching Cold," II, 462–734 (1665).

"New Experiments and Observations Made upon the Icy Noctiluca," IV, 469–495 (1682).

"New Experiments about the Preservation of Bodies in Vacuo Boyliano," IV, 145–149 (1674).

"New Experiments about the Relation betwixt Air and the Flamma Vitalis of Animals," III, 584–589 (1672).

"New Experiments Touching the Relation betwixt Flame and Air," III, 563–584 (1672).

"New Experiments Concerning the Relation between Light and Air, in Shining Wood and Fish," III, 157–169 (1668).

"New Experiments of the Positive or Relative Levity of Bodies under Water," III, 635–639 (1672).

"New Experiments Physico-mechanical, Touching the Spring of the Air," I, 1–117 (1660).

"New Experiments about the Weakened Spring, and Some Unobserved Effects of the Air," IV, 213–219 (1675).

"New Pneumatical Experiments about Respiration," III, 355–370 (1670).

"Observations and Experiments about the Saltness of the Sea," III, 764–780 (1674).

"Observations and Trials about the Resemblances and Differences between a Burning Coal and Shining Wood," III, 170–174 (1668).

"Occasional Reflections upon Several Subjects," II, 323–460 (1665).

"The Origin of Forms and Qualities, According to the Corpuscular Philosophy," III, 1–112 (1666).

"A Previous Hydrostatical Way of Estimating Ores," V, 489–507 (1690).

"A Proëmial Essay . . . with Some Considerations Touching Experimental Essays in General," I, 298–318 (1661).

"Of the Reconcileableness of Specific Medicines to the Corpuscular Philosophy," V, 74–129 (1685).

"Relations about the Bottom of the Sea," III, 349–354, 780–781 (1671, 1674).

422   Bibliography

"The Sceptical Chymist," I, 458–586 (1661).

"Short Memoirs for the Natural Experimental History of Mineral Waters," IV, 794–821 (1685).

"Some Considerations about the Reconcileableness of Reason and Religion," IV, 151–191 (1675).

"Some Considerations Touching the Style of the Holy Scriptures," II, 247–322 (1661).

"Some Considerations Touching the Usefulness of Experimental Natural Philosophy," II, 1–246 (1663); ". . . The Second Tome," III, 392–457 (1671).

"Some Motives and Incentives to the Love of God, Pathetically Discoursed of, in a Letter to a Friend [= "Seraphic Love"]," I, 243–293 (1659).

"Some Observations and Directions about the Barometer," II, 798–800 (1666).

"Some Observations about Shining Flesh, Both of Veal and of Pullet," III, 651–655 (1672).

"Some Specimens of an Attempt to Make Chymical Experiments Useful to Illustrate the Notions of the Corpuscular Philosophy," I, 354–376 (1661).

"Strange Reports," V, 604–609 (1691).

"Suspicions about Some Hidden Qualities in the Air," IV, 85–96 (1674).

"Of the Systematical or Cosmical Qualities of Things," III, 306–325 (1671).

"Of the Temperature of the Submarine Regions," III, 342–349 (1671).

"Of the Temperature of the Subterraneal Regions," III, 326–341 (1671).

"Two Essays, Concerning the Unsuccessfulness of Experiments," I, 318–353 (1661).

Other Writings

[1655] 1950. "An Epistolical Discourse . . . Inviting All True Lovers of Vertue and Mankind, to a Free and Generous Conmunication of Their Secrets and Receits in Physick," reprinted in Margaret E. Rowbottom, "The Earliest Published Writing of Robert Boyle," *Annals of Science* 6 (1950): 380–385 (orig. publ. in Samuel Hartlib, comp., *Chymical, Medicinal, and Chyrurgical Addresses* [London], 113–150).

1725. *The Philosophical Works,* ed. Peter Shaw, 3 vols. London.

[1744] 1969. "An Account of Philaretus [= Boyle] during His Minority," in Maddison 1969 (see under Secondary Sources), 2–45.

1991a. *The Early Essays and Ethics of Robert Boyle,* ed. John T. Harwood. Carbondale: Southern Illinois University Press.

1991b. "The Aretology or Ethicall Elements of Robert Boyle," in 1991a, 1–141.

1991c. "Of Sin," in 1991a, 143–168.

1991d. "Of Piety," in 1991a, 169–183.

1991e. "The Doctrine of Thinking," in 1991a, 185–202.

1991f. "The Dayly Reflection," in 1991a, 203–235.

1991g. "Of Time and Idleness," in 1991a, 237–248.

Early Modern and Related Primary Sources

Addison, Joseph, and Richard Steele, 1898. *The Tatler*, ed. George A. Aitken, 4 vols. London: Duckworth.
[Allestree, Richard], [1660] 1668. *The Gentleman's Calling*. London.
[Allott, Robert], 1599. *Wits Theater of the Little World*. London.
Anon., 1555. *The Institucion of a Gentleman*. London.
Anon., [1579, 1586] 1868. *Cyuile and Uncyuile Life*, in *Inedited Tracts: Illustrating the Manners, Opinions, and Occupations of Englishmen during the Sixteenth and Seventeenth Centuries . . .* , ed. W. C. Hazlitt. London: Roxburghe Library.
Ap-Robert, I., 1618. *The Younger Brother: His Apology. . . .* London.
Aristotle, 1984. *The Complete Works of Aristotle*, 2 vols., ed. Jonathan Barnes. Princeton, N.J.: Princeton University Press.
Ascham, Roger, 1570. *The Scholemaster*. London.
Ashley, Robert, 1947. *Of Honor*, ed. Virgil B. Heltzel (from 1607–1610 MS). San Marino, Calif.: Huntington Library.
Aubrey, John, 1957. *Aubrey's Brief Lives*, ed. Oliver Lawson Dick. Ann Arbor: University of Michigan Press.
———, 1972. *Aubrey on Education: A Hitherto Unpublished Manuscript by the Author of 'Brief Lives'*, ed. J. E. Stephens. London: Routledge & Kegan Paul.
Ault, Norman, ed., 1960. *Elizabethan Lyrics*. New York: Capricorn Books.
Bacon, Francis, 1614. *The Charge of Sir Francis Bacon Touching Duells*. London.
———, [1597] 1852. *The Moral and Historical Works of Lord Bacon, Including His Essays . . .* , ed. Joseph Devey. London: Henry G. Bohn.
———, 1857–1858a. *The Philosophical Works of Francis Bacon*, eds James Spedding, Robert Leslie Ellis and Douglas Denon Heath, 5 vols. London.
———, [1605] 1857–1858b. "The Advancement of Learning," in idem 1857–1858a, 3:253–491.
———, 1857–1858c. "Calor et Frigus," in idem 1857–1858a, 3:641–652.
———, [1623] 1857–1858d. "Of the Dignity and Advancement of Learning. Books II–IX," in idem 1857–1858a, 4: 273–498.
———, 1857–1858e. "The History of Dense and Rare," in idem 1857–1858a, 5: 337–400.
———, 1857–1858f. "The History of the Winds," in idem 1857–1858a, 5: 137–200.
———, [1623] 1857–1858g. "The New Organon," in idem 1857–1858a, 4: 39–248.
———, [1620] 1857–1858h. "Preparative towards a Natural and Experimental History [= *Parasceve*]," in idem 1857–1858a, 4: 249–263.
———, [1627] 1857–1858i. "Sylva Sylvarum: or, A Natural History. In Ten Centuries," in idem 1857–1858a, 2: 331–672.

Barrow, Isaac, 1830–1831. *The Works of Dr. Isaac Barrow*, 7 vols. London: A. J. Valpy.

Baxter, Richard, [1696] 1974. *Autobiography*, abridged by J. M. Lloyd Thomas, ed. N. H. Keeble. London: J. M. Dent, Everyman's Library.

Birch, Thomas, 1756–1757. *The History of the Royal Society of London . . .* , 4 vols. London.

———, [1744] 1772. "The Life of the Honourable Robert Boyle" (introduction to *The Works of the Honourable Robert Boyle*, ed. Thomas Birch, 2d ed., Vol. I, i–ccxxxviii. London: J. & F. Rivington).

Boyle, Richard, [comp. 1632] 1772. "Sir Richard Boyle, Knt. Earl of Corke, His True Remembrances," in Birch 1772 (see previous entry), vii-xi.

Brathwait, Richard, 1630. *The English Gentleman*. London.

———, 1631. *The English Gentlewoman*. London.

———, [comp. *ca.* 1630] 1821. *Some Rules and Orders for the Government of the House of an Earle*. London.

Britaine, William de, 1686. *Humane Prudence, or The Art by Which a Man May Raise Himself & Fortune to Grandeur*, 3d ed. London.

Browne, Thomas, 1646. *Pseudodoxia Epidemica: or, Enquiries into Very Many Received Tenents, and Commonly Presumed Truthes*. London.

———, 1940a. *The Religio Medici and Other Writings*, ed. C. H. Herford. London: J. M. Dent, Everyman's Library.

———, [1716; comp. *ca.* 1650] 1940b. "Christian Morals," in Browne 1940a, 231–287.

———, [1643] 1940c. "Religio Medici," in Browne 1940a, 1–89.

[Brydges, Grey?], 1620. *Horæ Subseciuæ. Observations and Discourses*. London.

Bryskett, Lodowick, [1606] 1970. *A Discourse of Civill Life*, ed. Thomas E. Wright. Northridge, Calif.: San Fernando Valley State College.

Budgell, Eustace, 1732. *Memoirs of the Life and Character of the Late Earl of Orrery, and of the Family of the Boyles. . . .* London.

Burnet, Gilbert, 1833a. *Lives, Characters, and an Address to Posterity*, ed. John Jebb. London: James Duncan.

———, 1833b. "Character of a Christian Philosopher, in a Sermon Preached January 7. 1691–2, at the Funeral of the Hon. Robert Boyle," in idem 1833a, 325–376.

———, 1833c. "The Life and Death of John [Wilmot,] Earl of Rochester," in idem 1833a, 165–278.

———, [1724] 1833d. *History of His Own Times*, 6 vols. Oxford: Oxford University Press.

———, 1902. *A Supplement to Burnet's History of My Own Time*, ed. H. C. Foxcroft. Oxford: Clarendon Press.

———, [1761; comp. *ca.* 1668] 1914. *Thoughts on Education*, ed. John Clarke. Aberdeen: Aberdeen University Press.

Burton, Robert, [1628] 1927. *The Anatomy of Melancholy*, eds Floyd Dell and Paul Jordan-Smith. New York: Tudor Publishing Co.

Butler, Samuel, 1908. *Characters and Passages from Note-books*, ed. A. R. Waller. Cambridge: Cambridge University Press.

Castiglione, Baldassare, [1528] 1959. *The Book of the Courtier*, trans. Charles S. Singleton. Garden City, N.Y.: Anchor Books.

Chamberlayne, Edward, 1673. *Angliæ Notitia; or the Present State of England . . .*, 7th ed., 2 vols. London.

[Charleton, Walter], 1669. *Two Discourses. I. Concerning the Different Wits of Men: II. Of the Mysteries of the Vintners.* London.

Chesterfield, Philip Dormer Stanhope, earl of, [1774] 1984. *Letters to His Son and Others.* London: J. M. Dent, Everyman's Library.

Christy, Miller, ed., [1631–1635] 1894. *The Voyages of Captain Luke Foxe of Hull, and Captain Thomas James of Bristol, in Search of a North-West Passage, in 1631–32,* 2 vols. London: Hakluyt Society.

Cicero, 1909. *Offices: De Officiis, Laelius, Cato Major and Select Letters.* London: J. M. Dent, Everyman's Library.

Cleland, James, 1612. *The Instruction of a Young Noble-man.* Oxford.

[Collins, Samuel], 1671. *The Present State of Russia, in a Letter to a Friend at London.* London.

Cowley, Abraham, 1661. *A Proposition for the Advancement of Experimental Philosophy.* London.

Dare, Josiah, [1672] 1929. *Counsellor Manners: His Last Legacy to His Son.* New York: Coward-McCann.

[Darrell, William], [1704–1712] 1723. *The Gentleman Instructed, in the Conduct of a Virtuous and Happy Life . . . ,* 8th ed. London.

[De Courtin, Antoine], [1671] 1685. *The Rules of Civility; or, Certain Ways of Deportment Observed amongst All Persons of Quality. . . .* London.

Defoe, Daniel, 1726. *The Complete English Tradesman.* London.

———, [comp. *ca.* 1729] 1890. *The Compleat English Gentleman,* ed. Karl D. Bülbring. London: David Nott.

Della Casa, Giovanni, [1558] 1958. *Galateo or the Book of Manners,* trans. R. S. Pine-Coffin. Harmondsworth: Penguin.

Descartes, René, 1955a. *The Philosophical Works of Descartes,* eds and trans. Elizabeth S. Haldane and G. R. T. Ross, 2 vols. New York: Dover.

———, [1637] 1955b. "Discourse on the Method," in idem 1955a, I, 79–130.

———, [1649] 1955c. "The Passions of the Soul," in idem 1955a, I, 329–427.

———, [1644] 1955d. "Principles of Philosophy," in idem 1955a, I, 201–302.

———, [1701] 1955e. "Rules for the Direction of the Mind," in idem 1955a, I, 1–77.

De Veer, Gerrit, [1598, 1599, 1605; English trans. 1609] 1876. *The Three Voyages of William Barents to the Arctic Regions (1594, 1595, and 1596),* 2d ed., ed. Koolemans Beynen. London: Hakluyt Society.

Dewhurst, Kenneth, 1981. *Willis's Oxford Casebook (1650–52).* Oxford: Sandford Publications.

Diogenes Laërtius, 1853. *The Lives and Opinions of Eminent Philosophers,* trans. C. D. Yonge. London: Henry G. Bohn.

Ellis, Clement, [1660] 1672. *The Gentile Sinner, or England's Brave Gentleman Character'd in a Letter to a Friend: Both As He Is, and As He Should Be,* 5th ed. Oxford.

Elyot, Thomas, [1531] 1962. *The Book Named The Governor,* ed. S. E. Lehmberg. London: J. M. Dent, Everyman's Library.

Emerson, Ralph Waldo, [1876] 1903. *English Traits.* Boston: Houghton, Mifflin.

Epictetus, 1616. *Epictetus His Manuell*, trans. J. Healey. London.

Erasmus, Desiderius, [1516] 1965. *The Education of a Christian Prince*, trans. Lester K. Born. New York: Octagon.

———, [1511] 1974. *Praise of Folly*, trans. Betty Radice. London: The Folio Society.

Evelyn, John, 1664. *Sylva, or A Discourse of Forest-Trees. . . .* London.

———, 1667. *Publick Employment and an Active Life Prefer'd to Solitude, and All Its Appanages. . . .* London.

———, 1854. *Diary and Correspondence of John Evelyn, F.R.S.*, 4 vols. London: Henry Colburn.

Ferne, John, 1586. *The Blazon of Gentrie*. London.

Ficino, Marsilio, [1489] 1989. *Three Books on Life*, ed. and trans. Carol V. Kaske and John R. Clark. Binghamton, N.Y.: Renaissance Society of America.

Filmer, Robert, [1648–1680] 1949. *Patriarcha and Other Political Works*, ed. Peter Laslett. Oxford: Basil Blackwell.

Frobisher, Martin, [1578] 1867. *The Three Voyages of Martin Frobisher. . . 1576–8*, ed. Richard Collinson. London: Hakluyt Society.

Fuller, Thomas, [1662] 1840. *The History of the Worthies of England*, new ed., ed. P. Austin Nuttall, 3 vols. London.

Gailhard, Jean, 1682. *Two Discourses. The First Concerning a Private Settlement at Home after Travel. The Second Concerning the Statesman, or Him Who Is in Publick Employments.* London.

[Gainsford, Thomas], 1616. *The Rich Cabinet Furnished with Varieties of Excellent Discriptions, Exquisite Characters, Witty Discourses, and Delightfull Histories, Deuine and Morall. . . . Wherevnto Is Annexed the Epitome of Good Manners, extracted from Mr. Iohn de la Casa.* London.

Galileo Galilei, 1957a. *Discoveries and Opinions of Galileo*, trans. Stillman Drake. Garden City, N.Y.: Doubleday Anchor.

———, [1623] 1957b. "The Assayer," in idem 1957a, 229–280 (excerpts).

———, [1615] 1957c. "Letter to the Grand Duchess Christina," in idem 1957a, 173–216.

———, [1613] 1957d. "Letters on Sunspots," in idem 1957a, 87–144 (excerpts).

———, [1610] 1957e. "The Starry Messenger," in idem 1957a, 21–58.

———, [1632] 1970. *Dialogue Concerning the Two Chief World Systems*, trans. Stillman Drake, 2d ed. Berkeley: University of California Press.

Gilbert, William, [1600] 1958. *De Magnete*, trans. P. Fleury Mottelay. New York: Dover.

Glanvill, Joseph, 1668. *Plus Ultra: or, the Progress and Advancement of Knowledge since the Days of Aristotle.* London.

———, 1676. *Essays on Several Important Subjects in Philosophy and Religion.* London.

———, [1665] 1885. *Scepsis Scientifica: or, Confest Ignorance, the Way to Science*, ed. John Owen. London: Kegan Paul, Trench.

Gouge, William, 1622. *Of Domesticall Duties*. London.

Grew, Nehemiah, 1682. *The Anatomy of Plants*. London.

Grierson, H. J. C., and G. Bullough, eds, 1934. *The Oxford Book of Seventeenth-Century Verse*. Oxford: Clarendon Press.

Guazzo, Stefano, [1581] 1925. *The Civile Conversation of M. Steeven Guazzo*, trans. George Pettie and Bartholomew Young, ed. Edward Sullivan, 2 vols. London: Constable and Co.

Hale, Matthew, 1676. *Contemplations Moral and Divine*. London.

Halley, Edmond, 1932. *Correspondence and Papers of Edmond Halley*, ed. Eugene Fairfield MacPike. Oxford: Clarendon Press.

Harrison, William, [1577] 1968. *The Description of England*, ed. Georges Edelen. Ithaca, N.Y.: Cornell University Press, Folger Shakespeare Library.

Harvey, William [1628–1651] 1989. *The Works of William Harvey, M.D.*, trans. Robert Willis. Philadelphia: University of Pennsylvania Press.

Harwood, John T., ed., 1991. *The Early Essays and Ethics of Robert Boyle*. Carbondale: Southern Illinois University Press.

Herbert, Edward, 1906. *The Autobiography of Edward, Lord Herbert of Cherbury*, 2d ed. rev., ed. Sidney Lee. London: George Routledge & Sons.

Hevelius, Johannes, 1665. *Prodromus Cometicus, Quo Historia, Cometa Anno 1664 Exorti Cursum.* . . . Gdansk.

———, 1666. *Descriptio Cometae Anno Aerae Christ. M.DC.LXV. Exorti . . . Cui Additus Est: Mantissa Prodromi Cometici.* Gdansk.

———, 1668. *Cometographia, Totam Naturam Cometarum.* . . . Gdansk.

Hobbes, Thomas, 1839–1845a. *The English Works of Thomas Hobbes*, ed. Sir William Molesworth, 11 vols. London: John Bohn.

———, [1662] 1839–1845b. "Considerations upon the Reputation, Loyalty, Manners, and Religion of Thomas Hobbes," in idem, 1839–1845a, IV, 409–440.

———, [1650] 1839–1845c. "Human Nature: or the Fundamental Elements of Policy," in idem 1839–1845a, IV, 1–76.

———, [1651] 1968. *Leviathan*, ed. C. B. Macpherson. Harmondsworth: Penguin.

———, [comp. *ca.* 1643] 1976. *Thomas White's 'De Mundo' Examined*, trans. Harold Whitmore Jones. London: Bradford University Press, in association with Crosby Lockwood Staples.

———, [1661] 1985. "Dialogus Physicus de Natura Aeris," trans. Simon Schaffer, in Shapin and Schaffer 1985, 345–391.

———, [1668] 1990. *Behemoth, or The Long Parliament*, ed. Ferdinand Tönnies. Chicago: University of Chicago Press.

Hooke, Robert, 1665. *Micrographia: or Some Physiological Descriptions of Minute Bodies Made by Magnifying Glasses*. London.

———, 1705a. *The Posthumous Works of Robert Hooke, M.D. S.R.S. Geom. Prof. Gresh. & c.*, ed. Richard Waller. London.

———, [1682] 1705b. "A Discourse of Comets," in Hooke 1705a, 149–190.

———, 1705c. "A General Scheme, or Idea of the Present State of Natural Philosophy," in Hooke 1705a, 1–70.

———, 1705d. "Lectures and Discourses of Earthquakes, and Subterraneous Eruptions," in Hooke 1705a, 210–450.

———, 1726. *Philosophical Experiments and Observations*, ed. William Derham. London.

———, [1679] 1931a. *Lectiones Cutlerianæ, or a Collection of Lectures: Physical, Mechanical, Geographical, & Astronomical Made before the Royal Society.* . . .

London. Facsimile reprint as Vol. VIII of Gunther, *Early Science in Oxford*.

———, [1674] 1931b. "Animadversions On the First Part of the *Machina Coelestis* of the Honourable, Learned, and deservedly Famous Astronomer Johannes Hevelius. . . . , in Hooke 1931a, 37–114.

———, [1678] 1931c. "Cometa," in Hooke 1931a, 209–328.

———, 1935. *The Diary of Robert Hooke M.A., M.D., F.R.S. 1672–1680*, eds Henry W. Robinson and Walter Adams. London: Taylor & Francis.

Hooker, Richard, [1593–1597] 1907. *Of the Laws of the Ecclesiastical Polity*, 2 vols. London: J. M. Dent, Everyman's Library.

Hume, David, [1739–1740] 1888. *A Treatise of Human Nature*, ed. L. A. Selby-Bigge. Oxford: Clarendon Press.

———, [1779] 1947. *Dialogues Concerning Natural Religion*, ed. Norman Kemp Smith. London: Collier Macmillan.

———, [1748] 1975. *Enquiry Concerning Human Understanding*, ed. L. A. Selby-Bigge, reprinted from 1777 edition. Oxford: Clarendon Press.

Hutcheson, Francis, 1755. *A System of Moral Philosophy*. London.

James I (king of England) 1603. *Basilikon Doron. Or His Maiesties Instructions to His Dearest Sonne, Henry the Prince*. London.

James, Thomas, [1633] 1894. *The Strange and Dangerous Voyage of Captaine Thomas James, in His Intended Discovery of the Northwest Passage into the South Sea*, in Christy 1894, Vol. II, pp. 447–627.

Johnson, Samuel, 1969. *The Rambler*, Vols. III-V of *Works*, eds. W. J. Bate and Albrecht B. Strauss. New Haven, Conn.: Yale University Press.

King, Gregory, 1696. *Natural and Political Observations and Conclusions upon the State and Condition of England*. London.

La Rochefoucauld, François, duc de, [1665] 1959. *The Maxims of La Rochefoucauld*, trans. Louis Kronenberger. New York: Random House.

Leeuwenhoek, Antoni Van, 1939–. *The Collected Letters of Antoni Van Leeuwenhoek*, eds. G. van Rijnbeck et al., 12 vols. Amsterdam/Lisse: Swets & Zeit-!inger.

Leibniz, Gottfried Wilhelm, [comp. *ca.* 1693–1696] 1949. *New Essays Concerning Human Understanding*, 3d ed., trans. Alfred Gideon Langley. La Salle, Ill.: Open Court.

Lingard, Richard, [1670] 1907. *A Letter of Advice to a Young Gentleman Leaving the University Concerning His Behaviour and Conversation in the World*, ed. Frank C. Erb. New York: McAuliffe & Booth.

Locke, John, [1690] 1812. "Some Thoughts Concerning Education," in idem, *Works*, 11th ed., 10 vols. London, Vol. IX, pp. 1–205.

———, [1690] 1959. *An Essay Concerning Human Understanding*, ed. Alexander Campbell Fraser, 2 vols. New York: Dover.

———, 1976–. *The Correspondence of John Locke*, ed. E. S. de Beer, 8 vols. Oxford: Clarendon Press.

———, [1690] 1988. *Two Treatises of Government*, ed. Peter Laslett, student edition. Cambridge: Cambridge University Press.

Lower, Richard, [1665] 1983. *Richard Lower's 'Vindicatio': A Defence of the Experimental Method*, facsimile edition and translation of *Diatribæ Thomæ Willisii*

M.D. . . . (London, 1665), ed. and trans. Kenneth Dewhurst. Oxford: Sandford Publications.

Machiavelli, Niccolò, [1532] 1952. *The Prince*, trans. Luigi Ricci. New York: Mentor.

Mackenzie, George, 1665. *A Moral Essay Preferring Solitude to Publick Employment, and All It's Appanages; Such as Fame, Command, Riches, Pleasures, Conversation, & c.* Edinburgh.

———, 1665. *Religio Stoici: With a Friendly Addresse to the Phanaticks of all Sects and Sorts.* Edinburgh.

———, 1667. *Moral Gallantry. A Discourse Wherein the Author Endeavours to Prove, That Point of Honour . . . Obliges Men to Be Vertuous. . . .* Edinburgh.

———, 1667. *A Moral Paradox: Maintaining That It Is Much Easier to Be Vertuous Then Vitious.* Edinburgh.

———, 1713. *Essays upon Several Moral Subjects.* London.

Markham, Francis, 1625. *The Booke of Honour. Or, Five Decads of Epistles of Honour.* London.

Markham, Gervase, 1595. *The Gentlemans Academie. Or, The Booke of S. Albans . . . Compiled by Iuliana Barnes, in the Year from the Incarnation of Christ 1486.* London.

Mason, Henry, 1624. *The New Art of Lying, Covered by Iesvites vnder the Vaile of Eqvivocation.* London.

Mayow, John, [1674] 1957. *Medico-physical Works, Being a Translation of Tractatus Quinque Medico-Physici.* Edinburgh: E. & S. Livingstone, for the Alembic Club.

Montaigne, Michel de, [1580–1588] 1965. *The Complete Essays of Montaigne*, trans. Donald M. Frame. Stanford, Calif.: Stanford University Press.

More, Henry, [1653] 1662. *An Antidote against Atheisme*, 3d ed. London.

———, 1671. *Enchiridion Metaphysicum.* London.

Mulcaster, Richard, 1581. *Positions Wherein Those Primitive Circumstances Be Examined, Which Are Necessarie for the Training Up of Children. . . .* London.

Newton, Isaac, [1730] 1952. *Opticks*, 4th ed New York: Dover Publications.

———, 1959–1977. *The Correspondence of Isaac Newton*, eds H. W. Turnbull, J. D. Scott, A. R. Hall, and Laura Tilling, 7 vols. Cambridge: Cambridge University Press.

———, 1967–. *The Mathematical Papers of Isaac Newton*, ed. D. T. Whiteside, 8 vols. Cambridge: Cambridge University Press.

Oldenburg, Henry, 1965–1986. *The Correspondence of Henry Oldenburg*, eds A. Rupert Hall and Marie Boas Hall, 13 vols. Madison: University of Wisconsin Press; London: Mansell; London: Taylor & Francis.

Orrery, Roger Boyle, earl of, 1937. *The Dramatic Works of Roger Boyle, Earl of Orrery*, ed. William Smith Clark II, 2 vols. Cambridge, Mass.: Harvard University Press.

Osborne, Francis, [1656–1658] 1896. *Advice to a Son, or, Directions for Your Better Conduct through the Various and Most Important Encounters of This Life*, ed. Edward Abbott Parry. London: David Nutt.

Papin, Denis, 1681. *A New Digester or Engine for Softning Bones, Containing the Description of Its Make and Use.* London.

Pascal, Blaise, [1663] 1937. *The Physical Treatises of Pascal: The Equilibrium of Liquids and The Weight of the Mass of the Air,* ed. Frederick Barry, trans. I. H. B. and A. G. H. Spiers. New York: Columbia University Press.

————, [1670, 1656–1657] 1941. *Pensées & Provincial Letters,* trans. W. F. Trotter and Thomas M'Crie. New York: Modern Library.

Peacham, Henry, [1622] 1962. *The Complete Gentleman . . . ,* ed. Virgil B. Heltzel. Ithaca, N.Y.: Cornell University Press, Folger Shakespeare Library.

Penn, William, 1915. *The Fruits of Solitude and Other Writings,* ed. Joseph Besse. London: J. M. Dent, Everyman's Library.

Petrie, Adam. 1720. *Rules of Good Deportment, or of Good Breeding.* Edinburgh.

[Petty, Sir William], [1648] 1745. *The Advice of W.P. to Mr. Samuel Hartlib, for the Management of Some Particular Parts of Learning,* reprinted in The Harleian Miscellany, Vol. VI, pp. 1–13. London: Harleian Society.

————, 1927. *The Petty Papers. Some Unpublished Writings of Sir William Petty Edited from the Bowood Papers by the Marquis of Lansdowne,* 2 vols. London: Constable.

Plato, 1961. *The Collected Dialogues,* eds Edith Hamilton and Huntington Cairns. Princeton, N.J.: Princeton University Press.

[Plattes, Gabriel], 1641. *A Description of the Famous Kingdom of Macaria; Shewing Its Excellent Government . . .* London. (Facsimile reprint in Webster 1979, 65–73.)

Powell, Thomas [1631] 1876. *Tom of All Trades, Or the Plaine Path-way to Refinement. . . ,* ed. Frederick J. Furnivall, New Shakspere Society, Series 6, Vol. II. London: The New Shakspere Society.

Power, Henry, 1664. *Experimental Philosophy.* London.

[Ramesey, William], 1676. *The Gentlemans Companion: or A Character of True Nobility, and Gentility. . . .* London.

Ray, John, 1670. *A Collection of English Proverbs.* Cambridge.

Rich, Mary, [1847?]. *Memoir of Lady Warwick: Also Her Diary, from A.D. 1666 to 1672.* London: Religious Tract Society.

————, 1848. *Autobiography of Mary Countess of Warwick,* ed. T. Crofton Croker. London: The Percy Society.

Rigaud, Stephen Jordan, ed., 1841. *Correspondence of Scientific Men of the Seventeenth Century . . . ,* 2 vols. Oxford: Oxford University Press.

Romei, Annibale, 1598. *The Courtiers Academie: Comprehending Seuen Seuerall Dayes Discourses . . . Translated into English by I. K.* London.

Rousseau, Jean-Jacques, [1782] 1979. *The Reveries of the Solitary Walker,* trans. and ed. Charles E. Butterworth. New York: New York University Press.

Scriba, Christoph J., ed., 1970. "The Autobiography of John Wallis, F.R.S.," *Notes and Records of the Royal Society* 25: 17–46.

Segar, William, 1975. *The Booke of Honor and Armes (1590) and Honor Military and Ciuill (1602),* facsimile reproductions. Delmar, N.Y.: Scholars' Facsimiles & Reprints.

Selden, John, 1610. *The Duello or Single Combat. . . .* London.

————, 1614. *Titles of Honor.* London.

————, [1689] 1927. *Table Talk,* ed. Frederick Pollock. London: Quaritch.

Shadwell, Thomas [1676] 1966. *The Virtuoso,* eds Marjorie Hope Nicolson and David Stuart Rodes. Lincoln: University of Nebraska Press.

Shaftesbury, Anthony Ashley Cooper, third earl of, [1711] 1964. *Characteristics of Men, Manners, Opinions, Times,* ed. John M. Robertson. Indianapolis: Bobbs-Merrill.

Shaw, Peter, 1725. "General Preface" to Robert Boyle, *The Philosophical Works,* ed. Shaw, 3 vols., Vol. I, pp. i–xvi. London.

Smith, Adam, [1759] 1976. *The Theory of Moral Sentiments,* eds D. D. Raphael and A. L. Macfie. Oxford: Clarendon Press.

Smith, Thomas, [1583] 1970. *De Republica Anglorum. The Maner of Governement or Policie of the Realme of England,* facsimile reproduction of 1583 orig. Menston: Scolar Press.

Sprat, Thomas, 1667. *The History of the Royal Society of London.* London.

Stafford, Antony, 1611. *Staffords Niobe: or His Age of Teares . . . ,* 2d ed. London.

———, 1634. *The Guide of Honour.* London.

Stanley, Thomas, 1660. *The History of Philosophy,* 3 vols. London.

Stevin, Simon, [1634] 1937. "Fourth and Fifth Books of Statics," trans. Ada Barry, appendix 1 in Pascal 1937, 135–158.

Stillingfleet, Edward, 1662. *Origines Sacræ, or a Rational Account of the Grounds of Christian Faith, as to the Truth and Divine Authority of the Scriptures, and the matters therein contained.* London.

Stubbe, Henry, 1670. *Legends No Histories.* London.

Sydenham, Thomas, 1848. *The Works of Thomas Sydenham, M.D.,* trans. and ed. R. G. Latham, 2 vols. London: Sydenham Society.

Tillotson, John, [1696] 1752. *The Works of the Most Reverend Dr. John Tillotson,* ed. Thomas Birch, 3 vols. London.

Trollope, Anthony, [1867] 1980. *The Last Chronicle of Barset.* Oxford: Oxford University Press.

Vives, Juan Luis, [1531] 1971. *On Education: A Translation of 'De Tradendis Disciplinis,'* trans. Foster Watson. Totowa, N.J.: Rowman and Littlefield.

Walker, Obadiah, 1673. *Of Education, Especially of Young Gentlemen.* Oxford.

Waller, Richard, 1705. "The Life of Dr. Robert Hooke," in Hooke 1705a, i–xxviii.

Wallis, John, 1693–1695. *Opera Mathematica,* 2 vols. Oxford.

[Ward, Seth], 1652. *A Philosophicall Essay towards an Eviction of the Being and Attributes of God, the Immortality of the Souls of Men, the Truth and Authority of Scripture.* Oxford.

Waterhouse, Edward, 1660. *A Discourse and Defence of Arms and Armory. . . .* London.

Webster, Charles, 1979. *Utopian Planning and the Puritan Revolution: Gabriel Plattes, Samuel Hartlib, and 'Macaria,'* Research Publications of the Wellcome Unit for the History of Medicine, Oxford, No. 2. Oxford: Wellcome Unit.

Wetenhall, Edward], 1684. *Enter into Thy Closet: or A Method and Order for Private Devotion,* 5th ed. London.

White, Adam, ed., 1855. *A Collection of Documents on Spitzbergen & Greenland . . . .* London: Hakluyt Society.

Wilkins, John, [1675] 1678. *Of the Principles and Duties of Natural Religion.* London.

———, 1802a. *The Mathematical and Philosophical Works of the Right Rev. John Wilkins,* 2 vols. London.

————, [1638] 1802b. "The Discovery of a New World; or, A Discourse Tending to Prove, That (It Is Probable) There May Be Another Habitable World in the Moon," in Wilkins 1802a, I, 1–130.

————, [1640] 1802c. "A Discourse Concerning a New Planet, Tending to Prove, That (It Is Probable) Our Earth Is One of the Planets," in Wilkins 1802a, I, 131–261.

Willughby, Francis, 1678. *The Ornithology*. London.

Wilson, Thomas, [comp. *ca.* 1601] 1936. *The State of England Anno Dom. 1600*, ed. F. J. Fisher, Camden Miscellany, Vol. XVI. London: Camden Society, pp. 1–47.

Wolseley, Charles, [1669] 1675. *The Unreasonableness of Atheism Made Manifest; In a Discourse, Written by the Command of a Person of Honour*, 3d ed. London.

Wood, Anthony, 1813–1820. *Athenae Oxoniensis*, 4 vols. London: Rivington.

Worthington, John, 1847–1886. *The Diary and Correspondence of Dr. John Worthington*, eds James Crossley and Richard Copley Christie, 3 vols. Manchester: The Chetham Society.

Wotton, Henry, [1651] 1938. *A Philosophical Survey of Education or Moral Architecture and The Aphorisms of Education*, ed. H. S. Kermode. London: Hodder & Stoughton, for the University Press of Liverpool.

Wotton, William, 1694. *Reflections upon Ancient and Modern Learning*. London.

Zouch, Thomas, ed., 1796. *Lives of Dr. John Donne, Sir Henry Wotton, Mr. Richard Hooker, Mr. George Herbert, and Dr. Robert Sanderson, by Izaak Walton*. York.

Secondary and Modern Sources

Adams, Percy G., 1962. *Travelers and Travel Liars 1660–1800*. Berkeley: University of California Press.

Agassi, Joseph, 1977. "Who Discovered Boyle's Law?" *Studies in History and Philosophy of Science* 8: 189–250.

————, 1977. "Robert Boyle's Anonymous Writings," *Isis* 68: 284–287.

Agnew, Jean-Christophe, 1986. *Worlds Apart: The Market and the Theater in Anglo-American Thought, 1550–1750*. Cambridge: Cambridge University Press.

Alexander, Peter, 1985. *Ideas, Qualities and Corpuscles: Locke and Boyle on the External World*. Cambridge: Cambridge University Press.

Amussen, Susan Dwyer, 1985. "Gender, Family and the Social Order, 1560–1725," in Fletcher and Stevenson 1985a, 196–217.

————, 1988. *An Ordered Society: Gender and Class in Early Modern England*. Oxford: Basil Blackwell.

Anderson, Judith H., 1984. *Biographical Truth: The Representation of Historical Persons in Tudor-Stuart Writing*. New Haven: Yale University Press.

Arendt, Hannah, 1958. *The Human Condition*. Chicago: University of Chicago Press.

Ashley, Maurice, 1954. *England in the Seventeenth Century*, 2d ed. Harmondsworth: Penguin.

Atkinson, J. Maxwell, and John Heritage, eds, 1984. *Structures of Social Action: Studies in Conversation Analysis*. Cambridge: Cambridge University Press.

Austin, J. L., 1962. *How to Do Things with Words.* Cambridge, Mass.: Harvard University Press.

Babb, Lawrence, 1951. *The Elizabethan Malady: A Study of Melancholia in English Literature from 1580 to 1642.* East Lansing: Michigan State University Press.

Bagley, Paul J., 1992. "On the Practice of Esotericism," *Journal of the History of Ideas* 53: 231–247.

Baldick, Robert, 1965. *The Duel: A History of Duelling.* London: Chapman and Hall.

Barber, Bernard, 1983. *The Logic and Limits of Trust.* New Brunswick, N.J.: Rutgers University Press.

———, 1987. "Trust in Science," *Minerva* 25: 123–134.

Barber, Charles, 1985. *The Theme of Honour's Tongue: A Study of Social Attitudes in the English Drama from Shakespeare to Dryden,* Gothenburg Studies in English, No. 58. Göteborg: Acta Universitatis Gothoburgensis.

Barker, Peter, and Bernard R. Goldstein, 1988. "The Role of Comets in the Copernican Revolution," *Studies in History and Philosophy of Science* 19: 299–319.

Barnes, Barry, 1971. "Making Out in Industrial Research," *Science Studies* 1: 157–175.

———, 1984. "Problems of Intelligibility and Paradigm Instances," in *Scientific Rationality: The Sociological Turn,* ed. James Robert Brown. Dordrecht: D. Reidel, pp. 113–125.

———, 1985. *About Science.* Oxford: Basil Blackwell.

———, 1986. "On Authority and Its Relationship to Power," in Law 1986, 180–195.

———, 1988. *The Nature of Power.* Cambridge: Polity Press.

———, 1989. "Ostensive Learning and Self-Referring Knowledge," in *Cognition and Social Worlds,* eds Angus Gellatly, Don Rogers, and John A. Sloboda, Keele Cognition Seminars, 2. Oxford: Clarendon Press, pp. 190–204.

Barnes, Barry, and Steven Shapin, eds, 1979. *Natural Order: Historical Studies of Scientific Culture.* London and Beverly Hills, Calif.: Sage.

Bazerman, Charles, 1988. *Shaping Written Knowledge: The Genre and Activity of the Experimental Article in Science.* Madison: University of Wisconsin Press.

Bechler, Zev, 1974. "Newton's 1672 Optical Controversies: A Study in the Grammar of Scientific Dissent," in Elkana 1974, 115–142.

Beck, Daniel A., 1986. "Miracle and the Mechanical Philosophy: The Theology of Robert Boyle in Its Historical Context." Ph.D. thesis, University of Notre Dame.

Becker, Howard S., 1960. "Notes on the Concept of Commitment," *American Journal of Sociology* 66: 32–40 (also in Becker 1970a, 261–273).

———, 1964. "Personal Change in Adult Life," *Sociometry* 27: 40–53 (also in Becker 1970a, 275–287).

———, 1967. "Whose Side Are We On?" *Social Problems* 14: 239–248 (also in Becker 1970a, 123–134).

———, 1967. "History, Culture and Subjective Experience: An Exploration of the Social Bases of Drug-induced Experiences," *Journal of Health and Social Behavior* 8: 163–176 (also in Becker 1970a, 307–327).

———, 1970a. *Sociological Work: Method and Substance.* Chicago: Aldine.

———, [1968] 1970b. "The Self and Adult Socialization," in Becker 1970a, 289–303.

———, 1982. *Art Worlds.* Berkeley: University of California Press.

———, 1986. *Doing Things Together.* Evanston, Ill.: Northwestern University Press.

Beier, Lucinda McCray, 1985. "In Sickness and in Health: A Seventeenth-Century Family's Experience," in Porter 1985, 101–128.

———, 1987. *Sufferers & Healers: The Experience of Illness in Seventeenth-Century England.* London: Routledge & Kegan Paul.

———, 1989. "Experience and Experiment: Robert Hooke, Illness and Medicine," in Hunter and Schaffer 1989, 235–252.

Beller, Mara, 1988. "Experimental Accuracy, Operationalism, and Limits of Knowledge—1925 to 1935," *Science in Context* 2: 147–162.

Benjamin, Andrew E., G. N. Cantor, and J. R. R. Christie, eds, 1987. *The Figural and the Literal: Problems of Language in the History of Science and Philosophy, 1630–1800.* Manchester: Manchester University Press.

Ben-Menahem, Yemima, 1988. "Models of Science: Fictions or Idealizations?" *Science in Context* 2: 163–175.

Bennett, J. A., 1975. "Hooke and Wren and the System of the World: Some Points towards an Historical Account," *British Journal for the History of Science* 8: 32–61.

———, 1980. "Robert Hooke as Mechanic and Natural Philosopher," *Notes and Records of the Royal Society* 35: 33–48.

———, 1986. "The Mechanics' Philosophy and the Mechanical Philosophy," *History of Science* 24: 1–28.

———, 1989. "Magnetical Philosophy and Astronomy from Wilkins to Hooke," in Taton and Wilson 1989, 222–230.

———, 1991. "The Challenge of Practical Mathematics," in Pumfrey, Rossi, and Slawinski 1991, 176–190.

Benson, Douglas, and John A. Hughes, 1983. *The Perspective of Ethnomethodology.* London: Longman.

Berger, Peter L., and Thomas Luckmann, [1966] 1971. *The Social Construction of Reality: A Treatise in the Sociology of Knowledge.* Harmondsworth: Penguin.

Béziat, Jean, 1875. "La vie et les travaux de Jean Hévélius," *Bulletino di Bibliografia e di Storia delle Scienze Matematiche e Fisiche* 8: 497–558, 589–669.

Biagioli, Mario, 1989. "The Social Status of Italian Mathematicians, 1450–1600," *History of Science* 27: 41–95.

———, 1990. "Galileo's System of Patronage," *History of Science* 28: 1–62.

———, 1990. "Galileo the Emblem Maker," *Isis* 81: 230–258.

———, 1992. "Scientific Revolution, Social Bricolage, and Etiquette," in Porter and Teich 1992, 11–54.

———, 1993. *Galileo, Courtier: The Practice of Science in the Culture of Absolutism.* Chicago: University of Chicago Press.

Bijker, Wiebe E., Thomas P. Hughes, and Trevor J. Pinch, eds, 1989. *The Social Construction of Technological Systems: New Directions in the Sociology and History of Technology.* Cambridge, Mass.: MIT Press.

Billacois, François, [1986] 1990. *The Duel: Its Rise and Fall in Early Modern France*, trans. Trista Selous. New Haven: Yale University Press.

Birley, Robert, 1958. "Robert Boyle's Headmaster at Eton," *Notes and Records of the Royal Society* 13: 104–114.

———, 1959. "Robert Boyle at Eton," *Notes and Records of the Royal Society* 14: 191.

Bloor, David, 1974. "Popper's Mystification of Objective Knowledge," *Science Studies* 4: 65–76.

———, 1982. "Durkheim and Mauss Revisited: Classification and the Sociology of Knowledge," *Studies in History and Philosophy of Science* 13: 267–297 (reprinted in Stehr and Meja 1984, 51–75).

———, 1983. *Wittgenstein: A Social Theory of Knowledge*. London: Macmillan.

———, 1984. "A Sociological Theory of Objectivity," in *Objectivity and Cultural Divergence*, ed. S. C. Brown. Cambridge: Cambridge University Press, pp. 229–245.

———, [1976] 1991. *Knowledge and Social Imagery*, 2d edition. Chicago: University of Chicago Press.

———, 1992. "Left and Right Wittgensteinians," in Pickering 1992, 266–282.

Blum, Alan F., 1971. "The Corpus of Knowledge as a Normative Order: Intellectual Critiques of the Social Order and Commonsense Features of Bodies of Knowledge," in *Knowledge and Control: New Directions for the Sociology of Education*, ed. Michael F. D. Young. London: Collier-Macmillan, pp. 117–132.

Bodewitz, Henk J. H. W., Henk Buurma, and Gerard H. de Vries, 1989. "Regulatory Science and the Social Management of Trust in Medicine," in Bijker, Hughes, and Pinch 1989, 243–259.

Bogen, David, and Michael Lynch, 1989. "Taking Account of the Hostile Native: Plausible Deniability and the Production of Conventional History in the Iran-Contra Hearings," *Social Problems* 36: 197–224.

Bok, Sissela, [1978] 1979. *Lying: Moral Choice in Public and Private Life*. New York: Vintage.

———, [1983] 1989. *Secrets: On the Ethics of Concealment and Revelation*. New York: Vintage.

Bolinger, Dwight, 1973. "Truth Is a Linguistic Question," *Language* 49: 539–550.

Brannigan, Augustine, and Michael Lynch, 1987. "On Bearing False Witness: Credibility as an Interactional Accomplishment," *Journal of Contemporary Ethnography* 16: 115–146.

Brauer, George C., Jr., 1959. *The Education of a Gentleman: Theories of Gentlemanly Education in England, 1660–1775*. New York: Bookman Associates.

Broad, William, and Nicholas Wade, 1982. *Betrayers of the Truth: Fraud and Deceit in the Halls of Science*. New York: Simon & Schuster.

Broadhead, Glenn J., 1980. "A Bibliography of the Rhetoric of Conversation in England, 1660–1800," *Rhetoric Society Quarterly*, 43–48.

Brown, Harcourt, [1934] 1967. *Scientific Organizations in Seventeenth Century France (1620–1680)*. New York: Russell & Russell.

Brown, Peter Lancaster, 1974. *Comets, Meteorites and Men*. London: Robert Hale.

Bryson, Anna, 1990. "The Rhetoric of Status: Gesture, Demeanour and the Image of the Gentleman in Sixteenth- and Seventeenth-Century England," in *Renaissance Bodies: The Human Figure in English Culture c. 1540–1660*, eds Lucy Gent and Nigel Llewellyn. London: Reaktion Books, pp. 136–153.

Bryson, Frederick Robertson, 1935. *The Point of Honor in Sixteenth-Century Italy: An Aspect of the Life of the Gentleman*, Publications of the Institute of French Studies. New York: Columbia University Press.

Burke, John G., ed., 1983. *The Uses of Science in the Age of Newton*. Berkeley: University of California Press.

Burke, Peter, 1978. *Popular Culture in Early Modern Europe*. London: Temple Smith.

———, 1987. *The Historical Anthropology of Early Modern Italy: Essays on Perception and Communication*. Cambridge: Cambridge University Press.

Burke, Peter, and Roy Porter, eds, 1987. *The Social History of Language*. Cambridge: Cambridge University Press.

Burns, R. M., 1981. *The Great Debate on Miracles: From Joseph Glanvill to David Hume*. Lewisburg, Pa.: Bucknell University Press.

Burtt, Edwin Arthur, [1924] 1954. *The Metaphysical Foundations of Modern Physical Science*. Garden City, N.Y.: Doubleday Anchor.

Butler, Martin, 1984. *Theatre and Crisis 1632–1642*. Cambridge: Cambridge University Press.

Butterfield, Herbert, [1949] 1965. *The Origins of Modern Science 1300–1800*, rev. ed. New York: Free Press.

Bynum, W. F., and Roy Porter, eds, 1985. *William Hunter and the Eighteenth-Century Medical World*. Cambridge: Cambridge University Press.

Callon, Michel, and Bruno Latour, 1992. "Don't Throw the Baby Out with the Bath School! A Reply to Collins and Yearley," in Pickering 1992, 343–368.

Camden, Carroll, [1952] 1975. *The Elizabethan Woman*, rev. ed. Mammaroneck, N.Y.: Paul P. Appel.

Campbell, Donald T., 1990. "Asch's Moral Epistemology for Socially Shared Knowledge," in *The Legacy of Solomon Asch: Essays in Cognition and Social Psychology*, ed. Irvin Rock. Hillsdale, N.J.: Lawrence Erlbaum, pp. 39–52.

Campbell, Richard, 1992. *Truth and Historicity*. Oxford: Clarendon Press.

Canfield, J. Douglas, 1989. *Word as Bond in English Literature from the Middle Ages to the Restoration*. Philadelphia: University of Pennsylvania Press.

Canny, Nicholas, 1982. *The Upstart Earl: A Study of the Social and Mental World of Richard Boyle First Earl of Cork 1566–1643*. Cambridge: Cambridge University Press.

Cantor, G. N., 1984. "Berkeley's *The Analyst* Revisited," *Isis* 75: 668–683.

Carrithers, Michael, 1985. "An Alternative Social History of the Self," in Carrithers, Collins, and Lukes 1985, 234–256.

Carrithers, Michael, Steven Collins, and Steven Lukes, eds, 1985. *The Category of the Person: Anthropology, Philosophy, History*. Cambridge: Cambridge University Press.

Cartwright, Nancy, 1983. *How the Laws of Physics Lie*. Oxford: Clarendon Press.

———, 1989. *Nature's Capacities and Their Measurement*. Oxford: Clarendon Press.

Caspari, Fritz, 1954. *Humanism and the Social Order in England.* Chicago: University of Chicago Press.

Centore, F. F., 1970. *Robert Hooke's Contributions to Mechanics: A Study in Seventeenth Century Natural Philosophy.* The Hague: M. Nijhoff.

Chapman, Allan, 1990. *Dividing the Circle: The Development of Critical Angular Measurement in Astronomy 1500–1850.* New York: Ellis Horwood.

Childs, Fenela Ann, 1984. "Prescriptions for Manners in English Courtesy Literature, 1690–1760, and Their Social Implications." D. Phil. thesis, Oxford University.

Christie, John R. R., 1989. "Laputa Revisited," in Christie and Shuttleworth 1989, 45–60.

Christie, John R. R., and Sally Shuttleworth, eds, 1989. *Nature Transfigured: Science and Literature, 1700–1900.* Manchester: Manchester University Press.

Chubin, Daryl E., 1990. "Scientific Malpractice and the Contemporary Politics of Knowledge," in Cozzens and Gieryn 1990, 144–163.

Clagett, Marshall, 1941. *Giovanni Marliani and Late Medieval Physics.* New York: Columbia University Press.

Clark, J. C. D., 1985. *English Society 1688–1832: Ideology, Social Structure and Political Practice during the Ancien Regime.* Cambridge: Cambridge University Press.

Clericuzio, Antonio, 1990. "A Redefinition of Boyle's Chemistry and Corpuscular Philosophy," *Annals of Science* 47: 561–589.

Coady, C. A. J., 1992. *Testimony: A Philosophical Study.* Oxford: Clarendon Press.

Cohen, I. Bernard, 1980. *The Newtonian Revolution.* Cambridge: Cambridge University Press.

Cole, Jonathan R., and Stephen Cole, 1972. "The Ortega Hypothesis," *Science* 178: 368–375.

———, 1973. *Social Stratification in Science.* Chicago: University of Chicago Press.

Collins, H. M., 1975. "The Seven Sexes: A Study in the Sociology of a Phenomenon, or the Replication of an Experiment in Physics," *Sociology* 9: 205–224.

———, 1981. "The Role of the Core-Set in Modern Science: Social Contingency with Methodological Propriety in Science," *History of Science* 19: 6–19.

———, 1981. "Son of Seven Sexes: The Social Destruction of a Physical Phenomenon," *Social Studies of Science* 11: 33–62.

———, 1981. "Understanding Science," *Fundamenta Scientiae* 2: 367–380.

———, 1983. "The Meaning of Lies: Accounts of Action and Participatory Research," in *Accounts and Action,* eds G. Nigel Gilbert and Peter Abell, Surrey Conference on Sociological Theory and Method, Vol. 1. Aldershot: Gower, pp. 69–76.

———, [1985] 1992. *Changing Order: Replication and Induction in Scientific Practice.* Chicago: University of Chicago Press.

Collins, H. M., and Steven Yearley, 1992. "Epistemological Chicken," in Pickering 1992, 301–326.

Collinson, Patrick, 1991. "Laudable Lying in the Age of Dissimulation [review of Zagorin 1990]," *Times Literary Supplement,* 1 March, 23.

Conant, James Bryant, [1948] 1970. "Robert Boyle's Experiments in Pneumatics," in *Harvard Case Histories in Experimental Science,* 2 vols. ed. James Bryant Conant. Cambridge, Mass.: Harvard University Press, Vol. I, pp. 1–63.

Cook, Harold J., 1986. *The Decline of the Old Medical Regime in Stuart London.* Ithaca, N.Y.: Cornell University Press.

——, 1989. "Physicians and the New Philosophy: Henry Stubbe and the Virtuosi-Physicians," in French and Wear 1989, 246–271.

Costello, William T., 1958. *The Scholastic Curriculum at Early Seventeenth-Century Cambridge.* Cambridge, Mass.: Harvard University Press.

Coulter, Jeff, 1975. "Perceptual Accounts and Interpretive Asymmetries," *Sociology* 17: 385–396.

——, 1979. *The Social Construction of Mind.* London: Macmillan.

Cozzens, Susan E., and Thomas F. Gieryn, eds, 1990. *Theories of Science in Society.* Bloomington: Indiana University Press.

Crawforth, M. A., 1987. "Instrument Makers in the London Guilds," *Annals of Science* 44: 319–377.

Crombie, A. C., 1952. *Augustine to Galileo: The History of Science A.D. 400–1650.* London: Falcon Press.

Cunningham, Andrew, 1989. "Thomas Sydenham: Epidemics, Experiment and the 'Good Old Cause,'" in French and Wear 1989, 164–190.

Curry, Patrick, ed., 1987. *Astrology, Science and Society: Historical Essays.* Woodbridge, Suffolk: Boydell & Brewer.

——, 1989. *Prophecy and Power: Astrology in Early Modern England.* Princeton, N.J.: Princeton University Press.

——, 1991. "Astrology in Early Modern England: The Making of a Vulgar Knowledge," in Pumfrey, Rossi, and Slawinski 1991, 274–291.

Curtis, Mark H., 1959. *Oxford and Cambridge in Transition 1558–1642: An Essay on the Changing Relations between the English Universities and English Society.* Oxford: Clarendon Press.

Daniels, Arlene Kaplan, 1987. "Invisible Work," *Social Problems* 34: 403–415.

Daston, Lorraine J., 1988. *Classical Probability in the Enlightenment.* Princeton: Princeton University Press.

——, 1988. "The Factual Sensibility," *Isis* 79: 452–470.

——, 1989. "Problems of Early Modern Quantification," unpublished paper delivered to the History of Science Society, Gainesville, Florida, October 1989.

——, 1991. "Marvelous Facts and Miraculous Evidence in Early Modern Europe," *Critical Inquiry* 18: 93–124.

——, 1991. "Baconian Facts, Academic Civility, and the Prehistory of Objectivity," *Annals of Scholarship* 8: 337–363.

——, 1992. "The Naturalized Female Intellect," *Science in Context* 5: 209–235.

Daston, Lorraine J., and Katharine Park, 1985. "Hermaphrodites in Renaissance France," *Critical Matrix: Princeton Working Papers in Women's Studies* 1, No. 5.

Davidson, Donald, 1984. *Inquiries into Truth and Interpretation.* Oxford: Clarendon Press.

——, 1990. "The Structure and Content of Truth," *Journal of Philosophy* 87: 279–328.

Davis, J. C., 1974. "The Levellers and Democracy," in Webster 1974, 70–78.

Dear, Peter, 1985. "*Totius in Verba:* Rhetoric and Authority in the Early Royal Society," *Isis* 76: 145–161.

———, 1987. "Jesuit Mathematical Science and the Reconstitution of Experience in the Early Seventeenth Century," *Studies in History and Philosophy of Science* 18: 133–175.

———, 1988. *Mersenne and the Learning of the Schools.* Ithaca, N.Y.: Cornell University Press.

———, 1990. "Miracles, Experiments, and the Ordinary Course of Nature," *Isis* 81: 663–683.

———, ed., 1991a. *The Literary Structure of Scientific Argument: Historical Studies.* Philadelphia: University of Pennsylvania Press.

———, 1991b. "Narratives, Anecdotes, and Experiments: Turning Experience into Science in the Seventeenth Century," in Dear 1991a, 135–163.

———, 1992. "From Truth to Disinterestedness in the Seventeenth Century," *Social Studies of Science* 22: 619–631.

Dennis, Michael Aaron, 1989. "Graphic Understanding: Instruments and Interpretation in Robert Hooke's *Micrographia*," *Science in Context* 3: 309–364.

De Waard, Cornélis, 1936. *L'expérience barométrique: ses antécédents et ses explications.* Thouars: J. Gamon.

Dewhurst, Kenneth, 1962. "Locke's Contribution to Boyle's Researches on the Air and on Human Blood," *Notes and Records of the Royal Society* 17: 198–206.

———, 1963. *John Locke (1632–1704), Physician and Philosopher: A Medical Biography.* London: Wellcome Historical Medical Library.

———, 1966. *Dr. Thomas Sydenham (1624–1689): His Life and Original Writings.* Berkeley: University of California Press.

Dijksterhuis, E. J., [1959] 1986. *The Mechanization of the World Picture: Pythagoras to Newton,* trans. C. Dikshoorn. Princeton, N.J.: Princeton University Press.

Dobell, Clifford, 1958. *Antony van Leeuwenhoek and His 'Little Animals': Being Some Account of the Father of Protozoology & Bacteriology and His Multifarious Discoveries in These Disciplines.* New York: Russell & Russell.

Doran, Madeleine, 1940. "On Elizabethan 'Credulity': With Some Questions Concerning the Use of the Marvelous in Literature," *Journal of the History of Ideas* 1: 151–176.

Douglas, Jack D., ed., 1970a. *Understanding Everyday Life: Toward the Reconstruction of Sociological Knowledge.* Chicago: Aldine.

———, 1970b. "Understanding Everyday Life," in J. Douglas 1970a, 3–44.

Douglas, Mary, 1975. *Implicit Meanings: Essays in Anthropology.* London: Routledge & Kegan Paul.

———, [1978] 1982. "Cultural Bias," in idem, *In the Active Voice.* London: Routledge & Kegan Paul, pp. 183–254.

———, 1986. *How Institutions Think.* Syracuse, N.Y.: Syracuse University Press.

———, 1986. *Risk Acceptability According to the Social Sciences,* Russell Sage Foundation, Social Research Perspectives, Occasional Reports on Current Topics, No. 11. New York: Russell Sage Foundation.

———, 1986. "The Social Preconditions of Radical Scepticism," in Law 1986, 68–87.

Drake, Stillman, 1985. "Galileo's Accuracy in Measuring Horizontal Projections," *Annali dell'Istituto e Museo di Storia della Scienze di Firenze* 10: 3–13.

Drew, Paul, and Anthony Wootton, eds, 1988. *Erving Goffman: Exploring the Interaction Order.* Cambridge: Polity Press.

Duffy, Eamon, 1981. "Valentine Greatrakes, the Irish Stroker: Miracle, Science and Orthodoxy in Restoration England," *Studies in Church History* 17: 251–273.

Duhem, Pierre, [1906] 1991. *The Aim and Structure of Physical Theory,* trans. Philip P. Wiener. Princeton, N.J.: Princeton University Press.

Dunn, John, 1988. "Trust and Political Agency," in Gambetta 1988, 73–93.

Durkheim, Émile, [1912] 1915. *The Elementary Forms of the Religious Life,* trans. Joseph Ward Swain. London: George Allen & Unwin.

———, [1933] 1960. *The Division of Labor in Society,* trans. George Simpson. Glencoe, Ill.: Free Press.

———, [1898] 1982. *The Rules of Sociological Method,* ed. Steven Lukes, trans. W. D. Halls. New York: Free Press.

Eamon, William, 1990. "From the Secrets of Nature to Public Knowledge," in Lindberg and Westman 1990, 333–365.

———, 1991. "Court, Academy, and Printing House: Patronage and Scientific Careers in Late Renaissance Italy," in Moran 1991a, 25–50.

Earle, Peter, 1989. *The Making of the English Middle Class: Business, Society and Family Life in London, 1660–1730.* London: Methuen.

Earle, William, [1955] 1968. *Objectivity: An Essay in Phenomenological Ontology.* Chicago: Quadrangle Books.

Einstein, Lewis, 1902. *The Italian Renaissance in England: Studies.* New York: Columbia University Press.

———, 1921. *Tudor Ideals.* London: G. Bell.

Ekman, Paul, 1985. *Telling Lies: Clues to Deceit in the Marketplace, Politics, and Marriage.* New York: W. W. Norton.

Elias, Norbert, [1939, 1969] 1978, 1983. *The Civilizing Process,* trans. Edmund Jephcott, 2 vols. [Vol. I = *The History of Manners;* Vol. II = *The Court Society*]. Oxford: Basil Blackwell.

———, 1991. *The Society of Individuals,* ed. Michael Schröter, trans. Edmund Jephcott. Oxford: Basil Blackwell.

Elkana, Yehuda, ed., 1974. *The Interaction between Science and Philosophy.* Atlantic Highlands, N.J.: Humanities Press.

Elster, Jon, 1989. *The Cement of Society: A Study of Social Order.* Cambridge: Cambridge University Press.

Elzinga, Aant, Jan Nolin, Rob Pranger, and Sune Sunesson, eds, 1990. *In Science We Trust? Moral and Political Issues of Science in Society,* Science and Technology Policy Studies, Vol. 2. Lund: Lund University Press.

Embree, Lester, ed., 1988a. *Worldly Phenomenology: The Continuing Influence of Alfred Schutz on North American Human Science,* Current Continental Research, 013. Washington: Center for Advanced Research in Phenomenology and University Press of America.

———, 1988b. "Schutz on Science," in Embree 1988a, 251–274.

'Espinasse, Margaret, 1956. *Robert Hooke.* London: Heinemann.

Ezrahi, Yaron, 1990. *The Descent of Icarus: Science and the Transformation of Contemporary Democracy.* Cambridge, Mass.: Harvard University Press.

Fairchilds, Cissie, 1984. *Domestic Enemies: Servants & Their Masters in Old Regime France*. Baltimore: Johns Hopkins University Press.

Feingold, Mordechai, 1984. *The Mathematicians' Apprenticeship: Science, Universities and Society in England, 1560–1640*. Cambridge: Cambridge University Press.

Fell-Smith, Charlotte, 1901. *Mary Rich, Countess of Warwick (1625–1678): Her Family & Friends*. London: Longmans, Green.

Findlen, Paula, 1989. "Museums, Collecting and Scientific Culture in Early Modern Italy." Ph.D. thesis, University of California at Berkeley.

———, 1989. "The Museum: Its Classical Etymology and Renaissance Genealogy," *Journal of the History of Collections* 1: 59–78.

———, 1990. "Jokes of Nature and Jokes of Knowledge: The Playfulness of Scientific Discourse in Early Modern Europe," *Renaissance Quarterly* 43: 292–331.

———, 1991. "The Economy of Scientific Exchange in Early Modern Italy," in Moran 1991a, 5–24.

———, in press. "The Limits of Civility and the Ends of Science."

Fisch, Harold, 1953. "The Scientist as Priest: A Note on Robert Boyle's Natural Theology," *Isis* 44: 252–265.

Fleck, Ludwik, [1935] 1979. *Genesis and Development of a Scientific Fact*, eds Thaddeus J. Trenn and Robert K. Merton, trans. Fred Bradley and Trenn. Chicago: University of Chicago Press.

Fletcher, Anthony, 1985. "Honour, Reputation and Local Officeholding in Elizabethan and Stuart England," in Fletcher and Stevenson 1985a, 92–115.

Fletcher, Anthony, and John Stevenson, eds, 1985a. *Order and Disorder in Early Modern England*. Cambridge: Cambridge University Press.

———, 1985b. "Introduction," in idem 1985a, 1–40.

Forrester, John, 1989. "Lying on the Couch," in Lawson and Appignanesi 1989, 145–165.

Foucault, Michel, 1977. "What Is an Author?" in idem, *Language, Counter-memory, Practice: Selected Essays and Interviews*, ed. Donald F. Bouchard, trans. Bouchard and Sherry Simon. Ithaca, N.Y.: Cornell University Press, pp. 113–138.

———, [1973] 1979. "Power and Norm: Notes," in *Michel Foucault: Power, Truth, Strategy*, eds M. Morris and P. Patton, Sydney: Feral Publications, pp. 59–66.

———, 1980. *Power/Knowledge: Selected Interviews and Other Writings 1972–1977*, ed. Colin Gordon, trans. Gordon, Leo Marshall, John Mepham, and Kate Soper. New York: Pantheon.

———, 1981. "The Order of Discourse," in *Untying the Text: A Post-structuralist Reader*, ed. Robert Young. London: Routledge & Kegan Paul, pp. 48–78.

Franco, Paul, 1990. *The Political Philosophy of Michael Oakeshott*. New Haven: Yale University Press.

Frank, Robert G., Jr., 1974. "The John Ward Diaries: Mirror of Seventeenth Century Science and Medicine," *Journal of the History of Medicine* 29: 147–179.

————, 1980. *Harvey and the Oxford Physiologists: Scientific Ideas and Social Interaction*. Berkeley: University of California Press.

Fraser, Antonia, 1984. *The Weaker Vessel: Woman's Lot in Seventeenth-Century England*. London: Weidenfeld and Nicolson.

French, Roger, and Andrew Wear, eds, 1989. *The Medical Revolution of the Seventeenth Century*. Cambridge: Cambridge University Press.

Fulton, John F., 1961. *A Bibliography of the Honourable Robert Boyle*, 2d ed. Oxford: Clarendon Press.

Gambetta, Diego, ed., 1988. *Trust: Making and Breaking Cooperative Relations*. Oxford: Basil Blackwell.

Garber, Daniel, 1992. *Descartes' Metaphysical Physics*. Chicago: University of Chicago Press.

Garfinkel, Harold, 1963. "A Conception of, and Experiments with, 'Trust' as a Condition of Stable Concerted Actions," in *Motivation and Social Interaction*, ed. O. J. Harvey. New York: Ronald Press, pp. 187–238.

————, 1967. *Studies in Ethnomethodology*. Englewood Cliffs, N.J.: Prentice-Hall.

————, ed., 1986. *Ethnomethodological Studies of Work*. London: Routledge & Kegan Paul.

Garfinkel, Harold, Michael Lynch, and Eric Livingston, 1981. "The Work of a Discovering Science Construed with Materials from the Optically Discovered Pulsar," *Philosophy of the Social Sciences* 11: 131–158.

Garrison, James W., 1987. "Newton and the Relation of Mathematics to Natural Philosophy," *Journal of the History of Ideas* 48: 609–627.

Geertz, Clifford, 1983a. *Local Knowledge: Further Essays in Interpretive Anthropology*. New York: Basic Books.

————, 1983b. "Blurred Genres: The Refiguration of Social Thought," in Geertz 1983a, 19–35.

————, 1983c. "Common Sense as a Cultural System," in Geertz 1983a, 73–93.

————, 1983d. "The Way We Think Now: Toward an Ethnography of Modern Thought," in Geertz 1983a, 147–163.

Gellner, Ernest, 1973. "Concepts and Society," in idem, *Cause and Meaning in the Social Sciences*, eds I. C. Jarvie and Joseph Agassi. London: Routledge & Kegan Paul, pp. 18–46.

————, 1985. "Relativism and Universals," in idem, *Relativism and the Social Sciences*. Cambridge: Cambridge University Press, pp. 83–100.

————, 1988. "Trust, Cohesion, and the Social Order," in Gambetta 1988, 142–157.

Giddens, Anthony, 1987. *Social Theory and Modern Sociology*. Cambridge: Polity Press.

————, 1988. "Goffman as a Systematic Social Theorist," in Drew and Wootton 1988, 250–279.

————, 1989. *The Consequences of Modernity*. Stanford, Calif.: Stanford University Press.

Gigerenzer, Gerd, et al., 1989. *The Empire of Chance: How Probability Changed Science and Everyday Life*. Cambridge: Cambridge University Press.

Ginzburg, Carlo, 1976. "High and Low: The Theme of Forbidden Knowledge in the Sixteenth and Seventeenth Centuries," *Past and Present* 73: 28–41.

———, 1991. "Checking the Evidence: The Judge and the Historian," *Critical Inquiry* 18: 79–92.

Goffman, Erving, [1959] 1969. *The Presentation of Self in Everyday Life*. London: Allen Lane, The Penguin Press.

———, 1967. *Interaction Ritual: Essays on Face-to-Face Behavior*. New York: Pantheon.

———, 1969. *Strategic Interaction*. Philadelphia: University of Pennsylvania Press.

———, 1971. *Relations in Public: Microstudies of the Public Order*. New York: Basic Books.

———, 1981. *Forms of Talk*. Philadelphia: University of Pennsylvania Press.

———, 1983. "Felicity's Condition," *American Journal of Sociology* 89: 1–53.

———, 1984. "The Interaction Order," *American Sociological Review* 48: 1–17.

———, [1963] 1986. *Stigma: Notes on the Management of Spoiled Identity*. New York: Touchstone.

Golinski, J. V., 1987. "Robert Boyle: Scepticism and Authority in Seventeenth-Century Chemical Discourse," in Benjamin, Cantor, and Christie 1987, 58–82.

———, 1989. "A Noble Spectacle: Research on Phosphorus and the Public Cultures of Science in the Early Royal Society," *Isis* 80: 11–39.

Gooday, Graeme, 1988. "Precision Measurement and the Genesis of Physics Teaching Laboratories in Victorian Britain," *British Journal for the History of Science* 21: 25–52.

Gooding, David, 1985. "'In Nature's School': Faraday as an Experimentalist," in *Faraday Rediscovered: Essays on the Life and Work of Michael Faraday, 1797–1867*, eds Gooding and Frank A. J. L. James. London: Macmillan, pp. 106–135.

Gooding, David, Trevor Pinch, and Simon Schaffer, eds, 1989. *The Uses of Experiment: Studies in the Natural Sciences*. Cambridge: Cambridge University Press.

Grafton, Anthony, and Lisa Jardine, 1986. *From Humanism to the Humanities: Education and the Liberal Arts in Fifteenth- and Sixteenth-Century Europe*. Cambridge, Mass.: Harvard University Press.

Grant, Robert, 1990. *Oakeshott*. London: Claridge Press.

Gratton, Carolyn, 1973. "Some Aspects of the Lived Experience of Interpersonal Trust," *Humanitas: Journal of the Institute of Man* 9: 273–296.

Greenblatt, Stephen, 1980. *Renaissance Self-fashioning: From More to Shakespeare*. Chicago: University of Chicago Press.

Grice, H. Paul, 1975. "Logic and Conversation," in *Syntax and Semantics. Volume 3: Speech Acts*, eds Peter Cole and Jerry L. Morgan. New York: Academic Press, pp. 43–58.

Griffin, Kim, 1973. "Interaction Variables of Interpersonal Trust," *Humanitas: Journal of the Institute of Man* 9: 297–315.

Grimshaw, Allen D., ed., 1990. *Conflict Talk: Sociolinguistic Investigations of Arguments in Conversations*. Cambridge: Cambridge University Press.

Gruber, Howard E., 1985. "From Epistemic Subject to Unique Creative Person at Work," *Archives de psychologie* 53: 167–185.

———, 1990. "The Cooperative Synthesis of Disparate Points of View," in *The Legacy of Solomon Asch: Essays in Cognition and Social Psychology*, ed. Irvin Rock. Hillside, N.J.: Lawrence Erlbaum, pp. 143–158.

Guerlac, Henry, 1981. *Newton on the Continent*. Ithaca, N.Y.: Cornell University Press.

Gunther, R. T., 1923–1967. *Early Science in Oxford*, 15 vols. Oxford: privately printed.

Hacking, Ian, 1975. *The Emergence of Probability: A Philosophical Study of Early Ideas about Probability, Induction and Statistical Inference*. Cambridge: Cambridge University Press.

———, 1983. *Representing and Intervening: Introductory Topics in the Philosophy of Natural Science*. Cambridge: Cambridge University Press.

Hagstrom, Warren O., [1965] 1975. *The Scientific Community*. Carbondale: Southern Illinois University Press.

———, 1976. "The Production of Culture in Science," *American Behavioral Scientist* 19: 753–768.

Hale, J. R., 1971. "Sixteenth-Century Explanations of War and Violence," *Past and Present* 51: 3–26.

Hall, A. Rupert, [1954] 1966. *The Scientific Revolution: The Formation of the Modern Scientific Attitude*, 2d ed. Boston: Beacon Press.

[Hall], Marie Boas, 1958. *Robert Boyle and Seventeenth-Century Chemistry*. Cambridge: Cambridge Univerity Press.

Hall, Marie Boas, 1965. "Oldenburg and the Art of Scientific Communication," *British Journal for the History of Science* 2: 278–290.

———, 1983. "Oldenburg, the *Philosophical Transactions*, and Technology," in J. G. Burke 1983, 21–47.

———, 1987. "Boyle's Method of Work: Promoting His Corpuscular Philosophy," *Notes and Records of the Royal Society* 41: 111–143.

———, 1991. *Promoting Experimental Learning: Experiment and the Royal Society 1660–1727*. Cambridge: Cambridge University Press.

———, 1992. "Frederic Slare, F.R.S. (1648–1727)," *Notes and Records of the Royal Society* 46: 23–41.

Hannaway, Owen, 1975. *The Chemists and the Word: The Didactic Origins of Chemistry*. Baltimore: Johns Hopkins University Press.

———, 1986. "Laboratory Design and the Aim of Science: Andreas Libavius versus Tycho Brahe," *Isis* 77: 585–610.

Hanson, Elizabeth, 1990. "Torture and Truth in Renaissance England," unpublished typescript.

Hardwig, John, 1991. "The Role of Trust in Knowledge," *Journal of Philosophy* 88: 693–708.

Harvey, Bill, 1981. "Plausibility and the Evaluation of Knowledge: A Case-Study of Experimental Quantum Mechanics," *Social Studies of Science* 11: 95–130.

Harvey, Cyril Pearce, 1958. *The Advocate's Devil*. London: Stevens.

Harvey, E. Ruth, 1975. *The Inward Wits: Psychological Theory in the Middle Ages and the Renaissance*. London: The Warburg Institute of the University of London.

Harwood, John T., 1991. "Science Writing and Writing Science: Robert Boyle and Rhetorical Theory," paper given to the Stalbridge Boyle Symposium, 14–16 December 1991.

Heal, Felicity, 1990. *Hospitality in Early Modern England.* Oxford: Clarendon Press.

Hecht, J. Jean, 1956. *The Domestic Servant Class in Eighteenth-Century England.* London: Routledge & Kegan Paul.

Heidegger, Martin, 1977. *Basic Writings,* ed. David Farrell Krell. San Francisco: Harper.

Heller, Thomas C., Morton Sosna, and David E. Wellbery, eds, 1986. *Reconstructing Individualism: Autonomy, Individuality, and the Self in Western Thought.* Stanford, Calif.: Stanford University Press.

Hempel, Carl G., 1966. *Philosophy of Natural Science.* Englewood Cliffs, N.J.: Prentice-Hall.

Henry, John, 1988. "The Origins of Modern Science: Henry Oldenburg's Contribution," *British Journal for the History of Science* 21: 103–110.

———, 1990. "Henry More versus Robert Boyle: The Spirit of Nature and the Nature of Providence," in *Henry More (1614–1687): Tercentenary Studies,* ed. Sarah Hutton. Dordrecht: Kluwer, pp. 55–76.

Heritage, John, 1984. *Garfinkel and Ethnomethodology.* Cambridge: Polity Press.

Hesse, Mary B., 1966. "Hooke's Vibration Theory and the Isochrony of Springs," *Isis* 57: 433–441.

Hetherington, Norriss S., 1972. "The Hevelius-Auzout Controversy," *Notes and Records of the Royal Society* 27: 103–106.

———, 1988. *Science and Objectivity: Episodes in the History of Astronomy.* Ames: Iowa State University Press.

Heyck, T. W., 1982. *The Transformation of Intellectual Life in Victorian England.* London: Croom Helm.

Heyd, Michael, 1984. "Robert Burton's Sources on Enthusiasm and Melancholy: From a Medical Tradition to Religious Controversy," *History of European Ideas* 5: 17–44.

Hill, Christopher, 1969. *Society and Puritanism in Pre-revolutionary England.* London: Panther.

———, 1975a. *The World Turned Upside Down: Radical Ideas during the English Revolution.* Harmondsworth: Penguin.

———, 1975b. *Change and Continuity in Seventeenth-century England.* Cambridge, Mass.: Harvard University Press.

———, 1975c. "A One-Class Society?" in Hill 1975b, 205–218.

———, 1975d. "Pottage for Freeborn Englishmen: Attitudes to Wage-Labour," in Hill 1975b, 219–238.

Holden, William P., 1954. *Anti-Puritan Satire 1572–1642,* Yale Studies in English, Vol. 126. New Haven: Yale University Press.

Hole, Christina, 1953. *The English Housewife in the Seventeenth Century.* London: Chatto & Windus.

Holmes, Geoffrey, 1982. *Augustan England: Professions, State and Society, 1680–1730.* London: George Allen & Unwin.

Holmes, Richard, 1985. *Firing Line.* London: Jonathan Cape.

Holzner, Burkart, 1973. "Sociological Reflections on Trust," *Humanitas: Journal of the Institute of Man* 9: 333–345.

———, 1978. "The Construction of Social Actors: An Essay on Social Identities," in Luckmann 1978, 291–310.

Houghton, Walter, 1942. "The English Virtuoso in the Seventeenth Century," *Journal of the History of Ideas* 3: 51–73, 190–219.

Howell, Roger, and David E. Brewster, 1974. "Reconsidering the Levellers: The Evidence of the *Moderate*," in Webster 1974, 79–100.

Hughes, David W., 1990. "Edmond Halley: His Interest in Comets," in Thrower 1990, 324–372.

Hull, David L., 1988. *Science as a Process: An Evolutionary Account of the Social and Conceptual Development of Science.* Chicago: University of Chicago Press.

Hunt, William, 1983. *The Puritan Moment: The Coming of Revolution in an English County.* Cambridge, Mass.: Harvard University Press.

———, 1990. "Civic Chivalry and the English Civil War," in *The Transmission of Culture in Early Modern Europe*, eds Anthony Grafton and Ann Blair. Philadelphia: University of Pennsylvania Press, pp. 204–237.

Hunter, Michael, 1981. *Science and Society in Restoration England.* Cambridge: Cambridge University Press.

———, 1982. *The Royal Society and Its Fellows 1660–1700: The Morphology of an Early Scientific Institution.* Chalfont St. Giles: British Society for the History of Science.

———, 1988. "Promoting the New Science: Henry Oldenburg and the Early Royal Society," *History of Science* 26: 165–181.

———, 1989. *Establishing the New Science: The Experience of the Early Royal Society.* Woodbridge, Suffolk: Boydell Press.

———, 1990. "Alchemy, Magic and Moralism in the Thought of Robert Boyle," *British Journal for the History of Science* 23: 387–410.

———, comp., 1992. *Letters and Papers of Robert Boyle: A Guide to the Manuscripts and Microfilm.* Bethesda, Md.: University Publications of America.

———, 1993. "Casuistry in Action: Robert Boyle's Confessional Interviews with Gilbert Burnet and Edward Stillingfleet, 1691," *Journal of Ecclesiastical History* 44: 80–98.

———, in press. "The Conscience of Robert Boyle: Functionalism, 'Dysfunctionalism' and the Task of Historical Understanding," in *Renaissance and Revolution: Humanists, Scholars, Craftsmen and Natural Philosophers in Early Modern Europe*, eds J. V. Field and Frank A. J. L. James. Cambridge: Cambridge University Press.

Hunter, Michael, and Simon Schaffer, eds, 1989. *Robert Hooke: New Studies.* Woodbridge, Suffolk: Boydell Press.

Hunter, Richard, and Ida Macalpine, 1959. "William Harvey and Robert Boyle," *Notes and Records of the Royal Society* 14: 115–127.

Husserl, Edmund, [1913] 1931. *Ideas: General Introduction to Pure Phenomenology*, trans. W. R. Boyce Gibson. London: George Allen & Unwin; New York: Macmillan.

Iliffe, Robert Charles, 1989. "'The Idols of the Temple': Isaac Newton and the Private Life of Anti-idolatry." Ph.D. thesis, Cambridge University.

————, 1991. "Author-Mongering: The 'Editor' between Producer and Consumer," unpublished typescript.

————, 1992. "'In the Warehouse': Privacy, Property and Priority in the Early Royal Society," *History of Science* 30: 29–68.

————, 1992. "Foreign Bodies: 'Strangers' and Natural Philosophy in the Restoration," unpublished typescript.

Ingegno, Alfonso, 1988. "The New Philosophy of Nature," in Schmitt et al. 1988, 236–263.

Istituto Nazionale di Studi sul Rinascimento, ed., 1982. *Scienze, credenze, occulte, livelli di cultura.* Florence: Leo S. Olschki.

Jacob, James R., 1972. "The Ideological Origins of Robert Boyle's Natural Philosophy," *Journal of European Studies* 2: 1–21.

————, 1977. *Robert Boyle and the English Revolution: A Study in Social and Intellectual Change.* New York: Burt Franklin.

————, 1977. "Boyle's Circle in the Protectorate: Revelation, Politics and the Millennium," *Journal of the History of Ideas* 38: 131–140.

————, 1978. "Boyle's Atomism and the Restoration Assault on Pagan Naturalism," *Social Studies of Science* 8: 211–233.

————, 1983. *Henry Stubbe, Radical Protestantism and the Early Enlightenment.* Cambridge: Cambridge University Press.

James, Mervyn, 1978. *English Politics and the Concept of Honour 1485–1642*, Past and Present Supplement, 3. Oxford: Past and Present Society.

————, 1986. *Society, Politics and Culture: Studies in Early Modern England.* Cambridge: Cambridge University Press.

James, William, [1907] 1991. *Pragmatism.* Buffalo, N.Y.: Prometheus.

Jardine, Nicholas, 1984. *The Birth of History and Philosophy of Science: Kepler's 'A Defence of Tycho against Ursus' with Essays on Its Provenance and Significance.* Cambridge: Cambridge University Press.

Johns, Adrian, 1991. "History, Science, and the History of the Book: The Making of Natural Philosophy in Early Modern England," *Publishing History* 30: 5–30.

————, 1992. "Wisdom in the Concourse: Natural Philosophy and the History of the Book in Early Modern England." Ph.D. thesis, Cambridge University.

————, 1993. "Ross versus Wilkins and the Meanings of Copernicanism," unpublished.

Johnston, Stephen, 1991. "Mathematical Practitioners and Instruments in Elizabethan England," *Annals of Science* 48: 319–344.

————, 1991. "Thomas Digges: Mathematician and Gentleman," unpublished typescript.

Jones, Gordon W., 1964. "Robert Boyle as a Medical Man," *Bulletin of the History of Medicine* 38: 139–152.

Jones, Irene, 1989. *Robert Boyle: Lord of the Manor of Stalbridge 1643–1691*, Sturminster Newton Museum, Booklet No. 4. Castle Cary, Somerset: Castle Cary Press.

Jones, J. R., 1979. *Country and Court: England, 1658–1714.* Cambridge, Mass.: Harvard University Press.

Jones, Richard Foster, [1936] 1982. *Ancients and Moderns: The Rise of the Scientific Movement in Seventeenth-Century England*, rev. ed. New York: Dover.

Jonsen, Albert R., and Stephen Toulmin, 1988. *The Abuse of Casuistry: A History of Moral Reasoning.* Berkeley: University of California Press.

Jordan, Kathleen, and Michael Lynch, 1992. "The Sociology of a Genetic Engineering Technique: Ritual and Rationality in the Performance of the 'Plasmid Prep,'" in *The Right Tools for the Job: At Work in Twentieth-Century Life Science,* eds Adele Clarke and Joan H. Fujimura. Princeton, N.J.: Princeton University Press, pp. 77–114.

Jordanova, Ludmilla, 1980. "Natural Facts: A Historical Perspective on Science and Sexuality," in *Nature, Culture and Gender,* eds Carol P. MacCormack and Marilyn Strathern. Cambridge: Cambridge University Press, pp. 42–69.

———, ed., 1986a. *Languages of Nature: Critical Essays on Science and Literature.* New Brunswick, N.J.: Rutgers University Press.

———, 1986b. "Naturalizing the Family: Literature and the Bio-medical Sciences in the Late Eighteenth Century," in Jordanova 1986a, 86–116.

———, 1989. *Sexual Visions: Images of Gender in Science and Medicine between the Eighteenth and Nineteenth Centuries.* Madison: University of Wisconsin Press.

Kaplan, Barbara Beigun, 1979. "The Medical Writings of Robert Boyle: Medical Philosophy in Mid–Seventeenth Century England." Ph.D. thesis, University of Maryland.

———, 1982. "Greatrakes the Stroker: The Interpretations of His Contemporaries," *Isis* 73: 178–185.

Kearney, Hugh F., 1970. *Scholars and Gentlemen: Universities and Society in Pre-industrial Britain 1500–1700.* Ithaca, N.Y.: Cornell University Press.

Keegan, John, 1976, *The Face of Battle.* New York: Viking.

Keller, Alex, 1976. "Renaissance Mathematical Duels," *History of Science* 14: 208–209.

Keller, Evelyn Fox, 1988. "Feminist Perspectives on Science Studies," *Science, Technology, & Human Values* 13: 235–249.

Kelso, Ruth, 1929. *The Doctrine of the English Gentleman in the Sixteenth Century.* University of Illinois Studies in Language and Literature, Vol. 14. Urbana: University of Illinois Press, pp. 1–288.

Kerr, Philip, ed., 1990. *The Penguin Book of Lies.* New York: Viking.

Keynes, Geoffrey, 1960. *A Bibliography of Dr. Robert Hooke.* Oxford: Clarendon Press.

Kiernan, V. G., [1986] 1989. *The Duel in European History: Honour and the Reign of Aristocracy.* Oxford: Oxford University Press.

King, Henry C., [1955] 1979. *The History of the Telescope.* New York: Dover.

King, Lester S., 1968. "Robert Boyle as an Amateur Physician," in Charles W. Bodemer and King, *Medical Investigation in Seventeenth Century England,* Papers Read at a Clark Library Seminar, October 14, 1967. Los Angeles: William Andrews Clark Memorial Library, pp. 27–49.

Kinsella, Noel A., 1973. "Some Psychological Dimensions of the Trusting Attitude," *Humanitas: Journal of the Institute of Man* 9: 253–271.

Kitcher, Philip, 1983. *The Nature of Mathematical Knowledge.* Oxford: Oxford University Press.

———, 1992. "Authority, Deference, and the Role of Individual Reason," in McMullin 1992, 244–271.

——, 1993. *The Advancement of Science: Science without Legend, Objectivity without Illusions.* New York: Oxford University Press.

Klibansky, Raymond, Erwin Panofsky, and Fritz Saxl, 1964. *Saturn and Melancholy: Studies in the History of Natural Philosophy, Religion, and Art.* London: Thomas Nelson.

Knorr-Cetina, Karin D., and Michael J. Mulkay, eds, 1983. *Science Observed: Perspectives on the Social Study of Science.* London: Sage.

Koyré, Alexandre, 1968a. *Metaphysics and Measurement: Essays in Scientific Revolution.* Cambridge, Mass.: Harvard University Press.

——, [1943] 1968b. "Galileo and Plato," in idem 1968a, 16–43.

——, [1953] 1968c. "An Experiment in Measurement," in idem 1968a, 89–117.

——, [1953] 1968d. "Pascal Savant," in idem 1968a, 131–156.

Kraye, Jill, 1988. "Moral Philosophy," in Schmitt et al. 1988, 303–386.

Kristeller, Paul Oskar, 1961. *Renaissance Thought: The Classic, Scholastic, and Humanist Strains.* New York: Harper Torchbook.

——, 1985. "The Active and Contemplative Life in Renaissance Humanism," in Vickers 1985, 133–152.

Kuhn, Thomas S., 1952. "Robert Boyle and Structural Chemistry in the Seventeenth Century," *Isis* 43: 12–36.

——, [1962] 1970. *The Structure of Scientific Revolutions,* 2d ed. Chicago: University of Chicago Press.

——, 1977a. *The Essential Tension: Selected Studies in Scientific Tradition and Change.* Chicago: University of Chicago Press.

——, [1961] 1977b. "The Function of Measurement in Modern Physical Science," in Kuhn 1977a, 178–224.

——, [1964] 1977c. "A Function for Thought Experiments," in Kuhn 1977a, 240–265.

——, [1976] 1977d. " Mathematical versus Experimental Traditions in the Development of Physical Science," in Kuhn, 1977a, 31–65.

Kussmaul, Ann, 1981. *Servants in Husbandry in Early Modern England.* Cambridge: Cambridge University Press.

Lakoff, Robin, 1972. "Language in Context," *Language* 48: 907–927.

Laqueur, Thomas, 1990. *Making Sex: Body and Gender from the Greeks to Freud.* Cambridge, Mass.: Harvard University Press.

Laslett, Peter, 1963. "The Face to Face Society," in idem, ed., *Philosophy, Politics and Society.* Oxford: Basil Blackwell, pp. 157–184.

——, [1965] 1988. *The World We Have Lost: Further Explored,* 3d ed. London: Routledge.

Latour, Bruno, 1987. *Science in Action: How to Follow Scientists and Engineers through Society.* Milton Keynes: Open University Press.

Latour, Bruno, and Steve Woolgar, [1979] 1986. *Laboratory Life: The [Social] Construction of Scientific Facts,* 2d (revised) ed. Princeton, N.J.: Princeton University Press.

Law, John, ed., 1986. *Power, Action and Belief: A New Sociology of Knowledge?,* Sociological Review Monograph No. 32. London: Routledge & Kegan Paul.

Lawrence, Christopher J., 1979. "The Nervous System and Society in the Scottish Enlightenment," in Barnes and Shapin 1979, 19–40.

Lawson, Hilary, and Lisa Appignanesi, eds, 1989. *Dismantling Truth: Reality in the Post-modern World.* London: Weidenfeld and Nicolson.

Leicester, Henry M., [1956] 1965. *The Historical Background of Chemistry.* New York: John Wiley.

Leites, Edmund, ed., 1988. *Conscience and Casuistry in Early Modern Europe.* Cambridge: Cambridge University Press.

Lémaine, Gerard, Gerard Darmon, and Saba El Nemer, 1982. *Noopolis: les laboratoires de recherche fondamentale: de l'atelier a l'usine.* Paris: CNRS.

Lewalski, Barbara Kiefer, 1979. *Protestant Poetics and the Seventeenth-Century Religious Lyric.* Princeton, N.J.: Princeton University Press.

Lindberg, David C., and Robert S. Westman, eds, 1990. *Reappraisals of the Scientific Revolution.* Cambridge: Cambridge University Press.

Lipmann, Otto, and Paul Plaut, eds, 1927. *Die Lüge in psychologischer, philosophischer, juristischer, historischer, soziologischer . . . Betrachtung.* Leipzig: Johann Ambrosius Barth.

Lloyd, G. E. R., 1983. *Science, Folklore and Ideology: Studies in the Life Sciences in Ancient Greece.* Cambridge: Cambridge University Press.

———, 1990. *Demystifying Mentalities.* Cambridge: Cambridge University Press.

Long, Pamela O., 1991. "The Openness of Knowledge: An Ideal and Its Context in 16th-Century Writings on Mining and Metallurgy," *Technology and Culture* 32: 318–355.

———, 1991. "Invention, Authorship, 'Intellectual Property,' and the Origin of Patents: Notes toward a Conceptual History," *Technology and Culture* 32: 846–884.

Luckmann, Thomas, ed., 1978. *Phenomenology and Sociology.* Harmondsworth: Penguin.

Luhmann, Niklas, 1979. *Trust and Power: Two Works,* trans. Howard Davis, John Raffan, and Kathryn Rooney, eds Tom Burns and Gianfranco Poggi. Chichester: John Wiley.

———, 1984. "The Differentiation of Advances in Knowledge: The Genesis of Science," in Stehr and Meja 1984, 103–148.

———, 1986. "The Individuality of the Individual: Historical Meanings and Contemporary Problems," in Heller, Sosna, and Wellbery 1986, 313–325.

———, 1988. "Familiarity, Confidence, Trust: Problems and Alternatives," in Gambetta 1988, 94–107.

Lynch, Michael, 1985. *Art and Artifact in Laboratory Science: A Study of Shop Work and Shop Talk in a Research Laboratory.* London: Routledge & Kegan Paul.

———, 1988. "Alfred Schutz and the Sociology of Science," in Embree 1988a, 71–100.

———, 1992. "Extending Wittgenstein: The Pivotal Move from Epistemology to the Sociology of Science," in Pickering 1992, 215–265.

———, 1993. *Scientific Practice and Ordinary Action: Ethnomethodological and Social Studies of Science.* Cambridge: Cambridge University Press.

Lynch, Michael, Eric Livingston, and Harold Garfinkel, 1983. "Temporal Order in Laboratory Work," in Knorr-Cetina and Mulkay 1983, 205–238.

Lyons, Henry, 1944. *The Royal Society 1660–1940: A History of Its Administration under Its Charters.* Cambridge: Cambridge University Press.

McCarthy, Thomas, 1973. "A Theory of Communicative Competence," *Philosophy of the Social Sciences* 3: 135–156.

MacDonald, Michael, 1981. *Mystical Bedlam: Madness, Anxiety, and Healing in Seventeenth-Century England.* Cambridge: Cambridge University Press.

Macfarlane, Alan, 1970. *The Family Life of Ralph Josselin, a Seventeenth-Century Clergyman: An Essay in Historical Anthropology.* Cambridge: Cambridge University Press.

———, 1979. *The Origins of English Individualism: The Family, Property and Social Transition.* New York: Cambridge University Press.

———, 1986. "Socio-economic Revolution in England and the Origin of the Modern World," in *Revolution in History,* eds Roy Porter and Mikuláš Teich. Cambridge: Cambridge University Press, pp. 145–166.

McGuire, J. E., 1972. "Boyle's Conception of Nature," *Journal of the History of Ideas* 33: 523–542.

McGuire, J. E., and P. M. Rattansi, 1966. "Newton and the 'Pipes of Pan,'" *Notes and Records of the Royal Society* 21: 108–143.

McGuire, J. E., and Martin Tamny, 1983. *Certain Philosophical Questions: Newton's Trinity Notebook.* Cambridge: Cambridge University Press.

———, 1985. "Newton's Astronomical Apprenticeship: Notes of 1664/5," *Isis* 76: 349–365.

McHugh, Peter, 1970. "On the Failure of Positivism," in J. Douglas 1970a, 320–335.

MacIntosh, J. J., 1991. "Locke and Boyle on Miracles and God's Existence," unpublished typescript.

———, 1992. "Robert Boyle's Epistemology: The Interaction between Scientific and Religious Knowledge," *International Studies in the Philosophy of Science* 6: 91–121.

MacIntyre, Alasdair, 1966. *A Short History of Ethics.* New York: Collier.

———, [1981] 1984. *After Virtue: A Study in Moral Theory,* 2d ed. Notre Dame, Ind.: University of Notre Dame Press.

McKeon, Michael, 1987. *The Origins of the English Novel.* Baltimore: Johns Hopkins University Press.

McKeon, Robert E., 1970. "Auzout, Adrien," in *Dictionary of Scientific Biography,* Vol. I, pp. 341–342.

Mackie, Fiona, 1985. *The Status of Everyday Life.* London: Routledge & Kegan Paul.

MacLachlan, Patricia A., 1974. "Papin, Denis," in *Dictionary of Scientific Biography,* Vol. X, pp. 292–293.

Maclean, Ian, 1980. *The Renaissance Notion of Woman: A Study in the Fortunes of Scholasticism and Medical Science in European Intellectual Life.* Cambridge: Cambridge University Press.

McMullin, Ernan, 1990. "Conceptions of Science in the Scientific Revolution," in Lindberg and Westman 1990, 27–92.

———, ed., 1992. *The Social Dimensions of Science.* Notre Dame, Ind.: University of Notre Dame Press.

Macpherson, C. B., 1964. *The Political Theory of Possessive Individualism: Hobbes to Locke.* Oxford: Oxford University Press.

————, 1974. "Harrington's 'Opportunity State,'" in Webster 1974, 23–53.

MacPike, Eugene Fairfield, 1937. *Hevelius, Flamsteed and Halley: Three Contemporary Astronomers and Their Mutual Relations.* London: Taylor & Francis.

Maddison, R. E. W., 1951. "Studies in the Life of Robert Boyle, F.R.S. Part I. Robert Boyle and Some of His Foreign Visitors," *Notes and Records of the Royal Society* 9: 1–35.

————, 1953. "Studies in the Life of Robert Boyle, F.R.S. Part III. The Charitable Disposal of Robert Boyle's Residuary Estate," *Notes and Records of the Royal Society* 10: 15–27.

————, 1954. "Studies in the Life of Robert Boyle, F.R.S. Part IV. Robert Boyle and Some of His Foreign Visitors," *Notes and Records of the Royal Society* 11: 38–53.

————, 1955. "Studies in the Life of Robert Boyle, F.R.S. Part V. Boyle's Operator: Ambrose Godfrey Hanckwitz," *Notes and Records of the Royal Society* 11: 159–188.

————, 1961. "The Plagiary of Francis Boyle," *Annals of Science* 17: 111–120.

————, 1961. "The Earliest Published Writing of Robert Boyle," *Annals of Science* 17: 165–173.

————, 1962. "The First Edition of Boyle's *Medicinal Experiments*," *Annals of Science* 18: 43–47.

————, 1963. "Studies in the Life of Robert Boyle, Part VI. The Stalbridge Period, 1645–55, and the Invisible College," *Notes and Records of the Royal Society* 18: 104–124.

————, 1965. "Studies in the Life of Robert Boyle, Part VII. The Grand Tour," *Notes and Records of the Royal Society* 20: 51–77.

————, 1969. *The Life of the Honourable Robert Boyle F.R.S.* London: Taylor & Francis.

Mahoney, Michael S., 1984. "Changing Canons of Mathematical and Physical Intelligibility in the Later 17th Century," *Historia Mathematica* 11: 417–423.

Maines, David R., ed., 1991. *Social Organization and Social Process: Essays in Honor of Anselm Strauss.* New York: Aldine de Gruyter.

Mandelbaum, Maurice, 1966. "Newton and Boyle and the Problem of 'Transdiction,'" in idem, *Philosophy, Science, and Sense Perception: Historical and Critical Studies.* Baltimore: Johns Hopkins University Press, pp. 61–117.

Mannheim, Karl, [1929] 1936. *Ideology and Utopia: An Introduction to the Sociology of Knowledge,* trans. Louis Wirth and Edward Shils. London: Kegan Paul, Trench, Trubner & Co.

Martin, Julian, 1992. *Francis Bacon, the State, and the Reform of Natural Philosophy.* Cambridge: Cambridge University Press.

Mason, John E., [1935] 1971. *Gentlefolk in the Making: Studies in the History of Courtesy Literature and Related Topics from 1531 to 1774.* New York: Octagon Books.

Mead, George Herbert, 1964. *Selected Writings,* ed. Andrew J. Reck. Chicago: University of Chicago Press.

Mendelson, Sara Heller, 1987. *The Mental World of Stuart Women: Three Studies.* Brighton: Harvester.

Merleau-Ponty, Maurice, 1964. *Sense and Non-sense,* trans. Hubert L. Dreyfus and Patricia Allen Dreyfus. Evanston, Ill.: Northwestern University Press.

Merton, Robert K., 1973a. *The Sociology of Science: Theoretical and Empirical Investigations*, ed. Norman W. Storer. Chicago: University of Chicago Press.

———, [1938] 1973b. "Science and the Social Order," in Merton 1973a, 254–266.

———, [1942] 1973c. "The Normative Structure of Science," in Merton 1973a, 267–278.

———, [1957] 1973d. "Priorities in Scientific Discovery," in Merton 1973a, 286–324.

———, 1976. *Sociological Ambivalence and Other Essays*. New York: Free Press.

Middleton, W. E. Knowles, 1966. *A History of the Thermometer and Its Uses in Meteorology*. Baltimore: Johns Hopkins University Press.

———, 1971. *The Experimenters: A Study of the Accademia del Cimento*. Baltimore: Johns Hopkins University Press.

Mills, C. Wright, 1940. "Situated Actions and Vocabularies of Motive," *American Sociological Review* 5: 904–913.

Mingay, G. E., 1976. *The Gentry: The Rise and Fall of a Ruling Class*. London: Longman.

Mitroff, Ian I., 1974. *The Subjective Side of Science: A Philosophical Inquiry into the Psychology of the Apollo Moon Scientists*. Amsterdam: Elsevier.

———, 1974. "Norms and Counter-norms in a Select Group of Apollo Moon Scientists: A Case Study of the Ambivalence of Scientists," *American Sociological Review* 39: 579–595.

Moran, Bruce T., 1977. "Princes, Machines and the Valuation of Precision in the Sixteenth Century," *Sudhoffs Archiv* 61: 209–228.

———, ed., 1991a. *Patronage and Institutions: Science, Technology, and Medicine at the European Court 1500–1750*. Woodbridge, Suffolk: Boydell Press.

———, 1991b. "Patronage and Institutions: Courts, Universities, and Academies in Germany; An Overview: 1550–1750," in Moran 1991a, 169–183.

More, Louis Trenchard, 1944. *The Life and Works of the Honourable Robert Boyle*. London: Oxford University Press.

Morgan, Edmund S., [1944] 1966. *The Puritan Family: Religion & Domestic Relations in Seventeenth-Century New England*, new ed. New York: Harper & Row.

Morgan, George W., 1973. "On Trusting," *Humanitas: Journal of the Institute of Man* 9: 237–251.

Morgan, John, 1986. *Godly Learning: Puritan Attitudes towards Reason, Learning, and Education, 1560–1640*. Cambridge: Cambridge University Press.

Morrah, Patrick, 1976. *Prince Rupert of the Rhine*. London: Constable.

Mukerji, Chandra, 1976. "Having the Authority to Know: Decision-Making in Student Film Crews," *Work and Occupations* 3: 63–87.

———, 1989. *A Fragile Power: Scientists and the State*. Princeton, N.J.: Princeton University Press.

Mullin, Jay, 1979. "Phenomenology and Friendship," in *Friends, Enemies, and Strangers: Theorizing in Art, Science, and Everyday Life*, eds. Alan Blum and Peter McHugh. Norwood, N.J.: Ablex, pp. 29–50.

Murdin, Lesley, 1985. *Under Newton's Shadow: Astronomical Practices in the Seventeenth Century*. Bristol: Adam Hilger.

Nagel, Thomas, 1986. *The View from Nowhere*. Oxford: Oxford University Press.

Naylor, Ronald H., 1976. "Galileo: Real Experiment and Didactic Demonstration," *Isis* 67: 398–419.

———, 1989. "Galileo's Experimental Discourse," in Gooding, Pinch, and Schaffer 1989, 117–134.

Neale, R. S., 1981. *Class in English History 1680–1850*. Oxford: Basil Blackwell.

Nelson, Benjamin, 1968. "Scholastic Rationales of 'Conscience', Early Modern Crises of Credibility, and the Scientific-Technocultural Revolutions of the 17th and 20th Centuries," *Journal for the Scientific Study of Religion* 7: 157–177.

Newman, William, 1987. "Newton's *Clavis* as Starkey's *Key*," *Isis* 78: 564–574.

Nieburg, H. L., 1966. *In the Name of Science*. Chicago: Quadrangle Books.

North, J. D., 1972. "Hevelius, Johannes," in *Dictionary of Scientific Biography*, Vol. VI, pp. 360–364.

Nowotny, Helga, 1990a. "Does It Only Need Good Men to Do Good Science? (Scientific Openness as Individual Responsibility)," in Nowotny 1990b, 95–106.

———, 1990b. *In Search of Usable Knowledge: Utilization Contexts and the Application of Knowledge*. Boulder, Colo.: Westview Press.

Noyes, Gertrude Elizabeth, 1937. *Bibliography of Courtesy and Conduct Books in Seventeenth-Century England*. New Haven, Conn.: Tuttle, Morehouse & Taylor.

Oakeshott, Michael, 1962a. *Rationalism in Politics and Other Essays*. New York: Basic Books.

———, 1962b. "Political Education," in idem 1962a, 111–136.

———, [1950] 1962c. "Rational Conduct," in idem 1962a, 80–110.

———, [1947] 1962d. "Rationalism in Politics," in idem 1962a, 1–36.

———, [1959] 1962e. "The Voice of Poetry in the Conversation of Mankind," in idem 1962a, 197–247.

———, [1933] 1966. *Experience and Its Modes*. Cambridge: Cambridge University Press.

Oakley, Francis, 1984. *Omnipotence, Covenant, & Order: An Excursion in the History of Ideas from Abelard to Leibniz*. Ithaca, N.Y.: Cornell University Press.

Obelkevich, James, 1987. "Proverbs and Social History," in Burke and Porter 1987, 43–72.

O'Brien, J. J., 1965. "Samuel Hartlib's Influence on Robert Boyle's Scientific Development," *Annals of Science* 21: 1–14, 257–276.

O'Connell, Joseph, 1993. "Metrology: The Creation of Universality by the Circulation of Particulars," *Social Studies of Science* 23: 129–173.

Oestreich, Gerhard, 1982. *Neostoicism and the Early Modern State*, eds Brigitta Oestreich and H. G. Koenigsberger, trans. David McLintock. Cambridge: Cambridge University Press.

Olesko, Kathryn M., 1991. *Physics as a Calling: Discipline and Practice in the Königsberg Seminar for Physics*. Ithaca, N.Y.: Cornell University Press.

Ophir, Adi, 1991. "A Place of Knowledge Re-created: The Library of Michel de Montaigne," *Science in Context* 4: 163–189.

Ophir, Adi, and Steven Shapin, 1991. "The Place of Knowledge: A Methodological Survey," *Science in Context* 4: 3–21.

Osler, Margaret J., 1992. "The Intellectual Sources of Robert Boyle's Philosophy of Nature: Gassendi's Voluntarism and Boyle's Physico-theological Project," in *Philosophy, Science, and Religion in England 1640–1700*, eds Richard Kroll, Richard Ashcraft, and Perez Zagorin. Cambridge: Cambridge University Press, pp. 178–198.

Osler, Margaret J., and Paul Lawrence Farber, eds, 1985. *Religion, Science, and Worldview: Essays in Honor of Richard S. Westfall*. Cambridge: Cambridge University Press.

Oster, Malcolm, 1992. "The Scholar and the Craftsman Revisited: Robert Boyle as Aristocrat and Artisan," *Annals of Science* 49: 255–276.

———, 1993. "Biography, Culture, and Science: The Formative Years of Robert Boyle," *History of Science* 31: 177–226.

Outram, Dorinda, 1978. "The Language of Natural Power: The *Éloges* of Georges Cuvier and the Public Language of Nineteenth Century Science," *History of Science* 18: 1978: 153–178.

———, 1984. *Georges Cuvier: Vocation, Science and Authority in Post-revolutionary France*. Manchester: Manchester University Press.

Palgrave, Mary E., 1901. *Mary Rich Countess of Warwick (1625–1678)*. London: J. M. Dent.

Palliser, D. M., 1983. *The Age of Elizabeth: England under the Later Tudors 1547–1603*. London: Longman.

Palm, L. C., 1989. "Leeuwenhoek and Other Dutch Correspondents of the Royal Society," *Notes and Records of the Royal Society* 43: 191–207.

Palm, L. C., and H. A. M. Snelders, eds, 1982. *Antoni van Leeuwenhoek 1632–1723*. Amsterdam: Rodopi.

Pannekoek, A., [1951] 1961. *A History of Astronomy*. New York: Interscience.

Park, Katharine, and Lorraine J. Daston, 1981. "Unnatural Conceptions: The Study of Monsters in Sixteenth- and Seventeenth-Century France and England," *Past and Present* 92: 20–54.

Partington, J. R., 1936. "Johann Baptista Van Helmont," *Annals of Science* 1: 359–384.

Partridge, Eric, 1959. *Origins: A Short Etymological Dictionary of Modern English*. New York: Macmillan.

Paul, Charles B., 1980. *Science and Immortality: The "Éloges" of the Paris Academy of Sciences (1699–1791)*. Berkeley: University of California Press.

Pickering, Andrew, ed., 1992. *Science as Practice and Culture*. Chicago: University of Chicago Press.

Pinch, Trevor J., 1981. "The Sun-Set: The Presentation of Certainty in Scientific Life," *Social Studies of Science* 11: 131–158.

———, 1985. "Towards an Analysis of Scientific Observation: The Externality and Evidential Significance of Observational Reports in Physics," *Social Studies of Science* 15: 3–36.

Pitt-Rivers, Julian, 1966. "Honour and Social Status," in *Honour and Shame: The Values of Mediterranean Society*, ed. J. G. Peristiany. Chicago: University of Chicago Press, pp. 21–77.

Pocock, J. G. A., 1957. *The Ancient Constitution and the Feudal Law: A Study of English Historical Thought in the Seventeenth Century*. Cambridge: Cambridge University Press.

————, 1975. *The Machiavellian Moment: Florentine Political Thought and the Atlantic Republican Tradition.* Princeton, N.J.: Princeton University Press.

Polanyi, Michael, 1958. *Personal Knowledge: Towards a Post-critical Philosophy.* Chicago: University of Chicago Press.

————, [1946] 1964. *Science, Faith and Society.* Chicago: University of Chicago Press.

————, 1969. *Knowing and Being,* ed. Marjorie Grene. Chicago: University of Chicago Press.

Pollner, Melvin, 1987. *Mundane Reason: Reality in Everyday and Sociological Discourse.* Cambridge: Cambridge University Press.

Pollock, Linda, 1992. *With Faith and Physic: The Life of a Tudor Gentlewoman: Lady Grace Mildmay, 1552–1620.* London: Collins and Brown.

Pomerantz, Anita M., 1984. "Giving a Source or Basis: The Practice in Conversation of Telling 'How I Know,'" *Journal of Pragmatics* 8: 607–625.

Popkin, Richard H., [1960] 1979. *The History of Scepticism from Erasmus to Spinoza,* rev. ed. Berkeley: University of California Press.

Popper, Karl R., [1945] 1950. *The Open Society and Its Enemies.* Princeton, N.J.: Princeton University Press.

————, 1972. *Objective Knowledge: An Evolutionary Approach.* Oxford: Clarendon Press.

————, [1963] 1974. *Conjectures and Refutations: The Growth of Scientific Knowledge,* 5th ed. London: Routledge & Kegan Paul.

————, 1976. *Unended Quest: An Intellectual Autobiography.* London: Fontana/Collins.

Porter, Roy, ed., 1985. *Patients and Practitioners: Lay Perceptions of Medicine in Pre-industrial Society.* Cambridge: Cambridge University Press.

————, 1987. "The Language of Quackery in England, 1660–1800," in Burke and Porter 1987, 73–103.

Porter, Roy, and Mikuláš Teich, eds, 1992. *The Scientific Revolution in National Context.* Cambridge: Cambridge University Press.

Porter, Theodore M., 1992. "Quantification and the Accounting Ideal in Science," *Social Studies of Science* 22: 633–652.

————, 1992. "Objectivity as Standardization: The Rhetoric of Impersonality in Measurement, Statistics, and Cost-Benefit Analysis," *Annals of Scholarship* 9: 19–59.

Principe, Lawrence M., 1990. "The Gold Process: Directions in the Study of Robert Boyle's Alchemy," in *Alchemy Revisited,* ed. Z. R. W. M. Von Martels. Leiden: E. J. Brill, pp. 200–205.

————, 1992. "Robert Boyle's Alchemical Secrecy: Codes, Ciphers and Concealments," *Ambix* 39: 63–74.

Prior, Moody E., 1957. "Bacon's Man of Science," in *Roots of Scientific Thought,* eds Philip P. Wiener and Aaron Noland. New York: Basic Books, pp. 382–389.

Pugliese, Patri Jones, 1982. "The Scientific Achievement of Robert Hooke: Method and Mechanics." Ph.D. thesis, Harvard University.

Pumfrey, Stephen, 1987. "Mechanizing Magnetism in Restoration England: The Decline of Magnetic Philosophy," *Annals of Science* 44: 1–22.

————, 1989. "'O tempora, O magnes!' A Sociological Analysis of the Discovery of Secular Magnetic Variation in 1634," *British Journal for the History of Science* 22: 181–214.

———, 1991. "Ideas above His Station: A Social Study of Hooke's Curatorship of Experiments," *History of Science* 29: 1–44.

Pumfrey, Stephen, Paolo L. Rossi, and Maurice Slawinski, eds, 1991. *Science, Culture and Popular Belief in Renaissance Europe*. Manchester: Manchester University Press.

Putnam, Hilary, 1975. "The Meaning of 'Meaning,'" in idem, *Mind, Language and Reality. Philosophical Papers, Volume 2*. Cambridge: Cambridge University Press, pp. 215–271.

Quine, Willard Van Orman, 1966. *The Ways of Paradox and Other Essays*. New York: Random House.

Ranger, Terence O., 1957. "Richard Boyle and the Making of an Irish Fortune, 1588–1614," *Irish Historical Studies* 10: 257–297.

Ravetz, Jerome R., 1971. *Scientific Knowledge and Its Social Problems*. Oxford: Clarendon Press.

Reeds, Karen M., 1976. "Renaissance Humanism and Botany," *Annals of Science* 33: 519–542.

Rees, Graham, 1975. "Francis Bacon's Semi-Paracelsian Cosmology," *Ambix* 22: 81–101, 161–173.

Reiss, Timothy J., 1982. *The Discourse of Modernism*. Ithaca, N.Y.: Cornell University Press.

Revel, Jacques, 1984. "Forms of Expertise: Intellectuals and 'Popular' Culture in France (1650–1800)," in *Understanding Popular Culture: Europe from the Middle Ages to the Nineteenth Century*, ed. Steven L. Kaplan. Amsterdam: Mouton, pp. 255–273.

———, 1989. "The Uses of Civility," in *A History of Private Life, Vol. III: Passions of the Renaissance*, ed. Roger Chartier, trans. Arthur Goldhammer. Cambridge, Mass.: Harvard University Press, Belknap Press, pp. 167–205.

Rich, Adrienne, 1979. *On Lies, Secrets, and Silence: Selected Prose 1966–1978*. New York: W. W. Norton.

Ringer, Fritz, 1992. "The Origins of Mannheim's Sociology of Knowledge," in McMullin 1992, 47–67.

Robinson, H. W., 1946. "The Administrative Staff of the Royal Society, 1663–1861," *Notes and Records of the Royal Society* 4: 193–205.

———, 1947. "Denis Papin (1647–1712)," *Notes and Records of the Royal Society* 5: 47–50.

Rogow, Arnold A., 1986. *Thomas Hobbes: Radical in the Service of Reaction*. New York: W. W. Norton.

Rorty, Richard, 1979. *Philosophy and the Mirror of Nature*. Princeton, N.J.: Princeton University Press.

———, 1989. "Science as Solidarity," in Lawson and Appignanesi 1989, 6–22 (also in Rorty 1991, 35–45).

———, 1991. *Objectivity, Relativism, and Truth, Philosophical Papers, Volume 1*. Cambridge: Cambridge University Press.

Rose, Mark, 1988. "The Author as Proprietor: *Donaldson v. Becket* and the Genealogy of Modern Authorship," *Representations* 23: 51–85.

Rosenberg, Charles E., 1976. *No Other Gods: On Science and American Social Thought.* Baltimore: Johns Hopkins University Press.

Rossi, Paolo, [1962] 1970. *Philosophy, Technology, and the Arts in the Early Modern Era,* trans. Salvator Attanasio, ed. Benjamin Nelson. New York: Harper & Row.

Roth, Julius A., 1966. "Hired Hand Research," *American Sociologist* 1: 190–196.

Ruby, Jane E., 1986. "The Origins of Scientific 'Law,'" *Journal of the History of Ideas* 47: 341–359.

Rudwick, Martin J. S., 1985. *The Great Devonian Controversy: The Shaping of Scientific Knowledge among Gentlemanly Specialists.* Chicago: University of Chicago Press.

Ruestow, Edward G., 1983. "Images and Ideas: Leeuwenhoek's Perception of the Spermatozoa," *Journal of the History of Biology* 16: 185–224.

Ruffner, James A., 1966. "The Background and Early Development of Newton's Theory of Comets." Ph.D. thesis, Indiana University.

———, 1971. "The Curved and the Straight: Cometary Theory from Kepler to Hevelius," *Journal of the History of Astronomy* 2: 178–194.

Sargent, Rose-Mary, 1989. "Scientific Experiment and Legal Expertise: The Way of Experience in Seventeenth-Century England," *Studies in History and Philosophy of Science* 20: 19–45.

Schaffer, Simon, 1984. "Making Certain," *Social Studies of Science* 14: 137–152.

———, 1987. "Godly Men and Mechanical Philosophers: Souls and Spirits in Restoration Natural Philosophy," *Science in Context* 1: 55–85.

———, 1988. "Astronomers Mark Time: Discipline and the Personal Equation," *Science in Context* 2: 115–145.

———, 1988. "Wallification: Thomas Hobbes on School Divinity and Experimental Pneumatics," *Studies in History and Philosophy of Science* 19: 275–298.

———, 1989. "Defoe's Natural Philosophy and the Worlds of Credit," in Christie and Shuttleworth 1989, 13–44.

———, 1990. "Measuring Virtue: Eudiometry, Enlightenment and Pneumatic Medicine," in *The Medical Enlightenment of the Eighteenth Century,* eds Andrew Cunningham and Roger French. Cambridge: Cambridge University Press, pp. 281–318.

———, 1992. "Self-Evidence," *Critical Inquiry* 18: 327–362.

———, 1992. "Late Victorian Metrology and Its Instrumentation: A Manufactory of Ohms," in *Invisible Connections: Instruments, Institutions, and Science,* eds Robert F. Bud and Susan E. Cozzens. Bellingham, Wash.: SPIE Optical Engineering Press, pp. 23–56.

———, 1992. "Experimental Subjects in the 1660s," unpublished typescript.

———, 1992. "'Accurate Measurement Is an English Science,'" unpublished typescript.

Schiebinger, Londa, 1989. *The Mind Has No Sex? Women in the Origins of Modern Science.* Cambridge, Mass.: Harvard University Press.

Schiffrin, Deborah, 1990. "The Management of a Co-operative Self during Argument: The Role of Opinions and Stories," in Grimshaw 1990, 241–259.

Schmitt, Charles B., Quentin Skinner, Eckhard Kessler, and Jill Kraye, eds, 1988. *The Cambridge History of Renaissance Philosophy.* Cambridge: Cambridge University Press.

Schuster, John A., 1984. "Methodologies as Mythic Structures: A Preface to the Future Historiography of Method," *Metascience* 1/2: 15–36.

———, 1986. "Cartesian Method as Mythic Speech: A Diachronic and Synchronic Analysis," in *The Politics and Rhetoric of Scientific Method: Historical Studies*, eds Schuster and Richard R. Yeo. Dordrecht: D. Reidel, pp. 33–95.

Schutz, Alfred, 1962–1966. *Collected Papers*, 3 vols. [Vol. I = *The Problem of Social Reality*, ed. Maurice Natanson; Vol. II = *Studies in Social Theory*, ed. Arvid Brodersen; Vol. III = *Studies In Phenomenological Philosophy*, ed. Ilse Schutz]. The Hague: Martinus Nijhoff.

———, 1970. *On Phenomenology and Social Relations: Selected Writings*, ed. Helmut R. Wagner. Chicago: University of Chicago Press.

Searle, John R., 1969. *Speech Acts: An Essay in the Philosophy of Language*. Cambridge: Cambridge University Press.

Seaver, Paul S., 1985. *Wallington's World: A Puritan Artisan in Seventeenth-Century London*. Stanford, Calif.: Stanford University Press.

Sennett, Richard, 1974. *The Fall of Public Man*. Cambridge: Cambridge University Press.

Shanahan, Timothy, 1988. "God and Nature in the Thought of Robert Boyle," *Journal of the History of Philosophy* 26: 547–569.

Shapin, Steven, 1980. "Social Uses of Science," in *The Ferment of Knowledge: Studies in the Historiography of Eighteenth-Century Science*, eds George S. Rousseau and Roy Porter. Cambridge: Cambridge University Press, pp. 93–139.

———, 1984. "Pump and Circumstance: Robert Boyle's Literary Technology," *Social Studies of Science* 14: 481–520.

———, 1987. "O Henry [essay review of Oldenburg, *Correspondence*]," *Isis* 78: 417–424.

———, 1988. "The House of Experiment in Seventeenth-Century England," *Isis* 79: 373–404.

———, 1988. "Robert Boyle and Mathematics: Reality, Representation, and Experimental Practice," *Science in Context* 2: 23–58.

———, 1988. "Closure and Credibility in 17th-Century Science," paper presented to Joint Conference of History of Science Society and British Society for the History of Science, Manchester, 11–15 July 1989, and reproduced in conference proceedings, pp. 147–154.

———, 1989. "Who Was Robert Hooke?" in Hunter and Schaffer 1989, 253–285.

———, 1989. "The Invisible Technician," *American Scientist* 77: 554–563.

———, 1991. " 'The Mind Is Its Own Place': Science and Solitude in Seventeenth-Century England," *Science in Context* 4: 191–218.

———, 1991. "'A Scholar and a Gentleman': The Problematic Identity of the Scientific Practitioner in Early Modern England," *History of Science* 29: 279–327.

———, 1992. "Discipline and Bounding: The History and Sociology of Science as Seen through the Externalism-Internalism Debate," *History of Science* 30: 333–369.

———, 1992. "Why the Public Ought to Understand Science-in-the-Making," *Public Understanding of Science* 1: 27–30.

————, 1993. "Personal Development and Intellectual Biography: The Case of Robert Boyle," *British Journal for the History of Science* 26: 335–345.

Shapin, Steven, and Barry Barnes, 1979. "Darwin and Social Darwinism: Purity and History," in Barnes and Shapin 1979, 125–142.

Shapin, Steven, and Simon Schaffer, 1985. *Leviathan and the Air-Pump: Hobbes, Boyle, and the Experimental Life.* Princeton, N.J.: Princeton University Press.

Shapiro, Barbara J., 1969. *John Wilkins, 1614–1672: An Intellectual Biography.* Berkeley: University of California Press.

————, 1969. "Law and Science in Seventeenth-Century England," *Stanford Law Review* 21: 727–766.

————, 1983. *Probability and Certainty in Seventeenth-Century England: A Study of the Relationships between Natural Science, Religion, History, Law, and Literature.* Princeton, N.J.: Princeton University Press.

————, 1986. "'To a Moral Certainty': Theories of Knowledge and Anglo-American Juries 1600–1850," *Hastings Law Journal* 38: 153–193 (a version appears as Shapiro 1991, ch. 1).

————, 1991. *"Beyond Reasonable Doubt" and "Probable Cause": Historical Perspectives on the Anglo-American Law of Evidence.* Berkeley: University of California Press.

Sharrock, W. W., 1974. "On Owning Knowledge," in R. Turner 1974, 45–53.

Shirley, John William, 1949. "The Scientific Experiments of Sir Walter Ralegh, the Wizard Earl, and the Three Magi in the Tower, 1603–1617," *Ambix* 4: 52–66.

Silver, Allan, 1985. "'Trust' in Social and Political Theory," in *The Challenge of Social Control: Citizenship and Institution Building in Modern Society: Essays in Honor of Morris Janowitz,* eds Gerald D. Suttles and Mayer N. Zald. Norwood, N.J.: Ablex, pp. 52–67.

Simmel, Georg, 1950. *The Sociology of Georg Simmel,* ed. and trans. Kurt H. Wolff. London: Collier-Macmillan; Glencoe, Ill.: Free Press.

————, [1907] 1978. *The Philosophy of Money,* trans. Tom Bottomore and David Frisby. London: Routledge & Kegan Paul.

Simon, Yves, 1962. *A General Theory of Authority.* Notre Dame, Ind.: Notre Dame University Press.

Simpson, A. D. C., 1989. "Robert Hooke and Practical Optics: Technical Support at a Scientific Frontier," in Hunter and Schaffer 1989, 33–61.

Skinner, Quentin, 1969. "Meaning and Understanding in the History of Ideas," *History and Theory* 8: 3–53.

Slaght, W. E., 1928. *Untruthfulness in Children: Its Conditioning Factors and Its Setting in Child Nature.* Iowa City: University of Iowa.

Smith, Hilda L., 1992. "Intellectual Bases for Feminist Analyses: The Seventeenth and Eighteenth Centuries," in *Women and Reason,* eds Elizabeth D. Harvey and Kathleen Okruhlik. Ann Arbor: University of Michigan Press, pp. 19–38.

Smith, Logan Pearsall, 1907. *The Life and Letters of Sir Henry Wotton,* 2 vols. Oxford: Clarendon Press.

Smith, Pamela H., 1991. "Curing the Body Politic: Chemistry and Commerce at Court, 1664–70," in Moran 1991a, 195–209.

————, in press. *Science and Culture in the Age of the Baroque: Johann Joachim*

Becher at the Courts of the Holy Roman Empire, 1635–82. Princeton, N.J.: Princeton University Press.

Smythe-Palmer, A., 1908. *The Ideal of a Gentleman, or A Mirror for Gentlefolks.* London: George Routledge; New York: E. P. Dutton.

Sommerville, Johann P., 1988. "The 'New Art of Lying': Equivocation, Mental Reservation, and Casuistry," in Leites 1988, 159–184.

Stallybrass, Peter, and Allon White, 1986. *The Politics and Poetics of Transgression.* Ithaca, N.Y.: Cornell University Press.

Star, Susan Leigh, 1991. "The Sociology of the Invisible: The Primacy of Work in the Writings of Anselm Strauss," in Maines 1991, 265–283.

Stehr, Nico, and Volker Meja, eds, 1984. *Society and Knowledge: Contemporary Perspectives in the Sociology of Knowledge.* New Brunswick, N.J.: Transaction Books.

Steneck, Nicholas H., 1982. "Greatrakes the Stroker: The Interpretations of Historians," *Isis* 73: 161–177.

Stewart, M. A., 1981. "Locke's Professional Contact with Robert Boyle," *Locke Newsletter* 12: 19–44.

Stewart, Walter W., and Ned Feder, 1987. "The Integrity of the Scientific Literature," *Nature* 325 (15 January): 207–214.

Stieb, Ernst W., 1964. "Robert Boyle's Medicina Hydrostatica and the Detection of Adulteration," in *Proceedings of the Tenth International Congress of the History of Science, Ithaca, 1962,* 2 vols. Paris: Hermann, Vol. II, pp. 841–845.

Stillinger, Jack, 1991. *Multiple Authorship and the Myth of Solitary Genius.* Oxford: Oxford University Press.

Stock, John T., 1969. *The Development of the Chemical Balance.* London: H.M.S.O.

Stone, Lawrence, 1965. *The Crisis of the Aristocracy 1558–1641.* Oxford: Clarendon Press.

———, 1977. *The Family, Sex and Marriage in England 1500–1800.* New York: Harper & Row.

———, 1990. "Radical Wisdom for Élite Boys," *Times Literary Supplement,* 2–8 March, 229–230.

Stone, Lawrence, and Jeanne C. Fawtier Stone, 1984. *An Open Elite? England 1540–1880.* Oxford: Clarendon Press.

Strong, P. M., 1988. "Minor Courtesies and Macro Structures," in Drew and Wootton 1988, 228–249.

Targosz, Karolina, 1977. "Johann Hevelius et ses démarches pour trouver des mécènes en France," *Revue d'histoire des sciences* 30: 25–41.

Taton, René, and Curtis Wilson, eds, 1989. *Planetary Astronomy from the Renaissance to the Rise of Astrophysics. Part A: Tycho Brahe to Newton,* The General History of Astronomy, Volume 2. Cambridge: Cambridge University Press.

Taylor, Charles, 1989. *Sources of the Self: The Making of Modern Identity.* Cambridge: Cambridge University Press; Cambridge, Mass.: Harvard University Press.

Temkin, Owsei, 1969. "Historical Reflections on a Scientist's Virtue," *Isis* 60: 427–438.

Thompson, E. P., 1971. "The Moral Economy of the English Crowd in the Eighteenth Century," *Past and Present* 50: 76–136.

————, 1991. *Customs in Common.* London: Merlin Press.

Thompson, Michael, Richard Ellis, and Aaron Wildavsky, 1990. *Cultural Theory.* Boulder, Colo.: Westview Press.

Thoren, Victor E., 1985. "Tycho Brahe as the Dean of a Renaissance Research Institute," in Osler and Farber 1985, 275–295.

————, 1990. *The Lord of Uraniborg: A Biography of Tycho Brahe.* Cambridge: Cambridge University Press.

Thorndike, Lynn, 1923–1958. *A History of Magic and Experimental Science,* 8 vols. New York: Columbia University Press.

Thrower, Norman J. W., ed., 1990. *Standing on the Shoulders of Giants: A Longer View of Newton and Halley.* Berkeley: University of California Press.

Todd, Margo, 1987. *Christian Humanism and the Puritan Social Order.* Cambridge: Cambridge University Press.

Toulmin, Stephen E., 1958. *The Uses of Argument.* Cambridge: Cambridge University Press.

Trevarthen, Colwyn, 1980. "The Foundations of Intersubjectivity: Development of Interpersonal and Cooperative Understanding in Infants," in *The Social Foundations of Language and Thought: Essays in Honor of Jerome S. Bruner,* ed. David R. Olson. New York: W. W. Norton, pp. 316–342.

Trevor-Roper, Hugh, 1988. "The Great Tew Circle," in idem, *Catholics, Anglicans and Puritans: Seventeenth Century Essays.* Chicago: University of Chicago Press, pp. 166–230.

Tribby, Jay, 1991. "Cooking (with) Clio and Cleo: Eloquence and Experiment in Seventeenth-Century Florence," *Journal of the History of Ideas* 52: 417–439.

————, 1991. "It's All *Sprezzatura* to Me!" paper presented to Conference on Civility, Court Society and Scientific Discourse at UCLA Center for 17th- and 18th-Century Studies, 12 October 1991.

————, 1992. "Body/Building: Living the Museum Life in Early Modern Europe," *Rhetorica* 10: 139–163.

Trilling, Lionel, 1972. *Sincerity and Authenticity.* Cambridge, Mass.: Harvard University Press.

Tryphon, Anastasia, Emiel Reith, Howard E. Gruber, Danielle Maurice, and Isabelle Sehl, 1989. "De l'ombre à l'objet: Rôle de l'âge, de l'objet et de l'interaction sociale dans la synthèse de points de vue," *Revue Canadienne de Psychologie* 43: 413–425.

Tully, James, 1988. "Governing Conduct," in Leites 1988, 12–71.

Turnbull, G. H., 1947. *Hartlib, Dury and Comenius: Gleanings from Hartlib's Papers.* London: Hodder & Stoughton, for University Press of Liverpool.

————, 1953. "Samuel Hartlib's Influence on the Early History of the Royal Society," *Notes and Records of the Royal Society* 10: 101–130.

————, 1953. "Peter Stahl, the First Public Teacher of Chemistry at Oxford," *Annals of Science* 9: 265–270.

Turner, A. J., 1973. "Mathematical Instruments and the Education of Gentlemen," *Annals of Science* 30: 51–88.

Turner, Roy, ed., 1974. *Ethnomethodology: Selected Readings.* Harmondsworth: Penguin.

Turner, Stephen P., 1990. "Forms of Patronage," in Cozzens and Gieryn 1990, 185–211.

Underdown, David E., 1985. *Revel, Riot, and Rebellion: Popular Politics and Culture in England 1603–1660*. Oxford: Clarendon Press.

———, 1985. "The Taming of the Scold: The Enforcement of Patriarchal Authority in Early Modern England," in Fletcher and Stevenson 1985a, 116–136.

Urbach, Peter, 1987. *Francis Bacon's Philosophy of Science: An Account and a Reappraisal*. LaSalle, Ill.: Open Court.

Ustick, W. L., 1933. "Changing Ideals of Aristocratic Character and Conduct in Seventeenth-Century England," *Modern Philosophy* 30: 147–166.

Van Berkel, K., 1982. "Intellectuals against Leeuwenhoek: Controversies about the Methods and Style of a Self-taught Scientist," in Palm and Snelders 1982, 187–209.

Van Helden, Albert, 1974. "Saturn and His Anses," *Journal for the History of Astronomy* 5: 105–121.

———, 1974. "'Annulo Cingitur': The Solution to the Problem of Saturn," *Journal for the History of Astronomy* 5: 155–174.

———, 1977. *The Invention of the Telescope* (Transactions of the American Philosophical Society, 67 [4]). Philadelphia: American Philosophical Society.

———, 1994. "Telescopes and Authority from Galileo to Cassini," *Osiris* 9: in press.

Van Leeuwen, Henry G., [1963] 1970. *The Problem of Certainty in English Thought, 1630–1690*, 2d ed. The Hague: Martinus Nijhoff.

Veblen, Thorstein, [1899] 1979. *The Theory of the Leisure Class*. Harmondsworth: Penguin.

Vickers, Brian, ed., 1985. *Arbeit, Musse, Meditation: Betrachtungen zur Vita Activa und Vita Contemplativa*. Zürich: Verlag der Fachvereine Zürich.

———, 1986. *Public and Private Life in the Seventeenth Century: The Mackenzie-Evelyn Debate*. Delmar, N.Y.: Scholars' Facsimiles & Reprints.

Vogt, George McGill, 1925. "Gleanings for the History of a Sentiment: Generositas Virtus, Non Sanguis," *Journal of English and Germanic Philology* 24: 102–124.

Walzer, Michael, 1965. *The Revolution of the Saints: A Study in the Origins of Radical Politics*. Cambridge, Mass.: Harvard University Press.

Warren, Leland E., 1983. "Turning Reality Round Together: Guides to Conversation in Eighteenth-Century England," *Eighteenth-Century Life* 8: 65–87.

Watson, Curtis Brown, 1960. *Shakespeare and the Renaissance Concept of Honor*. Princeton, N.J.: Princeton University Press.

Wear, Andrew, 1985. "Puritan Perceptions of Illness in Seventeenth Century England," in R. Porter 1985, 55–99.

Webber, Joan, 1968. *The Eloquent "I": Style and Self in Seventeenth-Century Prose*. Madison: University of Wisconsin Press.

Weber, Max, [1904–1905] 1958. *The Protestant Ethic and the Spirit of Capitalism*, trans. Talcott Parsons. New York: Charles Scribner's.

———, 1991a. *From Max Weber: Essays in Sociology*, eds H. H. Gerth and C. Wright Mills. London: Routledge.

———, 1991b. "Science as a Vocation," in Weber 1991a, 129–156.

Webster, Charles, 1965. "The Discovery of Boyle's Law and the Concept of the Elasticity of the Air in the Seventeenth Century," *Archive for History of Exact Sciences* 2: 441–502.

———, 1966. "Richard Towneley (1629–1707), the Towneley Group and Seventeenth-Century Science," *Transactions of the Historic Society of Lancashire and Cheshire* 118: 51–76.

———, ed., 1974. *The Intellectual Revolution of the Seventeenth Century.* London: Routledge & Kegan Paul.

———, 1975. *The Great Instauration: Science, Medicine, and Reform 1626–1660.* London: Duckworth.

———, 1979. *Utopian Planning and the Puritan Revolution: Gabriel Plattes, Samuel Hartlib, and 'Macaria,'* Research Publications of the Wellcome Unit for the History of Medicine, Oxford, No. 2. Oxford: Wellcome Unit.

———, 1982. "Paracelsus and Demons: Science as a Synthesis of Popular Belief," in Istituto Nazionale di Studi sul Rinascimento 1982, 3–20.

Weinstein, Arnold, 1981. *Fictions of the Self: 1550–1800.* Princeton, N.J.: Princeton University Press.

Weintraub, Karl Joachim, 1978. *The Value of the Individual: Self and Circumstance in Autobiography.* Chicago: University of Chicago Press.

Welbourne, Michael, 1986. *The Community of Knowledge,* Scots Philosophical Monographs, Number 9. Aberdeen: Aberdeen University Press.

Westfall, Richard S., 1980. *Never at Rest: A Biography of Isaac Newton.* Cambridge: Cambridge University Press.

Westman, Robert S., 1972. "The Comet and the Cosmos: Kepler, Mästlin and the Copernican Hypothesis," *Studia Copernicana* 5: 7–30.

———, 1980. "The Astronomer's Role in the Sixteenth Century: A Preliminary Study," *History of Science* 18: 105–147.

———, 1990. "Proof, Poetics, and Patronage: Copernicus's Preface to *De revolutionibus,*" in Lindberg and Westman 1990, 167–205.

Westrum, Ronald M., 1977. "Science and Social Intelligence about Anomalies: The Case of Unidentified Flying Objects," *Social Studies of Science* 7: 271–302.

Whigham, Frank, 1984. *Ambition and Privilege: The Social Tropes of Elizabethan Courtesy Literature.* Berkeley: University of California Press.

Wildeblood, Joan, and Peter Brinson, 1965. *The Polite World: A Guide to English Manners and Deportment from the Thirteenth to the Nineteenth Century.* London: Oxford University Press.

Wilkinson, Ronald Sterne, 1963. "George Starkey, Physician and Alchemist," *Ambix* 11: 121–152.

———, 1970. "The Hartlib Papers and Seventeenth-Century Chemistry. Part II," *Ambix* 17: 85–110.

Williams, Norman Lloyd, [1962] 1965. *Sir Walter Raleigh.* Harmondsworth: Penguin.

Wilson, Curtis, 1989. "Predictive Astronomy in the Century after Kepler," in Taton and Wilson 1989, 161–206.

Wintroub, Michael, n.d. "The Looking Glass of Facts," *History of Science,* in press.

Wittgenstein, Ludwig, 1956. *Remarks on the Foundations of Mathematics,* eds G. H. von Wright, R. Rhees, and G. E. M. Anscombe, trans. G. E. M. Anscombe. Oxford: Basil Blackwell.

————, 1967. *Zettel,* eds G. E. M. Anscombe and G. H. von Wright, trans. Anscombe, Oxford: Basil Blackwell.

————, 1972. *On Certainty,* eds G. E. M. Anscombe and G. H. von Wright, trans. Denis Paul and Anscombe. New York: Harper & Row.

————, 1976. *Philosophical Investigations,* trans. G. E. M. Anscombe. Oxford: Basil Blackwell.

Woolf, Patricia K., 1975. "The Second Messenger: Informal Communication in Cyclic AMP Research," *Minerva* 13: 349–373.

Wrightson, Keith, 1982. *English Society 1580–1680.* London: Hutchinson.

Wuthnow, Robert, 1987. *Meaning and Moral Order: Explorations in Cultural Analysis.* Berkeley: University of California Press.

Yeomans, Donald K., 1991. *Comets: A Chronological History of Observation, Science, Myth, and Folklore.* New York: John Wiley.

Zagorin, Perez, 1990. *Ways of Lying: Dissimulation, Persecution, and Conformity in Early Modern Europe.* Cambridge, Mass.: Harvard University Press.

Zilboorg, Gregory, 1941. *A History of Medical Psychology.* New York: W. W. Norton.

Ziman, John, 1968. *Public Knowledge: The Social Dimension of Science.* Cambridge: Cambridge University Press.

————, 1978. *Reliable Knowledge: An Exploration of the Grounds for Belief in Science.* Cambridge: Cambridge University Press.

Zimmerman, Don H., 1974. "Fact as a Practical Accomplishment," in R. Turner 1974, 128–143.

Zimmerman, Don H., and Melvin Pollner, 1970. "The Everyday World as a Phenomenon," in J. Douglas 1970a, 80–103.

Index

(This is a single index of persons and subjects. Material in notes, references to modern authors, and important early modern texts are only lightly indexed.)

Bacon, Francis: on academic philosophy, 173; on air, 344; on antiperistasis, 388; on assessment of veracity in communication, 221; on dueling, 107; on categories of falsehood, 103–4; on the constraints on the powerful, 100; on the credulity of traditional knowledge, 200–201; on distrust of new knowledge-claims, 196–97; on lying, 82, 93–94; specific gravity studies, 348–49; on subjecting nature to analysis, 247; on testimony, 205, 211, 217–18, 222, 234; on truth and interest, 224–25; on truthfulness of state servants, 99; on truth-telling, 73

Bacon, Robin, 378n.70, 404

Barnes, Barry, 13, 26, 28, 31n.89, 38–39, 387n.96

Barometers, 258, 385

Barrow, Isaac, 76

Baxter, Richard, 104, 182

Beale, John, 344

Becker, Howard, 14, 26n.70, 29n.80, 128, 406

Belief: bases of believability, 74–86; and assent, xxiii; religious belief, 320–21; and trust, 8; and truth, 4

Believability, bases of, 74–86

Bernard, Edward, 380

Biagioli, Mario, 121, 267n.63, 282n.103, 316

Biography: collective and individual, 127–30; and practical epistemology, xxviii

Birch, Thomas, 314

Bloor, David, 24n.66, 27n.73, 29

Bodin, Jean, 76

Bok, Sissela, 13

Borelli, Giovanni Alfonso, 267, 270, 279

Boyle, Francis, Viscount Shannon (Boyle brother), 131, 139–40, 142, 166n.127

Boyle, Katherine. See Ranelagh, Katherine

Boyle, Katherine Fenton (Boyle mother), 131

Boyle, Lewis, Viscount Kinalmeaky (Boyle brother), 138–39

Boyle, Mary. See Rich, Mary

Boyle, Richard, 1st earl of Cork (Boyle father): Robert Boyle on, 135; children of, 130–31; impoverishment by Irish rebellion, 142; life of, 132–35; plans for his sons, 48, 97, 139–41

Boyle, Richard, 2nd earl of Cork, Vis-

count Dungarvan, Baron Clifford, 1st earl of Burlington (Boyle brother), 131

Boyle, Robert, 126–92; on air, 345–47; on air-pressure, 258–59, 261; alleged courtship of, 164; amanuenses of, 358, 368; on antiperistasis, 387–88; applying himself to scientific pursuits, 172; assistants of, 372–78, 398; authorial identity of, 177–84, 223n.114; on authority, 202; authority of, 187, 304–5; Auzout's criticism of, 292–93, 299; 'Boyle's law,' 313, 322–30; on carnality, 165–66; on celibacy, 165–66; *Certain Physiological Essays,* 176–77, 293; on certainty, 121; chastity of, 164–65; as Christian gentleman, 149–50, 156–70; *The Christian Virtuoso,* 169; on the Christian virtuoso, 181–82, 191, 199, 291, 335; church office declined by, 168–69; *A Chymical Paradox,* 362; circumstantial style of narrating experiments, 317, 337; cold studies, 247–53; *Continuation of New Experiments Physico-mechanical,* 355–56; conversion experiences of, 158; cultural identity of, 136; "The Dayly Reflection," 150; death of, 144; disavowal of professional expert interest in knowledge, 180; *Discourse of Things above Reason,* 320; disengagement of self from texts of, 177–78; on disinterestedness, 176; early ethical writings of, 145–51; early life and family of, 130–43; at Eton, 140, 152n.69, 174, 314; on evidence appropriate to type of knowledge, 207; on exact citation, 117n.223; example of as check on skepticism, 301–2; *Excellency and Grounds of the Mechanical Hypothesis,* 330n.62; *The Excellency of Theology,* 169; on experience, 203n.32; *Experimenta & Observationes,* 177; experimental failures attributed to technicians, 389–91; and experimental natural philosophy, 126–27, 129, 143, 158–60, 175, 185, 191, 315; and experimental practice, 126, 175, 322, 326; experiments on flame and air, 386–87; *Experiments Touching Colours,* 177; explosions research, 391; factual testimony of, 291–302; *A Free Discourse against Customary Swearing,* 148; *A Free Inquiry,* 182; funeral sermon of, 185–88; on gentility, 145–51; as gentleman, xxviii, 130–32,

Papin, Denis, 356n.2; and air-pump experiments, 355–58; as Boyle's assistant, 326, 356–59, 361, 364, 372–73, 376, 379, 385; Huygens's recommendation of, 401–2; portrait of, 357
Paracelsus, Theophrast von Hohenheim, 235
Pascal, Blaise, 96, 337, 339–40, 385
Peacham, Henry: on Continental deceit, 97; on credibility of gentlemen, 69; on gentility and descent, 53; on gentility and labor, 50; on gentility and learning, 170; on gentility and wealth, 51; on the newly risen man of virtue, 61; on the purchase of arms and honor, 58; on virtue, 64
Pedantry, 116–19, 124, 173–75, 203, 221, 308–9, 317
Penn, William, 79, 82, 95
Perceptual competence: abilities of Hevelius, 273; and discrepancies in accounts, 32; errors of perception, 219, 265; of gentlemen, 75, 78; perceptual incompetence of common people, 77–78, 206–7, 219–21, 232, 264–66; presumption of competence a basis of manners, 36; and testimony, 205–6; of technicians, 384–87
Personal identity: Boyle's development of, 160, 191; and collective biography, 127–30; of experimental philosopher, 191; gentle identity and integrity, 42–64, 191; gentlemanly identity respecified by Boyle, 189; and knowledge-claims, 126; scholarly and gentle identities compared, 171; of servants, 404–5; and social interaction, 129; of technicians, 361–69
Personal providentialism, 157–60
Petit, Pierre, 267, 279
Petty, Maximilian, 405
Petty, William, 50, 53, 154–55
Phenomenology, xix, 28–30, 36, 259, 262
"Philaretus" (Boyle), 157
"Philosophicall Diary" (Boyle), 363
Philosophy: Bacon on academic philosophy, 173; Boyle on, 170–74; Common Sense philosophy, 12; commonsense realism, 29–31; early modern philosophers on authority and testimony, 198, 201–2; and the factual knowledge of artisans, 396; gentlemen as philosophers, 171; nominalism, 349; Oxford philo-

sophical circle, 143, 174; phenomenology, 28–30; pragmatism, 6; Scholasticism, 124, 236–37, 338, 349; and virtue, 171; Wilkins on academic philosophy, 175. *See also* Epistemology; Experimental natural philosophy; Ontology; Phenomenology
Physiognomy, 221–22, 236
Pinch, Trevor, 284n.108, 354n.121
Plagiarism, 182–84, 300–301
Plato, 70, 76, 311, 320
Plattes, Gabriel, 144n.49, 246
Plausibility: and assessment of testimony, 193–202, 212–13, 219-20, 228–31, 236–37, 244–45, 248–49, 265, 270, 287, 301–2, 307; and new knowledge-claims, 195–99; and trustworthiness, 21–22
Pocock, J. G. A., 60n.73
Polanyi, Michael, 25–26
Pollner, Melvin, 31
Popper, Sir Karl, 16, 24
Porter, Theodore, 14n.34
Power: divine, 331–32; and integrity, 100; social, 39; and truth, 36–38; and truth-telling, 65
Power, Henry, 260, 324n.44
Practical epistemology, xxvii–xxviii
Pragmatism, 6
Precision: in astronomy, 272–76, 290; courtesy texts on, 117–19, 351; in experimental philosophy, 341–54; as grounds for doubting testimony, 339; in mathematics, 351; normative character of, 311; in reports of factual knowledge, 310–11; in testimony, 233–34, 250–51, 253–54
Priests of nature, 159, 168
Princes (truthfulness of), 98–101
Probabilism: in discourse, xxvii, 114, 117–20, 214, 217, 228–29, 232–33; in natural philosophy, 120–21, 124–25, 175, 198, 207–9, 218, 224, 296, 308. *See also* Certainty; Moral certainty
Prodromus Cometicus (Hevelius), 273–74, 278
Proper motion (of comets), 267n.62, 271
Providentialism, 157–60, 250
Prudence, 103, 208, 238–42
Prudential maxims in assessing testimony, 211–27
Psychoanalytic theories of biography, 128
Putnam, Hilary, 23